Greens Sheriff Court and Sheriff Appeal Court Rules 2022/2023

Greens Sheriff Court and Sheriff Appeal Court Rules 2022/2023

REPRINTED FROM DIVISION D (COURTS, LOWER)
AND DIVISION S (SHERIFF APPEAL COURT
PRACTICE) OF THE PARLIAMENT HOUSE BOOK

W. GREEN

THOMSON REUTERS

Published in 2022 by Thomson Reuters, trading as W. Green.
Thomson Reuters is registered in England & Wales, Company No.1679046
Registered Office and address for service:
5 Canada Square, Canary Wharf, London, E14 5AQ
For further information on our products and services, visit *http://
www.sweetandmaxwell.co.uk*.

ISBN (print) 9780414105188

ISBN (e-book) 9780414105201

ISBN (print and e-book) 9780414105195

Printed and bound by CPI Group (UK) Ltd, Croydon, CR0 4YY
A CIP catalogue record for this book is available from the British Library.
For orders, go to: *http://www.tr.com/uki-legal-contact*; Tel: 0345 600 9355.

FSC
www.fsc.org
MIX
Paper from
responsible sources
FSC® C013604

Reprinted from the *Parliament House Book*, published in looseleaf form and updated five times a year by W. Green, the Scottish Law Publisher

The following paperback titles are also available in the series:

Annotated Rules of the Court of Session 2022/2023

Solicitors Professional Handbook 2022/2023

Parliament House Book consists of the following Divisions:

A Fees and Stamps

B Courts, Upper

C Court of Session Practice

D Courts, Lower

E Licensing

F Solicitors

G Legal Aid

H Bankruptcy and other Mercantile

I Companies

J Conveyancing, Land Tenure and Registration

K Family Law

L Landlord and Tenant

M Succession, Trusts, Liferents and Judicial Factors

S Sheriff Appeal Court Practice

Modifications to Court Practice During the COVID-19 Emergency

The Coronavirus (Scotland) Act 2020 came into force on 7 April 2020 and the Coronavirus (Scotland) (No.2) Act 2020 came into force on 27 May 2020. Schedule 4 of both of these Acts contained temporary modifications to the law relating to the justice system (both criminal and civil).

Briefly, the schedules provided that:

- electronic signatures on court documents would be permitted;
- electronic documents could be used in place of the actual documents;
- the requirement to physically attend court no longer applied, and
- anyone excused from personal attendance at court must instead appear by electronic means as directed by the court.

Since the pandemic, the conduct, management and disposal of civil court business has given rise to numerous temporary modifications to practice. In the sheriff court, each sheriffdom has issued guidance and directions to facilitate the continued handling and efficient disposal of business in their sheriffdoms in the light of the prevailing circumstances. These are frequently being reviewed and updated, and reference should be made to the Scottish Courts and Tribunal Services website where all such notices issued during the pandemic are published. See
https://www.scotcourts.gov.uk/coronavirus-orders-and-guidance.

MAIN TABLE OF CONTENTS

Volume 1

Volume 2

COURTS, LOWER: ACTS OF SEDERUNT, ETC AND SHERIFF APPEAL COURT PRACTICE

COURTS, LOWER: ACTS OF SEDERUNT, ETC

ACT OF SEDERUNT (SUMMARY APPLICATIONS, STATUTORY APPLICATIONS AND APPEALS ETC. RULES) 1999

(SI 1999/929)

19 March 1999.

ARRANGEMENT OF RULES

CHAPTER 1: GENERAL

The Lords of Council and Session, under and by virtue of the powers conferred on them by Schedule 1, paragraphs 24(1), 28D and 28(2), Schedule 2, paragraph 7 and Schedule 3, paragraph 13(3) to the Betting Gaming and Lotteries Act 1963, Schedule 2, paragraphs 33(1), 34(1), 45 and 47, and Schedule 9, paragraph 15 to the Gaming Act 1968, section 32 of the Sheriff Courts (Scotland) Act 1971, sections 66(5A) and 75 of the Sex Discrimination Act 1975, section 39(9) of the Licensing (Scotland) Act 1976, Schedule 3, paragraph 12 to the Lotteries and Amusements Act 1976, sections 136, 139, 146, 147, 152, 153, 182(3) and 185 of the Representation of the People Act 1983, sections 114(3), 204(3) and 231(3) of the Copyright, Designs and Patents Act 1988, section 19(3) of the Trade Marks Act 1994, section 46 of the Drug Trafficking Act 1994, Regulation 5(3) of the Olympics Association Right (Infringement Proceedings) Regulations 1995, and sections 31(5) and 48 of, and Schedule 1, paragraph 11 to, the Proceeds of Crime (Scotland) Act 1995 and of all other powers enabling them in that behalf, having approved draft rules submitted to them by the Sheriff Court Rules Council in accordance with section 34 of the Sheriff Courts (Scotland) Act 1971, do hereby enact and declare:

CHAPTER 1

GENERAL

Citation and commencement

1.1—(1)   This Act of Sederunt may be cited as the Act of Sederunt (Summary Applications, Statutory Applications and Appeals etc. Rules) 1999 and shall come into force on 1st July 1999.

(2)   This Act of Sederunt shall be inserted in the Books of Sederunt.

Interpretation

1.2—(1)[1]   In this Act of Sederunt, unless the context otherwise requires—

"the 2004 Act" means the Vulnerable Witnesses (Scotland) Act 2004;[2]

"enactment" includes an enactment comprised in, or in an instrument made under, an Act of the Scottish Parliament;

"Ordinary Cause Rules" means the First Schedule to the Sheriff Courts (Scotland) Act 1907;

"sheriff clerk" includes sheriff clerk depute; and

"summary application" has the meaning given by section 3(p) of the Sheriff Courts (Scotland) Act 1907.

(2)   Unless the context otherwise requires, any reference in this Act of Sederunt to a specified Chapter, Part or rule shall be construed as a reference to the Chapter, Part or rule bearing that number in this Act of Sederunt, and a reference to a specified paragraph, sub-paragraph or head shall be construed as a reference to the paragraph, sub-paragraph or head so numbered or lettered in the provision in which that reference occurs.

(3)   Any reference in this Act of Sederunt to a numbered Form shall, unless the context otherwise requires, be construed as a reference to the Form so numbered in Schedule 1 to this Act of Sederunt and includes a form substantially to the same effect with such variation as circumstances may require.

(4)[3]   In this Act of Sederunt, references to a solicitor include a reference to a member of a body which has made a successful application under section 25 of the Law Reform (Miscellaneous Provisions) (Scotland) Act 1990 but only to the extent that the member is exercising rights acquired by virtue of section 27 of that Act.

Revocation

1.3   The Acts of Sederunt mentioned in column (1) of Schedule 2 to this Act of Sederunt are revoked to the extent specified in column (3) of that Schedule.

---

[1] As amended by the Act of Sederunt (Ordinary Cause, Summary Application, Summary Cause and Small Claim Rules) Amendment (Miscellaneous) 2007 (SSI 2007/6), para.3(2) (effective January 29, 2007).

[2] As inserted by the Act of Sederunt (Ordinary Cause, Summary Application, Summary Cause and Small Claim Rules) Amendment (Vulnerable Witnesses (Scotland) Act 2004) (SSI 2007/463), r.3(2) (effective November 1, 2007).

[3] As inserted by the Act of Sederunt (Sheriff Court Rules Amendment) (Sections 25 to 29 of the Law Reform (Miscellaneous Provisions) (Scotland) Act 1990) 2009 (SSI 2009/164) r.3 (effective May 20, 2009).

Application

1.4 Unless otherwise provided in this Act of Sederunt or in any other enactment, any application or appeal to the sheriff shall be by way of summary application and the provisions of Chapter 2 of this Act of Sederunt shall apply accordingly.

Chapter 1A[1]

Lay Representation

Application and interpretation

1A.1.—(1) This Chapter is without prejudice to any enactment (including any other provision in these Rules) under which provision is, or may be, made for a party to a particular type of case before the sheriff to be represented by a lay representative.

(2) In this Chapter, a "lay representative" means a person who is not—

    (a) a solicitor;

    (b) an advocate, or

    (c) someone having a right to conduct litigation, or a right of audience, by virtue of section 27 of the Law Reform (Miscellaneous Provisions) (Scotland) Act 1990.

Lay representation for party litigants

1A.2.—[2](1) In any proceedings in respect of which no provision as mentioned in rule 1A.1(1) is in force, the sheriff may, on the request of a party litigant, permit a named individual (a "lay representative") to appear, along with the litigant, at a specified hearing for the purpose of representing the litigant at that hearing.

(2) An application under paragraph (1)—

    (a) is to be made orally on the date of the first hearing at which the litigant wishes a named individual to represent the litigant; and

    (b) is to be accompanied by a document, signed by the named individual, in Form A1.

(3) The sheriff may grant an application under paragraph (1) only if the sheriff is of the opinion that it would be in the interests of justice to grant it.

(4) It is a condition of permission granted by the sheriff that the lay representative does not receive directly or indirectly from the litigant any remuneration or other reward for his or her assistance.

(5) The sheriff may grant permission under paragraph (1) in respect of one or more specified hearings in the case; but such permission is not effective during any period when the litigant is legally represented.

(6) The sheriff may, of his or her own accord or on the motion of a party to the proceedings, withdraw permission granted under paragraph (1).

(6A) Where permission is granted under paragraph (1), the lay representative may do anything in the preparation or conduct of the hearing that the litigant may do.

(7) Where permission has been granted under paragraph (1), the litigant may—

---

[1] As inserted by the Act of Sederunt (Sheriff Court Rules) (Lay Representation) 2013 (SSI 2013/91) r.3 (effective April 4, 2013).

[2] As amended by the Act of Sederunt (Rules of the Court of Session, Sheriff Appeal Court Rules and Sheriff Court Rules Amendment) (Lay Representation) 2017 (SSI 2017/186) para.5 (effective 3 July 2017).

(a)   show the lay representative any document (including a court document); or

(b)   impart to the lay representative any information,

which is in his or her possession in connection with the proceedings without being taken to contravene any prohibition or restriction on the disclosure of the document or the information; but the lay representative is then to be taken to be subject to any such prohibition or restriction as if he or she were the litigant.

(8)   Any expenses incurred by the litigant in connection with lay representation under this rule are not recoverable expenses in the proceedings.

Chapter 2

Summary Application Rules

Part I

Interpretation

Interpretation

2.1   In this Chapter, unless the context otherwise requires—

"decree" includes any judgment, deliverance, interlocutor, act, order, finding or authority which may be extracted;

"defender" means any person other than the pursuer who is a party to a summary application; and

"pursuer" means any person making a summary application.

Part II

General Rules

Application

2.2   This Part applies to summary applications.

Lay support

2.2A—[1](1)   At any time during proceedings the sheriff may, on the request of a party litigant, permit a named individual to assist the litigant in the conduct of the proceedings by sitting beside or behind (as the litigant chooses) the litigant at hearings in court or in chambers and doing such of the following for the litigant as he or she requires—

(a)   providing moral support;

(b)   helping to manage the court documents and other papers;

(c)   taking notes of the proceedings;

(d)   quietly advising on—

(i)   points of law and procedure;

(ii)   issues which the litigant might wish to raise with the sheriff;

(iii)   questions which the litigant might wish to ask witnesses.

---

[1] As inserted by the Act of Sederunt (Sheriff Court Rules) (Miscellaneous Amendments) (No.2) 2010 (SSI 2010/416) r.3 (effective January 1, 2011).

(2)   It is a condition of such permission that the named individual does not receive from the litigant, whether directly or indirectly, any remuneration for his or her assistance.

(3)   The sheriff may refuse a request under paragraph (1) only if—

    (a)   the sheriff is of the opinion that the named individual is an unsuitable person to act in that capacity (whether generally or in the proceedings concerned); or

    (b)   the sheriff is of the opinion that it would be contrary to the efficient administration of justice to grant it.

(4)   Permission granted under paragraph (1) endures until the proceedings finish or it is withdrawn under paragraph (5); but it is not effective during any period when the litigant is represented.

(5)   The sheriff may, of his or her own accord or on the motion of a party to the proceedings, withdraw permission granted under paragraph (1); but the sheriff must first be of the opinion that it would be contrary to the efficient administration of justice for the permission to continue.

(6)   Where permission has been granted under paragraph (1), the litigant may—

    (a)   show the named individual any document (including a court document); or

    (b)   impart to the named individual any information,

which is in his or her possession in connection with the proceedings without being taken to contravene any prohibition or restriction on the disclosure of the document or the information; but the named individual is then to be taken to be subject to any such prohibition or restriction as if he or she were the litigant.

(7)   Any expenses incurred by the litigant as a result of the support of an individual under paragraph (1) are not recoverable expenses in the proceedings.

Relief from failure to comply with rules

2.3—(1)   The sheriff may relieve a party from the consequences of failure to comply with a provision in this Part which is shown to be due to mistake, oversight or other excusable cause, on such conditions as he thinks fit.

(2)   Where the sheriff relieves a party from the consequences of a failure to comply with a provision in this Part of these Rules under paragraph (1), he may make such order as he thinks fit to enable the summary application to proceed as if the failure to comply with the provision had not occurred.

The initial writ

2.4—(1)   Unless otherwise prescribed by any other enactment, a summary application shall be commenced by initial writ in Form 1.

(2)   The initial writ shall be written, typed or printed on A4 size paper of durable quality and shall not be backed or folded.

(3)   Where the pursuer has reason to believe that an agreement exists prorogating jurisdiction over the subject-matter of the summary application to another court, the initial writ shall contain details of that agreement.

(4)   Where the pursuer has reason to believe that proceedings are pending before another court involving the same cause of action and between the same parties as those named in the instance of the initial writ, the initial writ shall contain details of those proceedings.

(4A)[1] In an action which relates to a regulated agreement within the meaning given by section 189(1) of the Consumer Credit Act 1974 the initial writ shall include an averment that such an agreement exists and details of the agreement.

(5)   An article of condescendence shall be included in the initial writ averring—

(a)   the ground of jurisdiction; and

(b)   the facts upon which the ground of jurisdiction is based.

(6)   Where the residence, registered office or place of business, as the case may be, of the defender is not known and cannot reasonably be ascertained, the pursuer shall set out in the instance of the initial writ that the whereabouts of the defender are not known and aver in the condescendence what steps have been taken to ascertain his present whereabouts.

(7)   The initial writ shall be signed by the pursuer or his solicitor (if any) and the name and address of that solicitor shall be stated on the back of every service copy of that writ.

(8)   The initial writ shall include averments about those persons who appear to the pursuer to have an interest in the application and in respect of whom a warrant for citation is sought.

(9)[2] Where warrant to arrest on the dependence is sought, the initial writ shall include averments to justify the grant of such a warrant.

Order for intimation to interested persons by sheriff

2.5   The sheriff may make an order for intimation to any person who appears to him to have an interest in the summary application.

Time limits

2.6—(1)[3] This rule applies to a summary application where the time within which the application being an appeal under statute or an application in the nature of an appeal may be made is not otherwise prescribed.

(2)   An application to which this rule applies shall be lodged with the sheriff clerk within 21 days after the date on which the decision, order, scheme, determination, refusal or other act complained of was intimated to the pursuer.

(3)   On special cause shown, the sheriff may hear an application to which this rule applies notwithstanding that it was not lodged within the period prescribed in paragraph (2).

Warrants, forms and certificate of citation

2.7—[4](1)   Subject to paragraph (2), a warrant for citation or intimation may be signed by the sheriff or sheriff clerk.

---

[1] As inserted by the Act of Sederunt (Sheriff Court Rules) (Miscellaneous Amendments) 2009 (SSI 2009/294) r.3 (effective December 1, 2009) as substituted by the Act of Sederunt (Amendment of the Act of Sederunt (Sheriff Court Rules) (Miscellaneous Amendments) 2009) 2009 (SSI 2009/402) (effective November 30, 2009).

[2] As inserted by the Act of Sederunt (Ordinary Cause, Summary Application and Small Claim Rules) Amendment (Miscellaneous) 2004 (SSI 2004/197) para.3(2) (effective May 21, 2004).

[3] As amended by the Act of Sederunt (Ordinary Cause, Summary Application and Small Claim Rules) Amendment (Miscellaneous) 2004 (SSI 2004/197) para.3(3) (effective May 21, 2004).

[4] As amended by the Act of Sederunt (Ordinary Cause, Summary Application, Summary Cause and Small Claim Rules) Amendment (Miscellaneous) 2007 (SSI 2007/6), para.3(3) (effective January 29, 2007).

(1A)[1]   A warrant for arrestment on the dependence may be signed by the sheriff, if the sheriff considers it appropriate.

(2)   A warrant containing a period of notice shorter than the period of notice to be given to a defender under rule 3.6(1)(a) or (b), as the case may be, of the Ordinary Cause Rules or any other warrant which the sheriff clerk may not sign, shall be signed by the sheriff.

(3)   Where the sheriff clerk refuses to sign a warrant which he may sign, the party presenting the summary application may apply to the sheriff for the warrant.

(4)   Where citation is necessary—

(a)[2,3]   the warrant of citation shall, subject to paragraphs (5) and (7ZA)(a) and rule 3.18.3(1) (appeals under section 103J of the Local Government (Scotland) Act 1973), be in Form 2; and

(b)[4][5]   citation shall, subject to paragraphs (7) and (7ZA)(b) and rules 2.13 (service where address of person is not known) and 3.18.3(2) (appeals under section 103J of the Local Government (Scotland) Act 1973), be in Form 3.

(5)   Where a time to pay direction under the Debtors (Scotland) Act 1987 or a time order under the Consumer Credit Act 1974 may be applied for by the defender, the warrant of citation shall be in Form 4.

(6)   Where a warrant of citation in accordance with Form 4 is appropriate, there shall be served on the defender (with the initial writ and warrant) a notice in Form 5.

(7)   Where a time to pay direction under the Debtors (Scotland) Act 1987 or a time order under the Consumer Credit Act 1974 may be applied for by the defender, citation shall be in Form 6 which shall be attached to a copy of the initial writ and warrant of citation.

(7ZA)   In an application for enforcement of security over residential property within the meaning of Part IV of Chapter 3—

(a)   the warrant of citation will be in Form 6ZA;

(b)   citation will be in Form 6ZB which is to be attached to a copy of the initial writ,

Form 11C and warrant of citation.

(7A)   *[Repealed by the Act of Sederunt (Sheriff Court Rules) (Enforcement of Securities over Heritable Property) 2010 (SSI 2010/324) para.2 (effective September 30, 2010).]*

(8)   Where citation is necessary, the certificate of citation shall be in Form 7 which shall be attached to the initial writ.

(9)   Where citation is by a sheriff officer, one witness shall be sufficient for the execution of citation.

(10)   Where citation is by a sheriff officer, the certificate of citation shall be signed by the sheriff officer and the witness and shall state—

---

[1] As inserted by the Act of Sederunt (Ordinary Cause, Summary Application and Small Claim Rules) Amendment (Miscellaneous) 2004 (SSI 2004/197) para.3(4) (effective May 21, 2004).

[2] As amended by the Act of Sederunt (Summary Applications, Statutory Applications and Appeals etc. Rules) Amendment (No.2) (Local Government (Scotland) Act 1973) 2002 (SSI 2002/130) para.2(2) (effective March 8, 2002).

[3] As amended by the Act of Sederunt (Sheriff Court Rules)(Miscellaneous Amendments) 2013 (SSI 2013/135) para.2 (effective May 27, 2013).

[4] As amended by the Act of Sederunt (Summary Applications, Statutory Applications and Appeals etc. Rules) Amendment (No.2) (Local Government (Scotland) Act 1973) 2002 (SSI 2002/130) para.2(2) (effective March 8, 2002).

[5] As amended by the Act of Sederunt (Sheriff Court Rules)(Miscellaneous Amendments) 2013 (SSI 2013/135) para.2 (effective May 27, 2013).

    (a)   the method of citation; and

    (b)   where the method of citation was other than personal or postal citation, the full name and designation of any person to whom the citation was delivered.

   (11)   Where citation is executed under paragraph (3) of rule 2.11 (depositing or affixing by sheriff officer), the certificate shall include a statement—

    (a)   of the method of service previously attempted;

    (b)   of the circumstances which prevented such service being executed; and

    (c)   that a copy of the document was sent in accordance with the provisions of paragraph (4) of that rule.

Orders against which caveats may be lodged

   2.8 *[Omitted by Act of Sederunt (Sheriff Court Caveat Rules) 2006 (SI 2006/ 198), effective April 28, 2006]*

Form, lodging and renewal of caveats

   2.9 *[Omitted by Act of Sederunt (Sheriff Court Caveat Rules) 2006 (SI 2006/ 198), effective April 28, 2006]*

Postal service or intimation

   2.10—(1)   In any summary application in which service or intimation of any document or citation of any person may be by recorded delivery, such service, intimation or citation shall be by the first class recorded delivery service.

   (2)   Notwithstanding the terms of section 4(2) of the Citation Amendment (Scotland) Act 1882 (time from which period of notice reckoned), where service or intimation is by post, any period of notice contained in the warrant of citation shall run from the beginning of the day after the date of posting.

   (3)   On the face of the envelope used for postal service or intimation under this rule there shall be written or printed the following notice:—

    "This envelope contains a citation to or intimation from *(specify the court)*. If delivery cannot be made at the address shown it is to be returned immediately to:— The Sheriff Clerk *(insert address of sheriff clerk's office)*.".

   (4)   The certificate of citation or intimation in the case of postal service shall have attached to it any relevant postal receipts.

Service within Scotland by sheriff officer

   2.11—(1)   An initial writ, decree, charge, warrant or any other order or writ following upon such initial writ or decree served by a sheriff officer on any person shall be served—

    (a)   personally; or

    (b)   by being left in the hands of a resident at the person's dwelling place or an employee at his place of business.

   (2)   Where service is executed under paragraph (1)(b), the certificate of citation or service shall contain the full name and designation of any person in whose hands the initial writ, decree, charge, warrant or other order or writ, as the case may be, was left.

   (3)   Where a sheriff officer has been unsuccessful in executing service in accordance with paragraph (1), he may, after making diligent enquiries, serve the document question by—

    (a)   depositing it in that person's dwelling place or place of business; or (b)[1]   by leaving it at that person's dwelling place or place of business in such a way that it is likely to come to the attention of that person.

(4)   Subject to rule 2.18 (service of schedule of arrestment), where service is executed under paragraph (3), the sheriff officer shall, as soon as possible after such service, send a letter containing a copy of the document by ordinary first class post to the address at which he thinks it most likely that the person on whom service has been executed may be found.

(5)[2]   Where the firm which employs the sheriff officer has in its possession—

(a)   the document or a copy of it certified as correct by the pursuer's solicitor, the sheriff officer may serve the writ upon the defender without having the document or certified copy in his possession, in which case he shall if required to do so by the person on whom service is executed and within a reasonable time of being so required, show the document or certified copy to the person; or

(b)   a certified copy of the interlocutor pronounced allowing service of the document, the sheriff officer may serve the document without having in his possession the certified copy interlocutor if he has in his possession a facsimile copy of the certified copy interlocutor (which he shall show, if required, to the person on whom service is executed).

(6)[3]   Where service is executed under paragraphs (1)(b) or (3), the document and the citation or notice of intimation, as the case may be, must be placed in an envelope bearing the notice "This envelope contains a citation to or intimation from (*insert name of sheriff court*) " and sealed by the sheriff officer.

Service on persons furth of Scotland

2.12—[4, 5](1)   Subject to the following provisions of this rule, an initial writ, decree, charge, warrant or any other order or writ following upon such initial writ or decree served on a person furth of Scotland shall be served—

(a)   at a known residence or place of business in England, Wales, Northern Ireland, the Isle of Man, the Channel Islands or any country with which the United Kingdom does not have a convention providing for service of writs in that country—

(i)   in accordance with the rules for personal service under the domestic law of the place in which service is to be executed; or

(ii)   by posting in Scotland a copy of the document in question in a registered letter addressed to the person at his residence or place of business;

---

[1] As substituted by the Act of Sederunt (Sheriff Court Rules) (Miscellaneous Amendments) 2011 (SSI 2011/193) r.3 (effective April 4, 2011).

[2] As inserted by the Act of Sederunt (Ordinary Cause, Summary Application, Summary Cause and Small Claim Rules) Amendment (Miscellaneous) 2003 (SSI 2003/26), para.3(3) (effective 24 January 2003).

[3] As inserted by the Act of Sederunt (Sheriff Court Rules) (Miscellaneous Amendments) 2011 (SSI 2011/193) r.3 (effective 4 April 2011).

[4] As amended by the Act of Sederunt (Ordinary Cause, Summary Application, Summary Cause and Small Claim Rules) Amendment (Miscellaneous) 2003 (SSI 2003/26), para.3(4) (effective 24 January 2003).

[5] As amended and inserted by the Act of Sederunt (Ordinary Cause, Summary Application and Small Claim Rules) Amendment (Miscellaneous) 2004 (SSI 2004/197) (effective 21 May 2004), para.3(5) and substituted by the Act of Sederunt (Sheriff Court Ordinary Cause, Summary Application, Summary Cause and Small Claims Rules) Amendment (Council Regulation (EC) No. 1348 of 2000 Extension to Denmark) 2007 (SSI 2007/440) r.3(2) (effective 9 October 2007).

(b)[1] in a country which is a party to the Hague Convention on the Service Abroad of Judicial and Extra-Judicial Documents in Civil or Commercial Matters dated 15th November 1965 or the Convention in Schedule 1 or 3C to the Civil Jurisdiction and Judgments Act 1982—

    (i) by a method prescribed by the internal law of the country where service is to be executed for the service of documents in domestic actions upon persons who are within its territory;

    (ii)[2] by or through the central, or other appropriate, authority in the country where service is to be executed at the request of the Scottish Ministers;

    (iii) by or through a British Consular Office in the country where service is to be executed at the request of the Secretary of State for Foreign, Commonwealth and Development Affairs;

    (iv) where the law of the country in which the person resides permits, by posting in Scotland a copy of the document in a registered letter addressed to the person at his residence; or

    (v) where the law of the country in which service is to be executed permits, service by an *huissier*, other judicial officer or competent official of the country where service is to be executed; or

(c) in a country with which the United Kingdom has a convention on the service of writs in that country other than the conventions mentioned in sub-paragraph (b), by one of the methods approved in the relevant convention.

(1A)[3, 4] In a country to which the EC Service Regulation applies, service—

(a) may be effected by the methods prescribed in paragraph (1)(b)(ii) or (iii) only in exceptional circumstances; and

(b) is effected only if the receiving agency has informed the person that acceptance of service may be refused on the ground that the document has not been translated in accordance with paragraph (6).

(2) Any document which requires to be posted in Scotland for the purposes of this rule shall be posted by a solicitor or a sheriff officer, and on the face of the envelope there shall be written or printed the notice set out in rule 2.10(3).

(3) In the case of service by a method referred to in paragraph (1)(b)(ii) and (iii), the pursuer shall—

(a)[5, 6] send a copy of the writ and warrant of service with citation attached, or other document, as the case may be, with a request for service by the

---

[1] As amended by the Transfer of Functions (Secretary of State for Foreign, Commonwealth and Development Affairs) Order 2020 (SI 2020/942) Sch.1(2) para.14 (effective 30 September 2020).

[2] As substituted by the Act of Sederunt (Sheriff Court Rules) (Miscellaneous Amendments) 2011 (SSI 2011/193) r.6 (effective 4 April 2011).

[3] As amended and inserted by the Act of Sederunt (Ordinary Cause, Summary Application and Small Claim Rules) Amendment (Miscellaneous) 2004 (SSI 2004/197) (effective 21 May 2004), para.3(5) and substituted by the Act of Sederunt (Sheriff Court Ordinary Cause, Summary Application, Summary Cause and Small Claims Rules) Amendment (Council Regulation (EC) No. 1348 of 2000 Extension to Denmark) 2007 (SSI 2007/440) r.3(2) (effective 9 October 2007).

[4] As amended by the Act of Sederunt (Sheriff Court Rules) (Miscellaneous Amendments) (No.2) 2008 (SSI 2008/365) r.8(a) (effective 13 November 2008).

[5] As amended by the Act of Sederunt (Sheriff Court Rules) (Miscellaneous Amendments) 2011 (SSI 2011/193) r.7 (effective 4 April 2011).

[6] As amended by the Transfer of Functions (Secretary of State for Foreign, Commonwealth and Development Affairs) Order 2020 (SI 2020/942) Sch.1(2) para.14 (effective 30 September 2020).

method indicated in the request to the Scottish Ministers or, as the case may be, the Secretary of State for Foreign, Commonwealth and Development Affairs; and

(b) lodge in process a certificate signed by the authority which executed service stating that it has been, and the manner in which it was, served.

(4) In the case of service by a method referred to in paragraph (1)(b)(v), the pursuer or the sheriff officer shall—

(a) send a copy of the writ and warrant for service with citation attached, or other document, as the case may be, with a request for service by the method indicated in the request to the official in the country in which service is to be executed; and

(b) lodge in process a certificate of the official who executed service stating that it has been, and the manner in which it was, served.

(5) Where service is executed, in accordance with paragraph (1)(a)(i) or (1)(b)(i) other than on another party in the United Kingdom, the Isle of Man or the Channel Islands, the party executing service shall lodge a certificate by a person who is conversant with the law of the country concerned and who practises or has practised law in that country or is a duly accredited representative of the Government of that country, stating that the method of service employed is in accordance with the law of the place where service was executed.

(6) Every writ, document, citation or notice on the face of the envelope mentioned in rule 2.10(3) shall be accompanied by a translation in—

(a)[1] an official language of the country in which service is to be executed; or

(b) in a country to which the EC Service Regulation applies, a language of the member state of transmission that is understood by the person on whom service is being executed.

(7) A translation referred to in paragraph (6) shall be certified as correct by the person making it and the certificate shall—

(a) include his full name, address and qualifications; and

(b) be lodged with the execution of citation or service.

(8)[2] In this rule "the EC Service Regulation" means Regulation (EC) No. 1393/2007 of the European Parliament and of the Council of 13th November 2007 on the service in the Member States of judicial and extrajudicial documents in civil or commercial matters (service of documents), and repealing Council Regulation (EC) No. 1348/2000, as amended from time to time.

Service where address of person is not known

2.13—(1) Where the address of a person to be cited or served with a document is not known and cannot reasonably be ascertained, the sheriff shall grant warrant for citation or service upon that person by—

(a) the publication of an advertisement in Form 9 in a specified newspaper circulating in the area of the last known address of that person; or

(b) displaying on the walls of court a copy of the instance and crave of the initial writ, the warrant of citation and a notice in Form 10;

---

[1] As amended and inserted by the Act of Sederunt (Ordinary Cause, Summary Application and Small Claim Rules) Amendment (Miscellaneous) 2004 (SSI 2004/197) (effective 21 May 2004), para.3(5) and substituted by the Act of Sederunt (Sheriff Court Ordinary Cause, Summary Application, Summary Cause and Small Claims Rules) Amendment (Council Regulation (EC) No. 1348 of 2000 Extension to Denmark) 2007 (SSI 2007/440) r.3(2) (effective 9 October 2007).

[2] As substituted by the Act of Sederunt (Sheriff Court Rules) (Miscellaneous Amendments) (No.2) 2008 (SSI 2008/365) r.8(b) (effective 13 November 2008).

and any period of notice contained in the warrant of citation shall run from the date of publication of the advertisement or display on the walls of court, as the case may be.

(2)   Where service requires to be executed under paragraph (1), the pursuer shall lodge a service copy of the initial writ and a copy of any warrant of citation with the sheriff clerk from whom they may be uplifted by the person for whom they are intended.

(3)   Where a person has been cited or served in accordance with paragraph (1) and, after the summary application has commenced, his address becomes known, the sheriff may allow the initial writ to be amended subject to such conditions as to re-service, intimation, expenses or transfer of the summary application as he thinks fit.

(4)   Where advertisement in a newspaper is required for the purpose of citation or service under this rule, a copy of the newspaper containing the advertisement shall be lodged with the sheriff clerk by the pursuer.

(5)   Where display on the walls of court is required under paragraph (1)(b), the pursuer shall supply to the sheriff clerk for that purpose a certified copy of the instance and crave of the initial writ and any warrant of citation.

Persons carrying on business under trading or descriptive name

2.14—(1)   A person carrying on a business under a trading or descriptive name may be designed in the instance of the initial writ by such trading or descriptive name alone, and an extract of a—

(a)   decree pronounced in the sheriff court; or

(b)   decree proceeding upon any deed, decree arbitral, bond, protest of a bill, promissory note or banker's note or upon any other obligation or document on which execution may proceed, recorded in the sheriff court books,

against such person under such trading or descriptive name, shall be a valid warrant for diligence against such person.

(2)   An initial writ, decree, charge, warrant or any other order or writ following upon such initial writ or decree in a summary application in which a person carrying on business under a trading or descriptive name is designed in the instance of the initial writ by that name shall be served—

(a)   at any place of business or office at which such business is carried on within the sheriffdom of the sheriff court in which the cause is brought; or

(b)   where there is no place of business within that sheriffdom, at any place where such business is carried on (including the place of business or office of the clerk or secretary of any company, corporation or association or firm).

Endorsation unnecessary

2.15   An initial writ, decree, charge, warrant or any other order or writ following upon such initial writ or decree may be served, enforced or otherwise lawfully executed anywhere in Scotland without endorsation by a sheriff clerk and, if executed by a sheriff officer, may be so executed by a sheriff officer of the court which granted it or by a sheriff officer of the sheriff court district in which it is to be executed.

Re-service

2.16   Where it appears to the sheriff that there has been any failure or irregularity in citation or service on a person, he may order the pursuer to re-serve the initial writ on such conditions as the sheriff thinks fit.

No objection to regularity of citation, service or intimation

2.17—(1)   A person who appears in a summary application shall not be entitled to state any objection to the regularity of the execution of citation, service or intimation on him, and his appearance shall remedy any defect in such citation, service or intimation.

(2)   Nothing in paragraph (1) shall preclude a party from pleading that the court has no jurisdiction.

Service of schedule of arrestment

2.18   If a schedule of arrestment has not been personally served on an arrestee, the arrestment shall have effect only if a copy of the schedule is also sent by registered post or the first class recorded delivery service to—

    (a)   the last known place of residence of the arrestee; or

    (b)   if such a place of residence is not known, or if the arrestee is a firm or corporation, to the arrestee's principal place of business if known, or, if not known, to any known place of business of the arrestee,

and the sheriff officer shall, on the certificate of execution, certify that this has been done and specify the address to which the copy of the schedule was sent.

Form of schedule of arrestment on the dependence

2.18A.—[1](1)   An arrestment on the dependence shall be served by serving the schedule of arrestment on the arrestee in Form 10A.

(2)   A certificate of execution shall be lodged with the sheriff clerk in Form 10B.

Arrestment on dependence before service

2.19—(1)   An arrestment on the dependence of a summary application used before service shall cease to have effect if the initial writ is not served within 20 days from the date of arrestment and either—

    (a)   in the case where the pursuer is entitled to minute for decree in absence on the expiry of a period of notice contained in the warrant of citation, decree in absence has not been pronounced within 20 days after the expiry of the period of notice; or

    (b)   in the case where the pursuer is not entitled to minute for decree in absence prior to the first hearing of the summary application, there is no appearance by the pursuer at the first hearing and the summary application drops from the roll.

(2)   After such an arrestment has been executed, the party who executed it shall forthwith report the execution to the sheriff clerk.

---

[1] As inserted by the Act of Sederunt (Sheriff Court Rules Amendment) (Diligence) 2009 (SSI 2009/107) r.4 (effective April 22, 2009).

Movement of arrested property

2.20—(1)   Any person having an interest may apply by motion for a warrant authorising the movement of a vessel or cargo which is the subject of an arrestment to found jurisdiction or on the dependence of a summary application.

(2)   Where the court grants a warrant sought under paragraph (1), it may make such further order as it thinks fit to give effect to that warrant.

Transfer to another sheriff court

2.21—(1)   The sheriff may, on cause shown, remit a summary application to another sheriff court.

(2)   Subject to paragraph (4), where a summary application in which there are two or more defenders has been brought in the sheriff court of the residence or place of business of one of them, the sheriff may transfer the summary application to any other sheriff court which has jurisdiction over any of the defenders.

(3)   Subject to paragraph (4), where a plea of no jurisdiction is sustained, the sheriff may transfer the summary application to the sheriff court before which it appears to him the summary application ought to have been brought.

(4)   The sheriff shall not transfer a summary application to another sheriff court under paragraph (2) or (3) except—

(a)   on the motion of a party; and

(b)   where he considers it expedient to do so having regard to the convenience of the parties and their witnesses.

(5)   On making an or er under paragraph (1), (2) or (3), the sheriff—

(a)   shall state his reasons for doing so in the interlocutor; and

(b)   may make the order on such conditions as to expenses or otherwise as he thinks fit.

(6)   The court to which a summary application is transferred under paragraph (1), (2) or (3) shall accept the summary application.

(7)   A transferred summary application shall proceed in all respects as if it had been originally brought in the court to which it is transferred.

(8)   *[Repealed by the Act of Sederunt (Rules of the Court of Session, Sheriff Appeal Court Rules and Sheriff Court Rules Amendment) (Sheriff Appeal Court) 2015 (SSI 2015/419) r.9(2) (effective 1 January 2016; as to savings see SSI 2015/419 rule 20(5)(a)).]*

Applications for time to pay directions or time orders

2.22—[1](1)   This rule applies to a summary application in which—

(a)   a time to pay direction may be applied for under the Debtors (Scotland) Act 1987; or

(b)   a time order may be applied for under the Consumer Credit Act 1987.

(2)   A defender may apply for a time to pay direction or time order and, where appropriate, for recall or restriction of an arrestment—

(a)   by appearing and making the appropriate motion at a diet fixed for hearing of the summary application;

(b)[2]   except where the warrant of citation contains a shorter period of notice than the period of notice to be given to a defender under rule 3.6(1)(a) or

---

[1] As amended by the Act of Sederunt (Ordinary Cause, Summary Application, Summary Cause and Small Claim Rules) Amendment (Miscellaneous) 2007 (SSI 2007/6), para.3(4) (effective January 29, 2007).

[2] As amended by the Act of Sederunt (Sheriff Court Rules) (Miscellaneous Amendments) 2009 (SSI 2009/294) r.3 (effective December 1, 2009).

(b), as the case may be, of the Ordinary Cause Rules, by completing and returning the appropriate portion of Form 5 to the sheriff clerk at least 14 days before the first diet fixed for hearing of the summary application or the expiry of the period of notice or otherwise, as the case may be in the warrant of citation; or

(c) by application to the court at any stage before final decree.

(3)[1] On lodging an application under paragraph (2)(b), the defender shall send a copy of it to the pursuer by first class ordinary post.

(4)[2] Where the pursuer objects to the application of the defender lodged under paragraph (2)(b) he shall—

(a) complete and lodge with the sheriff clerk Form 5A prior to the date fixed for the hearing of the summary application; and

(b) send a copy of that form to the defender.

(5)[3] The sheriff clerk shall then fix a hearing in relation to the application under paragraph (2)(b) and intimate the hearing to the pursuer and the defender.

(6)[4] The sheriff may determine an application under paragraph (2)(c) without the defender having to appear.

Applications under the Mortgage Rights (Scotland) Act 2001

2.22A *[Repealed by the Act of Sederunt (Sheriff Court Rules) (Enforcement of Securities over Heritable Property) 2010 (SSI 2010/324) para.2 (effective September 30, 2010).]*

Remuneration of assessors

2.23 Where an assessor is appointed by the sheriff to assist him in determining the summary application, the remuneration to be paid to such assessor shall be part of the expenses of the application.

Deposits for expenses

2.24 Where, under any enactment, the sheriff requires the pursuer to deposit a sum of money to cover the expenses of an appeal under the enactment, such sum shall, subject to the provisions of that enactment, not exceed an amount which is twenty-five times the amount of the fee payable at that time in respect of lodging the initial writ.

When decrees extractable

2.25—(1) Subject to the following paragraphs—

(a) subject to sub-paragraph (c), a decree in absence may be extracted after the expiry of 14 days from the date of decree;

---

[1] Para.(3) substituted for paras (3)–(6) by the Act of Sederunt (Sheriff Court Rules) (Miscellaneous Amendments) 2009 (SSI 2009/294) r.3 (effective December 1, 2009).

[2] Para.(3) substituted for paras (3)–(6) by the Act of Sederunt (Sheriff Court Rules) (Miscellaneous Amendments) 2009 (SSI 2009/294) r.3 (effective December 1, 2009).

[3] Para.(3) substituted for paras (3)–(6) by the Act of Sederunt (Sheriff Court Rules) (Miscellaneous Amendments) 2009 (SSI 2009/294) r.3 (effective December 1, 2009).

[4] Para.(3) substituted for paras (3)–(6) by the Act of Sederunt (Sheriff Court Rules) (Miscellaneous Amendments) 2009 (SSI 2009/294) r.3 (effective December 1, 2009).

    (b)   subject to sub-paragraph (c), any decree pronounced in a defended summary application may be extracted at any time after whichever is the later of the following—

        (i)   the expiry of the period within which an application for leave to appeal may be made and no such application has been made;

        (ii)   the date on which leave to appeal has been refused and there is no right of appeal from such refusal;

        (iii)[1]   the expiry of the period within which an appeal may be made and no appeal has been made; or

        (iv)   the date on which an appeal has been finally disposed of; and

    (c)   where the sheriff has, in pronouncing decree, reserved any question of expenses, extract of that decree may be issued only after the expiry of 14 days from the date of the interlocutor disposing of the question of expenses unless the sheriff otherwise directs.

    (2)   The sheriff may, on cause shown, grant a motion to allow extract to be applied for and issued earlier than a date referred to in paragraph (1).

    (3)   In relation to a decree referred to in paragraph (1)(b) or (c), paragraph (2) shall not apply unless—

    (a)   the motion under that paragraph is made in the presence of the parties; or

    (b)   the sheriff is satisfied of proper intimation of the motion has been made in writing to every party not present at the hearing of the motion.

    (4)   Nothing in this rule shall affect the power of the sheriff to supersede extract.

Form of extract decree

2.26   The extract of a decree shall be in Form 11.

Form of warrant for execution

2.27   An extract of a decree on which execution may proceed shall include a warrant for execution in the following terms:— "This extract is warrant for all lawful execution hereon.".

Date of decree in extract

2.28—[2](1)   Where the Sheriff Appeal Court has adhered to the decision of the sheriff following an appeal, the date to be inserted in the extract decree as the date of decree shall be the date of the decision of the Sheriff Appeal Court.

    (2)   Where a decree has more than one date it shall not be necessary to specify in an extract what was done on each date.

Decrees in absence where defender furth of Scotland

2.29—(1)   Where a defender is domiciled in another part of the United Kingdom or in another Contracting State, the sheriff shall not grant decree in absence until it has been shown that the defender has been able to receive the initial writ in sufficient time to arrange for his defence or that all necessary steps have been taken to that end, and for the purposes of this paragraph—

---

[1] As amended by the Act of Sederunt (Rules of the Court of Session, Sheriff Appeal Court Rules and Sheriff Court Rules Amendment) (Sheriff Appeal Court) 2015 (SSI 2015/419) r.9(3) (effective 1 January 2016; as to savings see SSI 2015/419 rule 20(5)(a)).

[2] As amended by the Act of Sederunt (Rules of the Court of Session, Sheriff Appeal Court Rules and Sheriff Court Rules Amendment) (Sheriff Appeal Court) 2015 (SSI 2015/419) r.9(4) (effective 1 January 2016; as to savings see SSI 2015/419 rule 20(5)(a)).

(a) the question whether a person is domiciled in another part of the United Kingdom shall be determined in accordance with sections 41 and 42 of the Civil Jurisdiction and Judgments Act 1982;

(b) the question whether a person is domiciled in another Contracting State shall be determined in accordance with Article 52 of the Convention in Schedule 1 or 3C to that Act, as the case may be; and

(c) the term "Contracting State" has the meaning assigned in section 1 of that Act.

(2) Where an initial writ has keen served in a country to which the Hague Convention on the Service Abroad of Judicial and Extra-Judicial Documents in Civil or Commercial Matters dated 15th November 1965 applies, decree shall not be granted until it is established to the satisfaction of the sheriff that the requirements of Article 15 of the Convention have been complied with.

Motion procedure

2.30 Except where the sheriff otherwise directs, any motion relating to a summary application shall be made in accordance with, and regulated by, Chapter 15 of the Ordinary Cause Rules.

Power of sheriff to make orders

2.31 The sheriff may make such order as he thinks fit for the progress of a summary application in so far as it is not inconsistent with section 50 of the Sheriff Courts (Scotland) Act 1907.

Live links

2.32—[1](1) On cause shown, a party may apply by motion for authority for the whole or part of—

(a) the evidence of a witness or the party to be given; or

(b) a submission to be made,

through a live link.

(2) In paragraph (1)—

"witness" means a person who has been or may be cited to appear before the court as a witness, except a vulnerable witness within the meaning of section 11(1) of the 2004 Act;[2]

"submission" means any oral submission which would otherwise be made to the court by the party or his representative in person including an oral submission in support of a motion; and

"live link" means a live television link or such other arrangement as may be specified in the motion by which the witness, party or representative, as the case may be, is able to be seen and heard in the proceedings or heard in the proceedings and is able to see and hear or hear the proceedings while at a place which is outside the courtroom.

---

[1] As inserted by the Act of Sederunt (Ordinary Cause, Summary Application, Summary Cause and Small Claim Rules) Amendment (Miscellaneous) 2007 (SSI 2007/6), para.3(5) (effective January 29, 2007).

[2] As amended by the Act of Sederunt (Ordinary Cause, Summary Application, Summary Cause and Small Claim Rules) Amendment (Vulnerable Witnesses (Scotland) Act 2004) 2007 (SSI 2007/463), r.3(3) (effective November 1, 2007).

Enquiry when fixing hearing

2.33.[1]   Where the sheriff fixes a hearing he shall make enquiry whether there is
or is likely to be a vulnerable witness within the meaning of section 11(1) of the
2004 Act who is to give evidence at any proof or hearing, consider any child witness
notice or vulnerable witness application that has been lodged where no order has
been made and consider whether any order under section 12(1) of the 2004 Act
requires to be made.

Vulnerable witness procedure

2.34.[2]   Except where the sheriff otherwise directs, where a vulnerable witness is
to give evidence in a hearing of a summary application any child witness notice or
vulnerable application relating to the vulnerable witness shall be made in accordance with and regulated by Chapter 45 of the Ordinary Cause Rules.

Representation
2.35.—[3](1)   A party may be represented by any person authorised under any
enactment to conduct proceedings in the sheriff court in accordance with the terms
of that enactment.

(2)   The person referred to in paragraph (1) may do everything for the preparation and conduct of an action as may have been done by an individual conducting
his own action.

Expenses
2.36.—[4](1)   A party who—
  (a)   is or has been represented by a person authorised under any enactment to
         conduct proceedings in the sheriff court; and
  (b)   would have been found entitled to expenses if he had been represented by
         a solicitor or an advocate,
May be awarded expenses or outlays to which a party litigant may be found entitled
under the Litigants in Person (Costs and Expenses) Act 1975 or any enactment
under that Act.

Interventions by the CEHR
2.37.—[5](1)   In this rule and in rule 2.38, "the CEHR" means the Commission
for Equality and Human Rights.

(2)   The CEHR may apply to the sheriff for leave to intervene in any summary
application in accordance with this Rule.

---

[1] As inserted by the Act of Sederunt (Ordinary Cause, Summary Application, Summary Cause and
Small Claim Rules) Amendment (Vulnerable Witnesses (Scotland) Act 2004) 2007 (SSI 2007/463)
r.3(4) (effective November 1, 2007).

[2] As inserted by the Act of Sederunt (Ordinary Cause, Summary Application, Summary Cause and
Small Claim Rules) Amendment (Vulnerable Witnesses (Scotland) Act 2004) 2007 (SSI 2007/463),
r.3(4) (effective November 1, 2007).

[3] As inserted by the Act of Sederunt (Ordinary Cause, Summary Application, Summary Cause and
Small Claim Rules) Amendment (Miscellaneous) 2007 (SSI 2007/6), para.3(5) (effective January 29,
2007).

[4] As renumbered by the Act of Sederunt (Sheriff Court Rules) (Miscellaneous Amendments) 2008 (SSI
2008/223) r.14(2) (effective July 1, 2008).

[5] As inserted by the Act of Sederunt (Sheriff Court Rules) (Miscellaneous Amendments) 2008 (SSI
2008/223) r.5(2) (effective July 1, 2008).

(3)   An application for leave to intervene shall be by way of minute of intervention in Form 11AA and the CEHR shall—

    (a)   send a copy of it to all the parties; and

    (b)   lodge it in process, certifying that sub-paragraph (a) has been complied with.

(4)   A minute of intervention shall set out briefly—

    (a)   the CEHR's reasons for believing that the proceedings are relevant to a matter in connection with which the CEHR has a function;

    (b)   the issue in the proceedings which the CEHR wishes to address; and

    (c)   the propositions to be advanced by the CEHR and the CEHR's reasons for believing that they are relevant to the proceedings and that they will assist the sheriff.

(5)   The sheriff may—

    (a)   refuse leave without a hearing;

    (b)   grant leave without a hearing unless a hearing is requested under paragraph (6);

    (c)   refuse or grant leave after such a hearing.

(6)   A hearing, at which the applicant and the parties may address the court on the matters referred to in paragraph (8)(c) may be held if, within 14 days of the minute of intervention being lodged, any of the parties lodges a request for a hearing.

(7)   Any diet in pursuance of paragraph (6) shall be fixed by the sheriff clerk who shall give written intimation of the diet to the CEHR and all the parties.

(8)   The sheriff may grant leave only if satisfied that—

    (a)   the proceedings are relevant to a matter in connection with which the CEHR has a function;

    (b)   the propositions to be advanced by the CEHR are relevant to the proceedings and are likely to assist him; and

    (c)   the intervention will not unduly delay or otherwise prejudice the rights of the parties, including their potential liability for expenses.

(9)   In granting leave the sheriff may impose such terms and conditions as he considers desirable in the interests of justice, including making provision in respect of any additional expenses incurred by the parties as a result of the intervention.

(10)   The sheriff clerk shall give written intimation of a grant or refusal of leave to the CEHR and all the parties.

(11)   This rule is without prejudice to any other entitlement of the CEHR by virtue of having title and interest in relation to the subject matter of any proceedings by virtue of section 30(2) of the Equality Act 2006 or any other enactment to seek to be sisted as a party in those proceedings.

(12)   Nothing in this rule shall affect the power of the sheriff to make such other direction as he considers appropriate in the interests of justice.

(13)   Any decision of the sheriff in proceedings under this rule and rule 2.38 shall be final and not subject to appeal.

Form of intervention

2.38.—[1](1)   An intervention by the CEHR shall be by way of a written submission which (including any appendices) shall not exceed 5000 words.

(2)   The CEHR shall lodge the submission and send a copy of it to all the parties by such time as the sheriff may direct.

---

[1] As inserted by the Act of Sederunt (Sheriff Court Rules) (Miscellaneous Amendments) 2008 (SSI 2008/223) r.5(2) (effective July 1, 2008).

(3)   The sheriff may in exceptional circumstances—

(a)   allow a longer written submission to be made;

(b)   direct that an oral submission is to be made.

(4)   Any diet in pursuance of paragraph (3)(b) shall be fixed by the sheriff clerk who shall give written intimation of the diet to the CEHR and all the parties.

Interventions by the SCHR

2.39.—[1](1)   In this rule and in rules 2.40 and 2.41—

"the Act of 2006" means the Scottish Commission for Human Rights Act 2006;

"the SCHR" means the Scottish Commission for Human Rights.

(2)   An application for leave to intervene shall be by way of minute of intervention in Form 11AB and the SCHR shall—

(a)   send a copy of it to all the parties; and

(b)   lodge it in process, certifying that subparagraph (a) has been complied with.

(3)   In granting leave the sheriff may impose such terms and conditions as he considers desirable in the interests of justice, including making provision in respect of any additional expenses incurred by the parties as a result of the intervention.

(4)   The sheriff clerk shall give written intimation of a grant or refusal of leave to the SCHR and all the parties.

(5)   Any decision of the sheriff in proceedings under this rule and rules 2.40 and 2.41 shall be final and not subject to appeal.

Invitations to intervene

2.40.—[2](1)   An invitation to intervene under section 14(2)(b) of the Act of 2006 shall be in Form 11AC and the sheriff clerk shall send a copy of it to the SCHR and all the parties.

(2)   An invitation under paragraph (1) shall be accompanied by—

(a)   a copy of the pleadings in the proceedings; and

(b)   such other documents relating to those proceedings as the sheriff thinks relevant.

(3)   In issuing an invitation under section 14(2)(b) of the Act of 2006, the sheriff may impose such terms and conditions as he considers desirable in the interests of justice, including making provision in respect of any additional expenses incurred by the parties as a result of the intervention.

Form of intervention

2.41.—[3](1)   An intervention by the SCHR shall be by way of a written submission which (including any appendices) shall not exceed 5000 words.

(2)   The SCHR shall lodge the submission and send a copy of it to all the parties by such time as the sheriff may direct.

(3)   The sheriff may in exceptional circumstances—

(a)   allow a longer written submission to be made;

(b)   direct that an oral submission is to be made.

---

[1] As inserted by the Act of Sederunt (Sheriff Court Rules) (Miscellaneous Amendments) 2008 (SSI 2008/223) r.5(2) (effective July 1, 2008).

[2] As inserted by the Act of Sederunt (Sheriff Court Rules) (Miscellaneous Amendments) 2008 (SSI 2008/223) r.5(2) (effective July 1, 2008).

[3] As inserted by the Act of Sederunt (Sheriff Court Rules) (Miscellaneous Amendments) 2008 (SSI 2008/223) r.5(2) (effective July 1, 2008).

(4) Any diet in pursuance of paragraph (3)(b) shall be fixed by the sheriff clerk who shall give written intimation of the diet to the SCHR and all the parties.

Lodging audio or audio-visual recordings of children

2.42.—[1](1) In this rule "child" is a person under the age of 16 on the date of commencement of the proceedings and "children" shall be construed accordingly.

(2) Except where the sheriff otherwise directs, where a party seeks to lodge an audio or audio-visual recording of a child as a production in a summary application, this shall be done in accordance with and regulated by Chapter 50 of the Ordinary Cause Rules.

(3)[2] A party who has lodged a recording of a child shall—

(a) within 14 days after the final determination of the application, where no subsequent appeal has been made, or

(b) within 14 days after the disposal of any appeal made on the final determination of the application,

uplift the recording from process.

(4) Where a recording has not been uplifted as required by paragraph (3), the sheriff clerk shall intimate to—

(a) the solicitor who lodged the recording, or

(b) where no solicitor is acting, the party or such other party as seems appropriate,

that if he or she fails to uplift the recording within 28 days after the date of such intimation, it will be disposed of in such a manner as the sheriff directs.

Chapter 3

Rules on Applications under Specific Statutes

Part I

Administration of Justice (Scotland) Act 1972

Interpretation and application

3.1.1—[3](1) In this Part,

(a) "the Act" means the Administration of Justice (Scotland) Act 1972; and

(b) "listed items" means a list of the documents and other property which the applicant in terms of rule 3.1.2 wishes to be made the subject of the order.

(2) This Part applies to applications under section 1(1) of the Act.

Applications under section 1(1) of the Act

3.1.2—(1) An application for an order under section 1(1) of the Act (orders for inspection of documents and other property, etc.) shall be made by summary application where the proceedings in respect of which the application is made have not been commenced.

---

[1] As inserted by the Act of Sederunt (Sheriff Court Rules) (Miscellaneous Amendments) (No.3) 2012 (SSI 2012/271) para.3 (effective November 1, 2012).

[2] As amended by the Act of Sederunt (Rules of the Court of Session, Sheriff Appeal Court Rules and Sheriff Court Rules Amendment) (Sheriff Appeal Court) 2015 (SSI 2015/419) r.9(5) (effective 1 January 2016; as to savings see SSI 2015/419 rule 20(5)(a)).

[3] As amended by the Act of Sederunt (Summary Applications, Statutory Applications and Appeals etc. Rules) Amendment (No.2) (Administration of Justice (Scotland) Act 1972) 2000 (SSI 2000/387) (effective November 20, 2000).

(2)[1]   The summary application shall contain—

(a)   the listed items;

(b)   the address of the premises within which the applicant believes the listed items are to be found; and

(c)   the facts which give rise to the applicant's belief that, were the order not to be granted, the listed items, or any of them, would cease to be available for the purposes of section 1 of the Act.

Accompanying documents

3.1.3[2]   The applicant shall lodge with the summary application—

(a)   an affidavit supporting the averments in the summary application; and

(b)   an undertaking by the applicant that he—

(i)   will comply with any order of the sheriff as to payment of compensation if it is subsequently discovered that the order, or the implementation of the order, has caused loss to the respondent or, where the haver is not the respondent, to the haver;

(ii)   will bring within a reasonable time of the execution of the order any proceedings which he decides to bring; and

(iii)   will not, without leave of the sheriff, use any information, documents or other property obtained as a result of the order, except for the purpose of any proceedings which he decides to bring and to which the order relates.

Modification of undertakings

3.1.4[3]   The sheriff may, on cause shown, modify, by addition, deletion or substitution, the undertaking mentioned in rule 3.1.3.

Intimation and service of application

3.1.5—[4](1)   Before granting the summary application, the sheriff may order such intimation or service of the summary application to be given or executed, as the case may be, as he thinks fit.

(2)   Any person receiving intimation or service of the summary application by virtue of an order under paragraph (1) may appear and oppose the summary application.

---

[1] As inserted by the Act of Sederunt (Summary Applications, Statutory Applications and Appeals etc. Rules) Amendment (No.2) (Administration of Justice (Scotland) Act 1972) 2000 (SSI 2000/387) r.2(4) (effective November 20, 2000).

[2] As inserted by the Act of Sederunt (Summary Applications, Statutory Applications and Appeals etc. Rules) Amendment (No.2) (Administration of Justice (Scotland) Act 1972) 2000 (SSI 2000/387) r.2(4) (effective November 20, 2000).

[3] As inserted by the Act of Sederunt (Summary Applications, Statutory Applications and Appeals etc. Rules) Amendment (No.2) (Administration of Justice (Scotland) Act 1972) 2000 (SSI 2000/387) r.2(4) (effective November 20, 2000).

[4] As inserted by the Act of Sederunt (Summary Applications, Statutory Applications and Appeals etc. Rules) Amendment (No.2) (Administration of Justice (Scotland) Act 1972) 2000 (SSI 2000/387) r.2(4) (effective November 20, 2000).

Form of order

3.1.6[1] An order made under this Part shall—
  (a) be in Form 11A; and
  (b) include in addition a warrant of citation in Form 2.

Caution and other security

3.1.7[2] On granting, in whole or in part, the summary application the sheriff may order the applicant to find such caution or other security as he thinks fit.

Execution of an order

3.1.8[3] The order made in terms of rule 3.1.6 shall be served by the Commissioner in person and it shall be accompanied by a copy of the affidavit referred to in rule 3.1.3(a).

Duties of a Commissioner

3.1.9[4] The Commissioner appointed by the sheriff shall, on executing the order—
  (a) give to the haver a copy of the notice in Form 11B;
  (b) explain to the haver—
       (i) the meaning and effect of the order; and
       (ii) that he may be entitled to claim that some or all of the listed items are confidential or privileged;
  (c)[5] inform the haver of his right to seek legal advice and to ask the sheriff to vary or recall the order;
  (d) enter the premises and take all reasonable steps to fulfil the terms of the order;
  (e) where the order has authorised the recovery of any of the listed items, prepare an inventory of all the listed items to be recovered before recovering them; and
  (f) send any recovered listed items to the sheriff clerk to await the further order of the sheriff.

---

[1] As inserted by the Act of Sederunt (Summary Applications, Statutory Applications and Appeals etc. Rules) Amendment (No.2) (Administration of Justice (Scotland) Act 1972) 2000 (SSI 2000/387) r.2(4) (effective November 20, 2000).

[2] As inserted by the Act of Sederunt (Summary Applications, Statutory Applications and Appeals etc. Rules) Amendment (No.2) (Administration of Justice (Scotland) Act 1972) 2000 (SSI 2000/387) r.2(4) (effective November 20, 2000).

[3] As inserted by the Act of Sederunt (Summary Applications, Statutory Applications and Appeals etc. Rules) Amendment (No.2) (Administration of Justice (Scotland) Act 1972) 2000 (SSI 2000/387) r.2(4) (effective November 20, 2000).

[4] As inserted by the Act of Sederunt (Summary Applications, Statutory Applications and Appeals etc. Rules) Amendment (No.2) (Administration of Justice (Scotland) Act 1972) 2000 (SSI 2000/387) r.2(4) (effective November 20, 2000).

[5] As amended by the Act of Sederunt (Sheriff Court Rules) (Miscellaneous Amendments) (No.3) 2011 (SSI 2011/386) para.6 (effective November 28, 2011).

Confidentiality

3.1.10—[1](1)   Where confidentiality is claimed for any listed item, that listed item shall, where practicable, be enclosed in a sealed envelope.

(2)   A motion to have such a sealed envelope opened may be made by the party who obtained the order and he shall intimate the terms of the motion, by registered post or first class recorded delivery, to the person claiming confidentiality.

(3)   A person claiming confidentiality may oppose a motion made under paragraph (2).

Restrictions on service

3.1.11—[2](1)   Except on cause shown, the order may be served on Monday to Friday only, between the hours of 9am and 5pm only.

(2)   The order shall not be served at the same time as a search warrant granted in the course of a criminal investigation.

(3)   The Commissioner may be accompanied only by—

(a)   any person whom he considers necessary to assist him to execute the order;

(b)   such representatives of the applicant as are named in the order, and if it is likely that the premises will be occupied by an unaccompanied female and the Commissioner is not female, one of the people accompanying the Commissioner shall be female.

(4)   If it appears to the Commissioner when he comes to serve the order that the premises are occupied by an unaccompanied female and the Commissioner is neither female nor accompanied by a female, the Commissioner shall not enter the premises.

Right of haver to consult

3.1.12—[3](1)   The haver may seek legal or other professional advice of his or her choice.

(2)   Where the purpose of seeking this advice is to help the haver to decide whether to ask the sheriff to vary or recall the order, the haver may ask the Commissioner to delay starting the search for up to 2 hours or such other longer period as the Commissioner may permit.

(3)   Where the haver is seeking advice under this rule, he or she must—

(a)   inform the Commissioner and the applicant's agent of that fact;

(b)   not disturb or remove any listed items;

---

[1] As inserted by the Act of Sederunt (Summary Applications, Statutory Applications and Appeals etc. Rules) Amendment (No.2) (Administration of Justice (Scotland) Act 1972) 2000 (SSI 2000/387) r.2(4) (effective November 20, 2000).

[2] As inserted by the Act of Sederunt (Summary Applications, Statutory Applications and Appeals etc. Rules) Amendment (No.2) (Administration of Justice (Scotland) Act 1972) 2000 (SSI 2000/387) r.2(4) (effective November 20, 2000).

[3] As inserted by the Act of Sederunt (Summary Applications, Statutory Applications and Appeals etc. Rules) Amendment (No. 2) (Administration of Justice (Scotland) Act 1972) 2000 (SSI 2000/387) (effective November 20, 2000) and substituted by the Act of Sederunt (Sheriff Court Rules) (Miscellaneous Amendments) (No.3) 2011 (SSI 2011/386) para.6 (effective November 28, 2011).

(c)   permit the Commissioner to enter the premises, but not to start the search.

Part II

Betting and Gaming Appeals

[Revoked by the Act of Sederunt (Sheriff Court Rules) (Miscellaneous Amendments) 2008 (SSI 2008/223) para.14(3)(effective July 1, 2008).]

Part III

Coal Mining Subsidence Act 1991

Interpretation and application

3.3.1—(1)   In this Part—

"the Act" means the Coal Mining Subsidence Act 1991;

"agreement or consent" means the agreement or consent referred to in section 41 of the Act);

"person" means a person referred to in section 41 of the Act;

"any person with responsibility for subsidence affecting any land" has the meaning given in section 43 of the Coal Industry Act 1994.

(2)   This Part applies to proceedings under section 41 of the Act.

Applications under section 41 of the Act

3.3.2—(1)   An application under section 41 of the Act (disputes about withholding of agreement or consent) shall specify—

(a)   the person with whom any person with responsibility for subsidence affecting any land has reached agreement and from whom any person with responsibility for subsidence affecting any land obtained consent; and

(b)   the steps which have been taken to obtain the agreement or consent of the person who is withholding such agreement or consent.

(2)   An application under section 41 of the Act made in relation to the exercise of a power under section 5(3) or (5) of the Act, shall, when lodged with the sheriff clerk, be accompanied by the notice of proposed remedial action under section 4(2) of the Act.

Part IV[1]

Enforcement of Securities over Heritable Property

Section 1

Interpretation

3.4.1.   In this Part—

"the 1894 Act" means the Heritable Securities (Scotland) Act 1894;

"the 1970 Act" means the Conveyancing and Feudal Reform (Scotland) Act 1970;

---

[1] As substituted by the Act of Sederunt (Sheriff Court Rules) (Enforcement of Securities over Heritable Property) 2010 (SSI 2010/324) para.2 (effective September 30, 2010).

"application for enforcement of security over residential property" means any of the following—

(a) an application under section 24(1B) of the 1970 Act alone ("a 1970 Act only application");

(b) an application under section 5(1) of the 1894 Act, in a case falling within section 5(2) of that Act, alone ("an 1894 Act only application");

(c) an application under paragraphs (a) and (b) together ("a combined 1970 Act and 1894 Act application");

"entitled resident" means—

(a) in a 1970 Act only application, a person falling within the definition of that expression provided by section 24C of the 1970 Act;

(b) in an 1894 Act only application, a person falling within the definition of that expression provided by section 5D of the 1894 Act;

(c) in a combined 1970 Act and 1894 Act application, a person falling within either of those definitions;

"entitled resident application" means any of the following—

(a) an application under section 24B of the 1970 Act alone;

(b) an application under section 5C of the 1894 Act alone;

(c) an application under paragraphs (a) and (b) together.

"pre-action requirements" means—

(a) in a 1970 Act only application, the requirements specified in sections 24A(2) to (6) of the 1970 Act, together with any provision made under section 24A(8) of that Act;

(b) in an 1894 Act only application, the requirements specified in sections 5B(2) to (6) of the 1894 Act, together with any provision made under section 5B(8) of that Act;

(c) in a combined 1970 Act and 1894 Act application, both of those sets of requirements;

"a recall of decree application" means any of the following—

(a) an application under section 24D of the 1970 Act alone;

(b) an application under section 5E of the 1894 Act alone;

(c) an application under paragraphs (a) and (b) together.

Section 2

Disposal of applications under Part II of the 1970 Act for non-residential purposes

3.4.2.—(1) This rule applies to an application or counter-application made by virtue of paragraph (3)(2)(b) of the Act of Sederunt (Sheriff Court Rules) (Enforcement of Securities over Heritable Property) 2010.

(2) An interlocutor of the sheriff disposing of an application or counter-application is final and not subject to appeal except as to a question of title or as to any other remedy granted.

Section 3

Initial writ

3.4.3.—(1) An application for enforcement of security over residential property must include averments that the pre-action requirements have been complied with.

(2) The pursuer must lodge Form 11C with the initial writ.

(3)   The initial writ must specify the name and particulars of all persons known by the pursuer to be entitled residents; and crave warrant for intimation to such persons.

Section 4

Appointment of Hearing

3.4.4.   On an application being submitted under rule 3.4.3, the sheriff must—
   (a)   fix a hearing;
   (b)   appoint service and intimation of the initial writ and Form 11C.

Section 5

Answers
3.4.5.—(1)   Where a defender opposes an application, the sheriff may order answers to be lodged within such period that the sheriff specifies.
   (2)   The answers must—
   (a)   specify the name and particulars of all persons known by the defender to be entitled residents who have not already been named in the initial writ; and crave warrant for intimation to such persons; or
   (b)   state that to the best of the defender's knowledge there are no other entitled residents.

Section 6

Intimation to known entitled residents

3.4.6.   The sheriff must order that a copy of the initial writ together with a notice in Form 11D and Form 11E be intimated to all entitled residents referred to in rules 3.4.3(3) and 3.4.5(2)(a).

Section 7

Application to court by entitled residents
3.4.7.—(1)   This rule applies to an entitled resident application.
   (2)   Such application is to be made by lodging a minute in Form 11E in the principal application to which the application relates.
   (3)   On a Form 11E being lodged, the sheriff must—
   (a)   fix a hearing of the entitled resident application;
   (b)   order parties to lodge answers (where the sheriff considers it appropriate to do so) within such period that the sheriff specifies;
   (c)   order the applicant to serve upon every party and intimate to every entitled resident—
      (i)   a copy of the entitled resident application;
      (ii)   a note of the date, time and place of the hearing.

Section 8

Recall of decree
3.4.8.—(1)   This rule applies to a recall of decree application.
   (2)   Such application is to be made by lodging a minute in Form 11F.

(3)   On a Form 11F being lodged, the sheriff clerk must fix a hearing of the recall of decree application.

(4)   Where a hearing has been fixed under paragraph (3) the person seeking recall must, not less than seven days before the date fixed for the hearing, serve upon every party and intimate to every entitled resident—

  (a)   a copy of the recall of decree application;

  (b)   a note of the date, time and place of the hearing.

(4A)[1]   Where service or intimation under this rule is to be made to a party represented in the cause by a solicitor, a notice sent to such party's solicitor shall be held to be notice to the party.

(5)   At a hearing fixed under paragraph (3), the sheriff must recall the decree so far as not implemented and the hearing will then proceed as a hearing held under rule 3.4.4(a).

(6)   A minute for recall of a decree, when lodged and served or intimated in terms of this rule, will have the effect of preventing any further action being taken to enforce the decree.

(7)   If it appears to the sheriff that there has been any failure or irregularity in service or intimation of the minute for recall of a decree, the sheriff may order re-service or re-intimation of the minute (as the case may be) on such conditions as he or she thinks fit.

(8)   Where the person seeking recall does not appear or is not represented at the hearing for recall, the sheriff will pronounce an interlocutor ordaining that person to appear or be represented at a peremptory diet fixed by the sheriff to state whether or not that person intends to proceed with the person's defence or application, under certification that if that person fails to do so the sheriff may grant decree or make such other order or finding as the sheriff thinks fit.

(9)   The diet fixed in the interlocutor under paragraph (8) must not be less than 14 days after the date of the interlocutor unless the sheriff otherwise orders.

(10)   The sheriff must appoint a party to intimate to the person seeking recall a copy of the interlocutor and a notice in Form 11G.

(11)   Where a person on whom a notice and interlocutor has been intimated under paragraph (10) fails to appear or be represented at a diet fixed under paragraph (8) and to state his or her intention as required by that paragraph, the sheriff may grant decree of new or make such other order or finding as the sheriff thinks fit.

Part V

Copyright, Designs and Trade Marks

Interpretation

3.5.1   In this Part

  "the 1988 Act" means the Copyright, Designs and Patents Act 1988;

  "the 1994 Act" means the Trade Marks Act 1994; and

  "the 1995 Regulations" means the Olympics Association Right (Infringement Proceedings) Regulations 1995.

---

[1] As inserted by the Act of Sederunt (Sheriff Court Rules)(Miscellaneous Amendments) 2013 (SSI 2013/135) para.2 (effective May 27, 2013).

Orders for delivery up, forfeiture, destruction or other disposal

3.5.2 An application to the sheriff made under sections 99, 114, 195, 204, 230, 231 or 298 of the 1988 Act, under sections 16 or 19 of the 1994 Act or under Regulation 3 or 5 of the 1995 Regulations, shall be made—

    (a) by motion or incidental application, as the case may be, where proceedings have been commenced; or

    (b) by summary application where no proceedings have been commenced.

Service of notice on interested persons

3.5.3 Where an application has been made under section 114, 204, 231 or 298 of the 1988 Act, section 19 of the 1994 Act or Regulation 5 of the 1995 Regulations—

    (a) the application shall—

        (i) specify the name and address of any person known or believed by the applicant to have an interest in the subject matter of the application; or

        (ii) state that to the best of the applicant's knowledge and belief no other person has such an interest; and

    (b) the sheriff shall order that there be intimated to any person who has such an interest, a copy of the pleadings and any motion, incidental application or summary application, as the case maybe.

Procedure where leave of court required

3.5.4—(1) Where leave of the court is required under the 1988 Act before the action may proceed, the pursuer shall lodge along with the initial writ or summons a motion or incidental application, as the case may be, stating the grounds upon which leave is sought.

(2) The sheriff may hear the pursuer on the motion or incidental application and may grant or refuse it or make such other order in relation to it as he considers appropriate prior to determination.

(3) Where such motion or incidental application is granted, a copy of the sheriff's interlocutor shall be served upon the defender along with the warrant of citation.

Part VI

Drug Trafficking Act 1994

[Revoked by the Act of Sederunt (Summary Applications, Statutory Applications and Appeals etc. Rules) Amendment (No.5) (Proceeds of Crime Act 2002) 2002 (SSI 2002/563), para.2(3) (effective December 30, 2002), subject to savings outlined in para.2(3).]

Part VII

Licensing (Scotland) Act 1976

Interpretation and application

3.7.1—(1) In this Part, "the Act" means the Licensing (Scotland) Act 1976.

(2) This Part applies to appeals under section 39 of the Act.

Service

3.7.2 The appellant shall serve a copy of the initial writ on—
  (a) the clerk to the licensing board and the chief constable;
  (b) if he was the applicant at the hearing before the licensing board, upon all parties who appeared at the hearing; and
  (c) if he was an objector at the hearing, upon the applicant.

Statement of reasons of licensing board

3.7.3—(1) Where the appellant has received from the licensing board a statement of reasons for its decision, he shall lodge a copy thereof with the sheriff clerk along with the initial writ.

(2) The sheriff may, at any time prior to pronouncing a final interlocutor, require the licensing board to state the ground of refusal of an application and to give their reasons for finding such ground to be established.

Part VIII

Mental Health (Scotland) Act 1984

Interpretation and application

3.8.1—(1) In this Part, "the Act" means the Mental Health (Scotland) Act 1984.

(2) This Part applies to—
  (a) applications for admission submitted to a sheriff under section 21 of the Act;
  (b) guardianship applications submitted to a sheriff under section 40 of the Act; and
  (c) community care applications submitted under section 35A of the Act.

Appointment of hearing

3.8.2—(1) On an application being submitted, the sheriff shall appoint a hearing subject, in the case of an application for admission, to section 21(3A) of the Act.

(2) The sheriff may, where he considers it appropriate in all the circumstances, appoint that the hearing of an application shall take place in a hospital or other place.

Service of application

3.8.3—(1) The sheriff clerk shall serve or cause to be served on the patient a copy of the application, with the exception of any medical recommendation, together with a notice in Form 12.

(2) Where the patient is not a resident patient in a hospital, the notice and copy application shall be served on him personally by sheriff officer.

(3) Where the patient is a resident patient in a hospital, the notice and copy application shall be served together with a notice in Form 13 on his responsible medical officer—
  (a) by first class recorded delivery service; or
  (b) personally by sheriff officer.

(4) Where the patient is already the subject of a guardianship order, the notice and copy application (including any medical recommendations) shall, in addition to any other service required by this rule, be served on the guardian—
  (a) by first class recorded delivery service; or
  (b) personally a sheriff officer.

Duties of responsible medical officer

3.8.4—(1)   On receipt of a notice in Form 13 the responsible medical officer shall, subject to rule 3.8.5(1)—

(a)   deliver the notice in Form 12 to the patient; and

(b)   as soon as practicable thereafter, complete and return to the court a certificate of such delivery in Form 14.

(2)[1]   Where, in the opinion of the responsible medical officer, it would be prejudicial to the patient's health or treatment if the patient were to be present during the proceedings—

(a)   in an application to which rule 3.8.3(3) applies, the responsible medical officer shall set forth his reasons for his opinion in the certificate in Form 14; and

(b)   in any other case, the responsible medical officer or the special medical officer, as the case may be, shall set forth his reasons for his opinion in writing and send them to the sheriff clerk.

Appointment of curator ad litem

3.8.5—(1)   Where two medical certificates are produced stating that it would be prejudicial to the health or treatment of the patient if personal service were effected in terms of rule 3.8.3(2) or 3.8.4(1) the sheriff—

(a)   may dispense with such service; and

(b)   if he does so, shall appoint a curator ad litem to receive the application and represent the interest of that patient.

(2)   The sheriff may appoint a curator ad litem to represent the interests of the patient where he is satisfied that—

(a)   the patient should be excluded from the whole or any part of the proceedings under section 113(2) of the Act; or

(b)   in any other case, it is in all the circumstances appropriate to do so.

(3)   The sheriff clerk shall serve the application on the curator ad litem by handing, or sending by first class recorded delivery service, to him a copy of the application and of the order appointing him as the curator.

Appointment of solicitor by court

3.8.6   Where the patient has indicated that he wishes to be represented at the hearing but has not nominated a representative, the sheriff may appoint a solicitor to take instructions from the patient.

Intimation to representatives

3.8.7   Where in any proceedings under the Act, the sheriff clerk is aware that the patient is represented by any person and that representative would not otherwise receive intimation of any diet, a copy of the notice served on the patient shall be intimated to the representative by the sheriff clerk by first class recorded delivery service.

---

[1] As amended by SSI 2003/26, para.3(5) (clerical error).

Service by sheriff officer

3.8.8—(1)   Where a copy of an application and any notice has been served personally by sheriff officer, he shall prepare and return to the court an execution of such service setting forth in detail the manner and circumstances of such service.

(2)   Where a sheriff officer has been unable to effect personal service under this Part, he shall report to the court the reason why service was not effected.

Variation of conditions of community care order

3.8.9—(1)   Where, after consulting the persons referred to in subsections (1) and (2) of section 35D of the Act (variation of conditions of community care order), an application is made by the special medical officer for the variation of a community care order under that section, the special medical officer shall—

    (a)   complete Form 22 in Schedule 2 to the Mental Health (Prescribed Forms) (Scotland) Regulations 1996; and

    (b)   lodge that form with the sheriff clerk, together with a certified copy of the community care order to which the application for variation relates.

Hearing

3.8.10—(1)   Any hearing to determine an application under rule 3.8.9 shall take place within 28 days after receipt by the sheriff clerk of Form 22 and the community care order referred to in that rule.

(2)   Intimation of the date of the hearing referred to in paragraph (1) shall be given by the Stationery sheriff clerk by first class recorded delivery service to such persons as the sheriff may direct; and any intimation of such date to the patient shall be made personally by sheriff officer.

Appeal against community care order

3.8.11   An application by way of appeal for the revocation of a community care order under section 35F of the Act shall be in Form 15.

Part IX

Proceeds of Crime (Scotland) Act 1995

Interpretation and application

3.9.1—(1)   In this Part—

"the Act" means the Proceeds of Crime (Scotland) Act 1995; and
"administrator" means the person appointed under paragraph 1(1) of Schedule 1 to Act.

(2)   This Part applies to proceedings under sections 28, 29, 30, 31 and 33 of, and paragraphs 1, 2, 4, 6 and 12 of Schedule 1 to, the Act.

Service of restraint orders

3.9.2   Where the sheriff pronounces an interlocutor making a restraint order under section 28(1) of the Act (application for restraint order), the prosecutor shall serve a copy of that interlocutor on every person named in the interlocutor as restrained by the order.

Recall or variation of restraint orders

3.9.3.—(1)   An application to the sheriff under any of the following provisions of the Act shall be made by note in the process containing the interlocutor malting the restraint order to which the application relates—

    (a)   section 29(4) or (5) (recall of restraint orders in relation to realisable property);

    (b)   section 30(3) or (4) (recall of restraint orders in relation to forfeitable property);

    (c)   section 31(1) (variation or recall of restraint order).

(2)   In respect of an application by note under paragraph (1)(c) by a person having an interest for an order for variation or recall under section 31(1)(b) of the Act—

    (a)   *[Revoked by the Act of Sederunt (Ordinary Cause, Summary Application, Summary Cause and Small Claim Rules) Amendment (Miscellaneous) 2005 (SSI 2005/648) r.3(2) (effective January 2, 2006).]*

    (b)   the period of notice for lodging answers to the note shall be 14 days or such other period as the sheriff thinks fit.

Applications for interdict

3.9.4—(1)   An application to the sheriff under section 28(8) of the Act (interdict) may be made—

    (a)   in the application made under section 28(1) of the Act; or

    (b)   if made after a restraint order has been made, by note in the process of the application for that order.

(2)   An application under section 28(8) of the Act by note under paragraph (1)(b) shall not be intimated, served or advertised before that application is granted.

Applications in relation to arrestment

3.9.5—(1)   An application to the sheriff under section 33(1) of the Act (arrestment of property affected by restraint order by the prosecutor for warrant for arrestment may be made—

    (a)   in the application made under section 28(1) of the Act; or

    (b)   if made after a restraint order has been applied for, by note in the process of the application for that order.

(2)   An application to the sheriff under section 33(2) of the Act, to loose, restrict or recall an arrestment shall be made by note in the process of the application for the restraint order.

(3)   An application to the sheriff under section 33(4) of the Act (recall or restriction of arrestment) shall be made by note in the process containing the interlocutor making the restraint order to which the application relates.

Appeals to the Court of Session

3.9.6—(1)   This rule applies to appeals against an interlocutor of the sheriff refusing, varying or recalling or refusing to vary or recall a restraint order.

(2)   An appeal to which this rule applies shall be marked within 14 days after the date of the interlocutor concerned.

(3)   An appeal to which this rule applies shall be marked by writing a note of appeal on the interlocutor sheet, or other written record containing the interlocutor appealed against, or on a separate sheet lodged with the sheriff clerk, in the following terms:— "The applicant appeals to the Court of Session.".

(4)   A note of appeal to which this rule applies shall—

    (a)   be signed by the appellant;

    (b)   bear the date on which it is signed; and

    (c)   where the appellant is represented, specify the name and address of the solicitor or other agent who will be acting for him in the appeal.

(5)   The sheriff clerk shall transmit the process within 4 days after the appeal is marked to the Deputy Principal Clerk of Session.

(6)   Within the period specified in paragraph (5), the sheriff clerk shall—

    (a)   send written notice of the appeal to every other party; and

    (b)   certify on the interlocutor sheet that he has done so.

(7)   Failure of the sheriff clerk to comply with paragraph (6) shall not invalidate the appeal.

Applications for appointment of administrators

3.9.7—(1)   An application to the sheriff under paragraph 1 of Schedule 1 to the Act (appointment of administrators) shall be made—

    (a)   where made after a restraint order has been made, by note in the process of the application for that order; or

    (b)   in any other case, by summary application.

(2)   The notification to be made by the sheriff clerk under paragraph 1(3)(a) of Schedule 1 to the Act shall be made by intimation of a copy of the interlocutor to the person required to give possession of property to an administrator.

Incidental applications in an administration

3.9.8—(1)   An application to the sheriff under any of the following provisions of Schedule to the Act shall be made by note in the process of the application for appointment of the administrator—

    (a)   paragraph 1(1) with respect to an application after appointment of an administrator to require a person to give property to him;

    (b)   paragraph 1(4) (making or altering a requirement or removal of administrator);

    (c)   paragraph 1(5) (appointment of new administrator on death, resignation or removal of administrator);

    (d)   paragraph 2(1)(n) (directions as to functions of administrator);

    (e)   paragraph 4 (directions for application of proceeds).

(2)   An application to the sheriff under any of the following provisions of Schedule 1 to the Act shall be made in the application for appointment of an administrator under paragraph 1(1) of that Schedule or, if made after the application has been made, by note in the process—

    (a)   paragraph 2(1)(o) (special powers of administrator);

    (b)   paragraph 2(3) (vesting of property in administrator);

    (c)   paragraph 12 (order to facilitate the realisation of property).

Requirements where order to facilitate realisation of property considered

3.9.9   Where the sheriff considers making an order under paragraph 12 of Schedule 1 to the Act (order to facilitate the realisation of property)—

    (a)   the sheriff shall fix a date for a hearing in the first instance; and

    (b)   the applicant or noter, as the case may be, shall serve a notice in Form 16 on any person who has an interest in the property.

Documents for Accountant of Court

3.9.10—(1)   A person who has lodged any document in the process of an application for the appointment of an administrator shall forthwith send a copy of that document to the Accountant of Court.

(2)   The sheriff clerk shall transmit to the Accountant of Court any part of the process as the Accountant of Court may request in relation to an administration which is in dependence before the sheriff unless such part of the process is, at the time of request, required by the sheriff.

Procedure for fixing and finding caution

3.9.11   Rules 9 to 12 of the Act of Sederunt (Judicial Factors Rules) 1992 (fixing and finding caution in judicial factories) shall, with the necessary modifications, apply to the fixing and finding of caution by an administrator under this Part as they apply to the fixing and finding of caution by a judicial factor.

Administrator's title to act

3.9.12   An administrator appointed under this Part shall not be entitled to act until he has obtained a copy of the interlocutor appointing him.

Duties of administrator

3.9.13—(1)   The administrator shall, as soon as possible, but within three months after the date of his appointment, lodge with the Accountant of Court—

   (a)   an inventory of the property in respect of which he has been appointed;

   (b)   all vouchers, securities, and other documents which are in his possession; and

   (c)   a statement of that property which he has in his possession or intends to realise.

(2)   An administrator shall maintain accounts of his intromissions with the property in his charge and shall, subject to paragraph (3)—

   (a)   within six months after the date of his appointment; and

   (b)   at six monthly intervals after the first account during the subsistence of his appointment,

lodge with the Accountant of Court an account of his intromissions in such form, with such supporting vouchers and other documents, as the Accountant of Court may require.

(3)   The Accountant of Court may waive the lodging of an account where the administrator certifies that there have been no intromissions during a particular accounting period.

State of funds and scheme of division

3.9.14—(1)   The administrator shall—

   (a)   where there are funds available for division, prepare a state of funds after application of sums in accordance with paragraph 4(2) of Schedule 1 to the Act, and a scheme of division amongst those who held property which has been realised under the Act and lodge them and all relevant documents with the Accountant of Court; or

   (b)   where there are no funds available for division, prepare a state of funds only and lodge it with the Accountant of Court, and give to the Accountant of Court such explanations as he shall require.

(2)   The Accountant of Court shall—

   (a)   make a written report on the state of funds and any scheme of division including such observations as he considers appropriate for consideration by the sheriff; and

(b)   return the state of funds and any scheme of division to the administrator with his report.

(3)   The administrator shall, on receiving the report of the Accountant of Court—

(a)   lodge in process the report, the state of funds and any scheme of division;

(b)   intimate a copy of it to the prosecutor; and

(c)   intimate to each person who held property which has been realised under the Act a notice stating—

     (i)   that the state of funds and scheme of division or the state of funds only, as the case may be, and the report of the Accountant of Court, have been lodged in process; and

    (ii)   the amount for which that person has been ranked, and whether he is to be paid in full, or by a dividend, and the amount of it, or that no funds are available for payment.

Objections to scheme of division

3.9.15—(1)   A person wishing to be heard by the sheriff in relation to the distribution of property under paragraph 4(3) of Schedule 1 to the Act shall lodge a note of objection in the process to which the scheme of division relates within 21 days of the date of the notice intimated under rule 3.9.14(3)(c).

(2)   After the period for lodging a note of objection has expired and no note of objection has been lodged, the administrator may apply by motion for approval of the scheme of division and state of funds, or the state of funds only, as the case may be.

(3)   After the period for lodging a note of objection has expired and a note of objection has been lodged, the sheriff shall dispose of such objection after hearing any objector and the administrator and making such inquiry as he thinks fit.

(4)   If any objection is sustained to any extent, the necessary alterations shall be made to the state of funds and any scheme of division and shall be approved by the sheriff.

Application for discharge of administrator

3.9.16—(1)   Where the scheme of division is approved by the sheriff and the administrator delivered or conveyed to the persons entitled the sums or receipts allocated to them in the scheme, the administrator may apply for his discharge.

(2)   An application to the sheriff for discharge of the administrator shall be made by note in the process of the application under paragraph 1(1) of Schedule 1 to the Act.

Appeals against determination of outlays and remuneration

3.9.17   An appeal to the sheriff under paragraph 6(2) of Schedule 1 to the Act (appeal against a determination by the Accountant of Court) shall be made by note in the process of the application in which the administrator was appointed.

Part X

Rating (Disabled Persons) Act 1978

Interpretation and application

3.10.1—(1)   In this Part, "the Act" means the Rating (Disabled Persons) Act 1978.

(2)   This Part applies to appeals under section 6(5) or 6(5A) of the Act.

Appeals under section 6(5) or 6(5A) of the Act

3.10.2   Any appeal under this Part shall be lodged within 42 days of the date on which the application to the rating authority is refused by the authority.

Part XI

Representation of the People Act 1983

Interpretation and application
3.11.1—[1](1)   In this Part—

"sheriff clerk" means, except in rules 3.11.2, 3.11.22 and 3.11.23 the sheriff clerk of the sheriff court district where the trial of the election petition is to take place;
"the Act" means the Representation of the People Act 1983.
(2)   In this Part—
(a)   rules 3.11.2 to 3.11.21 apply to election petitions under the Act; and
(b)   rules 3.11.22 to 3.11.24 apply to registration appeals under section 56 of the Act where the appellant is a person—
(i)   whose entry in the register is an anonymous entry; or
(ii)   who has applied for such an entry.

Initiation of proceedings
3.11.2—(1)   The election petition shall be lodged with the sheriff clerk of a sheriff court district within which the election questioned has taken place.
(2)   The sheriff clerk shall without delay transmit it to the sheriff principal who shall forthwith appoint—
(a)   the time and place for trial of the petition;
(b)   the amount of the security to be given by the petitioner; and
(c)   if he thinks fit, answers to be lodged within a specified time after service.
(3)   Service in terms of section 136(3) of the Act (security for costs) shall be effected—
(a)   personally within—
(i)   5 days; or
(ii)   such other period as the sheriff principal may appoint, of the giving of security; or
(b)   by first class recorded delivery post within—
(i)   5 days; or
(ii)   such other period as the sheriff principal may appoint, of the giving of security.

Security for expenses by bond of caution
3.11.3—(1)   If the security proposed is in whole or in part by bond of caution, it shall be given by lodging with the sheriff clerk a bond for the amount specified by the sheriff principal.
(2)   Such bond shall—
(a)   recite the nature of the petition; and

---

[1] As substituted by the Act of Sederunt (Summary Applications, Statutory Applications and Appeals etc. Rules) Amendment (Registration Appeals) 2008 (SSI 2008/41), r.2(2) (effective March 17, 2008).

(b)   bind and oblige the cautioner and the petitioner jointly and severally, and their respective heirs, executors and successors whomsoever, that the petitioner shall make payment of all costs, charges and expenses that may be payable by him to any person by virtue of any order or decree pronounced in the petition.

(3)   The sufficiency of the cautioner must be attested to the satisfaction of the sheriff clerk, as in the case of judicial bonds of caution.

Objections to bond of caution

3.11.4—(1)   Objections to a bond of caution shall be lodged with the sheriff clerk within 14 days of service in terms of section 136(3) of the Act.

(2)   Objections shall be heard and disposed of by the sheriff clerk.

(3)   If any objection is allowed, it may be removed by a deposit of such sum of money as the sheriff clerk shall determine, made in the manner provided in rule 3.11.5 and within 5 days after the date of the sheriff clerk's determination.

Security by deposit

3.11.5—(1)   Security tendered in whole or in part by deposit of money shall be made in such bank the sheriff clerk may select.

(2)   The deposit receipt shall be—

(a)   taken in joint name of the petitioner and the sheriff clerk;

(b)   handed to the sheriff clerk; and

(c)   held by the sheriff clerk subject to the orders of the court in the petition.

Amendment of pleadings

3.11.6—(1)   Subject to paragraph (2), the sheriff principal shall have power at any stage to allow petition and any answers to be amended upon such condition as to expenses or otherwise as he shall think fit.

(2)   No amendment altering the ground upon which the election was questioned in the petition as presented shall be competent, except to the extent sanctioned by section 129(6) of the Act (time for presentation or amendment of petition questioning local election).

Notice of date and place of trial

3.11.7—(1)   The sheriff clerk shall, as soon as he receives intimation of the time and place fixed for trial—

(a)   display a notice thereof on the walls of his principal office; and

(b)   send by first class post one copy of such notice to—

    (i)   the petitioner;

    (ii)   the respondent;

    (iii)   the Lord Advocate; and

    (iv)   the returning officer.

(2)   The returning officer on receipt of notice from the sheriff clerk shall forthwith publish the time and place fixed for trial in the area for which the election questioned was held.

(3)   Subject to paragraph (4), display of a notice in accordance with paragraph (1)(a) shall be deemed to be notice in the prescribed manner within the meaning of section 139(1) of the Act (trial of petition) and such notice shall not be vitiated by any miscarriage of or relating to all or any copies sent by post.

(4)   At any time before the trial it shall be competent for any party interested to bring any miscarriage of notice sent by post before the sheriff principal, who shall deal therewith as he may consider fit.

Clerk of court

3.11.8   The sheriff clerk shall attend and act as clerk of court at the trial of the petition.

Shorthand writer's charges

3.11.9   The shorthand writer's charges, as approved by the sheriff principal, shall be paid in the first instance by the petitioner.

Appeals

3.11.10   The application to state a special case referred to in section 146(1) of the (special case for determination of the Court of Session) shall be made by minute in the petition proceedings.

List of votes objected to and of objections

3.11.11—(1)   When a petitioner claims the seat for an unsuccessful candidate, alleging that such candidate had a majority of lawful votes, he and the respondent shall, 5 days before the day fixed for the trial, respectively deliver to the sheriff clerk, and send by first class post to the other party and the Lord Advocate, a list of the votes intended to be objected to, and of the objections to each such vote.

(2)   The sheriff clerk shall allow inspection of such list to all parties concerned.

(3)   No evidence shall be allowed to be given against any vote or in support of any objection not specified in such list, except by leave of the sheriff principal granted upon such terms as to the amendment of the list, postponement of the trial, and payment of expenses as to him may seem fit.

Petition against undue return

3.11.12—(1)   When on the trial of a petition complaining of an undue return and claiming the office for some person, the respondent intends to give evidence to prove that that person was not duly elected, such respondent shall, 5 days before the day appointed for the trial, deliver to the sheriff clerk, and send by first class post to the petitioner and the Lord Advocate, a list of the objections to the election upon which he intends to rely.

(2)   No evidence shall be allowed to be given by a respondent in support of any objection to the election not specified in such list except by leave of the sheriff principal granted upon such terms as to the amendment of the list, postponement of the trial, and payment of expenses as to him may seem fit.

Prescribed officer

3.11.13   The sheriff clerk shall be the prescribed officer for the purposes of sections 143(1) (expense of witnesses) and 155(2) (neglect or refusal to pay costs) of the Act.

Leave to abandon

3.11.14—(1)   Application for leave to withdraw a petition in terms of section 147(1) of the Act (withdrawal of petition), shall be made by minute in Form 17 and shall be preceded by written notice of the intention to make it, sent by first class post to—

(a)   the respondent;

(b)   the Lord Advocate; and

(c)   the returning officer.

(2)   The returning officer shall forthwith publish the fact of his having received such notice in the area for which the election questioned was held.

(3)   The sheriff principal, upon the application being laid before him, shall by interlocutor, fix the time, not being earlier than 8 days after the date of the interlocutor, and place for hearing it.

(4)   The petitioner shall, at least 6 days before the day fixed for the hearing, publish in a newspaper circulating in the district named in the interlocutor a notice in Form 18.

Death of petitioner

3.11.15—(1)   In the event of the death of the sole petitioner, or of the last survivor of several petitioners, the sheriff clerk shall forthwith, upon the fact being brought to his knowledge, insert in a newspaper circulating in the district a notice in Form 19.

(2)   The time within which any person who might have been a petitioner in respect of the election may apply to the court by minute in the petition proceedings to be substituted as a petitioner shall be 21 days from the date of publication of such notice.

Notice by respondent that he does not oppose petition

3.11.16—(1)   Notice that a respondent does not intend to oppose a petition shall be given by leaving a written notice to that effect at the office of the sheriff clerk at least 6 days (exclusive of the day of leaving such notice) before the day fixed for the trial.

(2)   On such notice being left with the sheriff clerk, or on its being brought to his knowledge that a respondent other than a returning officer has died, resigned, or otherwise ceased to hold the office to which the petition relates, the sheriff clerk shall forthwith—

(a)   advertise the fact once in a newspaper circulating in the district; and

(b)   send intimation thereof by first class post to—

(i)   the petitioner;

(ii)   the Lord Advocate; and

(iii)   the returning officer, who shall publish the fact in the district.

(3)   The advertisement to be made by the sheriff clerk shall state the last day on which, under this Part, application to be admitted as a respondent to oppose the petition can be made.

Application to be admitted as respondent

3.11.17   Application to be admitted as a respondent to oppose a petition on the occurrence of any of the events mentioned in section 153(1) of the Act (withdrawal and substitution of respondents before trial) must be made by minute in the petition proceedings within 10 days after the date of publication of the advertisement mentioned in rule 3.11.16, unless the sheriff principal on cause shown sees fit to extend the time.

Public notice of trial not proceeding

3.11.18—(1)   This rule applies where after the notice of trial has been published the sheriff clerk receives notice

(a)   the petitioner's intention to apply for leave to withdraw;

(b)   the respondent's intention not to oppose;

(c)   the abatement of the petition by death; or

(d)   the occurrence of any of the events mentioned in section 153(1) of the Act.

(2)   Where this rule applies the sheriff clerk shall forthwith give notice by advertisement inserted once in a newspaper circulating in the district, that the trial will not proceed on the day fixed.

Notice to a party's agent sufficient

3.11.19   Where a party to proceedings under this Part is represented by a solicitor any reference to such party shall, where appropriate, be construed as a reference to the solicitor representing that party and a notice sent to his solicitor shall be held to be notice to the party.

Cost of publication

3.11.20   Where under this Part the returning officer or the sheriff clerk requires to have published a notice or advertisement, the cost shall be paid in the first instance by the petitioner or in the case of a notice under rule 3.11.15 from the estate of the sole or last surviving petitioner and shall form part of the general expenses of the petition.

Expenses

3.11.21   The expenses of petitions and other proceedings under the Act shall be taxed by the auditor of the sheriff court.

Application for serial number

3.11.22—[1](1)   Where a person desiring to appeal wishes to prevent his identity being disclosed he may, before lodging the appeal, apply to the sheriff clerk for a serial number to be assigned to him for all purposes connected with the appeal.

(2)   On receipt of an application for a serial number, the sheriff clerk shall assign such a number to the applicant and shall enter a note of it opposite the name of the applicant in the register of such serial numbers.

(3)   The contents of the register of serial numbers and the names of the persons to whom each number relates shall be treated as confidential by the sheriff clerk and shall not be disclosed to any person other than—

(a)   the sheriff;

(b)   the registration officer whose decision or determination is the subject of the appeal.

(4)   In this rule and in rule 3.11.23 "sheriff clerk" means the sheriff clerk of the sheriff court district in which the appeal is or is to be raised.

Confidentiality

3.11.23[2]   Unless the sheriff otherwise directs, all documents lodged in process of an appeal to which this rule applies are to be available only to the sheriff and the

---

[1] As inserted by the Act of Sederunt (Summary Applications, Statutory Applications and Appeals etc. Rules) Amendment (Registration Appeals) (SSI 2008/41), r.2(3) (effective March 17, 2008).

[2] As inserted by the Act of Sederunt (Summary Applications, Statutory Applications and Appeals etc. Rules) Amendment (Registration Appeals) (SSI 2008/41), r.2(3) (effective March 17, 2008).

parties; and such documents are to be treated as confidential by all persons involved in, or party to, the proceedings and by the sheriff clerk.

Hearing

3.11.24[1]   The hearing of an appeal to which this rule applies is to be in private.

Part XII

Requests or Applications under the Model Law on International Commercial Arbitration

Interpretation

3.12.1   In this Part, "the Model Law" means the United Nations Commission on International Trade Law Model Law on International Commercial Arbitration as set out in Schedule 7 to the Law Reform (Miscellaneous Provisions) (Scotland) Act 1990.

Application

3.12.2—(1)   Subject to sub-paragraph (2), any request or application which may be made to the sheriff under the Model Law shall be made by summary application.

(2)   Where proceedings involving the same arbitration and the same parties are already pending before the sheriff under this Part, a further application or request may be made by note in the same process.

(3)   The sheriff shall order service of such summary application or note to be made on such persons as he considers appropriate.

Recognition and enforcement of awards

3.12.3—(1)   There shall be lodged along with an application under Article 35 of the Model Law—

(a)   the original arbitration agreement or certified copy thereof;

(b)   the duly authenticated original award or certified copy thereof and

(c)   where appropriate, a duly certified translation in English of the agreement and award.

(2)   An application under this paragraph shall specify whether to the knowledge of the applicant—

(a)   the arbitral award has been recognised, or is being enforced, in any other jurisdiction; and

(b)   an application for setting aside or suspension of the arbitral award has been made to a court of the country in which or under whose law the award was made.

---

[1] As inserted by the Act of Sederunt (Summary Applications, Statutory Applications and Appeals etc. Rules) Amendment (Registration Appeals) (SSI 2008/41), r.2(3) (effective March 17, 2008).

(3)   Where the sheriff is satisfied that an arbitral award should be recognised and enforced, he shall so order and shall instruct the sheriff clerk to register the award in the Books of the Sheriff Court for execution.

Part XIII

Sex Discrimination Act 1975

[Omitted by the Act of Sederunt (Ordinary Cause, Summary Application, Summary Cause and Small Claim Rules) Amendment (Equality Act 2006 etc.) 2006 (SSI 2006/509) (effective November 3, 2006).]

Part XIV[1]

Access to Health Records Act 1990

Interpretation and application

3.14.1—(1)   In this Part—

"the Act" means the Access to Health Records Act 1990; and
"the Reg" means the Access to Health Records (Steps to Secure Compliance and Complaints Procedures) (Scotland) Regulations 1991.

(2)   This Part applies to applications under section 8(1) of the Act (applications to the court for order to comply with requirement of the Act).

Accompanying documents

3.14.2   An application shall specify those steps prescribed in the Regulations which have been taken by the person concerned to secure compliance with any requirement of the Act, and when lodged in process shall be accompanied by—

(a)   a copy of the application under section 3 of the Act (applications for access to a health record);
(b)   a copy of the complaint under regulation 3 or 4 of the Regulations (complaint about non-compliance with the Act); and
(c)   if applicable, a copy of the report under regulation 6 of the Regulations (report in response to complaint).

Time of making application

3.14.3   The application shall be made where the applicant—

(a)   has received a report in accordance with regulation 6 of the Regulations, within one year of the date of the report;

---

[1] As inserted by the Act of Sederunt (Summary Applications, Statutory Applications and Appeals etc. Rules) Amendment 2000 (SSI 2000/148), para.2(2) (effective July 3, 2000).

(b) has not received such a report, within 18 months of the date of the complaint.

Part XV

Race Relations Act 1976

[Omitted by the Act of Sederunt (Ordinary Cause, Summary Application, Summary Cause and Small Claim Rules) Amendment (Equality Act 2006 etc.) 2006 (SSI 2006/509) (effective November 3, 2006).]

Part XVI[1]

Adults with Incapacity (Scotland) Act 2000

Interpretation

3.16.1[2] In this Part—

"the 2000 Act" means the Adults with Incapacity (Scotland) Act 2000;

[3]"the 2003 Act" means the Mental Health (Care and Treatment) (Scotland) Act 2003;

"adult" means a person who is the subject of an application under the 2000 Act and—

(a) has attained the age of 16 years; or

(b)[4] in relation to an application for a guardianship order, will attain the age of 16 years within 3 months of the date of the application;

"authorised establishment" has the meaning ascribed to it in section 35(2) of the 2000 Act;

"continuing attorney" means a person on whom there has been conferred a power of attorney granted under section 15(1) of the 2000 Act;

[5, 6]"guardianship order" means an order made under—

(a) section 57(2)(c) or section 58(1A) of the Criminal Procedure (Scotland) Act 1995; or

(b) section 58(4) of the 2000 Act;

"incapable" has the meaning ascribed to it at section 1(6) of the 2000 Act, and "incapacity" shall be construed accordingly;

[7]"intervention order" means an order made under section 53(1) of the 2000 Act;

---

[1] As inserted by the Act of Sederunt (Summary Applications, Statutory Applications and Appeals etc. Rules) Amendment (Adults with Incapacity) 2001 (SSI 2001/142) r.3(2).

[2] As amended by the the Mental Health (Care and Treatment) (Scotland) Act 2003 (Modification of Subordinate Legislation) Order 2005 (SSI 2005/445) (effective October 5, 2005).

[3] Inserted by the the Mental Health (Care and Treatment) (Scotland) Act 2003 (Modification of Subordinate Legislation) Order 2005 (SSI 2005/445) (effective October 5, 2005).

[4] As substituted by the Act of Sederunt (Summary Applications, Statutory Applications and Appeals etc. Rules) Amendment (Adult Support and Protection (Scotland) Act 2007) 2008 (SSI 2008/111) r.3(1) (effective April 1, 2008).

[5] As amended by the Act of Sederunt (Summary Applications, Statutory Applications and Appeals etc. Rules) Amendment (No.3) (Adults with Incapacity) 2002 (SSI 2002/146) r.2(2).

[6] As amended by the Act of Sederunt (Summary Applications, Statutory Applications and Appeals etc. Rules Amendment) (Miscellaneous) 2013 (SSI 2013/293) r.2 (effective November 11, 2013).

[7] As amended by the Act of Sederunt (Summary Applications, Statutory Applications and Appeals etc. Rules) Amendment (No.3) (Adults with Incapacity) 2002 (SSI 2002/146) r.2(2).

"local authority" has the meaning ascribed to it by section 87(1) of the 2000 Act;[1]

"managers" has the meaning ascribed to it in paragraph 1 of Schedule 1 to the 2000 Act;

"Mental Welfare Commission" has the meaning ascribed to it by section 87(1) of the 2000 Act;[2]

"named person" has the meaning ascribed to it by section 329 of the Mental Health (Care and Treatment) (Scotland) Act 2003;[3]

"nearest relative" means, subject to section 87(2) of the 2000 Act, the person who would be, or would be exercising the functions of, the adult's nearest relative under sections 53 to 57 of the 1984 Act if the adult were a patient within the meaning of that Act and notwithstanding that the person neither is or was caring for the adult for the purposes of section 53(3) of that Act;

"power of attorney" includes a factory and commission;

"primary carer" means the person or organisation primarily engaged in caring for an adult;

"Public Guardian" shall be construed in accordance with section 6 of the 2000 Act; and

"welfare attorney" means a person on whom there has been conferred a power of attorney granted under section 16(1) of the 2000 Act.

Appointment of hearing

3.16.2 On an application or other proceedings being submitted under or in pursuance of the 2000 Act the sheriff shall—

(a) fix a hearing;

(b) order answers to be lodged (where he considers it appropriate to do so) within a period that he shall specify; and

(c) appoint service and intimation of the application or other proceedings.

Place, and privacy, of any hearing

3.16.3[4] The sheriff may, where he considers it appropriate in all the circumstances, appoint that the hearing of an application or other proceedings shall take place—

(a) in a hospital, or any other place than the court building;

(b) in private.

---

[1] As amended by the Act of Sederunt (Summary Applications, Statutory Applications and Appeals etc. Rules) Amendment (No.3) (Adults with Incapacity) 2002 (SSI 2002/146) r.2(2).

[2] As amended by the Act of Sederunt (Summary Applications, Statutory Applications and Appeals etc. Rules) Amendment (No.3) (Adults with Incapacity) 2002 (SSI 2002/146) r.2(2).

[3] As inserted by the Act of Sederunt (Summary Applications, Statutory Applications and Appeals etc. Rules) Amendment (Adult Support and Protection (Scotland) Act 2007) 2008 (SSI 2008/111) r.2(1) (effective April 1, 2008).

[4] As substituted by the Act of Sederunt (Ordinary Cause, Summary Application and Small Claim Rules) Amendment (Miscellaneous) 2004 (SSI 2004/197) para.3(7) (effective May 21, 2004).

Service of application and renewal proceedings[1]

3.16.4—(1)[2,3] Service of the application or other proceedings and subsequent proceedings, including proceedings for renewal of guardianship orders, shall be made in Form 20 on—

    (a) the adult;

    (b) the nearest relative of the adult;

    (c) the primary carer of the adult (if any);

    (d) the named person of the adult (if any);

    (e) any guardian, continuing attorney or welfare attorney of the adult who has any power relating to the application or proceedings;

    (f) the Public Guardian;

    (g) where appropriate, the Mental Welfare Commission;

    (h) where appropriate, the local authority;

    (i) where a guardianship order has been made under section 57(2)(c) or section 58(1A) of the Criminal Procedure (Scotland) Act 1995, to the Lord Advocate and, where the order was made by—

        (i) the High Court of Justiciary, to the Clerk of Justiciary; and

        (ii) a sheriff, to the sheriff clerk of the Sheriff Court in which the order was made;

    (j) any other person directed by the sheriff.

(2) Where the applicant is an individual person without legal representation service shall be effected by the sheriff clerk.

(3) Where the adult is in an authorised establishment the person effecting service shall not serve Form 20 on the adult under paragraph (1)(a) but shall instead serve Forms 20 and 21, together with Form 22, on the managers of that authorised establishment by—

    (a) first class recorded delivery post; or

    (b) personal service by a sheriff officer.

(4)[4] On receipt of Forms 20 and 21 in terms of paragraph (3) the managers of the authorised establishment shall, subject to rule 3.16.5—

    (a) immediately deliver the notice in Form 20 to the adult; and

    (b) as soon as practicable thereafter complete, and in any event before the date of the hearing specified in Form 20, and return to the sheriff clerk a certificate of such delivery in Form 22.

(5) Where the application or other proceeding follows on a remit under rule 3.16.9 the order for service of the application shall include an order for service on the Public Guardian or other party concerned.

(6)[5] Where the application is for an intervention order or a guardianship order, copies of the reports lodged in accordance with section 57(3) of the 2000 Act (reports to be lodged in court along with application) shall be served along with Form 20 or Forms 20, 21 and 22 as the case may be.

---

[1] As amended by the Act of Sederunt (Sheriff Court Rules)(Miscellaneous Amendments) (No.3) 2013 (SSI 2013/171) para.2 (effective June 25, 2013).

[2] As substituted by the Act of Sederunt (Sheriff Court Rules) (Miscellaneous Amendments) (No.3) 2013 (SSI 2013/171) r.2(2) (effective June 25, 2013).

[3] As amended by the Act of Sederunt (Summary Applications, Statutory Applications and Appeals etc. Rules Amendment) (Miscellaneous) 2013 (SSI 2013/293) r.2 (effective November 11, 2013).

[4] As amended by the Act of Sederunt (Summary Applications, Statutory Applications and Appeals etc. Rules Amendment) (Miscellaneous) 2013 (SSI 2013/293) r.2 (effective November 11, 2013).

[5] As amended by the Act of Sederunt (Summary Applications, Statutory Applications and Appeals etc. Rules) Amendment (No.3) (Adults with Incapacity) 2002 (SSI 2002/146) r.2(2).

Dispensing with service on adult

3.16.5—(1)   Where, in relation to any application or proceeding under or in pursuance of the 2000 Act, two medical certificates are produced stating that intimation of the application or other proceeding, or notification of any interlocutor relating to such application or other proceeding, would be likely to pose a serious risk to the health of the adult the sheriff may dispense with such intimation or notification.

(2)   Any medical certificates produced under paragraph (1) shall be prepared by medical practitioners independent of each other.

(3)[1]   In any case where the incapacity of the adult is by reason of mental disorder, one of the two medical practitioners must be a medical practitioner approved for the purposes of section 22(4) of the 2003 Act as having special experience in the diagnosis or treatment of mental disorder.

Hearing

3.16.6—(1)[2]   A hearing to determine any application or other proceeding shall take place within 28 days of the interlocutor fixing the hearing under rule 3.16.2 unless any person upon whom the application is to be served is outside Europe.

(2)   At the hearing referred to in paragraph (1) the sheriff may determine the application or other proceeding or may order such further procedure as he thinks fit.

Prescribed forms of application

3.16.7—(1)   An application submitted to the sheriff under or in pursuance of the 2000 Act, other than an appeal or remitted matter, shall be in Form 23.

(2)   An appeal to the sheriff under or in pursuance of the 2000 Act shall be in Form 24.

Subsequent applications

3.16.8—(1)[3]   Unless otherwise prescribed in the Part or under the 2000 Act, any application or proceedings subsequent to an initial application or proceeding considered by the sheriff including an application to renew an existing order, shall take the form of a minute lodged in the process.

(1ZA)[4]   Where a guardianship order has been made under section 57(2)(c) or section 58(1A) of the Criminal Procedure (Scotland) Act 1995, an application to renew it shall be made—

    (a)   on the first such application, in Form 23;

    (b)   on any subsequent application, in the form of a minute lodged in the process.

---

[1] As amended by the the Mental Health (Care and Treatment) (Scotland) Act 2003 (Modification of Subordinate Legislation) Order (SSI 2005/445) (effective October 5, 2005).

[2] As amended by the Act of Sederunt (Summary Applications, Statutory Applications and Appeals etc. Rules) Amendment (No.3) (Adults with Incapacity) 2002 (SSI 2002/146), r.2(2) (effective April 1, 2002).

[3] As amended by the Act of Sederunt (Summary Applications, Statutory Applications and Appeals etc. Rules) Amendment (No.3) (Adults with Incapacity) 2002 (SSI 2002/146) r.2(2) and the Act of Sederunt (Summary Applications, Statutory Applications and Appeals etc. Rules) Amendment (Adult Support and Protection (Scotland) Act 2007) 2008 (SSI 2008/111) r.3(2)(a) (effective April 1, 2008).

[4] As amended by the Act of Sederunt (Summary Applications, Statutory Applications and Appeals etc. Rules Amendment) (Miscellaneous) 2013 (SSI 2013/293) r.2 (effective November 11, 2013).

(1A)[1, 2] Except where the sheriff otherwise directs, any minute lodged under this rule shall be lodged in accordance with, and regulated by, Chapter 14 of the Ordinary Cause Rules.

(2) Where any subsequent application or proceedings under paragraph (1) above are made to a court in another sheriffdom the sheriff clerk shall transmit the court process to the court dealing with the current application or proceeding.

(3) Transmission of the process in terms of paragraph (2) shall be made within 4 days of it being requested by the sheriff clerk of the court in which the current application or proceedings have been raised.

(4)[3] Where the application is for renewal of a guardianship order, a copy of any report lodged under section 60 of the 2000 Act shall be served along with the minute.

(5) *[Repealed by the Act of Sederunt (Sheriff Court Rules)(Miscellaneous Amendments) (No.3) 2013 (SSI 2013/171) para.2 (effective June 25, 2013).]*

Remit of applications by the Public Guardian etc.

3.16.9 Where an application is remitted to the sheriff by the Public Guardian or by any other party authorised to do so under the 2000 Act the party remitting the application shall, within 4 days of the decision to remit, transmit the papers relating to the application to the sheriff clerk of the court where the application is to be considered.

Caution and other security[4]

3.16.10—[5](1) Where the sheriff requires a person authorised under an intervention order or any variation of an intervention order, or appointed as a guardian, to find caution he shall specify the amount and period within which caution is to be found in the interlocutor authorising or appointing the person or varying the order (as the case may be).

(1A)[6] The amount of caution specified by the sheriff in paragraph (1) may be calculated and expressed as a percentage of the value of the adult's estate.

(2) The sheriff may, on application made by motion before the expiry of the period for finding caution and on cause shown, allow further time for finding caution in accordance with paragraph (1).

(3) Caution shall be lodged with the Public Guardian.

(4) Where caution has been lodged to the satisfaction of the Public Guardian he shall notify the sheriff clerk.

---

[1] As amended by the Act of Sederunt (Summary Applications, Statutory Applications and Appeals etc. Rules) Amendment (No.3) (Adults with Incapacity) 2002 (SSI 2002/146) r.2(2) and the Act of Sederunt (Summary Applications, Statutory Applications and Appeals etc. Rules) Amendment (Adult Support and Protection (Scotland) Act 2007) 2008 (SSI 2008/111) r.3(2)(a) (effective April 1, 2008).

[2] As amended by the Act of Sederunt (Summary Applications, Statutory Applications and Appeals etc. Rules Amendment) (Miscellaneous) 2013 (SSI 2013/293) r.2 (effective November 11, 2013).

[3] As amended by the Act of Sederunt (Summary Applications, Statutory Applications and Appeals etc. Rules) Amendment (No.3) (Adults with Incapacity) 2002 (SSI 2002/146) r.2(2) and the Act of Sederunt (Summary Applications, Statutory Applications and Appeals etc. Rules) Amendment (Adult Support and Protection (Scotland) Act 2007) 2008 (SSI 2008/111) r.3(2)(a) (effective April 1, 2008).

[4] As amended by the Act of Sederunt (Summary Applications, Statutory Applications and Appeals etc. Rules) Amendment (Adult Support and Protection (Scotland) Act 2007) 2008 (SSI 2008/111) r.4 (effective April 1, 2008).

[5] As inserted by the Act of Sederunt (Summary Applications, Statutory Applications and Appeals etc. Rules) Amendment (No.3) (Adults with Incapacity) 2002 (SSI 2002/146), r.2(2).

[6] As inserted by the Act of Sederunt (Summary Applications, Statutory Applications and Appeals etc. Rules) Amendment (Adult Support and Protection (Scotland) Act 2007) 2008 (SSI 2008/111) r.4 (effective April 1, 2008).

(5)   The sheriff may at any time while a requirement to find caution is in force—

    (a)   increase the amount of, or require the person to find new, caution; or

    (b)   authorise the amount of caution to be decreased.

(6)[1]   Where the sheriff requires the person referred to in paragraph (1) to give security other than caution, the rules of Chapter 27 of the Ordinary Cause Rules shall apply with the necessary modifications.

Appointment of interim guardian

3.16.11[2]   An application under section 57(5) of the 2000 Act (appointment of interim guardian) may be made in the crave of the application for a guardianship order to which it relates or, if made after the submission of the application for a guardianship order, by motion in the process of that application.

Registration of intervention order or guardianship order relating to heritable property

3.16.12[3]   Where an application for an intervention order or a guardianship order seeks to vest in the person authorised under the order, or the guardian, as the case may be, any right to deal with, convey or manage any interest in heritable property which is recorded or capable of being recorded in the General Register of Sasines or is registered or capable of being registered in the Land Register of Scotland, the applicant must specify the necessary details of the property in the application to enable it to be identified in the Register of Sasines or the Land Register of Scotland, as the case may be.

Non-compliance with decisions of guardians with welfare powers

3.16.13—[4](1)   Where the court is required under section 70(3) of the 2000 Act to intimate an application for an order or warrant in relation to noncompliance with the decision of a guardian with welfare powers, the sheriff clerk shall effect intimation in Form 20 in accordance with paragraphs (2) and (3).

(2)   Intimation shall be effected—

    (a)   where the person is within Scotland, by first class recorded delivery post, or, in the event that intimation by first class recorded delivery post is unsuccessful, by personal service by a sheriff officer; or

    (b)   where the person is furth of Scotland, in accordance with rule 2.12 (service on persons furth of Scotland).

(3)   Such intimation shall include notice of the period within which any objection to the application shall be lodged.

---

[1] As inserted by the Act of Sederunt (Summary Applications, Statutory Applications and Appeals etc. Rules) Amendment (Adult Support and Protection (Scotland) Act 2007) 2008 (SSI 2008/111) r.4 (effective April 1, 2008).

[2] As inserted by the Act of Sederunt (Summary Applications, Statutory Applications and Appeals etc. Rules) Amendment (No.3) (Adults with Incapacity) 2000 (SSI 2002/146), r.2(2) (effective April 1, 2002).

[3] As inserted by the Act of Sederunt (Summary Applications, Statutory Applications and Appeals etc. Rules) Amendment (No.3) (Adults with Incapacity) 2002 (SSI 2002/146), r.2(2) (effective April 1, 2002).

[4] As inserted by the Act of Sederunt (Summary Applications, Statutory Applications and Appeals etc. Rules) Amendment (No.3) (Adults with Incapacity) 2002 (SSI 2002/146), r.2(2) (effective April 1, 2002).

Part XVII[1]

Anti-Terrorism, Crime and Security Act 2001

Interpretation

3.17.1   In this Part, any reference to a specified paragraph shall be construed as a reference to the paragraph bearing that number in Schedule 1 to the Anti-terrorism, Crime and Security Act 2001.

Applications for extended detention of cash or seized property

3.17.2—[2](1)   An application to the sheriff for an order under paragraph 3(2) (extended detention of seized cash) or paragraph 10D(1) (further detention of seized property) shall be made by summary application.

(2)   An application for any further order for the detention of cash under paragraph 3(2) or seized property under paragraph 10D(1) shall be made by minute in the original process and shall be proceeded with in accordance with sub-paragraph (3) below.

(3)   On the lodging of an application for any further order the sheriff shall—

    (a)   fix a date for determination of the application; and

    (b)   except where paragraph (4) below applies, order service of the application together with notice of such date for determination on any persons whom he considers may be affected.

(4)   This paragraph applies where the sheriff determines under paragraph 3(3A) or 10D(4) that the application is to be made and heard without notice.

Applications for release of detained cash or detained property

3.17.3—[3](1)   An application to the sheriff under—

    (a)   paragraph 5(2) (application for release of detained cash) or paragraph 9(1) (application by person who claims that cash belongs to that person) must be made—

        (i)   in the course of proceedings for an order under paragraph 3(2); or

        (ii)   where an order has been made under paragraph 3(2), by minute in the process of the application for that order;

    (b)   paragraph 10F (release of detained property) must be made—

        (i)   in the course of proceedings for an order under paragraph 10D(1); or

        (ii)   where an order has been made under paragraph 10D(1), by minute in the process of the application for that order;

    (c)   paragraph 10O (victims) must be made—

---

[1] As inserted by the Act of Sederunt (Summary Applications, Statutory Applications and Appeals etc. Rules) Amendment (Detention and Forfeiture of Terrorist Cash) 2002 (SSI 2002/ 129), para.2(2) (effective March 8, 2002).

[2] As amended by the Act of Sederunt (Rules of the Court of Session 1994 and Summary Applications, Statutory Applications and Appeals etc. Rules 1999 Amendment) (Proceeds of Crime) 2019 (SSI 2019/146) para.3 (effective 1 June 2019).

[3] As amended by the Act of Sederunt (Rules of the Court of Session 1994 and Summary Applications, Statutory Applications and Appeals etc. Rules 1999 Amendment) (Proceeds of Crime) 2019 (SSI 2019/146) para.3 (effective 1 June 2019).

         (i)   in the course of proceedings for an order under paragraph 10D(1) or 10G(2) (forfeiture); or

        (ii)   where an order under paragraph 10D(1) or 10G(2) has been made, by minute in the process of the application for that order.

(2)   On the lodging of such an application the sheriff shall—

    (a)   fix a date for a hearing; and

    (b)   order service of the application together with notice of such hearing on the procurator fiscal and any other person whom he considers may be affected by the granting of such an application.

Applications for forfeiture of detained cash or detained property

3.17.4—[1](1)   An application to the sheriff for an order under—

    (a)   paragraph 6(1)(b) (application for forfeiture of detained cash), where the court has made an order under paragraph 3(2);

    (b)   paragraph 10G(1)(b) (forfeiture), where the court has made an order under paragraph 10D(1),

must be made by minute in the process of the application for that order.

(2)   On the lodging of such an application the sheriff shall—

    (a)   fix a date for a hearing; and

    (b)   order service of the application together with notice of such hearing on any person whom he considers may be affected by the granting of such an application.

Applications for compensation

3.17.5—[2](1)   An application to the sheriff for an order under—

    (a)   paragraph 10(1) (compensation), where the court has made an order under paragraph 3(2);

    (b)   paragraph 10P(1) (compensation), where the court has made an order under paragraph 10D(1);

    (c)   paragraph 10Z7(2) (compensation), where the court has made an order under paragraph 10Q (application for account freezing order),

must be made by minute in the process of the application for that order.

(2)   On the lodging of such an application the sheriff shall—

    (a)   fix a date for a hearing; and

    (b)   order service of the application together with notice of such hearing on any person whom he considers may be affected by the granting of such an application.

---

[1] As amended by the Act of Sederunt (Rules of the Court of Session 1994 and Summary Applications, Statutory Applications and Appeals etc. Rules 1999 Amendment) (Proceeds of Crime) 2019 (SSI 2019/146) para.3 (effective 1 June 2019).

[2] As amended by the Act of Sederunt (Rules of the Court of Session 1994 and Summary Applications, Statutory Applications and Appeals etc. Rules 1999 Amendment) (Proceeds of Crime) 2019 (SSI 2019/146) para.3 (effective 1 June 2019).

Variation and recall of account freezing orders and applications to set aside forfeiture

3.17.6—[1](1)   An application to the sheriff for an order under paragraph 10T(1) (variation and setting aside of account freezing order) must be made by minute in the process of the application for that order.

(2)   An application to the sheriff for an order under paragraph 10Z (application to set aside forfeiture) must be made by summary application.

(3)   On the lodging of an application under paragraph (1) or (2) above the sheriff must—

    (a)   fix a date for a hearing; and

    (b)   order service of the application together with notice of such hearing on any person whom the sheriff considers may be affected by the granting of such an application.

Applications for forfeiture order

3.17.7—[2](1)   An application to the sheriff for an order under paragraph 10Z2(2)(b) (forfeiture order) must be made by minute in the process of the application for the associated account freezing order.

(2)   On the lodging of such an application the sheriff must—

    (a)   fix a date for a hearing; and

    (b)   order service of the application together with notice of such hearing on any person whom the sheriff considers may be affected by the granting of such an application.

Associated and joint property: transfer to Court of Session

3.17.8—[3](1)   This rule applies where the sheriff makes a transfer to the Court of Session under paragraph 10J (associated and joint property: default of agreement) of an application made under paragraph 10G(1)(b).

(2)   No later than 4 days after the sheriff has pronounced an interlocutor transferring the application to the Court of Session under paragraph 10J, the sheriff clerk must—

    (a)   send written notice of the transfer to the parties;

    (b)   certify on the interlocutor sheet that sub-paragraph (a) has been complied with; and

    (c)   transmit the process to the Deputy Principal Clerk of Session.

(3)   Failure by a sheriff clerk to comply with paragraph (2)(a) or (b) above does not affect the validity of the transfer.

Part XVIII[4]

---

[1] As inserted by the Act of Sederunt (Rules of the Court of Session 1994 and Summary Applications, Statutory Applications and Appeals etc. Rules 1999 Amendment) (Proceeds of Crime) 2019 (SSI 2019/146) para.3 (effective 1 June 2019).

[2] As inserted by the Act of Sederunt (Rules of the Court of Session 1994 and Summary Applications, Statutory Applications and Appeals etc. Rules 1999 Amendment) (Proceeds of Crime) 2019 (SSI 2019/146) para.3 (effective 1 June 2019).

[3] As inserted by the Act of Sederunt (Rules of the Court of Session 1994 and Summary Applications, Statutory Applications and Appeals etc. Rules 1999 Amendment) (Proceeds of Crime) 2019 (SSI 2019/146) para.3 (effective 1 June 2019).

[4] As inserted by the Act of Sederunt (Summary Applications, Statutory Applications and Appeals etc. Rules) Amendment (No.2) (Local Government (Scotland) Act 1973) 2002 (SSI 2002/130), r.2(3) (effective March 8, 2002).

Local Government (Scotland) Act 1973

Application

3.18.1— This Part applies to appeals to the sheriff principal under section 103J of the Local Government (Scotland) Act 1973 (appeals from the Accounts Commission for Scotland).

Appeals

3.18.2—(1) An appeal under this Part shall be made by summary application.

(2) A summary application made under paragraph (1) shall include grounds of appeal stating—

    (a) the finding or sanction or suspension being appealed;

    (b) reasons why the appeal should be allowed; and

    (c) the date of sending of the finding or imposition of the sanction or suspension concerned,

and shall be accompanied by a copy of such finding, sanction or suspension.

Warrant and form of citation

3.18.3—(1) A warrant for citation in an appeal under this Part shall be in Form 2A and shall state—

    (a) the date by which answers should be lodged; and

    (b) the date and time when the appeal will call.

(2) Citation in respect of a warrant granted under paragraph (1) shall be in Form 3A.

(3) Where a party on whom service has been made lodges answers under paragraph (1)(a) that party shall, at the same time, send a copy to the applicant.

(4) In Schedule 1 (forms)—

    (a) after Form 2 insert Form 2A; and

    (b) after Form 3 insert Form 3A,

as set out in the Schedule to this Act of Sederunt.

Part XIX[1]

Proceeds of Crime Act 2002

General

Interpretation and application

3.19.1.—[2, 3, 4](1) In this Part—

"the Act" means the Proceeds of Crime Act 2002;

---

[1] As inserted by the Act of Sederunt (Summary Applications, Statutory Applications and Appeals etc. Rules) Amendment (No.5) (Proceeds of Crime Act 2002) 2002 (SSI 2002/563), r.2(2) (effective December 30, 2002).

[2] As substituted by the Act of Sederunt (Summary Applications, Statutory Applications and Appeals etc. Rules) Amendment (No.6) (Proceeds of Crime Act 2002) 2003 (SSI 2003/98), r.2(2)(a) (effective February 24, 2003 for provisions specified in SSI 2003/98 para.1(1)(b)(ii); March 24, 2003 otherwise).

[3] As amended by the Act of Sederunt (Rules of the Court of Session 1994 and Summary Applications, Statutory Applications and Appeals etc. Rules 1999 Amendment) (Proceeds of Crime) 2019 (SSI 2019/146) r.3 (effective 1 June 2019).

"the 2005 Order" means the Proceeds of Crime Act 2002 (External Requests and Orders) Order 2005;

"external order" has the meaning set out in section 447(2) of the Act;

references to an administrator are to an administrator appointed under section 125(1) or 128(3);

a reference to a specified section is a reference to the section bearing that number in the Act; and any reference to a specified paragraph in a specified Schedule is a reference to the paragraph bearing that number in the Schedule of that number in the Act.

(2)   This Part applies to applications to the sheriff under Parts 3, 5 and 8 of the Act; but it only applies to applications under Part 8 in relation to property that is the subject of a—

    (a)   civil recovery investigation;

    (b)   detained cash investigation;

    (c)   detained property investigation;

    (d)   frozen funds investigation;

    (e)   *[Omitted by the Act of Sederunt (Rules of the Court of Session 1994 and Summary Applications, Statutory Applications and Appeals etc. Rules 1999 Amendment) (Proceeds of Crime) (No.2) 2019 (SSI 2019/405) r.3(2) (effective 28 December 2019).].*

(3)   This Part applies to applications to the sheriff under Parts 5A and 5B of the 2005 Order.

Recovery of cash or property in summary proceedings

Applications for extended detention of cash or further detention of seized property

3.19.2.—[1](1)   An application to the sheriff for an order under sections 295(2) and (7) (extended detention of seized cash) or 303L(1)(b) (further detention of seized property) shall be made by summary application.

(2)   An application for any further order for the detention of cash under section 295(2) or seized property under section 303L(1)(b) shall be made by minute in the process of the original application for extended detention of seized cash or seizure of property and shall be proceeded with in accordance with sub-paragraph (3) below.

(3)   On the lodging of an application for any further order the sheriff shall—

    (a)   fix a date for determination of the application; and

    (b)   order service of the application together with notice of such date for determination on any persons whom he considers may be affected.

Applications for release of detained cash or detained property

3.19.3.—[2](1)   An application to the sheriff under—

    (a)   section 297(3) (application for release of detained cash) must be made—

---

[4] As amended by the Act of Sederunt (Rules of the Court of Session 1994 and Summary Applications, Statutory Applications and Appeals etc. Rules 1999 Amendment) (Proceeds of Crime) No.2) 2019 (SSI 2019/405) r.3 (effective 28 December 2019).

[1] As amended by the Act of Sederunt (Rules of the Court of Session 1994 and Summary Applications, Statutory Applications and Appeals etc. Rules 1999 Amendment) (Proceeds of Crime) 2019 (SSI 2019/146) r.3 (effective 1 June 2019).

[2] As amended by the Act of Sederunt (Rules of the Court of Session 1994 and Summary Applications, Statutory Applications and Appeals etc. Rules 1999 Amendment) (Proceeds of Crime) 2019 (SSI 2019/146) para.3 (effective 1 June 2019).

   (i)   in the course of proceedings for an order under section 295(2); or
   (ii) where an order has been made under section 295(2), by minute in the process of the application for that order;
(b) section 301(1) (application by person who claims that cash belongs to that person) must be made—
   (i)   in the course of proceedings for an order under section 295(2) or 298 (forfeiture); or
   (ii) where an order has been made under section 295(2) or 298, by minute in the process of the application for that order;
(c) section 303N (release of detained property) must be made—
   (i)   in the course of proceedings for an order under section 303L(1)(b); or
   (ii) where an order has been made under section 303L(1)(b), by minute in the process of the application for that order;
(d) section 303V (victims and other owners) must be made—
   (i)   in the course of proceedings for an order under section 303L(1)(b) or 303O(3) (forfeiture); or
   (ii) where an order has been made under section 303L(1)(b) or 303O(3), by minute in the process of the application for that order.
(2) On the lodging of such an application the sheriff shall—
(a) fix a date for a hearing; and
(b) order service of the application together with notice of such hearing on the procurator fiscal and any other person whom he considers may be affected by the granting of such an application.

Applications for forfeiture of detained cash or detained property
   3.19.4.—[1](1) An application to the sheriff under—
(a) section 298(1)(b) (application by the Scottish Ministers for forfeiture of detained cash), where the court has made an order under section 295(2);
(b) section 303O(1)(b), where the court has made an order under section 303L(1)(b),
must be made by minute in the process of the application for that order.
   (1A)[2] In an application to the sheriff under article 213L(1) of the 2005 Order, a certified copy of the external order to be registered must be produced with the application.
   (2) On the lodging of such an application the sheriff shall—
(a) fix a date for a hearing; and
(b) order service of the application together with notice of such hearing on any person whom he considers may be affected by the granting of such an application.
   (3)[3] Where the sheriff grants an application under article 213L(1) of the 2005 Order, the sheriff clerk must register the certified copy of the external order.

---

[1] As amended by the Act of Sederunt (Rules of the Court of Session 1994 and Summary Applications, Statutory Applications and Appeals etc. Rules 1999 Amendment) (Proceeds of Crime) 2019 (SSI 2019/146) para.3 (effective 1 June 2019).
[2] As inserted by the Act of Sederunt (Rules of the Court of Session 1994 and Summary Applications, Statutory Applications and Appeals etc. Rules 1999 Amendment) (Proceeds of Crime) (No. 2) 2019 (SSI 2019/405) r.3(4)(a) (effective 28 December 2019).
[3] As inserted by the Act of Sederunt (Rules of the Court of Session 1994 and Summary Applications, Statutory Applications and Appeals etc. Rules 1999 Amendment) (Proceeds of Crime) (No. 2) 2019 (SSI 2019/405) r.3(4)(b) (effective 28 December 2019).

Variation and recall of account freezing orders and applications for forfeiture orders

3.19.4A.—[1, 2](1) An application to the sheriff for an order under section 303Z4(1)or article 213Z4 of the 2005 Order (variation and setting aside of account freezing order) must be made by minute in the process of the application for that order.

(2) An application to the sheriff for an order under section 303Z14(2) or article 213Z7(3) of the 2005 Order (forfeiture order) must be made by summary application.

(3) On the lodging of an application under paragraph (1) or (2) above the sheriff must—

(a) fix a date for a hearing;

(b) order service of the application together with notice of such hearing on any person whom the sheriff considers may be affected by the granting of such an application.

Applications for compensation

3.19.5.—[3](1) An application to the sheriff under—

(a) section 302(1A) (compensation), where the court has made an order under section 295(2);

(b) section 303W(1) (compensation), where the court has made an order under section 303L(1)(b);

(c) section 303Z18(2) (compensation), where the court has made an order under section 303Z3,

(d)[4] article 213Z11(2) of the 2005 Order (compensation), where the court has made an order under article 213Z3 of the 2005 Order (making of account freezing order),

must be made by minute in the process of the application for that order, and in any other case must be made by summary application.

(2) On the lodging of such an application the sheriff shall—

(a) fix a date for a hearing; and

(b) order service of the application together with notice of such hearing on any person whom he considers may be affected by the granting of such an application.

Associated and joint property: transfer to Court of Session

3.19.5A.—[5, 6](1) This rule applies where the sheriff makes a transfer to the Court of Session under section 303R or article 213O(1) of the 2005 Order (associ-

---

[1] As inserted by the Act of Sederunt (Rules of the Court of Session 1994 and Summary Applications, Statutory Applications and Appeals etc. Rules 1999 Amendment) (Proceeds of Crime) 2019 (SSI 2019/146) para.3 (effective 1 June 2019).

[2] As amended by the Act of Sederunt (Rules of the Court of Session 1994 and Summary Applications, Statutory Applications and Appeals etc. Rules 1999 Amendment) (Proceeds of Crime) (No. 2) 2019 (SSI 2019/405) r.3(5) (effective 28 December 2019).

[3] As amended by the Act of Sederunt (Rules of the Court of Session 1994 and Summary Applications, Statutory Applications and Appeals etc. Rules 1999 Amendment) (Proceeds of Crime) 2019 (SSI 2019/146) para.3 (effective 1 June 2019).

[4] As inserted by the Act of Sederunt (Rules of the Court of Session 1994 and Summary Applications, Statutory Applications and Appeals etc. Rules 1999 Amendment) (Proceeds of Crime) (No. 2) 2019 (SSI 2019/405) r.3(6) (effective 28 December 2019).

[5] As inserted by the Act of Sederunt (Rules of the Court of Session 1994 and Summary Applications, Statutory Applications and Appeals etc. Rules 1999 Amendment) (Proceeds of Crime) 2019 (SSI 2019/146) para.3 (effective 1 June 2019).

ated and joint property: default of agreement) of an application for an order under section 303O(1)(b) or article 213L(1) of the 2005 Order (forfeiture) respectively.

(2)   No later than 4 days after the sheriff has pronounced an interlocutor transferring the application to the Court of Session under section 303R or article 213O(1) of the 2005 Order the sheriff clerk must—

    (a)   send written notice of the transfer to the parties;

    (b)   certify on the interlocutor sheet that sub-paragraph (a) has been complied with; and

    (c)   transmit the process to the Deputy Principal Clerk of Session.

(3)   Failure by a sheriff clerk to comply with paragraph (2)(a) or (b) above does not affect the validity of the transfer.

Restraint and administration orders[1]

Service of restraint orders

3.19.6.   The intimation to be made by the prosecutor under section 121(3) shall be made by serving a copy of the interlocutor granting a restraint order on every person named in the interlocutor as restrained by the order.

Recall or variation of restraint orders

3.19.7.   An application to the sheriff under section 121(5) (variation or recall of restraint order) shall be made by minute in the process of the application for the restraint order.

Application for certification of domestic restraint order

3.19.7A.—[2](1)   In this rule—

    (a)   "the 2014 Regulations" means the Criminal Justice and Data Protection Protocol No. 36 Regulations 2014 and

    (b)   "domestic restraint order" and "specified information" have the meanings given by paragraph 1 of schedule 1 of the 2014 Regulations.

(2)   An application by the prosecutor for a certificate under paragraph 2 of schedule 1 of the 2014 Regulations (domestic restraint orders: certification) is made by minute and must—

    (a)   contain the specified information; and

    (b)   set out why the prosecutor considers that the property to which the application relates has been used or is likely to be used for the purposes of an offence or is the proceeds of an offence.

(3)   Where the court makes a certificate it must—

---

[6] As amended by the Act of Sederunt (Rules of the Court of Session 1994 and Summary Applications, Statutory Applications and Appeals etc. Rules 1999 Amendment) (Proceeds of Crime) (No. 2) 2019 (SSI 2019/405) r.3(7) (effective 28 December 2019).

[1] Inserted by the Act of Sederunt (Summary Applications, Statutory Applications and Appeals etc. Rules) Amendment (No.6) (Proceeds of Crime Act 2002) 2003 (SSI 2003/98), r.2(2)(b) (effective February 24, 2003 for provisions specified in SSI 2003/98 para.1(1)(b)(ii); March 24, 2003 otherwise).

[2] As inserted by the Act of Sederunt (Rules of the Court of Session 1994 and Summary Application Rules 1999 Amendment) (Serious Crime Prevention Orders etc.) 2016 (SSI 2016/319) r.3(2) (effective 12 December 2016).

(a) do so in the form annexed to Council Framework Decision 2003/577/JHA of 22 July 2003 on the execution in the European Union of orders freezing property or evidence; and

(b) provide in the domestic restraint order for notice to be given in accordance with paragraph 2(4) of schedule 1 to the 2014 Regulations.

Appeals to the Court of Session

3.19.8.—(1) An appeal against an interlocutor of the sheriff refusing, varying or recalling or refusing to vary or recall a restraint order shall be marked within 14 days after the date of the interlocutor concerned.

(2) Such an appeal shall be marked by writing a note of appeal on the interlocutor sheet, or other written record containing the interlocutor appealed against, or on a separate sheet lodged with the sheriff clerk, in the following terms—

"The applicant appeals to the Court of Session.".

(3) The note of appeal shall—

(a) be signed by the appellant;

(b) bear the date on which it is signed; and

(c) where the appellant is represented, specify the name and address of the solicitor or other agent who will be acting for him in the appeal.

(4) The sheriff clerk will transmit the process within 4 days after the appeal is marked to the Deputy Principal Clerk of Session.

(5) Within the period specified in paragraph (4), the sheriff clerk shall—

(a) send written notice of the appeal to every other party; and

(b) certify on the interlocutor sheet that he has done so.

(6) Failure of the sheriff clerk to comply with paragraph (5) shall not invalidate the appeal.

Applications in relation to arrestment

3.19.9.—(1) An application to the sheriff under section 124(1) (arrestment of property affected by restraint order) by the prosecutor for warrant for arrestment may be made—

(a) in the application made under section 121(2) (application for restraint order); or

(b) if made after a restraint order has been applied for, by minute in the process of the application for that order.

(2) An application to the sheriff under section 124(3) (recalling, loosing or restricting arrestment) or under section 124(6) (recall or restriction of arrestment) shall be made by minute in the process of the application for the restraint order.

Applications for appointment of administrators

3.19.10.—(1) An application to the sheriff under section 125(1) (appointment of management administrator) shall be made by minute in the process of the application for the restraint order.

(2) An application to the sheriff under section 128(2) (appointment of enforcement administrator) shall be made—

(a) where made after a restraint order has been made, by minute in the process of the application for that order; or

(b) in any other case, by summary application.

(3)   The notification to be made by the sheriff clerk under section 125(3) or 128(8) (as the case may be) shall be made by intimation of a copy of the interlocutor to the accused and the persons subject to the order.

Incidental applications in relation to an administration

3.19.11.   An application to the sheriff subsequent to the appointment of an administrator relating to any matter incidental to that appointment shall be made by minute in the process of the application in which the administrator was appointed.

Documents for Accountant of Court

3.19.12.—(1)   A person who has lodged any document in the process of an application for the appointment of an administrator shall forthwith send a copy of that document to the Accountant of Court.

(2)   The sheriff clerk shall transmit to the Accountant of Court any part of the process as the Accountant of Court may request in relation to an administration which is in dependence before the sheriff unless such part of the process is, at the time of request, required by the sheriff.

Procedure for fixing and finding caution

3.19.13.—(1)   The Accountant of Court shall forthwith, on receiving intimation of an application for the appointment of an administrator, fix the caution to be found in the event of appointment being made and shall notify the amount to the sheriff clerk and the applicant.

(2)   During the subsistence of the appointment of the administrator, the Accountant of Court may, at any time—

(a)   require the administrator to increase the amount of or find new or additional caution; or

(b)   authorise the administrator to decrease the amount of existing caution.

Time for finding caution

3.19.14.—(1)   Where the time within which caution is to be found is not stipulated in the interlocutor appointing the administrator, the time allowed for finding caution shall be, subject to paragraph (2) of this rule, limited to one calendar month from the date of the interlocutor.

(2)   The sheriff may, on application made before the expiry of the period for finding caution, and, on cause shown, allow further time for finding caution.

Procedure on finding caution

3.19.15.—(1)   Caution shall be lodged with the Accountant of Court.

(2)   Where caution has been found to the satisfaction of the Accountant of Court, he shall notify the sheriff clerk.

Issue of certified copy interlocutor

3.19.16.—(1)   A certified copy interlocutor of appointment of an administrator shall not be issued by the sheriff clerk until he receives notification from the Accountant of Court in accordance with rule 3.19.15(2).

Administrator's title to act

3.19.17.   An administrator shall not be entitled to act until he has obtained a certified copy of the interlocutor appointing him.

Accounts

3.19.18.—(1) An administrator shall maintain accounts of his intromissions with the property in his charge and shall, subject to paragraph (2)—

(a) within six months after the date of his appointment; and

(b) at six monthly intervals after the first account during the subsistence of his appointment,

lodge with the Accountant of Court an account of his intromissions in such form, with such supporting vouchers and other documents, as the Accountant of Court may require.

(2) The Accountant of Court may waive the lodging of an account where the administrator certifies that there have been no intromissions during a particular accounting period.

Application for discharge of administrator

3.19.19. An application to the sheriff for discharge of an administrator shall be made by minute in the process of the application in which the administrator was appointed.

Appeals against determination of outlays and remuneration

3.19.20. An appeal to the sheriff under paragraph 9(1) of Schedule 3 (appeal against a determination by the Accountant of Court) shall be made by minute in the process of the application in which the administrator was appointed.

Detention and realisation of seized property[1]

Discharge or variation of detention order

3.19.20A An application to the sheriff under section 127N(2) (discharge, variation and lapse of detention order) shall be made by minute in the process of the application for an order extending the period for which property may be detained under section 127J.

Appeals to the Court of Session

3.19.20B.—(1) This section shall apply to appeals against an interlocutor of the sheriff under the following sections—

(a) section 127O(1) or (2);

(b) section 131C(1), (2) or (4).

(2) An appeal shall be marked by writing a note of appeal on the interlocutor sheet, or other written record containing the interlocutor appealed against, or on a separate sheet lodged with the sheriff clerk, in the following terms—

The applicant [or affected person] appeals to the Court of Session.

(3) The note of appeal shall—

(a) be signed by the appellant;

(b) bear the date on which it is signed; and

(c) where the appellant is represented, specify the name and address of the solicitor or other agent who will be acting for him or her in the appeal.

---

[1] As inserted by the Act of Sederunt (Summary Applications, Statutory Applications and Appeals etc. Rules Amendment) (Policing and Crime Act 2009) 2013 (SSI 2013/241) r.2(2) (effective October 1, 2013).

(4)   The sheriff clerk shall transmit the process within 4 days after the appeal is marked to the Deputy Principal Clerk of Session.

(5)   Within the period specified in paragraph (4), the sheriff clerk shall—

(a)   send written notice of the appeal to every other party; and

(b)   certify on the interlocutor sheet that he or she has done so.

(6)   Failure of the sheriff clerk to comply with paragraph (5) shall not invalidate the appeal.

Civil recovery investigations[1]

Production orders

3.19.21.—(1)   An application to the sheriff under section 382(2) (order to grant entry to premises) may be made—

(a)   in the application for the production order; or

(b)   if made after the production order has been made, by minute in the process of the application for that order.

(2)   A report to the sheriff under section 385(4) (report of failure to bring production order made in relation to an authorised government department to the attention of the officer concerned) shall take the form of a letter to the sheriff clerk.

(3)   An application to the sheriff under section 386(4) (discharge or variation of a production order or an order to grant entry) shall be made by minute in the process of the application for the production order.

Search warrants

3.19.22.   An application to the sheriff under section 387(1) (search warrant) shall be in the form of a summary application.

Customer information orders

3.19.23.   An application under section 403(4) (discharge or variation of a customer information order) shall be made by minute in the process of the application for the customer information order.

Account monitoring orders

3.19.24.   An application under section 408(4) (discharge or variation of an account monitoring order) shall be made by minute in the process of the application for the account monitoring order.

Part XX[2]

---

[1] As inserted by the Act of Sederunt (Summary Applications, Statutory Applications and Appeals etc. Rules) Amendment (No.6) (Proceeds of Crime Act 2002) 2003 (SSI 2003/98), r.2(2)(b) (effective February 24, 2003 for provisions specified in SSI 2003/98 para.1(1)(b)(ii); March 24, 2003 otherwise).

[2] As inserted by the Act of Sederunt (Summary Applications, Statutory Applications and Appeals etc. Rules) Amendment (International Criminal Court) 2003 (SSI 2003/27), r.2(2) (effective January 24, 2003).

International Criminal Court (Scotland) Act 2001

General

Interpretation and application

3.20.1.—(1)   In this Part—

"the Act" means the International Criminal Court (Scotland) Act 2001;

"ICC crime" has the same meaning as in section 28(1) of the Act; and a reference to a specified section is a reference to the section bearing that number in the Act, and any reference to a specified paragraph in a specified schedule is a reference to the paragraph bearing that number in the schedule of that number to the Act.

(2)   This Part applies to applications to the sheriff under Parts 1 and 2 of schedule 5 to the Act.

Investigations of proceeds of ICC crime

Production or access orders

3.20.2.—(1)   An order under Part 1 of schedule 5 to the Act may be made by the sheriff on a summary application by a person authorised for the purpose under section 19 of the Act.

(2)   Any such application may be made on an ex parte application to a sheriff in chambers.

(3)   Any such application must set out reasonable grounds for suspecting—

    (a)   that a specified person has benefited from an ICC crime; and

    (b)   that the material to which the application relates is likely to be of substantial value (whether by itself or together with other material) to the investigation for the purposes of which the application is made.

(4)   Any application for variation or discharge of an order under Part 1 of schedule 5 to the Act shall be made by minute.

Search warrants

3.20.3.—(1)   On a summary application by a person authorised under section 19 of the Act to the sheriff sitting as a court of civil jurisdiction, the sheriff may issue a warrant under Part 2 of the Act.

(2)   Any such application must set out grounds sufficient to satisfy the sheriff—

    (a)   that a production or access order made in relation to material on the premises has not been complied with;

    (b)   that—

        (i)   there are reasonable grounds for suspecting that a specified person has benefited from an ICC crime;

        (ii)   there are grounds for making a production and access order in relation to material on the premises; and

        (iii)   it would not be appropriate to make a production and access order in relation to the material for any of the reasons specified in paragraph 10(4) of schedule 5 to the Act; or

    (c)   that—

        (i)   there are reasonable grounds for suspecting that a specified person has benefited from an ICC crime;

      (ii)   there are reasonable grounds for suspecting that there is material on the premises which cannot be particularised at the time of the application, but which—

            (aa)   relates to the specified person, or to the question of whether that person has benefited from an ICC crime, or to any question as to the extent or whereabouts of the proceeds of an ICC crime; and

            (bb)   is likely to be of substantial value (whether by itself or together with other material) to the investigation for the purposes of which the application is made; and

      (iii)   any of the circumstances specified in paragraph 10(6) of schedule 5 to the Act applies.

Part XXI[1]

Immigration And Asylum Act 1999

Interpretation

3.21.1. In this Part—

"the Act" means the Immigration and Asylum Act 1999; and
"an appeal" means an appeal to the sheriff under section 35A(1) or section 40B(1) of the Act.

Appeals
3.21.2.—(1) A person making an appeal against a decision by the Secretary of State to impose a penalty under section 32 or a charge under section 40 of the Act must, subject to paragraph (2), bring an appeal within 21 days after receiving the penalty notice or charge notice.

(2) Where the appellant has given notice of objection to the Secretary of State under section 35(4) or section 40A(3) of the Act within the time prescribed for doing so, he must bring an appeal within 21 days after receiving notice of the Secretary of State's decision under section 35(7) or section 40A(6) respectively of the Act in response to the notice of objection.

Part XXII[2]

Crime and Disorder Act 1998

[Revoked by the Act of Sederunt (Summary Applications, Statutory Applications and Appeals etc. Rules) Amendment (Antisocial Behaviour etc. (Scotland) Act 2004) 2004 (SSI 2004/455) r.2(2) (effective October 28, 2004: repeal has effect subject to transitional provisions specified in SSI 2004/455 r.2(3)).]

---

[1] As inserted by the Act of Sederunt (Summary Applications, Statutory Applications and Appeals etc. Rules) Amendment (Immigration and Asylum) 2003 (SSI 2003/261), r.2(2) (effective May 24, 2003).
[2] As inserted by the Act of Sederunt (Summary Applications, Statutory Applications and Appeals etc. Rules) Amendment (Standards Commission for Scotland) 2003 (SSI 2003/346), r.2(2) (effective July 4, 2003).

Part XXIII[1]

Ethical Standards in Public Life etc. (Scotland) Act 2000

Application

3.23.1. This Part applies to appeals to the sheriff principal under sections 22 (appeals from commission) or 26 (appeals by water industry commissioner) of the Ethical Standards in Public Life etc. (Scotland) Act 2000.

Appeals

3.23.2.—(1) An appeal under this Part shall be made by summary application.

(2) A summary application made under paragraph (1) shall include grounds of appeal stating—

> (a) which of the findings of, or sanction or suspension imposed by, the Standards Commission for Scotland is being appealed;
>
> (b) reasons why the appeal should be allowed; and
>
> (c) the date of the sending of that finding, or imposition of that sanction or suspension,

and shall be accompanied by a copy of that finding, sanction or suspension.

Warrant and form of citation

3.23.3.—(1) A warrant for citation in an appeal under this Part shall be in Form 2A, or a form as near thereto as circumstances permit, and shall state—

> (a) the date by which answers should be lodged; and
>
> (b) the date and time when the appeal will call.

(2) Citation in respect of a warrant granted under paragraph (1) shall be in Form 3A, or a form as near thereto as circumstances permit.

(3) Where a party on whom service has been made lodges answers under paragraph (1)(a) that party shall, at the same time, send a copy to the appellant.

Part XXIV[2]

International Protection of Adults

Interpretation

3.24.1. In this Part—

"the Act" means the Adults with Incapacity (Scotland) Act 2000;

"the Convention" means the Hague Convention of 13th January 2000 on the International Protection of Adults;

"international measure" means any measure taken under the law of a country other than Scotland for the personal welfare, or the protection of property, of an adult with incapacity, where—

---

[1] As inserted by the Act of Sederunt (Summary Applications, Statutory Applications and Appeals etc. Rules) Amendment (Standards Commission for Scotland) 2003 (SSI 2003/346), r.2(2) (effective July 4, 2003).

[2] As inserted by the Act of Sederunt (Summary Applications, Statutory Applications and Appeals etc. Rules) Amendment (International Protection of Adults) 2003 (SSI 2003/556), r.2(2) (effective November 14, 2003).

(a) jurisdiction in the other country was based on the adult's habitual residence there; or

(b) the other country and the United Kingdom were when that measure was taken parties to the Convention, and jurisdiction in that other country was based on a ground of jurisdiction in the Convention; and

"Public Guardian" shall be construed in accordance with section 6 (the public guardian and his functions) of the Act.

Application

3.24.2—(1) An application to register an international measure under paragraph 8(1) of schedule 3 to the Act shall be by summary application made under this Part.

(2) The original document making the international measure, or a copy of that document duly certified as such by an officer of the issuing or a requesting body, shall be lodged with an application under paragraph (1), together with (as necessary) an English translation of that document and that certificate.

(3) Any translation under paragraph (2) must be certified as a correct translation by the person making it, and the certificate must contain the full name, address and qualifications of the translator.

Intimation of application

3.24.3.—(1) The sheriff shall order intimation of an application to register an international measure—

(a) except where the sheriff is satisfied that the person to whom the international measure relates had an opportunity to be heard in the country where that measure was taken, to that person;

(b) which if registered would have the effect of placing the adult to whom the international measure relates in an establishment in Scotland, to the—

(i) Scottish Central Authority; and

(ii) Mental Welfare Commission;

(c) to the Public Guardian; and

(d) to any other person whom the sheriff considers appropriate.

(2) In this rule—

(a) "Scottish Central Authority" means an authority—

(i) designated under Article 28 of the Convention for the purposes of acting as such; or

(ii) appointed by the Scottish Ministers for the purposes of carrying out the functions to be carried out under schedule 3 of the Act by the Scottish Central Authority, where no authority is designated for the purposes of sub paragraph (i); and

(b)[1] "Mental Welfare Commission" means the Mental Welfare Commission for Scotland continued in being by section 4 of the Mental Health (Care and Treatment) (Scotland) Act 2003.

---

[1] As amended by the Mental Health (Care and Treatment) (Scotland) Act 2003 (Modification of Subordinate Legislation) Order 2005 (SSI 2005/445) Sch.1 para.29(1)(b) (effective October 5, 2005).

Notice to the Public Guardian

3.24.4.   The sheriff clerk shall within 7 days after the date of an order registering an international measure, provide the Public Guardian with—

    (a)   a copy of that order; and

    (b)   a copy of the international measure, and of any translation.

Register of recognised foreign measures

3.24.5.—(1)   There shall be a register of international measures ("the register") registered by order under this Part.

    (2)   The register shall include—

    (a)   the nature of the international measure;

    (b)   the date of the international measure;

    (c)   the date of the order under this Part granting recognition of the international measure;

    (d)   the name and address of—

        (i)   the person who applied for recognition of the international measure under this Part;

        (ii)   the person in respect of whom the international measure was taken; and

        (iii)   if applicable, the person on whom any power is conferred by the international measure; and

    (e)   a copy of the international measure, and of any translation.

    (3)   The Public Guardian shall maintain the register, and make it available during normal office hours for inspection by members of the public.

    (4)   The Public Guardian shall if requested by any person certify that an international measure registered under this Part has been entered in the register.

Part XXV[1]

Sexual Offences Act 2003

Interpretation

3.25.1.   In this Part—

"the Act" means the Sexual Offences Act 2003;

"main application" has the same meaning as in section 109(1) of the Act,[2] and words and expressions used in this Part and in the Act shall have the meanings given in the Act.

Time limit for service of a notice under section 99(3)

3.25.2.   If the person in respect of whom a notification order is sought wishes to serve on the applicant a notice under section 99(3) of the Act, that person must do so no later than 3 working days before the hearing date for the application for the relevant notification order.

---

[1] As inserted by the Act of Sederunt (Summary Applications, Statutory Applications and Appeals etc. Rules) Amendment (Sexual Offences Act 2003) 2004 (SSI 2004/222) r.2(2) (effective May 21, 2004).

[2] As inserted by the Act of Sederunt (Summary Applications, Statutory Applications and Appeals etc. Rules) Amendment (Protection of Children and Prevention of Sexual Offences (Scotland) Act 2005) 2005 (SSI 2005/473) r.2(2)(a) (effective October 7, 2005).

Time limit for service of a notice under section 106(11)

3.25.3. If the person in respect of whom a sexual offences prevention order is sought wishes to serve on the applicant a notice under section 106(11) of the Act, that person must do so no later than 3 working days before the hearing date for the application for the relevant sexual offences prevention order.

Time limit for service of a notice under section 116(6)

3.25.4. If the person in respect of whom a foreign travel order is sought wishes to serve on the applicant a notice under section 116(6) of the Act, that person must do so no later than 3 working days before the hearing date for the application for the relevant foreign travel order.

Variation, renewal or discharge of SOPOs

3.25.5.—[1](1) Where an application under section 108(1) of the Act for an order varying, renewing or discharging a sexual offences prevention order is made in a sheriff court other than the sheriff court in which the process relating to the sexual offences prevention order is held—

   (a)   the initial writ containing the application shall contain averments as to the sheriff court in which the process relating to the sexual offences prevention order is held;

   (b)   the sheriff clerk with whom the application is lodged shall notify the sheriff clerk of the sheriff court in which the process relating to the sexual offences prevention order is held; and

   (c)   the sheriff clerk of the sheriff court in which the process relating to the sexual offences prevention order is held shall, not later than 4 days after receipt of such notification, transfer the process relating to the sexual offences prevention order to the sheriff clerk of the sheriff court in which the application is made.

(2) For the purposes of paragraph (1), the sheriff court in which the process relating to the order is held is the sheriff court in which the sexual offences prevention order was granted or, where the process has been transferred under that paragraph, the last sheriff court to which the process has been transferred.

(3) A failure of the sheriff clerk to comply with paragraph (1) shall not invalidate the application.

Variation, renewal or discharge of FTOs

3.25.6.—[2](1) Subject to paragraph (2), an application under section 118 of the Act for an order varying, renewing or discharging a foreign travel order shall be made by minute in the process relating to the foreign travel order.

(2) Where an application under section 118(1) of the Act for an order varying, renewing or discharging a foreign travel order is made in a sheriff court other than the sheriff court in which the process relating to the foreign travel order is held—

   (a)   the application shall be made by summary application;

---

[1] As substituted by the Act of Sederunt (Summary Applications, Statutory Applications and Appeals etc. Rules) Amendment (Protection of Children and Prevention of Sexual Offences (Scotland) Act 2005) 2005 (SSI 2005/473) r.2(2)(b) (effective October 7, 2005).

[2] As substituted by the Act of Sederunt (Summary Applications, Statutory Applications and Appeals etc. Rules) Amendment (Protection of Children and Prevention of Sexual Offences (Scotland) Act 2005) 2005 (SSI 2005/473) r.2(2)(b) (effective October 7, 2005).

(b)   the initial writ containing the application shall contain averments as to the sheriff court in which the process relating to the foreign travel order is held;

(c)   the sheriff clerk with whom the application is lodged shall notify the sheriff clerk of the sheriff court in which the process relating to the foreign travel order is held; and

(d)   the sheriff clerk of the sheriff court in which the process relating to the foreign travel order is held shall, not later than 4 days after receipt of such notification, transfer the process relating to the foreign travel order to the sheriff clerk of the sheriff court in which the application is made.

(3)   For the purposes of paragraph (2), the sheriff court in which the process relating to the foreign travel order is held is the sheriff court in which the foreign travel order was granted or, where the process has been transferred under that paragraph, the last sheriff court to which the process has been transferred.

(4)   A minute under paragraph (1) shall be made in accordance with and regulated by Chapter 14 of the Ordinary Cause Rules.

(5)   A failure of the sheriff clerk to comply with paragraph (2) shall not invalidate the application.

Interim SOPOs

3.25.7.—[1](1)   Subject to paragraph (2), an application under section 109(2) of the Act for an interim sexual offences prevention order shall—

(a)   be made by crave in the initial writ containing the main application; and

(b)   once craved, be moved by motion to that effect.

(2)   Where an application under section 109(2) of the Act for an interim sexual offences prevention order is made in a sheriff court other than the sheriff court in which the main application was lodged, the application for an interim sexual offences prevention order shall be made by summary application.

(3)   The initial writ in a summary application under paragraph (2) shall contain averments as to the sheriff court in which the main application was lodged.

(4)   On receipt of a summary application under paragraph (2), the sheriff clerk shall notify the sheriff clerk of the sheriff court in which the main application was lodged.

(5)   There shall be produced with a summary application under paragraph (2) copies of the following documents, certified as correct by the applicant's solicitor or the sheriff clerk—

(a)   the initial writ containing the main application;

(b)   any answers to the main application; and

(c)   any interlocutors pronounced in the main application.

(6)   The sheriff clerk shall send a certified copy of any interlocutor disposing of a summary application under paragraph (2) to the sheriff clerk of the sheriff court in which the main application was lodged.

(7)   A failure of the sheriff clerk to comply with paragraph (4) or (6) shall not invalidate the main application or the summary application under paragraph (2).

---

[1] As inserted by the Act of Sederunt (Summary Applications, Statutory Applications and Appeals etc. Rules) Amendment (Protection of Children and Prevention of Sexual Offences (Scotland) Act 2005) 2005 (SSI 2005/473) r.2(2)(b) (effective October 7, 2005).

(8) Paragraphs (3) to (7) shall apply to an application for the variation, renewal or discharge of an interim sexual offences prevention order subject to the following modifications—

    (a) for references to a summary application under paragraph (2) there shall be substituted references to a summary application for the variation, renewal or discharge of an interim sexual offences prevention order;

    (b) references to the main application shall include references to any application for an interim sexual offences prevention order and any previous application for the variation, renewal or discharge of such an order; and

    (c) references to any interlocutors pronounced in the main application shall include any interlocutors pronounced in an application for an interim sexual offences prevention order or previous application for the variation, renewal or discharge of an interim sexual offences prevention order.".

Part XXVI

Protection of Children (Scotland) Act 2003

3.26.1.—3.26.6 *[Revoked by the Act of Sederunt (Rules of the Court of Session, Sheriff Appeal Court Rules and Sheriff Court Rules Amendment) (Sheriff Appeal Court) 2015 (SSI 2015/419) r.9(6) (effective 1 January 2016).]*

Part XXVII[1]

Antisocial Behaviour etc. (Scotland) Act 2004

Interpretation

3.27.1.—(1) In this Part—

"the Act" means the Antisocial Behaviour etc. (Scotland) Act 2004;

"ASBO" means an antisocial behaviour order under section 4(1) of the Act;

"interim ASBO" means an interim ASBO under section 7(2) of the Act;

"parenting order" means a parenting order under section 13 or 102 of the Act; and

"the Principal Reporter" means the Principal Reporter appointed under section 127 of the Local Government etc. (Scotland) Act 1994.

(2) Any reference to a section shall, unless the context otherwise requires, be a reference to a section of the Act.

Applications for variation or revocation of ASBO s to be made by minute in the original process

3.27.2.—(1) An application under section 5 (variation and revocation of antisocial behaviour orders) shall be made by minute in the original process of the application for the ASBO in relation to which the variation or revocation is sought.

---

[1] As inserted by the Act of Sederunt (Summary Applications, Statutory Applications and Appeals etc. Rules) Amendment (Antisocial Behaviour etc. (Scotland) Act 2004) 2004 (SSI 2004/455) r.2(4) (effective January 31, 2005 in relation to the provisions specified in SSI 2004/455 r.1(2)(a); April 4, 2005 in relation to the provisions specified in SSI 2004/455 r.1(2)(b); November 15, 2005 in relation to the provisions specified in SSI 2004/455 r.1(2)(c); October 28, 2004 otherwise).

(2)   Where the person subject to the ASBO is a child, a written statement containing the views of the Principal Reporter on the application referred to in rule 3.27.2(1) shall, where practicable, be lodged with that application.

Application for an interim ASBO

3.27.3.—(1)   An application for an interim ASBO shall be made by crave in the initial writ in which an ASBO is sought.

(2)   An application for an interim ASBO once craved shall be moved by motion to that effect.

(3)   The sheriff shall not consider an application for an interim ASBO until after the initial writ has been intimated to the person in respect of whom that application is made and, where that person is a child, a written statement containing the views of the Principal Reporter on that application has been lodged.

Notification of making etc. of ASBOs and interim ASBOs

3.27.4.   *[Repealed by the Act of Sederunt (Ordinary Cause and Summary Application Rules) Amendment (Miscellaneous) 2006 (SSI 2006/410) r.3(2) (effective August 18, 2006).]*

Parenting orders

3.27.5.—(1)   Where a sheriff is considering making a parenting order under section 13 (sheriffs power to make parenting order), the sheriff shall order the applicant for the ASBO to—

    (a)   intimate to any parent in respect of whom the parenting order is being considered—

        (i)   that the court is considering making a parenting order in respect of that parent;

        (ii)   that if that parent wishes to oppose the making of such a parenting order, he or she may attend or be represented at the hearing at which the sheriff considers the making of the parenting order;

        (iii)   the place, date and time of the hearing set out in sub-paragraph (a)(ii) above; and

        (iv)   that if that parent fails to appear and is not represented at the hearing, a parenting order may be made in respect of the parent; and

    (b)   serve on any parent in respect of whom the parenting order is being considered a copy of the initial writ in which the ASBO is sought.

(2)   Any parent in respect of whom a parenting order under section 13 is being considered may be sisted as a party to the action on their own motion, on the motion of either party or by the sheriff of his own motion.

Closure notice

3.27.6.—(1)   A closure notice served under section 27 (service etc.) shall be in the form of Form 25 and shall (in addition to the requirements set out in section 27(5))—

    (a)   state that it has been authorised by a senior police officer;

    (b)   specify the date, time and place of the hearing of the application for a closure order under section 28; and

    (c)   state that any person living on or having control of, responsibility for or an interest in the premises to which the closure notice relates who wishes to oppose the application should attend or be represented.

(2)   Certification of service of a copy of the closure notice to all persons identified in accordance with section 27(2)(b) shall be in the form of Form 26.

Application for closure orders

3.27.7.   An application to the sheriff for a closure order under section 28 shall be in the form of Form 27.

Application for extension of closure orders

3.27.8.   An application to the sheriff for an extension of a closure order under section 32 shall be by minute in the form of Form 28 lodged in the original process of the application for the closure order in relation to which the extension is sought and shall be lodged not less than 21 days before the closure order to which it relates is due to expire.

Application for revocation of closure order

3.27.9.   An application to the sheriff for revocation of a closure order under section 33 shall be by minute in the form of Form 29 lodged in the original process of the application for the closure order in relation to which the revocation is sought.

Application for access to premises

3.27.10.   An application to the sheriff for an order for access to premises under section 34 shall be by minute in the form of Form 30 lodged in the original process of the application for the closure order in relation to which the access order is sought.

Applications by summary application

3.27.11.   An application under section 35 (Reimbursement of expenditure), 63 (Appeal against graffiti removal notice) or 64 (Appeal against notice under section 61(4)) shall be by summary application.

3.27.12.   An application under section 71 (Failure to comply with notice: order as to rental income), 74 (Failure to comply with notice: management control order) or 97 (Appeals against notice under section 94) shall be by summary application.

Revocation and suspension of order as to rental income

3.27.13.   An application under section 73(2) for the revocation or suspension of an order relating to rental income shall be by minute lodged in the original process of the application for the order relating to rental income in relation to which the order for revocation or suspension is sought.

Revocation of management control order

3.27.14.   An application under section 76(1) for the revocation of a management control order shall be by minute lodged in the original process of the application for the management control order in relation to which the order for revocation is sought.

Review of parenting order

3.27.15.—(1)   An application under section 105(1) for revocation or variation of a parenting order shall be by minute lodged in the original process of the application for the parenting order in relation to which the order for revocation or variation is sought.

(2)   Where the court that made a parenting order makes an order under section 105(5) that court shall within 4 days transmit the original process relating to the parenting order to the court specified in that order.

Procedural requirements relating to parenting orders

3.27.16.   Where the sheriff is considering making a parenting order, or a revocation or variation of a parenting order, and it is practicable, having regard to the age and maturity of the child to—

    (a)   give the child an opportunity to indicate whether the child wishes to express views; and

    (b)   if the child so wishes, give the child an opportunity to express those views,

the sheriff shall order intimation in the form of Form 31 to the child in respect of whom the order was or is proposed to be made.

3.27.17.   Where the sheriff is considering making a parenting order or revoking or varying a parenting order and does not already have sufficient information about the child, the sheriff shall order intimation in the form of Form 32 to the local authority for the area in which the child resides.

Enforcement of local authorities' duties under section 71 of the Children (Scotland) Act 1995

3.27.18.   An application under section 71A(2) of the Children (Scotland) Act 1995 by the Principal Reporter shall be by summary application to the sheriff principal of the Sheriffdom in which the principal office of the local authority is situated.

Part XXVIII[1]

Land Reform (Scotland) Act 2003

Interpretation

3.28.1.   In this Part—

"the Act" means the Land Reform (Scotland) Act 2003.

Public notice of appeal against section 14(2) remedial notice

3.28.2.   Where an owner of land appeals by summary application undersection 14(4) of the Act against a notice served on him under section 14(2) of the Act, the owner must at the same time as, or as closely in time as practicable to, the lodging

---

[1] As inserted by the Act of Sederunt (Summary Applications, Statutory Applications and Appeals, etc. Rules) Amendment (Land Reform) (Scotland) Act 2005 (SSI 2005/61), r.2(2)(effective February 9, 2005).

of the application, advertise by publication of an advertisement in a newspaper circulating in the area of the land details of the application including details of the notice appealed against.

Restriction on number of persons being party to section 14(4) application

3.28.3. Persons interested in the exercise of access rights over the land to which a summary application under section 14(2) of the Act relates, and persons or bodies representative of such persons, may be parties to the summary application proceedings, but the court may order that any one or more of the persons or bodies who have the same interests and no others, may take an active part in the proceedings.

Public notice and restriction on number of parties to section 15 application

3.28.4. The provisions in rules 3.28.2 and 3.28.3 above apply with necessary modifications to a summary application appealing against a notice served under section 15(2) of the Act.

Public notice and restriction on number of parties to section 28 application

3.28.5.—(1) The provisions in rules 3.28.2 and 3.28.3 above apply with necessary modifications to a summary application for a declaration under section 28(1) or (2) of the Act.

(2) A summary application under section 28(1) or (2) of the Act may be made at any time.

Part XXIX[1]

Risk of Sexual Harm Orders

Interpretation

3.29.1. In this Part

"the Act" means the Protection of Children and Prevention of Sexual Offences (Scotland) Act 2005[5];

"main application" has the same meaning as in section 5 of the Act,

and words and expressions used in this Part and in the Act shall have the meanings given in the Act.

Variation, renewal or discharge of RSHOs

3.29.2.—(1) Subject to paragraph (2), an application under section 4(1) of the Act for an order varying, renewing or discharging a risk of sexual harm order shall be made by minute in the process relating to the risk of sexual harm order.

(2) Where an application under section 4(1) of the Act for an order varying, renewing or discharging a risk of sexual harm order is made in a sheriff court other than the sheriff court in which the process relating to the risk of sexual harm order is held—

    (a) the application shall be made by summary application;

    (b) the initial writ containing the application shall contain averments as to

---

[1] As inserted by Act of Sederunt (Summary Applications, Statutory Applications and Appeals etc. Rules) Amendment (Protection of Children and Prevention of Sexual Offences (Scotland) Act 2005) 2005 (SSI 2005/473) r.2(3) (effective October 7, 2005).

the sheriff court in which the process relating to the risk of sexual harm order is held;

(c)   the sheriff clerk with whom the application is lodged shall notify the sheriff clerk of the sheriff court in which the process relating to the risk of sexual harm order is held; and

(d)   the sheriff clerk of the sheriff court in which the process relating to the risk of sexual harm order is held shall, not later than 4 days after receipt of such notification, transfer the process relating to the risk of sexual harm order to the sheriff clerk of the sheriff court in which the application is made.

(3)   For the purposes of paragraph (2), the sheriff court in which the process relating to the risk of sexual harm order is held is the sheriff court in which the risk of sexual harm order was granted or, where the process has been transferred under that paragraph, the last sheriff court to which the process has been transferred.

(4)   A minute under paragraph (1) shall be made in accordance with and regulated by Chapter 14 of the Ordinary Cause Rules.

(5)   A failure of the sheriff clerk to comply with paragraph (2) shall not invalidate the application.

Interim RSHOs

3.29.3.—(1)   Subject to paragraph (2), an application under section 5(2) of the Act for an interim risk of sexual harm order shall—

(a)   be made by crave in the initial writ containing the main application; and

(b)   once craved, be moved by motion to that effect.

(2)   Where an application under section 5(2) of the Act for an interim risk of sexual harm order is made in a sheriff court other than the sheriff court in which the main application was lodged, the application for an interim risk of sexual harm order shall be made by summary application.

(3)   The initial writ in a summary application under paragraph (2) shall contain averments as to the sheriff court in which the main application was lodged.

(4)   On receipt of a summary application under paragraph (2), the sheriff clerk shall notify the sheriff clerk of the sheriff court in which the main application was lodged.

(5)   There shall be produced with a summary application under paragraph (2) copies of the following documents, certified as correct by the applicant's solicitor or the sheriff clerk:—

(a)   the initial writ containing the main application;

(b)   any answers to the main application; and

(c)   any interlocutors pronounced in the main application.

(6)   The sheriff clerk shall send a certified copy of any interlocutor disposing of a summary application under paragraph (2) to the sheriff clerk of the sheriff court in which the main application was lodged.

(7)   Rule 3.29.2 (variation, renewal or discharge of RSHOs) shall apply to an application for an order under section 5(6) of the Act for variation, renewal or discharge of an interim risk of sexual harm order subject to the following modifications:—

(a)   for references to section 4(1) of the Act there shall be substituted references to section 5(6) of the Act; and

(b)   for references to a risk of sexual harm order there shall be substituted references to an interim risk of sexual harm order.

(8) A failure of the sheriff clerk to comply with paragraph (4) or (6) shall not invalidate the main application or the summary application under paragraph (2).

Service of RSHOs

3.29.4.—(1) This rule applies to—

  (a) a risk of sexual harm order;

  (b) an interim risk of sexual harm order; and

  (c) an order varying or renewing an order mentioned in sub-paragraph (a) or (b).

(2)[1] The sheriff clerk shall serve a copy of the order on the person against whom it has effect.

(3)[2] For the purposes of paragraph (2), the copy of the order is served—

  (a) where the person against whom the order has effect is present in court when the order is made—

    (i) by giving it to the person and obtaining a receipt therefor;

    (ii) by sending it to the person by recorded delivery or registered post; or

    (iii) by causing it to be served by sheriff officer; or

  (b) where the person against whom the order has effect is not present in court when the order is made—

    (i) by sending it to the person by recorded delivery or registered post; or

    (ii) by causing it to be served by sheriff officer.

(4) A failure by the sheriff clerk to comply with this rule shall not invalidate the order.

Part XXX[3]

Mental Health (Care and Treatment) (Scotland) Act 2003

Interpretation

3.30.1. In this Part "the Act" means the Mental Health (Care and Treatment) (Scotland) Act 2003.

Applications for removal orders

3.30.2.—(1) An application under section 293 of the Act (removal order to place of safety) shall be lodged with the sheriff clerk who shall fix a date for hearing the application.

(2) An order fixing a hearing shall be intimated in such manner and within such timescales as may be prescribed by the sheriff.

---

[1] As substituted by the Act of Sederunt (Ordinary Cause and Summary Application Rules) Amendment (Miscellaneous) 2006 (SSI 2006/410) r.3(3) (effective August 18, 2006).

[2] As substituted by the Act of Sederunt (Ordinary Cause and Summary Application Rules) Amendment (Miscellaneous) 2006 (SSI 2006/410) r.3(3) (effective August 18, 2006).

[3] As inserted by Act of Sederunt (Summary Applications, Statutory Applications and Appeals etc. Rules) Amendment (Mental Health (Care and Treatment) (Scotland) Act 2003) 2005 (SSI 2005/504) r.2(2) (effective October 6, 2005).

Applications for recall or variation of removal orders

3.30.3.—(1)   An application under section 295 of the Act (recall or variation of removal order) shall be lodged with the sheriff clerk who shall fix a date for hearing the application.

(2)   An order fixing a hearing shall be intimated by the sheriff clerk in such manner and within such timescales as may be prescribed by the sheriff.

Remit to Court of Session

3.30.4.—(1)   Where the sheriff principal to whom an appeal is made remits the appeal to the Court of Session under section 320 of the Act (appeals), the sheriff clerk shall, within four days after the sheriff principal has pronounced the interlocutor remitting the appeal to the Court of Session, transmit the process to the Deputy Principal Clerk of Session.

(2)   On transmitting the process under paragraph (1), the sheriff clerk shall—

    (a)   send written notice of the remit and transmission of the process to each party; and

    (b)   certify on the interlocutor sheet that he has done so.

Part XXXI[1]

Football Banning Orders

Interpretation

3.31.1.   In this Part—

"the Act" means the Police, Public Order and Criminal Justice (Scotland) Act 2006;

"football banning order" means an order made under section 52(4) of the Act.

Applications for variation or termination of a football banning order

3.31.2.—(1)   An application under—

    (a)   section 57(1) of the Act for variation of a football banning order; or

    (b)   section 58(1) of the Act for termination of a football banning order, shall be made by minute in the process relating to the football banning order.

(2)   A minute under paragraph (1) shall be made in accordance with and regulated by Chapter 14 of the Ordinary Cause Rules.

Part XXXII[2]

Animal Health and Welfare

Interpretation

3.32.1.   In this Part—

"the 1981 Act" means the Animal Health Act 1981; and

---

[1] As inserted by the Act of Sederunt (Summary Applications, Statutory Applications and Appeals etc. (Rules) Amendment (Miscellaneous) 2006 (SSI 2006/437) r.2(2) (effective September 1, 2006).

[2] As inserted by the Act of Sederunt (Summary Applications, Statutory Applications and Appeals etc. Rules) Amendment (Miscellaneous) 2006 (SSI 2006/437) r.2(2) (effective September 1, 2006).

"the 2006 Act" means the Animal Health and Welfare (Scotland) Act 2006.

Interim orders

3.32.2.—(1) An application for an interim order under—

    (a)   section 28G(10) of the 1981 Act; or

    (b)   section 41(9) of the 2006 Act, or

    (c)[1]   section 48(9) of the Animal Welfare Act 2006,

shall be made by crave in the initial writ in which a seizure order is sought.

(2)   An application for an interim order once craved shall be moved by motion to that effect.

Interim orders pending appeal

3.32.3.   An application for an interim order under—

    (a)   section 28H(2) of the 1981 Act; or

    (b)   section 43(5) of the 2006 Act, or

    (c)[2]   section 49(5) of the Animal Welfare Act 2006,

where a seizure order is suspended or inexecutable shall be made by motion.

Part XXXIII[3]

The Equality Act 2010

Interpretation and application

3.33.1.—[4](1)   In this Part—

"the Commission" means the Commission for Equality and Human Rights; and "the 2010 Act" means the Equality Act 2010.

(2)   This Part applies to claims made by virtue of section 114(1) of the 2010 Act not including a claim for damages.

Intimation to Commission

3.33.2.[5]   The applicant shall, except where the applicant is the Commission, send a copy of the initial writ to the Commission by registered or recorded delivery post.

---

[1] As inserted by the Act of Sederunt (Summary Applications, Statutory Applications and Appeals etc. Rules) Amendment (Animal Welfare Act 2006) 2007 (SSI 2007/233) r.2(2) (effective March 26, 2007).

[2] As inserted by the Act of Sederunt (Summary Applications, Statutory Applications and Appeals etc. Rules) Amendment (Animal Welfare Act 2006) 2007 (SSI 2007/233) r.2(3) (effective March 26, 2007).

[3] As inserted by the Act of Sederunt (Ordinary Cause, Summary Application, Summary Cause and Small Claim Rules) Amendment (Equality Act 2006 etc.) 2006 (SSI 2006/509), (effective November 3, 2006). Chapter title amended by the Act of Sederunt (Sheriff Court Rules) (Equality Act 2010) 2010 (SSI 2010/340) para.3 (effective October 1, 2010).

[4] As substituted by the Act of Sederunt (Sheriff Court Rules) (Equality Act 2010) 2010 (SSI 2010/340) para.3 (effective October 1, 2010).

[5] As inserted by the Act of Sederunt (Sheriff Court Rules) (Miscellaneous Amendments) 2008 (SSI 2008/223) r.5(3)(b) (effective July 1, 2008).

Assessor

3.33.3.—(1) The sheriff may, of his own motion or on the motion of any party, appoint an assessor.

(2) The assessor shall be a person who the sheriff considers has special qualifications to be of assistance in determining the cause.

Taxation of Commission expenses

3.33.4. *[Omitted by the Act of Sederunt (Sheriff Court Rules) (Miscellaneous Amendments) 2008 (SSI 2008/223) r.5(3)(c) (effective July 1, 2008).]*

National security

3.33.5.—[1](1) Where, on a motion under paragraph (3) or of the sheriffs own motion, the sheriff considers it expedient in the interests of national security, the sheriff may—

  (a) exclude from all or part of the proceedings—

   (i) the pursuer;

   (ii) the pursuer's representatives;

   (iii) any assessors;

  (b) permit a pursuer or representative who has been excluded to make a statement to the court before the commencement of the proceedings or the part of the proceedings, from which he or she is excluded;

  (c) take steps to keep secret all or part of the reasons for his or her decision in the proceedings.

(2) The sheriff clerk shall, on the making of an order under paragraph (1) excluding the pursuer or the pursuer's representatives, notify the Advocate General for Scotland of that order.

(3) A party may apply by motion for an order under paragraph (1).

(4) The steps referred to in paragraph (1)(c) may include the following—

  (a) directions to the sheriff clerk; and

  (b) orders requiring any person appointed to represent the interests of the pursuer in proceedings from which the pursuer or the pursuer's representatives are excluded not to communicate (directly or indirectly) with any persons (including the excluded pursuer)—

   (i) on any matter discussed or referred to;

   (ii) with regard to any material disclosed,

during or with reference to any part of the proceedings from which the pursuer or the pursuer's representatives are excluded.

(5) Where the sheriff has made an order under paragraph (4)(b), the person appointed to represent the interests of the pursuer may apply by motion for authority to seek instructions from or otherwise communicate with an excluded person.

Transfer to Employment Tribunal

3.33.6.—[2](1) On transferring proceedings to an employment tribunal under section 140(2) of the 2010 Act, the sheriff—

  (a) shall state his or her reasons for doing so in the interlocutor; and

---

[1] As substituted by the Act of Sederunt (Sheriff Court Rules) (Equality Act 2010) 2010 (SSI 2010/340) para.3 (effective October 1, 2010).

[2] As inserted by the Act of Sederunt (Sheriff Court Rules) (Equality Act 2010) 2010 (SSI 2010/340) para.3 (effective October 1, 2010).

(b)   may make the order on such conditions as to expenses or otherwise as he or she thinks fit.

(2)   The sheriff clerk must, within 7 days from the date of such order—

(a)   transmit the relevant process to the Secretary of the Employment Tribunals (Scotland);

(b)   notify each party to the proceedings in writing of the transmission under subparagraph (a); and

(c)   certify, by making an appropriate entry on the interlocutor sheet, that he or she has made all notifications required under subparagraph (b).

(3)   Transmission of the process under paragraph (2)(a) will be valid notwithstanding any failure by the sheriff clerk to comply with paragraph (2)(b) and (c).

Transfer from Employment Tribunal

3.33.7.—[1](1)   On receipt of the documentation in proceedings which have been remitted from an employment tribunal under section 140(3) of the 2010 Act, the sheriff clerk must—

(a)   record the date of receipt on the first page of the documentation;

(b)   fix a hearing to determine further procedure not less than 14 days after the date of receipt of the process; and

(c)   forthwith send written notice of the date of the hearing fixed under subparagraph (b) to each party.

(2)   At the hearing fixed under paragraph (1)(b) the sheriff may make such order as he or she thinks fit to secure so far as practicable that the cause thereafter proceeds in accordance with these Rules.

Part XXXIV[2]

Licensing (Scotland) Act 2005

Appeals

3.34.—(1)   An appeal under section 131 of the Licensing (Scotland) Act 2005 is to be made by summary application.

(2)   An application under paragraph (1) must be lodged with the sheriff clerk of the sheriff court district in which the principal office of the Licensing Board is situated not later than 21 days after the relevant date.

(3)   In paragraph (2) "relevant date" means—

(a)   the date of the decision of the Licensing Board; or

(b)   where a statement of reasons has been required under section 51(2) of the 2005 Act, the date of issue of the statement of reasons.

Part XXXV[3]

---

[1] As inserted by the Act of Sederunt (Sheriff Court Rules) (Equality Act 2010) 2010 (SSI 2010/340) para.3 (effective October 1, 2010).

[2] As inserted by the Act of Sederunt (Summary Applications, Statutory Applications and Appeals etc. Rules) Amendment (Licensing (Scotland) Act 2005) 2008 (SSI 2008/9) r.2(2) (effective February 1, 2008) and substituted by the Act of Sederunt (Sheriff Court Rules) (Miscellaneous Amendments) (No.2) 2010 (SSI 2010/416) r.9 (effective December 13, 2010).

[3] As inserted by the Act of Sederunt (Summary Applications, Statutory Applications and Appeals etc. Rules) Amendment (Adult Support and Protection (Scotland) Act 2007) (No.2) 2008 (SSI 2008/335) r.2(2) (effective October 29, 2008).

Adult Support and Protection (Scotland) Act 2007

Interpretation

3.35.1. In this Part—

"the Act" means the Adult Support and Protection (Scotland) Act 2007;
"the adult at risk" has the same meaning as in section 3 of the Act.

Variation or recall of removal order

3.35.2.—(1) An application under section 17 of the Act (variation or recall of removal order) for variation or recall of a removal order shall be made by minute in the process relating to the removal order.

(2) A minute under paragraph (1) shall be made in accordance with and regulated by Chapter 14 of the Ordinary Cause Rules.

Applications—banning orders and temporary banning orders

3.35.3.—(1) Where in an application under subsection (1) of section 19 of the Act (banning orders) an order is sought under subsection (2)(a) or (b) of that section there shall, where appropriate and unless the sheriff otherwise directs, be lodged a plan which clearly identifies the area specified in the application.

(2) An application under section 21 of the Act (temporary banning orders) shall—

(a) be made by crave in the application for the banning order concerned; and

(b) once craved, be moved by motion to that effect.

(3) Where a temporary banning order is granted, the related application for a banning order shall be determined within 6 months of the date of the lodging of that application.

(4) An application under section 24(1)(a) of the Act (variation or recall of banning order) shall be made by minute in the process relating to the banning order.

(5) An application under section 24(1)(b) of the Act (variation or recall of temporary banning order) shall be moved by motion to that effect in the process relating to the application for the banning order concerned.

(6) A minute under paragraph (4) shall be made in accordance with and regulated by Chapter 14 of the Ordinary Cause Rules.

Attachment of power of arrest

3.35.4.—(1) The following documents shall be served under section 25(2) of the Act (powers of arrest) along with a power of arrest—

(a) a copy of the application for the order;

(b) a copy of the interlocutor granting the order and the power of arrest; and

(c) where the application to attach the power of arrest was made after the order was granted, a copy of the certificate of service of the order.

(2) The following documents shall be delivered to the chief constable in accordance with section 27(1) of the Act (notification to police)—

(a) a copy of the application for the order;

(b) a copy of the interlocutor granting the order;

(c) a copy of the certificate of service of the order; and

(d) where the application to attach the power of arrest was made after the order was granted—

    (i) where applicable, a copy of the application for the power of arrest;

    (ii) a copy of the interlocutor granting it; and

    (iii) a copy of the certificate of service of the power of arrest and the documents that required to be served along with it in accordance with section 25(2).

    (3) *[Revoked by the Act of Sederunt (Summary Applications, Statutory Applications and Appeals etc. Rules) Amendment (Adult Support and Protection (Scotland) Act 2007) (No.3) 2008 (SSI 2008/375) r.2(2) (effective November 20, 2008).]*

Notification to adult at risk etc.

3.35.5.[1] Where section 26(1)(b) of the Act (notification to the adult at risk etc. on the variation or recall of a banning order or temporary banning order) applies, the person prescribed for the purposes of section 26(2) is the sheriff clerk.

Certificate of delivery of documents

3.35.6.[2] Where a person is in any circumstances required to comply with section 26(2), 27(1) or 27(2) of the Act he shall, after such compliance, lodge in process a certificate of delivery in Form 34.

Warrants for entry

3.35.7.—(1) An application for a warrant for entry under section 38(2) of the Act (criteria for granting warrants of entry under section 7) shall be in Form 35.

    (2) The application may be granted without a hearing.

Applications for leave to appeal to the Sheriff Appeal Court

3.35.8.—(1) *[Omitted by the Act of Sederunt (Rules of the Court of Session, Sheriff Appeal Court Rules and Sheriff Court Rules Amendment) (Sheriff Appeal Court) 2015 (SSI 2015/419) r.9(7) (effective 1 January 2016; as to savings see SSI 2015/419 rule 20(5)(a)).]*

    (2) An application for leave to appeal against an interlocutor of the sheriff granting, or refusing to grant, a temporary banning order under section 51(2) of the Act shall be made within 7 days after the date of the interlocutor concerned.

    (3) *[Omitted by the Act of Sederunt (Rules of the Court of Session, Sheriff Appeal Court Rules and Sheriff Court Rules Amendment) (Sheriff Appeal Court) 2015 (SSI 2015/419) r.9(7) (effective 1 January 2016; as to savings see SSI 2015/419 rule 20(5)(a)).]*

Privacy of any hearing

3.35.9. The sheriff may, where he considers it appropriate in all the circumstances, appoint that the hearing of an application or other proceedings under this Part shall take place in private.

---

[1] As substituted by the Act of Sederunt (Summary Applications, Statutory Applications and Appeals etc. Rules) Amendment (Adult Support and Protection (Scotland) Act 2007) (No.3) 2008 (SSI 2008/375) r.2(3) (effective November 20, 2008).

[2] As substituted by the Act of Sederunt (Summary Applications, Statutory Applications and Appeals etc. Rules) Amendment (Adult Support and Protection (Scotland) Act 2007) (No.3) 2008 (SSI 2008/375) r.2(4) (effective November 20, 2008).

Part XXXVI[1]

UK Borders Act 2007

Interpretation

3.36.1. In this Part—

"the Act" means the UK Borders Act 2007; and

"an appeal" means an appeal to the sheriff under section 11(1) of the Act.

Appeals

3.36.2.—(1) Subject to paragraph (2), an appeal must be lodged with the sheriff clerk not later than 21 days after the date the penalty notice was received by the appellant.

(2) Where the appellant has given notice of objection under section 10(1) of the Act, an appeal must be lodged with the sheriff clerk not later than 21 days after the date that notice of the Secretary of State's decision under section 10(4) of the Act was received by the appellant.

Part XXXVII[2]

Employment Tribunals Act 1996

Conciliation: recovery of sums payable under compromises

3.37.1.—(1) An application to the sheriff for a declaration under section 19A(4) of the Employment Tribunals Act 1996 shall be made not later than 42 days from the date of issue of the certificate stating that a compromise has been reached.

(2) An application to the sheriff for a declaration under section 19A(4) of that Act is pending for the purposes of subsection (7) of that section from the date on which it is lodged with the sheriff clerk until the date upon which final judgment on the application has been extracted.

Part XXXVIII[3]

Counter-Terrorism Act 2008

Variation, renewal or discharge of foreign travel restriction order

3.38.—(1) Where an application under paragraph 9 of Schedule 5 to the Counter-Terrorism Act 2008 for an order varying, renewing or discharging a foreign travel restriction order is made in a sheriff court other than the sheriff court in which the process relating to the foreign travel restriction order is held—

    (a) the initial writ containing the application shall contain averments as to the sheriff court in which the process relating to the foreign travel restriction order is held;

---

[1] As inserted by the Act of Sederunt (Sheriff Court Rules) (Miscellaneous Amendments) (No.2) 2008 (SSI 2008/365) r.6 (effective November 25, 2006).

[2] As inserted by the Act of Sederunt (Summary Applications, Statutory Applications and Appeals etc. Rules) Amendment (Employment Tribunals Act 1996) 2009 (SSI 2009/109) r.2 (effective April 1, 2009).

[3] As inserted by the Act of Sederunt (Sheriff Court Rules) (Miscellaneous Amendments) 2009 (SSI 2009/294) r.18 (effective October 1, 2009).

(b) the sheriff clerk with whom the application is lodged shall notify the sheriff clerk of the sheriff court in which the process relating to the foreign travel restriction order is held; and

(c) the sheriff clerk of the sheriff court in which the process relating to the foreign travel restriction order is held shall, not later than 4 days after receipt of such notification, transfer the process relating to the foreign travel restriction order to the sheriff clerk of the sheriff court in which the application is made.

(2) For the purposes of paragraph (1), the sheriff court in which the process relating to the order is held is the sheriff court in which the foreign travel restriction order was granted or, where the process has been transferred under that paragraph, the last sheriff court to which the process has been transferred.

(3) A failure of the sheriff clerk to comply with paragraph (1) shall not invalidate the application.

Part XXXIX[1]

Public Health etc. (Scotland) Act 2008

Interpretation

3.39.1. In this Part—

"the Act" means the Public Health etc. (Scotland) Act 2008;
"an investigator" means a person appointed under section 21 of the Act;
"health board competent person" has the same meaning as in section 124 of the Act, and words and expressions used in this Part and in the Act shall have the same meaning given in the Act.

Application for a public health investigation warrant

3.39.2.—(1) An application made by an investigator for a warrant under section 27(2) of the Act (public health investigation warrants) shall be in Form 36.

(2) Where such a warrant is granted by the sheriff it shall be in Form 37.

Application for an order for medical examination

3.39.3.—(1) An application made by a health board for an order under section 34(1) of the Act (order for medical examination) shall be in Form 38.

(2) On receipt of an application mentioned in paragraph (1), the sheriff may order intimation of the application to such persons, within such a timescale and by such method as he sees fit.

(3) Where an order for a medical examination is granted by the sheriff it shall be in Form 39.

(4) Subject to the requirements of section 34(6)(b)(i) and (ii) of the Act, where an order for a medical examination is granted, the sheriff may direct that the order be notified to such persons, within such a timescale and by such method as he sees fit.

---

[1] As inserted by the Act of Sederunt (Summary Applications, Statutory Applications and Appeals etc. Rules) Amendment (Public Health etc. (Scotland) Act 2008) 2009 (SSI 2009/320) r.2 (effective October 1, 2009).

(5)   For the avoidance of doubt, the method of intimation or notification referred to in paragraphs (2) and (4) may include intimation or notification by telephone, email or facsimile transmission.

Application for a quarantine order

3.39.4.—(1)   An application made by a health board for a quarantine order under section 40(1) of the Act (quarantine orders) shall be in Form 40.

(2)   On receipt of an application mentioned in paragraph (1), the sheriff may order intimation of the application to such persons, within such a timescale and by such method as he sees fit.

(3)   Where a quarantine order is granted by the sheriff it shall be in Form 41.

(4)   Subject to the requirements of section 40(6)(b)(i) and (ii) of the Act, where a quarantine order is granted, the sheriff may direct that the order be notified to such persons, within such a timescale and by such method as he sees fit.

(5)   For the avoidance of doubt, the method of intimation or notification referred to in paragraphs (2) and (4) may include intimation or notification by telephone, email or facsimile transmission.

Application for a short term detention order

3.39.5.—(1)   An application made by a health board for a short term detention order under section 42(1) of the Act (order for removal to and detention in hospital) shall be in Form 42.

(2)   An application made by a health board for a short term detention order under section 43(1) of the Act (order for detention in hospital) shall be in Form 44.

(3)   On receipt of an application mentioned in paragraph (1) or (2), the sheriff may order intimation of the application to such persons, within such a timescale and by such method as he sees fit.

(4)   Where a short term detention order is granted by the sheriff under section 42(1) of the Act it shall be in Form 43.

(5)   Where a short term detention order is granted by the sheriff under section 43(1) of the Act it shall be in Form 45.

(6)   Subject to the requirements of sections 42(4)(b)(i) and (ii) and 43(4)(b)(i) and (ii) of the Act, where a short term detention order is granted under section 42(1) or 43(1) of the Act, the sheriff may direct that the order be notified to such persons, within such a timescale and by such method as he sees fit.

(7)   For the avoidance of doubt, the method of intimation or notification referred to in paragraphs (3) and (6) may include intimation or notification by telephone, email or facsimile transmission.

Application for an exceptional detention order

3.39.6.—(1)   An application made by a health board for an exceptional detention order under section 45(1) of the Act (exceptional detention order) shall be in Form 46.

(2)   On receipt of an application mentioned in paragraph (1), the sheriff may order intimation of the application to such persons, within such a timescale and by such method as he sees fit.

(3)   Where an exceptional detention order is granted by the sheriff it shall be in Form 47.

(4)   Subject to the requirements of section 45(4)(b)(i) and (ii) of the Act, where an exceptional detention order is granted, the sheriff may direct that the order be notified to such persons, within such a timescale and by such method as he sees fit.

(5)   For the avoidance of doubt, the method of intimation or notification referred to in paragraphs (2) and (4) may include intimation or notification by telephone, email or facsimile transmission.

Application for extension of a quarantine order, short term detention order or exceptional detention order

3.39.7.—(1)   An application made by a health board for an extension to a quarantine order, a short term detention order or an exceptional detention order under section 49(5) of the Act (extension of quarantine and hospital detention orders) shall be in Form 48.

(2)   On receipt of an application mentioned in paragraph (1), the sheriff may order intimation of the application to such persons, within such a timescale and by such method as he sees fit.

(3)   Where an order extending a quarantine order, a short term detention order or an exceptional detention order is granted by the sheriff it shall be in Form 49.

(4)   Subject to the requirements of section 49(10)(b)(i) and (ii) of the Act, where an order mentioned in paragraph (3) is granted, the sheriff may direct that the order be notified to such persons, within such a timescale and by such method as he sees fit.

(5)   For the avoidance of doubt, the method of intimation or notification referred to in paragraphs (2) and (4) may include intimation or notification by telephone, email or facsimile transmission.

Application for modification of a quarantine order, short term detention order or exceptional detention order

3.39.8.—(1)   An application made by a health board for an order modifying a quarantine order, a short term detention order or an exceptional detention order under section 51(1) of the Act (variation of quarantine and hospital detention orders) shall be in Form 50.

(2)   On receipt of an application mentioned in paragraph (1), the sheriff may order intimation of the application to such persons, within such a timescale and by such method as he sees fit.

(3)   Where an order modifying a quarantine order, a short term detention order or an exceptional detention order is granted by the sheriff it shall be in Form 51.

(4)   Subject to the requirements of section 51(5)(b)(i) and (ii) of the Act, where an order mentioned in paragraph (3) is granted, the sheriff may direct that the order be notified to such persons, within such a timescale and by such method as he sees fit.

(5)   For the avoidance of doubt, the method of intimation or notification referred to in paragraphs (2) and (4) may include intimation or notification by telephone, email or facsimile transmission.

Application for recall of an order granted in the absence of the person to whom it relates

3.39.9.—(1)   An application for recall of a quarantine order, a short term detention order or an exceptional detention order under section 59 of the Act (recall of orders granted in absence of persons to whom application relates) shall be in Form 52.

(2)   Subject to section 59(6) of the Act, on receipt of an application mentioned in paragraph (1), the sheriff may order intimation of the application to such persons, within such a timescale and by such method as he sees fit.

(3)   Where an order recalling a quarantine order, a short term detention order or an exceptional detention order is granted by the sheriff it shall be in Form 53.

(4)   Where an order mentioned in paragraph (3) is granted, the sheriff may direct that the order be notified to such persons, within such a timescale and by such method as he sees fit.

(5)   For the avoidance of doubt, the method of intimation or notification referred to in paragraphs (2) and (4) may include intimation or notification by telephone, email or facsimile transmission.

Intimation of applications in relation to a child

3.39.10.—(1)   This rule applies where an application is made under this Part and the person who it is proposed will be subject to the order is under 16.

(2)   On receipt of an application mentioned in paragraph (1), the sheriff may, in particular, order intimation of the application to a person who has day-to-day care or control of the person mentioned in paragraph (1).

Intimation of orders on the person to whom they apply

3.39.11.   Where a sheriff, in the absence of the person to whom it applies, grants—

(a)   a quarantine order under section 40(1) of the Act;

(b)   a short term detention order under section 42(1) of the Act;

(c)   an exceptional detention order under section 45 of the Act,

and the order is intimated to the person to whom it applies, a copy of Form 52 shall be delivered to that person along with the order.

Appeal to the sheriff against an exclusion order or a restriction order

3.39.12.—(1)   An appeal to the sheriff under section 61 of the Act (appeal against exclusion orders and restriction orders) in respect of an exclusion order or a restriction order shall be marked by lodging a note of appeal in Form 54.

(2)   On the lodging of a note of appeal, the sheriff clerk shall send a copy of the note of appeal to—

(a)   the health board competent person who made the exclusion order or restriction order; and

(b)   the person in relation to whom the order applies, where that person is not the appellant.

(3)   The sheriff shall make such order as he thinks fit in order to dispose of the appeal.

Application for a warrant to enter premises and take steps under Part 5 of the Act

3.39.13.—(1)   An application made by a local authority for a warrant under section 78(2) of the Act (warrant to enter and take steps) shall be in Form 55.

(2)   Where such a warrant is granted by the sheriff it shall be in Form 56.

Application for an order for disposal of a body

3.39.14.—(1)   An application made by a local authority for an order for the disposal of a body under section 93 of the Act (power of sheriff to order removal to mortuary and disposal) shall be in Form 57.

(2)   Where such an order is granted by the sheriff it shall be in Form 58.

Application for appointment of a single arbiter to determine a dispute in relation to compensation

3.39.15. An application under sections 30(6), 56(5), 57(3), 58(4) or 82(3) of the Act for the appointment of a single arbiter to determine a dispute in relation to compensation may be made by written application in the form of a letter addressed to the sheriff clerk.

Part XL[1]

Forced Marriage etc. (Protection and Jurisdiction) (Scotland) Act 2011

Interpretation

3.40.1. In this Part (except where the context otherwise requires) references to terms defined in Part 1 of the Forced Marriage etc. (Protection and Jurisdiction) (Scotland) Act 2011 have the same meaning here as given there.

Applications for leave for a forced marriage protection order

3.40.2.—(1) This rule applies where leave of the court is required to make an application for a forced marriage protection order.

(2) Leave shall be sought at the time of presenting the initial writ by letter addressed to the sheriff clerk.

(3) The letter shall include a statement of—

(a) the grounds on which leave is sought;

(b) whether or not the applicant has applied for legal aid.

(4) Where the applicant has applied for legal aid he or she must also present along with the initial writ written confirmation from the Scottish Legal Aid Board that it has determined, under regulation 7(2)(b) of the Civil Legal Aid (Scotland) Regulations 2002, that notification of the application should be dispensed with or postponed.

(5) An application under paragraph (2) shall not be served or intimated unless the sheriff otherwise directs.

(6) The sheriff may hear the pursuer on the application and may grant or refuse it or make such other order in relation to it as the sheriff considers appropriate.

(7) Where leave is granted, a copy of the interlocutor allowing leave must be served upon the defender along with the warrant of citation.

Applications for variation, recall or extension of a forced marriage protection order

3.40.3.—(1) An application for variation, recall or extension of a forced marriage protection order must be made by minute in the process relating to the forced marriage protection order.

(2) Except where the sheriff otherwise directs, any such minute must be lodged in accordance with, and regulated by, Chapter 14 of the Ordinary Cause Rules.

(3) Paragraph (4) applies where leave of the court is required under section 7(1)(d) or 8(3)(d) of the 2011 Act before an application for variation, or recall or extension of a forced marriage protection order may be made.

---

[1] As inserted by the Act of Sederunt (Sheriff Court Rules) (Miscellaneous Amendments) (No.3) 2011 (SSI 2011/386) para.7 (effective November 28, 2011).

(4)   Leave shall be sought at the time of presenting the minute by letter addressed to the sheriff clerk.

(5)   The letter shall include a statement of—

    (a)   the grounds on which leave is sought;

    (b)   whether or not the applicant has applied for legal aid.

(6)   Where the applicant has applied for legal aid he or she must also present along with the minute confirmation from the Scottish Legal Aid Board that it has determined, under regulation 7(2)(b) of the Civil Legal Aid (Scotland) Regulations 2002, that notification of the application should be dispensed with or postponed.

(7)   An application under paragraph (4) shall not be served or intimated unless the sheriff otherwise directs.

(8)   The sheriff may hear the applicant on the application and may grant or refuse it or make such other order in relation to it as the sheriff considers appropriate.

(9)   Where leave is granted, a copy of the interlocutor allowing leave must be intimated along with the minute.

PART XLI[1, 2, 3]

REPORTING RESTRICTIONS

Interpretation and application of this Part

3.41.1.—(1) This Part applies to orders which restrict the reporting of proceedings.

(2)   In this Part, "interested person" means a person—

    (a)   who has asked to see any order made by the sheriff which restricts the reporting of proceedings, including an interim order; and

    (b)   whose name is included on a list kept by the Lord President for the purposes of this Part.

Interim orders

3.41.2.—[4](1) Where the sheriff is considering making an order, the sheriff must first make an interim order.

(2)   The sheriff clerk shall immediately send a copy of the interim order to any interested person.

(3)   The sheriff shall specify in the interim order why the sheriff is considering making an order.

---

[1] As inserted by the Act of Sederunt (Sheriff Court Rules) (Miscellaneous Amendments) (No.3) 2011 (SSI 2011/386) para.8 (effective November 28, 2011).

[2] As amended by the Act of Sederunt (Sheriff Court Rules) (Miscellaneous Amendments) 2012 (SSI 2012/188) para.12 (effective August 1, 2012).

[3] As substituted by the Act of Sederunt (Rules of the Court of Session and Sheriff Court Rules Amendment No.3) (Reporting Restrictions) 2015 (SSI 2015/85) para.4 (effective April 1, 2015).

[4] As amended by the Act of Sederunt (Rules of the Court of Session 1994, Sheriff Appeal Court Rules and Sheriff Court Rules Amendment) (Reporting Restrictions) 2020 (SSI 2020/28) r.5(2) (effective 2 March 2020).

Representations

3.41.3.—[1](1) *[Repealed by the Act of Sederunt (Rules of the Court of Session 1994, Sheriff Appeal Court Rules and Sheriff Court Rules Amendment) (Reporting Restrictions) 2020 (SSI 2020/28) r.5(2) (effective 2 March 2020).]*

(2) An interested person who would be directly affected by the making of an order shall have an opportunity to make representations to the sheriff before an order is made.

(3) Representations shall—

(a) be made by letter addressed to the sheriff clerk;

(b) where an urgent hearing is sought, include reasons explaining why an urgent hearing is necessary;

(c) be lodged no later than 2 days after the interim order is sent to interested persons in accordance with rule 3.41.2(2).

(4) Where the period for lodging representations expires on a Saturday, Sunday, or public or court holiday, it shall be deemed to expire on the next day on which the sheriff clerk's office is open for civil court business.

(5) On representations being made—

(a) the sheriff shall appoint a date and time for a hearing—

(i) on the first suitable court day thereafter; or

(ii) where the sheriff is satisfied that an urgent hearing is necessary, at such earlier date and time as the sheriff may determine;

(b) the sheriff clerk shall—

(i) notify the date and time of the hearing to the parties to the proceedings and the person who has made representations; and

(ii) send a copy of the representations to the parties to the proceedings.

(6) Where no interested person makes representations in accordance with rule 3.41.3(2), the sheriff clerk shall put the interim order before the sheriff in chambers in order that the sheriff may resume consideration as to whether to make an order.

(7) Where the sheriff, having resumed consideration under rule 3.41.3(6), makes no order, the sheriff shall recall the interim order.

(8) Where the court recalls an interim order, the clerk of court shall immediately notify any interested person.

Notification of reporting restrictions

3.41.4.— Where the sheriff makes an order, the sheriff clerk shall immediately—

(a) send a copy of the order to any interested person;

(b) arrange for the publication of the making of the order on the Scottish Court Service website.

Applications for variation or revocation

3.41.5.—(1) A person aggrieved by an order may apply to the sheriff for its variation or revocation.

(2) An application shall be made by letter addressed to the sheriff clerk.

(3) On an application being made—

(a) the sheriff shall appoint the application for a hearing;

---

[1] As amended by the Act of Sederunt (Rules of the Court of Session 1994, Sheriff Appeal Court Rules and Sheriff Court Rules Amendment) (Reporting Restrictions) 2020 (SSI 2020/28) r.5(2) (effective 2 March 2020).

(b)　the sheriff clerk shall—

      (i)　notify the date and time of the hearing to the parties to the proceedings and the applicant;

      (ii)　send a copy of the application to the parties to the proceedings.

(4)　The hearing shall, so far as reasonably practicable, be before the sheriff who made the order.

Part XLII[1]

Regulation of Investigatory Powers Act 2000

Interpretation

3.42.1.　In this Part—

"the 2000 Act" means the Regulation of Investigatory Powers Act 2000; and words and expressions used in this Part and in the 2000 Act shall have the same meaning given in the 2000 Act.

Authorisations requiring judicial approval

3.42.2.—(1)　An application under section 23B(1) of the 2000 Act (procedure for judicial approval) for an order under section 23A(2) (authorisations requiring judicial approval)—

(a)　approving the grant or renewal of an authorisation; or

(b)　the giving or renewal of a notice,

shall be in Form 59, which must be signed by a solicitor on behalf of the local authority.

(2)　The application (and any order made in relation to it) must not be intimated to—

(a)　the person to whom the authorisation or notice which is the subject of the application or order relates; or

(b)　such person's representatives.

(3)　The application must be heard and determined by the sheriff in private.

(4)　Where an application is granted by the sheriff the order shall be in Form 60.

Part XLIII[2]

Proceeds of Crimes Act 2002 (External Investigations) Order 2013

Application of this Part

3.43.1.　This Part applies to applications to the sheriff under Part 2 of the Proceeds of Crime Act 2002 (External Investigations) Order 2013.

Applications

3.43.2.—(1)　An application under the following provisions shall be made by summary application—

(a)　article 40(1) (production orders);

---

[1] As inserted by the Act of Sederunt (Sheriff Court Rules) (Miscellaneous Amendments) (No.3) 2012 (SSI 2012/271) para.10 (effective November 1, 2012).

[2] As inserted by the Act of Sederunt (Summary Applications, Statutory Applications and Appeals etc. Rules Amendment) (Miscellaneous) 2013 (SSI 2013/293) r.3 (effective November 11; 2013).

(b) article 47(1) (search warrants);

(c) article 56(1) (customer information orders);

(d) article 63(1) (account monitoring orders).

(2) An application under the following provisions shall be made by minute in the process of the original application—

(a) article 46(2) (discharge or variation of a production order or an order to grant entry);

(b) article 62(2) (discharge or variation of a customer information order);

(c) article 67(2) (discharge or variation of an account monitoring order).

(3) An application under article 42(2) (order to grant entry) shall be made—

(a) in the application for the production order; or

(b) where the application is made after a production order is made, by minute in the process of the application for the production order.

Part XLIV[1]

Gender Recognition Act 2004

3.44.1. In this Part,—

"the 2004 Act" means the Gender Recognition Act 2004;

"full gender recognition certificate" and "interim gender recognition certificate" have the meanings assigned by section 25 of the 2004 Act;

"Gender Recognition Panels" is to be construed in accordance with Schedule 1 to the 2004 Act.

3.44.2.—(1) This rule applies where a party to a protected Scottish marriage who has been issued with an interim gender recognition certificate makes an application to the sheriff under section 4E of the 2004 Act for the issue of a full gender recognition certificate.

(2) The sheriff shall make an order for intimation of the application on the applicant's spouse, but no such order may be made unless there has been produced with the initial writ—

(a) an extract of the relevant entry in the register of marriages; and

(b) the interim gender recognition certificate or, failing that, a certified copy of the interim gender recognition certificate.

(3) For the purpose of this rule, a certified copy of an interim gender recognition certificate shall be a copy of that certificate sealed with the seal of the Gender Recognition Panels and certified to be a true copy by an officer authorised by the President of the Gender Recognition Panels.

(4) On the granting of the application the sheriff clerk shall give the applicant's spouse a certified copy of the full gender recognition certificate.

3.44.3. When a full gender recognition certificate has been issued on an application under section 4E of the 2004 Act, an application for a corrected gender recognition certificate under section 6 of the 2004 Act (Errors in certificates) shall be made by minute in the process in the application pursuant to which the full gender recognition certificate was issued.

---

[1] As inserted by the Act of Sederunt (Rules of the Court of Session and Sheriff Court Rules Amendment No. 2) (Marriage and Civil Partnership (Scotland) Act 2014) 2014 (SSI 2014/302) para.7 (effective December 16, 2014).

PART XLV[1]

MUTUAL RECOGNITION OF PROTECTION MEASURES IN CIVIL MATTERS

Interpretation

3.45.1.[2]   In this Part—

"the 2015 Act" means the Human Trafficking and Exploitation (Scotland) Act 2015;

"Article 5 certificate" means a certificate issued under Article 5 of the Regulation;

"Article 14 certificate" means a certificate issued under Article 14 of the Regulation;

"incoming protection measure" means a protection measure that has been ordered in a Member State other than the United Kingdom or Denmark;

"interim risk of sexual harm order" has the meaning given by section 5(2) of the Protection of Children and Prevention of Sexual Offences (Scotland) Act 2005;

"interim sexual offences prevention order" has the meaning given by section 109(2) of the Sexual Offences Act 2003;

"interim trafficking and exploitation prevention order" means an order made under section 24 of the 2015 Act;

"interim trafficking and exploitation risk order" means an order made under section 30 of the 2015 Act;

"Member State" means a Member State of the European Union;

"person causing the risk" has the meaning given by Article 3(3) of the Regulation;

"protected person" has the meaning given by Article 3(2) of the Regulation;

"protection measure" has the meaning given by Article 3(1) of the Regulation;

"registered post service" has the meaning given by section 125(1) of the Postal Services Act 2000;

"risk of sexual harm order" has the meaning given by section 2(1) of the Protection of Children and Prevention of Sexual Offences (Scotland) Act 2005;

"sexual offences prevention order" has the meaning given by section 106(1) of the Sexual Offences Act 2003;

"the Regulation" means Regulation (EU) No. 606/2013 of the European Parliament and of the Council of 12 June 2013 on mutual recognition of protection measures in civil matters.

"trafficking and exploitation prevention order" means an order made under section 18 of the 2015 Act;

"trafficking and exploitation risk order" means an order made under section 26 of the 2015 Act.

---

[1] As inserted by the Act of Sederunt Act of Sederunt (Rules of the Court of Session and Sheriff Court Rules Amendment No. 3) (Mutual Recognition of Protection Measures) 2014 (SSI 2014/371) para.4 (effective January 11, 2015).

[2] As amended by the Act of Sederunt (Summary Application Rules 1999 Amendment) (Trafficking Exploitation Orders) 2017 (SSI 2017/211) para.2(2)(a) (effective 30 June 2017 and 31 October 2017 subject to SSI 2017/211 para.1(3)).

Application of rules 3.45.3 to 3.45.9

3.45.2.   Rules 3.45.3 to 3.45.9 apply for the purpose of—

(a)   the issuing of an Article 5 certificate where the protection measure in respect of which the certificate is sought is—

    (i)   a sexual offences prevention order or an interim sexual offences prevention order; or

    (ii)   a risk of sexual harm order or an interim risk of sexual harm order; or

    (iii)[1,2]   a trafficking and exploitation prevention order or an interim trafficking and exploitation prevention order or a trafficking and exploitation risk order or an interim trafficking and exploitation risk order;

(b)   the rectification or withdrawal of such a certificate; and

(c)   the issuing of an Article 14 certificate subsequent to the issue of such a certificate.

Form of application for Article 5 certificate

3.45.3.   An application for the issue of an Article 5 certificate shall be made by lodging Form 61 in process.

Issue of Article 5 certificate

3.45.4.   The sheriff shall issue an Article 5 certificate where—

(a)   the order in respect of which the certificate is sought is a protection measure;

(b)   the person applying for the certificate is a protected person in respect of the protection measure;

(c)   the first condition specified in rule 3.45.5 is satisfied; and

(d)   the second condition specified in rule 3.45.5 is satisfied, if the protection measure is an interim order.

Conditions for issue of Article 5 certificate

3.45.5.—(1)   The first condition is that—

(a)   at the hearing when the order was granted, the person causing the risk was—

    (i)   personally present in court; or

    (ii)   represented by a solicitor or an advocate; or

(b)   the order has been—

    (i)   given or sent to the person causing the risk in accordance with section 112(3) of the Sexual Offences Act 2003; or

    (ii)   served on the person causing the risk in accordance with rule 3.29.4.

(2)   The second condition is that either paragraph (3) or (4) applies.

(3)   This paragraph applies where—

---

[1] As inserted by the Act of Sederunt (Summary Application Rules 1999 Amendment) (Trafficking Exploitation Orders) 2017 (SSI 2017/211) para.2(2)(b) (effective 30 June 2017 subject to SSI 2017/211 para.1(3)).

[2] As amended by the Act of Sederunt (Rules of the Court of Session 1994 and Summary Application Rules 1999 Amendment) (Miscellaneous) (SSI 2017/242) r.3(2) (effective 18 September 2017).

(a) the writ containing the crave for the order was intimated on the person causing the risk before the interim order was granted;

(b) the interim order was granted pursuant to an application intimated on the person causing the risk; and

(c) the person causing the risk had a sufficient opportunity to oppose the application, whether or not he or she did so.

(4) This paragraph applies where the sheriff is satisfied that the person causing the risk has had a sufficient opportunity to apply to have the interim order discharged.

(5) Where the sheriff requires to be satisfied that any writ, motion or interlocutor has been intimated for the purposes of this rule, it is for the person on whose behalf intimation has been given to lodge in process a certificate of intimation if such a certificate is not already in process.

Notice of issue of Article 5 certificate

3.45.6.—(1) Where the sheriff issues an Article 5 certificate, the sheriff clerk shall—

(a) give the protected person—
   (i) the certificate; and
   (ii) a certified copy of the interlocutor granting the protection measure; and

(b) give the person causing the risk notice of the issue of the certificate in accordance with paragraphs (2) to (4).

(2) Where the address of the person causing the risk is known, notice shall be given by sending that person—

(a) a notice in Form 62;

(b) a copy of the certificate; and

(c) a copy of the interlocutor granting the protection measure.

(3) Where the address of the person causing the risk is outwith the United Kingdom, the sheriff clerk shall send the documents mentioned in paragraph (2) by a registered post service.

(4) Where the address of the person causing the risk is not known, notice shall be given by displaying on the walls of court a notice in Form 63.

(5) In this rule, "Article 5 certificate" includes a rectified Article 5 certificate issued under Article 9(1)(a) of the Regulation.

Effect of variation of order

3.45.7. Where the order in respect of which an Article 5 certificate is sought has been varied prior to the issue of a certificate—

(a) the reference to the order in rule 3.45.4(a) is to the order as so varied; and

(b) the references to the interlocutor granting the protection measure in rule 3.45.6 include a reference to any interlocutor varying the order.

Application for rectification or withdrawal of Article 5 certificate

3.45.8.—(1) An application to the sheriff under Article 9 of the Regulation for rectification or withdrawal of an Article 5 certificate shall be made by lodging Form 64 in process.

(2) The sheriff may determine an application without a hearing unless the sheriff considers that a hearing is required.

Issue of Article 14 certificate

3.45.9.—(1)   An application for the issue of an Article 14 certificate shall be made by letter addressed to the sheriff clerk.

(2)   Where the sheriff issues an Article 14 certificate, the sheriff clerk shall send the certificate to the party on whose application the certificate was issued.

Form of applications relating to incoming protection measures

3.45.10.—(1)   The following applications shall be made by summary application—

(a)   an application for the adjustment of the factual elements of an incoming protection measure under Article 11 of the Regulation;

(b)   an application to refuse the recognition and, where applicable, the enforcement of an incoming protection measure under Article 13 of the Regulation;

(c)   a submission under Article 14(2) of the Regulation to suspend or withdraw the effects of the recognition and, where applicable, the enforcement of an incoming protection measure;

(d)   an application under section 1(1) of the Protection from Abuse (Scotland) Act 2001 for a power of arrest to be attached to an incoming protection measure;

(e)   an application under section 3(1) of the Domestic Abuse (Scotland) Act 2011 for a determination that an incoming protection measure is a domestic abuse interdict.

(2)   Where a process exists in relation to an incoming protection measure, an application mentioned in paragraph (1) shall be made by minute in that process.

Adjustment of incoming protection measure

3.45.11.—[1](1)   This rule applies for the purpose of an application under Article 11 of the Regulation to adjust the factual elements of an incoming protection measure.

(2)   Unless the sheriff considers that a hearing is required, the sheriff may—

(a)   dispense with intimation of the application; and

(b)   determine the application without a hearing.

(3)   Where necessary, the sheriff may grant decree in accordance with Scots law.

(4)   The sheriff clerk shall give the person causing the risk notice of the adjustment of the protection measure in accordance with paragraphs (5) to (7).

(5)   Where the address of the person causing the risk is known, notice shall be given by sending that person—

(a)   a notice in Form 65;

(b)   a copy of the interlocutor adjusting the factual elements of the protection measure.

(6)   Where the address of the person causing the risk is outwith the United Kingdom, the sheriff clerk shall send the documents mentioned in paragraph (5) by a registered post service.

(7)   Where the address of the person causing the risk is not known, notice shall be given by displaying on the walls of court a notice in Form 66.

---

[1] As amended by the Act of Sederunt (Rules of the Court of Session, Sheriff Appeal Court Rules and Sheriff Court Rules Amendment) (Sheriff Appeal Court) 2015 (SSI 2015/419) r.9(8) (effective 1 January 2016; as to savings see SSI 2015/419 rule 20(5)(a)).

(8)   An appeal against an interlocutor adjusting the factual elements of an incoming protection measure shall be made within 14 days after the date of the interlocutor concerned.

(9)   Where—

   (a)   the sheriff has dispensed with intimation of the application on the person causing the risk; and

   (b)   the person causing the risk has not appeared in the application,

the time within which the person causing the risk may make an appeal shall be reckoned from the date on which notice is given in accordance with paragraph (4).

Attachment of power of arrest to incoming protection measure

3.45.12.—(1)   In this rule, "the Act of 2001" means the Protection from Abuse (Scotland) Act 2001.

(2)   Where the sheriff attaches a power of arrest to a protection measure under section 1(2) of the Act of 2001, the following documents shall be served along with the power of arrest in accordance with section 2(1)—

   (a)   a copy of the protection measure;

   (b)   a copy of the Article 5 certificate issued by the issuing authority of the Member State of origin; and

   (c)   a copy of any interlocutor adjusting the factual elements of the protection measure.

(3)   After the power of arrest has been served, the following documents shall be delivered by the protected person to the chief constable of the Police Service of Scotland in accordance with section 3(1)—

   (a)   a copy of the protection measure;

   (b)   a copy of the Article 5 certificate issued by the issuing authority of the Member State of origin;

   (c)   a copy of any interlocutor adjusting the factual elements of the protection measure;

   (d)   a copy of the application for the attachment of the power of arrest;

   (e)   a copy of the interlocutor attaching the power of arrest;

   (f)   a copy of the certificate of service of the power of arrest and the documents that required to be served along with it in accordance with section 2(1) of the Act of 2001; and

   (g)   where a determination has previously been made in respect of the protection measure under section 3(1) of the Domestic Abuse (Scotland) Act 2011, a copy of the interlocutor making the determination.

(4)   An application under the following provisions of the Act of 2001 shall be made by minute in the process of the application in which the power of arrest was attached—

   (a)   section 2(3) (extension of power of arrest);

   (b)   section 2(7) (recall of power of arrest).

(5)   Where the sheriff extends the duration of, or recalls, a power of arrest, the person who obtained the extension, or the recall as the case may be, shall deliver a copy of the interlocutor granting the extension or the recall in accordance with section 3(1) of the Act of 2001.

(6)   Where the sheriff pronounces an interlocutor granting an application mentioned in rule 3.45.10(1)(a) to (c) in respect of an incoming protection measure to which a power of arrest is attached, the applicant shall deliver a copy of that interlocutor to the chief constable of the Police Service of Scotland in accordance with section 3(1) of the Act of 2001.

(7)   Where a person is required to comply with section 3(1) of the Act of 2001, that person shall, after complying with that section, lodge in process a certificate of delivery in Form 67.

Determination that incoming protection measure is a domestic abuse interdict

3.45.13.—(1)   This rule applies where the sheriff makes a determination that an incoming protection measure is a domestic abuse interdict.

(2)   A protected person who serves under 3(4) of the Domestic Abuse (Scotland) Act 2011 a copy of an interlocutor containing a determination under section 3(1) shall lodge in process a certificate of service.

(3)   Paragraph (4) applies where, in respect of the same protection measure—

(a)   a power of arrest under section 1 of the Protection from Abuse (Scotland) Act 2001 is in effect; and

(b)   a determination is made.

(4)   Where such a determination is made, the person who obtained the determination shall send to the chief constable of the Police Service of Scotland a copy of the interlocutor making the determination and the certificate of service.

(5)   Where a person is required by virtue of this rule to send documents to the chief constable of the Police Service of Scotland, that person must, after such compliance, lodge in process a certificate of sending in Form 68.

Part XLVI[1]

Counter-Terrorism and Security Act 2015

Interpretation

3.46.1.   In this Part—

"Schedule 1" means Schedule 1 to the Counter-Terrorism and Security Act 2015.

Applications for extended detention of travel documents

3.46.2.—[2](1)   An application to the sheriff for an order under paragraph 8(1) of Schedule 1 (extension of 14-day period by judicial authority) is to be in Form 69.

(1A)   Where an applicant seeks an order under paragraph 10(1) of Schedule 1 (order that specified information be withheld), the application for that order is to be included in Form 69.

(2)   On receipt of an application, the sheriff is to fix a date for the determination of the application.

(3)   The applicant must intimate the application to the person to whom it relates—

(a)   in Form 70, which is to be accompanied by a copy of the application; and

(b)   within the timescale and by the method specified by the sheriff.

(4)   Where—

(a)   at any time before intimation of an application, the sheriff grants an order under paragraph 10 of Schedule 1 (order that specified information be withheld); and

---

[1] As inserted by the Act of Sederunt (Rules of the Court of Session 1994 and Sheriff Court Rules Amendment) (No.3) (Miscellaneous) 2015 (SSI 2015/283) r.7(2) (effective 7 August 2015).

[2] Heading substituted by the Act of Sederunt (Rules of the Court of Session 1994 and Sheriff Court Rules Amendment) (Miscellaneous) 2016 (SSI 2016/102) r.4(2) (effective 21 March 2016).

(b) the information to which the order relates includes information contained in the application,

the sheriff may order intimation of the application under deletion of that information.

Further applications for extended detention of travel documents

3.46.3.[1] A further application under paragraph 8(1) of Schedule 1, by virtue of paragraph 12(1), is to be made by minute in the process relating to the extension of the 14-day period.

PART XLVII[2]

SERIOUS CRIME PREVENTION ORDERS

Interpretation

3.47.1. In this part—

"the 2007 Act" means the Serious Crime Act 2007;

"person who is the subject of a serious crime prevention order" is to be construed in accordance with section 1(6) of the 2007 Act;

"serious crime prevention order" has the meaning given by section 1(5) of the 2007 Act; and

"subject" means the person who is the subject of a serious crime prevention order.

Serious Crime Prevention Orders

3.47.2.—(1) An application by the Lord Advocate under section 8(aa) of the 2007 Act (limited class of applicants for making of orders) is to be made by summary application.

(2) When a summary application is lodged, the court must—

(a) fix a date for a hearing;

(b) order intimation of the application within 7 days to the person who is the proposed subject of the order; and

(c) order answers to be lodged within a period not exceeding 21 days.

(3) The application is to identify any person (other than the person who is the proposed subject of the order) in respect of whom the order sought may be likely to have a significant adverse effect or (as the case may be) state that there is no such person.

(4) A serious crime prevention order made under section 1 of the 2007 Act is to be made in Form 71.

(5) If the subject is not personally present or represented at the hearing at which the order is made, the applicant must serve a copy of the order on the subject.

Third party representations

3.47.3.—(1) Paragraphs (2) and (3) of this rule apply where a third party is identified by the applicant under rule 3.47.2(3).

---

[1] Heading substituted by the Act of Sederunt (Rules of the Court of Session 1994 and Sheriff Court Rules Amendment) (Miscellaneous) 2016 (SSI 2016/102) r.4(3) (effective 21 March 2016).

[2] As inserted by the Act of Sederunt (Rules of the Court of Session 1994 and Summary Application Rules 1999 Amendment) (Serious Crime Prevention Orders etc.) 2016 (SSI 2016/319) r.3(3) (effective 12 December 2016).

(2)   The court must order the applicant to intimate the application to any such third party within 7 days.

(3)   An application by a third party to make representations under section 9 of the 2007 Act is made by minute in the process within 14 days from the date of intimation.

(4)   The court may consider a minute by a third party, whether identified in accordance with rule 3.47.2(3), rule 3.47.4(2) or otherwise, without a hearing unless the third party requests a hearing or it seems to the court appropriate to fix a hearing.

(5)   If the court grants an application made in accordance paragraph (3) the court must—

    (a)   specify the manner in which representations are to be made; and

    (b)   intimate to the third party the date of any hearing fixed under rule 3.47.2(2)(a).

Variation or discharge of a serious crime prevention order

3.47.4.—(1)   An application to vary or discharge a serious crime prevention order is made in Form 72.

(2)   An application under paragraph (1) is to identify any person (other than the person who is the proposed subject of the order) in respect of whom the variation or discharge may be likely to have a significant adverse effect or (as the case may be) state that there is no such person known to the applicant.

(3)   When an application under paragraph (1) is lodged, the court must—

    (a)   fix a date for a hearing;

    (b)   order intimation of the application within 7 days—

        (i)   where the applicant is the relevant applicant authority, to the person who is the subject of the order; or

        (ii)   where the applicant is the person who is the subject of the order, to relevant applicant authority; or

        (iii)   where the applicant is any other person, to both the relevant applicant authority and the person who is the subject of the order; and

        (iv)   where a person is identified by the applicant under paragraph (2), to that person; and

    (c)   order answers to be lodged within a period not exceeding 21 days.

(4)   If the subject is not personally present or represented at the hearing at which the order is varied or discharged, the applicant must serve a copy of the varied order or, as the case may be, the interlocutor discharging the order, on the subject.

Part XLVIII[1]

Trafficking and Exploitation Orders

Interpretation

3.48.1.   In this Part—

"the 2015 Act" means the Human Trafficking and Exploitation (Scotland) Act 2015;

---

[1] As inserted by the Act of Sederunt (Summary Application Rules 1999 Amendment) (Trafficking Exploitation Orders) 2017 (SSI 2017/211) para.2 (effective 31 October 2017).

"trafficking and exploitation prevention order" means an order made under section 18 of the 2015 Act and

"trafficking and exploitation risk order" means an order made under section 26 of the 2015 Act.

Variation, renewal or discharge of trafficking and exploitation prevention orders

3.48.2.—(1) An application under section 23 of the 2015 Act to vary, renew or discharge a trafficking and exploitation prevention order is made by minute in the process relating to the application for the order.

(2) A minute under paragraph (1) is made in accordance with and regulated by Chapter 14 of the Ordinary Cause Rules.

(3) Where an application under section 23 of the 2015 Act to vary, renew or discharge an order is made in a sheriff court other than the sheriff court in which the process relating to the application for the order is held—

(a) it must be made by summary application;

(b) the initial writ containing the application must contain averments as to the sheriff court in which the process relating to the trafficking and exploitation prevention order is held;

(c) the sheriff clerk with whom the application is lodged must notify the sheriff clerk of the sheriff court in which the process relating to the trafficking and exploitation prevention order is held; and

(d) that sheriff clerk must, not later than 4 days after receipt of such notification, transfer the process relating to the trafficking and exploitation prevention order to the sheriff clerk of the sheriff court in which the application is made.

(4) For the purposes of paragraph (3), the sheriff court in which the process relating to the order is held is the sheriff court in which the trafficking and exploitation prevention order was granted or, where the process has been transferred under that paragraph, the last sheriff court to which the process has been transferred.

(5) A failure of the sheriff clerk to comply with paragraph (3) shall not invalidate the application.

Variation, renewal or discharge of a trafficking and exploitation risk order

3.48.3.—(1) An application under section 29 of the 2015 Act to vary, renew or discharge a trafficking an exploitation risk order is made by minute in the process relating to the application for the order.

(2) A minute under paragraph (1) is made in accordance with and regulated by Chapter 14 of the Ordinary Cause Rules.

(3) Where an application under section 29 of the 2015 Act to vary, renew or discharge an order is made in a sheriff court other than the sheriff court in which the process relating to the application for the order is held—

(a) it must be made by summary application;

(b) the initial writ containing the application must contain averments as to the sheriff court in which the process relating to the trafficking and exploitation risk order is held;

(c) the sheriff clerk with whom the application is lodged must notify the sheriff clerk of the sheriff court in which the process relating to the trafficking and exploitation risk order is held; and

(d) that sheriff clerk must, not later than 4 days after receipt of such notification transfer the process relating to the trafficking and exploitation risk order to the sheriff clerk of the sheriff court in which the application is made.

(4)   For the purposes of paragraph (3), the sheriff court in which the process relating to the order is held is the sheriff court in which the trafficking and exploitation risk order was granted, or where the process has been transferred under that paragraph, the last sheriff court to which the process has been transferred.

(5)   A failure of the sheriff clerk to comply with paragraph (3) shall not invalidate the application.

Part XLIX[1,2]

Illegal Working and Labour Market Enforcement Orders

Interpretation

3.49.1.   In this Part—

"the Act" means the Immigration Act 2016;

"application for compensation" means an application for compensation under paragraph 15 of schedule 6 of the Act; and

"illegal working compliance order" means an order made under paragraph 5 of schedule 6 of the Act.

Applications in relation to illegal working

3.49.2.—(1)   An application under any of the following paragraphs of schedule 6 of the Act—

(a)   paragraph 7 (extension of illegal working compliance orders);

(b)   paragraph 8 (variation or discharge of illegal working compliance orders);

(c)   paragraph 12 (access to other premises); and

(d)   paragraph 13 (reimbursement of costs),

is to be made by minute in the process relating to the illegal working compliance order.

(2)   A minute under paragraph (1) is to be made in accordance with and regulated by Chapter 14 of the Ordinary Cause Rules.

Applications for compensation

3.49.3.—(1)   Subject to paragraph (2), an application for compensation is to be made by minute in the process relating to the illegal working compliance order.

(2)   Where the illegal working closure notice under paragraph 1 of schedule 6 of the Act was cancelled under paragraph 3(1)(a) of that schedule, an application for compensation is to be made by summary application.

---

[1] Part XLIX inserted by the Act of Sederunt (Summary Applications, Statutory Applications and Appeals etc. Rules Amendment) (Illegal Working Orders) 2017 (SSI 2017/386) r.2(2) (effective 1 December 2017).

[2] As amended by the Act of Sederunt (Summary Applications, Statutory Applications and Appeals etc. Rules Amendment) (Labour Market Enforcement Orders) 2019 (SSI 2019/140) para.2 (effective 18 May 2019).

Labour market enforcement orders

3.49.4.—[1](1)   An application under section 19 of the Act is to contain details of any labour market enforcement order made under section 18 of the Act which is already in force in respect of the subject of the application.

(2)   An application under section 23 of the Act for variation or discharge of a labour market enforcement order made under section 18 of the Act is to be made by minute in the process relating to the order.

(3)   Where an application referred to in paragraph (2) is made in a sheriff court other than the sheriff court in which the process relating to the order is held—

    (a)   the sheriff clerk with whom the application is lodged is to notify the sheriff clerk of the sheriff court in which the process relating to the order is held; and

    (b)   the sheriff clerk of the sheriff court in which the process relating to the order is held is, not later than 4 days after receipt of such notification, to transfer the process relating to the order to the sheriff clerk of the sheriff court in which the application is made.

(4)   For the purposes of paragraph (3), the sheriff court in which the process relating to the order is held is the sheriff court in which the order was made or, where the process has been transferred under that paragraph, the last sheriff court to which the process has been transferred.

PART L[2]

TRANSFERS FROM THE LANDS TRIBUNAL FOR SCOTLAND TO THE SHERIFF UNDER THE
ELECTRONIC COMMUNICATIONS CODE

Interpretation

3.50.1.   In this Part "the Jurisdiction Regulations" means the Electronic Communications Code (Jurisdiction) Regulations 2017.

Transfer from Lands Tribunal for Scotland

3.50.2.—(1)   On receipt of the documentation in proceedings which have been transferred from the Lands Tribunal for Scotland to the sheriff under regulation 5 of the Jurisdiction Regulations, the sheriff clerk must record the date of receipt on the first page of the documentation.

(2)   Within 7 days of receipt of the documentation referred to in paragraph (1), the sheriff may make such order as he or she thinks fit to secure, so far as practicable, that the cause thereafter proceeds in accordance with these Rules.

(3)   An order under paragraph (2) may include—

    (a)   where the cause has not been intimated to the respondent before being transferred to the sheriff, an order for the applicant to make intimation of the cause to the respondent;

    (b)   where no response has been lodged by the respondent in the cause, an order for answers to be lodged;

---

[1] As amended by the Act of Sederunt (Summary Applications, Statutory Applications and Appeals etc. Rules Amendment) (Labour Market Enforcement Orders) 2019 (SSI 2019/140) para.2 (effective 18 May 2019).
[2] Part L inserted by the Act of Sederunt (Summary Applications, Statutory Applications and Appeals etc. Rules Amendment) (Transfer from Lands Tribunal for Scotland) 2017 (SSI 2017/459) r.2(2) (effective 19 January 2018).

(c)   an order for a hearing to determine further procedure.

PART LI[1]

DRUG DEALING TELECOMMUNICATIONS RESTRICTION ORDERS

Interpretation

3.51.1.   In this Part—

"the 2015 Act" means the Serious Crime Act 2015;

"DDTRO Regulations" means the Drug Dealing Telecommunications Restriction Orders Regulations 2017; and

unless the context otherwise requires, words and expressions used in this Part and in the 2015 Act or the DDTRO Regulations have the meaning given by the 2015 Act or the DDTRO Regulations, as the case may be.

Drug Dealing Telecommunications Restriction Orders

3.51.2.—(1)   An application under regulation 3 of the DDTRO Regulations (power to make a DDTRO) for a DDTRO—

(a)   is to be made by summary application in Form 73; and

(b)   must not be intimated to an affected person or their legal representative.

(2)   A DDTRO is to be made in Form 74.

(3)   An application for discharge, extension or variation of a DDTRO is to be made by an application in the process relating to the DDTRO in Form 75.

(4)   Where an application under paragraph (3) is made, the sheriff may make such orders as he or she thinks fit for dealing with the application, including an order—

(a)   requiring the applicant to intimate the application and any court order relating to it to any other person;

(b)   requiring any party to lodge answers; and

(c)   fixing a hearing on the application and any answers.

(5)   An application for a DDTRO must be heard and determined in private.

(6)   All proceedings in an application for discharge, extension or variation of a DDTRO must be heard and determined in public.

(7)   Rule 2.5 (order for intimation to interested persons by the sheriff) does not apply to applications under this Part.

(8)   Rule 2.30 (motion procedure), applying Chapter 15 of the Ordinary Cause Rules, applies to motions under this Part.

PART LII[2]

CARE HOMES: EMERGENCY INTERVENTION ORDERS

Interpretation

3.52.1.   In this Part—

---

[1] Part LI inserted by the Act of Sederunt (Summary Applications, Statutory Applications and Appeals etc. Rules Amendment) (Drug Dealing Telecommunications Restriction Orders) 2017 (SSI 2017/460) r.2(2) (effective 19 January 2018).

[2] Part LII inserted by the Act of Sederunt (Rules of the Court of Session 1994 and Sheriff Court Rules Amendment) (Miscellaneous) 2020 (SSI 2020/166) para.4 (effective 2 June 2020).

"the 2010 Act" means the Public Services Reform (Scotland) Act 2010 as modified by paragraph 17 (emergency intervention orders) of schedule 1 of the Coronavirus (Scotland) (No.2) Act 2020;

"emergency intervention order" has the meaning given by section 65A(2) (care homes: emergency intervention orders) of the 2010 Act.

Applications under section 65A of the 2010 Act

3.52.2.—(1)   An application for an emergency intervention order under section 65A(1) of the 2010 Act must be made by summary application.

(2)   An interim order under section 65A(3) of the 2010 Act must be sought by crave in the initial writ for the emergency intervention order.

(3)   An application under section 65A(13) of the 2010 Act for variation, extension or revocation of an emergency intervention order must be made by minute in the process for the emergency intervention order to which it relates.

(4)   An application under section 65A(14) of the 2010 Act for variation or recall of an interim order granted under section 65A(3) of that Act must be made by motion in the process of the emergency intervention order to which it relates.

PART LIII[1]

AGE OF CRIMINAL RESPONSIBILITY (SCOTLAND) ACT 2019

Application and interpretation of this Part

3.53.1.—(1)   This Part applies to applications under—

(a)   section 34 (application for order authorising search in relation to child under 12);

(b)   section 42 (application for child interview order);

(c)   section 61 (application for order authorising taking of prints and samples from child),

of the Age of Criminal Responsibility (Scotland) Act 2019.

(2)   In this Part, "the 2019 Act" means the Age of Criminal Responsibility (Scotland) Act 2019 and, unless the context otherwise requires, words and expressions used in this Part and in the 2019 Act have the meaning given by that Act.

Form of application

3.53.2.   An application under—

(a)   section 34 of the 2019 Act must be made in Form 76;

(b)   section 42 of the 2019 Act must be made in Form 77;

(c)   section 61 of the 2019 Act must be made in Form 78.

Processing of application

3.53.3.—(1)   On receipt by the court of an application to which this Part applies, it must be placed before the sheriff forthwith.

(2)   Rule 2.5 (order for intimation to interested persons by the sheriff) does not apply to applications to which this Part applies.

(3)   Where—

---

[1] As inserted by the Act of Sederunt (Summary Applications, Statutory Applications and Appeals etc. Rules 1999 and Sheriff Appeal Court Rules Amendment) (Age of Criminal Responsibility (Scotland) Act 2019) 2021 (SI 2021/452) art.2(2) (effective 17 December 2021).

(a) under sections 35(2), 43(2) or 62(2) (consideration of need for enquiry or hearing) of the 2019 Act, the sheriff considers it appropriate to enquire or hold a hearing;

(b) under sections 35(3), 43(3) or 62(3) (consideration of opportunity to make representations) of the 2019 Act, the sheriff considers that any of the persons mentioned in paragraphs (a) to (d) of those subsections should be given an opportunity to make representations,

the sheriff may make such order as the sheriff thinks fit in relation to that.

Form of order

3.53.4. An order under—

(a) section 36 (order authorising search in relation to child under 12) of the 2019 Act must be in Form 79;

(b) section 44(2) (child interview order) of the 2019 Act must be in Form 80;

(c) section 63 (order authorising taking of prints and samples from child) of the 2019 Act must be in Form 81.

Permission to appeal to Sheriff Appeal Court

3.53.5.—(1) An application for permission to appeal against a decision of the sheriff under sections 36, 44(2) or 63 of the 2019 Act must be made by motion.

(2) Within 1 day after permission to appeal has been granted by the sheriff, the court must transfer the process to the Clerk of the Sheriff Appeal Court.

SCHEDULE 1

Forms

Rule 1.2(3)

FORM A1[1, 2]

Rule 1A.2(2)(b)

Statement by prospective lay representative for Pursuer/Defender*

Case Ref. No.:

in the cause
SHERIFFDOM OF (*insert name of sheriffdom*)
AT (*insert place of sheriff court*)
[A.B.], (*insert designation and address*), Pursuer
against
[C.D.], (*insert designation and address*), Defender
Court ref. no:

Name and address of prospective lay representative who requests permission to represent party litigant:
Identify hearing(s) in respect of which permission for lay representation is sought:
The prospective lay representative declares that:

---

[1] As inserted by the Act of Sederunt (Sheriff Court Rules) (Lay Representation) 2013 (SSI 2013/91) r.3 (effective 4 April 2013).

[2] As amended by the Act of Sederunt (Rules of the Court of Session, Sheriff Appeal Court Rules and Sheriff Court Rules Amendment) (Lay Representation) 2017 (SSI 2017/186) para.5 (effective 3 July 2017).

(a)	I have no financial interest in the outcome of the case *or* I have the following financial interest in it:*
(b)	I am not receiving remuneration or other reward directly or indirectly from the litigant for my assistance and will not receive directly or indirectly such remuneration or other reward from the litigant.
(c)	I accept that documents and information are provided to me by the litigant on a confidential basis and I undertake to keep them confidential.
(d)	I have no previous convictions *or* I have the following convictions: (list convictions)*
(e)	I have not been declared a vexatious litigant under the Vexatious Actions (Scotland) Act 1898 *or* I was declared a vexatious litigant under the Vexatious Actions (Scotland) Act 1898 on [insert date].*

(Signed)
[Name of prospective lay representative]
[Date]

(Insert Place/Date)
The Sheriff grants/refuses* the application.

[Signed]
Sheriff Clerk
[Date]

*(*delete as appropriate)*

FORM 1

Rule 2.4(1)

Form of initial writ

SUMMARY APPLICATION UNDER (*title & section of statute or statutory instrument*)

INITIAL WRIT

SHERIFFDOM OF (*insert name of sheriffdom*)

AT (*insert place of sheriff court*)

[A.B.] (*design and state any special capacity in which the pursuer is suing*) Pursuer

against

[C.D.] (*design and state any special capacity in which the defender is being sued*) Defender

The Pursuer craves the court (*here state the specific decree, warrant or order sought*)

CONDESCENDENCE

(*State in numbered paragraphs the facts which form the ground of action*)

PLEAS-IN-LAW

(*State in numbered sentences*)

Signed
[A.B.], Pursuer
or [X.Y.], solicitor for the Pursuer
(*state designation and business address*)

FORM 2

Rule 2.7(4)(a)

[Form of warrant of citation]

(*Insert place and date*). Grants warrant to cite the defender (*insert name and address*) by serving upon him [*or* her] a copy of the writ and warrant [on a period of notice of (*insert period of notice*) days], [and ordains him [*or* her] to answer within the Sheriff Court House (*insert place of sheriff court*) [in Room No. ...., or in Chambers, *or otherwise, as the case may be*], on the .... day of .... at .... o'clock .... noon] [*or otherwise, as the case may be*] [and grants warrant to arrest on the dependence].

Signed
Sheriff [*or* sheriff clerk]

Rule 3.18.3(1)   FORM 2A[1]

Form of warrant of citation

(*Insert place and date*). Grants warrant to cite (*insert name and address of parties specified by sheriff principal*) by serving upon them a copy of the writ and warrant on a period of notice of 21 days and ordains them if they wish to oppose the application—

(a) to lodge answers within the period of notice; and

(b) to be represented within the Sheriff Court House (*insert place and address of sheriff court*) [in Room No..........., *or otherwise, as the case may be*], on the..........day of at..........o'clock.......... noon [*or otherwise, as the case may be*].

Signed
Sheriff [*or* sheriff clerk]

Rule 2.7(4)(b)   FORM 3

Form of citation for summary application
CITATION FOR SUMMARY APPLICATION
SHERIFFDOM OF (*insert name of sheriffdom*)
AT (*insert place of sheriff court*)
[A.B.], (*insert designation and address*) Pursuer
against
[C.D.], (*insert designation and address*) Defender
Court ref. no.

(*Insert place and date*). You [.CD.] are hereby served with this copy writ and warrant, and are required to answer it.

IF YOU ARE UNCERTAIN AS TO WHAT ACTION TO TAKE you should consult a solicitor. You may be eligible for legal aid depending on your income, and you can get information about legal aid from a solicitor. You may also obtain advice from any Citizens' Advice Bureau or other advice agency.

PLEASE NOTE THAT IF YOU DO NOTHING IN ANSWER TO THIS DOCUMENT the court may regard you as admitting the claim made against you and the pursuer may obtain decree against you in your absence.

Signed
[PQ.], Sheriff Officer,
or [X.Y] (*add designation and
business address*)

---

[1] Inserted by the Act of Sederunt (Summary Applications, Statutory Applications and Appeals etc. Rules) Amendment (No.2) (Local Government (Scotland) Act 1973) 2002 (SSI 2002/130) para.2(4) and Sch.

Solicitor for the Pursuer

Rule 3.18.3(2)   FORM 3A[1]

Form of citation for summary application
CITATION FOR SUMMARY APPLICATION
SHERIFFDOM OF (*insert name of sheriffdom*)
AT (*insert place of sheriff court*)
[A.B.], (*insert designation and address*), Applicant
against
[C.D.], (*insert designation and address*), Respondent
Court ref. no.

(*Insert place and date*). You [C.D.] are hereby served with this copy writ and warrant, and are required to answer it.

If you wish to oppose the application, you—

(a) must lodge answers with the sheriff clerk at (*insert place and address of sheriff court*) sheriff court, (*insert address*) not later than (*insert date*), and at the same time, send a copy of the answers to the Applicant; and

(b) should be represented within the Sheriff Court House (*insert place and address of sheriff court*) [in Room No..........., or otherwise, as the case may be] on the day of at.........o'clock.......... noon [*or otherwise as the case maybe*].

PLEASE NOTE THAT IF YOU DO NOTHING IN ANSWER TO THIS DOCUMENT the court may regard you as admitting the appeal and the Applicant may obtain decree against you in your absence.

Signed
[P.Q.], Sheriff Officer, or [X.Y.]
(*add designation and business address*)
Solicitor for the Applicant

Rule 2.7(5)   FORM 4[2]

Form of warrant of citation where time to pay direction or time order may be applied for

(*Insert place and date*). *Grants warrant to cite the defender (insert name and address*) by serving a copy of the writ and warrant, together with Form 5, [on a period of notice of (*insert period of notice) days*] and ordains him [*or* her] if he [*or* she]—

(a) intends to defend the action or make any claim [to answer within the Sheriff Court House (*insert place and address of sheriff court*) [in Room No..........., or in Chambers, *or otherwise, as the case may be*], on the.........day of.........at.........o'clock..........noon] [*or otherwise, as the case may be*] or

(b) admits the claim and intends to apply for a time to pay direction or time order (and where appropriate apply for recall or restriction of an arrestment) [either to appear at that diet and make such application or] to lodge the appropriate part of Form 5 duly completed with the sheriff clerk at (*insert place of sheriff court*) at least fourteen days before [the diet or the expiry of the period of notice *or otherwise*, as the case may be] [and grants warrant to arrest on the dependence].

Signed
Sheriff [*or* sheriff clerk]

---

[1] Inserted by the Act of Sederunt (Summary Applications, Statutory Applications and Appeals etc. Rules) Amendment (No.2) (Local Government (Scotland) Act 1973) 2002 (S.S.I. 2002 No. 130), para.2(4) and Sched.

[2] As amended by SSI 2007/6 (effective January 29, 2007) and SSI 2009/294 (effective December 1, 2009).

Rule 2.7(6) and 2.22(2)(b)   FORM 5[1, 2]

Form of notice to be served on defender where time to pay direction or time order may be applied for

Rule 2.7(6) and 2.22(2)(b)   ACTION RAISED BY

PURSUER   DEFENDER

AT...............SHERIFF COURT
(Including address)
COURT REF. NO.

THIS SECTION MUST BE COMPLETED BY THE PURSUER BEFORE SERVICE

(1) Time to pay directions

The Debtors (Scotland) Act 1987 gives you the right to apply to the court for a "time to pay direction" which is an order permitting you to pay any sum of money you are ordered to pay to the pursuer (which may include interest and court expenses) either by way of instalments or deferred lump sum. A deferred lump sum means that you must pay all the amount at one time within a period specified by the court.

When making a time to pay direction the court may recall or restrict an arrestment made on your property by the pursuer in connection with the action or debt (for example, your bank account may have been frozen).

(2) Time Orders

The Consumer Credit Act 1974 allows you to apply to the court for a "time order" during a court action, to ask the court to give you more time to pay a loan agreement. **A time order is similar to a time to pay direction, but can only be applied for where the court action is about a credit agreement regulated by the Consumer Credit Act.** The court has power to grant a time order in respect of a regulated agreement to reschedule payment of the sum owed. This means that a time order can change:

- the amount you have to pay each month
- how long the loan will last
- in some cases, the interest rate payable

A time order can also stop the creditor taking away any item bought by you on hire purchase or conditional sale under the regulated agreement, so long as you continue to pay the instalments agreed.

HOW TO APPLY FOR A TIME TO PAY DIRECTION OR TIME ORDER WHERE YOU ADMIT THE CLAIM AND YOU DO NOT WANT TO DEFEND THE ACTION

1. The appropriate application forms are attached to this notice. After completing the appropriate form it should be returned to the Sheriff Court at least fourteen days before the date of the first hearing or expiry of the period of notice or otherwise, as the case may be, in the warrant of citation. The address of the court is shown on page 1 of the application. No court fee is payable when lodging the application.

2. Before completing the application please read carefully the notes on how to

---

[1] As amended by SSI 2007/6 (effective January 29, 2007) and subtituted by Act of Sederunt (Sheriff Court Rules)(Miscellaneous Amendments) 2009 (SSI 2009/294) r.2 (effective December 1, 2009).

[2] As amended by the Act of Sederunt (Sheriff Court Rules)(Miscellaneous Amendments) 2011 (SSI 2011/193) r.10 (effective April 3, 2011).

complete the application. In the event of difficulty you may contact the court's civil department at the address above or any sheriff clerk's office, solicitor, Citizens Advice Bureau or other advice agency. Written guidance can also be obtained from the Scottish Court Service website (www.scotcourts.gov.uk).

WHAT WILL HAPPEN NEXT

If the pursuer objects to your application, a hearing will be fixed and the court will advise you in writing of the date and time.

If the pursuer does not object to your application, a copy of the court order for payment (called an extract decree) will be served on you by the pursuer's solicitor advising when instalment payments should commence or deferred payment be made.

Court ref. no.

APPLICATION FOR A TIME TO PAY DIRECTION UNDER THE DEBTORS (SCOTLAND) ACT 1987

*PART A   BY

*(This section must be completed by pursuer before service)

DEFENDER
In an action raised by
PURSUER

HOW TO COMPLETE THE APPLICATION
PLEASE WRITE IN INK USING BLOCK CAPITALS

PART A of the application will have been completed in advance by the pursuer and gives details of the pursuer and you as the defender.

PART B If you wish to apply to pay by instalments enter the amount and tick the appropriate box at B3(1). If you wish to apply to pay the full sum due in one deferred payment enter the period of deferment you propose at B3(2).

PART C Give full details of your financial position in the space provided.

PART D If you wish the court, when making the time to pay direction to recall or restrict an arrestment made in connection with the action, enter the appropriate details about what has been arrested and the place and date of the arrestment at D5, and attach the schedule of arrestment or copy.

Sign the application where indicated. Retain the copy initial writ and the form of notice which accompanied this application form as you may need them at a later stage. The application should be returned to the Sheriff Court at least fourteen days before the date of the first hearing or expiry of the period of notice or otherwise, as the case may be, in the warrant of citation. The address of the court is shown on page 1 of the application.

PART B   1. The applicant is a defender in the action brought by the above named pursuer.

2. The defender admits the claim and applies to the court for a time to pay direction.

3. The defender applies

(1) To pay by

instalments of £

(Tick one box only)

EACH WEEK   FORTNIGHT   MONTH
                   OR

(2) To pay the sum ordered in one payment within

WEEKS/MONTHS

Please state in this box why you say a time to pay direction should be made. In doing so, please consider the Note below.

NOTE

Under the 1987 Act, **the court is required to make a time to pay direction if satisfied that it is reasonable in the circumstances to do so, and having regard in particular to the following matters—**

The nature of and reasons for the debt in relation to which decree is granted or the order is sought Any action taken by the creditor to assist the debtor in paying the debt

The debtor's financial position The reasonableness of any proposal by the debtor to pay that debt

The reasonableness of any refusal or objection by the creditor to any proposal or offer by the debtor to pay the debt.

PART C   **4. Defender's financial position**

I am employed /self employed / unemployed

My net income is:	weekly, fortnightly or monthly	**My outgoings are:**	weekly, fortnightly or monthly
Wages	£	Mortgage/rent	£
State benefits	£	Council tax	£
Tax credits	£	Gas/electricity etc	£
Other	£	Food	£
		Credit and loans	£
		Phone	£
		Other	£
Total	£	Total	£

People who rely on your income (e.g. spouse/civil partner/ partner/ children) —how many

Here list all assets (if any) e.g. value of house; amounts in bank or building society accounts; shares or other investments:

Here list any outstanding debts:

PART D

5. The defender seeks to recall or restrict an arrestment of which the details are as follows (*please state, and attach the schedule of arrestment or copy*).

6. This application is made under sections 1(1) and 2(3) of the Debtors (Scotland) Act 1987.

Therefore the defender asks the court

*to make a time to pay direction

*to recall the above arrestment

*to restrict the above arrestment (*in which case state restriction wanted*)

Date (*insert date*)

Signed

Defender

Court ref. no.

APPLICATION FOR A TIME ORDER UNDER THE CONSUMER CREDIT ACT 1974

*PART A   By
***(This section must
be completed by
pursuer before
service)**

DEFENDER

In an action raised by

PURSUER

HOW TO COMPLETE THE APPLICATION
PLEASE WRITE IN INK USING BLOCK CAPITALS

PART A of the application will have been completed in advance by the pursuer and gives details of the pursuer and you as the defender.

PART B If you wish to apply to pay by instalments enter the amount and tick the appropriate box at B3. If you wish the court to make any additional orders, please give details at B4. Please give details of the regulated agreement at B5.

PART C Give full details of your financial position in the space provided.

Sign the application where indicated. Retain the copy initial writ and the form of notice which accompanied this application form as you may need them at a later stage. The application should be returned to the Sheriff Court at least fourteen days before the date of the first hearing or expiry of the period of notice or otherwise, as the case may be, in the warrant of citation. The address of the court is shown on page 1 of the application.

**PART
B**

1. The Applicant is a defender in the action brought by the above named pursuer.

I/WE WISH TO APPLY FOR A TIME ORDER under the Consumer Credit Act 1974

2. **Details of order(s) sought**

The defender wishes to apply for a time order under section 129 of the Consumer Credit Act 1974

The defender wishes to apply for an order in terms of section..........of the Consumer Credit Act 1974

3. Proposals for payment

I admit the claim and apply to pay the arrears and future instalments as follows:

By instalments of £..........per *week/fortnight/month

No time to pay direction or time to pay order has been made in relation to this debt.

4. Additional orders sought

The following additional order(s) is (are) sought: (*specify*)

The order(s) sought in addition to the time order is (are) sought for the following reasons:

5. Details of regulated agreement

(*Please attach a copy of the agreement if you have retained it and insert details of the agreement where known*)

(a) Date of agreement

(b) Reference number of agreement

(c) Names and addresses of other parties to agreement

(d) Name and address of person (if any) who acted as surety (guarantor) to the agreement

(e) Place where agreement signed (e.g. the shop where agreement signed, including name and address)

(f) Details of payment arrangements

i. The agreement is to pay instalments of £..........per week/ month

ii. The unpaid balance is £..........I do not know the amount of arrears

iii. I am £..........in arrears / I do not know the amount of arrears

PART C   **Defender's financial position**

I am employed /self employed / unemployed

	My net income is:	weekly, fortnightly or monthly	My outgoings are:	weekly, fortnightly or monthly
	Wages	£	Mortgage/rent	£
	State benefits	£	Council tax	£
	Tax credits	£	Gas/electricity etc	£
	Other	£	Food	£
			Credit and loans	£
			Phone	£
			Other	£
	Total	£	Total	£

People who rely on your income (e.g. spouse/civil partner/partner/ children)—how many

Here list all assets (if any) e.g. value of house; amounts in bank or building society accounts; shares or other investments:

Here list any outstanding debts:

Therefore the defender asks the court to make a time order

Date   Signed
                                            Defender

Rule 2.22(4)   FORM 5A[1]

Form of pursuer's response objecting to application for time to pay direction or time order

Court ref no:..........

SHERIFFDOM OF (*insert name of sheriffdom*)

AT (*insert place of sheriff court*)

PURSUER'S RESPONSE OBJECTING TO APPLICATION FOR TIME TO PAY DIRECTION OR TIME ORDER

in the cause

[A.B.], (*insert designation and address*), Pursuer

against

[C.D.], (*insert designation and address*), Defender

1. The pursuer received a copy application for a time to pay direction or time order lodged by the defender on (*date*).
2. The pursuer does not accept the offer.
3. The debt is (*please specify the nature of the debt*).
4. The debt was incurred on (*specify date*) and the pursuer has contacted the defender in relation to the debt on (*specify date(s)*).
*5. The contractual payments were (*specify amount*).
*6. (*Specify any action taken by the pursuer to assist the defender to pay the debt*).
*7. The defender has made payment(s) towards the debt of (*specify amount(s)*) on (*specify date(s)*).
*8. The debtor has made offers to pay (*specify amount(s)*) on (*specify date(s)*) which offer(s) was [were] accepted [*or* rejected] and (*specify amount*) was paid on (*specify date(s)*).
9. (*Here set out any information you consider relevant to the court's determination of the application*).

*delete as appropriate

(*Signed*)
Pursuer *or* Solicitor for pursuer
(*Date*)

---

[1] As inserted by the Act of Sederunt (Sheriff Court Rules) (Miscellaneous Amendments) 2009 (SSI 2009/294) r.2 (effective December 1, 2009).

Rule 2.7(7) FORM 6[1]

Form of citation where time to pay direction or time order may be applied for in summary application

SHERIFFDOM OF (*insert name of sheriffdom*)
AT (*insert place of sheriff court*)
[A.B.], (*insert designation and address*) Pursuer
against
[C.D.], (*insert designation and address*) Defender
Court ref. no.

(*Insert place and date*). You [CD.], are hereby served with this copy writ and warrant, together with Form 5 (application for time to pay direction in summary application).

Form 5 is served on you because it is considered that you may be entitled to apply for a time to pay direction or time order [and for the recall or restriction of an arrestment used on the dependence of the action or in security of the debt referred to in the copy writ]. See Form 5 for further details.

IF YOU ADMIT THE CLAIM AND WISH TO APPLY FOR A TIME TO PAY DIRECTION OR TIME ORDER, you must complete Form 5 and return it to the sheriff clerk at the above address at least 7 days before the hearing or the expiry of the period of notice or otherwise, as the case may be, in the warrant of citation.

IF YOU ADMIT THE CLAIM AND WISH TO AVOID A COURT ORDER BEING MADE AGAINST YOU, the whole sum claimed including interest and any expenses due should be paid to the pursuer or his solicitor by the court date.

IF YOU ARE UNCERTAIN AS TO WHAT ACTION TO TAKE you should consult a solicitor. You may be eligible for legal aid depending on your income, and you can get information about legal aid from a solicitor. You may also obtain advice from any Citizens' Advice Bureau, or other advice agency.

PLEASE NOTE THAT IF YOU DO NOTHING IN ANSWER TO THIS DOCUMENT the court may regard you as admitting the claim made against you and the pursuer may obtain decree against you in your absence.

Signed
[P.Q.], Sheriff Officer,
or [X.Y.] (*add designation and business address*)
Solicitor for the Pursuer

FORM 6ZA[2]

Rule 2.7(7ZA)(a)

Form of warrant of citation in an application to which rule 2.7(7ZA)(a) applies

(*Insert place and date*). Grants warrant to cite the defender (*insert name and address*) by serving a copy of the writ and warrant together with Form 6ZB and Form 11C [*on a period of notice of (*insert period of notice*) days] and ordains him [*or* her] if he [*or* she] intends to oppose the application—

To be present or represented at the diet on (*insert date and time*) within (*insert name and address of sheriff court*) [*or otherwise as the case may be*].

Signed
Sheriff [*or* sheriff clerk]

---

[1] As amended by the Act of Sederunt (Ordinary Cause, Summary Application, Summary Cause and Small Claim Rules) Amendment (Miscellaneous) 2007 (SSI 2007/6), para.3(6) (effective January 29, 2007).

[2] As inserted by the Act of Sederunt (Sheriff Court Rules) (Miscellaneous Amendments) 2013 (SSI 2013/135) para.2 (effective May 27, 2013).

(*delete as appropriate)

FORM 6ZB[1]

Rule 2.7(7ZA)(b)

Form of citation in an application to which rule 2.7(7ZA)(b) applies

SHERIFFDOM OF (*insert name of sheriffdom*)

AT (*insert place of sheriff court*)

[A.B.], (*insert designation and address*), Pursuer

Against

[C.D.], (*insert designation and address*), Defender

Court ref. no:

To: (*insert name and address of defender*)

Attached to this notice is a copy of an application by (*insert name of pursuer*) under [*insert reference to provision or provisions under which application is made*]. **IF THE APPLICATION IS GRANTED, THE PROPERTY AT (*INSERT ADDRESS OF SECURITY SUBJECTS*) MAY BE REPOSSESSED AND YOU WOULD NO LONGER HAVE THE RIGHT TO RESIDE THERE.**

The hearing will be held at (*insert name and address of sheriff court*) on (*insert date*) at (*insert time*).

IF YOU WISH TO OPPOSE THE APPLICATION you should be present or represented at the hearing.

IF YOU ARE UNCERTAIN AS TO WHAT ACTION TO TAKE you should consult a solicitor. You may be eligible for legal aid depending on your income, and you can get information about legal aid from a solicitor. You may also obtain advice from an approved lay representative, or any Citizens' Advice Bureau or other advice agency.

PLEASE NOTE THAT IF YOU DO NOTHING IN ANSWER TO THIS DOCUMENT the court may consider the application in the absence of you or your representative.

Signed

[P.Q.], Sheriff Officer,

or [X.Y.], (*add designation and business address*)

Solicitor for the Pursuer

FORM 6A

[Repealed by the Act of Sederunt (Sheriff Court Rules) (Enforcement of Securities over Heritable Property) 2010 (SSI 2010/324) para.2 (effective September 30, 2010).]

FORM 6B

[Repealed by the Act of Sederunt (Sheriff Court Rules) (Enforcement of Securities over Heritable Property) 2010 (SSI2010/324) para.2 (effective September 30, 2010).]

Rule 2.7(8)   FORM 7[2, 3, 4, 5]

Form of certificate of citation

CERTIFICATE OF CITATION

---

[1] As inserted by the Act of Sederunt (Sheriff Court Rules) (Miscellaneous Amendments) 2013 (SSI 2013/135) para.2 (effective May 27, 2013).

[2] Inserted by the Act of Sederunt (Amendment of Ordinary Cause Rules and Summary Applications, Statutory Applications and Appeals etc. Rules) Applications under the Mortgage Rights (Scotland) Act 2001) 2002 (SSI 2002/7), para.3(4) and Sch.2.

(Insert place and date) I, hereby certify that upon the day of I duly cited [CD.], Defender, to answer the foregoing writ. I did this by *(state method of service; [if by officer and not by post, add*: in the presence of [L.M.], *(insert designation)*, witness hereto with me subscribing;] *and where service executed by post state whether by registered post or the first class recorded delivery service).*

(In actions in which a time to pay direction or time order may be applied for, state whether Form 4 and Form 5 were sent in accordance with rule 2.7(5) and (6).)

(In applications for enforcement of security over residential property within the meaning of Part IV of Chapter 3 , state whether Forms 6ZA, 6ZB and 11C were provided in accordance with rule 2.7(7ZA)).

Signed
[P.Q.], Sheriff Officer
[L.M.], witness
or [X.Y.] *(add designation and business address)*
Solicitor for the Pursuer

Rule 2.9(1)   **FORM 8**

Form of caveat
[Repealed by the Act of Sederunt (Sheriff Court Caveat Rules) 2006 (SI 2006/ 198), effective April 28, 2006.]

Rule 2.13(1)(a)   **FORM 9**

Form of advertisement
NOTICE TO [C.D.]
Court ref. no.

An action has been raised in Sheriff Court by [A.B.], Pursuer calling as a Defender [CD.], whose last known address was *(insert last known address of defender).*

If [CD.] wishes to defend the action he [*or* she] should immediately contact the sheriff clerk *(insert address)* from whom the service copy initial writ may be obtained. If he [*or* she] fails to do so decree may pass against him [*or* her] [when the case calls in court on *(date)* or on the expiry of the period of notice *or otherwise, as the case may be in the warrant of citation*].

Signed
[X.Y.], *(add designation and business address)*
Solicitor for the Pursuer
or [P.Q.] *(add business address)*

Rule 2.13(1)(b)   **FORM 10**

Form of notice for walls of court
NOTICE TO [CD.]
Court ref. no.

An action has been raised in..........Sheriff Court by [A.B.], Pursuer calling as a Defender [CD.], whose last known address was *(insert last known address of defender).*

---

[3] As amended by the Act of Sederunt (Ordinary Cause, Summary Application, Summary Cause and Small Claim Rules) Amendment (Miscellaneous) 2007 (SSI 2007/6), para.3(6) (effective January 29, 2007).

[4] As amended by the Act of Sederunt (Sheriff Court Rules) (Enforcement of Securities over Heritable Property) 2010 (SSI 2010/324) para.2 (effective September 30, 2010).

[5] As amended by the Act of Sederunt (Sheriff Court Rules) (Miscellaneous Amendments) 2013 (SSI 2013/135) para.2 (effective May 27, 2013).

If [C.D.] wishes to defend the action he [or she] should immediately contact the sheriff clerk at (*insert address*) from whom the service copy initial writ may be obtained. If he [or she] fails to do so decree may pass against him [or her] [when the case calls in court on (*date*) or on the expiry of the period of notice *or otherwise, as the case may he in the warrant of citation*].

Date (*insert date*)

Signed
Sheriff clerk (*depute*)
Telephone no. (*insert telephone number of sheriff clerk's office*)

Rule 2.18A   FORM 10A[1]

Form of schedule of arrestment on the dependence
SCHEDULE OF ARRESTMENT ON THE DEPENDENCE

Date: (*date of execution*)
Time: (*time arrestment executed*)
To: (*name and address of arrested*)

IN HER MAJESTY'S NAME AND AUTHORITY AND IN NAME AND AUTHORITY OF THE SHERIFF.1, (*name*). Sheriff Officer, by virtue of:

- an initial writ containing warrant which has been granted for arrestment on the dependence of the action at the instance of (*name and address of pursuer*) against (*name and address of defender*) and dated (*date*);
- a counterclaim containing a warrant which has been granted for arrestment on the dependence of the claim by (*name and address of creditor*) againts (*name and address of debtor*) and dated (*date of warrant*);
- an order of the Sheriff at (*place*) dated (*dated of order*) granting warrant [for arrestment on the dependence of the action mised at the instance of (*name and address of pursuer*) against (*name and address of defender*).] [or for arrestment on the dependence of the claim in the counterclaim [or third party notice] by (*name and address of creditor*) against (*name and address of debtor*)].

arrest in your hands (i) the sum of (*amount*), in excess of the Protected Minimum Balance; where applicable (*see Note 1*), more or less, due by you to (*defender's name*)[*or name and address of common debtor i common debtor is not the defender*] or to any other person on his [or her] [or its] [or their] behalf, and (ii) all moveable things in your hands belonging or pertaining to the said (*name of common debtor*), to remain in your hands under arrestment until they are made forthcoming to (*name of pursuer*) [*or name and address of creditor if he is not the pursuer*] or until further order of the court.

This I do in the presence of (*name, occupation and address of witness*).

(*Signed*)
Sheriff Officer
(*Address*)

NOTE

1. This Schedule arrests in your hands (i) funds due by you to (*name of common debtor*) and (ii) goods or other moveables held by you for him. **You should not pay any funds to him or hand over any goods or other moveables to him without taking legal advice**.
2. This Schedule may be used to arrest a ship or cargo. If it is, you should

---

[1] As inserted by the Act of Sederunt (Sheriff Court Rules Amendment) (Diligence) 2009 (SSI 2009/107) (effective April 22, 2009).

consult your legal adviser about the effect of it.

3. The Protected Minimum Balance is the sum referred to in section 73F(4) of the Debtors (Scotland) Act 1987. This sum is currently set at [*insert current sum*]. The Protected Minimum Balance applies where the arrestment attaches funds standing to the credit of a debtor in an account held by a bank or other financial institution and the debtor is an individual. The Protected Minimum Balance does not apply where the account is held in the name of a company, a limited liability partnership, a partnership or an unincorporated association or where the account is operated by the debtor as a trading account.

4. Under section 73G of the Debtors (Scotland) Act 1987 you must also, within the period of 3 weeks beginning with the day on which the arrestment is executed, disclose to the creditor the nature and value of the funds and/or moveable property which have been attached. This disclosure must be in the form set out in Schedule 8 to the Diligence (Scotland) Regulations 2009. Failure to comply may lead to a financial penalty under section 73G of the Debtors (Scotland) Act 1987 and may also be dealt with as a contempt of court. You must, at the same time, send a copy of the disclosure to the debtor and to any person known to you who owns (or claims to own) attached property and to any person to whom attached funds are (or are claimed to be due), solely or in common with the debtor.

IF YOU WISH FURTHER ADVICE CONTACT ANY CITIZENS ADVICE BUREAU/LOCAL ADVICE CENTRE/SHERIFF CLERK OR SOLICITOR

Rule 2.18A   FORM 10B[1]

Form of certificate of execution of arrestment on the dependence
CERTIFICATE OF EXECUTION

I, (*name*), Sheriff Officer, certify that I executed an arrestment on the dependence, by virtue of an interlocutor of the Sheriff at (*place*) on (*date*) obtained at the instance of (*name and address of party arresting*) against (*name and address of defender*) on (*name of arrestee*)—

* by delivering the schedule of arrestment to (*name of arrestee or other person*) at (*place*) personally on (*date*).

* by leaving the schedule of arrestment with (*name and occupation of person with whom left*) at (*place*) on (*date*) [and by posting a copy of the schedule to the arrestee by registered post or first class recorded delivery to the address specified on the receipt annexed to this certificate].

* by depositing the schedule of arresment in (*place*) on (*date*). (*Specify that enquiry made and reasonable grounds exist for believing that the person on whom service is to be made resides at the place but is not available*) [and by posting a copy of the schedule to the arrestee by registered post or first class recorded delivery to the address specified on the receipt annexed to this certificate].

* by affixing the schedule of arrestment to the door at (*place*) on (*date*). (*Specify that enquiry made and that reasonable grounds exist for believing that the person on whom service is to be made resides at the place but is not available*) [and by posting a copy of schedule to the arrestee by registered post or first class recorded delivery to the address specified on the receipt annexed to this certificate].

---

[1] As inserted by the Act of Sederunt (Sheriff Court Rules Amendment) (Diligence) 2009 (SSI 2009/107) (effective April 22, 2009).

* by leaving the schedule of arrestment with (*name and occupation of person with whom left*) at (*place of business*) on (*date*) [and by posting a copy of schedule to the arrestee by registered post or first class recorded delivery to the address specified on the receipt annexed to this certificate].

* by depositing the schedule of arrestment at (*place of business*) on (*date*). (*Specify that enquiry made and that reasonable grounds exist for believing that the person on whom service is to be made carries on business at that place.*) [and by posting a copy of the schedule to the arrestee by registered post or first class recorded delivery to the address specified on the receipt annexed to this certificate].

* by affixing the schedule of arrestment to the door at (*place of business*) on (*date*). (*Specify that enquiry made and that reasonable grounds exist for believing that the person on whom service is to be made carries on business at that place.*) [and by posting a copy of schedule to the arrestee by registered post or first class recorded delivery to the address specified on the receipt annexed to this certificate].

* by leaving the schedule of arrestment at (*registered office*) on (*date*), in the hands of (*name of person*) [and by posting a copy of the schedule to the arrestee by registered post or first class recorded delivery to the address specified on the receipt annexed to this certificate].

* by depositing the schedule of arrestment at (*registered office*) on (*date*) [and by posting a copy of the schedule to the arrestee by registered post or first class recorded delivery to the address specified on the receipt annexed to this certificate].

* by affixing the schedule of arrestment to the door at (*registered office*) on (*date*) [and by posting a copy of the schedule to the arrestee by registered post or first class recorded delivery to the address specified on the receipt annexed to this certificate].

I did this in the presence of (*name, occupation and address of witness*).

(*Signed*)
Sheriff Officer
(*Address*)
(*Signed*)
(Witness)

*Delele where not applicable

NOTE

A copy of the Schedule of arrestment on the dependence is to be attached to this certificate.

Rule 2.26   FORM 11

Form of extract decree
EXTRACT DECREE

Sheriff Court   Court Ref. No.
Date of decree   *In absence
Pursuer(s)   Defender(s)
The Sheriff
and granted decree against the   for payment of expenses of £
This extract is warrant for all lawful execution hereon.
Date (*insert date*)   Sheriff clerk (*depute*)
*Delete as appropriate

Paragraph 5(4)

Rule 2.37(3)   FORM 11AA[1]

Form of minute of intervention by the Commission for Equality and Human Rights

SHERIFFDOM OF *(insert name of*   Court ref. no.
sheriffdom)

AT (insert place of sheriff court)

APPLICATION FOR LEAVE TO INTERVENE BY THE COMMISSION FOR EQUALITY AND HUMAN RIGHTS
in the cause
[A.B.] *(designation and address),* Pursuer
against
[CD.] *(designation and address),* Defender

[*Here set out briefly:*
(a)   the Commission's reasons for believing that the proceedings are relevant to a matter in connection with which the Commission has a function;
(b)   the issue in the proceedings which the Commission wishes to address; and
(c)   the propositions to be advanced by the Commission and the Commission's reasons for believing that they are relevant to the proceedings and that they will assist the court]

Rule 2.39(2)   FORM 11AB[2]

Form of minute of intervention by the Scottish Commission for Human Rights

SHERIFFDOM OF *(insert name of*   Court ref. no.
sheriffdom)

AT *(insert place of sheriff court)*

APPLICATION FOR LEAVE TO INTERVENE BY THE SCOTTISH COMMISSION FOR HUMAN RIGHTS
in the cause
[A.B.] *(designation and address),* Pursuer
against
[C.D.] *(designation and address),* Defender

[*Here set out briefly:*
(a)   *the issue in the proceedings which the Commission intends to address;*
(b)   *a summary of the submission the Commission intends to make.*]

Rule 2.40(1)   FORM 11AC[3]

Invitation to the Scottish Commission for Human Rights to intervene

SHERIFFDOM OF *(insert name of*   Court ref. no.
sheriffdom)

AT *(insert place of sheriff court)*

INVITATION TO THE SCOTTISH COMMISSION FOR HUMAN RIGHTS TO INTERVENE

---

[1] As inserted by the Act of Sederunt (Sheriff Court Rules) (Miscellaneous Amendments) 2008 (SSI 2008/223) para.5(4) (effective July 1, 2008).

[2] As inserted by the Act of Sederunt (Sheriff Court Rules) (Miscellaneous Amendments) 2008 (SSI 2008/223) para.5(4) (effective July 1, 2008).

[3] As inserted by the Act of Sederunt (Sheriff Court Rules) (Miscellaneous Amendments) 2008 (SSI 2008/223) para.5(4) (effective July 1, 2008).

in the cause

[A.B.] (*designation and address*), Pursuer

against

[C.D.] (*designation and address*), Defender

[*Here set out briefly:*

(a) *the facts, procedural history and issues in the proceedings*;

(b) *the issue in the proceedings on which the court seeks a submission*]

Rule 3.1.6   FORM 11A[1]

Form of order for recovery of documents etc. under the Administration of Justice (Scotland) Act 1972

SHERIFFDOM OF (*insert name of sheriffdom*)

AT (*insert place of sheriff court*)

in the Summary Application

of

[A.B.] (*designation and address*)

Applicant

against

[C.D.] (*designation and address*)

Respondent

Date: (*date of interlocutor*)

To: (*name and address of party or parties or named third party haver, from whom the documents and other property are sought to be recovered*)

THE SHERIFF having heard the applicant and being satisfied that it is appropriate to make an order under section 1 of the Administration of Justice (Scotland) Act 1972:

ORDERS the Summary Application to be served upon the person(s) named and designed in the application;

APPOINTS (*name and designation of Commissioner*) to be Commissioner of the court;

GRANTS commission and diligence;

ORDERS the Commissioner to explain to the haver on executing the order—

(1) the meaning and effect of the order;

(2) that the haver may be entitled to claim that certain of the documents and other property are confidential or privileged;

(3) that the haver has a right to seek legal or other professional advice of his or her choice and to apply to vary or recall the order;

and to give the haver a copy of the Notice in Form 11B of Schedule 1 to the Act of Sederunt (Summary Applications, Statutory Applications and Appeals etc. Rules) 1999.

GRANTS warrant to and authorises the said Commissioner, whether the haver has allowed entry or not—

(1) to enter, between the hours of 9am and 5pm on Monday to Friday, (*or, where the sheriff has found cause shown under* rule 3.1.11(1), *otherwise specify the time [and day]*) the premises at (*address of premises*) and any other place in Scotland owned or occupied by the haver at which it appears to the Commissioner that any of the items set out in the statement of facts in the application to the court (the "listed items") may be located;

---

[1] As substituted by the Act of Sederunt (Sheriff Court Rules) (Miscellaneous Amendments) (No.3) 2011 (SSI 2011/386) para.6 (effective November 28, 2011).

(2) to search for and take all other steps which the Commissioner considers necessary to take possession of or preserve (*specify the listed items*);

(3) to take possession of and to preserve all or any of the listed items and to consign them with the Sheriff Clerk at (*enter name and address of sheriff court*) to be held by him or her pending the further orders of the sheriff;

and for that purpose,

ORDERS the haver or his/her servants or agents to allow the Commissioner, any person whom the Commissioner considers necessary to assist him/her, and the Applicant's representatives to enter the premises named in the order and to allow them—

(1) to search for the listed items and take such other steps as the Commissioner considers it reasonable to take to execute the order;

(2) to remain in the premises until such time as the search is complete, including allowing them to continue the search on subsequent days if necessary.

FURTHER ORDERS the haver or his/her servants or agents—

(1) (*if appropriate*) to provide access to information stored on any computer owned or used by him/her by supplying or providing the means to overcome any and all security mechanisms inhibiting access thereto;

(2) to inform the Commissioner immediately of the whereabouts of the listed items;

(3) to provide the Commissioner with a list of the names and addresses of everyone to whom he or she has given any of the listed items;

and not to destroy, conceal or tamper with any of the listed items except in accordance with the terms of this order;

FURTHER AUTHORISES (*specify the representatives*) to be the sole representatives of the Applicant to accompany the Commissioner for the purpose of identification of the said documents and other property.

(Signed)

Sheriff

SCHEDULE TO THE ORDER
Undertakings given by the Applicant

The Applicant has given the following undertakings—

1. That he/she will comply with any order of the sheriff as to payment of compensation if it is subsequently discovered that the order, or the implementation of the order, has caused loss to the respondent or, where the respondent is not the haver, to the haver.

2. That he/she will bring within a reasonable time of the execution of the order any proceedings which he/she decides to bring.

3. That he/she will not, without leave of the sheriff, use any information, documents or other property obtained as a result of the order, except for the purpose of any proceedings which he/she decides to bring and to which the order relates.

(*or as modified under* rule 3.1.4)

Rule 3.1.9(a)   FORM 11B[1]

Notice to accompany order in Form 11A when served by Commissioner

IMPORTANT

NOTICE TO PERSON ON WHOM THIS ORDER IS SERVED

---

[1] As substituted by the Act of Sederunt (Sheriff Court Rules) (Miscellaneous Amendments) (No.3) 2011 (SSI 2011/386) para.6 (effective November 28, 2011).

1. This order orders you to allow the person appointed and named in the order as Commissioner to enter your premises to search for, examine and remove or copy the items mentioned in the order.
2. It also allows entry to the premises to any person appointed and named in the order as a representative of the person who has been granted the order and to any person accompanying the Commissioner to assist him/her.
3. No-one else is given authority to enter the premises.
4. You should read the order immediately.
5. You have the right to seek legal or other professional advice of your choice and you are advised to do so as soon as possible.
6. Consultation under paragraph 5 will not prevent the Commissioner from entering your premises for the purposes mentioned in paragraph 1 but if the purpose of your seeking advice is to help you to decide if you should ask the sheriff to vary or recall the order you are entitled to ask the Commissioner to delay searching the premises for up to 2 hours or such other longer period as the Commissioner may permit.
7. The Commissioner is obliged to explain the meaning and effect of the order to you.
8. The Commissioner is also obliged to explain to you that you are entitled to claim that the items, or some of them, are protected as confidential or privileged.
9. You are entitled to ask the sheriff to vary or recall the order provided that—
    (a) you take steps to do so at once; and
    (b) you allow the Commissioner, any person appointed as a representative of the person who has been granted the order and any person accompanying the Commissioner to assist him/her, to enter the premises meantime.
10. The Commissioner and the persons mentioned as representatives or assistants have a right to enter the premises even if you refuse to allow them to do so, unless—
    (a) you are female and alone in the premises and there is no female with the Commissioner (where the Commissioner is not herself female), in which case they have no right to enter the premises;
    (b) the Commissioner serves the order before 9am or after 5pm on a weekday or at any time on a Saturday or Sunday (except where the sheriff has specifically allowed this, which will be stated in the order);
    in which cases you should refuse to allow entry.
11. You are entitled to insist that there is no-one (*or* no-one other than X) present who could gain commercially from anything which might be read or seen on your premises.
12. You are required to hand over to the Commissioner any of the items mentioned in the order which are in your possession.
13. You may be found liable for contempt of court if you refuse to comply with the order.

Rule 3.4.3(2)   FORM 11C[1, 2]

---

[1] As inserted by the Act of Sederunt (Sheriff Court Rules) (Enforcement of Securities over Heritable Property) 2010 (SSI 2010/324) (effective September 30, 2010).
[2] As amended by the Act of Sederunt (Sheriff Court Rules) (Miscellaneous Amendments) 2013 (SSI 2013/135) para.2 (effective May 27, 2013).

Form of certificate of completion of pre-action requirements

Certificate of completion of pre-action requirements in an application under [insert reference to provision or provisions under which application is made] of the property at (*insert address of security subjects*).

in the cause

SHERIFFDOM OF (*insert name of sheriffdom*)

AT (*insert place of sheriff court*)

[A.B.], (*insert designation and address*), Pursuer

against

[C.D.], (*insert designation and address*), Defender

Court ref. no:

(Insert name of pursuer), pursuer and creditor in the security with (*insert name of defender*), the defender, in respect of the premises at (*insert address of security subjects*) aver(s) that the pre-action requirements, have been complied with (*tick boxes to confirm*)—

1. As soon as reasonably practicable upon the defender entering into default, the pursuer provided the defender with clear information about—[1]

   (a) the terms of the security;

   (b) the amount due to the pursuer under the security, including any arrears and any charges in respect of late payment, broken down so as to show—

      (i) the total amount of the arrears;

      (ii) the total outstanding amount due including any charges already incurred;

   (c) the nature and the level of any charges that may be incurred by virtue of the contract to which the security relates if the default is not remedied; and

   (d) any other obligation under the security in respect of which the defender is in default.

Please provide details of (a) the date on which the information mentioned in 1(a) was provided; and (b) how the requirements of 1(b), (c) and (d) were complied with including a copy of the information provided under those paragraphs:

---

[1] As amended by the Act of Sederunt (Sheriff Court Rules) (Miscellaneous Amendments) 2013 (SSI 2013/135) para.2 (effective May 27, 2013).

2. The pursuer has made reasonable efforts to agree with the defender proposals in respect of future payments to the pursuer under the security and the fulfilment of any other obligation under the security in respect of which the defender is in default, including—[1]

    (a) making reasonable attempts to contact the defender to discuss the default;

    (b) providing the defender with details of any proposals made by the pursuer, set out in such a way as to allow the defender to consider the proposal;

    (c) allowing the defender reasonable time to consider any proposals made by the pursuer;

    (d) notifying the defender within a reasonable time of any decision taken by the pursuer to accept or reject a proposal made by the defender and, where the pursuer rejects such proposal, the pursuer has provided reasons for rejecting the proposal in writing within 10 working days of notifying the defender it is rejecting the proposal;

    (e) considering the affordability of any proposal for the defender taking into account, where known to the pursuer, the defender's personal and financial circumstances.

    Provide details:

*3. Where the defender has failed to comply with a condition of an agreement reached with the pursuer in respect of any proposal and the defender has not previously failed to comply with a condition of the agreement—

    (a) the pursuer has given the defender notice in writing of its decision to make an application under [*insert reference to provision or provisions under which application is made*] and the ground of the proposed application before making the application;

    (b) the pursuer has not made an application before the expiry of 15 working days**, beginning with the date on which the defender is deemed to have received the notice referred to at paragraph (a);

    (c) the default by the defender in respect of which the application is intended to be made has not been remedied during that notice period.

    Provide details of the defender's failure to comply with a condition of the agreement:

    *Indicate here if not applicable

    **In this paragraph, "working day" means a day that is not a Saturday or Sunday, or any day that is a bank holiday under the Banking and Financial Dealings Act 1971 in any part of the United Kingdom.

4. The defender has not taken steps that are likely to result in—

    (a) the payment to the pursuer within a reasonable time of any arrears, or the whole amount, due to the pursuer under the security; and

    (b) fulfilment by the defender within a reasonable time of any other obligation under the security in respect of which the defender is in default.

---

[1] As amended by the Act of Sederunt (Sheriff Court Rules) (Miscellaneous Amendments) 2013 (SSI 2013/135) para.2 (effective May 27, 2013).

Indicate what (if any) steps have been taken by the defender and why those steps are not considered to be effective:

5. The pursuer has provided the defender with information about sources of advice and assistance in relation to management of debt, including—

    (a) where the security is regulated, any relevant information sheet published by the appropriate regulatory body;

    (b) a local citizens advice bureau or other advice organisation; and

    (c) the housing department of the local authority in whose area the property which is subject to the security is situated.

6. The pursuer has encouraged the defender to contact the iocal authority in whose area the security subjects are situated.

7. The pursuer has had regard to any guidance issued by the Scottish Ministers.

(Signed)

[X. Y,], (*add designation and business address*)

Pursuer's solicitor

Rule 3.4.6   FORM 11D[1]

Form of notice to entitled residents in an application for enforcement of security over residential property

Notice to an entitled resident in an application for repossession of the property at (*insert address of security subjects*).

SHERIFFDOM OF (*insert name of sheriffdom*)

AT (*insert place of sheriff court*)

[A.B.], (*insert designation and address*), Pursuer

against

[C.D.], (*insert designation and address*), Defender

Court ref. no:

To: (*insert name and address of entitled resident*)

Attached to this notice is a copy of an application by (*insert name of pursuer*) under [insert reference to provision or provisions under which application is made]. **IF THE APPLICATION IS GRANTED, THE PROPERTY AT (*INSERT ADDRESS OF SECURITY SUBJECTS*) MAY BE REPOSSESSED AND YOU WOULD NO LONGER HAVE THE RIGHT TO RESIDE THERE**. A Form 11E application form is also attached.

This Notice—

    (a) gives you warning that an application has been made to the sheriff court for an order which may affect your interest as an entitled resident under [*insert reference to relevant provision or provisions*] in the property at (*insert address of security subjects*); and

    (b) informs you that an entitled resident may apply to the court to continue the

---

[1] As inserted by the Act of Sederunt (Sheriff Court Rules) (Enforcement of Securities over Heritable Property) 2010 (SSI 2010/324) (effective September 30, 2010).

proceedings or make any other order [*insert reference to relevant provision or provisions*] of that Act.

IF YOU WISH TO MAKE AN APPLICATION FOR AN ORDER UNDER [INSERT REFERENCE TO RELEVANT PROVISION OR PROVISIONS] you should complete and lodge Form 11E with the sheriff clerk at (*insert name and address of sheriff court*).

IF YOU ARE UNCERTAIN AS TO WHAT ACTION TO TAKE you should consult a solicitor. You may be eligible for legal aid depending on your income, and you can get information about legal aid from a solicitor. You may also obtain advice from an approved lay representative, or any Citizens Advice Bureau or other advice agency.

PLEASE NOTE THAT IF YOU DO NOTHING IN ANSWER TO THIS DOCUMENT the court will consider the application in the absence of you or your representative.

> (Signed)
> [P.Q.], Sheriff Officer, or
> [X.Y.] (*add designation and business address*) Solicitor

Rules 3.4.6 and 3.4.7   FORM 11E[1, 2]

Form of application to court by entitled resident

Application to court by an entitled resident in proceedings for repossession of the property at (*insert address of security subjects*).

Sheriff Court:..........

Date:

Court ref. no.

1. This application is made [by/on behalf of] (*delete as appropriate*) (*insert name and address of entitled resident*).

2. The applicant is an entitled resident within the meaning of section 24C(1) of the Conveyancing and Feudal Reform (Scotland) Act 1970 and/or, as the case may be, section 5D of the Heritable Securities (Scotland) Act 1894 because his or her sole or main residence is the security subjects (in whole or in part) at (*insert address of security subjects) and (*tick one box as appropriate*)—

    (a) *he or she is the proprietor of the security subjects (where the proprietor is not the debtor in the security);* ☐

    (b) *her or she is the non-entitled spouse of the debtor or the proprietor of security subjects which are (in whole or in part) a matrimonial home;* ☐

    (c) *he or she is the non-entitled civil partner of the debtor or the proprietor of security subjects which are (in whole or in part) a family home;* ☐

    (d) *he or she is a person living together with the debtor or the proprietor as if* ☐

---

[1] As inserted by the Act of Sederunt (Sheriff Court Rules) (Enforcement of Securities over Heritable Property) 2010 (SSI 2010/324) (effective September 30, 2010).

[2] As amended by the Act of Sederunt (Rules of the Court of Session and Sheriff Court Rules Amendment No. 2) (Marriage and Civil Partnership (Scotland) Act 2014) 2014 (SSI 2014/302) r.7 (effective December 16, 2014).

they were married to each other;

(e) *he or she lived together with the debtor or the proprietor in a relationship* ☐
described in (d) and—

    (i) *the security subjects (in whole or in part) are not the sole or main residence of the debtor or the proprietor;*

    (ii) *he or she lived together with the debtor or the proprietor throughout the period of 6 months ending with the date on which the security subjects ceased to be the sole or main residence of the debtor or the proprietor; and*

    (iii) *the security subjects (in whole or in part) are the sole or main residence of a child aged under 16 who is a child of both parties in that relationship.*

3.   The applicant believes that the court should consider this application because *(insert relevant details)—*

4.   The applicant asks the court to make an order under section 24B(1) of the Conveyancing and Feudal Reform (Scotland) Act 1970 and/or section 5C(1) of the Heritable Securities (Scotland) Act 1894 for *(insert details of what you wish the court to do and why—)*

WHAT HAPPENS NEXT: When you lodge this form at the sheriff clerk's office, the sheriff will fix a hearing for all those with an interest to appear and be heard. You are required to serve upon every party and intimate to every entitled resident a copy of this form, together with details of the date, time and place of the hearing.

    IF YOU ARE UNCERTAIN AS TO WHAT ACTION TO TAKE you should consult a solicitor. You may be eligible for legal aid depending on your income, and you can get information about legal aid from a solicitor. You may also obtain advice from an approved lay representative or any Citizens Advice Bureau or other advice agency,

Date *(insert date)*   (Signed)
                              [P.Q.], (Applicant),
                              or [X.Y.], *(add designation and address of Applicant's representative)*

DIET ASSIGNED

    At *(insert place)* on *(insert date)*, the court assigns the *(insert date of hearing)* at *(insert time)* at *(insert name of sheriff court)* as a diet for hearing parties on the Form 11E application.

Date *(insert date)*   *(Signed)*
                              Sheriff Clerk

EXECUTION OF CITATION

    At *(insert place)* on *(insert date)*, I hereby certify that upon the *(insert date)*, I duly served upon every party and intimated to every entitled resident a copy of this Form HE application, together with details of the hearing. This I did by *(insert method of service/intimation)*.

Date *(insert date)*   *(Signed)*
                              [P.Q.], Sheriff Officer, or
                              [X.Y.] *(add designation and business address)* Applicant's Solicitor

Rule 3.4.8(2)   FORM 11F[1, 2]

Form of minute for recall of decree

Minute for recall of decree in an application for repossession of the property at (*insert address of security subjects*).

Sheriff Court:..........

Date:

Court ref. no.

A.B. (*pursuer*) against C.D. (*defender(s)*)

(*insert name*), being (*tick one box as appropriate*)—

The Pursuer*;	☐
The Defender*; or	☐

An entitled resident within the meaning of section 24C(1) of the Conveyancing and Feudal Reform (Scotland) Act 1970 and/or, as the case may be, section 5D of the Heritable Securities (Scotland) Act 1894 because my sole or main residence is the security subjects (in whole or in part) at (*insert address of security subjects*) and—*

(a)   *I am the proprietor of the security subjects (where the proprietor is not the debtor in the security);*   ☐

(b)   *I am the non-entitled spouse of the debtor or the proprietor of security subjects which are (in whole or in part) a matrimonial home;*   ☐

(c)   *I am the non-entitled civil partner of the debtor or the proprietor of security subjects which are (in whole or in part) a family home;*   ☐

(d)   *I am a person living with the debtor or the proprietor as if we were married to each other;*   ☐

(e)   *I am a person who lived together with the debtor or the proprietor in a relationship described in (d) and—*   ☐

    (i)   *the security subjects (in whole or in part) are not the sole or main residence of the debtor or the proprietor;*

    (ii)   *I lived together with the debtor or the proprietor throughout the period of 6 months ending with the date on which the security subjects ceased to be the sole or main residence of the debtor or the proprietor; and*

    (iii)   *the security subjects (in whole or in part) are the sole or main residence of a child aged under 16 who is a child of both parties in that relationship.*

moves the court to recall the decree pronounced on (*insert date*) in this case.

WHAT HAPPENS NEXT: When you lodge this form at the sheriff clerk's office, the sheriff clerk will fix a hearing for all those with an interest to appear and be heard. You are required to serve upon every party and intimate to every entitled resident a copy of this form, together with details of the date, time and place of the hearing.

---

[1] As inserted by the Act of Sederunt (Sheriff Court Rules) (Enforcement of Securities over Heritable Property) 2010 (SSI 2010/324) (effective September 30, 2010).

[2] As amended by the Act of Sederunt (Rules of the Court of Session and Sheriff Court Rules Amendment No. 2) (Marriage and Civil Partnership (Scotland) Act 2014) 2014 (SSI 2014/302) r.7 (effective December 16, 2014).

If you wish to proceed with this application for recall of decree **YOU MUST ATTEND OR BE REPRESENTED AT THAT HEARING.**

YOU ARE STRONGLY ADVISED TO SEEK IMMEDIATE LEGAL ADVICE FROM A SOLICITOR. You may be eligible for legal aid depending on your income, and you can get information about legal aid from a solicitor. You may also obtain advice from an approved lay representative or any Citizens Advice Bureau or other advice agency.

Date (*insert date*)

(*Signed*)

[P.Q.], (Applicant),

or [X.Y.], (*add designation and address of Applicant's representative*)

DIET ASSIGNED

At (*insert place*) on (*insert date*), the court assigns the (*insert date of hearing*) at (*insert time*) at (*insert name of sheriff court*) as a diet for hearing parties on the Form 11F application.

Date (*insert date*)

(*Signed*)

Sheriff Clerk

EXECUTION OF CITATION

At (*insert place*) on (*insert date*), I hereby certify that upon the (*insert date*), I duly served upon every party and intimated to every entitled resident a copy of this Form 11F application, together with details of the hearing. This I did by (*insert method of service/intimation*).

Date (*insert date*)

(*Signed*)

[P.Q.], Sheriff Officer, or

[X.Y.] (*add designation and business address*) Applicant's Solicitor

Rule 3.4.8(10)   FORM 11G[1]

Form of intimation where peremptory diet fixed in a recall of decree application

Intimation of peremptory diet fixed in an application for repossession of the property at (*insert address of security subjects*).

SHERIFFDOM OF (*insert name of sheriffdom*)

AT (*insert place of sheriff court*)

[A.B.], (*insert designation and address*), Pursuer

against

(C.D.], (*insert designation and address*), Defender

Court ref. no:

The court noted that you did not appear at the Hearing to consider your application for recall of decree on (*insert date*). In your absence the decree for repossession of the property at (*insert address of security subjects*) has been recalled. As a result of your non-appearance the sheriff has ordered that you appear or be represented on

---

[1] As inserted by the Act of Sederunt (Sheriff Court Rules) (Enforcement of Securities over Heritable Property) 2010 (SSI 2010/324) (effective September 30, 2010).

(*insert date*) at (*insert time*) within (*insert name and address of sheriff court*) in order to ascertain whether you intend to proceed with your defence or your application.

A copy of the order is attached.

When you appear you will be asked by the sheriff to state whether you intend to proceed with your defence or your application.

IF YOU ARE UNCERTAIN AS TO WHAT ACTION TO TAKE you should consult a solicitor. You may be eligible for legal aid depending on your income, and you can get information about legal aid from a solicitor. You may also obtain advice from an approved lay representative or any Citizens Advice Bureau or other advice agency.

PLEASE NOTE THAT IF YOU DO NOT APPEAR OR ARE NOT REPRE-SENTED AT THAT HEARING the sheriff may regard you as no longer wishing to proceed with your defence or your application arid the sheriff may award decree of new against you in your absence and you will not be allowed to make a further application for recall.

Date (*insert date*)

(*Signed*)

(*add designation and address*)

Rule 3.8.3(1) FORM 12

FORM OF NOTICE TO BE SERVED ON PERSON WHO IS SUBJECT OF HOSPITAL ORDER, GUARDIANSHIP ORDER OR COMMUNITY CARE ORDER PROCEEDINGS.

To [*name and address of patient*]

Attached to this notice is a copy of—

*an application to the managers of [*name of hospital*] for your admission to that hospital in accordance with section 21 of the Mental Health (Scotland) Act 1984.

*an application to the sheriff at [*name of Sheriff Court*] for a Community Care Order in accordance with section 35A of the Mental Health (Scotland) Act 1984.

*an application to the [*name of local authority*] for your reception into guardianship in accordance with Section 40 of the Mental Health (Scotland) Act 1984.

The hearing will be held at [*place*] .... **on** [*date*] .... **at** [*time*].

You may appear personally at the hearing of this application unless the court decides otherwise on medical recommendations.

In any event, if you are unable or do not wish to appear personally you may request any person to appear on your behalf.

If you do not appear personally or by representative, the sheriff will consider the application in the absence of you or your representative.

[*Signed*]
Sheriff Clerk

[*Place and date*]
*delete as appropriate

Rule 3.8.3(3) FORM 13

FORM OF NOTICE TO RESPONSIBLE MEDICAL OFFICER

To [*name and address of responsible medical officer*]

In accordance with the Mental Health (Scotland) Act 1984, a copy of the application and notice of hearing is sent with this notice.

1. You are requested to deliver it personally to [*name of patient*] and to explain the contents of it to him.

2. You are also required to arrange if the patient so wishes, for the attendance of [*name of patient*] at the hearing at [*place of hearing*] on [*date*] so that he may appear and be heard in person.

3. You are further requested to complete and return to me in the enclosed envelope the certificate appended hereto before the date of the hearing.

4. If in your opinion it would be prejudicial to the patient's health or treatment for him to appear and be heard personally you may so recommend in writing, with reasons on the certificate.

[*Signed*]
Sheriff Clerk

[*Place and date*]

Rule 3.8.4(1)(b) and   FORM 14
3.8.4(2)(a)

FORM OF CERTIFICATE OF DELIVERY BY RESPONSIBLE MEDICAL OFFICER

I, [*name and designation*], certify that—

1. I have on the..........day of..........personally delivered to [*name of patient*] a copy of the application and the intimation of the hearing; and have explained the contents or purport to him [*or* her].

2. The patient does [not] wish to attend the hearing.

3. The patient does [not] wish to be represented at the hearing [and has nominated [*name and address of representative*] to represent him].

4. I shall arrange for the attendance of the patient at the hearing [*or* in my view it would be prejudicial to the patient's health or treatment for him [*or* her] to appear and be heard in person for the following reasons [*give reasons*]].

[*Signature and designation*]

[*Address and date*]

Rule 3.8.11   FORM 15

FORM OF APPEAL FOR REVOCATION OF A COMMUNITY CARE ORDER UNDER SECTION 35F OF THE MENTAL HEALTH (SCOTLAND) ACT 1984
SHERIFFDOM OF (*insert name of sheriffdom*)
AT (*insert name of Sheriff Court*)

I, [*insert name and address of applicant*],

appeal to the sheriff for revocation of a community care order made on [*insert date of order*] on the following grounds:—

[*State grounds on which appeal is to proceed*]

The community care order was renewed under section 35C(5) of the Mental Health (Scotland) Act 1984 on [*insert date of renewal*] and is still in force.

The special medical officer specified in the community care order is [*insert name and address of special medical officer*].

[*Signed*]..........
Applicant..........
[*or* Solicitor for
Applicant]..........
[*Insert designation and address*]..........

Rule 3.9.9(b)   FORM 16

FORM OF NOTICE TO PERSON WITH INTEREST IN PROPERTY SUBJECT TO AN APPLICATION FOR AN ORDER UNDER PARAGRAPH 12 OF SCHEDULE 1 TO THE PROCEEDS OF CRIME (SCOTLAND) ACT 1995 IN THE SHERIFF COURT
in the
PETITION [*or* NOTE]
of
[A.B.] (*name and address*)
for an order under paragraph 12 of Schedule 1 to the Proceeds of Crime (Scotland) Act 1995
in respect of the estates of [CD.] (*name and address*)
Court Ref No.
Date: (*date of posting or other method of service*)
To: (name and address of person on whom notice is to be served)
This Notice—

(a) gives you warning that an application has been made to the sheriff court for an order which may affect your interest in property; and

(b) informs you that you have an opportunity to appear and make representations to the court before the application is determined.

TAKE NOTICE

1. That on (*date*) in the sheriff court at (*place*) a confiscation order was made under section 1 of the Proceeds of Crime (Scotland) Act 1995 in respect of [CD.] (name and address).

2. That on (*date*) the administrator appointed under paragraph 1(1)(a) of Schedule 1 to the Proceeds of Crime (Scotland) Act 1995 on (*date*) was empowered to realise property belonging to [CD.].

or

2. That on (*date*) the administrator was appointed under paragraph 1 (1)(b) of Schedule 1 to the Proceeds of Crime (Scotland) Act 1995 on (*date*) to realise property belonging to [CD.].

3. That application has been made by petition [or note] for an order under paragraph 12 of Schedule 1 to the Proceeds of Crime (Scotland) Act 1995 (*here set out briefly the nature of the order sought*). A copy of the petition [*or* note] is attached.

4. That you have the right to appear before the court in person or by counsel or other person having a right of audience and make such representations as you may have in respect of the order applied for. The court has fixed (*insert day and date fixed for hearing the application*), at (*insert time and place fixed for hearing*) as the time when you should appear to do this.

5. That if you do not appear or are not represented on the above date, the order applied for may be made in your absence.

IF YOU ARE UNCERTAIN ABOUT THE EFFECT OF THIS NOTICE, you should consult a Solicitor, Citizen's Advice Bureau or other local advice agency or adviser immediately.

(*Signed*) ....
Sheriff Officer ....
[*or* Solicitor [*or* Agent] for petitioner [*or* noter]] ....
(*Address*)..........

Rule 3.11.14(1)   FORM 17

Representation of the People Act 1983

In the petition questioning the election for the .... of ...., in which .... is petitioner and .... is respondent.

The petitioner desires to withdraw his petition on the following grounds [*state grounds*], and craves that a diet may be appointed for hearing his application. He has, in compliance, with rule 3.11.14 of the Act of Sederunt (Summary Applications, Statutory Applications and Appeals etc. Rules) 1999, given the written notice of his intention to present this application to the respondent, to the Lord Advocate, and to the returning officer.

[*To be signed by the petitioner or his solicitor.*]

Rule 3.11.14(4) FORM 18

Representation of the People Act 1983

In the petition questioning the election for the .... of ...., in which .... is the petitioner and .... is respondent.

Notice is hereby given that the above petitioner has applied for leave to withdraw his petition, and that the sheriff principal has, by interlocutor dated the .... day of ...., assigned the .... day of .... at .... o'clock .... noon within the .... as a diet for hearing the application.

Notice is further given that under the Act any person who might have been a petitioner in respect of the said election may at the above diet apply to the sheriff principal to be substituted as a petitioner.

[*To be signed by the petitioner or his solicitor.*]

Rule 3.11.15(1) FORM 19

Representation of the People Act 1983

In the petition questioning the election for the .... of ...., in which .... was the petitioner [*or* last surviving petitioner] and .... is the respondent.

Notice is hereby given that the above petition stands abated by the death of the petitioner [*or* last surviving petitioner], and that any person who might have been a petitioner in respect of the said election and who desires to be substituted as a petitioner must, within 21 days from this date, lodge with the undersigned sheriff clerk of [*name sheriff court district*], a minute craving to be so substituted.

Date (*insert date*)

[*To be signed by the sheriff clerk*]

Rule 3.16.4(1) FORM 20[1]

FORM OF NOTICE OF AN APPLICATION UNDER THE ADULTS WITH INCAPACITY (SCOTLAND) ACT 2000

To (*insert name and address*)

Attached to this notice is a copy of an application for (*insert type of application*) under the Adults with Incapacity (Scotland) Act 2000.

The hearing will be held at (insert place) on (insert date) at (insert time)

You may appear personally at the hearing of this application.

In any event, if you are unable or do not wish to appear personally you may appoint a legal representative to appear on your behalf.

---

[1] As inserted by the Act of Sederunt (Summary Applications, Statutory Applications and Appeals etc. Rules) Amendment (Adults with Incapacity) 2001 (SSI 2001/142), (effective April 2, 2001).

If you are uncertain as to what action to take you should consult a solicitor. You may be eligible for legal aid, and you can obtain information about legal aid from any solicitor. You may also obtain information from any Citizens Advice Bureau or other advice agency.

If you do not appear personally or by legal representative, the sheriff may consider the application in the absence of you or your legal representative.

(insert place and date)..........

(signed)..........

Sheriff Clerk ....

or

[P.Q.] Sheriff Officer ....

or

[X.Y.],Solicitor ....

Rule 3.16.4(3)　　　　　　　　FORM 21[1, 2]

FORM OF NOTICE TO MANAGERS

To *(insert name and address of manager)*

A copy of an application made under the Adults with Incapacity (Scotland) Act 2000 and notice of hearing is sent with this notice.

1. You are requested immediately on receipt to deliver it personally to (name of adult) and to explain the contents of it to him or her.

2. You are further requested to complete and return to the sheriff clerk in the enclosed envelope the certificate (Form 22) appended hereto before the date of the hearing.

(insert place and date)..........

(signed)..........

Sheriff Clerk ....

or

[P.Q.] Sheriff Officer ....

or

[X.Y.],Solicitor ....

Rule 3.16.4(4)　　　　　　　　FORM 22[3]

FORM OF CERTIFICATE OF DELIVERY BY MANAGER

I, *(insert name and designation)*, certify that—

I have on *(insert date)* personally delivered to (name of adult) a copy of the application and the intimation of the hearing and have explained the contents to him/her.

Date *(insert date)*..........

(signed)..........

Manager ....

(add designation and address)..........

---

[1] As inserted by the Act of Sederunt (Summary Applications, Statutory Applications and Appeals etc. Rules) Amendment (Adults with Incapacity) 2001 (SSI 2001/142), (effective April 2, 2001).

[2] As inserted by the Act of Sederunt (Summary Applications, Statutory Applications and Appeals etc. Rules Amendment) (Miscellaneous) 2013 (SSI 2013/293) r.2, (effective November 11, 2013).

[3] As inserted by the Act of Sederunt (Summary Applications, Statutory Applications and Appeals etc. Rules) Amendment (Adults with Incapacity) 2001 (SSI 2001/142), (effective April 2, 2001).

Rule 3.16.7(1)   FORM 23[1]

SUMMARY APPLICATION UNDER THE ADULTS WITH INCAPACITY (SCOTLAND) ACT 2000
SHERIFFDOM OF *(insert name of sheriffdom)*
AT *(insert place of Sheriff Court)*

[A.B.] *(design and state capacity in which the application is made)*, Pursuer

The applicant craves the court *(state here the specific order(s) sought by reference to the provisions in the Adults with Incapacity (Scotland) Act 2000 .)*

STATEMENTS OF FACT

(State in numbered paragraphs the facts on which the application is made, including:

1. *The designation of the adult concerned (if other than the applicant).*

(a) *the adult's nearest relative;*

(b) *the adult's primary carer;*

(ba) *the adult's named person;*

(c) *any guardian, continuing attorney or welfare attorney of the adult; and*

(d) *any other person who may have an interest in the application.*

3. *The adult's place of habitual residence and/or the location of the property which is the subject of the application.)*

(insert place and date) ....   *(signed)* ....

                                     [A.B.], Pursuer or

                                     [X.Y.], *(state designation and business address)*..........

                                     Solicitor for the Pursuer ....

Rule 3.16.7(2)   FORM 24[2]

APPEAL TO THE SHERIFF UNDER THE ADULTS WITH INCAPACITY (SCOTLAND) ACT 2000
SHERIFFDOM OF *(insert name of sheriffdom)*
AT *(insert place of Sheriff Court)*

[A.B.] *(design and state capacity in which the appeal is being made)*, Pursuer

This appeal is made in respect of *(state here the decision concerned, the date on which it was intimated to the pursuer, and refer to the relevant provisions in the Adults with Incapacity (Scotland) Act 2000).*

(State here, in numbered paragraphs:

1. *The designation of the adult concerned (if other than the applicant).*

2. *The designation of:*

(a) *the adult's nearest relative;*

(b) *the adult's primary carer;*

(ba) *the adult's named person;*

---

[1] As inserted by the Act of Sederunt (Summary Applications, Statutory Applications and Appeals etc. Rules) Amendment (Adults with Incapacity) 2001 (SSI 2001/142), (effective April 2, 2001) and amended by the Act of Sederunt (Summary Applications, Statutory Applications and Appeals etc. Rules) Amendment (Adult Support and Protection (Scotland) Act 2007) (SSI 2008/111) r.2(3) (effective April 1, 2008).

[2] As inserted by the Act of Sederunt (Summary Applications, Statutory Applications and Appeals etc. Rules) Amendment (Adults with Incapacity) 2001 (SSI 2001/142), r.3(3), (effective April 2, 2001) and amended by the Act of Sederunt (Summary Applications, Statutory Applications and Appeals etc. Rules) Amendment (Adult Support and Protection (Scotland) Act 2007) (SSI 2008/111) r.2(3) (effective April 1, 2008).

(c) *any guardian, continuing attorney or welfare attorney of the adult; and*

(d) *any other person who may have an interest in the application.*

3. *The adult's place of habitual residence and/or the location of the property which is the subject of the application.)*

The pursuer appeals against the decision on the following grounds (*state here in separate paragraphs the grounds on which the appeal is made*).

The pursuer craves the court (*state here orders sought in respect of appeal*).

(*insert place and date*) ....

(*signed*).........

[A.B.], Pursuer or

[X.Y.], (*state designation and business address*).........

Solicitor for the Pursuer ....

Rule 3.27.6(1)   FORM 25[1]

ANTISOCIAL BEHAVIOUR ETC. (SCOTLAND) ACT 2004
CLOSURE NOTICE

Section 27

1. The service of this closure notice is authorised by a senior police officer under section 26(1) of the Antisocial Behaviour etc. (Scotland) Act 2004 ("the Act").

2. The premises to which this closure notice relates are: (*specify premises*).

3. Access to those premises by any person other than—

(a) a person who habitually resides in the premises; or

(b) the owner of the premises,

is prohibited.

4. Failure to comply with this notice is an offence which may result in a fine of up to £2,500 or imprisonment for a term of up to 3 months (or both). The penalties may be higher for repeated failure to comply with this (or any other) closure notice.

5. An application for the closure of these premises will be made under section 28 of the Act and will be considered at (*insert place including Room No. if appropriate*) on the .... day of .... at .... am/pm.

6. On such an application as set out in paragraph 5 being made, the sheriff may make a closure order under section 29 of the Act in respect of these premises.

7. The effect of the Closure Order in respect of these premises would be to close the premises to all persons (other than any person expressly authorised access by the sheriff in terms of section 29(3) of the Act) for such period not exceeding 3 months as is specified in the order. Measures may be taken to ensure that the premises are securely closed against entry by any person.

8. If you live on or have control of, responsibility for or an interest in the premises to which this closure notice relates and wish to oppose the application for a closure order, you should attend or be represented at the hearing mentioned in paragraph 5 of this notice.

9. If you would like further information or advice about housing or legal matters you can contact—

(*specify at least two persons or organisations (including name and means of contacting) based in the locality of the promises who or which will be able to provide advice about housing and legal matters*). You also have a legal right to advice from your local authority should you be threatened with possible homelessness.

---

[1] Inserted by SSI 2004/455, para 5 and Sch. (effective October 28, 2004).

Rule 3.27.6(2)   FORM 26[1]

ANTISOCIAL BEHAVIOUR ETC. (SCOTLAND) ACT 2004
CERTIFICATION OF SERVICE

Section 27

I *(insert designation, including address and rank, of police officer)* certify that a copy of the closure notice which was authorised by *(insert designation of senior police officer)* on *(insert date on which closure notice was authorised)* in respect of *(insert details of the premises to which closure notice relates)* was served on: *(insert name and address of each person to whom a copy of the notice was given, including date)*

....
....
....
....
....

by *(insert designation, including address and rank, of police officer who served the copy or copies of the closure notice and, if more than one, indicate which police officer served a copy of the notice on which of the persons listed above).*

....
Signed
(insert designation, including rank, of police officer)

Rule 3.27.7   FORM 27[2]

ANTISOCIAL BEHAVIOUR ETC. (SCOTLAND) ACT 2004

Section 28

Sheriff Court.................... 20..........

(Court Ref No.)

PART A

APPLICATION FOR CLOSURE ORDER IN RESPECT OF PREMISES AT:

....
....
....

("the Premises")

PART B

1. This application is made [by/on behalf of] *(delete as appropriate)* *(insert name and rank of senior police officer)* of *(insert details of police force).*

2. Service of a closure notice on the Premises was authorised by *(insert details of senior police officer)* on the .... day of .... A copy of [the authorisation/ written confirmation of such authorisation] *(delete as appropriate)* is attached.

3. A copy of the closure notice was, on the .... day of ....,—

(a) fixed to:

(insert details of all locations in, or used as part of the Premises, to which a copy of the notice was fixed)

....
....
....
....

---

[1] Inserted by SSI 2004/455, para 5 and Sch. (effective October 28, 2004).
[2] Inserted by SSI 2004/455, para 5 and Sch. (effective October 28, 2004) and amended by SSI 2010/ 416 (effective December 13, 2010).

....

....

(b) given to:

(insert name and address of each person to whom a copy of the notice was given)

....

....

....

....

....

....

4. Certification in the prescribed form of service of the closure notice to the persons described at paragraph 3(b) above is attached.

5. This application is made on the following grounds:

(insert reasons for making application)

....

....

....

....

....

....

6. The following evidence is [attached/supplied] *(delete as appropriate)* in respect of this application *(insert short details of supporting evidence)*.

PART C

7. The applicant asks the court to—

(a) assign the hearing for the .... day of .... at .... am/pm; and

(b) make a closure order in respect of the Premises.

..........Signed

Senior Police Officer for [Police Force] (Applicant)

or [X.Y.] Solicitor for Senior Police Officer

(add designation and business address)

FORM OF INTERLOCUTOR

Sheriff Court .... 20..........

(Court Ref No.)

The sheriff having considered this application assigns .... at .... within .... as a hearing, this date having been previously intimated to known interested persons and published in the closure notice.

..........Signed

Sheriff

FORM OF INTERLOCUTOR

Sheriff Court .... 20..........

(Court Ref No.)

The sheriff having heard *(insert details of parties who attended the hearing)* and having considered the application [, being satisfied that the conditions mentioned in [section 30(2)] [section 30(2A)] of the Antisocial Behaviour etc. (Scotland) Act 2004 are met] *(delete as appropriate)* and having regard to the matters mentioned in section 30(3) of the Antisocial Behaviour etc. (Scotland) Act 2004 ("the Act"),

*1. makes an order under section 29(1) of the Act that the premises at *(insert details of premises)* are closed to all persons for a period of *(insert period)*.

*2. directs intimation of this interlocutor to *(insert details of all known interested persons)* and by posting a copy thereof at prominent places on the premises at *(indicate where copies have been posted)*.

*3. refuses to make a closure order in respect of the premises at *(insert details of premises)*.

*4. postpones the determination of the application until *(insert date)* at *(insert time)* within *(insert location)*.

*delete as appropriate

..........Signed

Sheriff

Rule 3.27.8   FORM 28[1]

ANTISOCIAL BEHAVIOUR ETC. (SCOTLAND) ACT 2004

Minute

Section 32

Application for extension of closure order

Sheriff Court ....: .... 20..........

(Court Ref No.)

PART A

PREMISES IN RESPECT OF WHICH CLOSURE ORDER HAS BEEN MADE:

....

....

....

("the Premises")

PART B

1. This application is made [by/on behalf of] *(delete as appropriate)* *(insert name and rank of senior police officer)* of *(insert details of police force)*.

2. A copy of the closure order made in respect of the Premises is attached. The closure order has effect until *(enter date)*.

3. The applicant believes that it is necessary to extend the period for which the closure order has effect for the purpose of preventing [relevant harm] [the commission of an exploitation offence] *(delete as appropriate)*, on the following grounds: *(specify reasons for extension)*.

4. *(Insert details of local authority)* has been consulted about the applicant's intention to make this application.

PART C

5. The applicant asks the court to—

(c) fix a hearing;

(d) order the applicant to intimate this application and the date of the hearing to such persons as the sheriff considers appropriate; and

(e) extend the closure order in respect of the Premises for a period of .... [months/days] *(delete as appropriate)* or for such period not exceeding 6 months as the court may consider appropriate.

..........Signed

Senior Police Officer for [Police Force] (Applicant)

or [X.Y.] Solicitor for Senior Police Officer

(add designation and business address)

FORM OF INTERLOCUTOR

Sheriff Court.................... 2..........

(Court Ref No.)

---

[1] Inserted by SSI 2004/455, para 5 and Sch. (effective October 28, 2004) and amended by SSI 2010/416 (effective December 13, 2010).

The sheriff having considered this minute orders the applicant to intimate this application and interlocutor to ...., assigns .... at .... within .... as a hearing and directs any person wishing to oppose the granting of the application to appear or be represented at the hearing to show cause why the application should not be granted.

..........Signed

Sheriff

FORM OF INTERLOCUTOR

Sheriff Court ....20..........

(Court Ref No.)

The sheriff having heard *(insert details of parties who attended the hearing)* [and] having considered this minute [and being satisfied that the condition mentioned in [section 32(1)] [section 32(1 A)] of the Antisocial Behaviour etc. (Scotland) Act 2004 is met] *(delete as appropriate)*,

*1. makes an order extending the closure order made under section 29(1) of the Antisocial Behaviour etc. (Scotland) Act 2004 in respect of the premises at *(insert details of premises)* for a period of *(insert period)*.

*2. directs intimation of this interlocutor to *(insert details of persons to whom sheriff considers it to he appropriate to intimate)* and by posting a copy thereof at prominent places on the premises at *(indicate where copies have been posted)*.

*3. refuses to make an order extending the closure order in respect of the premises at *(insert details of premises)*.

*4. postpones the determination of the application until *(insert date)* at *(insert time)* within *(insert location)*.

*delete as appropriate

..........Signed

Sheriff

Rule 3.27.9   FORM 29[1]

ANTISOCIAL BEHAVIOUR ETC. (SCOTLAND) ACT 2004

Minute

Section 33

Application for revocation of closure order

Sheriff Court .... 20..........

(Court Ref No.)

PART A

PREMISES IN RESPECT OF WHICH CLOSURE ORDER HAS BEEN MADE:

....

....

....

("the Premises")

The applicant is *(insert name and address of applicant)* who is:

*1. a senior police officer of the police force for the area within which the Premises (or part thereof) are situated.

*2. the local authority for the area within which the Premises or part thereof are situated.

---

[1] Inserted by SSI 2004/455, para 5 and Sch. (effective October 28, 2004) and amended by SSI 2010/416 (effective December 13, 2010).

*3. a person on whom a copy of the closure notice relating to the Premises in respect of which the closure order has effect was served under section 27(2)(b) or (3) of the Antisocial Behaviour etc. (Scotland) Act 2004.

*4. a person who has an interest in these premises but on whom the closure notice was not served.

*delete as appropriate.

PART B

1. A copy of the closure order made in respect of the Premises is attached.
2. The applicant believes that a closure order in respect of the Premises is no longer necessary to prevent [the occurrence of relevant harm][the commission of an exploitation offence] (*delete as appropriate*) for the following reasons (*specify grounds for application for revocation*).

PART C

3. The applicant asks the court to:
   (a) fix a hearing;
   (b) order the applicant to intimate this application and the date of the hearing to such persons as the sheriff considers appropriate and, where the applicant is not a senior police officer, to such senior police officer as the sheriff considers appropriate; and
   (c) order the revocation of the closure order.

..........Signed

Applicant (*include full designation*)

or [X.Y.] Solicitor for Applicant (*include full designation and business address*)

FORM OF INTERLOCUTOR

Sheriff Court.......... ....20...............

(Court Ref No.)

The sheriff having considered this minute orders the applicant to intimate this application and interlocutor to.........., assigns...........within...........as a hearing and directs any person wishing to oppose the granting of the application to appear or be represented at the hearing to show cause why the application should not be granted.

..........Signed

Sheriff

FORM OF INTERLOCUTOR

Sheriff Court...............20...........

(Court Ref No.)

The sheriff having heard (*insert details of parties who attended the hearing*) [and] having considered this minute [and being satisfied that a closure order is no longer necessary to prevent [the occurrence of relevant harm][the commission of an exploitation offence] (*delete as appropriate*),

*1. makes an order revoking the closure order made under section 29(1) of the Antisocial Behaviour etc. (Scotland) Act 2004 in respect of the premises at (insert details of the premises).

*2. directs intimation of this interlocutor to (insert details of persons to whom sheriff considers it to be appropriate to intimate).

*3. refuses to make an order revoking the closure order in respect of the premises at (insert details of the premises).

*4. postpones the determination of the application until (*insert date*) at (*insert time*) within (*insert location*).

*delete as appropriate

..........Signed

Sheriff

Rule 3.27.10   FORM 30[1]

ANTISOCIAL BEHAVIOUR ETC. (SCOTLAND) ACT 2004
Minute

Section 34

Application for access to premises in respect of which a closure order is in force

Sheriff Court.......... ....20..........

(Court Ref No.)

PART A

PREMISES IN RESPECT OF WHICH CLOSURE ORDER HAS BEEN MADE:

....

....

....

("the Premises")

PREMISES IN RESPECT OF WHICH APPLICATION FOR ACCESS IS BE-ING MADE:

....

....

....

PART B

1. A copy of the closure order made in respect of the Premises is attached. The closure order has effect until (*insert date*).

2. The applicant (*insert details of applicant*) [owns/occupies] (*delete as appropriate*) the following [part of] (delete as appropriate) building or structure in which the Premises are situated and in respect of which the closure order does not have effect.

PART C

3. The applicant asks the court to:

(a) fix a hearing;

(b) order the applicant to intimate this application and the date of the hearing to such persons as the sheriff considers appropriate and, where the applicant is not a senior police officer, to such senior police officer as the sheriff considers appropriate; and

(c) make an order allowing access (detail access provisions requested).

..........Signed

Applicant (*include full designation*)

or [X.Y.] Solicitor for Applicant (*include full designation and business address*)

FORM OF INTERLOCUTOR

Sheriff Court...............20..........

(Court Ref No.)

The sheriff having considered this minute orders the applicant to intimate this application and interlocutor to.........., assigns..........at..........within.......... as a hearing and directs any person wishing to oppose the granting of the application to appear or be represented at the hearing to show cause why the application should not be granted.

..........Signed

Sheriff

FORM OF INTERLOCUTOR

Sheriff Court...............20..........

(Court Ref No.)

---

[1] Inserted by SSI 2004/455, para 5 and Sch. (effective October 28, 2004).

The sheriff having heard (*insert details of parties who attended the hearing*) and having considered this minute,

*1. makes an order an order allowing (*insert name and address*)

....

....

....

access to the following part or parts of the premises at (*insert details of premises*) in relation to which a closure order has been made under section 29(1) of the Antisocial Behaviour etc. (Scotland) Act 2004: (*insert details of parts of premises to which access order is to apply*)

*2. directs intimation of this interlocutor to (*insert details of all known interested persons to whom the sheriff considers it to be appropriate to intimate*).

*3. refuses to make an access order in respect of the premises at (*insert details of premises*).

*4. postpones the determination of the application until (insert date) at (insert time) within (*insert location*).

*delete as appropriate

.... Signed

Sheriff

Rule 3.27.16   FORM 31

ANTISOCIAL BEHAVIOUR ETC. (SCOTLAND) ACT 2004 Section 13, 102 or 105

Intimation that court may make or revoke or vary a parenting order

Sheriff Court .... 20 ....

(Court Ref No.)

PART A

This part must be completed by the applicant's solicitor in language a child is capable of understanding

To **(1)**

The Sheriff (the person who has to decide about the parenting order) has been asked by **(2)** to decide:—

(a)   **(3)** and **(4)**;

(b)   **(5)**;

(c)   **(6)**.

If you want to tell the Sheriff what you think about the things **(2)** has asked the Sheriff to decide about your future you should complete Part B of this form and send it to the Sheriff Clerk at **(7)** by **(8)**. An envelope which does not need a postage stamp is enclosed for you to use to return the form.

IF YOU DO NOT UNDERSTAND THIS FORM OR IF YOU WANT HELP TO COMPLETE IT you may get free help from a SOLICITOR or contact the SCOTTISH CHILD LAW CENTRE ON the FREE ADVICE TELEPHONE LINE ON 0800 317 500.

If you return the form it will be given to the Sheriff. The Sheriff may wish to speak with you and may ask you to come and see him or her.

NOTES FOR COMPLETION

(1) Insert name and address of child.	(2) Insert description of party making the application to the court.
(3) Insert appropriate wording for parenting order sought.	(4) Insert appropriate wording, if relevant, for Antisocial Behaviour Order.

(5) Insert appropriate wording for contact.	(6) Insert appropriate wording for any other order sought or determinations to be made by sheriff.
(7) Insert address of sheriff clerk.	(8) Insert the date occurring 21 days after the date on which intimation is given.
(9) Insert court reference number.	(10) Insert name and address of parties to the action.

PART B

IF YOU WISH THE SHERIFF TO KNOW YOUR VIEWS ABOUT THE PARENTING ORDER YOU SHOULD COMPLETE THIS PART OF THE FORM

To the Sheriff Clerk, (7)

Court Ref. No. (9)

(10)..........

QUESTION (1): DO YOU WISH THE SHERIFF TO KNOW WHAT YOUR VIEWS ARE ABOUT THE PARENTING ORDER?

(PLEASE TICK BOX)

YES	
NO	

If you have ticked YES please also answer Question (2) or (3)

QUESTION (2): WOULD YOU LIKE A FRIEND, RELATIVE OR OTHER PERSON TO TELL THE SHERIFF YOUR VIEWS ABOUT THE PARENTING ORDER?

(PLEASE TICK BOX)

YES	
NO	

If you have ticked YES please write the name and address of the person you wish to tell the Sheriff your views in Box (A) below. You should also tell that person what your views are about the parenting order.

BOX A:	(NAME)			
	....			
	(ADDRESS)			
	....			
	....			
	....			
	Is this person—	A friend?		A relative?	
		A teacher?		Other?	

OR

QUESTION (3): WOULD YOU LIKE TO WRITE TO THE SHERIFF AND TELL HIM WHAT YOUR VIEWS ARE ABOUT THE PARENTING ORDER?

(PLEASE TICK BOX)

YES	
NO	

If you decide that you wish to write to the Sheriff you can write what your views are about the parenting order in Box (B) below or on a separate piece of paper. If you decide to write your views on a separate piece of paper you should send it along with this form to the Sheriff Clerk in the envelope provided.

BOX B:	WHAT I HAVE TO SAY ABOUT THE PARENTING ORDER:—

NAME: ....
   ADDRESS: ....
   DATE: ....

Rule 3.27.17   FORM 32[1]

ANTISOCIAL BEHAVIOUR ETC. (SCOTLAND) ACT 2004
Section 13, 102 or 105
Form of notice to local authority requesting a report in respect of a child
Sheriff Court.......... .... 20..........
(Court Ref No.)
To (*insert name and address*)

1. YOU ARE GIVEN NOTICE that in an action in the Sheriff Court at (*insert address*) an application for [the variation/revocation of] (*delete as appropriate*) a parenting order is being considered in respect of a parent of the child (*insert name of child*). A copy of the application is enclosed.

2. You are required to submit to the court a report on all the circumstances of the child, including but not limited to:—

(a) the current or proposed arrangements for the case and upbringing of the child;

(b) information about the family circumstances of the parent; and

(c) the likely effect of a parenting order on the family circumstances of the parent and the child.

3. This report should be sent to the Sheriff Court at .... on or before .... (*insert date*).

Date (*insert date*)
..........Signed:
Applicant (*include full designation*)
or [X.Y.] Solicitor for Applicant (*include full designation and business address*)
or Sheriff Clerk

Rule 3.34.2   FORM 33

NOTE OF APPEAL UNDER LICENSING (SCOTLAND) ACT 2005*[Repealed by the Act of Sederunt (Sheriff Court Rules) (Miscellaneous Amendments) (No.2) 2010 (SSI 2010/416) r.8 (effective December 13, 2010).]*

Rule 3.35.6   FORM 34[2]

---

[1] Inserted by SSI 2004/455, para 5 and Sch. (effective October 28, 2004).

[2] As inserted by the Act of Sederunt (Summary Applications, Statutory Applications and Appeals etc. Rules) Amendment (Adult Support and Protection (Scotland) Act 2007) (No.2) 2008 (SSI 2008/335) r.2(3) (effective October 29, 2008) and substituted by the Act of Sederunt (Summary Applications, Statutory Applications and Appeals etc. Rules) Amendment (Adult Support and Protection (Scotland) Act 2007) (No.3) 2008 (SSI 2008/375) para.2(5) (effective November 20, 2008).

Form of certificate of delivery of document under section 26(2), 27(1) or 27(2) of the Adult Support and Protection (Scotland) Act 2007

Court ref no:

(Insert place and date) I, (insert name and designation), hereby certify that on (date) I duly delivered to (insert name and address) (insert details of the document delivered). This I did by (state method of delivery).

Signed

(add designation and address or business address)

FORM 35[1]

FORM OF APPLICATION FOR WARRANT FOR ENTRY UNDER SECTION 38(2) OF THE ADULT SUPPORT AND PROTECTION (SCOTLAND) ACT 2007

SHERIFFDOM OF *(insert name of sheriffdom)*

AT *(insert place of sheriff court)*

[A.B.] *(design and state capacity in which the application is made)*, Applicant

The applicant craves the court to grant a warrant for entry in terms of sections 37 and 38(2) of the Adult Support and Protection (Scotland) Act 2007 to *(state address of specified place to which entry is sought)*.

Rule 3.39.2(1) FORM 36[2]

FORM OF APPLICATION FOR WARRANT UNDER SECTION 27 OF THE PUBLIC HEALTH ETC. (SCOTLAND) ACT 2008

SHERIFFDOM OF *(insert name of sheriffdom)*

AT *(insert place of sheriff court)*

[A.B.] (design and state address), Applicant

Order sought from the court

The applicant applies to the court to grant warrant to him:

1. to enter the premises at *(insert address of premises to which entry is sought)*.
2. to take with him any other person he may authorise and, if he has reasonable cause to expect any serious obstruction in obtaining access, a constable.
3. to take with him any equipment or materials required for any purpose for which the power of entry is being exercised.
4. to direct that those premises (or any part of them) are, or any thing in or on them is, to be left undisturbed (whether generally or in particular respects) for so long as he considers appropriate.
5. to exercise any of the powers conferred by sections 23, 24 and 25 of the Public Health etc. (Scotland) Act 2008 ("the Act").

Statement

*Delete as appropriate

1. This application is made pursuant to section 27 of the Act.
2. The applicant is an investigator duly appointed in terms of section 21(2) of the Act to carry out a public health investigation.
3. The said premises are*/are not* a dwellinghouse.
4. The said premises are within the jurisdiction of this court.
5. The applicant considers it necessary for the purpose of, or in connection with, a public health investigation to exercise the powers of entry available

---

[1] As inserted by the Act of Sederunt (Summary Applications, Statutory Applications and Appeals etc. Rules) Amendment (Adult Support and Protection (Scotland) Act 2007) (No.2) 2008 (SSI 2008/335) r.2(3) (effective October 29, 2008).

[2] As inserted by the Act of Sederunt (Summary Applications, Statutory Applications and Appeals etc. Rules) Amendment (Public Health etc. (Scotland) Act 2008) 2009 (SSI 2009/320) r.2 (effective October 1, 2009).

to him under section 22 of the Act, the other investigatory powers mentioned in section 23 of the Act, the power to ask questions mentioned in section 24 of the Act and any supplementary power mentioned in section 25 of the Act (*insert here a brief statement of reasons*).

*6. [*If the said premises are a dwellinghouse*] The applicant has in terms of section 26(2) of the Act given 48 hours notice of the proposed entry to a person who appears to be the occupier of the dwellinghouse and the period of notice has expired.

*7. The applicant is an investigator entitled to enter premises under section 22 of the Act and *the applicant has been refused entry to the said premises, or *the applicant reasonably anticipates that entry will be refused

OR

*7. The said premises are premises which the applicant is entitled to enter and they are unoccupied.

OR

*7. The said premises are premises which the applicant is entitled to enter and the occupier thereof is temporarily absent and there is urgency because (*here state briefly why there is urgency*).

OR

*7. The applicant is an investigator entitled to exercise a power under section 23 or 24 of the Act and

* has been prevented from exercising that power, or
* reasonably anticipates being prevented from exercising that power.

OR

*7 An application for admission to the said premises would defeat the object of the public health investigation.

8. In the circumstances narrated the applicant is entitled to the warrant sought and it should be granted accordingly.

(*signed*)

[A.B.] Applicant

or [X.Y.] (*add designation and business address*)

Solicitor for applicant

(*insert date*)

Rule 3.39.2(2)   FORM 37[1]

FORM OF WARRANT FOR A PUBLIC HEALTH INVESTIGATION

Sheriff Court...............20...............

(Court Ref. No.)

* *Delete as appropriate*

The sheriff, having considered an application made under section 27 of the Public Health etc. (Scotland) Act 2008 ("the Act") *[and productions lodged therewith] *[and (*where the premises referred to below are a dwellinghouse*) being satisfied that due notice has been given under section 26(2) of the Act and has expired],

Grants warrant to the applicant (*insert name*) as sought and authorises him:

(a)   to enter the premises at (*insert address*),

---

[1] As inserted by the Act of Sederunt (Summary Applications, Statutory Applications and Appeals etc. Rules) Amendment (Public Health etc. (Scotland) Act 2008) 2009 (SSI 2009/320) r.2 (effective October 1, 2009).

(b)   on entering the premises referred to at paragraph (a), to take—

    (i)   any other person authorised by him and, if he has reasonable cause to expect any serious obstruction in obtaining access, a constable; and

    (ii)   any equipment or materials required for any purpose for which the power of entry is being exercised,

(c)   to direct that—

    (i)   those premises (or any part of them) are; or

    (ii)   any thing in or on those premises is, to be left undisturbed (whether generally or in particular respects) for so long as he considers appropriate.

(d)   to exercise any power mentioned in sections 23 to 25 of the Act.

(signed)
Sheriff

Rule 3.39.3(1)   FORM 38[1]

FORM OF APPLICATION FOR MEDICAL EXAMINATION OF A PERSON UNDER SECTION 34 OF THE PUBLIC HEALTH ETC. (SCOTLAND) ACT 2008

SHERIFFDOM OF *(insert name of sheriffdom)*
AT *(insert place of sheriff court)*
[A.B.] *(design health board)*, Applicant

Order sought from the court

* *Delete as appropriate*

The applicant applies to the court to grant an order under section 34(1) of the Public Health etc. (Scotland) Act 2008 ("the Act") authorising the medical examination of *(insert name, address and date of birth of person to be medically examined)* ("the person").

*And (*if necessary, request any specialities in connection with the examination, about which the court's additional authority is sought pursuant to* section 34(3) of the Act).

Statement

Delete as appropriate

1.   This application is made pursuant to sections 33 and 34 of the Act.

2.   The person is present within the applicant's area. The applicant is a health board operating within the jurisdiction of this court. This court accordingly has jurisdiction.

3.   The person is aged 16 years or over.

OR

The person is under 16. The parent or other person who has day-to-day care or control of the person is *(insert name, address and relationship to the person)*.

4.

    (a)   The applicant *knows/*suspects that the person—

       *(i)   has an infectious disease, namely [*insert name of disease*];

       *(ii)   has been exposed to an organism which causes an infectious disease [*insert name of disease*];

     *(iii)   is contaminated; or

     *(iv)   has been exposed to a contaminant,

---

[1] As inserted by the Act of Sederunt (Summary Applications, Statutory Applications and Appeals etc. Rules) Amendment (Public Health etc. (Scotland) Act 2008) 2009 (SSI 2009/320) r.2 (effective October 1, 2009).

(insert here a brief statement indicating the basis upon which these matters are known or suspected by the applicant)

AND

(b)　It appears to the applicant that as a result—

(i)　there is or may be a significant risk to public health; and

(ii)　it is necessary, to avoid or minimise that risk, for the person to be medically examined.

(Insert here a brief statement indicating the reason why the applicant considers that there is or may be a significant risk to public health and that it is necessary, to avoid or minimise that risk, for the person to be medically examined).

5. The applicant proposes that the examination be carried out by *(insert proposed class or classes of health care professional).*

6. The applicant proposes that the examination be *(insert nature of the proposed examination).*

*7. The applicant has explained to the person—

(a)　that there is a significant risk to public health;

(b)　the nature of that risk; and

(c)　why the applicant considers it necessary for the proposed action to be taken in relation to that person.

OR

*7. The applicant states that the person is incapable of understanding any explanation of the matters referred to at section 31(3) of the Act *(state reason)* and has explained to *(insert name and address of a person mentioned in section 31(5)(a) or (b) of the Act and their relationship to the person)*—

(a)　that there is a significant risk to public health;

(b)　the nature of that risk; and

(c)　why the applicant considers it necessary for the proposed action to be taken in relation to that person.

OR

*7. The applicant states that no explanation has been given in relation to this application under section 31(3) or (5) of the Act because *(state why it was not reasonably practicable to do so).*

*8. The applicant states that *a response was made/*representations were made on behalf of the person in the following terms *(insert response or representations made).*

9. The applicant attaches to this application a certificate signed by a health board competent person which indicates that the competent person is satisfied as to the matters mentioned in statement 4 [*and *(in a case where medical examination of a group is sought)* that it is necessary, to avoid or minimise an actual or anticipated significant risk to public health, for all the persons in the group to be medically examined].

10. In the circumstances narrated the applicant is entitled to the order sought and it should be granted accordingly.

(signed)

[X.Y.] *(add designation and business address)*

Solicitor for applicant

(insert date)

FORM 39[1]

Rule 3.39.3(3)

FORM OF ORDER FOR A MEDICAL EXAMINATION

Sheriff Court...............

.... 20.......... at [*insert time*]

(Court Ref. No.)

The sheriff, having considered an application made under section 33(2) of the Public Health etc. (Scotland) Act 2008 ("the Act") *[and productions lodged therewith], and being satisfied as necessary as to the matters mentioned in section 34(2) of the Act,

1. Makes an order in terms of section 34(1) of the Act authorising the medical examination of (insert details of the person as given in the application) and authorises (insert the class or classes of health care professional by whom the medical examination is to be carried out) to carry out the examination,

*And (*add any additional matters to be dealt with in the order in terms of* section 34(3) of the Act).

2. Directs notification of this order (*insert details of method and timing of notice*) to (*the person to whom the order applies*)

*and (*the name and designation of any person to whom an explanation was given under* section 31(5) of the Act)

*and (*insert the name and designation of any other person whom the sheriff considers appropriate*).

* Delete *as appropriate*

(signed)

Sheriff

FORM 40[2]

Rule 3.39.4(1)

FORM OF APPLICATION FOR QUARANTINE ORDER UNDER SECTION 40 OF THE PUBLIC HEALTH ETC. (SCOTLAND) ACT 2008

SHERIFFDOM OF (*insert name of sheriffdom*)

AT (*insert place of sheriff court*)

[A.B.] (*design health board*), Applicant

Order sought from the court

* *Delete as appropriate*

The applicant applies to the court for a quarantine order under section 40(1) of the Public Health etc. (Scotland) Act 2008 ("the Act") authorising the quarantining of (*insert name, address and date of birth of person to be quarantined*) (*"the person"*) for a period of (*insert period*).

*and the person's removal to (*insert place of quarantine*) [by (*insert, if sought, the name and designation of a person mentioned in* section 4()(4)(d) of the Act)].

*authorising the taking in relation to the person of the following steps, namely *disinfection/

*disinfestation/*decontamination (*specify which steps are sought*)

*and imposing the following conditions in relation to the quarantine (insert conditions sought).

---

[1] As inserted by the Act of Sederunt (Summary Applications, Statutory Applications and Appeals etc. Rules) Amendment (Public Health etc. (Scotland) Act 2008) 2009 (SSI 2009/320) r.2 (effective October 1, 2009).

[2] As inserted by the Act of Sederunt (Summary Applications, Statutory Applications and Appeals etc. Rules) Amendment (Public Health etc. (Scotland) Act 2008) 2009 (SSI 2009/320) r.2 (effective October 1, 2009).

Statement

Delete as appropriate

1. This application is made pursuant to sections 39 and 40 of the Act.

2. The person is present within the applicant's area. The applicant is a health board operating within the jurisdiction of this court. This court accordingly has jurisdiction.

3. The person is aged 16 years or over.

OR

The person is under 16. The parent or other person who has day-to-day care or control of the person is (*insert name, address and relationship to the person*).

4. (a) The applicant *knows/*has reasonable grounds to suspect that the person—

*(i)   has an infectious disease, namely [*insert name of disease*];

*(ii) has been exposed to an organism which causes an infectious disease [*insert name of disease*];

*(iii) is contaminated; or

*(iv) has been exposed to a contaminant,

(*insert here a brief statement indicating the basis upon which these matters are known or suspected by the applicant*)

AND

(b) that as a result—

(i)   there is or may be a significant risk to public health; and

(ii) it is necessary, to avoid or minimise that risk, for the person to be quarantined. (*Insert here a brief statement indicating the reason why the applicant considers that there is or may be a significant risk to public health and that it is necessary, to avoid or minimise that risk, for the person to be quarantined*).

5. The applicant proposes that the person be quarantined at (*insert place and address*) *[and that he should be removed there by (*insert name and designation of person under* section 40(4) (d) of the Act)]. (*Indicate briefly why this is proposed*).

6. The applicant proposes that the person be quarantined for (*insert period of time*).

7. The applicant considers it necessary to *disinfect/*disinfest/*decontaminate the person (*insert details and reasons*).

*8. The applicant considers the conditions sought to be included in the order to be necessary because (*insert reasons*).

*9. The applicant has explained to the person—

(a)   that there is a significant risk to public health;

(b)   the nature of that risk; and

(c)   why the applicant considers it necessary for the proposed action to be taken in relation to that person.

OR

*9. The applicant states that the person is incapable of understanding any explanation of the matters referred to at section 31(3) of the Act (*state reason*) and has explained to (*insert name and address of a person mentioned in* section 31(5) (a) or (b) of the Act *and their relationship to the person*)—

(a)   that there is a significant risk to public health;

(b)   the nature of that risk; and

(c)   why the applicant considers it necessary for the proposed action to be taken in relation to that person.

OR

*9 The applicant states that no explanation has been given in relation to this application under section 31(3) or (5) of the Act because (*state why it was not reasonably practicable to do so*).

*10. The applicant states that *a response was made/*representations were made on behalf of the person in the following terms (*insert response or representations made*).

11. The applicant attaches to this application a certificate signed by a health board competent person which indicates that the competent person is satisfied as to the matters mentioned in statement 4.

12. In the circumstances narrated the applicant is entitled to the order sought and it should be granted accordingly.

> (*signed*)
> [X.Y.] (*add designation and business address*)
> Solicitor for applicant
> (*insert date*)

FORM 41[1]

Rule 3.39.4(3)

FORM OF QUARANTINE ORDER

Sheriff Court...............

.... 20..........at (*insert time*)

(Court Ref. No.)

The sheriff, having considered an application made under section 39(2) of the Public Health etc. (Scotland) Act 2008 ("the Act") *[and productions lodged therewith], and being satisfied as necessary as to the matters mentioned in section 40(2) of the Act,

1. Makes an order in terms of section 40(1) of the Act authorising the quarantining of (*insert details of the person as given in the application*) in (*insert the place in which the person is to be quarantined*) for a period of (insert the period for which the person is to be quarantined) and

Authorising the removal of (*insert name of the person*) to (*insert address at which the person is to be quarantined*)

Further (*insert any authorisation for disinfection/disinfestation/decontamination*),

(*Insert any conditions imposed by the order including the name and designation of any person authorised under* section 40(4) (d) of the Act *to effect a removal*), and

2. Directs notification of this order (*insert details of method and timing of notice*) to (the person to whom the order applies)

*and (*the name and designation of any person to whom an explanation was given under* section 31(5) of the Act)

*and (*insert the name and designation of any other person whom the sheriff considers appropriate*).

*Delete as appropriate

(*signed*)

Sheriff

FORM 42[2]

Rule 3.39.5(1)

---

[1] As inserted by the Act of Sederunt (Summary Applications, Statutory Applications and Appeals etc. Rules) Amendment (Public Health etc. (Scotland) Act 2008) 2009 (SSI 2009/320) r.2 (effective October 1, 2009).

[2] As inserted by the Act of Sederunt (Summary Applications, Statutory Applications and Appeals etc. Rules) Amendment (Public Health etc. (Scotland) Act 2008) 2009 (SSI 2009/320) r.2 (effective October 1, 2009).

FORM OF APPLICATION TO HAVE A PERSON REMOVED TO AND DETAINED IN HOSPITAL UNDER SECTION 42 OF THE PUBLIC HEALTH ETC. (SCOTLAND) ACT 2008

SHERIFFDOM OF (*insert name of sheriffdom*)

AT (*insert place of sheriff court*)

[A.B.] (*design health board*), Applicant

Order sought from the court

*Delete as appropriate

The applicant applies to the court for a short term detention order under section 42(1) of the Public Health etc. (Scotland) Act 2008 ("the Act") in respect of (*insert name, address and date of birth of person to be subject to the order*) ("the person").

1. authorising the person's removal to hospital *[by (*insert name and designation of a person mentioned in* section 42(1)(a) of the Act)] and the person's detention in hospital for the period of (*insert period*), and

2. authorising the taking in relation to the person of the following steps, namely *disinfection/ *disinfestation/*decontamination (*specify which steps are sought*).

Statement

*Delete as appropriate

1. This application is made pursuant to sections 41 and 42 of the Act.

2. The person is present within the applicant's area. The applicant is a health board operating within the jurisdiction of this court. This court accordingly has jurisdiction.

3. The person is aged 16 years or over.

OR

The person is under 16. The parent or other person who has day-to-day care or control of the person is (*insert name, address and relationship to the person*).

4. (a) The applicant knows that the person—

*(i)   has an infectious disease, namely [*insert name of disease*]; or

*(ii) is contaminated,

(*insert here a brief statement indicating the basis upon which these matters are known to the applicant*)

AND

(b) it appears to the applicant that as a result—

(i)   there is a significant risk to public health; and

(ii) it is necessary, to avoid or minimise that risk, for the person to be detained in hospital

(*Insert here a brief statement indicating the reason why the applicant considers that there is a significant risk to public health and that it is necessary, to avoid or minimise that risk, for the person to be detained in hospital*).

5. The applicant proposes that the person be detained at (*insert name and address of hospital*) *[and that he should be removed there by (*insert name and designation of person under* section 42(1)(a) of the Act *and indicate briefly why this is proposed*)].

6. The applicant proposes that the person be detained for (*insert period of time*).

7. The applicant considers it necessary to *disinfect,/*disinfest/*decontaminate the person (*insert details and reasons*).

*8. The applicant has explained to the person—

(a)   that there is a significant risk to public health;

(b)   the nature of that risk; and

(c)   why the applicant considers it necessary for the proposed action to be taken in relation to that person.

OR

*8. The applicant states that the person is incapable of understanding any explanation of the matters referred to at section 31(3) of the Act (*state reason*) and has explained to (*insert name and address of a person mentioned in* section 31(5)(a) or (b) of the Act *and their relationship to the person*)—
   (a)   that there is a significant risk to public health;
   (b)   the nature of that risk; and
   (c)   why the applicant considers it necessary for the proposed action to be taken in relation to that person.

OR

*8. The applicant states that no explanation has been given in relation to this application under section 31(3) or (5) of the Act because (*state why it was not reasonably practicable to do so*).

*9. The applicant states that *a response was made/*representations were made on behalf of the person in the following terms (*insert response or representations made*).

10. The applicant attaches to this application a certificate signed by a health board competent person which indicates that the competent person is satisfied as to the matters mentioned in statement 4.

11. In the circumstances narrated the applicant is entitled to the order sought and it should be granted accordingly.

(*signed*)
Solicitor for applicant
[X. Y.] (add designation and business address)
(insert date)

FORM 43[1]
Rule 3.39.5(4)
FORM OF SHORT TERM DETENTION ORDER—REMOVAL TO AND DETENTION IN HOSPITAL

Sheriff Court................
.... 20................ at (*insert time*)
(Court Ref. No.)

The sheriff, having considered an application made under section 41(2) of the Public Health etc. (Scotland) Act 2008 ("the Act") *[and productions lodged therewith], and being satisfied as necessary as to the matters mentioned in section 42(2) of the Act,

1. Makes an order in terms of section 42(1) of the Act authorising the short term detention in hospital of (*insert details of the person as given in the application*),

Authorising the removal of that person by (*specify person authorised to carry out removal in terms of* section 42(1)(a) of the Act) to (*specify hospital at which the person is to he detained, including the address*), there to be detained for (*insert period of detention*)

Further (*insert any authorisation for disinfectionjdisinfestationjdecontamination*), and

2. Directs notification of this order (*insert details of method and timing of notice*) to (*the person to whom the order applies*)

*and (*the name and designation of any person to whom an explanation was given under* section 31(5) of the Act)

---

[1] As inserted by the Act of Sederunt (Summary Applications, Statutory Applications and Appeals etc. Rules) Amendment (Public Health etc. (Scotland) Act 2008) 2009 (SSI 2009/320) r.2 (effective October 1, 2009).

*and (*insert the name and designation of any other person whom the sheriff considers appropriate*).

* *Delete as appropriate*
(signed)
Sheriff

FORM 44[1]

Rule 3.39.5(2)

FORM OF APPLICATION FOR A SHORT TERM DETENTION ORDER UNDER SECTION 43 OF THE PUBLIC HEALTH ETC. (SCOTLAND) ACT 2008

SHERIFFDOM OF (*insert name of sheriffdom*)
AT (*insert place of sheriff court*)
[A.B.] (*design health board*), Applicant

Order sought from the court

* *Delete as appropriate*

The applicant applies to the court for a short term detention order under section 43(1) of the Public Health etc. (Scotland) Act 2008 ("the Act") in respect of (*insert name, address and date of birth of person to be subject to the order*) ("the person").

1. authorising the person's detention in hospital for a period of (*insert period*), and

2. authorising the taking in relation to the person of the following steps, namely *disinfection/ *disinfestation/*decontamination (*specify which steps are sought*).

Statement

* *Delete as appropriate*

1. This application is made pursuant to sections 41 and 43 of the Act.

2. The person is present within the applicant's area. The applicant is a health board operating within the jurisdiction of this court. This court accordingly has jurisdiction.

3. The person is aged 16 years or over.

OR

The person is under 16. The parent or other person who has day-to-day care or control of the person is (*insert name, address and relationship to the person*).

4. (a) The applicant knows that the person—

*(i)   has an infectious disease, namely [*insert name of disease*]; or

*(ii)   is contaminated,

(*insert here a brief statement indicating the basis upon which these matters are known to the applicant*)

AND

(b) it appears to the applicant that as a result—

(i)   there is a significant risk to public health; and

(ii)   it is necessary, to avoid or minimise that risk, for the person to be detained in hospital.

(*Insert here a brief statement indicating the reason why the applicant considers that there is a significant risk to public health and that it is necessary, to avoid or minimise that risk, for the person to be detained in hospital*).

5. The person is currently in (*insert name and address of hospital*). The applicant proposes that the person be detained at (*insert name and address of hospital*).

6. The applicant proposes that the person be detained for (*insert period of time*).

---

[1] As inserted by the Act of Sederunt (Summary Applications, Statutory Applications and Appeals etc. Rules) Amendment (Public Health etc. (Scotland) Act 2008) 2009 (SSI 2009/320) r.2 (effective October 1, 2009).

7. The applicant considers it necessary to *disinfect/*disinfest/*decontaminate the person (*insert details and reasons*).

*8. The applicant has explained to the person—

(a)   that there is a significant risk to public health;

(b)   the nature of that risk; and

(c)   why the applicant considers it necessary for the proposed action to be taken in relation to that person.

OR

*8. The applicant states that the person is incapable of understanding any explanation of the matters referred to at section 31(3) of the Act (*state reason*) and has explained to (*insert name and address of a person mentioned in* section 31(5)(a) or (b) of the Act *and their relationship to the person*)—

(a)   that there is a significant risk to public health; Release 104: September 2009

(b)   the nature of that risk; and

(c)   why the applicant considers it necessary for the proposed action to be taken in relation to that person.

OR

*8. The applicant states that no explanation has been given in relation to this application under section 31(3) or (5) of the Act because {*state why it was not reasonably practicable to do so*).

*9. The applicant states that *a response was made/*representations were made on behalf of the person in the following terms (*insert response or representations made*).

10. The applicant attaches to this application a certificate signed by a health board competent person which indicates that the competent person is satisfied as to the matters mentioned in statement 4.

11. In the circumstances narrated the applicant is entitled to the order sought and it should be granted accordingly.

(*signed*)

[X.Y.] (*add designation and business address*)

Solicitor for applicant

(*insert date*)

FORM 45[1]

Rule 3.39.5(5)

FORM OF SHORT TERM DETENTION ORDER—DETENTION IN HOSPITAL

Sheriff Court...............

.... 20.......... at (*insert time*)

(Court Ref. No.)

The sheriff, having considered an application made under section 41(2) of the Public Health etc. (Scotland) Act 2008 ("the Act") *[and productions lodged therewith], and being satisfied as necessary as to the matters mentioned in section 43(2) of the Act,

1. Makes an order in terms of section 43(1) of the Act authorising the short term detention in hospital of (*insert details of the person as given in the application*) at (*insert name and address of hospital*) for (*insert period of detention*)

Further (*insert any authorisation for disinfection/disinfestationi/ decontamination*), and

---

[1] As inserted by the Act of Sederunt (Summary Applications, Statutory Applications and Appeals etc. Rules) Amendment (Public Health etc. (Scotland) Act 2008) 2009 (SSI 2009/320) r.2 (effective October 1, 2009).

2. Directs notification of this order (*insert details of method and timing of notice*) to (*the person to whom the order applies*)

*and (*the name and designation of any person to whom an explanation was given under* section 31(5) of the Act)

*and (*insert the name and designation of any other person whom the sheriff considers appropriate*).

Delete as appropriate

(*signed*)

Sheriff

FORM 46[1]

Rule 3.39.6(1)

FORM OF APPLICATION FOR EXCEPTIONAL DETENTION ORDER UNDER SECTION 45 OF THE PUBLIC HEALTH ETC. (SCOTLAND) ACT 2008

SHERIFFDOM OF (*insert name of sheriffdom*)

AT (*insert place of sheriff court*)

[A.B.] (*design health board*), Applicant

Order sought from the court

Delete as appropriate

The applicant applies to the court for an exceptional detention order under section 45(1) of the Public Health etc. (Scotland) Act 2008 ("the Act") in respect of (*insert name, address and date of birth of person to be subject to the order*) ("the person").

1. authorising the person's continued detention in hospital for a period of (*insert period*), and

2. authorising the taking in relation to the person of the following steps, namely ""disinfection/ *disinfestation/*decontamination (*specify which steps are sought*).

Statement

* *Delete as appropriate*

1. This application is made pursuant to sections 44 and 45 of the Act.

2. The person is presently detained in a hospital within the applicant's area by virtue of a short term detention order. The applicant is a health board operating within the jurisdiction of this court and applied for the short term detention order. This court accordingly has jurisdiction.

3. The person is aged 16 years or over.

OR

*The person is under 16. The parent or other person who has day-to-day care or control of the person is (*insert name, address and relationship to the person*).

4. The applicant is satisfied—

(a) that the person—

*(i)   has an infectious disease, namely [*insert name of disease*]; or

*(ii)   is contaminated,

AND

(b) that as a result there is a significant risk to public health,

(*insert here a brief statement indicating the basis upon which the applicant is satisfied of these matters*)

AND

---

[1] As inserted by the Act of Sederunt (Summary Applications, Statutory Applications and Appeals etc. Rules) Amendment (Public Health etc. (Scotland) Act 2008) 2009 (SSI 2009/320) r.2 (effective October 1, 2009).

(c) that it continues to be necessary, to avoid or minimise that risk, for the person to be detained in hospital (*insert here a brief statement indicating the reason why the applicant considers it necessary for the person to be detained in hospital*),

AND

(d) that it is necessary, to avoid or minimise that risk, for the person to be detained for a period exceeding the maximum period for which the person could be detained by virtue of the short term detention order were that order to be extended under section 49(5)(a) of the Act(*insert here a brief statement indicating the reason why the applicant considers it necessary for the person to be detained beyond that maximum period*).

5. The person is currently detained in (*insert name and address of hospital*) by virtue of a short term detention order granted on (*insert date*). The said order is extant until [*insert date*]. The applicant proposes that the person be detained at (*insert name and address of hospital*).

6. The applicant applies to the court to order that the person continue to be detained in (*insert name and address of hospital*) for (*insert period of time*) from (*insert date from which the order is to commence*).

7. The applicant considers it necessary to *disinfect/*disinfest/*decontaminate the person (*insert details and reasons*).

*8. The applicant has explained to the person—

(a)   that there is a significant risk to public health;

(b)   the nature of that risk; and

(c)   why the applicant considers it necessary for the proposed action to be taken in relation to that person.

OR

*8. The applicant states that the person is incapable of understanding any explanation of the matters referred to at section 31(3) of the Act (*state reason*) and has explained to (*insert name and address of a person mentioned in section 31(5) (a) or (b) of the Act and their relationship to the person*)—

(a)   that there is a significant risk to public health;

(b)   the nature of that risk; and

(c)   why the applicant considers it necessary for the proposed action to be taken in relation to that person.

OR

*8. The applicant states that no explanation has been given in relation to this application under section 31(3) or (5) of the Act because (*state why it was not reasonably practicable to do so*).

*9. The applicant states that *a response was made/*representations were made on behalf of the person in the following terms (*insert response or representations made*).

10. The applicant attaches to this application a certificate signed by a health board competent person which indicates that the competent person is satisfied as to the matters mentioned in statement 4.

11. In the circumstances narrated the applicant is entitled to the order sought and it should be granted accordingly.

(*signed*)
[X.Y.] (*add designation and business address*)
Solicitor for applicant
(*insert date*)

FORM 47 [1]

Rule 3.39.6(3)

FORM OF EXCEPTIONAL DETENTION ORDER

Sheriff Court.........

..........20..........at (insert time)

(Court Ref. No.)

The sheriff, having considered an application made under section 44(3) of the Public Health etc. (Scotland) Act 2008 ("the Act") *[and productions lodged therewith], and being satisfied as to the matters mentioned in section 45(2) of the Act,

1. Makes an exceptional detention order in terms of section 45(1) of the Act authorising the continued detention of (*insert details of the person as given in the application*) at (*insert name and address of hospital*) for (*insert period of detention*).

Further (*insert any authorisation for disinfection!disinfestation/decontamination*), and

2. Directs notification of this order (*insert details of method and timing of notice*) to (*the person to whom the order applies*)

*and (*the name and designation of any person to whom an explanation was given under* section 31(5) of the Act)

*and (*insert the name and designation of any other person whom the sheriff considers appropriate*).

* *Delete as appropriate*

(*signed*)

Sheriff

FORM 48 [2]

Rule 3.39.7(1)

FORM OF APPLICATION FOR EXTENSION OF A QUARANTINE ORDER, SHORT TERM DETENTION ORDER OR EXCEPTIONAL DETENTION ORDER UNDER SECTION 49 OF THE PUBLIC HEALTH ETC. (SCOTLAND) ACT 2008

SHERIFFDOM OF (*insert name of sheriffdom*)

AT (*insert place of sheriff court*)

[**A.B.**] (*design health hoard*), Applicant

Order sought from the court

Delete as appropriate

The applicant applies to the court to extend for a period of (insert period):

*the quarantine order granted on (*insert date*) in respect of (*insert name, address and date of birth of the person in respect of whom the order was granted*) ("the person") **OR**

*the short term detention order granted on (insert date) in respect of (*insert name, address and date of birth of the person*) ("the person") **OR**

*the exceptional detention order granted on (*insert date*) in respect of (*insert name, address and date of birth of the person*) ("the person").

Statement

Delete as appropriate

---

[1] As inserted by the Act of Sederunt (Summary Applications, Statutory Applications and Appeals etc. Rules) Amendment (Public Health etc. (Scotland) Act 2008) 2009 (SSI 2009/320) r.2 (effective October 1, 2009).

[2] As inserted by the Act of Sederunt (Summary Applications, Statutory Applications and Appeals etc. Rules) Amendment (Public Health etc. (Scotland) Act 2008) 2009 (SSI 2009/320) r.2 (effective October 1, 2009).

1. This application is made pursuant to section 49 of the Public Health etc. (Scotland) Act 2008.

2. The person is presently *quarantined/*detained in hospital within the applicant's area by virtue of *a quarantine order/*a short term detention order/*an exceptional detention order granted on (*insert date*) which expires on (*insert date*). This court accordingly has jurisdiction.

3. The person is aged 16 years or over.

OR

The person is under 16. The parent or other person who has day-to-day care or control of the person is (*insert name, address and relationship to the person*).

4. The applicant attaches to this application a certificate signed by a health board competent person which indicates that the competent person is satisfied as to the following matters:

*[*in relation to a proposed extension of a quarantine order*] That it is known, or there are reasonable grounds to suspect, that the person—

*(i)   has an infectious disease;

*(ii)   has been exposed to an organism which causes an infectious disease;

*(iii) is contaminated; or

*(iv)   has been exposed to a contaminant,

AND that as a result there is or may be significant risk to public health,

AND that it is necessary, to avoid or minimise that risk, for the person to continue to be quarantined.

OR

*[in relation to a proposed extension of a short term detention order or an exceptional detention order] That the person—

*(i)   has an infectious disease; or

*(ii)   is contaminated,

AND that as a result there is significant risk to public health,

AND that it is necessary, to avoid or minimise that risk, for the person to continue to be detained in hospital.

5. The court is asked to extend the order for a period of (*insert period*) from (*insert date from which the order is to commence*).

*6. An extension of the quarantine order, as sought, will not result in the person being quarantined for a continuous period exceeding 12 weeks.

OR

*6 An extension of the short term detention order, as sought, will not result in the person being detained in hospital for a continuous period exceeding 12 weeks.

OR

*6 An extension of the exceptional detention order, as sought, will not result in the person being detained in hospital for a continuous period exceeding 12 months.

7. In the circumstances narrated the applicant is entitled to the order sought and it should be granted accordingly.

(*signed*)

[X.Y.] (*add designation and business address*)
Solicitor for applicant
(*insert date*)

FORM 49[1]

Rule 3.39.7(3)

---

[1] As inserted by the Act of Sederunt (Summary Applications, Statutory Applications and Appeals etc. Rules) Amendment (Public Health etc. (Scotland) Act 2008) 2009 (SSI 2009/320) r.2 (effective October 1, 2009).

FORM OF ORDER EXTENDING A QUARANTINE ORDER, SHORT TERM DETENTION ORDER OR EXCEPTIONAL DETENTION ORDER

Sheriff Court..........

..........20..........at (*insert time*)

(Court Ref. No.)

The sheriff, having considered an application made under section 49(2) of the Public Health etc. (Scotland) Act 2008 ("the Act") and productions lodged therewith, and being satisfied as to the matters mentioned in section 49(6) of the Act,

1. Makes an order in terms of section 49(5) of the Act extending *the quarantine order/*the short term detention order/*the exceptional detention order which was granted in respect of (*insert details of the person as given in the application*) on (*insert date*) for a period of (*insert period*) and

2. Directs notification of this order (*insert details of method and timing of notice*) to (*the person to whom the order applies*)

*and (*the name and designation of any person to whom an explanation was given under* section 31(5) of the Act)

*and (*insert the name and designation of any other person whom the sheriff considers appropriate*).

* *Delete as appropriate*

(*signed*)

Sheriff

FORM 50[1]

Rule 3.39.8(1)

FORM OF APPLICATION FOR MODIFICATION OF A QUARANTINE ORDER, SHORT TERM DETENTION ORDER OR EXCEPTIONAL DETENTION ORDER UNDER SECTION 51 OF THE PUBLIC HEALTH ETC. (SCOTLAND) ACT 2008

SHERIFFDOM OF (*insert name of sheriffdom*)

AT (*insert place of sheriff court*)

[**A.B.**] (*design health hoard*), Applicant

Order sought from the court

Delete as appropriate

The applicant applies to the court to modify:

*the quarantine order granted on (insert date) in respect of (insert name, address and date of birth of the person in respect of whom the order was granted) ("the person") **OR**

*the short term detention order granted on (insert date) in respect of (insert name, address and date of birth of the person) ("the person") **OR**

*the exceptional detention order granted on (*insert date*) in respect of (*insert name, address and date of birth of the person*) ("the person")

by (*specify details of the modification sought*).

Statement

Delete as appropriate

1. This application is made pursuant to sections 50 and 51 of the Public Health etc. (Scotland) Act 2008.

---

[1] As inserted by the Act of Sederunt (Summary Applications, Statutory Applications and Appeals etc. Rules) Amendment (Public Health etc. (Scotland) Act 2008) 2009 (SSI 2009/320) r.2 (effective October 1, 2009).

2. The person is presently *quarantined/*detained in hospital within the applicant's area by virtue of *a quarantine order/*a short term detention order/*an exceptional detention order granted on (*insert date*) which expires on (*insert date*). This court accordingly has jurisdiction.

3. The person is aged 16 years or over.

OR

The person is under 16. The parent or other person who has day-to-day care or control of the person is (*insert name, address and relationship to the person*).

4. The applicant attaches to this application a certificate signed by a health board competent person which indicates that the competent person is satisfied as to the following matters:

*[*in relation to a proposed modification of a quarantine order*] That it is known, or there are reasonable grounds to suspect, that the person—

*(i)   has an infectious disease;

*(ii) has been exposed to an organism which causes an infectious disease;

*(iii) is contaminated; or

*(iv) has been exposed to a contaminant,

AND that as a result there is or may be significant risk to public health,

AND that it is necessary, to avoid or minimise that risk, for the person to continue to be quarantined.

OR

*[*in relation to a proposed modification of a short term detention order or an exceptional detention order*] That the person—

*(i)   has an infectious disease; or

*(ii) is contaminated,

AND that as a result there is significant risk to public health

AND that it is necessary, to avoid or minimise that risk, for the person to continue to be detained in hospital.

5. The modification is sought for the following reasons (*here insert a brief statement of reasons*).

6. In the circumstances narrated the applicant is entitled to the order sought and it should be granted accordingly.

(*signed*)

[X.Y.] (*add designation and business address*)
Solicitor for applicant
(*insert date*)

FORM 51 [1]

Rule 3.39.8(3)

FORM OF MODIFICATION OF A QUARANTINE ORDER, SHORT TERM
DETENTION ORDER OR EXCEPTIONAL DETENTION ORDER

Sheriff Court..........

..........20..........at [insert time]

(Court Ref. No.)

The sheriff, having considered an application made under section 50(2) of the Public Health etc. (Scotland) Act 2008 ("the Act") *[and productions lodged therewith], and being satisfied as to the matters mentioned in section 51(2) of the Act,

---

[1] As inserted by the Act of Sederunt (Summary Applications, Statutory Applications and Appeals etc. Rules) Amendment (Public Health etc. (Scotland) Act 2008) 2009 (SSI 2009/320) r.2 (effective October 1, 2009).

1. Makes an order in terms of section 51(1) of the Act modifying *the quarantine order/*the short term detention order/*the exceptional detention order which was granted in respect of (*insert details of the person as given in the application*) on (*insert date*), by

(*insert details of modification and, if applicable, name and designation of person considered appropriate under* section 51(4)(a)(iv) of the Act).

2. Directs notification of this order (*insert details of method and timing of notice*) to (*the person to whom the order applies*)

*and (*the name and designation of any person to whom an explanation was given under* section 31(5) of the Act)

*and (*insert the name and designation of any other person whom the sheriff considers appropriate*).

*Delete as appropriate

(*signed*)

Sheriff

FORM 52 [1]

Rule 3.39.9(1)

> Official use only
> Court ref:
> Date and time of receipt:

FORM OF APPLICATION FOR RECALL OF AN ORDER GRANTED IN THE ABSENCE OF THE PERSON TO WHOM IT APPLIES UNDER SECTION 59 OF THE PUBLIC HEALTH ETC. (SCOTLAND) ACT 2008

NOTES

This form should be used if you wish to apply to the sheriff for an order recalling a quarantine order OR a short term detention order OR an exceptional detention order which was made in the absence of the person to whom the order applies.

If you are the person to whom the order applies, you or your solicitor should complete and sign **PART A** and deliver it to the sheriff clerk of the sheriff court at which you wish to make your application.

If you are not the person to whom the order applies but instead are a person who has an interest in the welfare of the person to whom the order applies, you or your solicitor should complete and sign **PART B** and deliver it to the sheriff clerk of the sheriff court at which you wish to make your application.

Your application MUST be received by the sheriff clerk before the expiry of the period of 72 hours beginning with the time at which the order which you wish to be recalled was notified to you (or, as the case may be, the person to whom the order applies).

You should note that, despite the making of your application, the order which you wish recalled will REMAIN IN FORCE unless and until it is revoked by the sheriff.

Before determining your application the sheriff must give you and various other parties (who are specified in section 59(7) of the Act) the opportunity of making representations (whether orally or in writing) and of leading, or producing, evidence.

---

[1] As inserted by the Act of Sederunt (Summary Applications, Statutory Applications and Appeals etc. Rules) Amendment (Public Health etc. (Scotland) Act 2008) 2009 (SSI 2009/320) r.2 (effective October 1, 2009).

IF YOU ARE UNCERTAIN WHAT ACTION TO TAKE you should consult a solicitor. You may be entitled to legal aid depending on your financial circumstances, and you can get information about legal aid from a solicitor. You may also obtain advice from any Citizens Advice Bureau or other advice agency.

PART A

Sheriff Court (*Insert name of court*) | 1.

Details of applicant (*Insert full name, address and telephone number and, if available, e-mail address and fax number*) | 2.

Type of order you wish the sheriff to recall
(*Tick as appropriate*)

3.	Quarantine Order	☐
	Short Term Detention Order	☐
	Exceptional Detention Order	☐

Date of order (*Insert date of order you wish the sheriff to recall*) | 4.

Sheriff Court at which the order was made, if it was not the court specified in box 1 (*Insert name of court*) | 5.

If available, a copy of the order which you wish the sheriff to recall should be attached to this application.

Date and time at which the order was notified to you (*Insert date and exact time of day*) | 6.

I ask the sheriff to recall the order specified in boxes 3 and 4 on the following grounds:

(*State why you wish the order to be recalled. If necessary, continue on a separate sheet of paper*):

Signed:

Date:

(A solicitor should add his or her name and contact details)

PART B

Sheriff Court (*Insert name of court*)	1.

Details of applicant (*Insert full name, address and telephone number and, if available, email address and fax number*)	2.

Type of order you wish the sheriff to recall (*Tick as appropriate*)	3. Quarantine Order ☐ Short Term Detention Order ☐ Exceptional Detention Order ☐

Date of order (*Insert date of order you wish the sheriff to recall*)	4.

Sheriff Court at which the order was made, if it was not the court specified in box 1 (*Insert name of court*)	5.

Details of person to whom the order applies (*Insert name, address and telephone number and, if available, e-mail address and fax number*)	6.

If available, a copy of the order which you wish the sheriff to recall should be attached to this application.

Date and time at which the order was notified to the person named in box 6 (*Insert date and exact time of day*)	7.

I have an interest in the welfare of the person named in box 6 for the following reasons:

> (*State why you have an interest in the welfare of this person. If necessary, continue on a separate sheet of paper*):

I ask the sheriff to recall the order specified in boxes 3 and 4 on the following grounds:

> (*State why you wish the order to he recalled. If necessary, continue on a separate sheet of paper*):

Signed:
　Date:
　(A solicitor should add his or her name and contact details)

Rule 3.39.9(3)　　　　　　　　　　FORM 53[1]

FORM OF ORDER RECALLING A QUARANTINE ORDER, SHORT TERM DETENTION ORDER OR EXCEPTIONAL DETENTION ORDER

Sheriff Court...............
...............20..........
(Court Ref. No.)

The sheriff, having considered an application made under section 59(2) of the Public Health etc. (Scotland) Act 2008 for recall of *the quarantine order/*the short term detention order/*the exceptional detention order which was granted in respect of (*insert details of the person as given in the application*) on (*insert date*),

Refuses the application and Confirms the said order

OR

*Grants the application and Revokes the said order,

---

[1] As inserted by the Act of Sederunt (Summary Applications, Statutory Applications and Appeals etc. Rules) Amendment (Public Health etc. (Scotland) Act 2008) 2009 (SSI 2009/320) r.2 (effective October 1, 2009).

And Directs notification of this order (*insert details of method and timing of notice*) to *(*enter details of any other person whom the sheriff considers appropriate*).

*Delete as appropriate
(signed)
Sheriff

Rule 3.39.12(1)   FORM 54[1]

Official use only
Court ref:
Date and time of receipt:

FORM OF NOTE OF APPEAL UNDER SECTION 61 OF THE PUBLIC HEALTH ETC. (SCOTLAND) ACT 2008

NOTES

This form should be used if you wish to appeal to the sheriff under section 61 of the Public Health etc. (Scotland) Act 2008 in relation to an exclusion order OR a restriction order. A copy of the section is set out below.

If you are the person to whom the order applies, you or your solicitor should complete and sign PART A and deliver it to the sheriff clerk of the sheriff court at which you wish to appeal.

If you are not the person to whom the order applies but instead are a person who has an interest in the welfare of the person to whom the order applies, you or your solicitor should complete and sign PART B and deliver it to the sheriff clerk of the sheriff court at which you wish to appeal.

The form MUST be received by the sheriff clerk before the expiry of 14 days beginning with the day on which the order, modification or, as the case may be, decision against which you wish to appeal was made.

IF YOU ARE UNCERTAIN WHAT ACTION TO TAKE you should consult a solicitor. You may be entitled to legal aid depending on your financial circumstances, and you can get information about legal aid from a solicitor. You may also obtain advice from any Citizens Advice Bureau or other advice agency.

61 Appeal against exclusion orders and restriction orders

(1)   This section applies where a person is subject to—

    (a)   an exclusion order; or

    (b)   a restriction order.

(2)   A person mentioned in subsection (3) may appeal to the sheriff against—

    (a)   the making of the order;

    (b)   any conditions imposed by the order;

    (c)   any modification of the order under section 48(2); or

    (d)   a decision of a health board competent person under section 52(4) or 53(3) not to revoke the order.

(3)   The person referred to in subsection (2) is—

    (a)   the person in relation to whom the order applies; or

    (b)   any person who has an interest in the welfare or such a person.

(4)   An appeal under this section must be made before the expiry of the period of

---

[1] As inserted by the Act of Sederunt (Summary Applications, Statutory Applications and Appeals etc. Rules) Amendment (Public Health etc. (Scotland) Act 2008) 2009 (SSI 2009/320) r.2 (effective October 1, 2009).

14 days beginning with the day on which the order, modification or, as the case may be, decision appealed against is made.

(5) On an appeal under this section, the sheriff may—

   (a) confirm the order appealed against;

   (b) modify the order;

   (c) revoke the order;

   (d) confirm the decision appealed against;

   (e) quash that decision;

   (f) make such other order as the sheriff considers appropriate.

(6) In subsection (5)(b), "modify" is to be construed in accordance with section 48.

PART A

Sheriff Court (*Insert name of court*)   1.

Details of appellant (*Insert full name, address and telephone number and, if available, email address and fax number*)   2.

Type of order (*Tick as appropriate to indicate what type of order the appeal is about*)   3. Exclusion Order ☐ Restriction Order ☐

Date of order (*Insert date of order indicated in box 3*)   4.

Name and address of person who made the order (*Insert name and address. You should find this on the order*)   5.

If available, a copy of the order specified in boxes 3 and 4 should be attached to this application.

I appeal to the sheriff on the following grounds:

> (*State here with reasons*
> (*i*) *what it is about the order that you wish to appeal. You should specify at least one of the options given in* section 61(2).

> *(ii) what it is that you want the sheriff to do. You should specify one of the options given in* section 61(5). *If you choose the option given in* section 61(5)(f) *you should specify what order you wish the sheriff to make.*
> *If necessary, continue on a separate sheet of paper)*

Signed:

    Date:

    (A solicitor should add his or her name and contact details)

PART B

Sheriff Court (*Insert name of court*) | 1.

Details of appellant (*Insert full name, address and telephone number and, if available, email address and fax number*) | 2.

Type of order (*Tick as appropriate to indicate what type of order the appeal is about*) | 3. Exclusion Order
Restriction Order ☐

Date of order (*Insert date of order indicated in box 3*) | 4.

Name and address of person who made the order (*Insert name and address. You should find this on the order*) | 5.

Details of person to whom the order applies (*Insert full name, address and telephone number and, if available, email address and fax number*) | 6.

If available, a copy of the order specified in boxes 3 and 4 should be attached to this application.

    I have an interest in the welfare of the person named in box 6 for the following reasons:

> *(State why you have an interest in the welfare of this person. If necessary,*
> *continue on a separate sheet of paper)*:

I appeal to the sheriff on the following grounds:

> *(State here with reasons*
> *(i) what it is about the order that you wish to appeal. You should specify at least*
> *one of the options given in* section 61(2).
> *(ii) what it is that you want the sheriff to do. You should specify one of the options*
> *given in* section 61(5). *If you choose the option given in* section 61(5)(f) *you*
> *should specify what order you wish the sheriff to make.*
> *If necessary, continue on a separate sheet of paper)*

Signed:
Date:
(A solicitor should add his or her name and contact details)

Rule 3.39.13(1)   FORM 55[1]

FORM OF APPLICATION FOR WARRANT TO ENTER PREMISES AND
TAKE STEPS UNDER SECTION 78 OF THE PUBLIC HEALTH ETC.
(SCOTLAND) ACT 2008
SHERIFFDOM OF *(insert name of sheriffdom)*
AT *(insert place of sheriff court)*
[A.B.] (design and state address), Applicant

Order sought from the court

The applicant applies to the court to grant warrant to *(insert name)*, an officer of
the local authority

1. to enter the premises at *(insert address of premises to which entry is sought)*.
2. to take with him any other person he may authorise and, if he has reasonable
   cause to expect any serious obstruction in obtaining access, a constable.
3. to direct that those premises (or any part of them) are, or any thing in or on
   them is to be left undisturbed (whether generally or in particular respects)
   for so long as the officer considers appropriate.
4. to take any step mentioned in section 73(2) of the Public Health etc.
   (Scotland) Act 2008 ("the Act") or to remove any thing from the premises
   for the purpose of taking any such step at any other place.

Statement

*Delete as appropriate

1. This application is made pursuant to section 78 of the Act.
2. The applicant is a local authority and the said officer is an authorised officer
   within the meaning give in section 73(8) of the Act.
3. The said premises *are/*are not a dwellinghouse within the meaning given
   in section 26 of the Act.
4. The said premises are within the jurisdiction of this court.
5. The applicant considers it necessary that the authorised officer should
   exercise the powers of entry and take the other steps mentioned in section
   73(2) of the Act *(insert here a brief statement of reasons)*.

---

[1] As inserted by the Act of Sederunt (Summary Applications, Statutory Applications and Appeals etc.
Rules) Amendment (Public Health etc. (Scotland) Act 2008) 2009 (SSI 2009/320) r.2 (effective
October 1, 2009).

*6.   The authorised officer Release 104: September 2009

*has been refused entry to the said premises, or

   *reasonably anticipates that entry will be refused.

   OR

*6   The said premises are premises which the authorised officer is entitled to enter and they are unoccupied.

OR

*6   The said premises are premises which the authorised officer is entitled to enter and the occupier thereof is temporarily absent and there is urgency because (here state briefly why there is urgency).

OR

*6   The authorised officer

*has been prevented from taking any steps which he is entitled to take under Part 5 of the Act, or

*reasonably anticipates being prevented from taking any steps that he is entitled to take under Part 5 of the Act.

*7   [If the said premises are a dwellinghouse] The authorised officer has in terms of section 77(2) of the Act given 48 hours notice of the proposed entry to a person who appears to be the occupier of the dwellinghouse and the period of notice has expired.

8.   In the circumstances narrated the applicant is entitled to the warrant sought and it should be granted accordingly.

(signed)

[X.Y.[(add designation and business address)

Solicitor for applicant

(insert date)

Rule 3.39.13(2)   FORM 56[1]

FORM OF WARRANT TO ENTER PREMISES AND TAKE STEPS UNDER PART 5 OF THE PUBLIC HEALTH ETC. (SCOTLAND) ACT 2008

Sheriff Court...............

...............20 ....

(Court Ref. No.)

Delete as appropriate

The sheriff, having considered an application made under section 78 of the Public Health etc. (Scotland) Act 2008 ("the Act") *[and any productions lodged therewith], [*and (where the premises referred to below are a dwellinghouse) being satisfied that due notice has been given under section 77(2) of the Act and has expired],

   Grants warrant authorising the authorised person, (insert name):

(a)   to enter the premises at (insert address)

(b)   on entering the premises referred to at paragraph (a), to take any other person authorised by him and, if he has reasonable cause to expect any serious obstruction in obtaining access, a constable; and

(c)   to direct that:

   (i)   those premises (or any part of them) are; or

   (ii)   any thing in or on those premises is,

---

[1] As inserted by the Act of Sederunt (Summary Applications, Statutory Applications and Appeals etc. Rules) Amendment (Public Health etc. (Scotland) Act 2008) 2009 (SSI 2009/320) r.2 (effective October 1, 2009).

to be left undisturbed (whether generally or in particular respects) for so
long as he considers appropriate;

(d) to take any steps mentioned in section 73(2) of the Act; and

(e) to remove any thing from the premises for the purpose of taking any such
step at any other place.

(signed)

Sheriff

Rule 3.39.14(1)   FORM 57[1]

FORM OF APPLICATION FOR AN ORDER FOR DISPOSAL OF A BODY UNDER SECTION 93 OF THE PUBLIC HEALTH ETC. (SCOTLAND) ACT 2008

SHERIFFDOM OF (*insert name of sheriffdom*)

AT (*insert place of sheriff court*)

[A.B.] (*design local authority*), Applicant

Order sought from the court

* *Delete as appropriate*

*The applicant applies to the court to make an order authorising the applicant to
remove the body of (*insert name and date of birth of deceased person and address
of premises in which the body is being retained*) to a mortuary or other similar
premises and to dispose of that body before the expiry of (*insert period sought*).

OR

The applicant applies to the court to make an order authorising the applicant to
dispose of the body of (*insert name and date of birth of deceased person and address of premises in which the body is being retained*) as soon as reasonably
practicable.

Statement

* *Delete as appropriate*

1. This application is made pursuant to section 93 of the Public Health etc.
(Scotland) Act 2008.

2. The applicant's area falls within the jurisdiction of the court. The court accordingly has jurisdiction.

3. The body of the said (*insert details of deceased person*) is being retained in
(*insert name and address of premises*).

4. The applicant is a local authority in whose area the said premises are situated.

5. The applicant considers that the appropriate arrangements have not been
made for the disposal of the said body.

6. The applicant is satisfied that as a result there is a significant risk to public
health and it is necessary, to avoid or minimise that risk, for the body to be
appropriately disposed of.

*7 The applicant considers that the risk to public health is such that it is neces-
sary for the body to be disposed of immediately because (*insert here brief
reasons why immediate disposal of the body is sought*).

8. The applicant attaches to this application a certificate signed by a local
authority competent person which indicates that the competent person is
satisfied as to the matters mentioned in statements 3, 4, 5 and 6.

9. In the circumstances narrated the applicant is entitled to the order sought and
it should be granted accordingly.

---

[1] As inserted by the Act of Sederunt (Summary Applications, Statutory Applications and Appeals etc.
Rules) Amendment (Public Health etc. (Scotland) Act 2008) 2009 (SSI 2009/320) r.2 (effective
October 1, 2009).

(*signed*)
[X.Y.] (*add designation and business address*)
Solicitor for applicant
(*insert date*)

Rule 3.39.14(2)   FORM 58[1]
FORM OF ORDER FOR DISPOSAL OF A BODY
Sheriff Court...............
...............20..........
(Court Ref. No.)
*Delete as appropriate
The sheriff, having considered an application made under section 93 of the Public Health etc. (Scotland) Act 2008 and any productions lodged,
*Being satisfied that there is a significant risk to public health, makes an order authorising the applicant to remove the body of (*insert details of deceased person*) to a mortuary or other similar premises and to dispose of that body before the expiry of (*insert period sought*).
OR
* Being satisfied that the risk to public health is such that it is necessary for the body of (*insert details of deceased person*) to be disposed of immediately, makes an order authorising the applicant to dispose of the body as soon as reasonably practicable.
(*signed*)
Sheriff

FORM 59
Rule 3.42.2(1)
FORM OF APPLICATION FOR JUDICIAL APPROVAL UNDER SECTION 23B(1) OF THE REGULATION OF INVESTIGATORY POWERS ACT 2000
Court ref. no.
SHERIFFDOM OF (*insert name of sheriffdom*)
AT (*insert place of sheriff court*)
[A.B.], (*insert designation and address of local authority*), Applicant
Order sought from the court
*Delete as appropriate
The Applicant applies to the court under section 23B(1) of the Regulation of Investigatory Powers Act 2000 ("the Act") to grant an order under section 23A(2) of the Act approving [*[the grant or renewal of an authorisation] *or* [the giving or renewal of a notice]] to obtain communications data [*about (*insert name and address of person (if known) or other identifying details*] [*from (*insert name and address of postal or telecommunications operator from whom the communications data is to be obtained*)].
Statement
*Delete as appropriate
1. This application is made pursuant to section 23B(1) of the Act.

---

[1] As inserted by the Act of Sederunt (Summary Applications, Statutory Applications and Appeals etc. Rules) Amendment (Public Health etc. (Scotland) Act 2008) 2009 (SSI 2009/320) r.2 (effective October 1, 2009).

2. The Applicant is a local authority the area of which is situated within the jurisdiction of this court. This court accordingly has jurisdiction.

3.[1] [*Insert name and office, rank or position of relevant person*], a relevant person within the meaning of section 23A(6) of the Act, has—

*(a) granted or renewed an authorisation under section 22(3), (3B) or (3F) of the Act;

*(b) given or renewed a notice under section 22(4) of the Act

(*insert here a brief statement indicating when the authorisation or notice was given, granted or renewed and the terms of such authorisation or notice*)

4. At the time the relevant person [*[*granted or renewed] the authorisation under section [*22(3), (3B) or (3F)]] *or* [*[*gave or renewed] a notice under section 22(4)] of the Act there were reasonable grounds for believing that it was necessary to obtain communications data—

*(a) in the interests of national security;

*(b) for the purpose of preventing or detecting crime or of preventing disorder;

*(c) in the interests of the economic well-being of the United Kingdom;

*(d) in the interests of public safety;

*(e) for the purpose of protecting public health;

*(f) for the purpose of assessing or collecting any tax, duty, levy or other imposition, contribution or charge payable to a government department;

*(g) for the purpose, in an emergency, of preventing death or injury or any damage to a person's physical or mental health, or of mitigating any injury or damage to a person's physical or mental health; or

*(h) for any purpose (not falling within paragraphs (a) to (g)) which is specified for the purposes of section 22(2)(h) by an order made by the Secretary of State (*specify relevant details*).

(*insert here a brief statement indicating the basis upon which such grounds were believed to exist*)

5. At the time the relevant person [*[*granted or renewed] the authorisation under section [*22(3), (3B) or (3F)]] or [*[*gave or renewed] a notice under section 22(4)] of the Act there were reasonable grounds for believing that obtaining the data in question by the conduct authorised or required by the authorisation or notice was proportionate to what was sought to be achieved by so obtaining the data.

(*insert here a brief statement indicating the basis upon which so obtaining the data was believed to be proportionate*)

6. At the time that the authorisation or notice was given, granted or renewed the relevant conditions set out in section 23A(5)(a) or (c) of the Act were satisfied.

(*insert here a brief statement indicating the basis upon which the relevant conditions were satisfied*)

7. There remain reasonable grounds for believing that the matters referred to in paragraphs 4, 5 and 6 are satisfied in relation to the authorisation or notice.

(*insert here a brief statement indicating the basis for this averment*)

8. In the circumstances narrated the Applicant is entitled to the order sought and it should be granted accordingly.

> (*signed*)
>
> [X.Y.] (*add designation and business address*)

---

[1] As amended by the Act of Sederunt (Sheriff Court Rules)(Miscellaneous Amendments) 2013 (SSI 2013/135) para.6 (effective May 27, 2013).

Solicitor for Applicant

(*insert date*)

FORM 60[1]

Rule 3.42.2(4)

FORM OF ORDER UNDER SECTION 23A(2) OF THE REGULATION OF INVESTIGATORY POWERS ACT 2000

Sheriff Court ....

.... 20 ....

(Court Ref. No.)

Delete as appropriate

The sheriff, having considered an application made under section 23B(1) of the Regulation of Investigatory Powers Act 2000 ("the Act") for an order under section 23A(2) of the Act,

*Being satisfied as necessary as to the matters mentioned in section [*23A(3) or 23A(4)] of the Act:

1. Makes an order in terms of section 23A(2) of the Act [*approving the grant or renewal of the authorisation OR the giving or renewal of the notice].

[*2. Directs notification of this order by (insert details of method and timing of notice) to (insert name and address of postal or telecommunications operator from whom the communications data is to be obtained).]

OR

*Refuses to approve the [*grant or renewal of the authorisation concerned OR the giving or renewal of the notice concerned] [*and makes an order under section 23B(3) of the Act quashing the authorisation OR notice.]

*Delete as appropriate

(*signed*)

Sheriff

FORM 61[2,3]

Rule 3.45.3

APPLICATION FOR A CERTIFICATE UNDER ARTICLE 5 OF REGULATION (EU) NO. 606/2013 OF THE EUROPEAN PARLIAMENT AND OF THE COUNCIL OF 12TH JUNE 2013 ON MUTUAL RECOGNITION OF PROTECTION MEASURES IN CIVIL MATTERS

Sheriff Court ....

Court Ref. No. ....

1. The applicant is (*design*).
2. The applicant's date of birth is (*insert date of birth*).
3. The applicant's place of birth is (*insert place of birth*).
4. The address of the applicant to be used for notification purposes is (*insert address – the address given, which may be disclosed to the person against whom the protection measure was granted, must be an address to which any notification to the applicant can be sent*).
5. The application relates to a sexual offences prevention order (*or* an interim

---

[1] As amended by the Act of Sederunt (Sheriff Court Rules) (Miscellaneous Amendments) 2013 (SSI 2013/135) para.6 (effective May 27, 2013).

[2] As inserted by the Act of Sederunt Act of Sederunt (Rules of the Court of Session and Sheriff Court Rules Amendment No. 3) (Mutual Recognition of Protection Measures) 2014 (SSI 2014/371) para.4 (effective 11 January 2015).

[3] As amended by the Act of Sederunt (Summary Application Rules 1999 Amendment) (Trafficking Exploitation Orders) 2017 (SSI 2017/211) para.2(5) (effective 30 June 2017 and 31 October 2017 subject to SSI 2017/211 para.1(3)).

sexual offences prevention order, *or* a risk of sexual harm order *or* an interim risk of sexual harm order *or* trafficking and exploitation prevention order *or* interim trafficking and exploitation prevention order or trafficking and exploitation risk order *or* interim trafficking and exploitation risk order) granted on (*insert date of order*) in respect of (*insert name of person against whom protection measure was granted*).

6. The date of birth of the person against whom the order was granted is (*insert date of birth or "not known"*).

7. The place of birth of the person against whom the order was granted is (*insert place of birth or "not known"*).

8. The address of the person against whom the order was granted is (*insert address or "not known"*).

9. The applicant asks the court to issue a certificate pursuant to Article 5(1) of Regulation (EU) No. 606/2013 of the European Parliament and of the Civil Council of 12th June 2013 on mutual recognition of protection measures in civil matters in relation to the order referred to in paragraph 5.

Date (*insert date*)

(*Signed*)

[A.B. *or* C.D.]

[*or* Solicitor for Applicant]

(*add designation and business address*)

FORM 62[1]

Rule 3.45.6(2)(a)

NOTICE OF ISSUE OF CERTIFICATE UNDER ARTICLE 5 OF REGULATION (EU) NO. 606/2013 OF THE EUROPEAN PARLIAMENT AND OF THE COUNCIL OF 12TH JUNE 2013 ON MUTUAL RECOGNITION OF PROTECTION MEASURES IN CIVIL MATTERS

Sheriff Court ....

Court Ref No ....

Date: (*insert date of posting or other method of intimation*)

To: (*insert name and address of person causing the risk*)

A certificate has been issued to (*insert name of party to whom certificate was issued*) in accordance with Article 5(1) of Regulation (EU) No. 606/2013 of the European Parliament and of the Council of 12th June 2013 on mutual recognition of protection measures in civil matters. The certificate relates to an order granted by the sheriff on (*insert date of interlocutor containing protection measure*). A copy of the certificate and a copy of the order accompany this notice.

As a result of the issue of the certificate, (*insert name of person to whom certificate was issued*) can invoke the order in other Member States of the European Union.

If you consider that the certificate was wrongly issued, or that the certificate does not accurately reflect the terms of the order, you can apply to have the certificate withdrawn, or for the issue of a rectified certificate, by lodging an application in Form 64 with the sheriff clerk at the address below.

(*Signed*)

Sheriff Clerk

(*insert address and telephone number*)

---

[1] As inserted by the Act of Sederunt Act of Sederunt (Rules of the Court of Session and Sheriff Court Rules Amendment No. 3) (Mutual Recognition of Protection Measures) 2014 (SSI 2014/371) para.4 (effective January 11, 2015).

FORM 63[1]

Rule 3.45.6(4)

NOTICE FOR WALLS OF COURT OF ISSUE OF CERTIFICATE UNDER ARTICLE 5 OF REGULATION (EU) NO. 606/2013 OF THE EUROPEAN PARLIAMENT AND OF THE COUNCIL OF 12TH JUNE 2013 ON MUTUAL RECOGNITION OF PROTECTION MEASURES IN CIVIL MATTERS

Sheriff Court ....

Court Ref. No. ....

Date: (*insert date*)

To: (*insert name and address of person causing the risk*)

TAKE NOTICE

A certificate has been issued to (*insert name of party to whom certificate was issued*) in accordance with Article 5(1) of Regulation (EU) No. 606/2013 of the European Parliament and of the Council of 12th June 2013 on mutual recognition of protection measures in civil matters. The certificate relates to an order granted by the sheriff on (*insert date of interlocutor containing protection measure*) against (*insert name of person causing the risk*), whose last known address was (*insert last known address of person causing the risk*).

As a result of the issue of the certificate, (*insert name of person to whom certificate was issued*) can invoke the order in other Member States of the European Union.

If (*insert name of person causing the risk*) wishes to obtain a copy of the certificate and the order, that person should immediately contact the sheriff clerk at the address below.

If (*insert name of person causing the risk*) considers that the certificate was wrongly issued, or that the certificate does not accurately reflect the terms of the order, that person can apply to have the certificate withdrawn, or for the issue of a rectified certificate, by lodging an application in Form 64 with the sheriff clerk at the address below.

(Signed)

Sheriff Clerk

(insert address and telephone number)

FORM 64[2]

Rule 3.45.8(1)

APPLICATION FOR RECTIFICATION OR WITHDRAWAL OF A CERTIFICATE ISSUED UNDER ARTICLE 5 OF REGULATION (EU) NO. 606/2013 OF THE EUROPEAN PARLIAMENT AND OF THE COUNCIL OF 12TH JUNE 2013 ON MUTUAL RECOGNITION OF PROTECTION MEASURES IN CIVIL MATTERS

Sheriff Court ....

Court Ref No. ....

1. The applicant is (*design*).
2. On the application of (*insert name of person on whose application the certificate was issued*), the sheriff has issued a certificate in accordance with Article 5(1) of Regulation (EU) No. 606/2013 of the European Parliament

---

[1] As inserted by the Act of Sederunt Act of Sederunt (Rules of the Court of Session and Sheriff Court Rules Amendment No. 3) (Mutual Recognition of Protection Measures) 2014 (SSI 2014/371) para.4 (effective January 11, 2015).

[2] As inserted by the Act of Sederunt Act of Sederunt (Rules of the Court of Session and Sheriff Court Rules Amendment No. 3) (Mutual Recognition of Protection Measures) 2014 (SSI 2014/371) para.4 (effective 11 January 2015).

and of the Council of 12th June 2013 on mutual recognition of protection measures in civil matters.

3.　The certificate relates to a sexual offences prevention order [*or* an interim sexual offences protection order, *or* a risk of sexual harm order, *or* an interim risk of sexual harm order] granted by the sheriff on (*insert date of order*).

4.　The applicant considers that the certificate does not accurately reflect the terms of the order because: (*here specify nature of discrepancy*).

[*or* 4. The applicant considers that the certificate was wrongly issued because: (*here specify the reason the certificate was wrongly issued*).]

5.　The applicant asks the court to issue a rectified certificate [*or* to withdraw the certificate].

Date (*insert date*)

(*Signed*)

Applicant

[*or* Solicitor for Applicant]

(*add designation and business address*)

FORM 65[1]

Rule 3.45.11(5)(a)

NOTICE OF ADJUSTMENT OF A PROTECTION MEASURE UNDER ARTICLE 11 OF REGULATION (EU) NO. 606/2013 OF THE EUROPEAN PARLIAMENT AND OF THE COUNCIL OF 12TH JUNE 2013 ON MUTUAL RECOGNITION OF PROTECTION MEASURES IN CIVIL MATTERS

Sheriff Court ....

Court Ref No. ....

Date: (*insert date of posting or other method of intimation*)

To: (*insert name and address of person causing the risk*)

This notice relates to a protection measure ordered by (*insert name of issuing authority in Member State of origin*) in respect of which (*insert name of protected person*) is the protected person and you are the person causing the risk.

You are hereby given notice that, in exercise of the power conferred by Article 11(1) of Regulation (EU) No. 606/2013 of the European Parliament and of the Council of 12th June 2013 on mutual recognition of protection measures in civil matters, the sheriff has adjusted the factual elements of the protection measure. A copy of the order adjusting the protection measure accompanies this notice.

As a result of the adjustment, the protection measure falls to be recognised and enforced in the United Kingdom subject to the adjustment.

If you consider that the order adjusting the protection measure was wrongly granted, you have the right to appeal. If you are considering appealing, you are advised to consult a solicitor who will be able to give advice.

(*Signed*)

Sheriff Clerk

(*insert address and telephone number*)

FORM 66[2]

Rule 3.45.11(7)

---

[1] As inserted by the Act of Sederunt Act of Sederunt (Rules of the Court of Session and Sheriff Court Rules Amendment No. 3) (Mutual Recognition of Protection Measures) 2014 (SSI 2014/371) para.4 (effective 11 January 2015).

[2] As inserted by the Act of Sederunt Act of Sederunt (Rules of the Court of Session and Sheriff Court Rules Amendment No. 3) (Mutual Recognition of Protection Measures) 2014 (SSI 2014/371) para.4 (effective 11 January 2015).

NOTICE FOR WALLS OF COURT OF ADJUSTMENT UNDER ARTICLE 11 OF REGULATION (EU) NO. 606/2013 OF THE EUROPEAN PARLIAMENT AND OF THE COUNCIL OF 12TH JUNE 2013 ON MUTUAL RECOGNITION OF PROTECTION MEASURES

Sheriff Court ....

Court Ref. No. ....

Date: (*insert date*)

To: (*insert name of person causing the risk*)

This notice relates to a protection measure ordered by (*insert name of issuing authority in Member State of origin*) in respect of which (*insert name of protected person*) is the protected person and (*insert name of person causing the risk*) is the person causing the risk. That person's last known address is (*insert last known address of person causing the risk*).

(*Insert name of person causing the risk*) is hereby given notice that, in exercise of the power conferred by Article 11 of Regulation (EU) No. 606/2013 of the European Parliament and of the Council of 12th June 2013 on mutual recognition of protection measures in civil matters, the sheriff has adjusted the factual elements of the protection measure.

As a result of the adjustment, the protection measure falls to be recognised and enforced in the United Kingdom subject to the adjustment.

If (*insert name of person causing the risk*) wishes to obtain a copy of the order adjusting the protection measure, that person should immediately contact the sheriff clerk at the address below.

If (*insert name of person causing the risk*) considers that the order adjusting the protection measure was wrongly granted, that person has the right to appeal. If that person is considering appealing, that person is advised to consult a solicitor who will be able to give advice.

(*Signed*)

Sheriff Clerk

(*insert address and telephone number*)

FORM 67[1]

Rule 3.45.12(7)

FORM OF CERTIFICATE OF DELIVERY OF DOCUMENTS TO CHIEF CONSTABLE

(*insert place and date*) I, hereby certify that upon the day of I duly delivered to the chief constable of the Police Service of Scotland (*insert details of documents delivered*). This I did by (*state method of delivery*).

(Signed)

(*insert name and designation of person delivering documents*)

FORM 68[2]

Rule 3.45.13(5)

---

[1] As inserted by the Act of Sederunt Act of Sederunt (Rules of the Court of Session and Sheriff Court Rules Amendment No. 3) (Mutual Recognition of Protection Measures) 2014 (SSI 2014/371) para.4 (effective 11 January 2015).

[2] As inserted by the Act of Sederunt Act of Sederunt (Rules of the Court of Session and Sheriff Court Rules Amendment No. 3) (Mutual Recognition of Protection Measures) 2014 (SSI 2014/371) para.4 (effective 11 January 2015).

FORM OF CERTIFICATE OF SENDING OF DOCUMENTS TO CHIEF CONSTABLE

(*insert place and date*) I, hereby certify that upon the day of I duly sent to the chief constable of the Police Service of Scotland (*insert details of documents sent*). This I did by (*state method of delivery*).

(Signed)

(insert name and designation of person delivering documents)

FORM 69[1]

Form of application for extension of the 14-day period under paragraph 8(1) of Schedule 1 to the Counter-Terrorism and Security Act 2015
Rule 3.46.2(1)

SHERIFFDOM OF (*insert name of sheriffdom*)

AT (*insert place of sheriff court*)

[A.B.], (*insert designation, rank and address of applicant*)

APPLICANT

Order(s) sought from the court

1. The applicant applies to the sheriff under paragraph 8(1) of Schedule 1 to the Counter- Terrorism and Security Act 2015 to extend the period of retention of a travel document relating to (*insert name and address of person to whom the application relates*) ("the person") for a period of (*insert number of days*) from (*insert date of expiry of 14-day period*).

Withholding of specified information

2. The applicant applies to the sheriff for an order under paragraph 10(1) of Schedule 1 of the Act withholding the information specified in subparagraph (a) for the reasons set out in subparagraph (b).

(a) The specified information is (*insert details of the information to be withheld*)

(b) The reasons for withholding that information are (*insert reasons, by reference to paragraph 10(2) of Schedule 1 to the Act*).

Statement

1. This application is made under paragraph 8(1) of Schedule 1 to the Counter-Terrorism and Security Act 2015 ("the Act").

2. The applicant is a senior police officer (within the meaning of paragraph 1(5) of Schedule 1 to the Act.

3. The travel document to which the application relates is (*insert details of travel*

---

[1] As inserted by the Act of Sederunt (Rules of the Court of Session 1994 and Sheriff Court Rules Amendment) (No.3) (Miscellaneous) 2015 (SSI 2015/283) Sch.1 para.1 (effective 7 August 2015) and amended by the Act of Sederunt (Rules of the Court of Session 1994 and Sheriff Court Rules Amendment) (Miscellaneous) 2016 (SSI 2016/102) para.4 (effective 21 March 2016).

document).

4. The travel document was taken from the person at (*insert place*) on (*insert date*).

5. Authorisation for the retention of the document under paragraph 4 of Schedule 1 to the Act was given by (*insert name and rank of senior police officer who authorised retention*) on (*insert date*).

6. The travel document has since been retained while (*insert reason for retention of travel document by reference to paragraph 5(1) of Schedule 1 to the Act*).

7. (*Insert brief statement of steps taken by reference to paragraph 5(1) of Schedule 1 to the Act*).

(*signed*)
Applicant
[*or* Solicitor for applicant
(*add designation and business address*)]

FORM 70[1]
Form of intimation of application for extension of the 14-day period under paragraph 8(1) of Schedule 1 to the Counter-Terrorism and Security Act 2015
Rule 3.46.2(3)

SHERIFFDOM OF (*insert name of sheriffdom*)

AT (*insert place of sheriff court*)

[A.B.], (*insert designation, rank and address of applicant*

APPLICANT

(Place and date)

You (*insert designation and address*) are hereby given intimation of the attached application which was lodged with the sheriff clerk at (*insert place*) on (*insert date*).

The hearing of this application will take place at (*insert place and address of sheriff court*), on the .... day of .... at .... o'clock.

---

[1] As inserted by the Act of Sederunt (Rules of the Court of Session 1994 and Sheriff Court Rules Amendment) (No.3) (Miscellaneous) 2015 (SSI 2015/283) Sch.1 para.1 (effective 7 August 2015) and amended by the Act of Sederunt (Rules of the Court of Session 1994 and Sheriff Court Rules Amendment) (Miscellaneous) 2016 (SSI 2016/102) para.4 (effective 21 March 2016).

If you wish to oppose the application, you must —

(a) provide written representations to the court and the applicant by (*insert date*); or

(b) attend the hearing in person or be legally represented at it if you wish to make oral representations.

IF YOU ARE UNCERTAIN AS TO WHAT ACTION TO TAKE you should consult a solicitor. You may be eligible for legal aid depending on your income, and you can get information about legal aid from a solicitor. It might also be possible to obtain advice from any Citizens' Advice Bureau or other advice agency.

(*signed*)

Applicant

[*or* Solicitor for applicant

(*add designation and business address*)]

FORM 71[1]

Form of serious crime prevention order

Rule 3.47.2(4)

SHERIFFDOM OF (*insert name of sheriffdom*)

AT (insert place of sheriff court)

SERIOUS CRIME PREVENTION ORDER

Under section 1 of the Serious Crime Act 2007

Court: ....

Date: ....

Person who is the subject of the order: ....

Address: ....

Date of birth (if known): ....

THE SHERIFF:

1   having considered the application made by the Lord Advocate for a serious crime prevention order in respect of the subject; and

2.   having reasonable grounds to believe that making a serious crime prevention order would protect the public by preventing, restricting or disrupting involvement by the subject in serious crime in Scotland.

ACCORDINGLY, ORDERS that:

(*set out terms of the order*)

This order comes into force on (*date*). It ceases to be in force on (*date*).

(*where different provisions are to come into force, or to cease to be in force, on different dates, specify the dates in respect of each provision*).

---

[1] As inserted by the Act of Sederunt (Rules of the Court of Session 1994 and Summary Application Rules 1999 Amendment) (Serious Crime Prevention Orders etc.) 2016 (SSI 2016/319) Sch.1 para.1 (effective 12 December 2016).

(Signed)
Sheriff

FORM 72[1]

Form of application to vary or discharge a serious crime prevention order
Rule 3.47.4(1)

SHERIFFDOM OF *(insert name of sheriffdom)*
AT *(place)*
APPLICATION
of
[INSERT APPLICANT'S DETAILS]

APPLICANT

1. A copy of the serious crime prevention order which was made by the sheriff at *(place)* [*or* by the High Court sitting at *(place)*] on *(date)* is annexed to this application.
2. The serious crime prevention order has been varied as follows:- *(specify details of any previous variation).*]
3. The applicant is [the relevant applicant authority] or [the person who is the subject of the order] or [*specify details of any other person*] *(delete as appropriate).*
4. The applicant seeks to vary [*or* discharge] the serious crime prevention order for the following reasons:- *(here specify reasons).*

MAY IT THEREFORE PLEASE YOUR LORDSHIP:

thereafter, on being duly satisfied, to make an order varying [*or* discharging] the serious crime prevention order [by] *(here state the terms of the variation, if appropriate)* and to do further and otherwise as to your Lordship shall seem proper.

ACCORDING TO JUSTICE, etc.
(signed)
Solicitor for the applicant

FORM 73

Form of application for a drug dealing telecommunications restriction order under regulation 3 of the Drug Dealing Telecommunications Restriction Orders Regulations 2017

Rule 3.51.2(1)(a)
SHERIFFDOM OF *(insert name of sheriffdom)*

Court ref. no.

AT *(insert place of sheriff court)*
APPLICATION FOR A DRUG DEALING TELECOMMUNICATIONS RESTRICTION ORDER UNDER REGULATION 3 OF THE DRUG DEALING TELECOMMUNICATIONS RESTRICTION ORDERS REGULATIONS 2017
in the cause
[A.B.] *(insert designation and address)*
Applicant
Against
[C.D.] *(insert designation and address)*
Respondent
Order sought from the court

---

[1] As inserted by the Act of Sederunt (Rules of the Court of Session 1994 and Summary Application Rules 1999 Amendment) (Serious Crime Prevention Orders etc.) 2016 (SSI 2016/319) Sch.1 para.1 (effective 12 December 2016).

The applicant applies to the court for an order under regulation 3 of the Drug Dealing Telecommunications Restriction Orders Regulations 2017 to prevent or restrict the use in connection with drug dealing offences of the relevant item(s) listed in the schedule to this application.

Statement

1. This application is made under regulation 3 of the Drug Dealing Telecommunications Restriction Orders Regulations 2017.

2. The applicant is *[design the applicant]*.

3. *[Specify ground of jurisdiction, and the facts upon which the ground of jurisdiction is based]*. This court accordingly has jurisdiction.

4. The respondent is *[insert name and address of affected person, where that person is the communications provider for the purposes of this application, and (if known) the name and address of any other affected person or, if not known, the fact that that person's whereabouts are unknown and the steps taken to ascertain that person's whereabouts]*.

5. The applicant is satisfied that the relevant item(s) listed in the schedule to this application [has/have been, or is/are likely to have been, used] or [is/are likely to be used in the future] (*delete as appropriate*) in connection with drug dealing offences; and has reasonable grounds to believe that the order would prevent or restrict the use of a communication device in connection with drug dealing offences.

6. *[Specify the grounds upon which the order is sought and the relevant facts supporting those grounds.]*

7. The applicant seeks an order, in respect of the item(s) listed in the schedule which will *[specify the terms of the order sought, under reference to the item(s) listed]* and which will require to be complied with by *[specify time]* on *[specify date]*, or some other time and date as the court considers reasonable. The time and date suggested by the applicant are in all the circumstances reasonable.

8. The applicant requests the court to include in the order a provision to the effect that the applicant and a communications provider who is subject to the order may agree a date and time, at which the requirements of the order must be complied with, that is earlier than the date and time specified in the order.

Date (*insert date*)

(*Signed*)

Applicant

[or Solicitor for Applicant] *[add designation and business address]*

FORM 74

Form of a drug dealing telecommunication restriction order ("DDTRO") under the Drug Dealing Telecommunications Restriction Orders Regulations 2017

Rule 3.51.2(2)

SHERIFFDOM OF (*insert name of sheriffdom*)

Court ref. no.

AT (*insert place of sheriff court*)

The sheriff, having considered an application for an order under regulation 3 of the Drug Dealing Telecommunications Restriction Orders Regulations 2017 for a drug dealing telecommunications restriction order ("DDTRO") to prevent or restrict the use in connection with drug dealing offences of the relevant item(s) listed in the schedule to this application, and being satisfied that such an order should be made:

(i) make an order, in respect of the item(s) listed in the schedule to the application, that *[specify the terms of the order granted, under reference to the relevant item(s) listed]* which order is to be complied with by *[specify time]* on *[specify date]*;

(ii) directs notification of this order to C.D. (*specify the identity of the communications provider who is subject to this order*) by (*specify means of notification*);

(iii) further orders that the applicant and C.D. (*speify the identity of the communications provider who is subject to this order*) may agree a date and time at which the requirements of the order must be complied with that is earlier than the date and time specified in paragraph (i) of this order; and

(iv) directs the applicant to take reasonable steps to bring the making of the DDTRO to the attention of any affected person of whom the applicant is aware other than the communications provider.

Date (*insert date*)

(*Signed*)

Sheriff

FORM 75

Form of application for the discharge, extension or variation of a drug dealing telecommunications restriction order under regulation 10 of the Drug Dealing Telecommunications Restriction Orders Regulations 2017

Rule 3.51.2(3)

SHERIFFDOM OF (*insert name of sheriffdom*)

Court ref. no.

AT (*insert place of sheriff court*)

APPLICATION

by

[Specify designation and address of applicant]

FOR [DISCHARGE *or* EXTENSION *or* VARIATION] (*as the case may be*) OF A DRUG DEALING TELECOMMUNICATIONS RESTRICTION ORDER UNDER REGULATION 10 OF THE DRUG DEALING TELECOMMUNICATIONS RESTRICTION ORDERS REGULATIONS 2017

in the cause

[A.B.] (*insert designation and address*)

Applicant

against

[C.D.] (*insert designation and address*)

Respondent

Order sought from the court

The applicant applies to the court for [discharge *or* extension *or* variation] (*as the case may be*) of an order under regulation 3 of the Drug Dealing Telecommunications Restriction Orders Regulations 2017 made by the court on (*specify date*).

Statement

1. This application is made by *[specify whether the application is made by the applicant or respondent in the original application, or by any other affected person]*. It is made under regulation 10 of the Drug Dealing Telecommunications Restriction Orders Regulations 2017. The order made by the court on (*specify date*) provides that (*specify the terms of the order*).

2. The applicant seeks to discharge the terms of the order. *[OR (where the applicant seeks to extend or vary the terms of the order)* The applicant seeks to [extend *or* vary] the terms of the order (*as the case may be*) by (*specify the terms of the extension or variation sought).]*

3. The applicant seeks such *[a discharge or extension or variation]* of the order on the grounds that *[specify the grounds upon which the order is sought and the relevant facts supporting those grounds.]*

Date (*insert date*)

(*Signed*)

Applicant

[or Solicitor for Applicant] *[add designation and business address]*

Form 76[1]

Rule 3.53.2(a)

Form of application for an Order under section 36 of the Age of Criminal Responsibility (Scotland) Act 2019

SHERIFFDOM OF (*insert name of sheriffdom*)

Court Ref No:

At (*insert place if sheriff court*)

APPLICATION

by

[A.B.] (*insert designation and address of constable*)

Applicant

The applicant applies to the court for an order under section 36 of the Age of Criminal Responsibility (Scotland) Act 2019 ("the 2019 Act") authorising:

[1. A search of (*insert name, address and the date of birth of child to which the seach relates*) ("the child");]

[2. Entry to and search of the premises at (*insert address*) ("the premises");]

[3. Entry to and search of the vehicle (*insert such description to identify the vehicle to be searched including registration number or such other suitable identifier*) ("the vehicle"); and]

[4. The seizure of anything the constable may find [on the child,] [[or] on the premises,] [[or] in the vehicle] relevant to the investigation of the behavior to which the application relates.]

Statement

1. This application is made pursuant to section 34 of the 2019 Act.

2. The child in respect of whom the order is sought is (*insert name, address and date of birth*).

3. The child is [habitually resident within the area of the court] [[and] the behavior to which the applicant relates is suspected to have occured within the area of the court.] This court accordingly has jurisdiction.

4. A parent (which includes guardian and any person who has care of the child) of the child [is (*insert name and address*) *OR* is not known.].

5. The applicant has reasonable grounds to suspect that—

   a. the child [by behaving in a violent or dangerous way, has caused or risked causing serious physical harm to another person *OR* by behav-

---

[1] As inserted by the Act of Sederunt (Summary Applications, Statutory Applications and Appeals etc. Rules 1999 and Sheriff Appeal Court Rules Amendment) (Age of Criminal Responsibility (Scotland) Act 2019) 2021 (SI 2021/452) Sch.1 (effective 17 December 2021).

ing in a sexually violent or sexually coercive way, has caused or risked causing harm (whether physical or not) to another person]; and

  b. evidence relevant to the investigation of that behavior may be found [on the child,] [[or] on the premises] [[or] in the vehicle].

6. *(insert here a brief statement indicating the basis upon which these matters are known or suspected by the applicant).*

[7. The applicant has reasonable grounds to suspect that evidence relevant to the investigation of the behaviour to which the application relates may lost, disposed of, or tampered with, if an opportunity to make representations about this application was to be given to [the child,] [[or] a parent of the child,] [[or] any other person considered to have an interest in the application].

  (insert here a brief statement indicating the basis upon which these matters are known or suspected by the applicant).]

8. The applicant attaches to this application the following supporting evidence—

  (insert details).

9. In the circumstances narrated the applicant is entitled to the order(s) sought and such order(s) should be granted accordingly.

  (Signed)
  [P.Q.] *(Applicant)*
  or [X.Y.] *(add designation and business address)*
  Solicitor for Applicant
  (insert date)

Form 77[1]

Rule 3.53.2(b)

Form of application for an Order under section 44(2) of the Age of Criminal Responsibility (Scotland) Act 2019

SHERIFFDOM OF *(insert name of sheriffdom)*

Court Ref No:

AT *(insert place of sheriff court)*
APPLICATION
by
[A.B.] *(insert designation and address of constable)*

Applicant

The applicant applies to the court for an order under section 44(2) of the Age of Criminal Responsibility (Scotland) Act 2019 ("the 2019 Act") authorising:

1. An investigative interview of *(insert name, address and date of birth of child to which the investigative interview relates)* ("the child");

[2. *(specify any other action required in connection with the interview, in respect of which the court's authority is sought pursuant to section 44(5) of the 2019 Act).]*

Statement

1. This application is made pursuant to section 42 of the 2019 Act.

---

[1] As inserted by the Act of Sederunt (Summary Applications, Statutory Applications and Appeals etc. Rules 1999 and Sheriff Appeal Court Rules Amendment) (Age of Criminal Responsibility (Scotland) Act 2019) 2021 (SI 2021/452) Sch.1 (effective 17 December 2021).

2. The child in respect of whom the order is sought is (*insert name, address and date of birth*).

3. The child is [habitually resident within the area of the court] [[and] the behaviour to which the application relates is suspected to have occurred within the area of the court]. This court accordingly has jurisdiction.

4. A parent (which includes guardian and any person who has care of the child) of the child [is (*insert name and address*) OR is not known].

5. The applicant—

   a. has reasonable grounds to suspect that the child, while under 12 years of age, [by behaving in a violent or dangerous way, has caused or risked causing serious physical harm to another person OR by behaving in a sexually violent or sexually coercive way, has caused or risked causing harm (whether physical or not) to another person]; and

   b. considers that an investigative interview of the child in relation to the behaviour to which the application relates is necessary to properly investigate the child's behaviour and the circumstances surrounding it (including whether a person other than the child has committed an offence).

6. (*insert here a brief statement indicating the basis upon which these matters are known or suspected by the applicant*).

7. The applicant has determined that (*insert name of local authority*) is the relevant local authority in relation to the planning and conduct of the proposed investigative interview of the child. The applicant [has consulted that local authority about the making of this application and the provisional plans for the investigative interview OR has not consulted the local authority as it was not practicable to do so].

8. An investigative interview of the child [took place on OR was scheduled to take place on] (*insert date, time, location*) by virtue of section 40(1) of the 2019 Act. The child [[and] the child's parent (*insert name*)] withdrew their previously given agreement to the investigative interview of the child being conducted (*insert here a brief statement indicating when and how such an agreement was withdrawn*) [[and] failed to comply in a material respect with the plans drawn up for the investigative interview].

[9. Questioning of the child took place on (*insert date, time and location*) by virtue of section 54 of the 2019 Act, on the authority of (*insert name of authorising senior officer*).]

[10. The applicant has reasonable grounds to suspect that evidence relevant to the investigation of the behaviour to which the application relates may be lost, disposed of or tampered with, if an opportunity to make representations about this application was to be given to [the child] [[or] a parent of the child,] [[or] any other person considered to have an interest in the application.]

   (*insert here a brief statement indicating the basis upon which these matters are known or suspected by the applicant*).]

11. The applicant attaches to this application the following supporting evidence—

   (*insert details*).

   (*The provisional plans for the investigative interview of the child must be attached to this application*).

12. In the circumstances narrated the applicant is entitled to the order(s) sought

and such order(s) should be granted accordingly.

(Signed)

[P.Q.] *(Appplicant)*

or [X.Y.] *(add designation and business address)*

Solicitor for Applicant

(insert date)

Form 78[1]

Rule 3.53.2(c)

Form of application for an Order under section 63 of the Age of Criminal Responsibility (Scotland) Act 2019

SHERIFFDOM OF *(insert name of sheriffdom)*

Court Ref No:

AT *(insert place of sheriff court)*

APPLICATION

by

[A.B.] *(insert designation and address of constable)*

Applicant

The applicant applies to the court for an order under section 63 of the Age of Criminal Responsibility (Scotland) Act 2019 ("the 2019 Act") authorising:

1.   the taking of relevant physical data and/or relevant samples from *(insert name, address and date of birth of child)* ("the child");

      (insert details of data and/or samples to be taken, including, where relevant whether authority is sought to taken an intimate sample).

[2. and *(specify any other action required in connection with the taking of relevant physical data/samples from the child pursuant to section 63(4) and (6) of the 2019 Act).*]

Statement

1.   This application is made pursuant to section 61 of the 2019 Act.

2.   The child in respect of whom the order is sought is *(insert name, address and date of birth).*

3.   The child is [habitually resident within the area of the court] [[and the behaviour to which the application relates is suspected to have occurred within the area of the court.] This court accordingly has jurisdiction.

4.   A parent (which includes guardian and any person who has care of the child) of the child [is *(insert name and address and relationship to the child) OR* is not known].

5.   The applicant—

      a.   has reasonable grounds to suspect that the child, [by behaving in violent or dangerous way, has caused or risked causing serious physical harm to another person *OR* by behaving in a sexually violent or sexually coercive way, has caused or risked causing harm (whether physical or not) to another person]; and

      b.   considers that the taking of the relevant physical data or relevant sample from the child is necessary to properly investigate the child's behaviour and the circumstances surrounding it.

6.   *(insert here a brief statement indicating the basis upon which these matters are known or suspected by the applicant).*

---

[1] As inserted by the Act of Sederunt (Summary Applications, Statutory Applications and Appeals etc. Rules 1999 and Sheriff Appeal Court Rules Amendment) (Age of Criminal Responsibility (Scotland) Act 2019) 2021 (SI 2021/452) Sch.1 (effective 17 December 2021).

[7. Physical data or samples (*specify the data or sample taken*) were taken from the child on (*insert date, time, location*) by virtue of section 69 of the Act, and on the authority of (*insert name of authorising senior officer*).]

[8. The applicant proposes that the intimate sample(s) to be taken from the child is [are] taken by (*insert proposed class or classes of health care professional as per section 65(2) of the Act*).]

[9. The applicant has reasonable grounds to suspect that evidence relevant to the investigation of the behaviour to which the application relates may be lost, disposed of, or tampered with, if an opportunity to make representations about this application was to be given to [the child,] [[or] a parent of the child,] [[or] any other person considered to have an interest in the application].

(*insert here a brief statement indicating the basis upon which these matters are known or suspected by the applicant*).]

10. The applicant attaches to this application the following supporting evidence—

(*insert details*).

11. In the circumstances narrated the applicant is entitled to the order(s) sought and such order(s) should be granted accordingly.

(*Signed*)

[P.Q.] (*Appplicant*)

or [X.Y.] (*add designation and business address*)

Solicitor for Applicant

(*insert date*)

Form 79[1]

Rule 3.53.4(a)

Form of order authorising a search in relation to a child under 12

Sheriff Court:

.... 20 ....

Court Ref No:

Order sought from the court

The sheriff, having considered an application made by (*insert name of applicant*) for an order under section 36 of the Act of Criminal Responsibility (Scotland) Act 2019 ("the 2019 Act") in respect of (*insert name of child*), and productions lodged herewith, and being satisfied as necessary as to the matters mentioned in section 36(2) of the 2019 Act,

1. Makes an order in terms of section 36 of the 2019 Act authorising

*a search of (*insert details of the child as given in the application*);

*entry to and search of the premises (*insert details of premises as given in the application*);

*entry to and search of vehicle (*insert such description to identify the vehicle to he searched including any registration number or such other suitable identifier as given in the application*);

*the seizure of anything the constable may find on the child or on premises

---

[1] As inserted by the Act of Sederunt (Summary Applications, Statutory Applications and Appeals etc. Rules 1999 and Sheriff Appeal Court Rules Amendment) (Age of Criminal Responsibility (Scotland) Act 2019) 2021 (SI 2021/452) Sch.1 (effective 17 December 2021).

or in the vehicle relevant to the investigation of the behaviour to which the application relates.

2. Directs notification of this order *(insert details of method and timing of notice)* to *(insert the name and designation of any person other than the child whom the sheriff considers appropriate).*

This order comes into force on *(date).* It ceases to be in force on *(date).*

*Delete as appropriate

(signed)

Sheriff

Form 80[1]

Rule 3.53.4(b)

Form of Child Interview Order

Sheriff Court:

.... 20 ....

Court Ref No:

The sheriff, having considered an application made by *(insert name of applicant)* for an order under section 44(2) of the Act of Criminal Responsibility (Scotland) Act 2019 ("the 2019 Act") in respect of *(insert name of child)* and productions lodged therewith, and being satisfied as necessary as to the matters mentioned in section 44(2) of the 2019 Act,

1. Makes an order in terms of section 44(2) of the 2019 Act authorising:

*an investigative interview of *(insert details of the child as given in the application)* in relation to the behaviour to which the investigation relates;

*and (list any other action required in connection with the interview, about which the court's additional authority is sought pursuant to sections 44(5) and 44(6) of the 2019 Act).

2. Directs notification of this order *(insert details of method and timing of notice)* to *(insert the name and designation of any person other than the child whom the sheriff considers appropriate).*

This order comes into force on *(date).* It ceases to be in force on *(date).*

(where different provisions are to come into force, or to cease to he in force, on different dates, specify the dates in respect of each provision).

*Delete as appropriate

(signed)

Sheriff

Form 81[2]

Rule 3.53.4(c)

Order authorising taking of prints and samples from a child

Sheriff Court:

.... 20 ....

Court Ref No:

The sheriff, having considered an application made by *(insert name of applicant)* for an order under section 63 of the Act of Criminal Responsibility (Scotland) Act

---

[1] As inserted by the Act of Sederunt (Summary Applications, Statutory Applications and Appeals etc. Rules 1999 and Sheriff Appeal Court Rules Amendment) (Age of Criminal Responsibility (Scotland) Act 2019) 2021 (SI 2021/452) Sch.1 (effective 17 December 2021).

[2] As inserted by the Act of Sederunt (Summary Applications, Statutory Applications and Appeals etc. Rules 1999 and Sheriff Appeal Court Rules Amendment) (Age of Criminal Responsibility (Scotland) Act 2019) 2021 (SI 2021/452) Sch.1 (effective 17 December 2021).

2019 ("the 2019 Act") in respect of (*insert name of child*), and productions lodged herewith, and being satisfied as necessary as to the matters mentioned in section 63(2) of the 2019 Act,

1. Makes an order in terms of section 63 of the 2019 Act authorising
*the taking of the relevant physical data and/or physical samples specified in the application (*insert details physical data/samples to be taken, as given in the application*);
*the taking of the relevant intimate samples, as specified in the application (*insert details of intimate samples to be taken and class of person (as set out in section 65(2) of the 2019 Act) authorised to take said samples, as given in the application*).
*and (*add any additional matters to be dealt with in the order in terms of sections 63(4) and (6) of the 2019 Act*).

2. Directs notification of this order (*insert details of method and timing of notice*) to (*insert the name and designation of any person other than the child whom the sheriff considers appropriate*).

This order comes into force on (*date*). It ceases to be in force on (*date*).

(*where different provisions are to come into force, or to cease to be in force, on different dates, specify the dates in respect of each provision*).

*Delete as appropriate
(*signed*)
Sheriff

SCHEDULE 2

Revocations

Rule 1.3

(1) Act of Sederunt	(2) Reference	(3) Extent of Revocation
Codifying Act of Sederunt 1913	SR & O 1913/638	Book L, Chapter X (proceedings under the Representation of the People Act 1983)
Codifying Act of Sederunt 1913	SR & O 1913/638	Book L, Chapter XI (appeals to the Court under the Pilotage Act 1913)
Act of Sederunt Regulating Appeals under the Pharmacy and Poisons Act 1933	SR & O 1935/1313	The whole Act of Sederunt
Act of Sederunt (Betting, Gaming and Lotteries Act Appeals) 1965)	1965/1168	The whole Act of Sederunt
Act of Sederunt (Housing Appeals) 1966	1966/845	The whole Act of Sederunt
Act of Sederunt (Sheriff Court Procedure under Part IV of the Housing (Scotland) Act 1969) 1970	1970/1508	The whole Act of Sederunt
Act of Sederunt (Proceedings under Sex Discrimination Act 1975) 1976	1976/374	The whole Act of Sederunt

(1) Act of Sederunt	(2) Reference	(3) Extent of Revocation
Act of Sederunt (Proceedings under Sex Discrimination Act 1975) No 2 1976	1976/1851	The whole Act of Sederunt
Act of Sederunt (Proceedings under Sex Discrimination Act 1975) 1977	1977/973	The whole Act of Sederunt
Act of Sederunt (Appeals under the Licensing (Scotland) Act 1976) 1977	1977/1622	The whole Act of Sederunt
Act of Sederunt (Betting and Gaming Appeals) 1978	1978/229	The whole Act of Sederunt
Act of Sederunt (Appeals under the Rating (Disabled Persons) Act 1978) 1979	1979/446	The whole Act of Sederunt
Act of Sederunt (Copyright, Deisgns and Patents) 1990	1990/380	The whole Act of Sederunt
Act of Sederunt (Proceedings in the Sheriff Court under the Model Law on International Commercial Arbitration) 1991	1991/2214	The whole Act of Sederunt
Act of Sederunt (Coal Mining Subsidence Act 1991) 1992	1992/798	The whole Act of Sederunt
Act of Sederunt (Applications under Part III of the Criminal Justice (International Co-operation) Act 1990) 1992	1992/1077	The whole Act of Sederunt
Act of Sederunt (Sheriff Court Summary Application Rules) 1993	1993/3240	The whole Act of Sederunt
Act of Sederunt (Mental Health Rules) 1996	1996/2149	The whole Act of Sederunt
Act of Sederunt (Proceeds of Crime Rules) 1996	1996/2446	The whole Act of Sederunt

ACT OF SEDERUNT (SUMMARY CAUSE RULES) 2002

(SSI 2002/132)

The Lords of Council and Session, under and by virtue of the powers conferred by section 32 of the Sheriff Courts (Scotland) Act 1971 (a) and of all other powers enabling them in that behalf, having approved draft rules submitted to them by the Sheriff Court Rules Council in accordance with section 34 of the said Act of 1971, do hereby enact and declare:

Citation and commencement

1.—(1)   This Act of Sederunt may be cited as the Act of Sederunt (Summary Cause Rules) 2002 and shall come into force on 10th June 2002.

(2)   This Act of Sederunt shall be inserted in the Books of Sederunt.

Summary Cause Rules

2.[1]   The provisions of Schedule 1 to this Act of Sederunt shall have effect for the purpose of providing rules for a summary cause.

Transitional provision

3.   Nothing in Schedule 1 to this Act of Sederunt shall apply to a summary cause commenced before 10th June 2002 and any such action shall proceed according to the law and practice in force immediately before that date.

Revocation

4.   The Acts of Sederunt mentioned in column (1) of Schedule 2 to this Act of Sederunt are revoked to the extent specified in column (3) of that Schedule except—

(a)   in relation to any summary cause commenced before 10th June 2002; and

(b)   for the purposes of the Act of Sederunt (Small Claim Rules) 1988.

SCHEDULE 1

SUMMARY CAUSE RULES 2002

Paragraph 2

Arrangement of Rules

Chapter 1
Citation, interpretation and application

1.1.   Citation, interpretation and application

Chapter 2
Representation

2.1.   Representation

---

[1] As amended by the Act of Sederunt (Rules of the Court of Session 1994 and Sheriff Court Rules Amendment) (No.4) (Simple Procedure) 2016 (SSI 2016/315) para.4 (effective 28 November 2016).

Chapter 12
Summary decree

Chapter 13
Alteration of summons etc.

Chapter 14
Additional defender

Chapter 14A
Interventions by the Commission for Equality and Human Rights

Chapter 14B
Interventions by the Scottish Commission for Human Rights

Chapter 15
Application for sist of party and transference

Chapter 16
Transfer and remit of actions

Chapter 17
Productions and documents

Chapter 18
Recovery of evidence and attendance of witnesses

Chapter 18A
Vulnerable Witnesses (Scotland) Act 2004

Chapter 19
Challenge of documents

Chapter 20
European Court

Chapter 21
Abandonment

Glossary

Citation, interpretation and application

1.1—[1, 2](1)   These Rules may be cited as the Summary Cause Rules 2002.

(2)   In these Rules—

"the 1907 Act" means the Sheriff Courts (Scotland) Act 1907;

"the 1971 Act" means the Sheriff Courts (Scotland) Act 1971;

"the 1975 Act" means the Litigants in Person (Costs and Expenses) Act 1975;

"the 2004 Act" means the Vulnerable Witnesses (Scotland) Act 2004;[3]

"authorised lay representative" means a person to whom section 32(1) of the Solicitors (Scotland) Act 1980 (offence to prepare writs) does not apply by virtue of section 32(2)(a) of that Act;

"enactment" includes an enactment comprised in, or in an instrument made under, an Act of the Scottish Parliament;

"summary cause" has the meaning assigned to it by section 35(1) of the 1971 Act.

(3)   Any reference to a specified Chapter or rule shall be construed as a reference to the Chapter or rule bearing that number in these Rules, and a reference to a specified paragraph, subparagraph or head shall be construed as a reference to the paragraph, sub-paragraph or head so numbered or lettered in the provision in which that reference occurs.

(4)   A form referred to by number means the form so numbered in Appendix 1 to these Rules or a form substantially of the same effect with such variation as circumstances may require.

(4A)[4]   In these Rules, references to a solicitor include a reference to a member of a body which has made a successful application under section 25 of the Law Reform (Miscellaneous Provisions) (Scotland) Act 1990 but only to the extent that the member is exercising rights acquired by virtue of section 27 of that Act.

---

[1] As amended by the Act of Sederunt (Ordinary Cause, Summary Application, Summary Cause and Small Claim Rules) Amendment (Miscellaneous) 2007 (SSI 2007/6) r.4(2) (effective January 29, 2007).

[2] As amended by the Act of Sederunt (Rules of the Court of Session 1994 and Sheriff Court Rules Amendment) (No.4) (Simple Procedure) 2016 (SSI 2016/315) para.4 (effective 28 November 2016).

[3] As inserted by the Act of Sederunt (Ordinary Cause, Summary Application, Summary Cause and Small Claim Rules) Amendment (Vulnerable Witnesses (Scotland) Act 2004) 2007 (SSI 2007/463) r.4(2) (effective November 1, 2007).

[4] As inserted by the Act of Sederunt (Sheriff Court Rules Amendment) (Sections 25 to 29 of the Law Reform (Miscellaneous Provisions) (Scotland) Act 1990) 2009 (SSI 2009/164) r.4(2) (effective May 20, 2009).

(5)   The glossary in Appendix 2 to these Rules is a guide to the meaning of certain legal expressions used in these Rules, but is not to be taken as giving those expressions any meaning which they do not have in law generally.

Chapter 2

Representation

Representation

2.1.—[1](1)   A party may be represented by—

   (a)   an advocate;

   (b)   a solicitor;

   (c)   a person authorised under any enactment to conduct proceedings in the sheriff court, in accordance with the terms of that enactment; and

   (d)   subject to paragraphs (2) and (4), an authorised lay representative.

(2)   An authorised lay representative shall not appear in court on behalf of a party except at the hearing held in terms of rule 8.2(1) and, unless the sheriff otherwise directs, any subsequent or other calling where the action is not defended on the merits or on the amount of the sum due.

(3)   Subject to the provisions of this rule, the persons referred to in paragraph (1)(c) and (d) above may, in representing a party, do everything for the preparation and conduct of an action as may be done by an individual conducting his own action.

(4)   If the sheriff finds that the authorised lay representative is—

   (a)   not a suitable person to represent the party; or

   (b)   not in fact authorised to do so,

that person must cease to represent the party.

(5)[2]   A party may be represented by a person other than an advocate or solicitor at any stage of any proceedings under the Debtors (Scotland) Act 1987, if the sheriff is satisfied that that person is a suitable person to represent the party at that stage and is authorised to do so.

Lay support

2.2.—[3](1)   At any time during proceedings the sheriff may, on the request of a party litigant, permit a named individual to assist the litigant in the conduct of the proceedings by sitting beside or behind (as the litigant chooses) the litigant at hearings in court or in chambers and doing such of the following for the litigant as he or she requires—

   (a)   providing moral support;

   (b)   helping to manage the court documents and other papers;

   (c)   taking notes of the proceedings;

   (d)   quietly advising on—

       (i)   points of law and procedure;

       (ii)   issues which the litigant might wish to raise with the sheriff;

       (iii)   questions which the litigant might wish to ask witnesses.

---

[1] As amended by the Act of Sederunt (Ordinary Cause, Summary Application, Summary Cause and Small Claim Rules) Amendment (Miscellaneous) 2007 (SSI 2007/6) r.4(3) (effective January 29, 2007).

[2] As amended by the Act of Sederunt (Rules of the Court of Session, Sheriff Appeal Court Rules and Sheriff Court Rules Amendment) (Sheriff Appeal Court) 2015 (SSI 2015/419) r.11 (effective 1 January 2016; as to savings see SSI 2015/419 rule 20(6)(a)).

[3] As inserted by the Act of Sederunt (Sheriff Court Rules) (Miscellaneous Amendments) (No.2) 2010 (SSI 2010/416) r.4 (effective January 1, 2011).

(2) It is a condition of such permission that the named individual does not receive from the litigant, whether directly or indirectly, any remuneration for his or her assistance.

(3) The sheriff may refuse a request under paragraph (1) only if—

(a) the sheriff is of the opinion that the named individual is an unsuitable person to act in that capacity (whether generally or in the proceedings concerned); or

(b) the sheriff is of the opinion that it would be contrary to the efficient administration of justice to grant it.

(4) Permission granted under paragraph (1) endures until the proceedings finish or it is withdrawn under paragraph (5); but it is not effective during any period when the litigant is represented.

(5) The sheriff may, of his or her own accord or on the incidental application of a party to the proceedings, withdraw permission granted under paragraph (1); but the sheriff must first be of the opinion that it would be contrary to the efficient administration of justice for the permission to continue.

(6) Where permission has been granted under paragraph (1), the litigant may—

(a) show the named individual any document (including a court document); or

(b) impart to the named individual any information,

which is in his or her possession in connection with the proceedings without being taken to contravene any prohibition or restriction on the disclosure of the document or the information; but the named individual is then to be taken to be subject to any such prohibition or restriction as if he or she were the litigant.

(7) Any expenses incurred by the litigant as a result of the support of an individual under paragraph (1) are not recoverable expenses in the proceedings.

Chapter 2A[1]

Lay Representation

Application and interpretation

2A.1.—(1) This Chapter is without prejudice to any enactment (including any other provision in these Rules) under which provision is, or may be, made for a party to a particular type of case before the sheriff to be represented by a lay representative.

(2) In this Chapter, a "lay representative" means a person who is not—

(a) a solicitor;

(b) an advocate, or

(c) someone having a right to conduct litigation, or a right of audience, by virtue of section 27 of the Law Reform (Miscellaneous Provisions) (Scotland) Act 1990.

Lay representation for party litigants

2A.2.—[2](1) In any proceedings in respect of which no provision as mentioned in rule 2A.1(1) is in force, the sheriff may, on the request of a party litigant, permit a named individual (a "lay representative") to appear, along with the litigant, at a specified hearing for the purpose of representing the litigant at that hearing.

---

[1] As inserted by the Act of Sederunt (Sheriff Court Rules) (Lay Representation) 2013 (SSI 2013/91) r.4 (effective April 4, 2013).

[2] As amended by the Act of Sederunt (Rules of the Court of Session, Sheriff Appeal Court Rules and Sheriff Court Rules Amendment) (Lay Representation) 2017 (SSI 2017/186) para.6 (effective 3 July 2017).

(2)　An application under paragraph (1)—

    (a)　is to be made orally on the date of the first hearing at which the litigant wishes a named individual to represent the litigant; and

    (b)　is to be accompanied by a document, signed by the named individual, in Form A1.

(3)　The sheriff may grant an application under paragraph (1) only if the sheriff is of the opinion that it would be in the interests of justice to grant it.

(4)　It is a condition of permission granted by the sheriff that the lay representative does not receive directly or indirectly from the litigant any remuneration or other reward for his or her assistance.

(5)　The sheriff may grant permission under paragraph (1) in respect of one or more specified hearings in the case; but such permission is not effective during any period when the litigant is legally represented.

(6)　The sheriff may, of his or her own accord or on the motion of a party to the proceedings, withdraw permission granted under paragraph (1).

(6A)　Where permission is granted under paragraph (1), the lay representative may do anything in the preparation or conduct of the hearing that the litigant may do.

(7)　Where permission has been granted under paragraph (1), the litigant may—

    (a)　show the lay representative any document (including a court document); or

    (b)　impart to the lay representative any information,

which is in his or her possession in connection with the proceedings without being taken to contravene any prohibition or restriction on the disclosure of the document or the information; but the lay representative is then to be taken to be subject to any such prohibition or restriction as if he or she were the litigant.

(8)　Any expenses incurred by the litigant in connection with lay representation under this rule are not recoverable expenses in the proceedings.

Chapter 3

Relief from failure to comply with rules

Dispensing power of sheriff

3.1.—(1)　The sheriff may relieve any party from the consequences of any failure to comply with the provisions of these Rules which is shown to be due to mistake, oversight or other excusable cause, on such conditions as he thinks fit.

(2)　Where the sheriff relieves a party from the consequences of the failure to comply with a provision in these Rules under paragraph (1), he may make such order as he thinks fit to enable the action to proceed as if the failure to comply with the provision had not occurred.

Chapter 4

Commencement of action

Form of summons

4.1.—(1)　A summary cause action shall be commenced by summons, which shall be in Form 1.

(2)　The form of claim in a summons may be in one of Forms 2, 3, 4, 5, 6, 7, 8 or 9.

Statement of claim

4.2.　The pursuer must insert a statement of his claim in the summons to give the defender fair notice of the claim; and the statement must include—

    (a)　details of the basis of the claim including relevant dates; and

    (b)   if the claim arises from the supply of goods or services, a description of the goods or services and the date or dates on or between which they were supplied and, where relevant, ordered.

Actions relating to regulated agreements

4.2A.[1] In an action which relates to a regulated agreement within the meaning given by section 189(1) of the Consumer Credit Act 1974 the statement of claim shall include an averment that such an agreement exists and details of the agreement.

Defender's copy summons

4.3. A copy summons shall be served on the defender—
    (a)   where the action is for, or includes a claim for, payment of money—
        (i)   in Form 1a where an application for a time to pay direction under the Debtors (Scotland) Act 1987 or time order under the Consumer Credit Act 1974 may be applied for; or
        (ii) in Form 1b in every other case;
    (b)   where the action is not for, and does not include a claim for, payment of money, in Form 1c; or
    (c)   in an action of multiplepoinding, in Form 1d.

Authentication and effect of summons

4.4.—(1) A summons shall be authenticated by the sheriff clerk in some appropriate manner except where—
    (a)   he refuses to do so for any reason;
    (b)   the defender's address is unknown; or
    (c)   a party seeks to alter the normal period of notice specified in rule 4.5(2); or
    (d)[2] a warrant for arrestment on the dependence, or to found jurisdiction, is sought.

  (2) If any of paragraphs (1)(a) to (d) applies, the summons shall be authenticated by the sheriff, if he thinks it appropriate.

  (3) The authenticated summons shall be warrant for—
    (a)   service on the defender; and
    (b)   where the appropriate warrant has been sought in the summons—
        (i)   arrestment on the dependence; or
        (ii) arrestment to found jurisdiction,
    as the case may be.

  (4)[3, 4] Where a warrant for arrestment to found jurisdiction, is sought, averments to justify that warrant must be included in the statement of claim.

Period of notice

4.5.—(1) An action shall proceed after the appropriate period of notice of the summons has been given to the defender prior to the return day.

---

[1] As inserted by the Act of Sederunt (Sheriff Court Rules) (Miscellaneous Amendments) 2009 (SSI 2009/294) r.4 (effective December 1, 2009) as substituted by the Act of Sederunt (Amendment of the Act of Sederunt (Sheriff Court Rules) (Miscellaneous Amendments) 2009) 2009 (SSI 2009/402) (effective November 30, 2009).

[2] As inserted by the Act of Sederunt (Ordinary Cause, Summary Application and Small Claim Rules) Amendment (Miscellaneous) (SSI 2004/197) r.4(2) (effective May 21, 2004).

[3] As inserted by the Act of Sederunt (Ordinary Cause, Summary Application and Small Claim Rules) Amendment (Miscellaneous) (SSI 2004/197) r.4(2) (effective May 21, 2004).

[4] As substituted by the Act of Sederunt (Sheriff Court Rules) (Miscellaneous Amendments) 2009 (SSI 2009/294) r.7 (effective October 1, 2009).

(2) The appropriate period of notice shall be—

(a) 21 days where the defender is resident or has a place of business within Europe; or

(b) 42 days where the defender is resident or has a place of business outwith Europe.

(3) The sheriff may, on cause shown, shorten or extend the period of notice on such conditions as to the form of service as he may direct, but in any case where the period of notice is reduced at least two days' notice must be given.

(4) If a period of notice expires on a Saturday, Sunday, public or court holiday, the period of notice shall be deemed to expire on the next day on which the sheriff clerk's office is open for civil court business.

(5) Notwithstanding the terms of section 4(2) of the Citation Amendment (Scotland) Act 1882, where service is by post the period of notice shall run from the beginning of the day next following the date of posting.

(6) The sheriff clerk shall insert in the summons—

(a) the return day, which is the last day on which the defender may return a form of response to the sheriff clerk; and

(b) the calling date, which is the date set for the action to call in court.

(7)[1] The calling date shall be 14 days after the return day.

Intimation

4.6. Any provision in these Rules requiring papers to be sent to or any intimation to be made to any party, applicant or claimant shall be construed as if the reference to the party, applicant or claimant included a reference to the solicitor representing that party, applicant or claimant.

Chapter 4A[2, 3]

Personal Injury Pre-action Protocol

Application and interpretation

4A.1.—(1) This Chapter applies to an action of damages for, or arising from, personal injuries.

(2) In this Chapter "the Protocol" means the Personal Injury Pre-Action Protocol set out in Appendix 1B, and references to the "aims of the Protocol", "requirements of the Protocol" and "stages of the Protocol" are to be construed accordingly.

Requirement to comply with the Protocol

4A.2. In any case where the Protocol applies, the court will normally expect parties to have complied with the requirements of the Protocol before proceedings are commenced.

Consequences of failing to comply with the Protocol

4A.3.—(1) This rule applies where the sheriff considers that a party ("party A")—

(a) failed, without just cause, to comply with the requirements of the Protocol; or

(b) unreasonably failed to accept an offer in settlement which was—

---

[1] As amended by the Act of Sederunt (Sheriff Court Rules) (Miscellaneous Amendments) 2009 (SSI 2009/294) r.7 (effective December 1, 2009).

[2] As inserted by the Act of Sederunt (Sheriff Court Rules Amendment) (Personal Injury Pre-Action Protocol) 2016 (SSI 2016/215) para.3 (effective 28 November 2016).

[3] As amended by the Act of Sederunt (Rules of the Court of Session 1994 and Sheriff Court Rules Amendment) (No. 2) (Miscellaneous) 2016 (SSI 2016/229) para.3 (effective 28 November 2016).

    (i)   made in accordance with the Protocol; and

    (ii) lodged as a tender during the period beginning with the commencement of proceedings and ending with the lodging of defences.

(2) The sheriff may, on the sheriff's own motion, or on the motion of any party, take any steps the sheriff considers necessary to do justice between the parties, and may in particular—

    (a)   sist the action to allow any party to comply with the requirements of the Protocol;

    (b)   make an award of expenses against party A;

    (c)   modify an award of expenses; or

    (d)   make an award regarding the interest payable on any award of damages.

(3) A motion made by a party under paragraph (2) must include a summary of—

    (a)   the steps taken by parties under the Protocol with a view to settling the action; and

    (b)   that party's assessment of the extent to which parties have complied with the requirements of the Protocol.

(4) In considering what steps (if any) to take under paragraph (2), the sheriff must take into account—

    (a)   the nature of any breach of the requirements of the Protocol; and

    (b)   the conduct of the parties during the stages of the Protocol.

(5) In assessing the conduct of the parties, the sheriff must have regard to the extent to which that conduct is consistent with the aims of the Protocol.

(6) This rule does not affect any other enactment or rule of law allowing the sheriff to make or modify awards regarding expenses and interest."

Chapter 5

Register of Summary Causes, service and return of the summons

Register of Summary Causes

5.1.—(1) The sheriff clerk shall keep a register of summary cause actions and incidental applications made in such actions, which shall be known as the Register of Summary Causes.

(2) There shall be entered in the Register of Summary Causes a note of all actions, together with a note of all minutes under rule 24.1(1) (recall of decree) and the entry for each action or minute must contain the following particulars where appropriate:—

    (a)   the names, designations and addresses of the parties;

    (b)   whether the parties were present or absent at any hearing, including an inspection, and the names of their representatives;

    (c)   the nature of the action;

    (d)   the amount of any claim;

    (e)   the date of issue of the summons;

    (f)   the method of service;

    (g)   the return day;

    (h)   the calling date;

    (i)   whether a form of response was lodged and details of it;

    (j)   the period of notice if shortened or extended in accordance with rule 4.5(3);

    (k)   details of any minute by the pursuer regarding an application for a time to pay direction or time order, or minute by the pursuer requesting decree or other order;

    (l)   details of any interlocutors issued;

   (m)   details of the final decree and the date of it; and

    (n)   details of any variation or recall of a decree.

(3)   There shall be entered in the Register of Summary Causes in the entry for the action to which they relate details of incidental applications including, where appropriate—

    (a)   whether parties are present or absent at the hearing of the application, and the names of their representatives;

    (b)   the nature of the application; and

    (c)   the interlocutor issued or order made.

(4)   The Register of Summary Causes must be—

    (a)   authenticated in some appropriate manner by the sheriff in respect of each day any order is made or application determined in an action; and

    (b)   open for inspection during normal business hours to all concerned without fee.

(5)   The Register of Summary Causes may be kept in electronic or documentary form.

Persons carrying on business under trading or descriptive name

5.2.—(1) A person carrying on a business under a trading or descriptive name may sue or be sued in such trading or descriptive name alone.

(2)   An extract of—

    (a)   a decree pronounced in an action; or

    (b)   a decree proceeding upon any deed, decree arbitral, bond, protest of a bill, promissory note or banker's note or upon any other obligation or document on which execution may proceed, recorded in the sheriff court books, against such person under such trading or descriptive name shall be a valid warrant for diligence against such person.

(3)   A summons, decree, charge or other document following upon such summons or decree in an action in which a person carrying on business under a trading or descriptive name sues or is sued in that name may be served—

    (a)   at any place of business or office at which such business is carried on within the sheriffdom of the sheriff court in which the action is brought; or

    (b)   if there is no place of business within that sheriffdom, at any place where such business is carried on (including the place of business or office of the clerk or secretary of any company, corporation or association or firm).

Form of service and certificate thereof

5.3.—(1) Subject to rule 5.5 (service where address of defender is unknown), a form of service in Form 11 must be enclosed with the defender's copy summons.

(2)   After service has been effected a certificate of execution of service in Form 12 must be prepared and signed by the person effecting service.

(3)   When service is by a sheriff officer, the certificate of execution of service must—

    (a)   be signed by him; and

    (b)   specify whether the service was personal or, if otherwise, the mode of service and the name of any person to whom the defender's copy summons was delivered.

(4)   If service is effected in accordance with rule 5.4(2), the certificate must also contain a statement of—

    (a)   the mode of service previously attempted; and

(b)   the circumstances which prevented such service from being effected.

Service within Scotland by sheriff officer

5.4.—(1)   A sheriff officer may validly serve any summons, decree, charge or other document following upon such summons or decree issued in an action by—

(a)   personal service; or

(b)   leaving it in the hands of—

(i)   a resident at the person's dwelling place; or

(ii)   an employee at the person's place of business.

(2)   If a sheriff officer has been unsuccessful in effecting service in accordance with paragraph (1), he may, after making diligent inquiries, serve the document—

(a)   by depositing it in the person's dwelling place or place of business by means of a letter box or by other lawful means; or

(b)[1]   by leaving it at that person's dwelling place or place of business in such a way that it is likely to come to the attention of that person.

(3)   Subject to the requirements of rule 6.1 (service of schedule of arrestment), if service is effected in accordance with paragraph (2), the sheriff officer must thereafter send by ordinary post to the address at which he thinks it most likely that the person may be found a letter containing a copy of the document.

(4)   In proceedings in or following on an action, it shall be necessary for any sheriff officer to be accompanied by a witness except where service, citation or intimation is to be made by post.

(5)   Where the firm which employs the sheriff officer has in its possession—

(a)   the document or a copy of it certified as correct by the pursuer's solicitor, the sheriff officer may serve the document upon the defender without having the document or certified copy in his possession (in which case he shall if required to do so by the person on whom service is executed and within a reasonable time of being so required, show the document or certified copy to the person); or

(b)   a certified copy of the interlocutor pronounced allowing service of the document, the sheriff officer may serve the document without having in his possession the certified copy interlocutor if he has in his possession a facsimile copy of the certified copy interlocutor (which he shall show, if required, to the person on whom service is executed).

(6)[2]   Where service is executed under paragraphs (1)(b) or (2), the document and the citation or notice of intimation, as the case may be, must be placed in an envelope bearing the notice "This envelope contains a citation to or intimation from (*insert name of sheriff court*)" and sealed by the sheriff officer.

Service on persons whose address is unknown

5.5.—(A1)[3]   Subject to rule 6.A7, this rule applies to service where the address of a person is not known.

(1)   If the defender's address is unknown to the pursuer and cannot reasonably be ascertained by him, the sheriff may grant warrant to serve the summons—

(a)   by the publication of an advertisement in Form 13 in a newspaper circulating in the area of the defender's last known address; or

---

[1] As substituted by the Act of Sederunt (Sheriff Court Rules) (Miscellaneous Amendments) 2011 (SSI 2011/193) r.4 (effective April 4, 2011).

[2] As inserted by the Act of Sederunt (Sheriff Court Rules) (Miscellaneous Amendments) 2011 (SSI 2011/193) r.4 (effective April 4, 2011).

[3] As inserted by the Act of Sederunt (Sheriff Court Rules) (Miscellaneous Amendments) 2009 (SSI 2009/294) r.11 (effective October 1, 2009).

(b)   by displaying on the walls of court a notice in Form 14.

(2)   Where a summons is served in accordance with paragraph (1), the period of notice, which must be fixed by the sheriff, shall run from the date of publication of the advertisement or display on the walls of court, as the case may be.

(3)   If service is to be effected under paragraph (1), the pursuer must lodge a service copy of the summons with the sheriff clerk.

(4)   The defender may uplift from the sheriff clerk the service copy of the summons lodged in accordance with paragraph (3).

(5)   If display on the walls of court is required under paragraph (1)(b), the pursuer must supply to the sheriff clerk for that purpose a completed copy of Form 14.

(6)   In every case where advertisement in a newspaper is required for the purpose of service, a copy of the newspaper containing said advertisement must be lodged with the sheriff clerk.

(7)   If service has been made under this rule and thereafter the defender's address becomes known, the sheriff may allow the summons to be amended and, if appropriate, grant warrant for reservice subject to such conditions as he thinks fit.

Service by post

5.6.—(A1)   [Repealed by the Act of Sederunt (Sheriff Court Rules) (Miscellaneous Amendments) 2009 (SSI 2009/294) r.11 (effective October 1, 2009).]

(1)   If it is competent to serve or intimate any document or to cite any person by recorded delivery, such service, intimation or citation, must be made by the first class recorded delivery service.

(2)   On the face of the envelope used for postal service under this rule, there must be written or printed a notice in Form 15.

(3)   The certificate of execution of postal service must have annexed to it any relevant postal receipt.

Service on persons outwith Scotland

5.7.—(1)   If any summons, decree, charge or other document following upon such summons or decree, or any charge or warrant, requires to be served outwith Scotland on any person, it must be served in accordance with this rule.

(2)   If the person has a known home or place of business in—

(a)   England and Wales, Northern Ireland, the Isle of Man or the Channel Islands; or

(b)   any country with which the United Kingdom does not have a convention providing for service of writs in that country,

the document must be served either—

(i)   by posting in Scotland a copy of the document in question in a registered letter addressed to the person at his residence or place of business; or

(ii)   in accordance with the rules for personal service under the domestic law of the place in which the document is to be served.

(3)   Subject to paragraph (4), if the document requires to be served in a country which is a party to the Hague Convention on the Service Abroad of Judicial and Extra-Judicial Documents in Civil or Commercial Matters dated 15th November 1965 or the European Convention on Jurisdiction and Enforcement of Judgments in Civil and Commercial Matters as set out in Schedule 1 or 3C to the Civil Jurisdiction and Judgments Act 1982, it must be served—

(a)   by a method prescribed by the internal law of the country where service is to be effected for the service of documents in domestic actions upon persons who are within its territory;

(b)[1] by or through a British consular authority at the request of the Secretary of State for Foreign, Commonwealth and Development Affairs;

(c)[2] by or through a central authority in the country where service is to be effected at the request of the Scottish Ministers;

(d) where the law of the country in which the person resides permits, by posting in Scotland a copy of the document in a registered letter addressed to the person at his residence; or

(e) where the law of the country in which service is to be effected permits, service by an *huissier*, other judicial officer or competent official of the country where service is to be made.

(4)[3] If the document requires to be served in a country to which the EC Service Regulation applies, service—

(a) may be effected by the methods prescribed in paragraph (3)(b) or (c) only in exceptional circumstances; and

(b) is effected only if the receiving agency has informed the person that acceptance of service may be refused on the ground that the document has not been translated in accordance with paragraph (12).

(5) If the document requires to be served in a country with which the United Kingdom has a convention on the service of writs in that country other than the conventions specified in paragraph (3) or the regulation specified in paragraph (4), it must be served by one of the methods approved in the relevant convention.

(6) Subject to paragraph (9), a document which requires to be posted in Scotland for the purposes of this rule must be posted by a solicitor or a sheriff officer, and the form of service and certificate of execution of service must be in Forms 11 and 12 respectively.

(7) On the face of the envelope used for postal service under this rule there must be written or printed a notice in Form 15.

(8) Where service is effected by a method specified in paragraph (3)(b) or (c), the pursuer must—

(a)[4,5] send a copy of the summons and warrant for service with form of service attached, or other document, with a request for service to be effected by the method indicated in the request to the Scottish Ministers or, as the case may be, the Secretary of State for Foreign, Commonwealth and Development Affairs; and

(b) lodge in process a certificate of execution of service signed by the authority which has effected service.

(9) If service is effected by the method specified in paragraph (3)(e), the pursuer must—

(a) send to the official in the country in which service is to be effected a copy

---

[1] As amended by the Transfer of Functions (Secretary of State for Foreign, Commonwealth and Development Affairs) Order 2020 (SI 2020/942) Sch.1(2) para.15 (effective 30 September 2020).

[2] As substituted by the Act of Sederunt (Sheriff Court Rules) (Miscellaneous Amendments) 2011 (SSI 2011/193) r.6 (effective 4 April 2011).

[3] As substituted by Act of Sederunt (Ordinary Cause, Summary Application, Summary Cause and Small Claim Rules) Amendment (Miscellaneous) 2004 (SSI 2004/197) r.4(3)(a) (effective 21 May 2004) and amended by the Act of Sederunt (Sheriff Court Rules) (Miscellaneous Amendments) (No.2) 2008 (SSI 2008/365) r.9(a) (effective 13 November 2008).

[4] As amended by the Act of Sederunt (Sheriff Court Rules) (Miscellaneous Amendments) 2011 (SSI 2011/193) r.7 (effective 4 April 2011).

[5] As amended by the Transfer of Functions (Secretary of State for Foreign, Commonwealth and Development Affairs) Order 2020 (SI 2020/942) Sch.1(2) para.15 (effective 30 September 2020).

of the summons and warrant for service, with citation attached, or other document, with a request for service to be effected by delivery to the defender or his residence; and

(b) lodge in process a certificate of execution of service by the official who has effected service.

(10)   Where service is executed in accordance with paragraph (2)(b)(ii) or (3)(a) other than on another party in—

(a) the United Kingdom;
(b) the Isle of Man; or
(c) the Channel Islands, the party executing service must lodge a certificate stating that the form of service employed is in accordance with the law of the place where the service was executed.

(11)   A certificate lodged in accordance with paragraph (10) shall be given by a person who is conversant with the law of the country concerned and who—

(a) practises or has practised law in that country; or
(b) is a duly accredited representative of the government of that country.

(12)[1]   Every summons or document and every citation and notice on the face of the envelope referred to in paragraph (7) must be accompanied by a translation in an official language of the country in which service is to be executed, unless English is—

(a) an official language of the country in which service is to be executed; or
(b) in a country to which the EC Service Regulation applies, a language of the member state of transmission that is understood by the person on whom service is being executed.

(13)   A translation referred to in paragraph (12) must be certified as a correct translation by the person making it and the certificate must contain the full name, address and qualifications of the translator and be lodged along with the execution of such service.

(14)[2]   In this rule "the EC Service Regulation" means Regulation (EC) No. 1393/ 2007 of the European Parliament and of the Council of 13th November 2007 on the service in the Member States of judicial and extrajudicial documents in civil or commercial matters (service of documents), and repealing Council Regulation (EC) No. 1348/2000, as amended from time to time.

Endorsation by sheriff clerk of defender's residence not necessary

5.8.   Any summons, decree, charge or other document following upon a summons or decree may be served, enforced or otherwise lawfully executed in Scotland without endorsation by a sheriff clerk and, if executed by a sheriff officer, may be so executed by a sheriff officer of the court which granted the summons, or by a sheriff officer of the sheriff court district in which it is to be executed.

Contents of envelope containing defender's copy summons

5.9.   Nothing must be included in the envelope containing a defender's copy summons except—

(a) the copy summons;
(b) a response or other notice in accordance with these Rules; and

---

[1] As substituted for existing text by the Act of Sederunt (Ordinary Cause, Summary Application, Summary Cause and Small Claim Rules) Amendment (Miscellaneous) 2004 (SSI 2004/197) r.4(3)(b) (effective 21 May 2004) and by the Act of Sederunt (Sheriff Court Rules) (Miscellaneous Amendments) (No.2) 2008 (SSI 2008/365) r.9(a) (effective 13 November 2008).

[2] As substituted by the Act of Sederunt (Sheriff Court Rules) (Miscellaneous Amendments) (No.2) 2008 (SSI 2008/365) r.9(b) (effective 13 November 2008).

(c) any other document approved by the sheriff principal.

Re-service

5.10.—(1) If it appears to the sheriff that there has been any failure or irregularity in service upon a defender, the sheriff may order the pursuer to re-serve the summons on such conditions as he thinks fit.

(2) If re-service has been ordered in accordance with paragraph (1) or rule 5.5(7) the action shall proceed thereafter as if it were a new action.

Defender appearing barred from objecting to service

5.11.—(1) A person who appears in an action shall not be entitled to state any objection to the regularity of the execution of service or intimation on him and his appearance shall remedy any defect in such service or intimation.

(2) Nothing in paragraph (1) shall preclude a party pleading that the court has no jurisdiction.

Return of summons

5.12.—(1) If any appearance in court is required on the calling date in respect of any party—

(a) the summons; and

(b) the relevant certificate of execution of service, shall be returned to the sheriff clerk not later than two days before the calling date.

(2) If no appearance by any party is required on the calling date, only the certificate of execution of service need be returned to the sheriff clerk, not later than two days before the calling date.

(3) If the pursuer fails to proceed in accordance with paragraph (1) or (2) as appropriate, the sheriff may dismiss the action.

Chapter 6[1]

Interim Diligence

Interpretation

6.A1. In this Chapter—

"the 1987 Act" means the Debtors (Scotland) Act 1987; and
"the 2002 Act" means the Debt Arrangement and Attachment (Scotland) Act 2002.

Application for interim diligence

6.A2.—(1) The following shall be made by incidental application—

(a) an application under section 15D(1) of the 1987 Act for warrant for diligence by arrestment or inhibition on the dependence of an action or warrant for arrestment on the dependence of an admiralty action;

(b) an application under section 9C of the 2002 Act for warrant for interim attachment.

(2) Such an application must be accompanied by a statement in Form 15a.

(3) A certified copy of an interlocutor granting an application under paragraph (1) shall be sufficient authority for execution of the diligence concerned.

---

[1] Chapter renamed and rr.6.A1–6.A7 inserted by the Act of Sederunt (Sheriff Court Rules Amendment) (Diligence) 2008 (SSI 2008/121) r.6 (effective April 1, 2008).

Effect of authority for inhibition on the dependence

6.A3.—(1) Where a person has been granted authority for inhibition on the dependence of an action, a certified copy of the interlocutor granting the application may be registered with a certificate of execution in the Register of Inhibitions and Adjudications.

[1](2) A notice of a certified copy of an interlocutor granting authority for inhibition under rule 6.A2 may be registered in the Register of Inhibitions and Adjudications; and such registration is to have the same effect as registration of a notice of inhibition under section 155(2) of the Titles to Land Consolidation (Scotland) Act 1868.

Recall etc of arrestment or inhibition

6.A4.—(1) An application by any person having an interest—

    (a) to loose, restrict, vary or recall an arrestment or an interim attachment; or

    (b) to recall, in whole or in part, or vary, an inhibition,

shall be made by incidental application.

(1A)[2] An incidental application under paragraph (1) shall—

    (a) specify the name and address of each of the parties;

    (b) where it relates to an inhibition, contain a description of the inhibition including the date of registration in the Register of Inhibitions and Adjudications.

(2) Paragraph (1) does not apply to an application made orally at a hearing under section 15K that has been fixed under section 15E(4) of the Act of 1987.

Incidental applications in relation to interim diligence, etc.

6.A5. An application under Part 1A of the 1987 Act or Part 1A of the 2002 Act other than mentioned above shall be made by incidental application.

Form of schedule of inhibition on the dependence

6.A6. *[Revoked by the Act of Sederunt (Sheriff Court Rules Amendment) (Diligence) 2009 (SSI 2009/107) r.5 (effective April 22, 2009).]*

Service of inhibition on the dependence where address of defender not known

6.A7.—(1) Where the address of a defender is not known to the pursuer, an inhibition shall be deemed to have been served on the defender if the schedule of inhibition is left with or deposited at the office of the sheriff clerk of the sheriff court district where the defender's last known address is located.

(2) Where service of an inhibition on the dependence is executed under paragraph (1), a copy of the schedule of inhibition shall be sent by the sheriff officer by first class post to the defender's last known address.

Form of schedule of arrestment on the dependence

6.A8.—(1)[3] An arrestment on the dependence shall be served by serving the schedule of arrestment on the arrestee in Form 15b.

(2) A certificate of execution shall be lodged with the sheriff clerk in Form 15c.

---

[1] As substituted by the Act of Sederunt (Sheriff Court Rules Amendment) (Diligence) 2009 (SSI 2009/107) r.5 (effective April 22, 2009).
[2] As inserted by the Act of Sederunt (Rules of the Court of Session and Sheriff Court Rules Amendment No.2) (Miscellaneous) 2014 (SSI 2014/192) r.4 (December 8, 2014).
[3] As inserted by the Act of Sederunt (Sheriff Court Rules Amendment) (Diligence) 2009 (SSI 2009/107) r.5 (effective April 22, 2009).

Service of schedule of arrestment

6.1. If a schedule of arrestment has not been personally served on an arrestee, the arrestment shall have effect only if a copy of the schedule is also sent by registered post or the first class recorded delivery service to—

    (a)   the last known place of residence of the arrestee; or

    (b)   if such place of residence is not known, or if the arrestee is a firm or corporation, to the arrestee's principal place of business if known, or, if not known, to any known place of business of the arrestee,

and the sheriff officer must, on the certificate of execution, certify that this has been done and specify the address to which the copy of the schedule was sent.

Arrestment before service

6.2.—(1)[1] An arrestment to found jurisdiction used prior to service shall cease to have effect, unless the summons is served within 21 days from the date of execution of the arrestment.

(2) When such an arrestment as is referred to in paragraph (1) has been executed, the party using it must forthwith report the execution to the sheriff clerk.

Recall and restriction of arrestment

6.3—(1) The sheriff may order that an arrestment on the dependence of an action or counterclaim shall cease to have effect if the party whose funds or property are arrested—

    (a)   pays into court; or

    (b)   finds caution to the satisfaction of the sheriff clerk in respect of, the sum claimed together with the sum of £50 in respect of expenses.

(2) Without prejudice to paragraph (1), a party whose funds or property are arrested may at any time apply to the sheriff to exercise his powers to recall or restrict an arrestment on the dependence of an action or counterclaim, with or without consignation or caution.

(3) An application made under paragraph (2) must be intimated by the applicant to the party who instructed the arrestment.

(4) On payment into court in accordance with paragraph (1), or if the sheriff recalls or restricts an arrestment on the dependence of an action in accordance with paragraph (2) and any condition imposed by the sheriff has been complied with, the sheriff clerk must—

    (a)   issue to the party whose funds or property are arrested a certificate in Form 16 authorising the release of any sum or property arrested to the extent ordered by the sheriff; and

    (b)   send a copy of the certificate to—

        (i)   the party who instructed the arrestment; and

        (ii)   the party who has possession of the funds or property that are arrested.

Chapter 7

Undefended action

Undefended action

7.1.—(1) Subject to paragraphs (4), (5) and (6), where the defender has not lodged a form of response on or before the return day—

    (a)   the action shall not require to call in court on the calling date; and

---

[1] As amended by the Act of Sederunt (Sheriff Court Rules Amendment) (Diligence) 2008 (SSI 2008/ 121) r.6(5) (effective April 1, 2008).

(b)   the pursuer must lodge a minute in Form 17 before the sheriff clerk's office closes for business on the second day before the calling date.

(2)   If the pursuer does not lodge a minute in terms of paragraph (1), the sheriff must dismiss the action.

(3)   If the sheriff is not prepared to grant the order requested in Form 17, the sheriff clerk must—

(a)   fix a date, time and place for the pursuer to be heard; and

(b)   inform the pursuer of—

(i)   that date, time and place; and

(ii)   the reasons for the sheriff wishing to hear him.

(4)   Where no form of response has been lodged in an action—

(a)   for recovery of possession of heritable property; or

(b)   of sequestration for rent, the action shall call in court on the calling date and the sheriff shall determine the action as he thinks fit.

(5)   Where no form of response has been lodged in an action of multiplepoinding the action shall proceed in accordance with rule 27.9(1)(a).

(6)   Where no form of response has been lodged in an action of count, reckoning and payment the action shall proceed in accordance with rule 29.2.

(7)   If the defender does not lodge a form of response in time or if the sheriff is satisfied that he does not intend to defend the action on the merits or on the amount of the sum due, the sheriff may grant decree with expenses against him.

Application for time to pay direction or time order

7.2.—(1)   If the defender admits the claim, he may, where competent—

(a)   make an application for a time to pay direction (including, where appropriate, an application for recall or restriction of an arrestment) or a time order by completing the appropriate part of the form of response contained in the defender's copy summons and lodging it with the sheriff clerk on or before the return day; or

(b)   lodge a form of response indicating that he admits the claim and intends to apply orally for a time to pay direction (including, where appropriate, an application for recall or restriction of an arrestment) or time order.

(1A)[1]   The sheriff clerk must on receipt forthwith intimate to the pursuer a copy of any response lodged under paragraph (1).

(2)[2]   Where the defender has lodged an application in terms of paragraph (1)(a), the pursuer may intimate that he does not object to the application by lodging a minute in Form 18 before the time the sheriff clerk's office closes for business on the day occurring 9 days before the calling date stating that he does not object to the defender's application and seeking decree.

(3)   If the pursuer intimates in accordance with paragraph (2) that he does not object to the application—

(a)   the sheriff may grant decree on the calling date;

(b)   the parties need not attend; and

(c)   the action will not call in court.

---

[1] As inserted by the Act of Sederunt (Sheriff Court Rules) (Miscellaneous Amendments) 2009 (SSI 2009/294) r.4 (effective December 1, 2009).

[2] As substituted by the Act of Sederunt (Sheriff Court Rules) (Miscellaneous Amendments) 2009 (SSI 2009/294) r.4 (effective December 1, 2009).

(4)[1] If the pursuer wishes to oppose the application for a time to pay direction or time order made in accordance with paragraph (1)(a) he must before the time the sheriff clerk's office closes for business on the day occurring 9 days before the calling date—

    (a) lodge a minute in Form 19; and

    (b) send a copy of that minute to the defender.

(5) Where the pursuer objects to an application in terms of paragraph (1)(a) or the defender has lodged a form of response in accordance with paragraph (1)(b), the action shall call on the calling date when the parties may appear and the sheriff must decide the application and grant decree accordingly.

(6) The sheriff shall decide an application in accordance with paragraph (5) whether or not any of the parties appear.

(7) Where the defender has lodged an application in terms of paragraph (1)(a) and the pursuer fails to proceed in accordance with either of paragraphs (2) or (4) the sheriff may dismiss the claim.

Decree in actions to which the Hague Convention or Civil Jurisdiction and Judgements Act 1982 apply

7.3.—(1) If the summons has been served in a country to which the Hague Convention on the Service Abroad of Judicial and Extra-Judicial Documents in Civil or Commercial Matters dated 15th November 1965 applies, decree must not be granted until it is established to the satisfaction of the sheriff that the requirements of Article 15 of that Convention have been complied with.

(2) Where a defender is domiciled in another part of the United Kingdom or in another Contracting State, the sheriff shall not grant decree until it has been shown that the defender has been able to receive the summons in sufficient time to arrange his defence or that all necessary steps have been taken to that end.

(3) For the purposes of paragraph (2)—

    (a) the question whether a person is domiciled in another part of the United Kingdom shall be determined in accordance with sections 41 and 42 of the Civil Jurisdiction and Judgments Act 1982;

    (b) the question whether a person is domiciled in another Contracting State shall be determined in accordance with Article 52 of the Convention in Schedule 1 or 3C to that Act; and

    (c) the term "Contracting State" has the meaning assigned in section 1 of that Act.

Chapter 8

Defended action

Response to summons

8.1.—(1) If the defender intends—

    (a) to challenge the jurisdiction of the court or the competency of the action;

    (b) to defend the action (whether as regards the amount claimed or otherwise); or

    (c) state a counterclaim,

he must complete and lodge with the sheriff clerk on or before the return day the form of response contained in the defender's copy summons including a statement of his response which gives fair notice to the pursuer.

---

[1] As substituted by the Act of Sederunt (Sheriff Court Rules) (Miscellaneous Amendments) 2009 (SSI 2009/294) r.4 (effective December 1, 2009).

(2) The sheriff clerk must upon receipt intimate to the pursuer a copy of any response lodged under paragraph (1).

Procedure in defended action

8.2.—(1) Where the defender has lodged a form of response in accordance with rule 8.1(1) the action will call in court for a hearing.

(2) The hearing shall be held on the calling date.

(3) The sheriff may continue the hearing to such other date as he considers appropriate.

(4) The defender must either be present or be represented at the hearing.

(5) Where the defender—

    (a) does not appear or is not represented; and

    (b) the pursuer is present or is represented,

decree may be granted against the defender in terms of the summons.

(6) Where at the hearing—

    (a) the pursuer does not appear or is not represented; and

    (b) the defender is present or represented, the sheriff shall dismiss the action and may grant decree in terms of any counterclaim.

(7) If all parties fail to appear at the hearing, the sheriff shall, unless sufficient reason appears to the contrary, dismiss the action and any counterclaim.

Purpose of hearing

8.3.—(1) If, at the hearing, the sheriff is satisfied that the action is incompetent or that there is a patent defect of jurisdiction, he must grant decree of dismissal in favour of the defender or, if appropriate, transfer the action in terms of rule 16.1(2).

(2) At the hearing, the sheriff shall—

    (a) ascertain the factual basis of the action and any defence, and the legal basis on which the action and defence are proceeding; and

    (b) seek to negotiate and secure settlement of the action between the parties.

(3) If the sheriff cannot secure settlement of the action between the parties, he shall—

    (a) identify and note on the summons the issues of fact and law which are in dispute;

    (b) note on the summons any facts which are agreed;

    (c) where it appears that the claim as stated or any defence stated in response to it is not soundly based in law in whole or in part, hear parties forthwith on that matter and may grant decree in favour of any party; and

    (d) if satisfied that the claim and any defence have or may have a sound basis in law and that the dispute between the parties depends upon resolution of disputed issues of fact, fix a diet of proof or, alternatively, if satisfied that the claim and any defence have a sound basis in law and that the facts of the case are sufficiently agreed, hear parties forthwith on the merits of the action and may grant decree in whole or in part in favour of any party.

    (e)[1] enquire whether there is or is likely to be a vulnerable witness within the meaning of section 11(1) of the 2004 Act who is to give evidence at any proof or hearing, consider any child witness notice or vulnerable witness

---

[1] As inserted by the Act of Sederunt (Ordinary Cause, Summary Application, Summary Cause and Small Claim Rules) Amendment (Vulnerable Witnesses (Scotland) Act 2004) 2007 (SSI 2007/463) r.4(3) (effective November 1, 2007).

application that has been lodged where no order has been made and consider whether any order under section 12(1) of the 2004 Act requires to be made.

(4)   Where the sheriff fixes a proof, the sheriff clerk shall make up a folder for the case papers.

Remit to person of skill

8.4.—(1)   The sheriff may, on an incidental application by any party or on a joint application, remit to any person of skill, or other person, to report on any matter of fact.

(2)   If a remit under paragraph (1) is made by joint application or of consent of all parties, the report of such person shall be final and conclusive with respect to the matter of fact which is the subject of the remit.

(3)   If a remit under paragraph (1) is made—

   (a)   on the application of one of the parties, the expenses of its execution must, in the first instance, be met by that party; or

   (b)   on a joint application or of consent of all parties, the expenses must, in the first instance, be met by the parties equally, unless the sheriff otherwise orders.

Inspection and recovery of documents

8.5.—(1)   Each party shall, within 28 days after the date of the fixing of a proof, intimate to every other party, and lodge with the sheriff clerk, a list of documents, which are or have been in his possession or control which he intends to use or put in evidence at the proof, including the whereabouts of those documents.

(2)   A party who has received a list of documents from another party under paragraph (1) may inspect those documents which are in the possession or control of the party intimating the list at a time and place fixed by that party which is reasonable to both parties.

(3)   Nothing in this rule shall affect—

   (a)   the law relating, or the right of a party to object, to the inspection of a document on the ground of privilege or confidentiality; or

   (b)   the right of a party to apply under rule 18.1 for a commission and diligence for recovery of documents or under rule 18.3 for an order under section 1 of the Administration of Justice (Scotland) Act 1972.

Exchange of lists of witnesses

8.6.—(1)   Within 28 days after the date of the fixing of a proof, each party shall intimate to every other party, and lodge with the sheriff clerk, a list of witnesses, including any skilled witnesses, whom he intends to call to give evidence.

(2)   A party who seeks to call as a witness a person not on his list intimated and lodged under paragraph (1) shall, if any other party objects to such a witness being called, seek leave of the sheriff to call that person as a witness; and such leave may be granted on such conditions, if any, as the sheriff thinks fit.

(3)[1]   The list of witnesses intimated under paragraph (1) shall include the name, occupation (where known) and address of each intended witness and indicate whether the witness is considered to be a vulnerable witness within the meaning of section 11(1) of the 2004 Act and whether any child witness notice or vulnerable witness application has been lodged in respect of that witness.

---

[1] As amended by the Act of Sederunt (Ordinary Cause, Summary Application, Summary Cause and Small Claim Rules) Amendment (Vulnerable Witnesses (Scotland) Act 2004) 2007 (SSI 2007/463) r.4(4) (effective November 1, 2007).

Exchange of reports of skilled witnesses

8.7.—(1) Not less than 28 days before the diet of proof, a party shall—

    (a) disclose to every other party in the form of a written report the substance of the evidence of any skilled person whom he intends to call as a witness; and

    (b) lodge a copy of that report in process.

(2) Except on special cause shown, a party may only call as a skilled witness any person the substance of whose evidence has been disclosed in accordance with paragraph (1).

Evidence generally

8.8. Where possible, the parties shall agree photographs, sketch plans, and any statement or document not in dispute.

Notices to admit and notices of non-admission

8.8A.—[1](1) At any time after a form of response has been lodged, a party may intimate to any other party a notice or notices calling on him or her to admit for the purposes of that cause only—

    (a) such facts relating to an issue averred in the statement of claim or form of response as may be specified in the notice;

    (b) that a particular document lodged with the sheriff clerk and specified in the notice is—

        (i) an original and properly authenticated document; or

        (ii) a true copy of an original and properly authenticated document.

(2) Where a party on whom a notice is intimated under paragraph (1)—

    (a) does not admit a fact specified in the notice, or

    (b) does not admit, or seeks to challenge, the authenticity of a document specified in the notice,

he or she must, within 21 days after the date of intimation of the notice under paragraph (1), intimate a notice of non-admission to the party intimating the notice to him or her under paragraph (1) stating that he or she does not admit the fact or document specified.

(3) A party who fails to intimate a notice of non-admission under paragraph (2) will be deemed to have admitted the fact or document specified in the notice intimated to him or her under paragraph (1); and such fact or document may be used in evidence at a proof if otherwise admissible in evidence, unless the sheriff, on special cause shown, otherwise directs.

(4) The party serving a notice under paragraph (1) or (2) must lodge a copy of it with the sheriff clerk.

(5) A deemed admission under paragraph (3) must not be used—

    (a) against the party by whom it was deemed to be made other than in the cause for the purpose for which it was deemed to be made; or

    (b) in favour of any person other than the party by whom the notice was given under paragraph (1).

(6) The sheriff may, at any time, allow a party to amend or withdraw an admission made by him or her on such conditions, if any, as the sheriff thinks fit.

(7) A party may, at any time, withdraw in whole or in part a notice of non-admission by intimating a notice of withdrawal.

---

[1] As inserted by the Act of Sederunt (Sheriff Court Rules) (Miscellaneous Amendments) 2010 (SSI 2010/279) r.6 (effective July 29, 2010).

Hearing parts of action separately

8.9.—(1) In any action which includes a claim for payment of money, the sheriff may—

(a)   of his own accord; or

(b)   on the incidental application of any party,

order that proof on liability or any specified issue be heard separately from proof on any other issue and determine the order in which the proofs shall be heard.

(2) The sheriff shall pronounce such interlocutor as he thinks fit at the conclusion of the first proof of any action ordered to be heard in separate parts under paragraph (1).

Returning borrowed parts of process before proof

8.10. All parts of process which have been borrowed must be returned to process not later than noon on the day preceding the proof.

Conduct of proof

8.11 The pursuer must lead in the proof unless the sheriff, on the incidental application of any of the parties which has been intimated to the other parties not less than seven days before the diet of proof, directs otherwise.

Administration of oath or affirmation to witness

8.12. The sheriff must administer the oath to a witness in Form 20 or, where the witness elects to affirm, the affirmation in Form 21.

Noting of evidence, etc.

8.13.—(1) The sheriff who presides at the proof may make a note of any facts agreed by the parties since the hearing held in terms of rule 8.2(1).

(2) The parties may, and must if required by the sheriff, lodge a joint minute of admissions of the facts upon which they have reached agreement.

(3) The sheriff must—

(a)   make for his own use notes of the evidence led at the proof, including any evidence the admissibility of which is objected to, and of the nature of any such objection; and

(b)   retain these notes until after any appeal has been disposed of.

Parties to be heard at close of proof

8.14.—(1) After all the evidence has been led relevant to the particular proof, the sheriff must hear parties on the evidence.

(2) At the conclusion of that hearing, the sheriff may—

(a)   pronounce his decision; or

(b)   reserve judgment.

Objections to admissibility of evidence

8.15. If in the course of a proof an objection is made to the admissibility of any evidence and that line of evidence is not abandoned by the party pursuing it, the sheriff must except where—

(a)   he is of the opinion that the evidence is clearly irrelevant or scandalous; or

(b)   *[Revoked by the Act of Sederunt (Rules of the Court of Session, Sheriff Appeal Court Rules and Sheriff Court Rules Amendment) (Sheriff Appeal Court) 2015 (SSI 2015/419) r.11 (effective 1 January 2016; as to savings see SSI 2015/419 rule 20(6)(a)).]*

Incidental appeal against rulings on confidentiality of evidence and production of documents

8.16. *[Revoked by the Act of Sederunt (Rules of the Court of Session, Sheriff Appeal Court Rules and Sheriff Court Rules Amendment) (Sheriff Appeal Court) 2015 (SSI 2015/419) r.11 (effective 1 January 2016; as to savings see SSI 2015/419 rule 20(6)(a)).]*

Application for time to pay direction or a time order in defended action

8.17. A defender in an action which proceeds as defended may, where it is competent to do so, make a incidental application or apply orally at any hearing, at any time before decree is granted, for a time to pay direction (including where appropriate, an order recalling or restricting an arrestment on the dependence) or time order.

Pronouncement of decision

8.18.—(1) If the sheriff pronounces his decision at the end of the hearing held in terms of rule 8.2(1) or any proof, he must state briefly the grounds of his decision, including the reasons for his decision on any question of law or of admissibility of evidence.

(2) If the sheriff pronounces his decision after reserving judgement, he must give to the sheriff clerk within 28 days—

    (a) a statement of his decision; and

    (b) a brief note of the matters mentioned in paragraph (1).

(3) The sheriff clerk must send copies of the documents mentioned in paragraphs (2)(a) and (b) to each of the parties.

Chapter 9

Incidental applications and sists

General

9.1.—(1) Except where otherwise provided, any incidental application in an action may be made—

    (a) orally with the leave of the sheriff during any hearing of the action; or

    (b) by lodging the application in written form with the sheriff clerk.

(2) An application lodged in accordance with paragraph (1)(b) may only be heard after not less than two days' notice has been given to the other party.

(3) Where the party receiving notice of an incidental application lodged in accordance with paragraph (1)(b) intimates to the sheriff clerk and the party making the application that the application is not opposed, the application shall not require to call in court unless the sheriff so directs.

(4) Any intimation made under paragraph (3) shall be made not later than noon on the day before the application is due to be heard.

Application to sist action

9.2.—(1) Where an incidental application to sist an action is made, the reason for the sist—

    (a) shall be stated by the party seeking the sist; and

    (b) shall be recorded in the Register of Summary Causes and on the summons.

(2)   Where an action has been sisted, the sheriff may, after giving parties an opportunity to be heard, recall the sist.

Chapter 10

Counterclaim

Counterclaim

10.1.—(1)   If a pursuer intends to oppose a counterclaim, he must lodge answers within seven days of the lodging of the form of response.

(2)   The pursuer must at the same time as lodging answers intimate a copy of any answers to every other party.

(3)[1]   The defender may apply for warrant for interim diligence in respect of a counterclaim.

(4)–(5)   *[Repealed by the Act of Sederunt (Sheriff Court Rules) (Miscellaneous Amendments) 2009 (SSI 2009/294) r. 11 (effective October 1, 2009).]*

Chapter 11

Third party procedure

Application for third party notice

11.1.—(1)   Where in an action a defender claims that—

(a)   he has in respect of the subject matter of the action a right of contribution, relief or indemnity against any person who is not a party to the action; or

(b)   a person whom the pursuer is not bound to call as a defender should be made a party to the action along with the defender in respect that such person is—

(i)   solely liable, or jointly or jointly and severally liable with the defender to the pursuer in respect of the subject matter of the action; or

(ii)   liable to the defender in respect of the claim arising from or in connection with the liability, if any, of the defender to the pursuer,

he may apply by incidental application for an order for service of a third party notice upon that other person.

(2)   An application for service of a third party notice shall be made at the time when the defender lodges a form of response, unless the sheriff on cause shown shall permit a later application.

(3)   Where—

(a)   a pursuer against whom a counterclaim is made; or

(b)   a third party convened in the action,

seeks, in relation to the claim against him, to make against a person who is not a party, a claim mentioned in paragraph (1) as a claim which could be made by a defender against a third party, he shall apply by incidental application for an order for service of a third party notice; and rules 11.2 and 11.3 shall, with the necessary modifications, apply to such a claim as they apply in relation to a counterclaim by a defender.

Procedure

11.2.—(1)   If an application in terms of rule 11.1 is granted, the sheriff shall—

(a)   fix a date on which he will regulate further procedure; and

(b)   grant warrant to serve on the third party—

---

[1] As amended by the Act of Sederunt (Sheriff Court Rules) (Miscellaneous Amendments) 2009 (SSI 2009/294) r.11 (effective October 1, 2009).

    (i)   a copy of the summons;

    (ii) a copy of the grounds upon which it is claimed that the third party is liable; and

    (iii) a notice in Form 22 and a copy of Form 23.

(2) A copy of the third party notice, and any certificate of execution of service, shall be lodged by the defender before the hearing fixed under paragraph (1)(a).

(3) A third party seeking to answer the claim against him shall complete and lodge the form of response no later than seven days before the hearing fixed under paragraph (1)(a).

(4) The sheriff clerk must upon receipt intimate to the other parties a copy of any response lodged under paragraph (3).

Warrants for diligence on third party notice

11.3.—(1)[1] A defender who applies for an order for service of a third party notice may apply for—

    (a)   a warrant for arrestment to found jurisdiction;

    (b)   a warrant for interim diligence,

which would have been permitted had the warrant been sought in an initial writ in a separate action.

(1A)[2] On an application under paragraph (1)(a) being made—

    (a)   the sheriff may grant the application if he thinks it appropriate; and

    (b)   the sheriff shall not grant the application unless averments to justify the warrant sought have been made.

(2) A certified copy of the interlocutor granting warrant for diligence shall be sufficient authority for execution of the diligence.

Chapter 12

Summary decree

Application of chapter

12.1. This chapter applies to any action other than an action of multiplepoinding.

Application for summary decree

12.2.—(1) A pursuer may at any time after a defender has lodged a form of response apply by incidental application for summary decree against any defender on the ground that there is no defence to the action or any part of it.

(2) In applying for summary decree the pursuer may ask the sheriff to dispose of the whole or part of the subject matter of the action.

(3) The pursuer shall intimate an application under paragraph (1) by registered or recorded delivery post to every other party not less than seven days before the date fixed for the hearing of the application.

(4) On an application under paragraph (1), the sheriff may ordain any party, or a partner, director, officer or office-bearer of any party—

    (a)   to produce any relevant document or article; or

    (b)   to lodge an affidavit in support of any assertion of fact made in the action or at the hearing of the incidental application.

---

[1] As substituted by the Act of Sederunt (Sheriff Court Rules) (Miscellaneous Amendments) 2009 (SSI 2009/294) r.11 (effective October 1, 2009).

[2] As inserted by the Act of Sederunt (Ordinary Cause, Summary Application, Summary Cause and Small Claim Rules) Amendment (Miscellaneous) 2004 (SSI 2004/197) r.4(5) (effective May 21, 2004) and amended by the Act of Sederunt (Sheriff Court Rules) (Miscellaneous Amendments) 2009 (SSI 2009/294) r.11 (effective October 1, 2009).

(5) Notwithstanding the refusal of an application for summary decree, a subsequent application may be made on a change of circumstances.

Summary decree in a counterclaim etc.

12.3. Rule 12.2 shall apply with the necessary modifications to an application by any other party for summary decree.

Chapter 13

Alteration of summons etc.

Alteration of summons etc.

13.1.—(1) The sheriff may, on the incidental application of a party, allow amendment of the summons, form of response, counterclaim or answers to a counterclaim and adjust the note of disputed issues at any time before final judgment is pronounced on the merits.

(2) In an undefended action, the sheriff may order the amended summons to be re-served on the defender on such period of notice as he thinks fit.

(3) Paragraph (1) includes amendment for the following purposes:-

    (a) increasing or reducing the sum claimed;

    (b) seeking a different remedy from that originally sought;

    (c) correcting or supplementing the designation of a party;

    (d) enabling a party to sue or be sued in a representative capacity; and

    (e) sisting a party in substitution for, or in addition to, the original party.

(4) Where an amendment sists an additional or substitute defender to the action the sheriff shall order such service and regulate further procedure as he thinks fit.

Chapter 14

Additional defender

Additional defender

14.1—(1) Any person who has not been called as a defender may apply by incidental application to the sheriff for leave to enter an action as a defender, and to state a defence.

(2) An application under this rule must specify—

    (a) the applicant's title and interest to enter the action; and

    (b) the grounds of the defence which he proposes to state.

(3) On the lodging of an application under this rule—

    (a) the sheriff must appoint a date for hearing the application; and

    (b) the applicant must forthwith serve a copy of the application and of the order for a hearing on the parties to the action.

(4) After hearing the applicant and any party to the action the sheriff may, if he is satisfied that the applicant has shown title and interest to enter the action, grant the application.

(5) Where an application is granted under paragraph (4)—

    (a) the applicant shall be treated as a defender; and

    (b) the sheriff must forthwith consider whether any decision already taken in the action on the issues in dispute between the parties requires to be reconsidered in light of the terms of the application.

(6)[1] Paragraph (5)(b) does not apply to a personal injuries action raised under Chapter 34.

---

[1] As inserted by the Act of Sederunt (Summary Cause Rules Amendment) (Personal Injuries Actions) 2012 (SSI 2012/144) para.2 (effective September 1, 2012).

(7)[1] Where an application is granted under paragraph (4) in a personal injuries action raised under Chapter 34, the sheriff may make such further order as the sheriff thinks fit.

Chapter 14A[2]

Interventions by the Commission for Equality and Human Rights

Interpretation

14A.1. In this Chapter "the CEHR" means the Commission for Equality and Human Rights.

Interventions by the CEHR

14A.2.—(1) The CEHR may apply to the sheriff for leave to intervene in any summary cause action in accordance with this Chapter.

(2) This Chapter is without prejudice to any other entitlement of the CEHR by virtue of having title and interest in relation to the subject matter of any proceedings by virtue of section 30(2) of the Equality Act 2006 or any other enactment to seek to be sisted as a party in those proceedings.

(3) Nothing in this Chapter shall affect the power of the sheriff to make such other direction as he considers appropriate in the interests of justice.

(4) Any decision of the sheriff in proceedings under this Chapter shall be final and not subject to appeal.

Applications to intervene

14A.3.—(1) An application for leave to intervene shall be by way of minute of intervention in Form 23A and the CEHR shall-

   (a) send a copy of it to all the parties; and

   (b) lodge it in process, certifying that subparagraph (a) has been complied with.

(2) A minute of intervention shall set out briefly—

   (a) the CEHR's reasons for believing that the proceedings are relevant to a matter in connection with which the CEHR has a function;

   (b) the issue in the proceedings which the CEHR wishes to address; and

   (c) the propositions to be advanced by the CEHR and the CEHR's reasons for believing that they are relevant to the proceedings and that they will assist the sheriff.

(3) The sheriff may—

   (a) refuse leave without a hearing;

   (b) grant leave without a hearing unless a hearing is requested under paragraph (4);

   (c) refuse or grant leave after such a hearing.

(4) A hearing, at which the applicant and the parties may address the court on the matters referred to in paragraph (6)(c) may be held if, within 14 days of the minute of intervention being lodged, any of the parties lodges a request for a hearing.

(5) Any diet in pursuance of paragraph (4) shall be fixed by the sheriff clerk who shall give written intimation of the diet to the CEHR and all the parties.

(6) The sheriff may grant leave only if satisfied that—

---

[1] As inserted by the Act of Sederunt (Summary Cause Rules Amendment) (Personal Injuries Actions) 2012 (SSI 2012/144) para.2 (effective September 1, 2012).
[2] As inserted by the Act of Sederunt (Sheriff Court Rules) (Miscellaneous Amendments) 2008 (SSI 2008/223) r.6(2) (effective July 1, 2008). Originally named Chapter 13B Interventions by the Scottish Commission for Human Rights in a possible drafting error.

(a) the proceedings are relevant to a matter in connection with which the CEHR has a function;

(b) the propositions to be advanced by the CEHR are relevant to the proceedings and are likely to assist him; and

(c) the intervention will not unduly delay or otherwise prejudice the rights of the parties, including their potential liability for expenses.

(7) In granting leave the sheriff may impose such terms and conditions as he considers desirable in the interests of justice, including making provision in respect of any additional expenses incurred by the parties as a result of the intervention.

(8) The sheriff clerk shall give written intimation of a grant or refusal of leave to the CEHR and all the parties.

Form of intervention

14A.4.—(1) An intervention shall be by way of a written submission which (including any appendices) shall not exceed 5000 words.

(2) The CEHR shall lodge the submission and send a copy of it to all the parties by such time as the sheriff may direct.

(3) The sheriff may in exceptional circumstances-

(a) allow a longer written submission to be made;

(b) direct that an oral submission is to be made.

(4) Any diet in pursuance of paragraph (3)(b) shall be fixed by the sheriff clerk who shall give written intimation of the diet to the CEHR and all the parties.

Chapter 14B[1]

Interventions by the Scottish Commission for Human Rights

Interpretation

14B.1. In this Chapter—

"the Act of 2006" means the Scottish Commission for Human Rights Act 2006; and

"the SCHR" means the Scottish Commission for Human Rights.

Applications to intervene

14B.2.—(1) An application for leave to intervene shall be by way of minute of intervention in Form 23B and the SCHR shall—

(a) send a copy of it to all the parties; and

(b) lodge it in process, certifying that subparagraph (a) has been complied with.

(2) In granting leave the sheriff may impose such terms and conditions as he considers desirable in the interests of justice, including making provision in respect of any additional expenses incurred by the parties as a result of the intervention.

(3) The sheriff clerk shall give written intimation of a grant or refusal of leave to the SCHR and all the parties.

(4) Any decision of the sheriff in proceedings under this Chapter shall be final and not subject to appeal.

Invitations to intervene

14B.3.—(1) An invitation to intervene under section 14(2)(b) of the Act of 2006 shall be in Form 23C and the sheriff clerk shall send a copy of it to the SCHR and all the parties.

---

[1] As inserted by the Act of Sederunt (Sheriff Court Rules) (Miscellaneous Amendments) 2008 (SSI 2008/223) r.6(2) (effective July 1, 2008).

(2)   An invitation under paragraph (1) shall be accompanied by—

  (a)   a copy of the pleadings in the proceedings; and

  (b)   such other documents relating to those proceedings as the sheriff thinks relevant.

(3)   In issuing an invitation under section 14(2)(b) of the Act of 2006, the sheriff may impose such terms and conditions as he considers desirable in the interests of justice, including making provision in respect of any additional expenses incurred by the parties as a result of the intervention.

Form of intervention

14B.4.—(1)   An intervention shall be by way of a written submission which (including any appendices) shall not exceed 5000 words.

(2)   The SCHR shall lodge the submission and send a copy of it to all the parties by such time as the sheriff may direct.

(3)   The sheriff may in exceptional circumstances—

  (a)   allow a longer written submission to be made;

  (b)   direct that an oral submission is to be made.

(4)   Any diet in pursuance of paragraph (3)(b) shall be fixed by the sheriff clerk who shall give written intimation of the diet to the SCHR and all the parties.

Chapter 15

Application for sist of party and transference

Application for sist of party and transference

15.1.—(1)   If a party dies or becomes legally incapacitated while an action is depending, any person claiming to represent that party or his estate may apply by incidental application to be sisted as a party to the action.

(2)   If a party dies or becomes legally incapacitated while an action is depending and the provisions of paragraph (1) are not invoked, any other party may apply by incidental application to have the action transferred in favour of or against, as the case may be, any person who represents that party or his estate.

Chapter 16

Transfer and remit of actions

Transfer to another court

16.1.—(1)   The sheriff may transfer an action to any other sheriff court, whether in the same sheriffdom or not, if the sheriff considers it expedient to do so.

(2)   If the sheriff is satisfied that the court has no jurisdiction, he may transfer the action to any sheriff court in which it appears to the sheriff that it ought to have been brought.

(3)   An action so transferred shall proceed in all respects as if it had been brought originally in the court to which it is transferred.

Remit from summary cause to ordinary cause

16.2.—[1](1)   If the sheriff makes a direction that an action is to be treated as an ordinary cause, the sheriff must, at the time of making that direction—

  (a)   direct the pursuer to lodge an initial writ and intimate it to every other party, within 14 days of the date of this direction;

---

[1] As substituted by the Act of Sederunt (Rules of the Court of Session 1994 and Sheriff Court Rules Amendment) (No. 2) (Personal Injury and Remits) 2015 (SSI 2015/227) r.9 (effective September 22, 2015).

(b) direct the defender to lodge defences within 28 days of the date of the direction; and

(c) fix a date and time for an Options Hearing and that date is to be the first suitable court day occurring not sooner than ten weeks, or such lesser period as the sheriff considers appropriate, after the last date for lodging the initial writ.

(2) Where a direction is made under paragraph (1) in relation to a personal injuries action within the meaning of Chapter 34 (action of damages for, or arising from, personal injuries)—

(a) the action is to proceed as a personal injuries action within the meaning of Part A1 of Chapter 36 of the Ordinary Cause Rules 1993 in Schedule 1 to the 1907 Act and in particular—

(i) the initial writ is to be lodged in the form specified by rule 36.B1 (form of initial writ);

(ii) the defences are to be lodged in accordance with rule 9.6 (defences) as modified by rule 36.E1(5) (no note of pleas-in-law);

(b) paragraph (1)(c) does not apply.

Remit from summary cause to all-Scotland sheriff court

16.2A.—[1](1) This rule applies where a party applies for an action to be treated as an ordinary cause and transferred to the all-Scotland sheriff court.

(2) Where the sheriff—

(a) directs that the action is to be treated as an ordinary cause; and

(b) certifies that the importance or difficulty of the proceedings makes it appropriate to transfer the action to the all-Scotland sheriff court,

the sheriff must make an order transferring the action to that court.

(3) In this rule—

(a) "all-Scotland sheriff court" means the sheriff court specified in the All-Scotland Sheriff Court (Sheriff Personal Injury Court) Order 2015(a) so far as the court is constituted by a sheriff sitting in the exercise of the sheriff's all-Scotland jurisdiction for the purpose of dealing with civil proceedings of a type specified in that Order;

(b) the reference to a sheriff's all-Scotland jurisdiction is to be construed in accordance with section 42(3) of the Courts Reform (Scotland) Act 2014.

Remits from ordinary cause to summary cause

16.2B.[2,3] If the sheriff directs that an ordinary cause or small claim is to be treated as an action under these Rules—

(a) the initial writ is to be deemed to be a summary cause summons;

(b) the sheriff must specify the next step of procedure to be followed in the action.

---

[1] As inserted by the Act of Sederunt (Rules of the Court of Session 1994 and Sheriff Court Rules Amendment) (No. 2) (Personal Injury and Remits) 2015 (SSI 2015/227) r.9 (effective September 22, 2015).

[2] As inserted by the Act of Sederunt (Rules of the Court of Session 1994 and Sheriff Court Rules Amendment) (No. 2) (Personal Injury and Remits) 2015 (SSI 2015/227) r.9 (effective September 22, 2015).

[3] As amended by the Act of Sederunt (Rules of the Court of Session 1994 and Sheriff Court Rules Amendment) (No.4) (Simple Procedure) 2016 (SSI 2016/315) para.4 (effective 28 November 2016).

Remit from Court of Session

16.3.[1] On receipt of the process in an action which has been remitted from the Court of Session under section 93 of the Courts Reform (Scotland) Act 2014 (remit of cases from the Court of Session), the sheriff clerk must—

(a) record the date of receipt in the Register of Summary Causes;

(b) fix a hearing to determine further procedure on the first court day occurring not earlier than 14 days after the date of receipt of the process; and

(c) forthwith send written notice of the date of the hearing fixed under paragraph (b) to each party.

Chapter 17

Productions and documents

Lodging of productions

17.1.—(1) A party who intends to rely at a proof upon any documents or articles in his possession, which are reasonably capable of being lodged with the court, must—

(a) lodge them with the sheriff clerk together with a list detailing the items no later than 14 days before the proof; and

(b) at the same time send a copy of the list to the other party.

(2) The documents referred to in paragraph (1) include any affidavit or other written statement admissible under section 2 (1) of the Civil Evidence (Scotland) Act 1988.

(3) A party lodging a document under this rule must send a copy of it to every other party, unless it is not practicable to do so.

(4) Subject to paragraph (5), only documents or articles produced—

(a) in accordance with paragraph (1) (and, if it was a document to which rule 8.5 (1) applies, was on the list lodged in accordance with that rule);

(b) at a hearing under rule 8.2; or

(c) under rule 18.2 (2) or (3), may be used or put in evidence.

(5) Documents other than those mentioned in paragraph (4) may be used or put in evidence only with the—

(a) consent of the parties; or

(b) permission of the sheriff on cause shown, and on such terms as to expenses or otherwise as to him seem proper.

Copy productions

17.2.—(1) A copy of every production, marked with the appropriate number of process of the principal production, must be lodged for the use of the sheriff at a proof not later than 48 hours before the diet of proof.

(2) Each copy production consisting of more than one sheet must be securely fastened together by the party lodging it.

Borrowing of productions

17.3.—(1) Any productions borrowed must be returned not later than noon on the day preceding the date of the proof.

(2) A receipt for any production borrowed must be entered in the list of productions and that list must be retained by the sheriff clerk.

(3) Subject to paragraph (4), productions may be borrowed only by—

---

[1] As amended by the Act of Sederunt (Rules of the Court of Session 1994 and Sheriff Court Rules Amendment) (No. 2) (Personal Injury and Remits) 2015 (SSI 2015/227) r.9 (effective September 22, 2015).

    (a)   a solicitor; or

    (b)   his authorised clerk for whom he shall be responsible.

  (4) A party litigant or an authorised lay representative may borrow a production only with permission of the sheriff and subject to such conditions as the sheriff may impose.

  (5) Productions may be inspected within the office of the sheriff clerk during normal business hours, and copies may be obtained by a party litigant, where practicable, from the sheriff clerk.

Penalty for failure to return productions

  17.4.—(1) If a solicitor has borrowed a production and fails to return it for any diet at which it is required, the sheriff may impose upon such solicitor a fine not exceeding £50.

  (2) A fine imposed under paragraph (1) shall—

    (a)   be payable to the sheriff clerk; and

    (b)   be recoverable by civil diligence.

  (3) An order imposing a fine under this rule shall not be subject to review except that the sheriff who granted it may, on cause shown, recall it.

Documents lost or destroyed

  17.5.—(1) This rule applies to any—

    (a)   summons;

    (b)   form of response;

    (c)   answers to a counterclaim;

    (d)   third party notice or answers to a third party notice;

    (d)   Register of Summary Causes; or

    (e)   other document lodged with the sheriff clerk in connection with an action.

  (2) Where any document mentioned in paragraph (1) is—

    (a)   lost; or

    (b)   destroyed,

a copy of it, authenticated in such manner as the sheriff may require, may be substituted and shall, for the purposes of the action including the use of diligence, be equivalent to the original.

Documents and productions to be retained in custody of sheriff clerk

  17.6.—(1) This rule applies to all documents or other productions which have at any time been lodged or referred to during a hearing or proof.

  (2) The sheriff clerk must retain in his custody any document or other production mentioned in paragraph (1) until—

    (a)   after the expiry of the period during which an appeal is competent; and

    (b)   any appeal lodged has been disposed of.

  (3) Each party who has lodged productions in an action shall—

    (a)   after the final determination of the claim, where no appeal has been lodged, within 14 days after the appeal period has expired; or

    (b)   within 14 days after the disposal of any appeal lodged on the final determination of the action, uplift the productions from the sheriff clerk.

  (4) Where any production has not been uplifted as required by paragraph (3), the sheriff clerk shall intimate to—

    (a)   the solicitor who lodged the production; or

    (b)   where no solicitor is acting, the party himself or such other party as seems appropriate, that if he fails to uplift the production within 28 days after the date of such intimation, it will be disposed of in such manner as the sheriff directs.

Chapter 18

Recovery of evidence and attendance of witnesses

Diligence for recovery of documents

18.1.—(1) At any time after a summons has been served, a party may make an incidental application in writing to the sheriff to grant commission and diligence to recover documents.

(2) A party who makes an application in accordance with paragraph (1) must list in the application the documents which he wishes to recover.

(3) A copy of the incidental application made under paragraph (1) must be intimated by the applicant to—

(a) every other party; and

(b) where necessary, the Advocate General for Scotland or the Lord Advocate (and if there is any doubt, both).

(4) The Advocate General for Scotland and the Lord Advocate may appear at the hearing of any incidental application under paragraph (1).

(5) The sheriff may grant commission and diligence to recover those documents in the list mentioned in paragraph (2) which he considers relevant to the action.

Optional procedure before executing commission and diligence

18.2.—(1) Any party who has obtained a commission and diligence for the recovery of documents may, at any time before executing it, serve by first class recorded delivery post on the person from whom the documents are sought to be recovered (or on his known solicitor or solicitors) an order with certificate attached in Form 24.

(2) Documents recovered in response to an order under paragraph (1) must be sent to, and retained by, the sheriff clerk who shall, on receiving them, advise the parties that the documents are in his possession and may be examined within his office during normal business hours.

(3) If the party who served the order is not satisfied that full production has been made under the specification, or that adequate reasons for non-production have been given, he may execute the commission and diligence in normal form, notwithstanding his adoption in the first instance of the foregoing procedure by order.

(4) At the commission, the commissioner shall—

(a) administer the appropriate oath or affirmation to any clerk and any shorthand writer appointed for the commission; and

(b) administer to the haver the oath in Form 20, or where the haver elects to affirm, the affirmation in Form 21.

(5) Documents recovered under this rule may be tendered as evidence at any hearing or proof without further formality, and rules 18.4(2), (3) and (4) shall apply to such documents.

Optional procedure before executing commission and diligence – personal injuries actions

18.2A.—[1](1) This rule applies to actions to which Chapter 34 applies (action of damages for, or arising from, personal injuries) but only where each party is legally represented.

(2) Any party who has obtained a commission and diligence for the recovery of documents may, at any time before executing it, serve by first class recorded delivery post on the solicitor or solicitors of the person from whom the documents are sought to be recovered an order with certificate attached in Form 10B.

(3) Documents recovered in response to an order under paragraph (2) must be sent to, and retained by, the party who obtained the order who must, on receiving them, advise the parties that the documents are in his possession and may be examined within his office during normal business hours.

(4) If the party who served the order is not satisfied that full production has been made under the specification, or that adequate reasons for non-production have been given, he may execute the commission and diligence in normal form, notwithstanding his adoption in the first instance of the foregoing procedure by order.

(5) At the commission, the commissioner must—

(a) administer the appropriate oath or affirmation to any clerk and any shorthand writer appointed for the commission; and

(b) administer to the haver the oath in Form 20, or where the haver elects to affirm, the affirmation in Form 21.

(6) Documents recovered under this rule may be tendered as evidence at any hearing or proof without further formality, and rules 18.4(2), (3) and (4) shall apply to such documents.

Applications for orders under section 1 of the Administration of Justice (Scotland) Act 1972

18.3—(1) An application by a party for an order under section 1 of the Administration of Justice (Scotland) Act 1972, must be made by incidental application in writing.

(2) At the time of lodging an incidental application under paragraph (1), a specification of—

(a) the document or other property sought to be inspected, photographed, preserved, taken into custody, detained, produced, recovered, sampled or experimented with or upon, as the case may be; or

(b) the matter in respect of which information is sought as to the identity of a person who might be a witness or a defender, must be lodged in process.

(3) A copy of the specification lodged under paragraph (2) and the incidental application made under paragraph (1) must be intimated by the applicant to—

(a) every other party;

(b) any third party haver; and

(c) where necessary, the Advocate General for Scotland or the Lord Advocate (and if there is any doubt, both).

(4) If the sheriff grants an incidental application under paragraph (1) in whole or in part, he may order the applicant to find such caution or give such other security as he thinks fit.

(5) The Advocate General for Scotland and the Lord Advocate may appear at the hearing of any incidental application under paragraph (1).

---

[1] As inserted by the Act of Sederunt (Rules of the Court of Session, Ordinary Cause Rules and Summary Cause Rules Amendment) (Miscellaneous) 2014 (SSI 2014/152) r.4 (effective July 7, 2014).

Confidentiality

18.4—(1)[1] Confidentiality may be claimed for any evidence sought to be recovered under rule 18.2, rule 18.2A or 18.3.

(2) Where confidentiality is claimed under paragraph (1), the documents or property in respect of which confidentiality is claimed shall be enclosed in a separate, sealed packet.

(3) A sealed packet referred to in paragraph (2) shall not be opened except by authority of the sheriff obtained on the incidental application of the party who sought the commission and diligence or order.

(4) The incidental application made under paragraph (3) must be intimated by the applicant to the party or parties from whose possession the documents specified in the commission and diligence or order were obtained.

(5) Any party received intimation under paragraph (4) may appear at the hearing of the application.

Preservation and obtaining of evidence

18.5—(1) Evidence in danger of being lost may be taken to be retained until required and, if satisfied that it is desirable so to do, the sheriff may, upon the application of any party at any time, either take it himself or grant authority to a commissioner to take it.

(2) The interlocutor granting such a commission shall be sufficient authority for citing the witness to appear before the commission.

(3) The evidence of any witness who—

(a) is resident beyond the sheriffdom;

(b) although resident within the sheriffdom, resides at some place remote from the court in which the proof is to be held; or

(c) is by reason of illness, age, infirmity or other sufficient cause unable to attend the proof, may be taken in the same manner as is provided in paragraph (1).

(4) On special cause shown, evidence may be taken from any witness or haver on a ground other than one mentioned in paragraph (1) or (3).

(5) Evidence taken under paragraph (1), (3) or (4) may be taken down by—

(a) the sheriff;

(b) the commissioner; or

(c) a clerk or shorthand writer nominated by the sheriff or commissioner, and such evidence may be recorded in narrative form or by question and answer as the sheriff or commissioner shall direct and the extended notes of such evidence certified by such clerk or shorthand writer shall be the notes of such oral evidence.

(6) At the commission, the commissioner shall or where the sheriff takes evidence himself, the sheriff shall—

(a) administer the appropriate oath or affirmation to any clerk and any shorthand writer appointed for the commission; and

(b) administer to the witness the oath in Form 20, or where the witness elects to affirm, the affirmation in Form 21.

---

[1] As amended by the Act of Sederunt (Rules of the Court of Session, Ordinary Cause Rules and Summary Cause Rules Amendment) (Miscellaneous) 2014 (SSI 2014/152) r.4 (effective July 7, 2014).

Warrants for production of original documents from public records

18.6—(1) If a party seeks to obtain from the keeper of any public record production of the original of any register or deed in his custody for the purposes of an action, he must apply to the sheriff by incidental application.

(2) Intimation of an incidental application under paragraph (1) must be given to the keeper of the public record concerned at least seven days before the incidental application is lodged.

(3) In relation to a public record kept by the Keeper of the Registers of Scotland or the Keeper of the Records of Scotland—

(a) where it appears to the sheriff that it is necessary for the ends of justice that an incidental application under this rule should be granted, he must pronounce an interlocutor containing a certificate to that effect; and

(b) the party applying for production may apply by letter (enclosing a copy of the interlocutor duly certified by the sheriff clerk), addressed to the Deputy Principal Clerk of Session, for an order from the Court of Session authorising the Keeper of the Registers or the Keeper of the Records, as the case may be, to exhibit the original of any register or deed to the sheriff.

(4) The Deputy Principal Clerk of Session must submit the application sent to him under paragraph (3) to the Lord Ordinary in chambers who, if satisfied, shall grant a warrant for production or exhibition of the original register or deed sought.

(5) A certified copy of the warrant granted under paragraph (4) must be served on the keeper of the public record concerned.

(6) The expense of the production or exhibition of such an original register or deed must be met, in the first instance, by the party who applied by incidental application under paragraph (1).

Letter of request

18.7—(1)[1] Subject to paragraph (7), this rule applies to an application for a letter of request to a court or tribunal outside Scotland to obtain evidence of the kind specified in paragraph (2), being evidence obtainable within the jurisdiction of that court or tribunal, for the purpose of an action depending before the sheriff.

(2) An application to which paragraph (1) applies may be made in relation to a request—

(a) for the examination of a witness;

(b) for the inspection, photographing, preservation, custody, detention, production or recovery of, or the taking of samples of, or the carrying out of any experiment on or with, a document or other property, as the case may be;

(c) for the medical examination of any person;

(d) for the taking and testing of samples of blood from any person; or

(e) for any other order for obtaining evidence, for which an order could be obtained from the sheriff.

(3) Such an application must be made by minute in Form 25 together with a proposed letter of request in Form 25a.

(4) It shall be a condition of granting a letter of request that any solicitor for the applicant, or a party litigant, as the case may be, is to be personally liable, in the first instance, for the whole expenses which may become due and payable in respect of the letter of request to the court or tribunal obtaining the evidence and to any wit-

---

[1] As amended by the Act of Sederunt (Taking of Evidence in the European Community) 2003 (SSI 2003/601) r.5(2) (effective January 1, 2004).

ness who may be examined for the purpose; and he must consign into court such sum in respect of such expenses as the sheriff thinks fit.

(5)   Unless the court or tribunal to which a letter of request is addressed is a court or tribunal in a country or territory—

(a)   where English is an official language; or

(b)   in relation to which the sheriff clerk certifies that no translation is required, then the applicant must, before the issue of the letter of request, lodge in process a translation of that letter and any interrogatories and cross-interrogatories into the official language of that court or tribunal.

(6)[1]   The letter of request when issued, any interrogatories and cross-interrogatories and the translations (if any) must be forwarded by the sheriff clerk to the Scottish Ministers or to such person and in such manner as the sheriff may direct.

(7)[2]   This rule does not apply to any request for the taking of evidence under Council Regulation (EC) No. 1206/2001 of 28th May 2001 on cooperation between the courts of the Member States in the taking of evidence in civil or commercial matters.

Taking of evidence in the European Community

18.7A.—[3](1)   This rule applies to any request—

(a)   for the competent court of another Member State to take evidence under Article 1.1(a) of the Council Regulation; or

(b)   that the court shall take evidence directly in another Member State under Article 1.1(b) of the Council Regulation.

(2)   An application for a request under paragraph (1) shall be made by minute in Form 25B, together with the proposed request in form A or I (as the case may be) in the Annex to the Council Regulation.

(3)   In this rule, "the Council Regulation" means Council Regulation (EC) No. 1206/2001 of 28th May 2001 on cooperation between the courts of the Member States in the taking of evidence in civil or commercial matters.

Citation of witnesses

18.8.—(1)   The citation of a witness or haver must be in Form 26 and the certificate of it must be in Form 26a.

(2)   A party shall be responsible for securing the attendance of his witnesses or havers at a hearing and shall be personally liable for their expenses.

(3)   The summons or the copy served on the defender shall be sufficient warrant for the citation of witnesses and havers.

(4)   The period of notice given to witnesses or havers cited in terms of paragraph (3) must be not less than seven days.

(5)   A witness or haver shall be cited—

(a)   by registered post or the first class recorded delivery service by the solicitor for the party on whose behalf he is cited; or

(b)   by a sheriff officer—

(i)   personally;

---

[1] As substituted by the Act of Sederunt (Sheriff Court Rules) (Miscellaneous Amendments) 2011 (SSI 2011/193) r.8 (effective April 4, 2011).
[2] As inserted by the Act of Sederunt (Taking of Evidence in the European Community) 2003 (SSI 2003/601) r.5(2) (effective January 1, 2004).
[3] As inserted by the Act of Sederunt (Taking of Evidence in the European Community) 2003 (SSI 2003/601) r.5(3) (effective January 1, 2004).

    (ii)   by a citation being left with a resident at the person's dwelling place or an employee at his place of business;

    (iii) by depositing it in that person's dwelling place or place of business;

    (iv) by affixing it to the door of that person's dwelling place or place of business; or

    (v)   by registered post or the first class recorded delivery service.

(6) Where service is effected under paragraph (5) (b) (iii) or (iv), the sheriff officer shall, as soon as possible after such service, send by ordinary post to the address at which he thinks it most likely that the person may be found, a letter containing a copy of the citation.

Citation of witnesses by party litigants

18.9.—(1) Where a party to an action is a party litigant he shall—

    (a) not later than 28 days before the diet of proof apply to the sheriff by incidental application to fix caution for expenses in such sum as the sheriff considers reasonable having regard to the number of witnesses he proposes to cite and the period for which they may be required to attend court; and

    (b) before instructing a solicitor or a sheriff officer to cite a witness, find caution in the sum fixed in accordance with paragraph (1).

(2) A party litigant who does not intend to cite all the witnesses referred to in his application under paragraph 1(a), may apply by incidental application for variation of the amount of caution.

Witnesses failing to attend

18.10.—(1) A hearing must not be adjourned solely on account of the failure of a witness to appear unless the sheriff, on cause shown, so directs.

(2) A witness or haver who fails without reasonable excuse to answer a citation after having been properly cited and offered his travelling expenses if he has asked for them may be ordered by the sheriff to pay a penalty not exceeding £250.

(3) The sheriff may grant decree for payment of a penalty imposed under paragraph (2) above in favour of the party on whose behalf the witness or haver was cited.

(4) The sheriff may grant warrant for the apprehension of the witness or haver and for bringing him to court.

(5) A warrant mentioned in paragraph (4) shall be effective in any sheriffdom without endorsation and the expenses of it may be awarded against the witness or haver.

Chapter 18A[1]

Vulnerable Witnesses (Scotland) Act 2004

Interpretation

18A.1. In this Chapter—

"child witness notice" has the meaning given in section 12(2) of the 2004 Act;
"review application" means an application for review of arrangements for vulnerable witnesses pursuant to section 13 of the 2004 Act;

---

[1] As inserted by the Act of Sederunt (Ordinary Cause, Summary Application, Summary Cause and Small Claim Rules) Amendment (Vulnerable Witnesses (Scotland) Act 2004) 2007 (SSI 2007/463) r.4(5) (effective November 1, 2007).

"vulnerable witness application" has the meaning given in section 12(6) of the 2004 Act.

Child Witness Notice

18A.2. A child witness notice lodged in accordance with section 12(2) of the 2004 Act shall be in Form 26B.

Vulnerable Witness Application

18A.3. A vulnerable witness application lodged in accordance with section 12(6) of the 2004 Act shall be in Form 26C.

Intimation

18A.4.—(1) The party lodging a child witness notice or vulnerable witness application shall intimate a copy of the child witness notice or vulnerable witness application to all the other parties to the proceedings and complete a certificate of intimation.

(2) A certificate of intimation referred to in paragraph (1) shall be in Form 26D and shall be lodged with the child witness notice or vulnerable witness application.

Procedure on lodging child witness notice or vulnerable witness application

18A.5.—(1) On receipt of a child witness notice or vulnerable witness application, the sheriff may—

   (a)   make an order under section 12(1) or (6) of the 2004 Act without holding a hearing;
   (b)   require further information from any of the parties before making any further order;
   (c)   fix a date for a hearing of the child witness notice or vulnerable witness application.

(2) The sheriff may, subject to any statutory time limits, make an order altering the date of the proof or other hearing at which the child or vulnerable witness is to give evidence and make such provision for intimation of such alteration to all parties concerned as he deems appropriate.

(3) An order fixing a hearing for a child witness notice or vulnerable witness application shall be intimated by the sheriff clerk—

   (a)   on the day the order is made; and
   (b)   in such manner as may be prescribed by the sheriff,

to all parties to the proceedings and such other persons as are named in the order where such parties or persons are not present at the time the order is made.

Review of arrangements for vulnerable witnesses

18A.6.—(1) A review application shall be in Form 26E.

(2) Where the review application is made orally, the sheriff may dispense with the requirements of paragraph (1).

Intimation of review application

18A.7.—(1) Where a review application is lodged, the applicant shall intimate a copy of the review application to all other parties to the proceedings and complete a certificate of intimation.

(2) A certificate of intimation referred to in paragraph (1) shall be in Form 26F and shall be lodged together with the review application.

Procedure on lodging a review application

18A.8.—(1) On receipt of a review application, the sheriff may—

   (a)   if he is satisfied that he may properly do so, make an order under section

13(2) of the 2004 Act without holding a hearing or, if he is not so satisfied, make such an order after giving the parties an opportunity to be heard;

(b)   require of any of the parties further information before making any further order;

(c)   fix a date for a hearing of the review application.

(2) The sheriff may, subject to any statutory time limits, make an order altering the date of the proof or other hearing at which the child or vulnerable witness is to give evidence and such provision for intimation of such alteration to all parties concerned as he deems appropriate.

(3) An order fixing a hearing for a review application shall be intimated by the sheriff clerk—

(a)   on the day the order is made; and

(b)   in such manner as may be prescribed by the sheriff,

to all parties to the proceedings and such other persons as are named in the order where such parties or persons are not present at the time the order is made.

Determination of special measures

18A.9. When making an order under section 12(1) or (6) or 13(2) of the 2004 Act the sheriff may, in light thereof, make such further orders as he deems appropriate in all the circumstances.

Intimation of an order under section 12(1) or (6) or 13(2)

18A.10. An order under section 12(1) or (6) or 13(2) of the 2004 Act shall be intimated by the sheriff clerk—

(a)   on the day the order is made; and

(b)   in such manner as may be prescribed by the sheriff,

to all parties to the proceedings and such other persons as are named in the order where such parties or persons are not present at the time the order is made.

Taking of evidence by commissioner

18A.11.—(1) An interlocutor authorising the special measure of taking evidence by a commissioner shall be sufficient authority for the citing the witness to appear before the commissioner.

(2) At the commission the commissioner shall—

(a)   administer the oath de fideli administratione to any clerk appointed for the commission; and

(b)   administer to the witness the oath in Form 20, or where the witness elects to affirm, the affirmation in Form 21.

(3) The commission shall proceed without interrogatories unless, on cause shown, the sheriff otherwise directs.

Commission on interrogatories

18A.12.—(1) Where interrogatories have not been dispensed with, the party citing or intending to cite the vulnerable witness shall lodge draft interrogatories in process.

(2) Any other party may lodge cross-interrogatories.

(3) The interrogatories and cross-interrogatories, when adjusted, shall be extended and returned to the sheriff clerk for approval and the settlement of any dispute as to their contents by the sheriff.

(4) The party who cited the vulnerable witness shall—

(a)   provide the commissioner with a copy of the pleadings (including any adjustments and amendments), the approved interrogatories and any cross-interrogatories and a certified copy of the interlocutor of his appointment;

   (b)   instruct the clerk; and

   (c)   be responsible in the first instance for the fee of the commissioner and his clerk.

(5) The commissioner shall, in consultation with the parties, fix a diet for the execution of the commission to examine the witness.

Commission without interrogatories

18A.13. Where interrogatories have been dispensed with, the party citing or intending to cite the vulnerable witness shall—

   (a)   provide the commissioner with a copy of the pleadings (including any adjustments and amendments) and a certified copy of the interlocutor of his appointment;

   (b)   fix a diet for the execution of the commission in consultation with the commissioner and every other party;

   (c)   instruct the clerk; and

   (d)   be responsible in the first instance for the fees of the commissioner and his clerk.

Lodging of video record and documents

18A.14.—(1) Where evidence is taken on commission pursuant to an order made under section 12(1) or (6) or 13(2) of the 2004 Act the commissioner shall lodge the video record of the commission and relevant documents with the sheriff clerk.

(2) On the video record and any documents being lodged the sheriff clerk shall—

   (a)   note—

       (i)   the documents lodged;

      (ii)   by whom they were lodged; and

     (iii)   the date on which they were lodged, and

   (b)   intimate what he has noted to all parties concerned.

Custody of video record and documents

18A.15.—(1) The video record and documents referred to in rule 18A.14 shall, subject to paragraph (2), be kept in the custody of the sheriff clerk.

(2) Where the video record of the evidence of a witness is in the custody of the sheriff clerk under this rule and where intimation has been given to that effect under rule 18A.14(2), the name and address of that witness and the record of his evidence shall be treated as being in the knowledge of the parties; and no party shall be required, notwithstanding any enactment to the contrary—

   (a)   to include the name of that witness in any list of witnesses; or

   (b)   to include the record of his evidence in any list of productions.

Application for leave for party to be present at the commission

18A.16. An application for leave for a party to be present in the room where the commission proceedings are taking place shall be by incidental application..

(2) In rule 37.1(2) (live links) at the end of the definition of "witness" there shall be inserted the following—

    ", except a vulnerable witness within the meaning of section 11(1) of the 2004 Act.".

(3) In Appendix 1—

   (a)   for Form 26 there shall be substituted the form in Part 1 of Schedule 2 to this Act of Sederunt; and

(b) after Form 26A there shall be inserted the forms set out in Part 2 of Schedule 2 to this Act of Sederunt.

Chapter 19

Challenge of documents

Challenge of documents

19.1.—(1) If a party relies on a deed or other document to support his case, any other party may object to the deed or document without having to bring an action of reduction.

(2) If an objection is made, the sheriff may order the objector, if an action of reduction would otherwise have been competent, to find caution or to consign with the sheriff clerk a sum of money as security.

Chapter 20

European Court

Interpretation of rules 20.2 to 20.5

20.1.—(1) In rules 20.2 to 20.5—

"the European Court" means the Court of Justice of the European Communities;

"reference" means a reference to the European Court for—

(a) a preliminary ruling under Article 234 of the E.E.C. Treaty, Article 150 of the Euratom Treaty or Article 41 of the E.C.S.C. Treaty; or

(b) a ruling on the interpretation of the Conventions, as defined in section 1(1) of the Civil Jurisdiction and Judgments Act 1982, under Article 3 of Schedule 2 to that Act.

(2) The expressions "E.E.C. Treaty", "Euratom Treaty" and "E.C.S.C. Treaty" have the meanings assigned respectively in Schedule 1 to the European Communities Act 1972.

Application for reference

20.2.—(1) The sheriff may, on the application of a party or of his own accord make a reference.

(2) A reference must be made in the form of a request for a preliminary ruling of the European Court in Form 27.

Preparation of case for reference

20.3.—(1) If the sheriff decides that a reference shall be made, he must within four weeks draft a reference.

(2) On the reference being drafted, the sheriff clerk must send a copy to each party.

(3) Within four weeks after the date on which copies of the draft have been sent to parties, each party may—

(a) lodge with the sheriff clerk; and

(b) send to every other party, a note of any adjustments he seeks to have made in the draft reference.

(4) Within 14 days after the date on which any such note of adjustments may be lodged, the sheriff, after considering any such adjustments, must make and sign the reference.

(5) The sheriff clerk must forthwith intimate the making of the reference to each party.

Sist of action

20.4.—(1) Subject to paragraph (2), on a reference being made, the action must, unless the sheriff when making the reference otherwise orders, be sisted until the European Court has given a preliminary ruling on the question referred to it.

(2) The sheriff may recall a sist made under paragraph (1) for the purpose of making an interim order which a due regard to the interests of the parties may require.

Transmission of reference

20.5. A copy of the reference, certified by the sheriff clerk, must be transmitted by the sheriff clerk to the Registrar of the European Court.

Chapter 21

Abandonment

Abandonment of action

21.1.—(1) A pursuer may before an order granting absolvitor or dismissing the action has been pronounced, offer to abandon the action.

(2) Where the pursuer offers to abandon the action in accordance with paragraph (1), the sheriff clerk shall, subject to the approval of the sheriff, fix the amount of the defender's expenses to be paid by the pursuer in accordance with rule 23.3 and the action must be continued to the first appropriate court occurring not sooner than 14 days after the amount has been fixed.

(3) If before the continued diet the pursuer makes payment to the defender of the amount fixed under paragraph (2), the sheriff must dismiss the action unless the pursuer consents to absolvitor.

(4) If before the continued diet the pursuer fails to pay the amount fixed under paragraph (2), the defender shall be entitled to decree of absolvitor with expenses.

Chapter 22

Decree by default

Decree by default

22.1.—(1) If, after a proof has been fixed under rule 8.3(3)(d), a party fails to appear at a hearing where required to do so, the sheriff may grant decree by default.

(2) If all parties fail to appear at a hearing or proof where required to do so, the sheriff must, unless sufficient reason appears to the contrary, dismiss the action and any counterclaim.

(3) If, after a proof has been fixed under rule 8.3(3)(d), a party fails to implement an order of the court, the sheriff may, after giving him an opportunity to be heard, grant decree by default.

(4) The sheriff shall not grant decree by default solely on the ground that a party has failed to appear at the hearing of an incidental application.

Chapter 22A[1]

Dismissal of Action due to Delay

Dismissal of action due to delay

22A.1.—(1) Any party to an action may, while that action is depending before the court, apply by written incidental application to the court to dismiss the action due to inordinate and inexcusable delay by another party or another party's agent in progressing the action, resulting in unfairness.

---

[1] As inserted by the Act of Sederunt (Sheriff Court Rules) (Miscellaneous Amendments) 2009 (SSI 2009/294) r.15 (effective October 1, 2009).

(2)[1] An application under paragraph (1) shall include a statement of the grounds on which it is proposed that the application should be allowed.

(3) In determining an application made under this rule, the court may dismiss the action if it appears to the court that—

(a) there has been an inordinate and inexcusable delay on the part of any party or any party's agent in progressing the action; and

(b) such delay results in unfairness specific to the factual circumstances, including the procedural circumstances, of that action.

(4) In determining whether or not to dismiss an action under paragraph (3), the court shall take account of the procedural consequences, both for the parties and for the work of the court, of allowing the action to proceed.

(5) Rule 9.1 shall, with the necessary modifications, apply to an application under paragraph (1).

Chapter 23

Decrees, extracts, execution and variation

Decree

23.1. The sheriff must not grant decree against—

(a) a defender or a third party in respect of a claim; or

(b) a pursuer in respect of a counterclaim, under any provision of these Rules unless satisfied that a ground of jurisdiction exists.

Final decree

23.2.[2, 3] The final decree of the sheriff shall be granted, where expenses are awarded, only after expenses have been dealt with in accordance with rules 23.3, 23.3A and 23.3B.

Expenses

23.3.—[4, 5, 6](1)[7] Subject to rule 23.3A and paragraphs (2) to (4), the sheriff clerk must, with the approval of the sheriff, assess the amount of expenses including the fees and outlays of witnesses awarded in any cause, in accordance with the applicable statutory table of fees.

(2) A party litigant, who is not represented by a solicitor or advocate and who would have been entitled to expenses if he had been so represented, may be awarded any outlays or expenses to which he might be found entitled by virtue of the 1975 Act or any enactment under that Act.

---

[1] As amended by the Act of Sederunt (Sheriff Court Rules) (Miscellaneous Amendments) 2010 (SSI 2010/279) r.7 (effective July 29, 2010).

[2] As substituted by the Act of Sederunt (Summary Cause Rules) (Amendment) 2002 (SSI 2002/516) r.2(2) (effective January 1, 2003).

[3] As amended by the Act of Sederunt (Rules of the Court of Session, Sheriff Appeal Court Rules and Sheriff Court Rules Amendment) (Sheriff Appeal Court) 2015 (SSI 2015/419) r.11 (effective 1 January 2016; as to savings see SSI 2015/419 rule 20(6)(a)).

[4] As amended by the Act of Sederunt (Summary Cause Rules) (Amendment) 2002 (SSI 2002/516) r.2(3) (effective January 1, 2003).

[5] As amended by the Act of Sederunt (Ordinary Cause, Summary Application, Summary Cause and Small Claim Rules) Amendment (Miscellaneous) 2007 (SSI 2007/6) r.4(4) (effective January 29, 2007).

[6] As amended by the Act of Sederunt (Rules of the Court of Session, Sheriff Appeal Court Rules and Sheriff Court Rules Amendment) (Sheriff Appeal Court) 2015 (SSI 2015/419) r.11 (effective 1 January 2016; as to savings see SSI 2015/419 rule 20(6)(a)).

[7] As amended by the Act of Sederunt (Sheriff Court Rules Amendment) (Sections 25 to 29 of the Law Reform (Miscellaneous Provisions) (Scotland) Act 1990) 2009 (SSI 2009/164) r.4(3) (effective May 20, 2009).

(3)   A party who is or has been represented by an authorised lay representative or a person authorised under any enactment to conduct proceedings in the sheriff court and who would have been found entitled to expenses if he had been represented by a solicitor or an advocate may be awarded any outlays or expenses to which a party litigant might be found entitled in accordance with paragraph (2).

(4)   A party who is not an individual, and—

      (i)   is or has been represented by an authorised lay representative or a person authorised under any enactment to conduct proceedings in the sheriff court;

      (ii)   if unrepresented, could not represent itself; and

      (iii)   would have been found entitled to expenses if it had been represented by a solicitor or an advocate,

may be awarded any outlays to which a party litigant might be found entitled under the 1975 Act or any enactment made under that Act.

(5)   Except where an account of expenses is allowed to be taxed under rule 23.3A, in every case including an appeal where expenses are awarded, the sheriff clerk shall hear the parties or their solicitors on the claims for expenses including fees, if any, and outlays.

(6)   Except where the sheriff has reserved judgment or where he orders otherwise, the hearing on the claim for expenses must take place immediately upon the decision being pronounced.

(7)   When that hearing is not held immediately, the sheriff clerk must—

    (a)   fix the date, time and place when he shall hear the parties or their solicitors; and

    (b)   give all parties at least 14 days' notice in writing of the hearing so fixed.

(8)   The party awarded expenses must—

    (a)   lodge his account of expenses in court at least seven days prior to the date of any hearing fixed under paragraph (7); and

    (b)   at the same time forward a copy of that account to every other party.

(9)   The sheriff clerk must—

    (a)   fix the amount of the expenses; and

    (b)   report his decision to the sheriff in open court for his approval at a diet which the sheriff clerk has intimated to the parties.

(10)   The sheriff, after hearing parties or their solicitors if objections are stated, must pronounce final decree including decree for payment of expenses as approved by him.

(11)   *[Revoked by the Act of Sederunt (Rules of the Court of Session, Sheriff Appeal Court Rules and Sheriff Court Rules Amendment) (Sheriff Appeal Court) 2015 (SSI 2015/419) r.11 (effective 1 January 2016; as to savings see SSI 2015/419 rule 20(6)(a)).]*

(12)   Failure by—

    (a)   any party to comply with any of the foregoing provisions of this rule; or

    (b)   the successful party or parties to appear at the hearing on expenses, must be reported by the sheriff clerk to the sheriff at a diet which the sheriff clerk has intimated to the parties.

(13)   In either of the circumstances mentioned in paragraphs (12)(a) or (b), the sheriff must, unless sufficient cause be shown, pronounce decree on the merits of the action and find no expenses due to or by any party.

(14)   A decree pronounced under paragraph (13) shall be held to be the final decree for the purposes of these Rules.

(15) The sheriff may, if he thinks fit, on the application of the solicitor of any party to whom expenses may be awarded, made at or before the time of the final decree being pronounced, grant decree in favour of that solicitor for the expenses of the action.

Taxation

23.3A.—(1)[1] Either—

(a) the sheriff, on his own motion or on the motion of any party; or

(b) the sheriff clerk on cause shown,

may allow an account of expenses to be taxed by the auditor of court instead of being assessed by the sheriff clerk under rule 23.3.

(2) Where an account of expenses is lodged for taxation, the account and process shall be transmitted by the sheriff clerk to the auditor of court.

(3) The auditor of court shall—

(a) assign a diet of taxation not earlier than 7 days from the date he receives the account from the sheriff clerk; and

(b) intimate that diet forthwith from to the party who lodged the account.

(4) The party who lodged the account of expenses shall, on receiving intimation from the auditor of court under paragraph (3)—

(a) send a copy of the account; and

(b) intimate the date, time and place of the diet of taxation, to every other party.

(5) After the account has been taxed, the auditor of court shall transmit the process with the account and his report to the sheriff clerk.

(6) Where the auditor of court has reserved consideration of the account at the date of the taxation, he shall intimate his decision to the parties who attended the taxation.

(7) Where no objections are lodged under rule 23.3B (objections to auditor's report), the sheriff may grant decree for the expenses as taxed.

23.3B.— Objections to auditor's report

(1)[2] A party may lodge a note of objections to an account as taxed only where he attended the diet of taxation.

(2) Such a note shall be lodged within 7 days after—

(a) the diet of taxation; or

(b) where the auditor of court reserved consideration of the account under paragraph (6) of rule 23.3A, the date on which the auditor of court intimates his decision under that paragraph.

(3) The sheriff shall dispose of the objection in a summary manner, with or without answers.

Correction of interlocutor or note

23.4. At any time before extract, the sheriff may correct any clerical or incidental error in an interlocutor or note attached to it.

Taxes on funds under control of the court

23.5.—(1) Subject to paragraph (2), in an action in which money has been consigned into court under the Sheriff Court Consignations (Scotland) Act 1893, no decree, warrant or order for payment to any person shall be granted until there has

---

[1] As inserted by the Act of Sederunt (Summary Cause Rules) (Amendment) 2002 (SSI 2002/516) r.2(4) (effective January 1, 2003).

[2] As inserted by the Act of Sederunt (Summary Cause Rules) (Amendment) 2002 (SSI 2002/516) r.2(4) (effective January 1, 2003).

been lodged with the sheriff clerk a certificate by an authorised officer of the Inland Revenue stating that all taxes or duties payable to the Commissioners of Inland Revenue have been paid or satisfied.

(2)   In an action of multiplepoinding, it shall not be necessary for the grant of a decree, warrant or order for payment under paragraph (1) that all of the taxes or duties payable on the estate of a deceased claimant have been paid or satisfied.

Extract of decree

23.6.—(1)   Extract of a decree signed by the sheriff clerk may be issued only after the lapse of 14 days from the granting of the decree unless the sheriff on application orders earlier extract.

(2)   In an action (other than an action to which rule 30.2 applies) where an appeal has been lodged, the extract may not be issued until the appeal has been disposed of.

(3)   The extract decree—

    (a)   may be written on the summons or on a separate paper;

    (b)   may be in one of Forms 28 to 28k; and

    (c)   shall be warrant for all lawful execution.

Charge

23.7.—(1)   The period for payment specified in any charge following on a decree for payment granted in an action shall be—

    (a)   14 days if the person on whom it is served is within the United Kingdom; and

    (b)   28 days if he is outside the United Kingdom or his whereabouts are unknown.

(2)   The period in respect of any other form of charge on a decree in an action shall be 14 days.

Service of charge where address of defender is unknown

23.8.—(1)   If the address of a defender is not known to the pursuer, a charge shall be deemed to have been served on the defender if it is—

    (a)   served on the sheriff clerk of the sheriff court district where the defender's last known address is located; and

    (b)   displayed by the sheriff clerk on the walls of court for the period of the charge.

(2)   On receipt of such a charge, the sheriff clerk must display it on the walls of court and it must remain displayed for the period of the charge.

(3)   The period specified in the charge shall run from the first date on which it was displayed on the walls of court.

(4)   On the expiry of the period of charge, the sheriff clerk must endorse a certificate in Form 29 on the charge certifying that it has been displayed in accordance with this rule and must then return it to the sheriff officer by whom service was executed.

Diligence on decree in actions for delivery

23.9.—(1)   In an action for delivery, the court may, when granting decree, grant warrant to search for and take possession of goods and to open shut and lockfast places.

(2)   A warrant granted under paragraph (1) shall only apply to premises occupied by the defender.

Applications in same action for variation, etc. of decree

23.10.—(1)   If by virtue of any enactment the sheriff, without a new action being initiated, may order that—

(a) a decree granted be varied, discharged or rescinded; or

(b) the execution of that decree in so far as it has not already been executed be sisted or suspended,

the party requesting the sheriff to make such an order must do so by lodging a minute to that effect, setting out briefly the reasons for the application.

(2) On the lodging of such a minute by the pursuer, the sheriff clerk must grant warrant for service upon the defender (provided that the pursuer has returned the extract decree).

(3) On the lodging of such a minute by the defender, the sheriff clerk must grant warrant for service upon the pursuer ordaining him to return the extract decree and may, where appropriate, grant interim sist of execution of the decree.

(4) Subject to paragraph (5), the minute shall not be heard in court unless seven days' notice of the minute and warrant has been given to the other parties by the party lodging the minute.

(5) The sheriff may, on cause shown, alter the period of seven days referred to in paragraph (4) but may not reduce it to less than two days.

(6) This rule shall not apply to any proceedings under the Debtors (Scotland) Act 1987 or to proceedings which may be subject to the provisions of that Act.

Chapter 23A[1]

Qualified One-Way Costs Shifting

Application and interpretation of this Chapter

23A.1.—(1) This Chapter applies in civil proceedings, where either or both—

(a) an application for an award of expenses is made to the sheriff;

(b) such an award is made by the sheriff.

(2) Where this Chapter applies—

(a) rules 21.1(2) to (4) (abandonment of action);

(b) any common law rule entitling a pursuer to abandon an action, to the extent that it concerns expenses,

are disapplied.

(3) Where the sheriff would be entitled to make an award of expenses, and before expenses are dealt with in terms of rules 23.3 (expenses), 23.3A (taxation) and 23.3B (objections to auditor's report), the sheriff is to have regard to rules 23A.2 and 23A.3.

(4) In this Chapter—

"the Act" means the Civil Litigation (Expenses and Group Proceedings) (Scotland) Act 2018;

"the applicant" has the meaning given in rule 23A.2(1), and "applicants" is construed accordingly;

"civil proceedings" means civil proceedings to which section 8 of the Act (restriction on pursuer's liability for expenses in personal injury claims) applies.

---

[1] Inserted by Act of Sederunt (Rules of the Court of Session 1994, Sheriff Appeal Court Rules and Sheriff Court Rules Amendment) (Qualified One-Way Costs Shifting) 2021 (SSI 2021/226) (effective 30 June 2021).

Application for an award of expenses

23A.2.—(1) Where proceedings have been brought by a pursuer, another party to the action ("the applicant") may make an application to the sheriff for an award of expenses to be made against the pursuer, on one or more of the grounds specified in either or both—

(a) section 8(4)(a) to (c) of the Act;

(b) paragraph (2) of this rule.

(2) The grounds specified in this paragraph, which are exceptions to section 8(2) of the Act, are as follows—

(a) failure by the pursuer to obtain an award of damages greater than the sum offered by way of a tender lodged in process;

(b) unreasonable delay on the part of the pursuer in accepting a sum offered by way of a tender lodged in process;

(c) abandonment of the action by the pursuer in terms of rule 21.1, or at common law.

Award of expenses

23A.3.—(1) Subject to paragraph (2), the determination of an application made under rule 23A.2(1) is at the discretion of the sheriff.

(2) Where, having determined an application made under rule 23A.2(1), the sheriff makes an award of expenses against the pursuer on the ground specified in either rule 23A.2(2)(a) or (b)—

(a) the pursuer's liability is not to exceed the amount of expenses the applicant has incurred after the date of the tender;

(b) the liability of the pursuer to the applicant, or applicants, lodging the tender is to be limited to an aggregate sum, payable to all applicants (if more than one) of 75% of the amount of damages awarded to the pursuer and that sum is to be calculated without offsetting against those expenses any expenses due to the pursuer by the applicant, or applicants, before the date of the tender;

(c) the sheriff is to order that the pursuer's liability is not to exceed the sum referred to in sub-paragraph (b), notwithstanding that any sum assessed by the Sheriff Clerk, or by the Auditor of Court as payable under the tender procedure may be greater;

(d) where the award of expenses is in favour of more than one applicant the sheriff, failing agreement between the applicants, is to apportion the award of expenses recoverable under the tender procedure between them.

(3) In the event that the sheriff makes an award of expenses against the pursuer on the ground other than that specified in rule 23A.2(2)(c), the sheriff may make such orders in respect of expenses, as it considers appropriate, including—

(a) making an award of decree of dismissal dependant on payment of expenses by the pursuer within a specified period of time;

(b) provision for the consequences of failure to comply with any conditions applied by the court.

Procedure

23A.4.—(1) An application under rule 23A.2(1)—

(a) is to be made by incidental application, in writing, and Chapter 9 (incidental applications and sists) otherwise applies to incidental applications under this Chapter;

(b) may be made at any stage in the case prior to assessment of the amount of expenses to be awarded in the cause, in terms of rule 23.3, an order for an account of expenses to be taxed in terms of rule 23.3A or a finding by the sheriff that expenses in the cause are to be awarded as not due to or by any party.

(2) Where an application under rule 23A.2(1) is made, the sheriff may make such orders as the sheriff thinks fit for dealing with the application, including an order—

(a) requiring the applicant to intimate the application to any other person;
(b) requiring any party to lodge a written response;
(c) requiring the lodging of any document;
(d) fixing a hearing.

Award against legal representatives

23A.5. Section 8(2) of the Act does not prevent the sheriff from making an award of expenses against a pursuer's legal representative in terms of section 11 (awards of expenses against legal representatives) of the Act.".

Chapter 24

Recall of decree

Recall of decree

24.1.—[1](1) A party may apply for recall of a decree granted under any of the following provisions—

(a) rule 7.1; or
(b) paragraph (5), (6) or (7) of rule 8.2.

(2) The application is to be by minute in Form 30, which must be lodged with the sheriff clerk.

(3) The application must include where appropriate (and if not already lodged with the sheriff clerk), the proposed defence or the proposed answer to the counterclaim.

(4) A party may apply for recall of a decree in the same action on one occasion only.

(5) A minute for recall of a decree of dismissal must be lodged within 14 days of the date of decree.

(6) Subject to paragraphs (7) to (9), a minute for recall of any other kind of decree may be lodged at any time before the decree is fully implemented.

(7) Subject to paragraphs (8) and (9), where a charge or arrestment has been executed following the decree, the minute must be lodged within 14 days of that execution (or the first such execution where there has been more than one).

(8) Subject to paragraph (9), in the case of a party seeking recall who was served with the action under rule 5.7, the minute must be lodged—

(a) within a reasonable time of such party having knowledge of the decree against him or her; but
(b) in any event, within one year of the date of decree.

(9) Where the decree includes a decree for removing from heritable property to which section 216(1) of the Bankruptcy and Diligence etc. (Scotland) Act 2007 applies, the minute may be lodged at any time before the defender has been removed from the subjects or premises.

(10) On the lodging of a minute for recall of a decree, the sheriff clerk must fix a date, time and place for a hearing of the minute.

---

[1] As substituted by the Act of Sederunt (Sheriff Court Rules) (Miscellaneous Amendments) 2011 (SSI 2011/193) r.16 (effective April 4, 2011).

(11) Where a hearing has been fixed under paragraph (10), the party seeking recall must, not less than 7 days before the date fixed for the hearing, serve upon the other party—

(a) a copy of the minute in Form 30a; and

(b) a note of the date, time and place of the hearing.

(12) At a hearing fixed under paragraph (10), the sheriff must recall the decree so far as not implemented and the hearing must then proceed as a hearing held under rules 8.2(3) to (7) and 8.3.

(13) A minute for recall of a decree, when lodged and served in terms of this rule, will have the effect of preventing any further action being taken by the other party to enforce the decree.

(14) On receipt of the copy minute for recall of a decree, any party in possession of an extract decree must return it forthwith to the sheriff clerk.

(15) If it appears to the sheriff that there has been any failure or irregularity in service of the minute for recall of a decree, the sheriff may order re-service of the minute on such conditions as the sheriff thinks fit.

Chapter 25

Appeals

Appeals: application for stated case

25.1.—[1](1) An appeal to the Sheriff Appeal Court, other than an appeal to which rule 25.4 applies, must be in Form 31 lodged with the sheriff clerk not later than 14 days after the date of final decree—

(a) requesting a stated case; and

(b) specifying the point of law upon which the appeal is to proceed.

(2) The appellant must, at the same time as lodging Form 31, intimate a copy of it to every other party.

(3) The sheriff must, within 28 days of the lodging of Form 31, issue a draft stated case containing—

(a) findings in fact and law or, where appropriate, a narrative of the proceedings before him;

(b) appropriate questions of law; and

(c) a note stating the reasons for his decisions in law,

and the sheriff clerk must send a copy of the draft stated case to the parties.

(4) In an appeal where questions of admissibility or sufficiency of evidence have arisen, the draft stated case must contain a description of the evidence led at the proof to which these questions relate.

(5) Within 14 days of the issue of the draft stated case—

(a) a party may lodge with the sheriff clerk a note of any adjustments which he seeks to make;

(b) a respondent may state any point of law which he wishes to raise in the appeal; and

(c) the note of adjustment and, where appropriate, point of law must be intimated to every other party.

---

[1] As amended by the Act of Sederunt (Rules of the Court of Session, Sheriff Appeal Court Rules and Sheriff Court Rules Amendment) (Sheriff Appeal Court) 2015 (SSI 2015/419) r.11 (effective 1 January 2016; as to savings see SSI 2015/419 rule 20(6)(a)).

(6) The sheriff may, on the motion of a party or of his own accord, and must where he proposes to reject any proposed adjustment, allow a hearing on adjustments and may provide for such further procedure under this rule prior to the hearing of the appeal as he thinks fit.

(7) The sheriff must, within 14 days after—

(a) the latest date on which a note of adjustments has been or may be lodged; or

(b) where there has been a hearing on adjustments, that hearing, and after considering such note and any representations made to him at the hearing, state and sign the case.

(8) If the sheriff is temporarily absent from duty for any reason, the sheriff principal may extend any period specified in paragraphs (3) or (7) for such period or periods as he considers reasonable.

(9) The stated case signed by the sheriff must include questions of law, framed by him, arising from the points of law stated by the parties and such other questions of law as he may consider appropriate.

(10) After the sheriff has signed the stated case, the appeal is to proceed in accordance with Chapter 29 of the Act of Sederunt (Sheriff Appeal Court Rules) 2015.

Effect of and abandonment of appeal

25.2. *[Revoked by the Act of Sederunt (Rules of the Court of Session, Sheriff Appeal Court Rules and Sheriff Court Rules Amendment) (Sheriff Appeal Court) 2015 (SSI 2015/419) r.11 (effective 1 January 2016; as to savings see SSI 2015/419 rule 20(6)(a)).]*

Hearing of appeal

25.3. *[Revoked by the Act of Sederunt (Rules of the Court of Session, Sheriff Appeal Court Rules and Sheriff Court Rules Amendment) (Sheriff Appeal Court) 2015 (SSI 2015/419) r.11 (effective 1 January 2016; as to savings see SSI 2015/419 rule 20(6)(a)).]*

Appeal in relation to a time to pay direction

25.4.—[1](1) This rule applies to appeals to the Sheriff Appeal Court or to the Court of Session which relate solely to any application in connection with a time to pay direction.

(2) Rule 25.1 shall not apply to appeals under this rule.

(3) An application for leave to appeal against a decision in an application for a time to pay direction or any order connected therewith must—

(a) be made in Form 32 within seven days of that decision, to the sheriff who made the decision; and

(b) must specify the question of law upon which the appeal is to proceed.

(4) If leave to appeal is granted, the appeal must be lodged in Form 33 and intimated by the appellant to every other party within 14 days of the order granting leave and the sheriff must state in writing his reasons for his original decision.

(5) *[Revoked by the Act of Sederunt (Rules of the Court of Session, Sheriff Appeal Court Rules and Sheriff Court Rules Amendment) (Sheriff Appeal Court) 2015 (SSI 2015/419) r.11 (effective 1 January 2016; as to savings see SSI 2015/419 rule 20(6)(a)).]*

---

[1] As amended by the Act of Sederunt (Rules of the Court of Session, Sheriff Appeal Court Rules and Sheriff Court Rules Amendment) (Sheriff Appeal Court) 2015 (SSI 2015/419) r.11 (effective 1 January 2016; as to savings see SSI 2015/419 rule 20(6)(a)).

Sheriff to regulate interim possession

25.5—(1) Notwithstanding an appeal, the sheriff shall have power—

(a)   to regulate all matters relating to interim possession;

(b)   to make any order for the preservation of any property to which the action relates or for its sale, if perishable;

(c)   to make any order for the preservation of evidence; or

(d)   to make in his discretion any interim order which a due regard for the interests of the parties may require.

(2)   An order under paragraph (1) shall not be subject to review except by the appellate court at the hearing of the appeal.

Provisions for appeal in actions for recovery of heritable property to which rule 30.2 applies

25.6.   In an action to which rule 30.2 applies—

(a)   it shall not be competent to shorten or dispense with the period for appeal specified in rule 25.1;

(b)   it shall be competent to appeal within that period for appeal irrespective of the early issue of an extract decree; and

(c)[1]   the lodging of a Form 31 shall not operate so as to suspend diligence unless the sheriff directs otherwise.

Appeal to the Court of Session

25.7.   *[Revoked by the Act of Sederunt (Rules of the Court of Session, Sheriff Appeal Court Rules and Sheriff Court Rules Amendment) (Sheriff Appeal Court) 2015 (SSI 2015/419) r.11 (effective 1 January 2016; as to savings see SSI 2015/419 rule 20(6)(a)).]*

Chapter 26

Management of damages payable to persons under legal disability

Orders for payment and management of money

26.1.—(1)   In an action of damages in which a sum of money becomes payable, by virtue of a decree or an extra-judicial settlement, to or for the benefit of a person under legal disability (other than a person under the age of 18 years), the sheriff shall make such order regarding the payment and management of that sum for the benefit of that person as he thinks fit.

(2)   Any order required under paragraph (1) shall be made on the granting of decree for payment or of absolvitor.

Methods of management

26.2.   In making an order under rule 26.1(1), the sheriff may—

(a)   order the money to be paid to—

(i)   the Accountant of Court; or

(ii)   the guardian of the person under legal disability, as trustee, to be applied, invested or otherwise dealt with and administered under the directions of the sheriff for the benefit of the person under legal disability;

(b)   order the money to be paid to the sheriff clerk of the sheriff court district in which the person under legal disability resides, to be applied, invested

---

[1] As amended by the Act of Sederunt (Rules of the Court of Session, Sheriff Appeal Court Rules and Sheriff Court Rules Amendment) (Sheriff Appeal Court) 2015 (SSI 2015/419) r.11 (effective 1 January 2016; as to savings see SSI 2015/419 rule 20(6)(a)).

or otherwise dealt with and administered, under the directions of the sheriff of that district, for the benefit of the person under legal disability; or

(c) order the money to be paid directly to the person under legal disability.

Subsequent orders

26.3.—(1) If the sheriff has made an order under rule 26.1(1), any person having an interest may apply for an order under rule 26.2, or any other order for the payment or management of the money, by incidental application.

(2) An application for directions under rule 26.2(a) or (b) may be made by any person having an interest by incidental application.

Management of money paid to sheriff clerk

26.4.—(1) A receipt in Form 35 by the sheriff clerk shall be a sufficient discharge in respect of the amount paid to him under rules 26.1 to 26.3.

(2) The sheriff clerk shall, at the request of any competent court, accept custody of any sum of money in an action of damages ordered to be paid to, applied, invested or otherwise dealt with by him, for the benefit of a person under legal disability.

(3) Any money paid to the sheriff clerk under rules 26.1 to 26.3 must be paid out, applied, invested or otherwise dealt with by the sheriff clerk only after such intimation, service and enquiry as the sheriff may order.

(4) Any sum of money invested by the sheriff clerk under rules 26.1 to 26.3 must be invested in a manner in which trustees are authorised to invest by virtue of the Trustee Investments Act 1961.

Management of money payable to children

26.5. If the sheriff has made an order under section 13 of the Children (Scotland) Act 1995, an application by a person for an order by virtue of section 11(1)(d) of that Act must be made in writing.

Chapter 27

Action of multiplepoinding

Application of Chapter

27.1. This Chapter applies to an action of multiplepoinding.

Application of other rules

27.2.—(1) Rule 8.1 shall not apply to an action of multiplepoinding.

(2) Rules 8.2 to 8.17 shall only apply to an action of multiplepoinding in accordance with rule 27.7.

Pursuer in multiplepoinding

27.3. An action of multiplepoinding may be raised by any party holding or having an interest in or claim on the fund or subject *in medio*.

Parties

27.4. The pursuer must call as defenders—

(a) all persons so far as known to him as having an interest in the fund or subject *in medio*; and

(b) where he is not the holder of the fund or subject, the holder of that fund or subject.

Statement of fund or subject in medio

27.5.—(1) Where the pursuer is the holder of the fund or subject *in medio* he shall include a statement of the fund or subject in his statement of claim.

(2) Where the pursuer is not the holder of the fund or subject *in medio*, the holder shall, before the return day—

  (a) lodge with the sheriff clerk a statement in Form 5a providing—
    (i) a statement of the fund or subject;
    (ii) a statement of any claim or lien which he may profess to have on the fund or subject; and
    (iii)[1] a list of all persons known to him as having an interest in the fund or subject; and
  (b) intimate the statement in Form 5a to the pursuer, the defenders and all persons listed in the statement as having an interest in the fund or subject.

Response to summons

27.6.—(1) If a defender intends to—

  (a) challenge the jurisdiction of the court or the competency of the action;
  (b) object to the extent of the fund or subject *in medio*; or
  (c) make a claim on the fund, he must complete and lodge with the sheriff clerk on or before the return day the form of response contained in the defender's copy summons as appropriate, including a statement of his response which gives fair notice to the pursuer.

(2) The sheriff clerk must upon receipt intimate to the pursuer a copy of any response lodged under paragraph (1).

Procedure where response lodged

27.7. Where in a form of response a defender states a defence in accordance with rule 27.6(1)(a)—

  (a) the provisions of rules 8.2 to 8.17 shall, with the necessary modifications, apply to the resolution of the issues raised under that sub-paragraph; and
  (b) rules 27.8 to 27.10 shall apply only once those issues have been so dealt with.

Objections to fund or subject in medio

27.8.—(1) If objections to the fund or subject *in medio* have been lodged, the sheriff must, after disposal of any defence—

  (a) fix a hearing; and
  (b) state the order in which the claimants shall be heard at the hearing.

(2) If no objections to the fund or subject in medio have been lodged, or if objections have been lodged and disposed of, the sheriff may approve the fund or subject and if appropriate find the holder liable only in one single payment.

Claims hearing

27.9.—(1) This rule applies where—

  (a) no defence or objection to the extent of the fund or subject in medio has been stated;
  (b) any defence stated has been repelled; or
  (c) any such objection stated has been dealt with.

(2) The sheriff must—

  (a) order claims in Form 5b to be lodged within 14 days; and
  (b) must fix a claims hearing at which all parties may appear or be represented.

(3) The sheriff clerk must intimate to the parties, the order for claims and the date and time of any claims hearing fixed in terms of paragraph (2).

---

[1] As substituted by SSI 2003/26, r.4(3) (clerical error).

Procedure at claims hearing

27.10.—(1) If there is no competition between the claimants who appear at the claims hearing, the sheriff may order the holder of the fund or subject *in medio*, or the sheriff clerk if it is consigned with him in terms of rule 27.12, to make it over to the claimants in terms of their claims or otherwise and subject to such provisions as to expenses as he directs.

(2) If the sheriff is unable at the claims hearing to resolve competing claims, he shall pronounce an order—

    (a) fixing a date, time and place for a further hearing; and

    (b) regulating the nature and scope of the hearing and the procedure to be followed.

(3) The sheriff may require that evidence be led at the further claims hearing fixed under paragraph (2).

(4) The sheriff clerk must intimate to all claimants the date, time and place of any hearing fixed under paragraph (2).

(5) At the conclusion of the claims hearing or the further claims hearing fixed under paragraph (2), the sheriff may either pronounce his decision or reserve judgement in which case he must give his decision in writing within 28 days and the sheriff clerk must forthwith intimate it to the parties.

(6) In giving his decision under paragraph (5) the sheriff—

    (a) must dispose of the action;

    (b) may order the holder of the fund or subject *in medio*, or the sheriff clerk if it is consigned with him in terms of rule 27.12, to make it over to such claimants and in such quantity or amount as he may determine; and

    (c) must deal with all questions of expenses.

Advertisement

27.11. If it appears to the sheriff at any stage in the multiplepoinding that there may be other potential claimants who are not parties to the action, he may order such advertisement or intimation of the order for claims as he thinks proper.

Consignation and discharge of holder

27.12.—(1) At any stage in an action of multiplepoinding the sheriff may order that—

    (a) the fund or subject *in medio* be consigned in the hands of the sheriff clerk; or

    (b) any subject *in medio* be sold and the proceeds of sale consigned in the hands of the sheriff clerk.

(2) After such consignation the holder of the fund or subject may apply for his exoneration and discharge.

(3) The sheriff may allow the holder of the fund or subject, on his exoneration and discharge, his expenses out of the fund as a first charge on the fund.

Chapter 28

Action of furthcoming

Expenses included in claim

28.1. The expenses of bringing an action for furthcoming, including the expenses of the arrestment, shall be deemed to be part of the arrestor's claim which may be paid out of the arrested fund or subject.

Chapter 29

Action of count, reckoning and payment

Response to summons

29.1. If a defender wishes to admit liability to account in an action for count, reckoning and payment, this must be stated on the form of response.

Accounting hearing

29.2.—(1) This rule applies where in an action of count, reckoning and payment—

(a) no form of response has been lodged;

(b) the defender has indicated on the form of response that he admits liability to account;

or

(c) any defence stated has been repelled.

(2) Where paragraph 1(a) or (b) applies, the pursuer must lodge with the sheriff clerk a minute in Form 17 before close of business on the second day before the calling date.

(3) If the pursuer does not lodge a minute in accordance with paragraph (2), the sheriff must dismiss the action.

(4) Where the pursuer has lodged a minute in accordance with paragraph (2), or any defence stated has been repelled, the sheriff shall pronounce an order—

(a) for the lodging of accounts within 14 days and objections within such further period as the sheriff may direct;

(b) fixing a date, time and place for an accounting hearing; and

(c) regulating the nature and scope of the accounting hearing and the procedure to be followed.

(5) The sheriff may require that evidence be led at an accounting hearing fixed under paragraph (4) to prove the accounts and in support of any objection taken.

(6) The sheriff clerk must intimate to all claimants the date, time and place of any hearing fixed under paragraph (4).

Chapter 30

Recovery of possession of heritable property

Action raised under section 38 of the 1907 Act

30.1. An action for the recovery of possession of heritable property made in terms of section 38 of the 1907 Act may be raised by—

(a) a proprietor;

(b) his factor; or

(c) any other person authorised by law to pursue a process of removing.

Action against persons in possession of heritable property without right or title

30.2.—(1) Subject to paragraph (2), this rule applies only to an action for recovery of possession of heritable property against a person or persons in possession of heritable property without right or title to possess the property.

(2) This rule shall not apply with respect to a person who has or had a title or other right to occupy the heritable property and who has been in continuous occupation since that title or right is alleged to have come to an end.

(3) Where the name of a person in occupation of a heritable property is not known and cannot reasonably be ascertained, the pursuer shall call that person as a defender by naming him as an "occupier".

(4) Where the name of a person in occupation of the heritable property is not known and cannot reasonably be ascertained, the summons shall be served (whether or not it is also served on a named person), unless the sheriff otherwise directs, by an officer of the court—

  (a) affixing a copy of the summons and a citation in Form 11 addressed to "the occupiers" to the main door or other conspicuous part of the premises, and if practicable, depositing a copy of each of those documents in the premises; or

  (b) in the case of land only, inserting stakes in the ground at conspicuous parts of the occupied land to each of which is attached a sealed transparent envelope containing a copy of the summons and a citation in Form 11 addressed to "the occupiers".

(5) In an action to which this rule applies, the sheriff may in his discretion, and subject to rule 25.6, shorten or dispense with any period of time provided anywhere in these rules.

(6) An application by a party under this rule to shorten or dispense with any period may be made orally and the provisions in rule 9.1 shall not apply, but the sheriff clerk must enter details of any such application in the Register of Summary Causes.

Effect of decree

30.3. When decree for the recovery of possession is granted, it shall have the same force and effect as—

  (a) a decree of removing;
  (b) a decree of ejection;
  (c) a summary warrant of ejection;
  (d) a warrant for summary ejection in common form; or
  (e) a decree pronounced in a summary application for removing, in terms of sections 36, 37 and 38 respectively of the 1907 Act.

Preservation of defender's goods and effects

30.4.[1] When decree is pronounced, the sheriff may give such directions as he deems proper for the preservation of the defender's goods and effects.

Action of removing where fixed term of removal

30.5.—(1) Subject to section 21 of the Agricultural Holdings (Scotland) Act 1991—

  (a) if the tenant has bound himself to remove by writing, dated and signed—

---

[1] As amended by the Act of Sederunt (Ordinary Cause, Summary Application, Summary Cause and Small Claim Rules) Amendment (Miscellaneous) 2007 (SSI 2007/6) r.4(6) (effective January 29, 2007).

     (i)   within 12 months after the term of removal; or

    (ii)   where there is more than one ish, after the ish first in date to remove, an action of removing may be raised at any time; and

  (b)   if the tenant has not bound himself, an action of removing may be raised at any time, but—

     (i)   in the case of a lease of lands exceeding two acres in extent for three years and upwards, an interval of not less than one year nor more than two years must elapse between the date of notice of removal and the term of removal first in date;

    (ii)   in the case of a lease of lands exceeding two acres in extent, whether written or oral, held from year to year or under tacit relocation, or for any other period less than three years, an interval of not less than six months must elapse between the date of notice of removal and the term of removal first in date; and

   (iii)   in the case of a house let with or without land attached not exceeding two acres in extent, as also of land not exceeding two acres in extent without houses, as also of mills, fishings, shootings, and all other heritable subjects excepting land exceeding two acres in extent and let for a year or more, 40 days at least must elapse between the date of notice of removal and the term of removal first in date.

(2)   In any defended action of removing, the sheriff may order the defender to find caution for violent profits.

Form of notices and letter

   30.6.—(1) A notice under section 34, 35 or 36 of the 1907 Act must be in Form 3a.

   (2) A notice under section 37 of the 1907 Act must be in Form 3b.

   (3) A letter of removal must be in Form 3c.

Giving notice of removal

   30.7.—(1) A notice under section 34, 35, 36, 37 or 38 of the 1907 Act may be given by—

  (a)   a sheriff officer;

  (b)   the person entitled to give such notice; or

  (c)   the solicitor or factor of such person,

posting the notice by registered post or the first class recorded delivery service at any post office within the United Kingdom in time for it to be delivered at the address on the notice before the last date on which by law such notice must be given, addressed to the person entitled to receive such notice, and bearing the address of that person at the time, if known, or, if not known, to the last known address of that person.

   (2) A sheriff officer may also give notice under any section of the 1907 Act mentioned in paragraph (1) in any manner in which he may serve an initial writ; and, accordingly, rule 5.4 shall, with the necessary modifications, apply to the giving of notice under this paragraph as it applies to service of a summons.

Evidence of notice to remove

   30.8.—(1) It shall be sufficient evidence that notice has been given if—

  (a)   a certificate of the sending of notice under rule 30.7 dated and endorsed on the lease or an extract of it, or on the letter of removal, is signed by the sheriff officer or the person sending the notice, his solicitor or factor; or

(3) In the definition of "personal injuries action", "personal injuries" includes any disease or impairment, whether physical or mental.

Raising a personal injuries action

Form of summons

34.2.—(1) In a personal injuries action the form of claim to be inserted in box 4 of Form 1 (summary cause summons) shall be in Form 2 (form of claim in a summons for payment of money).

(2) The pursuer must, instead of stating the details of claim in box 7 of Form 1, attach to Form 1 a statement of claim in Form 10 (form of statement of claim in a personal injuries action), which must give the defender fair notice of the claim and include—

(a) a concise statement of the grounds of the claim in numbered paragraphs relating only to those facts necessary to establish the claim;

(b) the names of every medical practitioner from whom, and every hospital or other institution in which, the pursuer or, in an action in respect of the death of a person, the deceased, received treatment for the personal injuries.

(3) A summons may include—

(a) an application for warrants for intimation so far as permitted under these Rules; and

(b) a specification of documents containing such of the calls in Form 10b (form of order of court for recovery of documents etc.) as the pursuer considers appropriate.

Defender's copy summons

34.3.—(1) A copy summons shall be served on the defender—

(a) in Form 1e where an application for a time to pay direction under the Debtors (Scotland) Act 1987 may be applied for; or

(b) in Form 1f in every other case,

in each case, including a copy statement of claim in Form 10.

(2) A form of response in Form 10a shall accompany the defender's copy summons when it is served on the defender.

Response to summons

34.4.—(1) If a defender intends to—

(a) challenge the jurisdiction of the court or the competency of the action;

(b) defend the action (whether as regards the amount claimed or otherwise); or

(c) state a counterclaim,

the defender must complete and lodge with the sheriff clerk on or before the return day the form of response contained in the defender's copy summons and Form 1 stating, in a manner which gives the pursuer fair notice, the grounds of fact and on which the defender intends to resist the claim.

(2) A counterclaim may include—

(a) an application for warrants for intimation so far as permitted under Rules; and

(b) a specification of documents containing such of the calls in Fo the defender considers appropriate.

(3) The sheriff clerk must, upon receipt, intimate to the pursuer a response lodged under paragraph (1).

(b) an acknowledgement of the notice is endorsed on the lease or an extract of it, or on the letter of removal, by the party in possession or his agent.

(2) If there is no lease, a certificate of the sending of such notice must be endorsed on a copy of the notice or letter of removal.

30.9[1] Where, in response to a summons for the recovery of heritable property which includes a claim for payment of money, a defender makes a written application about payment, he shall not thereby be taken to be admitting the claim for recovery of possession of the heritable property.

Chapter 30A

Execution of deeds relating to heritage

Form of application under section 87 of the Courts Reform (Scotland) Act 2014

30A.1.[2] An application for an order for execution under section 87 (power of sheriff to order sheriff clerk to execute deed relating to heritage) of the Courts Reform (Scotland) Act 2014 may be made—

(a) by a claim in the summons;

(b) where no such claim has been made, by incidental application to amend the summons; or

(c) where final decree has been pronounced, by lodging a minute in the process of the action to which the application relates.

Chapter 31

Action of sequestration for rent

[Repealed by the Act of Sederunt (Sheriff Court Rules Amendment) (Diligence) 2008 (SSI 2008/121) r.2(1)(b) (effective April 1, 2008).]

Chapter 32

Action for aliment

Recall or variation of decree for aliment

32.1.—(1) Applications for the recall or variation of any decree for payment of aliment pronounced in the small debt court under the Small Debt Acts or in a summary cause under the 1971 Act must be made by summons.

(2) The sheriff may make such interim orders in relation to such applications or in relation to actions brought under section 3 of the Sheriff Courts (Civil Jurisdiction and Procedure) (Scotland) Act 1963 as he thinks fit.

(3) In paragraph (1) "the Small Debt Acts" means and includes the Small Debt (Scotland) Acts 1837 to 1889 and Acts explaining or amending the same.

Warrant and forms for intimation

32.2. In the summons in an action brought under section 3 of the Sheriff Courts (Civil Jurisdiction and Procedure) (Scotland) Act 1963, the pursuer must include an application for a warrant for intimation—

(a) in an action where the address of the defender is not known to the pursuer and cannot reasonably be ascertained, to—

---

[1] As inserted by the Act of Sederunt (Sheriff Court Rules) (Miscellaneous Amendments) 2008 (SSI 2008/223) r.8 (effective July 1, 2008).

[2] As inserted by the Act of Sederunt (Rules of the Court of Session 1994 and Sheriff Court Rules Amendment) (No. 2) (Miscellaneous) 2016 (SSI 2016/229) para.3 (effective 28 November 2016).

(i) every child of the marriage between the parties who has reached the age of 16 years; and

(ii) one of the next-of-kin of the defender who has reached that age,

unless the address of such a person is not known to the pursuer and cannot reasonably be ascertained, and a notice of intimation in Form 36 must be attached to the copy of the summons intimated to any such person; or

(b) in an action where the defender is a person who is suffering from a mental disorder, to—

(i) those persons mentioned in paragraphs (a)(i) and (ii), unless the address of such person is not known to the pursuer and cannot reasonably be ascertained; and

(ii) the guardian of, the defender, if one has been appointed, and a notice in Form 37 must be attached to the copy of the summons intimated to any such person.

Chapter 33

Child Support Act 1991

Interpretation of rules 33.2 to 33.4

33.1. In rules 33.2 to 33.4 below—

"the 1991 Act" means the Child Support Act 1991;

"child" has the meaning assigned in section 55 of the 1991 Act;

"claim relating to aliment" means a crave for decree of aliment in relation to a child or for recall or variation of such a decree; and

"maintenance calculation" has the meaning assigned in section 54 of the 1991 Act.

Statement of claim

33.2.—(1) Any summons or counterclaim which contains a claim relating to aliment and to which section 8(6), (7), (8) or (10) of the 1991 Act applies must—

(a) state, where appropriate—

(i) that a maintenance calculation under section 11 of the 1991 Act (maintenance calculations) is in force;

(ii) the date of the maintenance calculation;

(iii) the amount and frequency of periodical payments of child support maintenance fixed by the maintenance calculation; and

(iv) the grounds on which the sheriff retains jurisdiction under section 8(6), (7), (8) or (10) of the 1991 Act; and

(b) unless the sheriff on cause shown otherwise directs, be accompanied by any document issued by the Secretary of State to the party intimating the making of the maintenance calculation referred to in sub-paragraph (a).

(2) Any summons or counterclaim which contains a claim relating to aliment and to which section 8(6), (7), (8) or (10) of the 1991 Act does not apply must include a statement—

(a) that the habitual residence of the absent parent, person with care or qualifying child, within the meaning of section 3 of the 1991 Act, is outwith the United Kingdom; or

(b) that the child is not a child within the meaning of section 55 of the 1991 Act.

(3) A summons or counterclaim which involves parties in respect of whom a decision has been made in any application, review or appeal under the 1991 Act must—

(a) include in the statement of claim statements to the effect that such a decision has been made and give details of that decision; and

(b) unless the sheriff on cause shown otherwise directs, be accompanied by any document issued by the Secretary of State to the parties intimating that decision.

Effect of maintenance calculations

33.3.—(1) On receiving notification that a maintenance calculation has been made, cancelled or has ceased to have effect so as to affect an order of a kind prescribed for the purposes of section 10 of the 1991 Act, the sheriff clerk must enter in the Register of Summary Causes in respect of that order a note to that effect.

(2) The note mentioned in paragraph (1) must state that—

(a) the order ceases or ceased to have effect from the date two days after the making of the maintenance calculation; or

(b) the maintenance calculation has been cancelled or has ceased to have effect.

Effect of maintenance calculations on extracts of decrees relating to aliment

33.4—(1) Where a decree relating to aliment is affected by a maintenance calculation, any extract of that decree issued by the sheriff clerk must be endorsed with the following certificate:—

"A maintenance calculation having been made under the Child Support Act 1991 on (*insert date*), this order, in so far as it relates to the making or securing of periodical payments to or for the benefit of (*insert name(s) of child/children*), ceases to have effect from (*insert date two days after the date on which the maintenance calculation was made*).".

(2) Where a decree relating to aliment has ceased to have effect on the making of a maintenance calculation and that maintenance calculation is later cancelled or ceases to have effect, any extract of that order issued by the sheriff clerk must be endorsed also with the following certificate:—

"The jurisdiction of the child support officer under the Child Support Act 1991 having terminated on (*insert date*), this order, in so far as it relates to (*insert name(s) of child/children*), again shall have effect as of (*insert date of termination of child support officer's jurisdiction*).".

Chapter 34[1]

Action of Damages for, or Arising from, Personal Injuries

Application and interpretation

Application and interpretation of this Chapter

34.1.—(1) This Chapter applies to a personal injuries action.

(2) In this Chapter—

"personal injuries action" means an action of damages for, or arising from, personal injuries or death of a person from personal injuries;

"personal injuries procedure" means the procedure that applies to a personal injuries action as established by rules 34.7 to 34.11;

"1982 Act" means the Administration of Justice Act 1982.

---

[1] As substituted by the Act of Sederunt (Summary Cause Rules Amendment) (Personal Injuries Actions) 2012 (SSI 2012/144) para.2 (effective September 1, 2012; not applicable to an action raised before September 1, 2012).

(4)   Within 7 days of receipt of intimation under paragraph (3), the pursuer shall return to the sheriff clerk the summons and the relevant certificate of execution of service.

Inspection and recovery of documents

34.5.—(1)   This rule applies where the summons or counterclaim in a personal injuries action contains a specification of documents by virtue of rule 34.2(3)(b) or rule 34.4(2)(b).

(2)   On the summons being authenticated or counterclaim received, an order granting commission and diligence for the production and recovery of the documents mentioned in the specification shall be deemed to have been granted and the sheriff clerk shall certify Form 10b to that effect by attaching thereto a docquet in Form 10c (form of docquet etc.).

(3)   An order which is deemed to have been granted under paragraph (2) shall be treated for all purposes as an interlocutor granting commission and diligence signed by the sheriff.

(4)   The pursuer or defender in the case of a counterclaim may serve an order under paragraph (2) and the provisions of Chapter 18 (recovery of evidence and attendance of witnesses) shall thereafter apply, subject to any necessary modifications, as if the order were an order obtained on an incidental application made under rule 18.1 (diligence for recovery of documents).

(5)   Nothing in this rule shall affect the right of a party to apply under rule 18.1 for a commission and diligence for recovery of documents or under rule 18.3 for an order under section 1 of the Administration of Justice (Scotland) Act 1972 in respect of any document or other property whether or not mentioned in the specification annexed to the summons.

Personal injuries action: application of other rules

Application of other rules

34.6.—(1)   The following rules do not apply to a personal injuries action—
rule 4.1(2) (form of claim in a summons);
rule 4.2 (statement of claim);
rule 4.3 (defender's copy summons);
rule 8.1 (response to summons);
rule 8.2 (procedure in defended action);
rule 8.3 (purpose of hearing);
rule 8.5 (inspection and recovery of documents);
rule 8.6 (exchange of lists of witnesses);
rule 8.13(1) (noting of evidence, etc.).

(2)   In the application of Chapter 11 (third party procedure)—
   (a)   rule 11.1(2) (application for third party notice) shall not apply;
   (b)   in the application of rule 11.2(1) (procedure) a copy of Form 10 and any timetable already issued in terms of rule 34.7(1)(c) shall also be served on the third party; and
   (c)   where a third party lodges a form of response under rule 11.2(3), any timetable already issued under rule 34.7(1)(c) shall apply to the third party.

(3)   In respect of adjustments to the parties' respective statements made in accordance with the timetable issued under rule 34.7(1)(c), the requirement under rule 13.1 (alteration of summons etc.) to make an incidental application in respect of such adjustments shall not apply.

(4) In relation to an action proceeding in accordance with personal injuries procedure references elsewhere in these Rules to the statement of claim in the summons shall be construed as references to the statement required under rule 34.2(2) and the numbered paragraphs of that statement.

Personal injuries procedure

Allocation of diets and timetables

34.7.—(1) The sheriff clerk shall, on the lodging of the form of response in pursuance of rule 34.4(1) or, where there is more than one defender, the first lodging of a form of response—

(a) discharge the hearing assigned to take place on the calling date specified in the summons;

(b) allocate a diet for proof of the action, which shall be no earlier than 4 months (unless the sheriff on cause shown directs an earlier diet to be fixed) and no later than 9 months from the date of the first lodging of the form of response; and

(c) issue a timetable stating—

    (i) the date of the diet mentioned in subparagraph (b); and

    (ii) the dates no later than which the procedural steps mentioned in paragraph (2) are to take place.

(2) Those procedural steps are—

(a) application for a third party notice under rule 11.1;

(b) the pursuer serving a commission for recovery of documents under rule 34.5;

(c) the parties adjusting their respective statements;

(d) the pursuer lodging with the sheriff clerk a statement of valuation of claim;

(e) the pursuer lodging with the sheriff clerk a certified adjusted statement of claim;

(f) the defender (and any third party to the action) lodging with the sheriff clerk a certified adjusted response to statement of claim;

(g) the defender (and any third party to the action) lodging with the sheriff clerk a statement of valuation of claim;

(h) the parties lodging with the sheriff clerk a list of witnesses together with any productions upon which they wish to rely; and

(i) the pursuer lodging with the sheriff clerk the minute of the pre-proof conference.

(3) The dates mentioned in paragraph (1)(c)(ii) are to be calculated by reference to periods specified in Appendix 1A, which, with the exception of the period specified in rule 34.10(2), the sheriff principal may vary for his or her sheriffdom or for any court within his or her sheriffdom.

(4) A timetable issued under paragraph (1)(c) shall be in Form 10d and shall be treated for all purposes as an interlocutor signed by the sheriff; and so far as the timetable is inconsistent with any provision in these Rules which relates to a matter to which the timetable relates, the timetable shall prevail.

(5)[1] Where a party fails to comply with any requirement of a timetable other than that referred to in rule 34.10(3), the sheriff clerk may fix a date and time for the parties to be heard by the sheriff.

---

[1] As amended by the Act of Sederunt (Rules of the Court of Session, Ordinary Cause Rules and Summary Cause Rules Amendment) (Miscellaneous) 2014 (SSI 2014/152) r.4 (effective July 7, 2014).

(6)   The relevant parties must lodge with the sheriff clerk the following documents by the date specified in the timetable and intimate that fact to the other parties at the same time—

    (a)   in the case of the pursuer, a certified adjusted statement of claim; and

    (b)   in the case of the defender (and any third party to the action), a certified adjusted response to statement of claim.

(7)   The pursuer shall, on lodging the certified adjusted statement of claim required by paragraph (6)(a), apply by incidental application to the sheriff, craving the court—

    (a)   to allow parties a preliminary proof on specified matters;

    (b)   to allow a proof; or

    (c)   to make some other specified order.

(8)   The application lodged under paragraph (7) shall specify the anticipated length of the preliminary proof, or proof, as the case may be.

(9)   In the event that any party proposes to crave the court to make any order other than an order allowing a proof under paragraph (7)(b), that party shall, on making or opposing (as the case may be) the pursuer's application, specify the order to be sought and give full notice of the grounds of their application or their grounds of opposition to such application.

(10)   *[As repealed by the Act of Sederunt (Rules of the Court of Session, Ordinary Cause Rules and Summary Cause Rules Amendment) (Miscellaneous) 2014 (SSI 2014/152) r.4 (effective July 7, 2014).]*

(11)   A party who seeks to rely on the evidence of a person not on his or her list lodged in accordance with paragraph (2)(h) must, if any other party objects to such evidence being admitted, seek leave of the sheriff to admit that evidence whether it is to be given orally or not; and such leave may be granted on such conditions, if any, as the sheriff thinks fit.

(12)   The list of witnesses intimated in accordance with paragraph (2)(h) must include the name, occupation (where known) and address of each intended witness and indicate whether the witness is considered to be a vulnerable witness within the meaning of section 11(1) of the 2004 Act and whether any child witness notice or vulnerable witness application has been lodged in respect of that witness.

(13)   A production which is not lodged in accordance with paragraph (2)(h) shall not be used or put in evidence at proof unless—

    (a)   by consent of the parties; or

    (b)   with the leave of the sheriff on cause shown and on such conditions, if any, as to expenses or otherwise as the sheriff thinks fit.

(14)   In a cause which is one of a number of causes arising out of the same cause of action, the sheriff may—

    (a)   on the application of a party to that cause; and

    (b)   after hearing parties to all those causes,

appoint that cause or any part of those causes to be the leading cause and to sist the other causes pending the determination of the leading cause.

(15)   In this rule, "pursuer" includes additional pursuer or applicant as the case may be.

Applications for sist or for variation of timetable

34.8.—(1)   The action may be sisted or the timetable varied by the sheriff on the incidental application of any party to the action.

(2)   An application under paragraph (1)—

    (a)   shall be placed before the sheriff; and

(b)[1]   shall be granted only on cause shown.

(3)   Any sist of an action in terms of this rule shall be for a specific period.

(4)   Where the timetable issued under rule 34.7(1)(c) is varied under this rule, the sheriff clerk shall issue a revised timetable in Form 10d.

(5)   A revised timetable issued under paragraph (4) shall have effect as if it were a timetable issued under rule 34.7(1)(c) and any reference in this Chapter to any action being taken in accordance with the timetable shall be construed as a reference to its being taken in accordance with the timetable as varied under this rule.

Statements of valuation of claim

34.9.—(1)   Each party to the action shall make a statement of valuation of claim in Form 10e.

(2)   A statement of valuation of claim (which shall include a list of supporting documents) shall be lodged with the sheriff clerk.

(3)   Each party shall, on lodging a statement of valuation of claim—

   (a)   intimate the list of documents included in the statement of valuation of claim to every other party; and

   (b)   lodge each of those documents with the sheriff clerk.

(4)   Nothing in paragraph (3) shall affect—

   (a)   the law relating to, or the right of a party to object to, the recovery of a document on the ground of privilege or confidentiality; or

   (b)   the right of a party to apply under rule 18.1 for a commission and diligence for recovery of documents or under rule 18.3 for an order under section 1 of the Administration of Justice (Scotland) Act 1972.

(5)   Without prejudice to rule 34.11(2), where a party has failed to lodge a statement of valuation of claim in accordance with a timetable issued under rule 34.7(1)(c), the sheriff may, at any hearing under paragraph (5) of that rule—

   (a)   where the party in default is the pursuer, dismiss the action; or

   (b)   where the party in default is the defender, grant decree against the defender for an amount not exceeding the pursuer's valuation.

Pre-proof conferences

34.10.—(1)   For the purposes of this rule, a pre-proof conference is a conference of the parties, which shall be held not later than four weeks before the date assigned for the proof—

   (a)   to discuss settlement of the action; and

   (b)   to agree, so far as is possible, the matters which are not in dispute between them.

(2)   Subject to any variation of the timetable in terms of rule 34.8, a joint minute of a pre-proof conference, made in Form 10f, shall be lodged with the sheriff clerk by the pursuer not later than three weeks before the date assigned for proof.

(3)   Where a joint minute in Form 10f has not been lodged in accordance with paragraph (2) and by the date specified in the timetable the sheriff clerk must fix a date and time for the parties to be heard by the sheriff.

(4)   If a party is not present during the pre-proof conference, the representative of such party shall have access to the party or another person who has authority to commit the party in settlement of the action.

---

[1] As amended by the Act of Sederunt (Rules of the Court of Session, Ordinary Cause Rules and Summary Cause Rules Amendment) (Miscellaneous) 2014 (SSI 2014/152) r.4 (effective July 7, 2014).

Incidental hearings

34.11.—(1) Where the sheriff clerk fixes a date and time for a hearing under rules 34.7(5) or (10) or rule 34.10(3), the sheriff clerk must—

  (a) fix a date not less than seven days after the date of the notice referred to in subparagraph (b);

  (b) give notice to the parties to the action—

    (i) of the date and time of the hearing; and

    (ii) requiring the party in default to lodge with the sheriff clerk a written explanation as to why the timetable has not been complied with and to intimate a copy to all other parties not less than two clear working days before the date of the hearing.

  (2) At the hearing, the sheriff—

  (a) must consider any explanation provided by the party in default;

  (b) may award expenses against that party; and

  (c) may make any other appropriate order, including decree of dismissal.

Personal injuries action: additional provisions

Intimation to connected persons in certain actions of damages

34.12.—(1) This rule applies to an action of damages in which, following the death of any person from personal injuries, damages are claimed—

  (a) in respect of the injuries from which the deceased died; or

  (b) in respect of the death of the deceased.

  (2) In this rule "connected person" means a person, not being a party to the action, who has title to sue the defender in respect of the personal injuries from which the deceased died or in respect of his or her death.

  (3) The pursuer shall state in the summons, as the case may be—

  (a) that there are no connected persons;

  (b) that there are connected persons, being the persons specified in the application for warrant for intimation; or

  (c) that there are connected persons in respect of whom intimation should be dispensed with on the ground that—

    (i) the names or whereabouts of such persons are not known to, and cannot reasonably be ascertained by, the pursuer; or

    (ii) such persons are unlikely to be awarded more than £200 each.

  (4) Where the pursuer makes a statement in accordance with paragraph (3)(b), the summons shall include an application for warrant for intimation to any such persons.

  (5) A notice of intimation in Form 10g shall be attached to the copy of the summons, where intimation is given on a warrant under paragraph (4).

  (6) Where the pursuer makes a statement in accordance with paragraph (3)(c), the summons shall include an application for an order to dispense with intimation.

  (7) In determining an application under paragraph (6), the sheriff shall have regard to—

  (a) the desirability of avoiding a multiplicity of actions; and

  (b) the expense, inconvenience or difficulty likely to be involved in taking steps to ascertain the name or whereabouts of the connected person.

  (8) Where the sheriff is not satisfied that intimation to a connected person should be dispensed with, the sheriff may—

  (a) order intimation to a connected person whose name and whereabouts are known;

(b) order the pursuer to take such further steps as the sheriff may specify in the interlocutor to ascertain the name or whereabouts of any connected person; and

(c) order advertisement in such manner, place and at such times as the sheriff may specify in the interlocutor.

(9) Where the name or whereabouts of a person, in respect of whom the sheriff has dispensed with intimation on a ground specified in paragraph (3)(c), subsequently becomes known to the pursuer, the pursuer shall apply to the sheriff by incidental application for a warrant for intimation to such a person; and such intimation shall be made in accordance with paragraph (5).

(10) A connected person may apply by incidental application to be sisted as an additional pursuer to the action.

(11) An application under paragraph (10) shall also seek leave of the sheriff to adopt the existing grounds of action and to amend the summons and statement of claim.

(12) Where an application under paragraph (10) is granted, any timetable already issued under rule 34.7(1)(c)—

(a) shall apply to such connected person; and

(b) must be intimated to such person by the sheriff clerk.

(13) Where a connected person to whom intimation is made—

(a) does not apply to be sisted as an additional pursuer to the action;

(b) subsequently raises a separate action against the same defender in respect of the same personal injuries or death; and

(c) would, apart from this rule, be awarded the expenses or part of the expenses of that action,

such person shall not be awarded those expenses except on cause shown.

Provisional damages for personal injuries

34.13.—(1) In this rule—

"further damages" means the damages referred to in section 12(4)(b) of the 1982 Act; and

"provisional damages" means the damages referred to in section 12(4)(a) of the 1982 Act.

(2) An application for an order under section 12(2)(a) of the 1982 Act (application for provisional damages) shall be made by including in the summons a claim for provisional damages in Form 10h, and where such application is made, a concise statement as to the matters referred to in paragraphs (a) and (b) of section 12(1) of that Act must be included in the statement of claim.

(3) An application for further damages by a pursuer in respect of whom an order has been made under section 12(2)(b) of the 1982 Act (application for further damages) shall be made by lodging an incidental application with the sheriff clerk in Form 10i, which shall include—

(a) a claim for further damages;

(b) a concise statement of the facts supporting that claim;

(c) an application for warrant to serve the incidental application on—

(i) every other party; and

(ii) where such other parties are insured or otherwise indemnified, their insurer or indemnifier, if known to the pursuer; and

(d) a request for the sheriff to fix a hearing on the application.

(4) A notice of intimation in Form 10j shall be attached to every copy of the incidental application served on a warrant granted under paragraph (3)(c).

(5) At the hearing fixed under paragraph (3)(d), the sheriff may determine the application or order such further procedure as the sheriff thinks fit.

Mesothelioma actions: special provisions

34.14.—[1](1) This rule applies where liability to a relative of the pursuer may arise under section 5 of the Damages (Scotland) Act 2011 (discharge of liability to pay damages: exception for mesothelioma).

(2) On settlement of the pursuer's claim, the pursuer may apply by incidental application for all or any of the following—

(a) a sist for a specified period;

(b) discharge of any diet;

(c) where the action is one to which the personal injuries procedure applies, variation of the timetable issued under rule 34.7(1)(c).

(3) Paragraphs (4) to (7) apply where an application under paragraph (2) has been granted.

(4) As soon as reasonably practicable after the death of the pursuer, any agent who immediately prior to the death was instructed in a cause by the deceased pursuer shall notify the court of the death.

(5) The notification under paragraph (4) shall be by letter to the sheriff clerk and shall be accompanied by a certified copy of the death certificate relative to the deceased pursuer.

(6) A relative of the deceased may apply by incidental application for the recall of the sist and for an order for further procedure.

(7) On expiration of the period of any sist pronounced on an application under paragraph (2), the sheriff clerk may fix a date and time for the parties to be heard by the sheriff.

Chapter 35

Electronic transmission of documents

Extent of provision

35.1.—(1) Any document referred to in these rules which requires to be—

(a) lodged with the sheriff clerk;

(b) intimated to a party; or

(c) sent by the sheriff clerk,

may be in electronic or documentary form, and if in electronic form may be lodged, intimated or sent by e-mail or similar means.

(2) Paragraph (1) does not apply to any certificate of execution of service, citation or arrestment, or to a decree or extract decree of the court.

(3) Where any document is lodged by e-mail or similar means the sheriff may require any principal document to be lodged.

---

[1] In relation to any action raised in respect of any death occurring before July 7, 2011, rule 34.14 of the Summary Cause Rules shall be construed in accordance with art.4 of the Damages (Scotland) Act 2011 (Commencement, Transitional Provisions and Savings) Order 2011.

Time of lodgement

35.2. The time of lodgement, intimation or sending shall be the time when the document was sent or transmitted.

Chapter 36[1]

The Equality Act 2010

Interpretation and application

36.1.—[2](1)   In this Chapter—

"the Commission" means the Commission for Equality and Human Rights; and "the 2010 Act" means the Equality Act 2010.

(2)   This Chapter applies to claims made by virtue of section 114(1) of the 2010 Act including a claim for damages.

Intimation to Commission[3]

36.2. The pursuer shall send a copy of the summons to the Commission by registered or recorded delivery post.

Assessor

36.3.—(1)   The sheriff may, of his own motion or on the incidental application of any party, appoint an assessor.

(2)   The assessor shall be a person who the sheriff considers has special qualifications to be of assistance in determining the cause.

Taxation of Commission expenses

36.4.   *[Repealed by the Act of Sederunt (Sheriff Court Rules) (Miscellaneous Amendments) 2008 (SSI 2008/223) r.6(3)(c) (effective July 1, 2008).]*

National security

36.5.—[4](1)   Where, on an incidental application under paragraph (3) or of the sheriff's own motion, the sheriff considers it expedient in the interests of national security, the sheriff may—

   (a)   exclude from all or part of the proceedings—

      (i)   the pursuer;

      (ii)   the pursuer's representatives;

      (iii)   any assessors;

   (b)   permit a pursuer or representative who has been excluded to make a statement to the court before the commencement of the proceedings or the part of the proceedings, from which he or she is excluded;

   (c)   take steps to keep secret all or part of the reasons for his or her decision in the proceedings.

(2)   The sheriff clerk shall, on the making of an order under paragraph (1) excluding the pursuer or the pursuer's representatives, notify the Advocate General for Scotland of that order.

---

[1] As inserted by the Act of Sederunt (Ordinary Cause, Summary Application, Summary Cause and Small Claim Rules) Amendment (Equality Act 2006 etc.) 2006 (SSI 2006/509) r.4(2) (effective November 3, 2006). Chapter title amended by the Act of Sederunt (Sheriff Court Rules) (Equality Act 2010) 2010 (SSI 2010/340) para.4 (effective October 1, 2010).

[2] As substituted by the Act of Sederunt (Sheriff Court Rules) (Equality Act 2010) 2010 (SSI 2010/340) para.4 (effective October 1, 2010).

[3] As substituted by the Act of Sederunt (Sheriff Court Rules) (Miscellaneous Amendments) 2008 (SSI 2008/223) r.6(3)(b) (effective July 1, 2008).

[4] As substituted by the Act of Sederunt (Sheriff Court Rules) (Equality Act 2010) 2010 (SSI 2010/340) para.4 (effective October 1, 2010).

(3)   A party may make an incidental application for an order under paragraph (1).

(4)   The steps referred to in paragraph (1)(c) may include the following—

 (a)   directions to the sheriff clerk; and

 (b)   orders requiring any person appointed to represent the interests of the pursuer in proceedings from which the pursuer or the pursuer's representatives are excluded not to communicate (directly or indirectly) with any persons (including the excluded pursuer)—

  (i)   on any matter discussed or referred to;

  (ii)   with regard to any material disclosed,

during or with reference to any part of the proceedings from which the pursuer or the pursuer's representatives are excluded.

(5)   Where the sheriff has made an order under paragraph (4)(b), the person appointed to represent the interests of the pursuer may make an incidental application for authority to seek instructions from or otherwise communicate with an excluded person.

(6)   The sheriff may, on the application of a party intending to lodge an incidental application in written form, reduce the period of notice of two days specified in rule 9.1(2) or dispense with notice.

(7)   An application under paragraph (6) shall be made in the written incidental application, giving reasons for such reduction or dispensation.

Transfer to Employment Tribunal

36.6.—[1](1)   On transferring proceedings to an employment tribunal under section 140(2) of the 2010 Act, the sheriff —

 (a)   shall state his or her reasons for doing so in the interlocutor; and

 (b)   may make the order on such conditions as to expenses or otherwise as he or she thinks fit.

(2)   The sheriff clerk must, within 7 days from the date of such order—

 (a)   transmit the relevant process to the Secretary of the Employment Tribunals (Scotland);

 (b)   notify each party to the proceedings in writing of the transmission under subparagraph (a); and

 (c)   certify, by making an appropriate entry in the Register of Summary Causes, that he or she has made all notifications required under subparagraph (b).

(3)   Transmission of the process under paragraph (2)(a) will be valid notwithstanding any failure by the sheriff clerk to comply with paragraph (2)(b) and (c).

Transfer from Employment Tribunal

36.7.—[2](1)   On receipt of the documentation in proceedings which have been remitted from an employment tribunal under section 140(3) of the 2010 Act, the sheriff clerk must—

 (a)   record the date of receipt on the first page of the documentation;

 (b)   fix a hearing to determine further procedure not less than 14 days after the date of receipt of the process; and

 (c)   forthwith send written notice of the date of the hearing fixed under subparagraph (b) to each party.

---

[1] As inserted by the Act of Sederunt (Sheriff Court Rules) (Equality Act 2010) 2010 (SSI 2010/340) para.4 (effective October 1, 2010).

[2] As inserted by the Act of Sederunt (Sheriff Court Rules) (Equality Act 2010) 2010 (SSI 2010/340) para.4 (effective October 1, 2010).

(2)   At the hearing fixed under paragraph (1)(b) the sheriff may make such order as he or she thinks fit to secure so far as practicable that the cause thereafter proceeds in accordance with these Rules.

Chapter 37[1]

Live Links

37.1.—(1)   On cause shown, a party may apply by incidental application for authority for the whole or part of—

(a)   the evidence of a witness or the party to be given; or

(b)   a submission to be made,

through a live link.

(2)   in paragraph (1)—

"witness" means a person who has been or may be cited to appear before the court as a witness except a vulnerable witness within the meaning of section 11(1) of the Act of 2004;[2]

"submission" means any oral submission which would otherwise be made to the court by the party or his representative in person including an oral submission in support of an incidental application; and

"live link" means a live television link or such other arrangement as may be specified in the incidental application by which the witness, party or representative, as the case may be, is able to be seen and heard in the proceedings or heard in the proceedings and is able to see and hear or hear the proceedings while at a place which is outside the court room.

Appendix 1

FORMS

Rule 1.1(4)

Rule 4.1(1)[3, 4]

FORM A1

Rule 2A.2(2)(b)

Statement by prospective lay representative for Pursuer/Defender*

Case Ref. No.:

in the cause

SHERIFFDOM OF (*insert name of sheriffdom*)

AT (*insert place of sheriff court*)

[A.B.], (*insert designation and address*), Pursuer

against

[C.D.], (*insert designation and address*), Defender

Court ref. no:

---

[1] As inserted by the Act of Sederunt (Ordinary Cause, Summary Application, Summary Cause and Small Claim Rules) Amendment (Miscellaneous) 2007 (SSI 2007/6) r.4(7) (effective January 29, 2007).

[2] As amended by the Act of Sederunt (Ordinary Cause, Summary Application, Summary Cause and Small Claim Rules) Amendment (Vulnerable Witnesses (Scotland) Act 2004) 2007 (SSI 2007/463) r.4(6) (effective November 1, 2007).

[3] As inserted by the Act of Sederunt (Sheriff Court Rules) (Lay Representation) 2013 (SSI 2013/91) r.4 (effective April 4, 2013).

[4] As amended by the Act of Sederunt (Rules of the Court of Session, Sheriff Appeal Court Rules and Sheriff Court Rules Amendment) (Lay Representation) 2017 (SSI 2017/186) para.6 (effective 3 July 2017).

	Name and address of prospective lay representative who requests permission to represent party litigant:

Name and address of prospective lay representative who requests permission to represent party litigant:

Identify hearing(s) in respect of which permission for lay representation is sought:

The prospective lay representative declares that:

(a)	I have no financial interest in the outcome of the case *or* I have the following financial interest in it:*
(b)	I am not receiving remuneration or other reward directly or indirectly from the litigant for my assistance and will not receive directly or indirectly such remuneration or other reward from the litigant.
(c)	I accept that documents and information are provided to me by the litigant on a confidential basis and I undertake to keep them confidential.
(d)	I have no previous convictions *or* I have the following convictions: (list convictions)*
(e)	I have not been declared a vexatious litigant under the Vexatious Actions (Scotland) Act 1898 *or* I was declared a vexatious litigant under the Vexatious Actions (Scotland) Act 1898 on [insert date].*

(Signed)
[Name of prospective lay representative]
[Date]

(Insert Place/Date)
The Sheriff grants/refuses* the application.

[*Signed*]
Sheriff Clerk
[Date]

(*delete as appropriate)[1]
FORM 1
Summons

FORM 1

Summary Cause Summons

Action for/of

(state type, e.g. payment of money)

		OFFICIAL USE ONLY
		SUMMONS No.

Sheriff Court (name, address, e-mail and telephone no.)	1	
Name and address of person raising the action (**pursuer**)	2	
Name and address of person against whom action raised (**defender, arrestee, etc.**)	3	
Name(s) and address(s) of any interested party (eg.	3a	

---

[1] As amended by the Act of Sederunt (Sheriff Court Rules Amendment) (Diligence) 2008 (SSI 2008/121) r.6(6) (effective April 1, 2008) and by the Act of Sederunt (Summary Cause Rules Amendment) (Personal Injuries Actions) 2012 (SSI 2012/144) para.2 (effective September 1, 2012).

connected person)		

Claim (form of decree or other order sought)	4	

Name, full address, telephone no, and e-mail address of pursuer's solicitor or representative (if any) acting in the case	5	

Fee Details (Enter these only if forms sent electronically to court)	5a	

6

RETURN DAY	20		
CALLING DATE	20	at	**am.**

*Sheriff Clerk to delete as appropriate

The pursuer is authorised to serve a copy summons in form *1a/1b/ 1c/1d/1e/1f, on the defender, and give intimation to any interested party, not less than * 21/42 days before the **RETURN DAY** shown in the box above. The summons is warrant for service, and for citation of witnesses to attend court on any future date at which evidence may be led.

Court Authentication

Sheriff clerk depute (name)   Date:.......... 20

NOTE: The pursuer should complete boxes 1 to 5a above and box 7 on page 2. The sheriff clerk will complete box 6.

---

7.   **STATE DETAILS OF CLAIM HERE (all cases) and PARTICULARS OF ARREST-MENT (furthcoming actions only)**

(To be completed by the pursuer. If space is insufficient, a separate sheet may be attached)

The details of the claim are:...............

FOR OFFICIAL USE ONLY

Sheriff's notes as to:

1. Issues of fact and law in dispute

2. Facts agreed

3. Reasons for any final disposal at the hearing held on the calling date.

```
┌─────────────────────────────────────────────────────────┐
│                                                         │
│                                                         │
│                                                         │
│                                                         │
│                                                         │
│                                                         │
│                                                         │
└─────────────────────────────────────────────────────────┘
```

[1, 2]

FORM 1a

Rule 4.3(a)

Defender's copy summons—claim for or including payment of money where time to pay direction or time order may be applied for

┌────────────────────────────┐
│ **OFFICIAL USE ONLY**   │
│ **SUMMONS No.**   │
└────────────────────────────┘

Summary Cause Summons
Action for/of
(state type, e.g. payment of money)
DEFENDER'S COPY: Claim for or including payment of money (where time to pay direction or time order may be applied for)

Sheriff Court (name, address, e-mail and telephone no.)	1	
Name and address of person raising the action (**pursuer**)	2	
Name and address of person against whom action raised (**defender, arrestee, etc.**)	3	
Name(s) and address(es) of any interested party (e.g. connected person)	3a	

---

[1] As amended by the Act of Sederunt (Sheriff Court Rules Amendment) (Diligence) 2008 (SSI 2008/121) r.6(8) (effective April 1, 2008) and substituted by the Act of Sederunt (Sheriff Court Rules) (Miscellaneous Amendments) 2009 (SSI 2009/294) r.4 (effective December 1, 2009).

[2] As amended by the Act of Sederunt (Sheriff Court Rules) (Miscellaneous Amendments) 2011 (SSI 2011/193) r.11 (effective April 4, 2011) and by the Act of Sederunt (Summary Cause Rules Amendment) (Personal Injuries Actions) 2012 (SSI 2012/144) para.2 (effective September 1, 2012).

Claim (form of decree 4
or other order sought)

Name, full address, 5
telephone no., and
e-mail address of
pursuer's solicitor or
representative (if any)
acting in the case

6 | RETURN DAY | 20 |
| CALLING DATE | 20 | at | am. |

NOTE: You will find details of claim on page 2.

PAGE 1

7.   STATEMENT OF CLAIM

    PARTICULARS OF ARRESTMENT (furthcoming actions only)

    (To be completed by the pursuer. If space is insufficient, a separate sheet may be attached)

    The details of the claim are:

8.   **SERVICE ON DEFENDER**

    (PLACE)...............   **(DATE)..........**

    To:...............   **(Defender)..........**

    You are hereby served with a copy of the above summons.

                                         Solicitor/sheriff officer
                                         delete as appropriate

```

```

NOTE: The pursuer should complete boxes 1 to 6 on page 1, the statement of claim in box 7 on page 2 and section A on page 6 before service on the defender. The person serving the Summons will complete box 8, above.

PAGE 2

WHAT MUST I DO ABOUT THIS SUMMONS?

The RETURN DAY (on page 1 of this summons) is the deadline by which you need to reply to the court. You must send the correct forms back (see below for details) by this date if you want the court to hear your case. If you do not do this, in most cases there will not be a hearing about your case and the court will make a decision in your absence.

The CALLING DAY (on page 1 of this summons) is the date for the court hearing.

Note: If your case is about **recovery of possession of heritable property** (eviction) there will be a hearing even if you do not send back the forms, so you should attend court on the calling date. If you make an application for time to pay in such a case and the court accepts your application, it may still make an order for eviction, so you should attend court if you wish to defend the action for eviction.

You should decide whether you wish to dispute the claim and/or whether you owe any money or not, and how you wish to proceed. Then, look at the 5 options listed below. Find the one that covers your decision and follow the instructions given there.

If you are not sure what you need to do, contact the sheriff clerk's office before the return day. Written guidance can also be obtained from the Scottish Court Service website (www.scotcourts.gov.uk).

OPTIONS

1. **ADMIT LIABILITY FOR THE CLAIM and settle it with the pursuer now.**

   If you wish to avoid the possibility of a court order passing against you, you should settle the claim (including any question of expenses) with the pursuer or his representative **in good time before the return day**. Please do not send any payment direct to the court. Any payment should be made to the pursuer or his representative.

2. **ADMIT LIABILITY FOR THE CLAIM and make** written **application to pay by instalments or by** deferred **lump sum.**

   Complete Box 1 of section B on page 6 of this form and return pages 6, 8 and 9 to the court to arrive on or before the return day. You should then contact the court to find out whether or not the pursuer has accepted your offer. If he has not accepted it, the case will then call in court on the calling date, when the court will decide how the amount claimed is to be paid.

   NOTE: If you fail to return pages 6, 8 and 9 as directed, or if, having returned them, you fail to attend or are not represented at the calling date if the case is to call, the court may decide the claim in your absence.

3. **ADMIT LIABILITY FOR THE CLAIM and attend at court to make application to pay by instalments or deferred lump sum.**

   Complete Box 2 on page 6. Return page 6 to the court so that it arrives on or before the return day.

PAGE 3

You must attend personally, or be represented, at court on the calling date. Your representative may be a Solicitor, or someone else having your authority. It may be helpful if you or your representative bring pages 1 and 2 of this form to the court.

830

NOTE: **If you fail to return page 6 as directed, or if, having returned it, you fail to attend or are not represented at the calling date, the court may decide the claim in your absence.**

4.   **DISPUTE THE CLAIM and attend at court to do any of the following:**

- Challenge the jurisdiction of the court or the competency of the action
- Defend the action (whether as regards the sum claimed or otherwise)
- State a counterclaim

Complete Box 3 on page 6. Return page 6 to the court so that it arrives **on or before the return day. You must attend personally, or be represented, at court on the calling date**.

Your representative may be a solicitor, or someone else having your authority. It may be helpful if you or your representative bring pages 1 and 2 of this form to the court.

NOTE: **If you fail to return page 6 as directed, or if, having returned it, you fail to attend or are not represented at the calling date, the court may decide the claim in your absence.**

WRITTEN NOTE OF PROPOSED DEFENCE

You must send to the court by the return day a written note of any proposed defence, or intimate that you intend to dispute the sum claimed or wish to dispute the court's jurisdiction. You must also attend or be represented at court on the calling date.

5.   **ADMIT LIABILITY FOR THE CLAIM and make written application for a time order under the Consumer Credit Act 1974.**

Complete Box 4 on page 6 and return pages 6 and 10 to 12 to the court to arrive on or before the return day. You should then contact the court to find out whether or not the pursuer has accepted your offer. Where you have been advised that the pursuer has not accepted your offer then the case will call in court on the calling date. You should appear in court on the calling date as the court will decide how the amount claimed is to be paid.

NOTE: If you fail to return pages 6 and 10 to 12 as directed, or if, having returned them, you fail to attend or are not represented at the calling date if the case is to call, the court may decide the claim in your absence.

PLEASE NOTE

If you do nothing about this summons, the court will almost certainly, where appropriate, grant decree against you and order you to pay the pursuer the sum claimed, including any interest and expenses found due.

YOU ARE ADVISED TO KEEP PAGES 1 AND 2, AS THEY MAY BE USEFUL AT A LATER STAGE OF THE CASE.

PAGE 4

Notes:

(1)   **Time to pay directions**

The Debtors (Scotland) Act 1987 gives you the right to apply to the court for a "time to pay direction". This is an order which allows you to pay any sum which the court orders you to pay either in instalments or by deferred lump sum. A "deferred lump sum" means that you will be ordered by the court to pay the whole amount at one time within a period which the court will specify.

If the court makes a time to pay direction it may also recall or restrict any arrestment made on your property by the pursuer in connection with the action or debt (for example, your bank account may have been frozen).

No court fee is payable when making an application for a time to pay direction.

If a time to pay direction is made, a copy of the court order (called an extract decree) will be sent to you by the pursuer telling you when payment should start or when it is you have to pay the lump sum.

If a time to pay direction is not made, and an order for immediate payment is made against you, an order to pay (called a charge) may be served on you if you do not pay.

(2) **Determination of application**

Under the 1987 Act, the court is required to make a time to pay direction if satisfied that it is reasonable in the circumstances to do so, and having regard in particular to the following matters—

- The nature of and reasons for the debt in relation to which decree is granted
- Any action taken by the creditor to assist the debtor in paying the debt
- The debtor's financial position
- The reasonableness of any proposal by the debtor to pay that debt
- The reasonableness of any refusal or objection by the creditor to any proposal or offer by the debtor to pay the debt.

(3) **Time Orders**

The Consumer Credit Act 1974 allows you to apply to the court for a "time order" during a court action, to ask the court to give you more time to pay a loan agreement. **A time order is similar to a time to pay direction, but can only be applied for where the court action is about a credit agreement regulated by the Consumer Credit Act**. The court has power to grant a time order in respect of a regulated agreement to reschedule payment of the sum owed. This means that a time order can change:

- the amount you have to pay each month
- how long the loan will last
- in some cases, the interest rate payable

A time order can also stop the creditor taking away any item bought by you on hire purchase or conditional sale under the regulated agreement, so long as you continue to pay the instalments agreed.

No court fee is payable when making an application for a time order.

PAGE 5

SECTION A

This section must be completed before service

| Summons No |
| Return Day |
| Calling Date |

SHERIFF COURT (Including address)

PURSUER'S FULL NAME AND ADDRESS

DEFENDER'S FULL NAME AND ADDRESS

SECTION B   **DEFENDER'S RESPONSE TO THE SUMMONS**

** **Delete those boxes which do not apply**

832

**Box 1	**ADMIT LIABILITY FOR THE CLAIM and make <u>written</u> application to pay by instalments or by <u>deferred</u> lump sum.** I do not intend to defend the case but admit liability for the claim. I wish to make a written application about payment. I have completed the application form on pages 8 and 9.
**Box 2	**ADMIT LIABILITY FOR THE CLAIM and <u>attend at court</u> to make application to pay by instalments or deferred lump sum.** I admit liability for the claim. I intend to appear or be represented at court on the calling date.
**Box 3	**DISPUTE THE CLAIM (or the amount due) and attend at court** *I intend to challenge the jurisdiction of the court. *I intend to challenge the competency of the action. *I intend to defend the action. *I wish to dispute the amount due only. *I apply for warrant to serve a third party notice (see page 14). I intend to appear or be represented in court on the calling date. .... *I attach a note of my proposed defence/counterclaim. *delete as necessary
**Box 4	**ADMIT LIABILITY FOR THE CLAIM and apply for a time order under the** Consumer Credit Act 1974. I do not intend to defend the case but admit liability for the claim. I wish to apply for a time order under the Consumer Credit Act 1974. I have completed the application form on pages 10 to 12.

PAGE 6

WRITTEN NOTE OF PROPOSE DEFENCE / COUNTERCLAIM

State which facts in the statement of claim are admitted:

833

State briefly any facts regarding the circumstances of the claim on which you intent to rely:

State details of counterclaim, if any:

PLEASE REMEMBER: You must send your response to the court to **arrive on or before the return day** if you have completed a response in Section B. If you have admitted the claim, please do not send any payment direct to the court. **Any payments you wish to make should be made to the pursuer or his solicitor**.

Page 7

APPLICATION IN WRITING FOR A TIME TO PAY DIRECTION UNDER THE DEBTORS (SCOTLAND) ACT 1987

I WISH TO APPLY FOR A TIME TO PAY DIRECTION

I admit the claim and make application to pay as follows:

(1) By instalments of £ .... per *week / fortnight / month

OR

(2) In one payment within .... *weeks / months from the date of the court order.

The debt is for (*specify the nature of the debt*) and has arisen (*here set out the reasons the debt has arisen*)

Please also state why you say a time to pay direction should be made. In doing so, please consider the Notes (1) and (2) on page 5.

To help the court please provide details of your financial position in the boxes below.

I am employed / self-employed / unemployed
*Please also indicate whether payment/receipts are weekly, fortnightly or monthly

My outgoings are:	*Weekly / fortnightly/ monthly		My net income is	*Weekly / fortnightly/ monthly
Rent/mortgage	£		Wages/pensions	£
Council tax	£		State benefits	£
Gas/electricity etc	£		Tax credits	£
Food	£		Other	£
Loans and credit agreements	£			
Phone	£			
Other	£			
Total	£		Total	£

People who rely on your income (e.g. spouse/ civil partner/ partner/chil-dren)— how many

Page 8

Please list details of all capital held, e.g. value of house; amount in savings account, shares or other investments:

I am of the opinion that the payment offer is reasonable for the following reason(s):

Here set out any information you consider relevant to the court's determination of the application. In doing so, please consider Note (2) on page 5.

*APPLICATION FOR RECALL OR RESTRICTION OF AN ARRESTMENT

I seek the recall or restriction of the arrestment of which the details are as follows:

Date:

*Delete if inapplicable

Page 9

835

	APPLICATION FOR A TIME ORDER UNDER THE CONSUMER CREDIT ACT 1974
	By
	DEFENDER
	In an action raised by
	PURSUER
	PLEASE WRITE IN INK USING BLOCK CAPITALS
	If you wish to apply to pay by instalments enter the amount at box 3. If you wish the court to make any additional orders, please give details at box 4. Please give details of the regulated agreement at box 5 and details of your financial position in the spaces provided below box 5. Sign and date the application where indicated. You should ensure that your application arrives at the court along with the completed page 6 on or before the return day.
	1. The Applicant is a defender in the action brought by the above named pursuer. **I/WE WISH TO APPLY FOR A TIME ORDER under the Consumer Credit Act 1974**
	2. **Details of order(s) sought** The defender wishes to apply for a time order under section 129 of the Consumer Credit Act 1974 The defender wishes to apply for an order in terms of section .... of the Consumer Credit Act 1974
	3. **Proposals for payment** I admit the claim and apply to pay the arrears and future instalments as follows: By instalments of £ .... per *week/fortnight/month No time to pay direction or time to pay order has been made in relation to this debt.
	4. **Additional orders sought** The following additional order(s) is (are) sought: (*specify*)

<table>
<tr><td></td><td>The order(s) sought in addition to the time order is (are) sought for the following reasons:</td></tr>
</table>

	The order(s) sought in addition to the time order is (are) sought for the following reasons:
	5. Details of regulated agreement *(Please attach a copy of the agreement if you have retained it and insert details of the agreement where known)* (a) Date of agreement (b) Reference number of agreement
	(c) Names and addresses of other parties to agreement (d) Name and address of person (if any) who acted as surety (guarantor) to the agreement (e) Place where agreement signed (e.g. the shop where agreement signed, including name and address) (f) Details of payment arrangements i. The agreement is to pay instalments of £ .... per week/month ii. The unpaid balance is £ .... / I do not know the amount of arrears iii. I am £ .... in arrears / I do not know the amount of arrears

PAGE 11

	Defender's financial position			
	I am employed /self employed / unemployed			
	My net income is:	weekly, fortnightly or monthly	**My outgoings are:**	weekly, fortnightly or monthly
	Wages	£	Mortgage/rent	£
	State benefits	£	Council tax	£
	Tax credits	£	Gas/electricity etc	£
	Other	£	Food	£
			Credit and loans	£
			Phone	£
			Other	£
	Total	£	Total	£
	People who rely on your income (e.g. spouse/civil partner/partner/children)—how many			
	Here list all assets (if any) e.g. value of house; amounts in bank or building society accounts; shares or other investments:....................			
	Here list any outstanding debts:....................			
	Therefore the defender asks the court to make a time order			
	Date:..............		Signed:..............	
			Defender:..............	

APPLICATION FOR SERVICE OF A THIRD PARTY NOTICE
NOTE:
You can apply to have another party added to the action if:

(A)   **You think that, as regards the matter which the action is about, that other party has a duty to:**

                                       1. Indemnify you; or
                                       2. Make a contribution in respect of the matter; or
                                       3. Relieve you from any responsibility as regards it.

                                                   or

(B)   **You think that other party is:**
                                       1. Solely liable to the pursuer; or
                                       2. Liable to the pursuer along with you; or
                                       3. Has a liability to you as a result of the pursuer's claim against you.

You may apply for warrant to found jurisdiction if you wish to do so.

FORM OF APPLICATION

(TO BE RETURNED TO THE COURT ALONG WITH YOUR RESPONSE)

I request the court to grant warrant for service of a third party notice on the following party:

Name: ....

Address: ....

The reason I wish a third party notice to be served on the party mentioned above is as follows:
(Give details below of the reasons why you wish the party to be made a defender in the action.)

*__*I apply for warrant to found jurisdiction

*delete as appropriate

Date: ....

[blank box]

FORM 1b

Rule 4.3(a)

Defender's copy summons - claim for or including payment of money (where time to pay direction or time order may not be applied for)

FORM 1b

Summary Cause Summons
Action for/of

(state type, e.g. payment of money)

| OFFICIAL USE ONLY |
| SUMMONS No. |

DEFENDER'S COPY: Claim for or including payment of money (where time to pay direction or time order may not be applied for)

Sheriff Court (name, address, e-mail and telephone no.)	**1**	
Name and address of person raising the action (**pursuer**)	**2**	
Name and address of person against whom action raised (**defender, arrestee, etc.**)	**3**	
Name(s) and address(s) of any interested party (e.g. connected person)	**3a**	
Claim (Form of decree or other order sought)	**4**	
Name, full address, telephone no., and e-mail address of pursuer's solicitor or representative (if any)	**5**	

---

[1] As amended by the Act of Sederunt (Sheriff Court Rules Amendment) (Diligence) 2008 (SSI 2008/121) r.6(8) (effective April 1, 2008) and by the Act of Sederunt (Summary Cause Rules Amendment) (Personal Injuries Actions) 2012 (SSI 2012/144) para.2 (effective September 1, 2012).

6	RETURN DAY	20		
	CALLING DATE	20	at	am.

NOTE: You will find details of claim on page 2.

PAGE 1

7.	**STATEMENT OF CLAIM**

7. STATEMENT OF CLAIM

PARTICULARS OF ARRESTMENT (furthcoming actions only.)

(To be completed by the pursuer. If space is insufficient, a separate sheet may be attached)

The details of the claim are:

8. SERVICE ON DEFENDER

(Place)..............   (Date)..........

To:..............   (defender)..........

You are hereby served with a copy of the above summons.

Solicitor / sheriff officer

delete as appropriate

NOTE: The pursuer should complete boxes 1 to 6 on page 1, the statement of claim in box 7 on page 2 and section A on page 5 before service on the defender. The person serving the Summons will complete box 8.

WHAT MUST I DO ABOUT THIS SUMMONS?

Decide whether you wish to dispute the claim, or admit any liability for the claim and whether you owe any money or not, and how you wish to proceed. Thereafter, look at the 2 options listed below. Find the one which covers your decision and follow the instructions given there. You will find the RETURN DAY and the CALLING DATE on page one of the summons.

Written guidance on summary cause procedure can be obtained from the sheriff clerk at any sheriff clerk's office. Further advice can also be obtained by contacting any of the following:

Citizen's Advice Bureau, Consumer Advice Centre, Trading Standards or Consumer Protection Department or a Solicitor. (Addresses can be found in the guidance booklets)

Options

1. ADMIT LIABILITY FOR THE CLAIM and settle it with the pursuer now.

If you wish to avoid the possibility of a court order passing against you, you should settle the claim (including any question of expenses) with pursuer or his representative **in good time before the return day**. Please do not send any payment direct to the court. Any payment should be made to the pursuer or his representative.

2. DISPUTE THE CLAIM and attend at court to do any of the following:

- Challenge the jurisdiction of the court or the competency of the action
- Defend the action
- Dispute the sum claimed
- State a counterclaim

Complete Section B on page 4. Return your response to the court so that it arrives **on or before the return day. You must attend personally, or be represented, at court on the calling date.**

Your representative may be a solicitor, or someone else having your authority. It may be helpful if you or your representative bring pages 1 and 2 of this form to the court.

NOTE: If you fail to return your response as directed, or if, having returned it, you fail to attend or are not represented at the calling date, the court will almost certainly decide the claim in your absence.

Written Note of Proposed Defence

You must send to the court by the return day a written note of any proposed defence, or intimate that you intend to dispute the sum claimed or wish to challenge the court's jurisdiction. You must also attend or be represented at court on the calling date.

Please Note:

If you do nothing about this summons, the court will almost certainly, where appropriate, grant decree against you and order you to pay the pursuer the sum claimed, including any interest and expenses found due.

You Are Advised to Keep Pages 1 And 2, as They May Be Useful at a Later Stage of the Case.

SECTION A
This section must
be completed
before service

Summons No
Return Day
Calling Date

SHERIFF COURT (Including address)

PURSUER'S FULL NAME AND ADDRESS

DEFENDER'S FULL NAME AND ADDRESS

SECTION B   **DEFENDER'S RESPONSE TO THE SUMMONS**

DISPUTE THE CLAIM (or the amount due) and attend at court

* I intend to challenge the jurisdiction of the court.

* I intend to challenge the competency of the action.

* I intend to defend the claim.

* I wish to dispute the amount due only.

* I apply for warrant to serve a third party notice (see page 6).

* I intend to appear or be represented in court on the calling date.

....

* I attach a note of my proposed defence/counterclaim (see page 5).

* *delete as necessary*

WRITTEN NOTE OF PROPOSED DEFENCE / COUNTERCLAIM

State which facts in the statement of claim are admitted:

State briefly any facts regarding the circumstances of the claim on which you
intend to rely:

State details of counterclaim, if any:

PLEASE REMEMBER: You must send your response to the court to **arrive on or
before the return day** if you have completed a response in Section B. If you have
admitted the claim, please do not send any payment direct to the court. **Any payments you wish to make should be made to the pursuer or his solicitor.**

APPLICATION FOR SERVICE OF A THIRD PARTY NOTICE

NOTE:

You can apply to have another party added to the action if:

**(A) You think that, as regards the matter which the action is about, that
other party has a duty to:**

1. Indemnify you; or
2. Make a contribution in respect of the matter; or
3. Relieve you from any responsibility as regards it.

or

(B) You think that other party is:

4. Solely liable to the pursuer; or
5. Liable to the pursuer along with you; or
6. Has a liability to you as a result of the pursuer's claim against you.

You may apply for warrant to found jurisdiction if you wish to doso.

FORM OF APPLICATION

(TO BE RETURNED TO THE COURT ALONG WITH YOUR RESPONSE)

**I request the court to grant warrant for service of a third party notice on
the following party:**

Name:...............

Address:..............

**The reason I wish a third party notice to be served on the party mentioned
above is as follows:** (Give details below of the reasons why you wish the party
to be made a defender in the action.)

* I apply for warrant to found jurisdiction

* delete as appropriate

```
┌─────────────────────────────────────────────────────────┐
│                                                         │
│                                                         │
│                                                         │
│                                                         │
└─────────────────────────────────────────────────────────┘
```

FORM 1c[1]

Defender's copy summons — non monetary claim
Rule 4.3(b)

FORM 1c

OFFICIAL USE ONLY
SUMMONS No.

Summary Cause Summons
Action for/of
(state type, e.g. delivery)

DEFENDER'S COPY: Non Monetary Claim

Sheriff Court (name, address, e-mail and telephone no.)	1	
Name and address of person raising the action (**pursuer**)	2	
Name and address of Person against whom Action raised (**defender**)	3	
Claim (Form of decree or other order sought)	4	
Name, full address, telephone no, and e-mail address of pursuer's solicitor or representative (if any)	5	

6	**RETURN DAY**	20
	CALLING DATE	20 at am.

NOTE: You will find details of claim on page 2.

7.	**STATE DETAILS OF CLAIM HERE OR ATTACH A STATEMENT OF CLAIM**
	(to be completed by the pursuer. If space is insufficient, a separate sheet may be attached)
	The details of the claim are:

---

[1] As amended by the Act of Sederunt (Sheriff Court Rules Amendment) (Diligence) 2008 (SSI 2008/121) r.6(8) (effective April 1, 2008).

---

8. **SERVICE ON DEFENDER**

(Place)...............   (Date).........

To:...............   (defender)

You are hereby served with a copy of the above summons.

                              * Solicitor / sheriff officer
                              (delete as appropriate)

NOTE: The pursuer should complete boxes 1 to 6 on page 1, the statement of claim in box 7 on page 2 and section A on page 5 before service on the defender. The person serving the Summons will complete box 8.

WHAT MUST I DO ABOUT THIS SUMMONS?

Decide whether you wish to dispute the action and how you wish to proceed. Thereafter, look at the 2 options listed below. Find the one which covers your decision and follow the instructions given there. You will find the RETURN DAY and the CALLING DATE on page one of the summons.

Written guidance on summary cause procedure can be obtained from the sheriff clerk at any sheriff clerk's office. Further advice can also be obtained by contacting any of the following:

Citizen's Advice Bureau, Consumer Advice Centre, Trading Standards or Consumer Protection Department or a Solicitor. (Addresses can be found in the guidance booklets)

Options

1. ADMIT LIABILITY FOR THE CLAIM and settle it with the pursuer now.

If you wish to avoid the possibility of a court order passing against you, you should settle the claim (including any liability for expenses) with the pursuer or his representative in good time before the return day.

2. DISPUTE THE CLAIM and attend at court to do any of the following:

*   Challenge the jurisdiction of the court or the competency of the action
*   Defend the action
*   State a counterclaim

Complete Section B on page 4. Return page 4 to the court so that it arrives **on or before the return day. You must attend personally, or be represented, at court on the calling date.**

Your representative may be a solicitor, or someone else having your authority. It may be helpful if you or your representative bring pages 1 and 2 of this form to the court.

NOTE: If you fail to return page 4 as directed, or if, having returned it, you fail to attend or are not represented at the calling date, the court will almost certainly decide the claim in your absence.

Written Note of Proposed Defence

You must send to the court by the return day a written note of any proposed defence, or intimate that you wish to challenge the jurisdiction of the court. You must also attend or be represented at court on the calling date.

Please Note

If you do nothing about this summons, the court will almost certainly, where appropriate, grant decree against you, including any interest and expenses found due.

You Are Advised to Keep Pages 1 And 2, as They May Be Useful at a Later Stage of the Case.

SECTION A
This section must
Be completed
Before service

Summons No
Return Day
Calling Date

SHERIFF COURT (Including address)

PURSUER'S FULL NAME AND ADDRESS

DEFENDER'S FULL NAME AND ADDRESS

SECTION B   **DEFENDER'S RESPONSE TO THE SUMMONS**

DISPUTE THE CLAIM and attend at court

* I intend to challenge the jurisdiction of the court.

* I intend to challenge the competency of the court.

* I wish to defend the action.

* I apply for warrant to serve a third party notice (see page 6).

I intend to appear or be represented in court on the calling date.

*I attach a note of my proposed defence/counterclaim (see page 5).

* delete as necessary

WRITTEN NOTE OF PROPOSED DEFENCE / COUNTERCLAIM

State which facts in the statement of claim are admitted:

State briefly any facts regarding the circumstances of the claim on which you intend to rely:

State details of counterclaim, if any:

PLEASE REMEMBER: You must send your response to the court to **arrive** on or **before the return day** if you have completed a response in Section B.

APPLICATION FOR SERVICE OF A THIRD PARTY NOTICE
NOTE:

You can apply to have another party added to the action if:

(A) You think that, as regards the matter which the action is about, that other party has a duty to:

1. Indemnify you; or
2. Make a contribution in respect of the matter; or
3. Relieve you from any responsibility as regards it.

or

(B) You think that other party is:

4. Solely liable to the pursuer; or

5. Liable to the pursuer along with you; or

6. Has a liability to you as a result of the pursuer's claim against you.

You may apply for warrant to found jurisdiction if you wish to do so.

Form of Application

(TO BE RETURNED TO THE COURT ALONG WITH YOUR RESPONSE)

I request the court to grant warrant for service of a third party notice on the following party:

Name:...............

Address:...............

The reason I wish a third party notice to be served on the party mentioned above is as follows:
(Give details below of the reasons why you wish the party to be made a defender in the action.)

* I apply for warrant to found jurisdiction

delete as appropriate

FORM 1d

Defender's copy summons - multiplepoinding

Rule 4.3(c)

FORM 1d

Summary Cause Summons

Action of Multiplepoinding

DEFENDER'S COPY

Sheriff Court (name, address, e-mail and telephone no.)	**1**	
Name and address of person raising the action (**pursuer**)	**2**	
Name and address of person against whom action raised (**defenders**)	**3**	
Claim (Form of decree or other order sought - see Form 5)	**4**	
Name, full address, telephone no., and e-mail address of pursuer's solicitor (if any)	**5**	

6	**RETURN DAY** 20
	CALLING DATE 20 at am.

NOTE: You will find details of claim on page 2.

7.	STATE DETAILS OF CLAIM HERE OR ATTACH A STATEMENT OF CLAIM
	(to be completed by the pursuer. If space is insufficient, a separate sheet may be attached)
	The details of the claim are:

8. **SERVICE ON DEFENDER**

(Place)............... (Date).........

To:............... (Defender.)

You are hereby served with the above summons. The pursuer has been authorised by the court to serve it on you.

Solicitor / sheriff officer
(delete as appropriate)

NOTE: The Pursuer should complete boxes 1 to 6 on page 1, the statement of claim in box 7 on page 2 and section A on page 5 before service on the defender. The person serving the Summons will complete box 8.

WHAT MUST I DO ABOUT THIS SUMMONS?

Decide whether you wish to dispute the action and how you wish to proceed. Thereafter, look at the 2 options listed below. Find the one which covers your decision and follow the instructions given there. You will find the RETURN DAY and the CALLING DATE on page one of the summons.

Written guidance on summary cause procedure can be obtained from the sheriff clerk at any sheriff clerk's office. Further advice can also be obtained by contacting any of the following:

Citizen's Advice Bureau, Consumer Advice Centre, Trading Standards or Consumer Protection Department or a solicitor. (Addresses can be found in the guidance booklets)

OPTIONS

1. ADMIT LIABILITY FOR THE CLAIM and settle it with the pursuer now.

If you wish to avoid the possibility of a court order passing against you, you should attempt to settle the claim (including any liability for expenses) with the pursuer or his Solicitor **in good time before the return day**.

2. DISPUTE THE CLAIM and attend at court to do any of the following:

- Challenge the jurisdiction of the court or the competency of the action.
- Object to the extent of the fund or subject detailed in the statement of claim on page 2.
- Make a claim on the fund or subject.

Complete Section B on page 4. Return page 4 to the court so that it arrives **on or before the return day. You must attend personally, or be represented, at court on the calling date**.

Your representative may be a Solicitor, or someone else having your authority. It may be helpful if you or your representative bring pages 1 and 2 of this form to the court.

NOTE: If you fail to return page 4 as directed, or if, having returned it, you fail to attend or are not represented at the calling date, the court will almost certainly deal with the action in your absence.

NOTES:

1. If you do nothing about this summons, the court will almost certainly deal with the action in your absence.

2. **IF YOU ARE THE HOLDER OF THE FUND,** you must complete the enclosed form 5a and send it to the sheriff clerk before the return day. You must

also, before the return day, send a copy of form 5a to the pursuer, the other defenders in the action and to all the persons you have listed in form 5a as having an interest in the fund or subject.

YOU ARE ADVISED TO KEEP PAGES 1 AND 2, AS THEY MAY BE USEFUL AT A LATER STAGE OF THE CASE.

SECTION A
This section
must be
completed
Before service

Summons No

Return Day

Calling Date

SHERIFF
COURT (Including address)

PURSUER'S
FULL NAME
AND ADDRESS

DEFENDER'S
FULL NAME
AND ADDRESS

SECTION B

DEFENDER'S RESPONSE TO THE SUMMONS

DISPUTE THE CLAIM and attend at court

I intend to:

* (1) Challenge the jurisdiction of the court or the competency of the action.
* (2) Object to the extent of the fund or subject detailed in the statement of claim.
* (3) Make a claim on the fund or subject.

I intend to appear or be represented in court on the calling date.

* *delete as necessary*

Please give below brief details of your reason(s) for disputing the claim in accordance with your response to 1, 2 or 3 above:

FORM 1e

FORM 1e

| OFFICIAL USE ONLY |
| SUMMONS No. |

Rule 34.3(1)(a)

Summary Cause Summons—Personal Injuries Action

DEFENDER'S COPY: Claim for payment of money in a personal injuries action (where time to pay direction may be applied for)

Sheriff Court (name, address, e-mail and telephone no.)	**1**	
Name and address of person raising the action (**pursuer**)	**2**	
Name and address of person against whom action raised (**defender, arrestee, etc.**)	**3**	
Name(s) and address(es) of any interested party (e.g. connected person)	**3a**	
Claim (form of decree of other order sought)	**4**	
Name, full address, telephone no., and e-mail address of pursuer's solicitor or representative	**5**	

---

[1] As inserted by the Act of Sederunt (Summary Cause Rules Amendment) (Personal Injuries Actions) 2012 (SSI 2012/144) para.2 (effective September 1, 2012; not applicable to an action raised before September 1, 2012).

(if any) acting in
the case

6	RETURN DAY	20		
	CALLING DATE	20	at	am.

NOTE: You will find details of the claim in the attached Form 10 (statement of claim in a personal injuries action).

PAGE 1

7.	**STATEMENT OF CLAIM**
	(Pursuer to attach copy Form 10 (statement of claim in a personal injuries action))
	The details of the claim are as stated in the attached copy Form 10.

8.	**SERVICE ON DEFENDER**
	(Place)............... **(Date)..........**
	To:............... **(Defender)..........**
	You are hereby served with a copy of the above summons.
	Solicitor / sheriff officer
	delete as appropriate

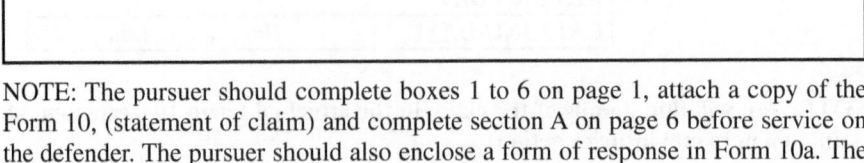

NOTE: The pursuer should complete boxes 1 to 6 on page 1, attach a copy of the Form 10, (statement of claim) and complete section A on page 6 before service on the defender. The pursuer should also enclose a form of response in Form 10a. The person serving the Summons will complete box 8, above.

PAGE 2

WHAT MUST I DO ABOUT THIS SUMMONS?

The RETURN DAY (on page 1 of this summons) is the deadline by which you need to reply to the court. You must send the correct forms back (see below for details) by this date if you want the court to hear your case. If you do not do this, in most cases there will not be a hearing about your case and the court will make a decision in your absence.

The CALLING DAY (on page 1 of this summons) is the date when the court will deal with your case should you not respond to this summons, or the date of the court hearing should you admit the claim and the court is required to consider your application to pay the sum claimed by instalments or by deferred lump sum.

You should decide whether you wish to dispute the claim and/or whether you owe any money or not, and how you wish to proceed. Then, look at the 4 options listed below. Find the one that covers your decision and follow the instructions given there.

You may have a policy of insurance that could indemnify you against this claim. This could be motor, home contents, buildings, travel or some other form of liability insurance that may offer cover to meet legal costs to defend this claim or to meet any claim against you that is admitted or proved. If you believe you have any such insurance cover, you should **immediately** contact your insurer and take steps to forward to them details of this claim.

IF YOU ARE UNCERTAIN WHAT ACTION TO TAKE you should consult a solicitor. You may also obtain advice from a Citizens Advice Bureau or other advice agency. Alternatively, if you are not sure what you need to do, contact the sheriff clerk's office before the return day. Written guidance is available from the Scottish Court Service website (www.scotcourts.gov.uk).

OPTIONS

1. ADMIT LIABILITY FOR THE CLAIM and settle it with the pursuer now.

If you wish to avoid the possibility of a court order passing against you, you should settle the claim (including any question of expenses) with the pursuer or their representative **in good time before the return day.** Please do not send any payment direct to the court. Any payment should be made to the pursuer or their representative.

2. ADMIT LIABILITY FOR THE CLAIM and make written application to pay by instalments or by deferred lump sum.

Complete Box 1 of section B on page 6 of this form and return pages 6, 7 and 8 to the court **to arrive on or before the return day.** You should then contact the court to find out whether or not the pursuer has accepted your offer. If the pursuer has not accepted it, the case will then call in court on the calling date, when the court will decide how the amount claimed is to be paid.

NOTE: If you fail to return pages 6, 7 and 8 as directed, or if, having returned them, you fail to attend or are not represented at the calling date if the case is to call, the court may decide the claim in your absence.

3. ADMIT LIABILITY FOR THE CLAIM and attend at court to make application to pay by instalments or deferred lump sum.

Complete Box 2 of section B on page 6 of this form. Return page 6 to the court so that it arrives **on or before the return day.**

PAGE 3

You must attend personally, or be represented, at court on the calling date. Your representative may be a solicitor, or someone else having your authority. It may be helpful if you or your representative bring pages 1 and 2 of this Form and Form 10 to the court.

NOTE: If you fail to return page 6 as directed, or if, having returned it, you fail to attend or are not represented at the calling date, the court may decide the claim in your absence.

4. DISPUTE THE CLAIM for any of the following reasons:
- Challenge the jurisdiction of the court or the competency of the action;
- Defend the action;
- Dispute the sum claimed; or
- State a counterclaim.

You must complete Box 3 of Section B on page 6 and the attached form of response in Form 10a, stating in a manner which gives the pursuer fair notice, the grounds of fact and law on which you intend to resist the claim, or counterclaim, and return these to the court so that they arrive **on or before the return day.** Thereafter, the case **will not** call in court on the calling date and you do not require to attend or be represented at court on that date. The sheriff clerk will send to you or your representative a timetable confirming the anticipated date for the hearing of evidence and the dates by which various procedural matters must be undertaken. Your representative may be a solicitor or someone else having your authority.

NOTE: If you fail to return page 6 and the completed Form 10a as directed, the case may call on the calling date, and the court may decide the claim in your absence.

PLEASE NOTE

If you do nothing about this summons, the court will almost certainly, where appropriate, grant decree against you and order you to pay the pursuer the sum claimed, including any interest and expenses found due.

YOU ARE ADVISED TO KEEP PAGES 1 AND 2 AND FORM 10, AS THEY MAY BE USEFUL AT A LATER STAGE OF THE CASE.

PAGE 4

Notes:

(1) Time to pay directions

The Debtors (Scotland) Act 1987 gives you the right to apply to the court for a "time to pay direction". This is an order which allows you to pay any sum which the court orders you to pay either in instalments or by deferred lump sum. A "deferred lump sum" means that you will be ordered by the court to pay the whole amount at one time within a period which the court will specify.

If the court makes a time to pay direction it may also recall or restrict any arrestment made on your property by the pursuer in connection with the action or debt (for example, your bank account may have been frozen).

No court fee is payable when making an application for a time to pay direction.

If a time to pay direction is made, a copy of the court order (called an extract decree) will be sent to you by the pursuer telling you when payment should start or when it is you have to pay the lump sum.

If a time to pay direction is not made, and an order for immediate payment is made against you, an order to pay (called a charge) may be served on you if you do not pay.

(2) Determination of application

Under the 1987 Act, the court is required to make a time to pay direction if satisfied that it is reasonable in the circumstances to do so, and having regard in particular to the following matters—

- The nature of and reasons for the debt in relation to which decree is granted
- Any action taken by the creditor to assist the debtor in paying the debt
- The debtor's financial position
- The reasonableness of any proposal by the debtor to pay that debt
- The reasonableness of any refusal or objection by the creditor to any proposal or offer by the debtor to pay the debt.

PAGE 5

SECTION A

This section must be completed before service

	Summons No
	Return Day
	Calling Date

SHERIFF COURT
(Including address)

PURSUER'S FULL NAME AND ADDRESS

DEFENDER'S FULL NAME AND ADDRESS

SECTION B   **DEFENDER'S RESPONSE TO THE SUMMONS**
** **Delete those boxes which do not apply**

**Box 1

> **ADMIT LIABILITY FOR THE CLAIM and make written application to pay by instalments or by deferred lump sum**.
>
> I do not intend to defend the case but admit liability for the claim.
>
> I wish to make a written application about payment.

854

	I have completed the application form on pages 7 and 8.
**Box 2	**ADMIT LIABILITY FOR THE CLAIM and attend at court to make application to pay by instalments or deferred lump sum.** I admit liability for the claim. I intend to appear or be represented at court on the calling date.
**Box 3	**DISPUTE THE CLAIM (or the amount due)** *I intend to challenge the jurisdiction of the court. *I intend to challenge the competency of the action. *I intend to defend the action/state a counterclaim. *I wish to dispute the amount due only. *I apply for warrant to serve a third party notice (see page 10). *delete as necessary .... I attach completed Form 10a stating my proposed defence/counterclaim.

PLEASE REMEMBER: You must send your response to the court to **arrive on or before the return day** if you have completed a response in Section B. If you have admitted the claim, please do not send any payment direct to the court. **Any payments you wish to make should be made to the pursuer or their solicitor.**

PAGE 6

APPLICATION IN WRITING FOR A TIME TO PAY DIRECTION UNDER THE DEBTORS (SCOTLAND) ACT 1987

I WISH TO APPLY FOR A TIME TO PAY DIRECTION

I admit the claim and make application to pay as follows:

(1) By instalments of £ .... per *week / fortnight / month

OR

(2) In one payment within .... *weeks / months from the date of the court order.

The debt is for (*specify the nature of the debt*) and has arisen (*here set out the reasons the debt has arisen*)

Please also state why you say a time to pay direction should be made. In doing so, please consider the Notes (1) and (2) on page 5.

To help the court please provide details of your financial position in the boxes below.

I am employed / self-employed / unemployed
*Please also indicate whether payment/receipts are weekly, fortnightly or monthly

My outgoings are:	*Weekly / fortnightly/ monthly		My net income is	*Weekly / fortnightly/ monthly
Rent/ mortgage	£		Wages/ pensions	£
Council tax	£		State benefits	£
Gas/ electricity etc	£		Tax credits	£
Food	£		Other	£
Loans and credit agree-ments	£			
Phone	£			
Other	£			
Total	£		Total	£

People who rely on your income (e.g. spouse/civil partner/ partner/ children)— how many

PAGE 7

Please list details of all capital held, e.g. value of house; amount in savings account, shares or other investments:

I am of the opinion that the payment offer is reasonable for the following reason(s):

Here set out any information you consider relevant to the court's determination of the application. In doing so, please consider Note (2) on page 5.

*APPLICATION FOR RECALL OR RESTRICTION OF AN ARREST-MENT

I seek the recall or restriction of the arrestment of which the details are as follows:

*Delete if inapplicable

Date:

PAGE 8

APPLICATION FOR SERVICE OF A THIRD PARTY NOTICE
NOTE:
You can apply to have another party added to the action if:

(A)   **You think that, as regards the matter which the action is about, that other party has a duty to:**

1. Indemnify you; or
2. Make a contribution in respect of the matter; or
3. Relieve you from any responsibility as regards it.

or

(B)   **You think that other party is:**
1. Solely liable to the pursuer; or
2. Liable to the pursuer along with you; or
3. Has a liability to you as a result of the pursuer's claim against you.

You may apply for warrant to found jurisdiction if you wish to do so.

PAGE 9

FORM OF APPLICATION

(TO BE RETURNED TO THE COURT ALONG WITH YOUR RESPONSE)

I request the court to grant warrant for service of a third party notice on the following party:

Name:...............

Address:...............

The reason I wish a third party notice to be served on the party mentioned above is as follows:

(Give details below of the reasons why you wish the party to be made a defender in the action.)

*I apply for warrant to found jurisdiction

delete as appropriate

Date:...............

PAGE 10[1]
FORM 1f

Form 1f

---

[1] As inserted by the Act of Sederunt (Summary Cause Rules Amendment) (Personal Injuries Actions) 2012 (SSI 2012/144) para.2 (effective September 1, 2012; not applicable to an action raised before September 1, 2012).

Rule 34.3(1)(b)

Summary Cause Summons—Personal Injuries Action

DEFENDER'S COPY: Claim for payment of money in a personal injuries action (where time to pay direction may be applied for)

Sheriff Court (name, address, e-mail and telephone no.)	**1**	
Name and address of person raising the action (**pursuer**)	**2**	
Name and address of person against whom action raised (**defender, arrestee, etc.**)	**3**	
Name(s) and address(es) of any interested party (e.g. connected person)	**3a**	
Claim (form of decree of other order sought)	**4**	
Name, full address, telephone no., and e-mail address of pursuer's solicitor or representative (if any) acting in the case	**5**	

6	**RETURN DAY** 20
	CALLING DATE 20 at am.

NOTE: You will find details of the claim in the attached Form 10 (statement of claim in a personal injuries action).

PAGE 1

7.	**STATEMENT OF CLAIM**

(Pursuer to attach copy Form 10 (statement of claim in a personal injuries action))

The details of the claim are as stated in the attached copy Form 10.

---

8. **SERVICE ON DEFENDER**

(Place)...............   **(Date)..........**

To:...............   **(Defender)..........**

You are hereby served with a copy of the above summons.

Solicitor / sheriff officer
delete as appropriate

NOTE: The pursuer should complete boxes 1 to 6 on page 1, attach a copy of the Form 10, (statement of claim) and complete section A on page 6 before service on the defender. The pursuer should also enclose a form of response in Form 10a. The person serving the Summons will complete box 8, above.

PAGE 2

WHAT MUST I DO ABOUT THIS SUMMONS?

The RETURN DAY (on page 1 of this summons) is the deadline by which you need to reply to the court. You must send the correct forms back (see below for details) by this date if you want the court to hear your case. If you do not do this, in most cases there will not be a hearing about your case and the court will make a decision in your absence.

The CALLING DAY (on page 1 of this summons) is the date when the court will deal with your case should you not respond to this summons.

You should decide whether you wish to dispute the claim and/or whether you owe any money or not, and how you wish to proceed. Then, look at the 2 options listed on the next page. Find the one that covers your decision and follow the instructions given there.

You may have a policy of insurance that could indemnify you against this claim. This could be motor, buildings, travel or some other form of liability insurance that may offer cover to meet legal costs to defend this claim or to meet any claim against you that is admitted or proved. If you believe you have any such insurance cover, you should **immediately** contact your insurer and take steps to forward to them details of this claim.

IF YOU ARE UNCERTAIN WHAT ACTION TO TAKE you should consult a solicitor. You may also obtain advice from a Citizens Advice Bureau or other advice agency. Alternatively, if you are not sure what you need to do, contact the sheriff clerk's office before the return day. Written guidance is available from the Scottish Court Service website (www.scotcourts.gov.uk).

PAGE 3

OPTIONS

1. ADMIT LIABILITY FOR THE CLAIM and settle it with the pursuer now.

If you wish to avoid the possibility of a court order passing against you, you should settle the claim (including any question of expenses) with the pursuer or their representative **in good time before the return day.** Please do not send any payment direct to the court. Any payment should be made to the pursuer or their representative.

2. DISPUTE THE CLAIM for any of the following reasons:
- Challenge the jurisdiction of the court or the competency of the action;
- Defend the action;
- Dispute the sum claimed; or
- State a counterclaim.

You must complete Section B on page 5 and the attached form of response in Form 10a, stating in a manner which gives the pursuer fair notice, the grounds of fact and law on which you intend to resist the claim, or counterclaim, and return these to the court so that they arrive **on or before the return day**. Thereafter, the case **will not** call in court on the calling date and you do not require to attend or be represented at court on that date. The sheriff clerk will send to you or your representative a timetable confirming the anticipated date for the hearing of evidence and the dates by which various procedural matters must be undertaken. Your representative may be a solicitor or someone else having your authority.

NOTE: If you fail to return page 5 and the completed Form 10a as directed, the case may call on the calling date, and the court may decide the claim in your absence.

PLEASE NOTE

If you do nothing about this summons, the court will almost certainly, where appropriate, grant decree against you and order you to pay the pursuer the sum claimed, including any interest and expenses found due.

YOU ARE ADVISED TO KEEP PAGES 1 AND 2 AND FORM 10, AS THEY MAY BE USEFUL AT A LATER STAGE OF THE CASE.

Page 4

SECTION A

This section must be completed before service

	Summons No
	Return Day
	Calling Date

SHERIFF COURT
(Including address)

PURSUER'S FULL NAME AND ADDRESS

DEFENDER'S FULL NAME AND ADDRESS

SECTION B **DEFENDER'S RESPONSE TO THE SUMMONS**

** **Delete those boxes which do not apply**

> **DISPUTE THE CLAIM (or the amount due)**
>
> *I intend to challenge the jurisdiction of the court.
>
> *I intend to challenge the competency of the action.
>
> *I intend to defend the action/state a counterclaim.
>
> *I wish to dispute the amount due only.
>
> *I apply for warrant to serve a third party notice (see page 6).
>
> *delete as necessary
>
> ....
>
> I attach completed Form 10a stating my proposed defence/counterclaim.

PLEASE REMEMBER: You must send your response to the court to **arrive on or before the return day** if you have completed a response in Section B. If you have admitted the claim, please do not send any payment direct to the court. **Any payments you wish to make should be made to the pursuer or their solicitor.**

PAGE 5

APPLICATION FOR SERVICE OF A THIRD PARTY NOTICE
NOTE:
You can apply to have another party added to the action if:

(A)	**You think that, as regards the matter which the action is about, that other party has a duty to:**	
	1.	Indemnify you; or
	2.	Make a contribution in respect of the matter; or
	3.	Relieve you from any responsibility as regards it.
		or
(B)	**You think that other party is:**	
	1.	Solely liable to the pursuer; or
	2.	Liable to the pursuer along with you; or
	3.	Has a liability to you as a result of the pursuer's claim against you.

You may apply for warrant to found jurisdiction if you wish to do so.
PAGE 6

FORM OF APPLICATION

(TO BE RETURNED TO THE COURT ALONG WITH YOUR RESPONSE)

I request the court to grant warrant for service of a third party notice on the following party:

Name:..............

Address:..............

The reason I wish a third party notice to be served on the party mentioned above is as follows:

(Give details below of the reasons why you wish the party to be made a defender in the action.)

*I apply for warrant to found jurisdiction

delete as appropriate

Date:...............

PAGE 7

Rule 4.1(2)   FORM 2

Form of claim in a summons for payment of money..........The pursuer claims from the defender(s) the sum of £..........with..........interest on that sum at the rate of..........annually from the date of service, together with the expenses of bringing the action.

Rule 4.1(2)   FORM 3

Form of claim in a summons for recovery of possession of heritable property The pursuer claims that, in the circumstances described in the statement contained on page 2 of this copy summons, he is entitled to recover possession of the property at (*address*), and that you refuse or delay to remove from said property.

The pursuer therefore asks the court to grant a decree against you, removing you, and your family, sub-tenants and dependants (if any) with your goods and possessions from the said property.

The pursuer also claims from you the expenses of bringing the action.

Rule 30.6(1)   FORM 3A

Form of notice of removal under sections 34, 35 or 36 of the Sheriff Courts (Scotland) Act 1907

To: (*name, designation and address of party in possession*)

You are hereby required to remove from (*describe subjects*) at the term of (*or, if different terms, state them and the subjects to which they apply*), in terms of (*describe lease, terms of letter of removal or otherwise*).

(date)   *(signature, designation and address)*

Rule 30.6(2)   FORM 3B

Form of notice of removal under section 37 of the Sheriff Courts (Scotland) Act 1907

NOTICE OF REMOVAL UNDER SECTION 37 OF THE SHERIFF COURTS (SCOTLAND) ACT 1907

To:...............
(name, designation and address)
You are hereby required to remove from *(describe subjects)* at the term of *(Whitsunday or Martinmas), (date)*.

(date)   signature, designation and address)*

Rule 30.6(3)   FORM 3C

Form of letter of removal

To: *(name, designation and address)*...............*(place and date)*. I am to remove from (describe subjects by usual name or give a short description sufficient for identification) at the term of *(insert term and date)*.

(date)   *(signature, designation and address)*

Rule 4.1(2)   FORM 4

Form of claim in a summons of sequestration for rent
[Repealed by the Act of Sederunt (Sheriff Court Rules Amendment) (Diligence) 2008 (SSI 2008/121) r.2(1)(b) (effective April 1, 2008).]

Rule 31.2(2)   FORM 4A

Notice informing defender of right to apply for certain orders under the Debtors (Scotland) Act 1987
[Repealed by the Act of Sederunt (Sheriff Court Rules Amendment) (Diligence) 2008 (SSI 2008/121) r.2(1)(b) (effective April 1, 2008).]

Rule 31.2(2)   FORM 4B

Certificate of Sequestration
[Repealed by the Act of Sederunt (Sheriff Court Rules Amendment) (Diligence) 2008 (SSI 2008/121) r.2(1)(b) (effective April 1, 2008).]

Rule 4.1(2)   FORM 5

Form of claim in a summons of multiplepoinding
The pursuer claims that, in the circumstances described in the statement contained on page 2 of this copy summons, the *(state party)* is the holder of a fund *(or subject)* valued at £.......... on which competing claims are being made by the defenders.

The pursuer therefore asks the court to grant a decree finding the holder of the said fund or subject liable to make payment of, or to deliver, same to the party found by the court to be entitled thereto.

The pursuer also asks that the expenses of bringing the action be deducted from the value of the said fund or subject before payment is made.

Rule 27.5(2)(a)   **FORM 5A**

Form of statement by holder of fund or subject when not the pursuer

(1) I, *(name, address)*, hereby state that the fund or subject in the summary cause summons raised at the instance of AB *(design)* against CD, *(EF and GH) (design)* is as follows: *(description and details of fund or subject)*.

(2) I have the following claim or lien on said fund or subject (give details, including a reference to any document founded upon in support of the claim).

(3) I am aware that the persons listed below have an interest in the said fund/subject:

(list names and addresses)

(4) I certify that I have today intimated a copy of this statement to each of the persons contained in the list at (3) above.

(date)

Rule 27.9(2)(a)   **FORM 5B**

Form of claim on the fund or subject in action of multiplepoinding

I, EF, claim to be preferred on the fund in the multiplepoinding raised in the name of AB against CD, EF etc. for the sum of £.......... by reason of *(state ground of claim, including a reference to any document founded upon in support thereof)* with interest thereon from *(date)*.

I also claim any appropriate court expenses which I may incur by appearing in this action.

(signature)

Rule 4.1(2)   **FORM 6**

Form of claim in a summons of furthcoming

The pursuer claims that, in the circumstances described in the statement contained on page 2 of this copy summons, the said *(name of common debtor)* is due to him the sum of £...........

He further claims that he has lawfully arrested in the hands of the said *(name of arrestee)* the goods or money valued at £.......... and described in the said statement of claim, which ought to be made furthcoming to him.

He therefore asks the court to order that you make furthcoming and deliver to him the said arrested goods or money or so much thereof as will satisfy *(or part satisfy)* the said sum of £.......... owing to him.

The pursuer also claims from you the expenses of bringing this action. If the value of the arrested funds are insufficient to meet the sum owing to the pursuer plus the expenses of the action, the pursuer claims those expenses from the said *(name of common debtor)*.

Rule 4.1(2)   **FORM 7**

Form of claim in a summons for delivery

The pursuer claims that, in the circumstances described in the statement contained on page 2 of this copy summons, he has right to the possession of the article(s) described therein.

He therefore asks the court to grant a decree ordering you to deliver the said articles to the pursuer.

Alternatively, if you do not deliver said articles, the pursuer asks the court to grant a decree ordering you to pay to him the sum of £.......... with interest on that sum at the rate of.......... % annually from *(date)* until payment.

The pursuer also claims from you the expenses of bringing the action.

Rule 4.1(2)   **FORM 8**

Form of claim in a summons for implement of an obligation

The pursuer claims that, in the circumstances described in the statement contained on page 2 of this copy summons, you are obliged to

He therefore asks the court to grant a decree ordering you to implement the said obligation.

Alternatively, if you do not fulfil the obligation, the pursuer asks the court to grant a decree ordering you to pay to him the sum of £.......... with interest on that sum at the rate of.......... % annually from (*date*) until payment.

The pursuer also claims from you the expenses of bringing the action.

Rule 4.1(2)   **FORM 9**

Form of claim in a summons for count, reckoning and payment

The pursuer claims that, in the circumstances described in the statement contained on page 2 of this copy summons, you have intromitted with (*describe briefly the fund or estate*), in which he has an interest.

He therefore asks the court to grant a decree ordering you to produce a full account of your intromissions therewith, and for payment to him of the sum of £.........., or such other sum as appears to the court to be the true balance due by you, with interest thereon at the rate of.......... % annually from (*date*) until payment.

Alternatively, if you do not produce such an account, the pursuer asks the court to grant a decree ordering you to pay to him the said sum of £.......... with interest thereon at the rate of.......... % annually from (*date*) until payment.

The pursuer also claims from you the expenses of bringing the action.

Rule 34.2(2)   **FORM 10**[1]

Form of statement of claim in a personal injuries action

1. The pursuer is (*state designation, address, occupation, date of birth and National Insurance number (where applicable) of the pursuer*). (*In an action arising out of the death of a relative state designation of the deceased and relation to the pursuer*).
2. The defender is (*state designation, address and occupation of the defender*).
3. The court has jurisdiction to hear this claim against the defender because (*state briefly ground of jurisdiction*).
4. (*State briefly the facts necessary to establish the claim*).
5. (*State briefly the personal injuries suffered and the heads of claim. Give names and addresses of medical practitioners and hospitals or other institutions in which the person injured received treatment*).
6. (*State whether claim based on fault at common law or breach of statutory duty; if breach of statutory duty, state provision of enactment*).

Rules 34.3(2) and 34.4(1)   **FORM 10A**[2]

Form of response (action for damages: personal injuries)

Court ref. no:

---

[1] As inserted by the Act of Sederunt (Summary Cause Rules Amendment) (Personal Injuries Actions) 2012 (SSI 2012/144) para.2 (effective September 1, 2012; not applicable to an action raised before September 1, 2012).

[2] As inserted by the Act of Sederunt (Summary Cause Rules Amendment) (Personal Injuries Actions) 2012 (SSI 2012/144) para.2 (effective September 1, 2012; not applicable to an action raised before September 1, 2012).

SHERIFFDOM OF (*insert name of sheriffdom*)
AT (*insert place of sheriff court*)
in the cause
[A.B.], (*insert name and address*), Pursuer
against
[C.D.], (*insert name and address*), Defender
RESPONSE TO STATEMENT OF CLAIM

Question	Response

Question

1. Is it intended to dispute the description and designation of the pursuer? If so, why?

2. Is the description and designation of the defender disputed? If so, why?

3. Is there any dispute that the court has jurisdiction to hear the claim? If so, why?

4. (a) State which facts in paragraph 4 of the statement of claim are admitted.

(b) State any facts regarding the circumstances of the claim upon which the defender intends to rely.

5. (a) State whether the nature and extent of the pursuer's injuries is disputed and whether medical reports can be agreed.

(b) If the defender has a medical report upon which he or she intends to rely to contradict the pursuer's report in any way, state the details.

(c) State whether the claims for other losses are disputed in whole or in part.

6. (a) Does the defender accept that the common law duty or duties in the statement of claim were incumbent upon them in the circumstances? If not, state why.

(b) Does the defender accept that the statutory duty or duties alleged in the statement of claim were incumbent upon them in the circumstances? If not, state why.

(c) State any other provisions or propositions upon which the defender proposes to rely in relation to the question of their liability for the accident including, if appropriate, details of any allegation of contributory negligence.

(d) Does the defender allege that the accident was caused by any other wrongdoer? If so, give details.

(e) Does the defender allege that they are entitled to be indemnified or relieved

868

Question	Response
from any liability they might have to the pursuer? If so, give details.	
7. Does the defender intend to pursue a counterclaim against the pursuer? If so, give details.	

(Insert date)   *(signature, designation and address)*

Rules 34.2(3)(b) and 34.4(2)(b)   **FORM 10B**[1, 2]

Form of order of court for recovery of documents in personal injuries action

Court ref. no:

SHERIFFDOM OF *(insert name of sheriffdom)*
AT *(insert place of sheriff court)*
SPECIFICATION OF DOCUMENTS
in the cause
[A.B.], *(insert name and address, or, as the case may be, the party who obtained the order.)*, Pursuer
against
[C.D.], *(insert name and address)*, Defender

To: *(insert name and address of party or parties from whom the following documents are sought to be recovered).*

You are hereby required to produce to the sheriff clerk at *(insert address)* within seven days of the service on you of this Order:

[Insert such of the following calls as are required]

1. All books, medical records, reports, charts, X-rays, notes and other documents of *(specify the name of each medical practitioner or general practitioner practice named in summons in accordance with* rule 34.2(2)(b)), and relating to the pursuer *[or, as the case may be, the deceased]* from *(insert date)*, in order that excerpts may be taken therefrom at the sight of the Commissioner of all entries showing or tending to show the nature, extent and cause of the pursuer's *[or, as the case may be, the deceased's]* injuries when he or she attended his or her doctor on or after *(specify date)* and the treatment received by him or her since that date.

2. All books, medical records, reports, charts, X-rays, notes and other documents of *(specify, in separate calls, the name of each hospital or other institution named in summons in accordance with* rule 34.2(2)(b)), and relating to the pursuer *[or, as the case may be, the deceased]* from *(insert date)*, in order that excerpts may be taken therefrom at the sight of the Commissioner of all entries showing or tending to show the nature, extent and cause of the pursuer's *[or, as the case may be, the deceased's]* injuries when he or she was admitted to that institution on or about *(specify date)*, the treatment received by him or her since that date and his or her certificate of discharge, if any.

3. The medical records and capability assessments held by the defender's occupational health department relating to the pursuer *[or, as the case may be, the deceased]*, except insofar as prepared for or in contemplation of litigation, in order that excerpts may be taken therefrom at the sight of the Commissioner of all entries

---

[1] As inserted by the Act of Sederunt (Summary Cause Rules Amendment) (Personal Injuries Actions) 2012 (SSI 2012/144) para.2 (effective September 1, 2012; not applicable to an action raised before September 1, 2012).

[2] As amended by the Act of Sederunt (Rules of the Court of Session, Ordinary Cause Rules and Summary Cause Rules Amendment) (Miscellaneous) 2014 (SSI 2014/152) r.4 (effective July 7, 2014).

showing or tending to show the nature and extent of any injuries, symptoms and conditions from which the pursuer [or, as the case may be, the deceased] was suffering and the nature of any assessment and diagnosis made thereof on or subsequent to (specify date).

4. All wage books, cash books, wage sheets, computer records and other earnings information relating to the pursuer [or, as the case may be, the deceased] (N.I. number (specify number)) held by or on behalf of (specify employer), for the period (specify dates commencing not earlier than 26 weeks prior to the date of the accident or the first date of relevant absence, as the case may be) in order that excerpts may be taken therefrom at the sight of the Commissioner of all entries showing or tending to show—

(a)   the pursuer's [or, as the case may be, the deceased's] earnings, both gross and net of income tax and employee National Insurance Contributions, over the said period;

(b)   the period or periods of the pursuer's [or, as the case may be, the deceased's] absence from employment over the said period and the reason for absence;

(c)   details of any increases in the rate paid over the period (specify dates) and the dates on which any such increases took effect;

(d)   the effective date of, the reasons for and the terms (including any terms relative to any pension entitlement) of the termination of the pursuer's [or, as the case may be, the deceased's] employment;

(e)   the nature and extent of contributions (if any) to any occupational pension scheme made by the pursuer [or, as the case may be, the deceased] and his or her employer;

(f)   the pursuer's present entitlement (if any) to any occupational pension and the manner in which said entitlement is calculated.

5. All accident reports, memoranda or other written communications made to the defender or anyone on his or her behalf by an employee of the defender who was present at or about the time at which the pursuer [or, as the case may be, the deceased] sustained the injuries in respect of which the summons in this cause was issued and relevant to the matters contained in the statement of claim.

6. Any assessment current at the time of the accident referred to in the summons or at the time of the circumstances referred to in the summons giving rise to the cause of action (as the case may be) undertaken by or on behalf of the defender for the purpose of regulation 3 of the Management of Health and Safety at Work Regulations 1992 and subsequently regulation 3 of the Management of Health and Safety at Work Regulations 1999 [or (specify the regulations or other legislative provision under which the risk assessment is required)] in order that excerpts may be taken therefrom at the sight of the Commissioner of all entries relating to the risks posed to workers [or (specify the matters set out in the statement of claim to which the risk assessment relates)].

7. Failing principals, drafts, copies or duplicates of the above or any of them.

Date (insert date of posting or other   (Insert signature, name and business
method of service)   address of the agent for the pursuer)

NOTES:

1. The documents recovered will be considered by the parties to the action and they may or may not be lodged with the sheriff clerk. A written receipt will be given or sent to you by the sheriff clerk, who may thereafter allow them to be inspected by the parties. The party in whose possession the documents are will be responsible for their safekeeping.

2. Payment may be made, within certain limits, in respect of claims for outlays incurred in relation to the production of documents. Claims should be made in writing to the person who has obtained an order that you produce the documents.

3. If you claim that any of the documents produced by you is **confidential** you must still produce such documents but may place them in a separate sealed packet by themselves, marked "CONFIDENTIAL". Any party who wishes to open the sealed packet must apply to the sheriff by incidental application. A party who makes such an application must intimate the application to you.

4. Subject to paragraph 3 above, you may produce these documents by sending them by registered post or by recorded delivery service, or by hand delivery to the sheriff clerk at (*insert address*).

CERTIFICATE

I hereby certify with reference to the above order of the sheriff at (*insert name of sheriff court*) in the case (*insert court reference number*) and the enclosed specification of documents, served on me and marked respectively X and Y—

1. That the documents which are produced and which are listed in the enclosed inventory signed by me and marked Z, are all the documents in my possession falling within the specification.

or

That I have no documents in my possession falling within the specification.

2. That, to the best of my knowledge and belief, there are in existence other documents falling within the specification, but not in my possession. These documents are as follows—(*describe them by reference to the descriptions of documents in the specification*). They were last seen by me on or about (*date*), at (*place*), in the hands of (*insert name and address of the person*).

or

That I know of the existence of no documents in the possession of any person, other than me, which fall within the specification.

(*Insert date*)   (*Signed*)

                                                                       (*Name and address*)

Rule 34.5(2)   **FORM 10C**[1]

Form of docquet for deemed grant of recovery of documents in a personal injuries action

Court ref. no:

Court (*insert court*)

Commission and diligence for the production and recovery of the documents called for in this specification of documents is deemed to have been granted.

Date (*insert date*)   (*Signed*)

                                                                 Sheriff Clerk (depute)

Rule 34.7(1)(c) and (4)   **FORM 10D**[2]

---

[1] As inserted by the Act of Sederunt (Summary Cause Rules Amendment) (Personal Injuries Actions) 2012 (SSI 2012/144) para.2 (effective September 1, 2012; not applicable to an action raised before September 1, 2012).

[2] As inserted by the Act of Sederunt (Summary Cause Rules Amendment) (Personal Injuries Actions) 2012 (SSI 2012/144) para.2 (effective September 1, 2012; not applicable to an action raised before September 1, 2012).

Form of timetable

Court ref. no:

TIMETABLE
in the cause
[A.B.], (*insert name and address*), Pursuer
against
[C.D.], (*insert name and address*), Defender
This timetable has effect as if it were an interlocutor of the sheriff.

1. The diet allocated for the proof in this action will begin on (*date*). Subject to any variation under rule 34.8, this order requires the parties to undertake the conduct of this action within the periods specified in paragraphs 2 to 10 below.

2. An application under rule 11.1 (third party procedure) shall be made by (*date*).

3. Where the pursuer has obtained a commission and diligence for the recovery of documents by virtue of rule 34.5, the pursuer shall serve the order not later than (*date*).

4. For the purposes of rule 34.7(2)(c), the adjustment period shall end on (*date*).

5. The pursuer shall lodge with the sheriff clerk a statement of valuation of claim under rule 34.9 not later than (*date*).

6. The pursuer shall lodge with the sheriff clerk a certified adjusted statement of claim not later than (*date*).

7. The defender (and any third party to the action) shall lodge with the sheriff clerk a certified adjusted response to statement of claim not later than (*date*).

8. The defender (and any third party to the action) shall lodge with the sheriff clerk a statement of valuation of claim under rule 34.9 not later than (*date*).

9. Not later than (*date*) the parties shall lodge with the sheriff clerk lists of witnesses and productions.

10. Not later than (*date*) the pursuer shall lodge with the sheriff clerk a pre-proof minute under rule 34.10.

(*Insert date*)   (*Signed*)
                                         Sheriff Clerk (depute)

Rule 34.9   **FORM 10E**[1]

Form of statement of valuation of claim

Court ref. no:

SHERIFFDOM OF (*insert name of sheriffdom*)
AT (*insert place of sheriff court*)
STATEMENT OF VALUATION OF CLAIM
in the cause
[A.B.], (*insert name and address*), Pursuer
against
[C.D.], (*insert name and address*), Defender

Head of Claim	Components	Valuation
Solatium	Past	£x
	Future	£x
Interest on past solatium	Percentage applied to past	£x

---

[1] As inserted by the Act of Sederunt (Summary Cause Rules Amendment) (Personal Injuries Actions) 2012 (SSI 2012/144) para.2 (effective September 1, 2012; not applicable to an action raised before September 1, 2012).

Head of Claim	Components	Valuation
	solatium (*state percentage rate*)	
Past wage loss	Date from which wage loss claimed: (*date*)	£x
	Date to which wage loss claimed: (*date*)	
	Rate of net wage loss (*per week, per month or per annum*)	
Interest on past wage loss	Percentage applied to past wage loss: (*state percentage rate*)	£x
Future wage loss	Multiplier: (*state multiplier*)	£x
	Multiplicand: (*state multiplicand and show how calculated*)	
	Discount factor applied (if appropriate): (*state factor*)	
	Or specify any other method of calculation	
Past services	Date from which services claimed: (*date*)	£x
	Date to which services claimed: (*date*)	
	Nature of services: (............)	
	Person by whom services provided: (............)	
	Hours per week services provided: (............)	
	Net hourly rate claimed: (..........)	
	Total amount claimed: (..........)	
	Interest	
Future loss of capacity to provide personal services	Multiplier: (*insert multiplier*)	£x
	Multiplicand: (*insert multiplicand, showing how calculated*)	
Needs and other expenses	One off	£x
	Multiplier: (*insert multiplier*)	
	Multiplicand: (*insert multiplicand*)	
	Interest	
Any other heads as appropriate (*specify*)		£x

Head of Claim	Components	Valuation
Total		£x (*insert total valuation of claim*)
List of Supporting Documents:—		

(*Insert date*) (*Signed*)
(*Name and address*)

Rule 34.10(2) **FORM 10F**[1]

Minute of pre-proof conference

Court ref. no.:

SHERIFFDOM OF (*insert sheriffdom*)
AT (*insert place of sheriff court*)
JOINT MINUTE OF PRE-PROOF CONFERENCE
in the cause
[*A.B.*], Pursuer
against
[*C.D.*], Defender

[E.F.] for the pursuer and
[G.H.] for the defender hereby state to the court:

1. That the pre-proof conference was held in this case [*at (place) or by (telephone conference or video conference or other remote means)*] on [*date*].

2. That the following persons were present—
(*State names and designations of persons attending conference*)

3. That the following persons were available to provide instructions by telephone or video conference—
(*State names and designations or persons available to provide instructions by telephone or video conference*)

4. That the persons participating in the conference discussed settlement of the action.

5. That the following questions were addressed—

Section 1

		Yes	No
1.	Is the diet of proof still required?		
2.	If the answer to question 1 is "yes", does the defender admit liability? (If "no", complete section 2) If yes, does the defender plead contributory negligence? If yes, is the degree of contributory negligence agreed?		

---

[1] As inserted by the Act of Sederunt (Summary Cause Rules Amendment) (Personal Injuries Actions) 2012 (SSI 2012/144) para.2 (effective September 1, 2012; not applicable to an action raised before September 1, 2012).

		Yes	No
	If yes, state % degree of fault attributed to the pursuer.		
3.	If the answer to question 1 is "yes", is the quantum of damages agreed? (If "no", complete section 3)		

Section 2

[To be inserted only if the proof is still required]

It is estimated that the hearing will last *[insert number]* *[days/hours]*.

NB. If the estimate is more than one day then this should be brought to the attention of the sheriff clerk. This may affect prioritisation of the case.

During the course of the pre-proof conference, the pursuer called on the defender to agree certain facts, questions of law and matters of evidence.

Those calls, and the defender's responses, are as follows—

Call	Response	
	Admitted	*Denied*
1.		
2.		
3.		
4.		

During the course of the pre-proof conference, the defender called on the pursuer to agree certain facts, questions of law and matters of evidence.

Those calls, and the pursuer's responses, are as follows—

Call	Response	
	Admitted	*Denied*
1.		
2.		
3.		
4.		

Section 3

Quantum of damages

Please indicate where agreement has been reached on an element of damages

Head of claim	Components	Not agreed	Agreed at
Solatium	Past Future		
Interest on past solatium	Percentage applied to past solatium (*state percentage*)		
Past wage loss	Date from which wage loss claimed Date to which wage loss claimed		

Head of claim	Components	Not agreed	Agreed at
	Rate of net wage loss (*per week, per month or per annum*)		
Interest on past wage loss			
Future wage loss	Multiplier Multiplicand (*showing how calculated*)		
Past necessary services	Date from which services claimed Date to which services claimed Hours per week services provided Net hourly rate claimed		
Past personal services	Date from which services claimed Date to which services claimed Hours per week services provided Net hourly rate claimed		
Interest on past services			
Future necessary services	Multiplier Multiplicand (*showing how calculated*)		
Future personal services	Multiplier Multiplicand (*showing how calculated*)		
Needs and other expenses	One off Multiplier Multiplicand (*showing how calculated*)		
Any other heads as appropriate (specify)			

(Insert date of signature)   *(Signed by each party/his or her solicitor)*

Rule 34.12(5)   **FORM 10G**[1]

Form of intimation to connected persons

Court ref. no:

SHERIFFDOM OF *(insert sheriffdom)*
AT *(insert place of sheriff court)*
in the cause
[*A.B.*], Pursuer
against
[*C.D.*], Defender

To: *(insert name and address as in warrant)*

You are hereby given notice that an action has been raised in the above sheriff court against *(insert name of defender)*, by your *(insert relationship, e.g. father, brother or other relative as the case may be)*. A copy of the summons is attached.

It is believed that you may have a title or interest to sue *(name of defender)* in this action, which is based upon *(the injuries from which the late (insert name and designation) died) (or the death of the late (insert name and designation))*. You may therefore be entitled to enter this action as an additional pursuer. This may be done by lodging an incidental application with the sheriff clerk at *(insert address of sheriff court)*.

If you wish to appear as a party in the action, or are uncertain about what action to take, you should contact a solicitor. You may, depending on your financial circumstances, be entitled to legal aid, and you can get information about legal aid from a solicitor.

You may also obtain advice from any Citizen's Advice Bureau, other advice agency or any sheriff clerk's office.

(Insert date of signature)   *(Signed)*

                                        (Solicitor for the pursuer)

Rule 34.13(2)   **FORM 10H**[2]

Form of claim for provisional damages

Court ref. no:

SHERIFFDOM OF *(insert sheriffdom)*
AT *(insert place of sheriff court)*
in the cause
[*A.B.*], Pursuer
against
[*C.D.*], Defender

For payment to the pursuer by the defender of the sum of *(amount in words and figures)* as provisional damages under section 12(2)(a) of the Administration of Justice Act 1982.

(Statements to include that there is a risk that the pursuer will as result of the act or omission which gave rise to the cause of action develop serious disease or serious deterioration of condition in the future; and that the defender was, at the time of

---

[1] As inserted by the Act of Sederunt (Summary Cause Rules Amendment) (Personal Injuries Actions) 2012 (SSI 2012/144) para.2 (effective September 1, 2012; not applicable to an action raised before September 1, 2012).

[2] As inserted by the Act of Sederunt (Summary Cause Rules Amendment) (Personal Injuries Actions) 2012 (SSI 2012/144) para.2 (effective September 1, 2012; not applicable to an action raised before September 1, 2012).

the act or omission which gave rise to the cause of action, a public authority, public corporation or insured or otherwise indemnified in respect of the claim).

(Insert date of signature)   *(Signed)*

                                                (Solicitor for the pursuer)

Rule 34.13(3)   **FORM 10I**[1]

Form of application for further damages

                                                Court ref. no:

SHERIFFDOM OF *(insert sheriffdom)*
AT *(insert place of sheriff court)*
APPLICATION FOR FURTHER DAMAGES
in the cause
[*A.B.*], Pursuer
against
[*C.D.*], Defender

The pursuer claims payment from the defender of the sum *(insert amount* in words and figures*)* as further damages under section 12(2)(b) of the Administration of Justice Act 1982.

(Insert concise statement of facts supporting claim for further damages).

The pursuer requests the sheriff to fix a hearing on this incidental application and applies for warrant to serve the application on—

(Here state names and addresses of other parties to the action; and, where such other parties are insured or otherwise indemnified, their insurers or indemnifiers, if known to the pursuer).

(Insert date of signature)   *(Signed)*

                                                (Solicitor for the pursuer)

Rule 34.13(4)   **FORM 10J**[2]

Form of application for further damages

                                                Court ref. no:

SHERIFFDOM OF *(insert sheriffdom)*
AT *(insert place of sheriff court)*
APPLICATION FOR FURTHER DAMAGES
in the cause
[*A.B.*], Pursuer
against
[*C.D.*], Defender

To:

TAKE NOTICE

(Pursuer's name and address), pursuer, raised an action against *(defender's name and address)*, defender, in the sheriff court at *(insert name of sheriff court)*.

---

[1] As inserted by the Act of Sederunt (Summary Cause Rules Amendment) (Personal Injuries Actions) 2012 (SSI 2012/144) para.2 (effective September 1, 2012; not applicable to an action raised before September 1, 2012).

[2] As inserted by the Act of Sederunt (Summary Cause Rules Amendment) (Personal Injuries Actions) 2012 (SSI 2012/144) para.2 (effective September 1, 2012; not applicable to an action raised before September 1, 2012).

In the action, the sheriff on (*date*) made an award of provisional damages in accordance with section 12(2)(a) of the Administration of Justice Act 1982 in favour of the pursuer against (*you* or *name of party*). [The sheriff specified that the pursuer may apply for an award of further damages under section 12(2)(b) of that Act at any time before (*date*)]. The pursuer has applied by incidental application for an award of further damages against you [or name of party]. A copy of the incidental application is attached.

A hearing on the incidental application has been fixed for (*date and time*) at (*place of sheriff court*). If you wish to be heard on the incidental application, you should attend or be represented at court on that date.

(*Insert date of signature*)   (*Signed*)

                                                (*Solicitor for the pursuer*)

Rule 5.3(1)   **FORM 11**

Form of service

XY, you are hereby served with a copy of the above (or attached) summons.

                                    (*signature of solicitor or sheriff officer*)

Rule 5.3(2)   **FORM 12**

Form of certificate of execution of service

Case name:

                                                        Court ref: no:

(*Place and date*)...............

I,..........,hereby certify that on the..........day of.........., 20..........,I duly cited XY to answer the foregoing summons. This I did by (*set forth the mode of service*).

(*Signature of solicitor or sheriff officer*)

Rule 5.5(1)(a)   **FORM 13**

Service on person whose address is unknown Form of advertisement

A summary cause action has been raised in the sheriff court at..........by AB, pursuer against CD, defender, whose last known address was..........

If the said CD wishes to defend the action he should immediately contact the sheriff clerk's office at the above court.

Address of court:

Telephone no:

Fax no:

E-mail address:

Rule 5.5(1)(b)   **FORM 14**

Service on person whose address is unknown

Form of notice to be displayed on the walls of court

A summary cause action has been raised in this court by AB, pursuer against CD, defender, whose last known address was...............

If the said CD wishes to defend the action he should immediately contact the sheriff clerk's office.

(*Date*)   Displayed on the walls of court
                        of this date.

                                            Sheriff clerk depute

Rule 5.6(2)   **FORM 15**

Service by post—form of notice
This letter contains a citation to or intimation from the sheriff court at..........
If delivery cannot be made the letter must be returned immediately to the sheriff clerk at (*insert full address*).

Rule 6.A2(2)   **FORM 15A**[1]

Statement to accompany application for interim diligence
DEBTORS (SCOTLAND) ACT 1987 Section 15D [or DEBT ARRANGEMENT AND ATTACHMENT (SCOTLAND) ACT 2002 Section 9C]
Sheriff Court:...............
In the Cause (Cause Reference No.)
[A.B.] (*designation and address*)

Pursuer

against
[C.D.] (*designation and address*)

Defender

STATEMENT

1. The applicant is the pursuer [*or* defender] in the action by [A.B] (*design*) against [C.D.] (*design*).

2. [The following persons have an interest [*specify names and addresses*].]

3. The application is [*or* is not] seeking the grant under section 15E(1) of the 1987 Act of warrant for diligence [or section 9D(1) of the 2002 Act of interim attachment] in advance of a hearing on the application.

4. [*Here provide such other information as may be prescribed by regulations made by the Scottish Ministers under* section 15D(2)(d) of the 1987 Act *or* 9C(2)(d,) of the 2002 Act]

(*Signed*)
Solicitor [*or* Agent] for A.B. [*or* C.D.]
(*include full designation*)

Rule 6.A8   **FORM 15B**[2]

Form of schedule of arrestment on the dependence
SCHEDULE OF ARRESTMENT ON THE DEPENDENCE

Rule 6.A8   **FORM 15C**[3]

Form of certificate of execution of arrestment on the dependence
CERTIFICATE OF EXECUTION

* by affixing the schedule of arrestment to the door at (*place*) on (*date*). (*Specify that enquiry made and that reasonable grounds exist for believing that the person on whom service is to be made resides at the place but is not available*) [and by posting a copy of the schedule to the arrestee by registered post or first class recorded delivery to the address specified on the receipt annexed to this certificate].

---

[1] As inserted by the Act of Sederunt (Sheriff Court Rules Amendment) (Diligence) 2008 (SSI 2008/121) r.6(9) (effective April 1, 2008).

[2] As inserted by the Act of Sederunt (Sheriff Court Rules Amendment) (Diligence) 2008 (SSI 2008/121) r.6(9) (effective April 1, 2008) and substituted by the Act of Sederunt (Sheriff Court Rules Amendment) (Diligence) 2009 (SSI 2009/107) (effective April 22, 2009).

[3] As inserted by the Act of Sederunt (Sheriff Court Rules Amendment) (Diligence) 2008 (SSI 2008/121) r.6(9) (effective April 1, 2008) and substituted by the Act of Sederunt (Sheriff Court Rules Amendment) (Diligence) 2009 (SSI 2009/107) (effective April 22, 2009).

* by leaving the schedule of arrestment with (*name and occupation of person with whom left*) at (*place of business*) on (*date*).[and by posting a copy of the schedule to the arrestee by registered post or first class recorded delivery to the address specified on the receipt annexed to this certificate].

* by depositing the schedule of arrestment at (*place of business*) on (*date*). (*Specify that enquiry made and that reasonable grounds exist for believing that the person on whom service is to be made carries on business at that place.*) [and by posting a copy of the schedule to the arrestee by registered post or first class recorded delivery to the address specified on the receipt annexed to this certificate].

* by affixing the schedule of arrestment to the door at (*place of business*) on (*date*). (*Specify that enquiry made and that reasonable grounds exist for believing that the person on whom service is to be made carries on business at that place.*) [and by posting a copy of the schedule to the arrestee by registered post or first class recorded delivery to the address specified on the receipt annexed to this certificate].

* by leaving the schedule of arrestment at (*registered office*) on (*date*), in the hands of (*name of person*) [and by posting a copy of the schedule to the arrestee by registered post or first class recorded delivery to the address specified on the receipt annexed to this certificate].

* by depositing the schedule of arrestment at (*registered office*) on (*date*) [and by posting a copy of the schedule to the arrestee by registered post or first class recorded delivery to the address specified on the receipt annexed to this certificate].

* by affixing the schedule of arrestment to the door at (*registered office*) on (*date*). [and by posting a copy of the schedule to the arrestee by registered post or first class recorded delivery to the address specified on the receipt annexed to this certificate].

I did this in the presence of (*name, occupation and address of witness*).

(*Signed*)
Sheriff Officer
(*Address*)
(*Signed*)
(Witness)

*Delete where not applicable

NOTE

A copy of the Schedule of arrestment on the dependence is to be attached to this certificate.

Rule 6.3(4)(a)   **FORM 16**

Recall or restriction of arrestment
Certificate authorising the release of arrested funds or property
Sheriff court, (*place*)...............
Court ref. no.:..........AB (pursuer) against CD (defender)

I, (*name*), hereby certify that the sheriff on (*date*) authorised the release of the funds or property arrested on the *dependence of the action/counterclaim/third party notice to the following extent:

(*details of sheriff's order*)

(*Date*)   Sheriff clerk depute

*delete as appropriate
Copy to:
Party instructing arrestment
Party possessing arrested funds/property

Rule 7.1(1)   **FORM 17**

Form of minute—no form of response lodged by defender

Sheriff court, (*place*)...............

Calling date:..............

In respect that the defender(s) has/have failed to lodge a form of response to the summons, the pursuer respectfully craves the court to make the orders specified in the following case(s):

Court ref. No   Name(s) of defender(s)   Minute(s)

Rule 7.1(2)   FORM 18[1]

Form of minute—pursuer not objecting to application for a time to pay direction or time order

Sheriff court, (*place*)...............

Court ref. no.:..............

Name(s) of defender(s)..............

Calling date:..............

I do not object to the defender's application for

*a time to pay direction

*recall or restriction of an arrestment

*a time order

The pursuer requests the court to grant decree or other order in terms of the following minute(s)

*delete as appropriate

FORM 19[2]

Rule 7.2(4)

Form of minute—pursuer opposing an application for a time to pay direction or time order

Sheriff court (place):...............

Court ref no:...............

Name(s) of defender(s):..............

Calling date:..............

I oppose the defender's application for

*a time to pay direction

*recall or restriction of arrestment

*a time order

* delete as appropriate

1. The debt is (*please specify the nature of the debt*).

2. The debt was incurred on (*specify date*) and the pursuer has contacted the defender in relation to the debt on (*specify date(s)*).

*3. The contractual payments were (*specify amount*).

*4. (*Specify any action taken by the pursuer to assist the defender to pay the debt*).

*5. The defender has made payment(s) towards the debt of (*specify amount(s)*) on (*specify date(s)*).

---

[1] As amended by the Act of Sederunt (Ordinary Cause, Summary Application, Summary Cause and Small Claim Rules) Amendment (Miscellaneous) 2003 (SSI 2003/26) r.4(4)(b) (effective January 24, 2003).

[2] As substituted by the Act of Sederunt (Sheriff Court Rules) (Miscellaneous Amendments) 2009 (SSI 2009/294) r.4 (effective December 1, 2009)

*6. The debtor has made offers to pay (*specify amount(s)*) on (*specify date(s)*) which offer(s) was [were] accepted] [or rejected] and (*specify amount*) was paid on (*specify date(s)*).

7. (*Here set out any information you consider relevant to the court's determination of the application*).

8. The pursuer requests the court to grant decree.

* *delete as appropriate*

(*Signed*)
Pursuer [*or* Solicitor for Pursuer]
(*Date*)

Rule 8.12

FORM 20
Form of oath for witnesses

I swear by Almighty God that I will tell the truth, the whole truth and nothing but the truth.

Rule 8.12

FORM 21
Form of affirmation for witnesses

I solemnly, sincerely and truly declare and affirm that I will tell the truth, the whole truth and nothing but the truth.

Rule 11.2(1)(b)(iii)

FORM 22
Form of third party notice

Court ref. no.

SHERIFF COURT, (*place*)

THIRD PARTY NOTICE
in the cause
(AB) (*insert designation and address*), pursuer
against
(CD) (*insert designation and address*), defender

To (EF)

You are given notice by (CD) of an order granted by the sheriff at (*insert place of court*) in which (AB) is the pursuer and (CD) is the defender. A copy of the order is enclosed herewith.

In the action, the pursuer claims from the defender (*insert a brief account of the circumstances of the claim*) as more fully appears in the copy summons enclosed.

The defender claims that,...............(* *delete as appropriate*).

*if he is liable to the pursuer, you are liable to relieve him wholly/partially of his liability, as more fully appears in the copy grounds upon which the defender relies for this, which are also enclosed.

*he is not liable to the pursuer for the claim made against him. He maintains that any liability to the pursuer in respect of this claim rests solely on you, as more fully appears in the copy grounds upon which the defender relies for this, which are also enclosed.

*if he is liable to the pursuer in respect of this claim, he shares that liability with you, as more fully appears in the copy grounds upon which the defender relies for this, which are also enclosed.

*You are liable to him in respect of the claim, as more fully appears in the copy grounds upon which the defender relies for this, which are also enclosed.

If you wish to resist the claim(s) made by the defender as detailed above, you must—

(a) return the form of response enclosed to the sheriff clerk at (*address*) by (*date seven days before the date of hearing*); and

(b) attend or be represented at a hearing on (*date and time*).

(*Date*)...............(*Signature of person serving notice*)

Rule 11.2(1)(b)(iii)

FORM 23

Form of response to third party notice

in the cause

(AB) (*insert designation and address*), pursuer

against

(CD) (*insert designation and address*), defender

I wish to answer the claim made against me by (CD), defender. (*here state briefly the grounds of opposition to the defender's claim.*)

(*date*)

Rule 14A.3(1)

FORM 23A[1]

Form of minute of intervention by the Commission for Equality and Human Rights

SHERIFF COURT, (place)..........Court ref. no...........

APPLICATION FOR LEAVE TO INTERVENE BY THE COMMISSION FOR EQUALITY AND HUMAN RIGHTS

in the cause

[A.B.] (designation and address), Pursuer

against

[C.D.] (designation and address), Defender

[Here set out briefly:

(a) the Commission's reasons for believing that the proceedings are relevant to a matter in connection with which the Commission has a function;

(b) the issue in the proceedings which the Commission wishes to address; and

(c) the propositions to be advanced by the Commission and the Commission's reasons for believing that they are relevant to the proceedings and that they will assist the court.]

Rule 14B.2(1)

FORM 23B[2]

Form of minute of intervention by the Scottish Commission for Human Rights

SHERIFF COURT, (place)..........Court ref. no...........

APPLICATION FOR LEAVE TO INTERVENE BY THE SCOTTISH COMMISSION FOR HUMAN RIGHTS

in the cause

[A.B.] (designation and address), Pursuer

against

[C.D.] (designation and address), Defender

[Here set out briefly:

(a) the issue in the proceedings which the Commission intends to address; and

(b) a summary of the submission the Commission intends to make.]

Rule 14B.3(1)

---

[1] As inserted by the Act of Sederunt (Sheriff Court Rules) (Miscellaneous Amendments) 2008 (SSI 2008/223) Sch.3 (effective July 1, 2008).

[2] As inserted by the Act of Sederunt (Sheriff Court Rules) (Miscellaneous Amendments) 2008 (SSI 2008/223) Sch.3 (effective July 1, 2008).

FORM 23C[1]
Invitation to the Scottish Commission for Human Rights to intervene
SHERIFF COURT, (place).........Court ref. no...........
INVITATION TO THE SCOTTISH COMMISSION FOR HUMAN RIGHTS TO INTERVENE
in the cause

[A.B.] (designation and address), Pursuer

against

[C.D.] (designation and address), Defender

[Here set out briefly:

(a)   the facts, procedural history and issues in the proceedings;

(b)   the issue in the proceedings on which the court seeks a submission.]

Rule 18.2(1)

FORM 24[2]
Order by the court and certificate in optional procedure for recovery of documents

Sheriff Court, (*place and address*)

In the cause (*court ref. no.*)

in which

AB (*design*) is the pursuer

and

CD (*design*) is the defender

To: (*name and designation of party or haver from whom the documents are sought to be recovered.*)

You are required to produce to the sheriff clerk at (*address*) within..........days of the service upon you of this order:

(1) This order itself (which must be produced intact);

(2) The certificate marked 'B' attached;

(3) All documents within your possession covered by the specification which is enclosed; and

(4) A list of those documents. You can produce the items listed above either:

(a) by delivering them to the sheriff clerk at the address shown above; or

(b) sending them to the sheriff clerk by registered or recorded delivery post.

(*date*)..........(*Signature, name, address and designation of person serving order*)

PLEASE NOTE:

If you claim confidentiality for any of the documents produced by you, you must still produce them. However, they may be placed in a separate envelope by themselves, marked "confidential". The court will, if necessary, decide whether the envelope should be opened or not.

Claims for necessary outlays within certain specified limits may be paid. Claims should be made in writing to the person who has obtained an order that you produce the documents.

CERTIFICATE
B

Sheriff Court, (*place and address*)

In the cause (*court ref. no.*)

in which

AB (*design*) is the pursuer

---

[1] As inserted by the Act of Sederunt (Sheriff Court Rules) (Miscellaneous Amendments) 2008 (SSI 2008/223) Sch.3 (effective July 1, 2008).

[2] As substituted by Act of Sederunt (Ordinary Cause, Summary Application, Summary Cause and Small Claim Rules) Amendment (Miscellaneous) 2005 (SSI 2005/648) (effective January 2, 2006).

and

CD (*design*) is the defender.

Order for recovery of documents dated..........

With reference to the above order and relative specification of documents, I certify:

delete as appropriate

*that the documents produced herewith and the list signed by me which accompanies them are all the documents in my possession which fall under the specification.

* I have no documents in my possession falling under the specification.

* I believe that there are other documents falling within the specification which are not in my possession. These documents are (*list the documents as described in the specification*) These documents were last seen by me on (*date*) in the possession of (*name and address of person/company, if known*).

* I know of no documents falling within the specification which are in the possession of any other person.

(*name*) (*date*)

Rule 18.7(3)

FORM 25

Form of minute in an application for letter of request

Sheriff Court, (*place and address*)

MINUTE

for (*designation*)

In the cause (court ref. no.)

in which

AB (*design*) is the pursuer

and

CD (*design*) is the defender.

The minuter states to the court that the evidence specified in the proposed letter of request lodged with this minute is required for the purpose of this cause. The minuter respectfully asks the court to issue a letter of request in terms of the proposed letter of request to (*central authority of the country or territory in which the evidence is to be obtained*) in order to obtain the evidence so specified.

(*designation of minuter*)

Rule 18.7(3)

FORM 25A

Form of letter of request

PART A—items to be included in every letter of request

1.	Sender	(*Identity and address*).......... ....
2.	Central authority of the requested state	(*Identity and address*).......... ....
3.	Persons to whom the executed request is to be returned	(*Identity and address*).......... ....
4.	The undersigned applicant has the honour to submit the following request:	
5.	a. Requesting Judicial authority	(*Identity and address*).......... ....

b. To the competent authority   (*the requested state*)..........

....

6.   Names and addresses of the parties and
     their representatives
     a. pursuer   ....
     b. defender   ....
     c. other parties   ....
7.   Nature and purpose of the proceedings   ....
     and summary of the facts

....

8.   Evidence to be obtained or other   ....
     judicial act to be performed

....

PART B—items to be completed where applicable

9.   Identity and address of any person to   ....
     be examined

....

10. Questions to be put to the person to be   (*or, see attached list*)..........
     examined, or statement of the subject
     matter about which they are to be
     examined

....

....

....

11. Documents or other property to be   (*specify whether to be produced,*
     inspected   *copied,*
                                         valued etc.)................
12. Any requirement that the evidence be   (*in the event that the evidence can-*
     given on oath or affirmation and any   *not be taken in the manner*
     special form to be used   *requested, specify whether it is to*
                                          be taken in such manner as
                                          provided by local law for the
                                          formal taking of evidence)

13. Special methods or procedure to be fol-   ....
     lowed

....

14. Request for notification of the time and   ....
     place for the execution of the request
     and identity and address of any person
     to be notified

....

....

....

15. Request for attendance or participation   ....
     of judicial personnel of the requesting

887

authority at the execution of the letter
of request

....

....

....

16. Specification of privilege or duty to   ....
    refuse to give evidence under the law
    of the state of origin

....

....

17. The fees and expenses incurred will be   *(identity and address)*..........
    borne by

....

PART C—to be included in every letter of request

18. Date of request, signature and seal of   ....
    the requesting authority

....

Rule 18.7A(2)

FORM 25B[1]

Form of minute in application for taking of evidence in the European Community
Sheriff Court, (*place and address*)

MINUTE
for (*designation*)
In the cause (court ref. no.)
in which
AB (*design*) is the pursuer
and
CD (*design*) is the defender.

The minuter states to the court that the evidence specified in the proposed Form A
[or Form I] lodged with this minute is required for the purpose of this cause. The
minuter respectfully asks the court to issue that Form to (*specify the applicable
court, tribunal, central body or competent authority*) in order to obtain the evidence
specified.

Signed (*designation of minuter*)

Rule 18.8(1)

FORM 26[2]

Form of citation of witness or haver

(*date*)

CITATION

SHERIFFDOM OF (*insert name of sheriffdom*)

AT (*insert place of sheriff court*)

TO *[A.B.]* (design)

---

[1] As inserted by the Act of Sederunt (Taking of Evidence in the European Community) 2003 (SI 2003/
601).

[2] As substituted by the Act of Sederunt (Ordinary Cause, Summary Application, Summary Cause and
Small Claim Rules) Amendment (Vulnerable Witnesses (Scotland) Act 2004) 2007 (SSI 2007/463)
(effective November 1, 2007).

(Name) who is pursuing/defending a case against *(name)* *[or is a (specify) in the case of (name) against (name)]* has asked you to be a witness. You must attend the above sheriff court on *(insert date)* at *(insert time)* for that purpose, *[and bring with you (specify documents)]*.

If you
* would like to know more about being a witness
* are a child under the age of 16
* think you may be a vulnerable witness within the meaning of section 11(1) of the Vulnerable Witnesses (Scotland) Act 2004 (that is someone the court considers may be less able to give their evidence due to mental disorder or fear or distress connected to giving your evidence at the court hearing).

you should contact *(specify the solicitor acting for the party or the party litigant citing the witness)* for further information.

If you are a vulnerable witness (including a child under the age of 16) then you should be able to use a special measure (such measures include use of a screen, a live TV link or a supporter, or a commissioner) to help you give evidence.

Expenses

You may claim back money which you have had to spend and any earnings you have lost within certain specified limits, because you have to come to court on the above date. These may be paid to you if you claim within specified time limits. Claims should be made to the person who has asked you to attend court. Proof of any loss of earnings should be given to that person.

If you wish your travelling expenses to be paid before you go to court, you should apply for payment to the person who has asked you to attend court.

Failure to attend

It is very important that you attend court and you should note that failure to do so may result in a warrant being granted for your arrest. In addition, if you fail to attend without any good reason, having requested and been paid your travelling expenses, you may be ordered to pay a penalty not exceeding £250.

If you have any questions about anything in this citation, please contact *(specify the solicitor acting for the party or the party litigant citing the witness)* for further information.

Signed

[P.Q.] Sheriff Officer

or [X.Y.], *(add designation and business address)*

Solicitor for the pursuer *[or defender] [or (specify)]*

Rule 18.8(1)

FORM 26A

Form of certificate of witness citation

I certify that on *(date)* I duly cited AB *(design)* to attend at *(name of court)* on *(date)* at *(time)* as a witness for the *(design party)* in the action at the instance of CD *(design)* against EF *(design)* (and I required him to bring with him ....). This I did by ....

(Signature of solicitor or sheriff officer)

Rule 18A.2

FORM 26B[1, 2]

---

[1] As inserted by the Act of Sederunt (Ordinary Cause, Summary Application, Summary Cause and Small Claim Rules) Amendment (Vulnerable Witnesses (Scotland) Act 2004) 2007 (SSI 2007/463) (effective November 1, 2007).

[2] As amended by the Act of Sederunt (Rules of the Court of Session 1994 and Sheriff Court Rules Amendment) (No.3) (Miscellaneous) 2015 (SSI 2015/283) r.5(2) (effective 1 September 2015).

Form of child witness notice
VULNERABLE WITNESSES (SCOTLAND) ACT 2004 SECTION 12

Received the..........day of.........20
(Date of receipt of this notice)
..............(signed)
Sheriff Clerk

CHILD WITNESS NOTICE

Sheriff Court...............20

Court Ref. No.

1. The applicant is the pursuer [or defender] in the action by [A.B.] *(design)* against [C.D.] *(design)*.

2. The applicant has cited *[or intends to cite]* [E.F.] *(date of birth)* as a witness.

3. [E.F.] is a child witnesses under section 11 of the Vulnerable Witnesses (Scotland) Act 2004 [and was under the age of eighteen on the date of the commencement of proceedings].

4. The applicant considers that the following special measure[s] is [are] the most appropriate for the purpose of taking the evidence of [E.F.] *[or that [E.F.] should give evidence without the benefit of any special measure]:*—
(delete as appropriate and specify any special measure(s) sought).

5. [(a) The reason] [s] this [these] special measure[s] is [are] considered the most appropriate is [are] as follows:—
(here specify the reason(s) for the special measure(s) sought).

OR

[(b) The reason] [s] it is considered that [E.F.] should give evidence without the benefit of any special measure is [are]:—
(here explain why it is felt that no special measures are required).

6. [E.F.] and the parent[s] of *[or person[s] with parental responsibility for]* [E.F.] has [have] expressed the following view[s] on the special measure[s] that is [are] considered most appropriate *[or the appropriateness of [E.F.] giving evidence without the benefit of any special measure]:*—
(delete as appropriate and set out the views(s) expressed and how they were obtained)

7. Other information considered relevant to this application is as follows:—
(here set out any other information relevant to the child witness notice).

8. The applicant asks the court to —

(a) consider this child witness notice;

(b) make an order authorising the special measure[s] sought;
or

(c) make an order authorising the giving of evidence by [E.F.] without the benefit of special measures.

(delete as appropriate)

(Signed)
[A.B. *or* C.D.]
[or Representative of A.B. *[or C.D.]] (include full designation)*

NOTE: This form should he suitably adapted where section 16 of the Act of 2004 *applies.*

FORM 26C[1]
Form of vulnerable witness application

---

[1] As inserted by the Act of Sederunt (Ordinary Cause, Summary Application, Summary Cause and Small Claim Rules) Amendment (Vulnerable Witnesses (Scotland) Act 2004) 2007 (SSI 2007/463) (effective November 1, 2007).

The sheriff

and granted decree against..........the for payment of expenses of £..........against the (name of party).

This extract is warrant for all lawful execution thereon.

Date   Sheriff clerk depute

*delete as appropriate

FORM 28A
Form of extract decree–payment

Rule 23.6(3)

Sheriff Court	Court ref. no.
Date of decree	*in absence
Pursuer(s)	Defender(s)

The sheriff granted decree against the..........for payment to the..........the undernoted sums:

(1) Sum(s) decerned for: £

(2) Interest at per cent per year from (date) until payment.

(3) Expenses of £..........against the (name of party).

*A time to pay direction was made under section 1(1) of the Debtors (Scotland) Act 1987.

*A time order was made under section 129(1) of the Consumer Credit Act 1974.

*The amount is payable by instalments of £percommencing within

*days/weeks/months of intimation of this extract decree.

*The amount is payable by lump sum within*days/weeks/months of intimation of this extract decree.

This extract is warrant for all lawful execution thereon.

Date   Sheriff clerk depute

*delete as appropriate

FORM 28B[1]
Form of extract decree—recovery of possession of heritable property (no rent arrears)

Rule 23.6(3)

Sheriff Court	Court ref. no.
Date of decree	*in absence
Pursuer(s)	Defender(s)

The sheriff

(1) granted warrant for ejecting the defender (and others mentioned in the summons) from the premises at.........., such ejection being not sooner than (date) at 12 noon.

(2) granted decree against the defender for payment to the pursuer of the sum of £.......... of expenses.

This extract is warrant for all lawful execution thereon.

---

[1] As amended by the Act of Sederunt (Sheriff Court Rules) (Miscellaneous Amendments) 2012 (SSI 2012/188) para.11 (effective August 1, 2012).

Rule 18A.3
VULNERABLE WITNESSES (SCOTLAND) ACT 2004 Section 12

Received the..........day of..........20..........
(Date of receipt of this notice)
..........(signed)
Sheriff Clerk

VULNERABLE WITNESS APPLICATION

Sheriff Court................ ....20..........

Court Ref. No.

1. The applicant is the pursuer [or defender] in the action by [A.B] (design) against [C.D.] (design).

2. The applicant has cited [or intends to cite] [E.F.] (date of birth) as a witness.

3. The applicant considers that [E.F.] is a vulnerable witness under section 11(1)(b) of the Vulnerable Witnesses (Scotland) Act 2004 for the following reasons:—

(here specify reasons witness is considered to be a vulnerable witness).

4. The applicant considers that the following special measure[s] is [are] the most appropriate for the purpose of taking the evidence of [E.F.]:—

(specify any special measure(s) sought).

5. The reason[s] this [these] special measure[s] is [are] considered the most appropriate is [are] as follows:—

(here specify the reason(s) for the special measures(s) sought).

6. [E.F.] has expressed the following view[s] on the special mcasure[s] that is [are] considered most appropriate:—

(set out the views expressed and how they were obtained).

7. Other information considered relevant to this application is as follows:—

(here set out any other information relevant to the vulnerable witness application).

8. The applicant asks the court to—

(a) consider this vulnerable witness application;

(b) make an order authorising the special measure[s] sought.

(Signed)
[A.B. or CD]
[or Representative of A.B. [or C.D.]] (include full designation)
NOTE: This form should be suitably adapted where section 16 of the Act of 2004 applies.

FORM 26D

Form of certificate of intimation[1]

Rule 18A.4(2)
VULNERABLE WITNESSES (SCOTLAND) ACT 2004 Section 12
CERTIFICATE OF INTIMATION

Sheriff Court.................... 20

Court Ref. No.

I certify that intimation of the child witness notice [or vulnerable witness application] relating to (insert name of witness) was made to (insert names of parties or solicitors for parties, as appropriate) by (insert method of intimation; where intimation is by facsimile transmission, insert fax number to which intimation sent) on (insert dale of intimation).

---

[1] As inserted by the Act of Sederunt (Ordinary Cause, Summary Application, Summary Cause and Small Claim Rules) Amendment (Vulnerable Witnesses (Scotland) Act 2004) 2007 (SSI 2007/463) (effective November 1, 2007).

Date:..........

(*Signed*)
Solicitor/or Sheriff Officer
(*include full business designation*)

FORM 26E[1]
Form of application for review

Rule 18A.6(1)
VULNERABLE WITNESSES (SCOTLAND) ACT 2004 Section 13

Received the...........day of..........20..........
(*date of receipt of this notice*)
...............(*signed*)
Sheriff Clerk

APPLICATION FOR REVIEW OF ARRANGEMENTS FOR VULNERABLE
WITNESS

Sheriff Court....................20.....

Court Ref. No.

1. The applicant is the pursuer *[or* defender] in the action by [A.B.] (*design*) against [C.D.] (*design*).
2. A proof *[or* hearing] is fixed for (*date*) at (*time*).
3. [E.F.] is a witness who is to give evidence at, or for the purposes of, the proof *[or* hearing]. [E.F.] is a child witness *[or* vulnerable witness] under section 11 of the Vulnerable Witnesses (Scotland) Act 2004.
4. The current arrangements for taking the evidence of [E.F.] are (*here specify current arrangements*).
5. The current arrangements should be reviewed as (*here specify reasons for review*).
6. [E.F.] [and the parent[s] of *[or* person[s] with parental responsibility for] [E.F.]] has [have] expressed the following view[s] on [the special measure[s] that is [are] considered most appropriate] *[or* the appropriateness of [E.F.] giving evidence without the benefit of any special measure]:–
(*delete as appropriate and set out the view(s) expressed and how they were obtained*).
7. The applicant seeks (here specify the order sought).

(*Signed*)
[A.B. or C.D.]
[or Representative of A.B. *[or* C.D.]] (*include full designation*)
NOTE: *This form should be suitably adapted where* section 16 of the Act of 2004 *applies.*

FORM 26F[2]
Form of certificate of intimation

Rule 18A.7(2)
VULNERABLE WITNESSES (SCOTLAND) ACT 2004 Section 13
CERTIFICATE OF INTIMATION

Sheriff Court.........................20..........

Court Ref. No.

---

[1] As inserted by the Act of Sederunt (Ordinary Cause, Summary Application, Summary Cause and Small Claim Rules) Amendment (Vulnerable Witnesses (Scotland) Act 2004) 2007 (SSI 2007/463) (effective November 1, 2007).

[2] As inserted by the Act of Sederunt (Ordinary Cause, Summary Application, Summary Cause and Small Claim Rules) Amendment (Vulnerable Witnesses (Scotland) Act 2004) 2007 (SSI 2007/463) (effective November 1, 2007).

I certify that intimation of the review application relating to (*insert name of witness*) was made to (*insert names of parties or solicitors for parties, as appropriate*) by (*insert method of intimation; where intimation is by facsimile transmission, insert fax number to which intimation sent*) on (*insert date of intimation*).
Date:..........

(*Signed*)
Solicitor *[or* Sheriff Officer]
(*include full business designation*)

FORM 27
Form of reference to the European Court

Rule 20.2(2)

REQUEST
for
PRELIMINARY RULING
of
THE COURT OF JUSTICE OF THE EUROPEAN COMMUNITIES
from
THE SHERIFFDOM OF (*insert name of sheriffdom*) at (*insert place of court*)
In the cause
AB (*insert designation and address*),

Pursuer

Against
CD (*insert designation and address*)

Defender

(*Here set out a clear and succinct statement of the case giving rise to the request for a ruling of the European Court in order to enable the European Court to consider and understand the issues of Community law raised and to enable governments of Member states and other interested parties to submit observations. The statement of the case should include*:
(a) *particulars of the parties*;
(b) *the history of the dispute between the parties*;
(c) *the history of the proceedings*;
(d) *the relevant facts as agreed by the parties or found by the court or, falling such agreement or finding, the contentions of the parties on such facts*;
(e) *the nature of the issues of law and fact between the parties*;
(f) *the Scots law, so far as relevant*;
(g) *the Treaty provisions or other acts, instruments or rules of Community law concerned*;
(h) *an explanation of why the reference is being made*).
The preliminary ruling of the Court of Justice of the European Communities is accordingly requested on the following questions:
1,2,etc. (*Here set out the question(s) on which the ruling is sought, identifying the Treaty provisions or other acts, instruments or rules of Community law concerned.*)
Dated..........the..........day of..........20

FORM 28
Form of extract decree–basic

Rule 23.6(3)

Sheriff Court
Date of decree
Pursuer(s)

Court ref. no.
*in absence
Defender(s)

Rule 18A.3
VULNERABLE WITNESSES (SCOTLAND) ACT 2004 Section 12
Received the..........day of..........20..........
(*Date of receipt of this notice*)
..........(*signed*)
Sheriff Clerk
VULNERABLE WITNESS APPLICATION
Sheriff Court............... ....20..........

Court Ref. No.

1. The applicant is the pursuer *[or defender]* in the action by [A.B] (*design*) against [C.D.] (*design*).

2. The applicant has cited *[or intends to cite]* [E.F.] (*date of birth*) as a witness.

3. The applicant considers that [E.F.] is a vulnerable witness under section 11(1)(b) of the Vulnerable Witnesses (Scotland) Act 2004 for the following reasons:—

(*here specify reasons witness is considered to be a vulnerable witness*).

4. The applicant considers that the following special measure[s] is [are] the most appropriate for the purpose of taking the evidence of [E.F.]:—

(*specify any special measure(s) sought*).

5. The reason[s] this [these] special measure[s] is [are] considered the most appropriate is [are] as follows:—

(*here specify the reason(s) for the special measures(s) sought*).

6. [E.F.] has expressed the following view[s] on the special mcasure[s] that is [are] considered most appropriate:—

(*set out the views expressed and how they were obtained*).

7. Other information considered relevant to this application is as follows:—

(*here set out any other information relevant to the vulnerable witness application*).

8. The applicant asks the court to—

(a)   consider this vulnerable witness application;

(b)   make an order authorising the special measure[s] sought.

(*Signed*)
[A.B. or CD]
[or Representative of A.B. [or C.D.]] (include full designation)
NOTE: This form should be suitably adapted where section 16 of the Act of 2004 applies.

FORM 26D

Form of certificate of intimation[1]

Rule 18A.4(2)
VULNERABLE WITNESSES (SCOTLAND) ACT 2004 Section 12
CERTIFICATE OF INTIMATION
Sheriff Court.................... 20

Court Ref. No.

I certify that intimation of the child witness notice *[or vulnerable witness application]* relating to (*insert name of witness*) was made to (*insert names of parties or solicitors for parties, as appropriate*) by (*insert method of intimation; where intimation is by facsimile transmission, insert fax number to which intimation sent*) on (*insert dale of intimation*).

---

[1] As inserted by the Act of Sederunt (Ordinary Cause, Summary Application, Summary Cause and Small Claim Rules) Amendment (Vulnerable Witnesses (Scotland) Act 2004) 2007 (SSI 2007/463) (effective November 1, 2007).

Date:..........

(*Signed*)
Solicitor/or Sheriff Officer
(*include full business designation*)

FORM 26E[1]
Form of application for review

Rule 18A.6(1)
VULNERABLE WITNESSES (SCOTLAND) ACT 2004 Section 13

Received the...........day of..........20.........
(*date of receipt of this notice*)
...............(*signed*)
Sheriff Clerk

APPLICATION FOR REVIEW OF ARRANGEMENTS FOR VULNERABLE
WITNESS

Sheriff Court....................20.....

Court Ref. No.

1. The applicant is the pursuer *[or* defender] in the action by [A.B.] (*design*) against [C.D.] (*design*).
2. A proof *[or* hearing] is fixed for (*date*) at (*time*).
3. [E.F.] is a witness who is to give evidence at, or for the purposes of, the proof *[or* hearing]. [E.F.] is a child witness *[or* vulnerable witness] under section 11 of the Vulnerable Witnesses (Scotland) Act 2004.
4. The current arrangements for taking the evidence of [E.F.] are (*here specify current arrangements*).
5. The current arrangements should be reviewed as (*here specify reasons for review*).
6. [E.F.] [and the parent[s] of *[or* person[s] with parental responsibility for] [E.F.]] has [have] expressed the following view[s] on [the special measure[s] that is [are] considered most appropriate] *[or* the appropriateness of [E.F.] giving evidence without the benefit of any special measure]:–
   (*delete as appropriate and set out the view(s) expressed and how they were obtained*).
7. The applicant seeks (here specify the order sought).

(*Signed*)
[A.B. or C.D.]
[or Representative of A.B. *[or* C.D.]] (*include full designation*)
NOTE: This form should be suitably adapted where section 16 of the Act of 2004
applies.

FORM 26F[2]
Form of certificate of intimation

Rule 18A.7(2)
VULNERABLE WITNESSES (SCOTLAND) ACT 2004 Section 13
CERTIFICATE OF INTIMATION

Sheriff Court.........................20..........

Court Ref. No.

---

[1] As inserted by the Act of Sederunt (Ordinary Cause, Summary Application, Summary Cause and Small Claim Rules) Amendment (Vulnerable Witnesses (Scotland) Act 2004) 2007 (SSI 2007/463) (effective November 1, 2007).
[2] As inserted by the Act of Sederunt (Ordinary Cause, Summary Application, Summary Cause and Small Claim Rules) Amendment (Vulnerable Witnesses (Scotland) Act 2004) 2007 (SSI 2007/463) (effective November 1, 2007).

I certify that intimation of the review application relating to (*insert name of witness*) was made to (*insert names of parties or solicitors for parties, as appropriate*) by (*insert method of intimation; where intimation is by facsimile transmission, insert fax number to which intimation sent*) on (*insert date of intimation*).

Date:..........

(*Signed*)
Solicitor [*or* Sheriff Officer]
(*include full business designation*)
FORM 27
Form of reference to the European Court

Rule 20.2(2)

REQUEST
for
PRELIMINARY RULING
of
THE COURT OF JUSTICE OF THE EUROPEAN COMMUNITIES
from
THE SHERIFFDOM OF (*insert name of sheriffdom*) at (*insert place of court*)
In the cause
AB (*insert designation and address*),

Pursuer

Against
CD (*insert designation and address*)

Defender

(*Here set out a clear and succinct statement of the case giving rise to the request for a ruling of the European Court in order to enable the European Court to consider and understand the issues of Community law raised and to enable governments of Member states and other interested parties to submit observations. The statement of the case should include*:

(a) *particulars of the parties*;
(b) *the history of the dispute between the parties*;
(c) *the history of the proceedings*;
(d) *the relevant facts as agreed by the parties or found by the court or, falling such agreement or finding, the contentions of the parties on such facts*;
(e) *the nature of the issues of law and fact between the parties*;
(f) *the Scots law, so far as relevant*;
(g) *the Treaty provisions or other acts, instruments or rules of Community law concerned*;
(h) *an explanation of why the reference is being made*).

The preliminary ruling of the Court of Justice of the European Communities is accordingly requested on the following questions:

1,2,etc. (*Here set out the question(s) on which the ruling is sought, identifying the Treaty provisions or other acts, instruments or rules of Community law concerned.*)

Dated..........the..........day of..........20

FORM 28
Form of extract decree–basic

Rule 23.6(3)

Sheriff Court	Court ref. no.
Date of decree	*in absence
Pursuer(s)	Defender(s)

893

The sheriff

and granted decree against..........the for payment of expenses of £..........against the (name of party).

This extract is warrant for all lawful execution thereon.

Date   Sheriff clerk depute

*delete as appropriate

FORM 28A
Form of extract decree–payment

Rule 23.6(3)

Sheriff Court	Court ref. no.
Date of decree	*in absence
Pursuer(s)	Defender(s)

The sheriff granted decree against the..........for payment to the..........the undernoted sums:

(1) Sum(s) decerned for: £
(2) Interest at per cent per year from (date) until payment.
(3) Expenses of £..........against the (name of party).

*A time to pay direction was made under section 1(1) of the Debtors (Scotland) Act 1987.

*A time order was made under section 129(1) of the Consumer Credit Act 1974.

*The amount is payable by instalments of £percommencing within

*days/weeks/months of intimation of this extract decree.

*The amount is payable by lump sum within*days/weeks/months of intimation of this extract decree.

This extract is warrant for all lawful execution thereon.

Date   Sheriff clerk depute

*delete as appropriate

FORM 28B[1]
Form of extract decree—recovery of possession of heritable property (no rent arrears)

Rule 23.6(3)

Sheriff Court	Court ref. no.
Date of decree	*in absence
Pursuer(s)	Defender(s)

The sheriff

(1) granted warrant for ejecting the defender (and others mentioned in the summons) from the premises at.........., such ejection being not sooner than (date) at 12 noon.
(2) granted decree against the defender for payment to the pursuer of the sum of £.......... of expenses.

This extract is warrant for all lawful execution thereon.

---

[1] As amended by the Act of Sederunt (Sheriff Court Rules) (Miscellaneous Amendments) 2012 (SSI 2012/188) para.11 (effective August 1, 2012).

Date   Sheriff clerk depute

Rule 23.6(3)

FORM 26BA[1]

Form of extract decree—recovery of possession of heritable property in accordance with section 16(5A) of the Housing (Scotland) Act 2001 (non-payment of rent)

Sheriff Court	Court ref no.
Date of decree	* in absence
Pursuer(s)	Defender(s)

The sheriff—

(1) granted warrant for ejecting the defender (and others mentioned in the summons) from the premises at (*insert address of premises*) on (*insert date*) and specified a period of (*number*) (*days/weeks/months**) from that date as the period for which the pursuer's right to eject shall have effect.

(2) granted decree against the defender for payment to the pursuer of the undernoted sums:

    (a) Sum(s) decerned for: £(*insert sum*).

    (b) Interest at (*insert rate of interest*) per cent per year from (*insert date*) until payment.

    (c) Expenses of £(*insert amount*) against the (*insert name of party*).

*A time to pay direction was made under section 1(1) of the Debtors (Scotland) Act 1987.

*The amount is payable by instalments of £(*insert sum*) per (*insert period*) commencing within (*insert timescale*) *days/weeks/months of intimation of this extract decree.

The amount is payable by lump sum within (*insert timescale*) *days/weeks/months of intimation of this extract decree.

This extract is warrant for all lawful execution thereon.

Date   (Sheriff clerk depute)

delete as appropriate

FORM 28BB[2, 3]

Rule 23.6(3)

Form of extract decree—recovery of possession of heritable property in other cases
(non-payment of rent)

Sheriff Court	Court ref no.
Date of decree	*in absence
Pursuer(s)	Defender(s)

The sheriff—

(1) granted warrant for ejecting the defender (and others mentioned in the summons) from the premises at (*insert address of premises*), such ejection being not sooner than (*insert date*) at 12 noon.

---

[1] As inserted by the Act of Sederunt (Sheriff Court Rules) (Miscellaneous Amendments) 2012 (SSI 2012/188) para.11 (effective August 1, 2012).

[2] As inserted by the Act of Sederunt (Sheriff Court Rules) (Miscellaneous Amendments) 2013 (SSI 2013/135) para.3 (effective May 27, 2013).

[3] As amended by the Act of Sederunt (Sheriff Court Rules) (Miscellaneous Amendments) (No.3) 2013 (SSI 2013/171) para.5 (effective June 25, 2013).

(2)   granted decree against the defender for payment to the pursuer of the undernoted sums:

    (a)   Sum(s) decerned for: £*(insert sum)*.

    (b)   Interest at *(insert rate of interest)* per cent per year from *(insert date)* until payment.

    (c)   Expenses of £*(insert amount)* against the *(insert name of party)*.

*A time to pay direction was made under section 1(1) of the Debtors (Scotland) Act 1987.

The amount is payable by instalments of £(insert sum)* per *(insert period)* commencing within *(insert timescale)* *days/weeks/months of intimation of this extract decree.

* The amount is payable by lump sum within *(insert timescale)* *days/weeks/months of intimation of this extract decree.

This extract is warrant for all lawful execution thereon.

Date   *(Sheriff clerk depute)*

delete as appropriate

FORM 28C

Form of extract decree and warrant to sell in sequestration for rent and sale
Rule 23.6(3)

[Repealed by the Act of Sederunt (Sheriff Court Rules Amendment) (Diligence) 2008 (SSI 2008/121) r.2(1)(b) (effective April 1, 2008).]

FORM 28D

Form of extract—warrant for ejection and to re-let in sequestration for rent and sale
Rule 23.6(3)

[Repealed by the Act of Sederunt (Sheriff Court Rules Amendment) (Diligence) 2008 (SSI 2008/121) r.2(1)(b) (effective April 1, 2008).]

FORM 28E

Form of extract decree—furthcoming
Rule 23.6(3)

Sheriff Court	Court ref. no.
Date of decree	*in absence
Date of original decree	
Pursuer(s)	
Defender(s)/Arrestee(s)	
Common debtor	

The sheriff granted decree

(1)   against the arrestee(s) for payment of £, or such other sum(s) as may be owing by the arrestee(s) to the common debtor(s) by virtue of the original decree mentioned above in favour of the pursuer(s) against the common debtor(s).

(2)   for expenses of £

*payable out of the arrested fund.

  *payable by the common debtor.

  delete as appropriate

This extract is warrant for all lawful execution thereon.

Date   Sheriff clerk depute

FORM 28F

Form of extract decree—delivery
Rule 23.6(3)

Sheriff Court   Court ref. no.

Date of decree   *in absence

Pursuer(s)

Defender(s)

The sheriff granted decree against the defender
- (1)   for delivery to the pursuer of (*specify articles*)
- (2)   for expenses of £

*Further, the sheriff granted warrant to officers of court to (1) open shut and lockfast places occupied by the defender and (2) search for and take possession of said goods in the possession of the defender.

    delete as appropriate

This extract is warrant for all lawful execution thereon.

Date   Sheriff clerk depute

FORM 28G

Form of extract decree—delivery—payment failing delivery

    Rule 23.6(3)

Sheriff Court   Court ref. no.

Date of decree   *in absence

Pursuer(s)

Defender(s)

The sheriff, in respect that the defender has failed to make delivery in accordance with the decree granted in this court on (*date*), granted decree for payment against the defender of the undernoted sums:
- (1)   Sum(s) decerned for: £.........., being the alternative crave claimed.
- (2)   Interest at..........per cent per year from (*date*) until payment.
- (3)   Expenses of £..........against the (*name of party*).

*A time to pay direction was made under section 1(1) of the Debtors (Scotland) Act 1987.

    *A time order was made under section 129(1) of the Consumer Credit Act 1974.

    *The amount is payable by instalments of £..........per...........commencing within..........*days/weeks/months..........of intimation of this extract decree.

    *The amount is payable by lump sum within..........*days/weeks/months of intimation of this extract decree.

    delete as appropriate

This extract is warrant for all lawful execution thereon.

Date   Sheriff clerk depute

FORM 28H

Form of extract decree—aliment

    Rule 23.6(3)

Sheriff Court   Court ref. no.

Date of decree   *in absence

Pursuer(s)

Defender(s)

The sheriff

Granted decree against the defender for payment to the pursuer of aliment at the rate of £.......... per *week/month.
*delete as appropriate
This extract is warrant for all lawful execution thereon.

Date   Sheriff clerk depute

FORM 28I
Form of extract decree—ad factum praestandum
Rule 23.6(3)

Sheriff Court   Court ref. no.
Date of decree   *in absence
Pursuer(s)
Defender(s)

The sheriff
(1) ordained the defender(s)
(2) granted decree for payment of expenses of £against the defender(s).
*delete as appropriate
This extract is warrant for all lawful execution thereon.

Date   Sheriff clerk depute

FORM 28J
Form of extract decree—absolvitor
Rule 23.6(3)

Sheriff Court   Court ref. no.
Date of decree   *in absence
Pursuer(s)
Defender(s)

The sheriff
(1) absolved the defender(s)
(2) granted decree for payment of expenses of £.......... against the
*delete as appropriate
This extract is warrant for all lawful execution thereon.

Date   Sheriff clerk depute

FORM 28K
Form of extract decree—dismissal
Rule 23.6(3)

Sheriff Court   Court ref. no.
Date of decree   *in absence
Pursuer(s)
Defender(s)

The sheriff
(1) dismissed the action against the defender(s)
*(2) granted decree for payment of expenses of £.......... against the
*(3) found no expenses due to or by either party
*delete as appropriate

This extract is warrant for all lawful execution thereon.

Date   Sheriff clerk depute

FORM 29
Form of certificate by sheriff clerk
Service of charge where address of defender is unknown

Rule 23.8(4)

I certify that the foregoing charge was displayed on the walls of court on (*date*) and that it remained so displayed for a period of (*period of charge*) from that date.

(*date*)   Sheriff clerk depute

FORM 30[1]
Minute for recall of decree

Rule 24.1(1)

Sheriff Court: (place)
Court ref. no.:

AB (*pursuer*) against CD (*defender(s)*)

The *(*pursuer/defender/third party*) moves the court to recall the decree pronounced on (*date*) in this case * and in which execution of a charge/arrestment was effected on (*date*)

*Proposed defence/answer:

*delete as appropriate

Rule 24.1(6)(a)

FORM 30A[2]
Minute for recall of decree—service copy

Sheriff Court:..........(*place*)

Court ref. no.:..........

AB (*pursuer*) against CD (*defender(s)*)

The *(*pursuer/defender/third party*) moves the court to recall the decree pronounced on (*date*) in this case * and in which execution of a charge/arrestment was effected on (*date*)

*Proposed defence/answer:

*delete as appropriate

NOTE: You must return the summons to the sheriff clerk at the court mentioned at the top of this form by (*insert date 2 days before the date of the hearing.*)

Rule 25.1(1)

FORM 31[3]
Form of application for stated case

SHERIFF COURT (*place*)

Court ref. no..........AB (pursuer) against CD (defender)

The pursuer/defender appeals the sheriff's interlocutor of (*date*) to the Sheriff Appeal Court and requests the sheriff to state a case.

---

[1] As amended by the Act of Sederunt (Sheriff Court Rules) (Miscellaneous Amendments) 2011 (SSI 2011/193) r.16 (effective April 4, 2011).

[2] As amended by the Act of Sederunt (Sheriff Court Rules) (Miscellaneous Amendments) 2011 (SSI 2011/193) r.16 (effective April 4, 2011).

[3] As amended by the Act of Sederunt (Rules of the Court of Session, Sheriff Appeal Court Rules and Sheriff Court Rules Amendment) (Sheriff Appeal Court) 2015 (SSI 2015/419) r.11 (effective 1 January 2016; as to savings see SSI 2015/419 rule 20(6)(a)).

The point(s) of law upon which the appeal is to proceed is/are: (*give brief statement*)

(*date*)

Rule 25.4(3)(a)

FORM 32[1]

Application for leave to appeal against time to pay direction

SHERIFF COURT (*place*)

Court ref. no........... AB (pursuer) against CD (defender)

The pursuer/defender requests the sheriff to grant leave to appeal the decision made on (*date*) in respect of the defender's application for a time to pay direction to the Sheriff Appeal Court/Court of Session.

The point(s) of law upon which the appeal is to proceed is/are: (*give brief statement*)

(*date*)

Rule 25.4(4)

FORM 33[2]

Appeal against time to pay direction

SHERIFF COURT (*place*)

Court ref. no........... AB (pursuer) against CD (defender)

The pursuer/defender appeals the decision made on (*date*) in respect of the defender's application for a time to pay direction to the Sheriff Appeal Court/Court of Session.

(*date*)

Rule 25.7(1)

FORM 34

Application for certificate of suitability for appeal to the Court of Session

[Repealed by the Act of Sederunt (Rules of the Court of Session, Sheriff Appeal Court Rules and Sheriff Court Rules Amendment) (Sheriff Appeal Court) 2015 (SSI 2015/419) r.11 (effective 1 January 2016; as to savings see SSI 2015/419 rule 20(6)(a)).]

Rule 26.4(1)

FORM 35

Form of receipt for money paid to the sheriff clerk

In the sheriff court of (*name of sheriffdom*) at (*place of sheriff court*).

In the cause (*state names of parties or other appropriate description*)

AB (*designation*) has this day paid into court the sum of £........., being a payment made in terms of rule 26(4)(1) of the Summary Cause Rules 2002.

*Custody of this money has been accepted at the request of (*insert name of court making the request*)

**delete as appropriate*

(Date)   Sheriff clerk depute

Rule 32.2(a)

FORM 36

Action for aliment

Form of notice of intimation to children and next of kin where address of defender is unknown

---

[1] As amended by the Act of Sederunt (Rules of the Court of Session, Sheriff Appeal Court Rules and Sheriff Court Rules Amendment) (Sheriff Appeal Court) 2015 (SSI 2015/419) r.11 (effective 1 January 2016; as to savings see SSI 2015/419 rule 20(6)(a)).

[2] As amended by the Act of Sederunt (Rules of the Court of Session, Sheriff Appeal Court Rules and Sheriff Court Rules Amendment) (Sheriff Appeal Court) 2015 (SSI 2015/419) r.11 (effective 1 January 2016; as to savings see SSI 2015/419 rule 20(6)(a)).

Court ref. no.

To: (*insert name and address as in warrant*)

You are hereby given notice that an action for aliment has been raised against (*name*), your (*insert relationship, e.g, father, brother or other relative as the case may be*). A copy of the summons is enclosed.

If you know of his/her present address, you are requested to inform the sheriff clerk at (*insert full address*) in writing immediately.

If you wish to appear as a party in the action, or are uncertain about what action to take, you should contact a solicitor. You may, depending on your financial circumstances, be entitled to legal aid, and you can get information about legal aid from a solicitor.

You may also obtain advice from any Citizen's Advice Bureau, other advice agency or any sheriff clerk's office.

Rule 32.2(b)

FORM 37

Action for aliment

Form of notice of intimation to children, next of kin and guardian where defender suffers from mental disorder

Court ref. no.

To: (*insert name and address as in warrant*)

You are hereby given notice that an action for aliment has been raised against (*name*), your (*insert relationship, e.g, father or other relative, or ward, as the case may be*). A copy of the summons is enclosed.

If you wish to appear as a party in the action, or are uncertain about what action to take, you should contact a solicitor immediately. You may, depending on your financial circumstances, be entitled to legal aid, and you can get information about legal aid from a solicitor.

You may also obtain advice from any Citizen's Advice Bureau, other advice agency or any sheriff clerk's office.

Appendix 1B[1,2]

THE PERSONAL INJURY PRE-ACTION PROTOCOL

Application of the Protocol

1. This Protocol applies to claims for damages for, or arising from personal injuries, unless:

   (a)   the claimant reasonably estimates that the total liability value of the claim, exclusive of interest and expenses, exceeds £25,000;

   (b)   the accident or other circumstance giving rise to the liability occurred before 28th November 2016;

   (c)   the claimant is not represented by a solicitor during the stages of the Protocol; or

   (d)   the injuries for which damages are claimed—

       (i)   arise from alleged clinical negligence;

       (ii)   arise from alleged professional negligence; or

       (iii)   take the form of a disease.

In this paragraph—

---

[1] As inserted by the Act of Sederunt (Sheriff Court Rules Amendment) (Personal Injury Pre-Action Protocol) 2016 (SSI 2016/215) para.3 (effective 28 November 2016).

[2] As amended by the Act of Sederunt (Rules of the Court of Session 1994 and Sheriff Court Rules Amendment) (No. 2) (Miscellaneous) 2016 (SSI 2016/229) para.3 (effective 28 November 2016).

"clinical negligence" has the same meaning as in rule 36.C1 of the Ordinary Cause Rules 1993; and

"disease" includes—

    (a)   any illness, physical or psychological; and

    (b)   any disorder, ailment, affliction, complaint, malady or derangement, other than a physical or psychological injury solely caused by an accident or other similar single event.

Definitions

2. In this Protocol:

"claimant" means the person who is seeking damages from the defender;

"defender" means the person against whom a claim is made.

"next-day postal service which records delivery" means a postal service which—

    (a)   seeks to deliver documents or other things by post no later than the next working day in all or the majority of cases; and

    (b)   provides for the delivery of documents or other things by post to be recorded.

Aims of the Protocol

3. The aims of the Protocol are to assist parties to avoid the need for, or mitigate the length and complexity of, civil proceedings by encouraging:

- the fair, just and timely settlement of disputes prior to the commencement of proceedings; and
- good practice, as regards:
  - early and full disclosure of information about the dispute;
  - investigation of the circumstances surrounding the dispute; and
  - the narrowing of issues to be determined through litigation in cases which do not reach settlement under the Protocol.

Protocol rules

4. Where, in the course of completing the stages of the Protocol, the claimant reasonably estimates that the total value of the claim, exclusive of interest and expenses, has increased beyond £25,000, the claimant must advise the defender that the Protocol threshold has been exceeded. Parties may agree to continue following the stages of the Protocol on a voluntary basis with a view to facilitating settlement before commencing proceedings.

5. Anything done or required to be done by a party under this Protocol may be done by a solicitor, insurer or other representative dealing with the claim for, or on behalf of, that party.

6. Where a party is required under this Protocol to intimate or send a document to another party, the document may be intimated or sent to the solicitor, insurer or other representative dealing with the claim for, or on behalf of, that party.

7. Documents that require to be intimated or sent under the Protocol, should, where possible, be intimated or sent by email using an email address supplied by the claimant or defender. Alternatively, such documents are to be sent or intimated using a next-day postal service which records delivery.

8. Where there is a number of days within which or a date by which something has to be done (including being sent or intimated), it must be done or sent so that it will be received before the end of that period or that day.

9. The claimant is expected to refrain from commencing proceedings unless:

- all stages of the Protocol have been completed without reaching settlement;

- the defender fails to complete a stage of the Protocol within the specified period;
- the defender refuses to admit liability, or liability is admitted on the basis that the defender does not intend to be bound by the admission in any subsequent proceedings;
- the defender admits liability but alleges contributory negligence and the fact or level of contributory negligence is disputed by the claimant (see paragraph 18).
- settlement is reached but the defender fails to pay damages and agreed expenses/outlays within 5 weeks of settlement (see paragraph 35 below); or
- it is necessary to do so for time-bar reasons (in which case, proceedings should be commenced and a sist applied for to allow the stages of the Protocol to be followed).

10. Parties are expected to co-operate generally with each other with a view to fulfilling the aims of the Protocol.

The stages of the Protocol

11. *Stage 1 – issuing of Claim Form*

The claimant must send a Claim Form to the defender as soon as sufficient information is available to substantiate a claim. The Claim Form should contain a clear summary of the facts on which the claim is based, including allegations of negligence, breaches of common law or statutory duty and an indication of injuries suffered and financial loss incurred. A suggested template for the Claim Form can be found in Annex A at the end of this Appendix.

12. *Stage 2 – the defender's acknowledgement of Claim Form*

The defender must acknowledge the Claim Form within 21 days of receipt.

13. *Stage 3 – the defender's investigation of the claim and issuing of Response*

The defender has a maximum of three months from receipt of the Claim Form to investigate the merits of the claim. The defender must send a reply during that period, stating whether liability is admitted or denied, giving reasons for any denial of liability, including any alternative version of events relied upon. The defender must confirm whether any admission made is intended to be a binding admission. Paragraph 9 above confirms that the claimant may raise proceedings if a non-binding admission is made.

14. If the defender denies liability, in whole or in part, they must disclose any documents which are relevant and proportionate to the issues in question at the same time as giving their decision on liability.

15. Paragraph 14 does not apply to documents that would never be recoverable in the course of proceedings, or that the defender would not be at liberty to disclose in the absence of an order from the court.

16. A suggested list of documents which are likely to be material in different types of claim is included in Annex B at the end of this Appendix.

17. If an admission of liability is made under this Protocol, parties will be expected to continue to follow the stages of the Protocol, where:

- the admission is made on the basis that the defender is to be bound by it (subject to the claim subsequently being proved to be fraudulent); and
- the admission is accepted by the claimant.

18. *Stage 4 – disclosure of documents and reports following admission of liability*

Where the defender admits liability to make reparation under the Protocol but alleges contributory negligence, the defender must give reasons supporting the allegations and disclose the documents which are relevant and proportionate to the issue of contributory negligence. The claimant must respond to the allegation of contributory negligence before proceedings are raised.

19. Medical reports are to be instructed by the claimant at the earliest opportunity but no later than 5 weeks from the date the defender admits, in whole or part, liability (unless there is a valid reason for not obtaining a report at this stage).

20. Any medical report on which the claimant intends to rely must be disclosed to the other party within 5 weeks from the date of its receipt. Similarly, any medical report on which the defender intends to rely must be disclosed to the claimant within 5 weeks of receipt.

21. Parties may agree an extension to the issuing of medical reports if necessary.

22. *Stage 5 – issuing of Statement of Valuation of Claim*
The claimant must send a Statement of Valuation of Claim to the defender (in the same form as Form P16 in Appendix 1 of the Ordinary Cause Rules), together with supporting documents. The Statement of Valuation of Claim should be sent as soon as possible following receipt of all the other relevant information, including medical reports, wage slips, etc.

23. If the defender considers that additional information is required in order to consider whether to make an offer in settlement, the defender may request additional information from the claimant. Any such request is to be made promptly following receipt of the Statement of Valuation of Claim and supporting documents. The claimant must provide the information requested within 14 days of receipt of the request.

24. *Stage 6 – offer of settlement*
Any offer in settlement to be made by the defender may be made within 5 weeks from the date of receipt of the Statement of Valuation of Claim, medical reports and supporting evidence (including any additional information requested under paragraph 23).

25. Where the claimant's injuries are minor and no formal medical treatment is sought, a settlement offer may be made in the absence of medical evidence; otherwise, settlement offers may only be made following the submission of satisfactory medical evidence of injury.

26. An offer in settlement is only valid for the purposes of this Protocol if it includes an offer to pay expenses in accordance with the expenses provisions (at paragraphs 30-33) in the event of acceptance.

27. *Stage 7 – claimant's response to offer of settlement*
If a settlement offer is made, the claimant must either accept the offer or issue a reasoned response within 14 days of receipt of the offer. Alternatively, if the claimant considers that additional information is required to allow full and proper consideration of the settlement offer, the claimant may make a request for additional information from the defender within 14 days of the receipt of the offer.

28. Where additional information or documentation is requested to allow the claimant to give full and proper consideration to the settlement offer, the claimant must accept the offer or issue a reasoned response within 21 days of receipt of the additional information or documentation.

29. In any reasoned response issued, the claimant must:
- reject the offer outright, giving reasons for the rejection; or
- reject the offer and make a counter-offer, giving reasons.

30. The expenses to be paid to the claimant in the event of settlement comprise—
    (a) a payment in respect of the claimant's liability for solicitors' fees calculated in accordance with paragraph 31, and
    (b) reimbursement of all other reasonably incurred outlays.

31. The payment in respect of liability for solicitors' fees is the sum of—

(a) £546;

(b) 3.5% of the total amount of agreed damages up to £25,000;

(c) 25% of that part of the agreed damages up to £3,000;

(d) 15% of the excess of the agreed damages over £3,000 up to £6,000;

(e) 7.5% of the excess of the agreed damages over £6,000 up to £12,000;

(f) 5% of the excess of the agreed damages over £12,000 up to £18,000;

(g) 2.5% of the excess of the agreed damages over £18,000; and

(h) a figure corresponding to the VAT payable on the sum of the foregoing.

32. Where an expert report has been instructed, any associate agency fee is not a reasonably incurred outlay for the purpose of paragraph 30(b).

33. Any deduction from damages in accordance with section 7 of the Social Security (Recovery of Benefits) Act 1997 is to be disregarded for the purpose of paragraph 31.

34. *Stage 8 – stocktaking period*

The claimant must not raise proceedings until at least 14 days after the defender receives the claimant's reasoned response (even in cases where the settlement offer is rejected outright). This period allows parties to take stock of their respective positions and to pursue further settlement negotiations if desired.

35. *Stage 9 – payment*

Damages and Protocol expenses must be paid within 5 weeks of settlement (with interest payable thereafter at the judicial rate).

Annex A

1. This form is to be used where the details of the defender's insurers are known:

Pre-Action Protocol Claim Form
TO: (*name of insurance company*)
FROM: (*name of solicitor and firm representing claimant*)
DATE: (*date of issue of Claim Form*)
This is a claim which we consider to be subject to the terms of the Personal Injury Pre-Action Protocol as set out in the Act of Sederunt (Sheriff Court Rules Amendment) (Personal Injury Pre- Action Protocol) 2016. **Please acknowledge receipt of this claim within 21 days of the date of this Form.**
CONTACT: (*postal and email address of solicitor representing claimant*)

Claimant's details	
Claimant's Full Name	
Claimant's Full Address	
Claimant's Date of Birth	
Claimant's Payroll or Reference Number	
Claimant's Employer (name and address)	
Claimant's National Insurance Number	

Details of Claim
We are instructed by the above named to claim damages in connection with: [*state nature of accident* an accident at work/road traffic accident/tripping ac-

cident] on [Xth] day of [year] at [*state place of accident* – which must be sufficiently detailed to establish location].

The circumstances of the accident are:-

[*provide brief outline and simple explanation* e.g. defective machine, vicarious liability].

Your insured failed to:- [*provide brief details of the common law and/or statutory breaches*].

Our client's injuries are as follows:- [*provide brief outline*].

i. Our client received treatment for the injuries at [*give name and address of GP/ treating hospital*].

[In cases of road accidents...]

ii. Our client's motor insurers are:-

Our client is still suffering from the effects of his/her injury. We invite you to participate with us in addressing his/her immediate needs by use of rehabilitation. He/she is employed as [*insert occupation*] and has had the following time off work [*provide dates of absence*]. His/her approximate weekly income is [*insert if known*].

Reports
We are obtaining a police report and will let you have a copy of same upon your undertaking to meet half the fee.
At this stage of our enquiries we would expect the undernoted documents to be relevant to this claim. (...)

2. This form is to be used where the details of the defender's insurers are not known:

Pre -Action Protocol Claim Form
TO: (*name of defender*)
FROM: (*name of solicitor and firm representing claimant*)
DATE: (*date of issue of Claim Form*)
This is a claim which we consider to be subject to the terms of the Personal Injury Pre-Action Protocol as set out in the Act of Sederunt (Sheriff Court Rules Amendment) (Personal Injury Pre- Action Protocol) 2016. **You should acknowledge receipt of this claim and forward it to your Insurers as soon as possible, asking them to contact us within 21 days of the date of this Form.**
CONTACT: (*postal and email address of solicitor representing claimant*)

Claimant's details	
Claimant's Full Name	
Claimant's Full Address	
Claimant's Payroll or Reference Number	
Claimant's Employer (name and address)	

We are instructed by the above named to claim damages in connection with: [*state nature of accident* an accident at work/road traffic accident/tripping accident] on [Xth] day of [year] at [*state place of accident* – which must be sufficiently detailed to establish location].

The circumstances of the accident are:-
[*provide brief outline and simple explanation* e.g. defective machine, vicarious liability].
You failed to:- [*provide brief details of the common law and/or statutory breaches*].
Our client's injuries are as follows:- [*provide brief outline*].
i. Our client received treatment for the injuries at [*give name and address of GP/ treating hospital*].
[In cases of road accidents...]
ii. Our client's motor insurers are:-
Our client is still suffering from the effects of his/her injury. We invite you to participate with us in addressing his/her immediate needs by use of rehabilitation. He/she is employed as [*insert occupation*] and has had the following time off work [*provide dates of absence*]. His/her approximate weekly income is [*insert if known*].

Reports
We are obtaining a police report and will let you have a copy of same upon your undertaking to meet half the fee.
At this stage of our enquiries we would expect the undernoted documents to be relevant to this claim. (...)

ANNEX B – STANDARD DISCLOSURE

Road Traffic Cases

1. **Section A – cases where liability is at issue**
   (i)   Documents identifying nature, extent and location of damage to defender's vehicle where there is any dispute about point of impact.
   (ii) MOT certificate where relevant.
   (iii) Maintenance records where vehicle defect is alleged or it is alleged by defender that there was an unforeseen defect which caused or contributed to the accident.

Section B - accidents involving a potential defender's commercial vehicle
   (i)   Tachograph charts or entry from individual control book, where relevant.
   (ii) Maintenance and repair records required for operators' licence where vehicle defect is alleged or it is alleged by defender that there was an unforeseen defect which caused or contributed to the accident.

Section C - cases against local authorities where a highway design defect is alleged
   (i)   Documents produced to comply with section 39 of the Road Traffic Act 1988 in respect of the duty designed to promote road safety to include studies into road accidents in the relevant area and documents relating to measures recommended to prevent accidents in the relevant area.

Road/footway tripping claims

2. Documents from the Highway Authority or local authority for a period of 12 months prior to the accident–
   (i)   Records of inspection for the relevant stretch of road/footway.

(ii)   Maintenance records including records of independent contractors working in relevant area.

(iii) Statement of the Roads Authority's policy under the Code of Practice for Highway Maintenance Management (2005) or alternatively records of the Minutes of Highway Authority or Local Authority meetings where maintenance or repair policy has been discussed or decided.

(iv)   Records of complaints about the state of roads/footway at the accident locus for a 12 month period prior to the accident.

(v)   Records of other accidents which have occurred on the relevant stretch of road/footway within 12 months of the accident.

Workplace claims – general

3.

(i)   Accident book entry.

(ii)   First aider report.

(iii) Surgery record.

(iv)   Foreman/supervisor accident report.

(v)   Safety representatives' accident report.

(vi)   RIDDOR (Reporting of Injuries, Disease and Dangerous Occurrences Regulations 2013) report to the Health and Safety Executive (HSE).

(vii) Other communications between defenders and HSE.

(viii) Minutes of Health and Safety Committee meeting(s) where accident/matter considered.

(ix)   Report to the Department for Work and Pensions.

(x)   Documents listed above relative to any previous accident/matter identified by the claimant and relied upon as proof of negligence.

(xi)   Earnings information where defender is employer.

Workplace claims -

4. Documents produced to comply with requirements of the Management of Health and Safety at Work Regulations 1991/3242

(i)   Pre-accident Risk Assessment required by Regulation 3.

(ii)   Post-accident Re-Assessment required by Regulation 3.

(iii) Accident Investigation Report prepared in implementing the requirements of Regulation 5.

(iv)   Health Surveillance Records in appropriate cases required by Regulation 6.

(v)   Information provided to employees under Regulation 10.

(vi)   Documents relating to the employee's health and safety training required by Regulation 13.

Workplace claims – Disclosure where specific regulations apply

5. Section A – Manual Handling Operations Regulations 1992/2793

(i)   Manual Handling Risk Assessment carried out to comply with the requirements of Regulation 4(1)(b)(i).

(ii)   Re-assessment carried out post-accident to comply with requirements of Regulation 4(1)(b)(i).

(iii) Documents showing the information provided to the employee to give general indications related to the load and precise indications on the weight of the load and the heaviest side of the load if the centre of gravity was not positioned centrally to comply with Regulation 4(1)(b)(iii).

(iv) Documents relating to training in respect of manual handling operations and training records.

(v) All documents showing or tending to show the weight of the load at the material time.

Section B – Personal Protective Equipment at Work Regulations 1992/2966

(i) Documents relating to the assessment of Personal Protective Equipment to comply with Regulation 6.

(ii) Documents relating to the maintenance and replacement of Personal Protective Equipment to comply with Regulation 7.

(iii) Record of maintenance procedures for Personal Protective Equipment to comply with Regulation 7.

(iv) Records of tests and examinations of Personal Protective Equipment to comply with Regulation 7.

(v) Documents providing information, instruction and training in relation to the Personal Protective Equipment to comply with Regulation 9.

(vi) Instructions for use of Personal Protective Equipment to include the manufacturers' instructions to comply with Regulation 10.

Section C – Workplace (Health Safety and Welfare) Regulations 1992/3004

(i) Repair and maintenance records required by Regulation 5.

(ii) Housekeeping records to comply with the requirements of Regulation 9.

(iii) Hazard warning signs or notices to comply with Regulation 17.

Section D – Provision and Use of Work Equipment Regulations 1998/2306

(i) Manufacturers' specifications and instructions in respect of relevant work equipment establishing its suitability to comply with Regulation 4.

(ii) Maintenance log/maintenance records required to comply with Regulation 5.

(iii) Documents providing information and instructions to employees to comply with Regulation 8.

(iv) Documents provided to the employee in respect of training for use to comply with Regulation 9.

(v) Any notice, sign or document relied upon as a defence to alleged breaches of Regulations 14 to 18 dealing with controls and control systems.

(vi) Instruction/training documents issued to comply with the requirements of Regulation 22 insofar as it deals with maintenance operations where the machinery is not shut down.

(vii) Copies of markings required to comply with Regulation 23.

(viii) Copies of warnings required to comply with Regulation 24.

Section E – Lifting Operations and Lifting Equipment Regulations 1998/2307

(i) All documents showing the weight of any load to establish lifting equipment of adequate strength and stability to comply with Regulation 4.

(ii) All notices and markings showing the safe working load of machinery and accessories to comply with Regulation 7.

(iii) All documents showing lifting operations have been planned by a competent person, appropriately supervised and carried out in a safe manner to comply with Regulation 8.

(iv) All defect reports to comply with Regulation 10.

Section F – Pressure Systems Safety Regulations 2000/128

(i) Information and specimen markings provided to comply with the requirements of Regulation 5.

(ii) Written statements specifying the safe operating limits of a system to comply with the requirements of Regulation 7.

(iii) Copy of the written scheme of examination required to comply with the requirements of Regulation 8.

(iv) Examination records required to comply with the requirements of Regulation 9.

(v) Instructions provided for the use of operator to comply with Regulation 11.

(vi) Records kept to comply with the requirements of Regulation 14.

Section G – Control of Substances Hazardous to Health Regulations 2002/2677

(i) Risk assessment carried out to comply with the requirements of Regulation 6.

(ii) Reviewed risk assessment carried out to comply with the requirements of Regulation 6.

(iii) Copy labels from containers used for storage handling and disposal of carcinogenics to comply with the requirements of Regulation 7.

(iv) Warning signs identifying designation of areas and installations which may be contaminated by carcinogenics to comply with the requirements of Regulation 7.

(v) Documents relating to the assessment of the Personal Protective Equipment to comply with Regulation 7.

(vi) Documents relating to the maintenance and replacement of Personal Protective Equipment to comply with Regulation 7.

(vii) Record of maintenance procedures for Personal Protective Equipment to comply with Regulation 7.

(viii) Records of tests and examinations of Personal Protective Equipment to comply with Regulation 7.

(ix) Documents providing information, instruction and training in relation to the Personal Protective Equipment to comply with Regulation 7.

(x) Instructions for use of Personal Protective Equipment to include the manufacturers' instructions to comply with Regulation 7.

(xi) Air monitoring records for substances assigned a maximum exposure limit or occupational exposure standard to comply with the requirements of Regulation 7.

(xii) Maintenance examination and test of control measures records to comply with Regulation 9.

(xiii) Monitoring records to comply with the requirements of Regulation 10.

(xiv) Health surveillance records to comply with the requirements of Regulation 11.

(xv) Documents detailing information, instruction and training including training records for employees to comply with the requirements of Regulation 12.

    (xvi)   Labels and Health and Safety data sheets supplied to the employers to comply with the CLP (Classification, Labelling and Packaging) Regulations.

Section H – Control of Noise at Work Regulations 2005/1643

    (i)   Any risk assessment records required to comply with the requirements of Regulation 5.

    (ii)   Manufacturers' literature in respect of all ear protection made available to claimant to comply with the requirements of Regulation 7.

    (iii)   Health surveillance records relating to the claimant to comply with the requirements of Regulation 9.

    (iv)   All documents provided to the employee for the provision of information to comply with Regulation 10.

Section I – Construction (Design and Management) Regulations 2015/51

    (i)   All documents showing the identity of the principal contractor, or a person who controls the way in which construction work is carried out by a person at work, to comply with the terms of Regulation 5.

    (ii)   Notification of a project form (HSE F10) to comply with the requirements of Regulation 6.

    (iii)   Construction Phase Plan to comply with requirements of Regulation 12.

    (iv)   Health and Safety file to comply with the requirements of Regulations 4 and 12.

    (v)   Information and training records provided to comply with the requirements of Regulations 4, 14 and 15.

    (vi)   Records of consultation and engagement of persons at work to comply with the requirements of Regulation 14.

    (vii)   All documents and inspection reports to comply with the terms of Regulations 22, 23 and 24.

Appendix IA[1]

SCHEDULE OF TIMETABLE UNDER PERSONAL INJURIES PROCEDURE

Steps referred to under rule 34.7(1)(c)	Period of time within which action must be carried out*
Application for a third party notice under rule 11.1 (rule 34.7(2)(a))	Not later than 28 days after the form of response has been lodged
Pursuer serving a commission for recovery of documents under rule 34.5 (rule 34.7(2)(b))	Not later than 28 days after the form of response has been lodged
Parties adjusting their respective statements (rule 34.7(2)(c))	Not later than 8 weeks after the form of response has been lodged
Pursuer lodging a statement of valuation of claim (rule 34.7(2)(d))	Not later than 8 weeks after the form of response has been lodged
Pursuer lodging a certified adjusted statement of claim (rule 34.7(2)(e))	Not later than 10 weeks after the form of response has been lodged
Defender (and any third party to the	Not later than 10 weeks after the form of response has been

---

[1] As inserted by the Act of Sederunt (Summary Cause Rules Amendment) (Personal Injuries Actions) 2012 (SSI 2012/144) para.2 (effective September 1, 2012; not applicable to an action raised before September 1, 2012).

Steps referred to under rule 34.7(1)(c)	Period of time within which action must be carried out*
action) lodging a certified adjusted response to statement of claim (rule 34.7(2)(f))	lodged
Defender (and any third party to the action) lodging a statement of valuation of claim (rule 34.7(2)(g))	Not later than 12 weeks after the form of response has been lodged
Parties lodging a list of witnesses together with any productions on which they wish to rely (rule 34.7(2)(h))	Not later than 8 weeks before the date assigned for the proof
Pursuer lodging the minute of the pre-proof conference (rule 34.7(2)(i))	Not later than 21 days before the date assigned for the proof
*NOTE: Where there is more than one defender in an action, references in the above table to the form of response having been lodged should be read as references to the first lodging of a form of response.	

Appendix 2[1]

GLOSSARY

Absolve

To find in favour of and exonerate the defender.

Absolvitor

An order of the court granted in favour of and exonerating the defender which means that the pursuer is not allowed to bring the same matter to court again.

Action of count, reckoning and payment

A legal procedure for requiring someone to account for their dealings with assets under their stewardship. For example, a trustee might be subject to such an action.

Action of furthcoming

A final stage of diligence or enforcement. It results in whatever has been subject to arrestment being made over to the person who is suing. For example, where a bank account has been arrested this results in the appropriate amount being transferred to the pursuer.

Appellant

A person making an appeal against the sheriff's decision. This might be the pursuer or the defender.

Arrestee

A person subject to an arrestment.

Arrestment on the dependence

A court order to freeze the goods or bank account of the defender until the court has heard the case.

Arrestment to found jurisdiction

A court order to used against a person who has goods or other assets in Scotland to give the court jurisdiction to hear a case. This is achieved by preventing anything being done with the goods or assets until the case has been disposed of.

Authorised lay representative

A person other than a lawyer who represents a party to a summary cause.

Calling date

The date on which the case will first be heard in court.

Cause

Another word for case or claim.

Caution (pronounced kay-shun)

A security, usually a sum of money, given to ensure that some obligation will be carried out.

Certificate of execution of service

The document recording that an application to, or order or decree of, the court for service of documents has been effected.

Charge

---

[1] As amended by the Act of Sederunt (Rules of the Court of Session 1994 and Sheriff Court Rules Amendment) (No.4) (Simple Procedure) 2016 (SSI 2016/315) para.4 (effective 28 November 2016).

An order to obey a decree of a court. A common type is one served on the defender by a sheriff officer on behalf of the pursuer who has won a case demanding payment of a sum of money.

Claim

The part of the summons which sets out the legal remedy which the pursuer is seeking.

Commission and diligence

Authorisation by the court for someone to take the evidence of a witness who cannot attend court or to obtain the production of documentary evidence. It is combined with a diligence authorising the person appointed to require the attendance of the witness and the disclosure of documents.

Consignation

The deposit in court, or with a third party, of money or an article in dispute.

Continuation

An order made by the sheriff postponing the completion of a hearing until a later date or dates.

Contribution, Right of

The right of one person who is legally liable to pay money to someone to claim a proportionate share from others who are also liable.

Counterclaim

A claim made by a defender in response to the pursuer's case and which is not necessarily a defence to that case. It is a separate but related case against the pursuer which is dealt with at the same time as the pursuer's case.

Damages

Money compensation payable for a breach of contract or some other legal duty.

Declarator of irritancy of a lease

A decision of a court finding that a tenant has failed to observe a term of a lease which may lead to the termination of the lease.

Decree

An order of the court containing the decision of the case in favour of one of the parties and granting the remedy sought or disposing of the case.

Decree of ejection

A decree ordering someone to leave land or property which they are occupying. For example, it is used to remove tenants in arrears with their rent.

Decree of removing

A court order entitling someone to recover possession of heritable property and ordering a person to leave land which he is occupying. For example, it is used to remove tenants in arrears with their rent.

Defender

Person against whom a summary cause is started.

Deliverance

A decision or order of a court.

Diet

Date for a court hearing.

Diligence

The collective term for the procedures used to enforce a decree of a court. These include arrestment of wages, goods or a bank account.

Dismissal

An order bringing to an end the proceedings in a summary cause. It is usually possible for a new summary cause to be brought if not time barred.

Domicile

The place where a person is normally resident or where, in the case of a company, it has its place of business or registered office.

Execution of service

See *Certificate of execution of service*.

Execution of a charge

The intimation of the requirement to obey a decree or order of a court.

Execution of an arrestment

The carrying out of an order of arrestment.

Expenses

The costs of a court case.

Extract decree

The document containing the order of the court made at the end of the summary cause. For example, it can be used to enforce payment of a sum awarded.

Fund in medio

See *Multiplepoinding*.

Haver

A person who holds documents which are required as evidence in a case.

Heritable property

Land and buildings as opposed to moveable property.

Huissier

An official in France and some other European countries who serves court documents.

Incidental application

An application that can be made during the course of a summary cause for certain orders. Examples are applications for the recovery of documents or to amend the statement of claim.

Interlocutor

The official record of the order or judgment of a court.

Interrogatories

Written questions put to someone in the course of a court case and which must be answered on oath.

Intimation

Giving notice to another party of some step in a summary cause.

Jurisdiction

The authority of a court to hear particular cases.

Ish

The date on which a lease terminates.

Letter of request

A document issued by the sheriff court requesting a foreign court to take evidence from a specified person within its jurisdiction or to serve Scottish court documents on that person.

Messenger at arms

Officers of court who serve documents issued by the Court of Session.

Minute

A document produced in the course of a case in which a party makes an application or sets out his position on some matter.

Minute for recall

A form lodged with the court by one party asking the court to recall a decree.

Multiplepoinding (pronounced "multiple pinding")

A special type of summary cause in which the holder of property, etc. (referred to as the fund*in medio*) requires claimants upon it to appear and settle claims in court. For example, where the police come into possession of a stolen car of which two or more people claim to be owner this procedure could be used.

Options Hearing

A preliminary stage in an ordinary cause action.

Ordinary cause

Another legal procedure for higher value cases available in the sheriff court.

Party litigant

A person who conducts his own case.

Process

The court file containing the collection of documents relating to a case.

Productions

Documents or articles which are used in evidence.

Pursuer

The person who starts a summary cause.

Recall of an arrestment

A court order withdrawing an arrestment.

Restriction of an arrestment

An order releasing part of the money or property arrested.

Recall of a decree

An order revoking a decree which has been granted.

Recovery of documents

The process of obtaining documentary evidence which is not in the possession of the person seeking it (e.g. hospital records necessary to establish the extent of injuries received in a road accident).

Remit between procedures

A decision of the sheriff to transfer the summary cause to another court procedure i.e. ordinary cause procedure.

Respondent

When a decision of the sheriff is appealed against, the person making the appeal is called the appellant. The other side in the appeal is called the respondent.

Return day

The date by which the defender must send a written reply to the court and, where appropriate, the pursuer must return the summons to court.

Schedule of arrestment

The list of items which may be arrested.

Serve / service

Sending a copy of the summons or other court document to the defender or another party.

Sheriff clerk

The court official responsible for the administration of the sheriff court.

Sheriff officer

A person who serves court documents and enforces court orders.

Simple procedure

Simple procedure is a court process designed to provide a speedy, inexpensive and informal way to resolve disputes.

Sist of action

The temporary suspension of a court case by court order.

Sist as a party

To add another person as a litigant in a case.

Specification of documents

A list lodged in court of documents for the recovery of which a party seeks a court order.

Stated case[1]

An appeal procedure where the sheriff sets out his findings and the reasons for his decision and states the issues on which the decision of the Sheriff Appeal Court is requested.

Statement of claim

The part of the summons in which pursuers set out details of their cases against defenders.

Summons

The form which must be filled in to begin a summary cause.

Time to pay direction

A court order for which a defender who is an individual may apply permitting a sum owed to be paid by instalments or by a single payment at a later date.

Time order

A court order which assists debtors who have defaulted on an agreement regulated by the Consumer Credit Act 1974 (c.39) and which may be applied for during a court action.

Warrant for diligence

Authority to carry out one of the diligence procedures.

Writ

A legally significant writing.

SCHEDULE 2

REVOCATIONS

Paragraph 4

[*Not reprinted.*]

---

[1] As amended by the Act of Sederunt (Rules of the Court of Session, Sheriff Appeal Court Rules and Sheriff Court Rules Amendment) (Sheriff Appeal Court) 2015 (SSI 2015/419) r.11 (effective 1 January 2016; as to savings see SSI 2015/419 rule 20(6)(a)).

ACT OF SEDERUNT (SIMPLE PROCEDURE) 2016

(SSI 2016/200)

D2.51

28 November 2016.

In accordance with section 4 of the Scottish Civil Justice Council and Criminal Legal Assistance Act 2013, the Court of Session has, taking into consideration the matters in section 75 of the Courts Reform (Scotland) Act 2014, approved draft rules submitted to it by the Scottish Civil Justice Council with such modifications as it thinks appropriate.

The Court of Session therefore makes this Act of Sederunt under the powers conferred by section 14(7) of the Scottish Commission for Human Rights Act 2006, section 104(1) of the Courts Reform (Scotland) Act 2014 and all other powers enabling it to do so.

Citation and commencement, etc.

1.—(1)   This Act of Sederunt may be cited as the Act of Sederunt (Simple Procedure) 2016.

D2.51.1

(2)   It comes into force on 28th November 2016.

(3)   A certified copy is to be inserted in the Books of Sederunt.

The Simple Procedure Rules

2.—(1)   Schedule 1 contains rules for simple procedure cases and may be cited as the Simple Procedure Rules.

D2.51.2

(2)   A form referred to in the Simple Procedure Rules means—

   (a)   the form with that name in Schedule 2, or

   (b)[1]   an electronic version of the form with that name in Schedule 2, adapted for use by the Scottish Courts and Tribunals Service with—

      (i)   the portal on its website, or

      (ii)   the internet interface to its case management system.

(3)   Where the Simple Procedure Rules require a form to be used, that form may be varied where the circumstances require it.

Interpretation of the Simple Procedure Rules

3.—[2](1)   In the Simple Procedure Rules—

D2.51.3

   "a case where the expenses of a claim are capped" means a simple procedure case—

      (a)   to which an order made under section 81(1) of the Courts Reform (Scotland) Act 2014 applies; or

      (b)   [[3]]

   "a decision which absolves the respondent" means a decree of absolvitor;

   "a decision which orders the respondent to deliver something to the claimant" means a decree for delivery or for recovery of possession;

---

[1] As substituted by the Act of Sederunt (Simple Procedure Amendment) (Civil Online) 2022 (SSI 2022/81) r.2(2) (effective 31 March 2022).

[2] As amended by the Act of Sederunt (Rules of the Court of Session 1994 and Sheriff Court Rules Amendment) (No. 4) (Simple Procedure) 2016 (SSI 2016/315) para.7 (effective 28 November 2016).

[3] Omitted by the Act of Sederunt (Rules of the Court of Session 1994 and Sheriff Court Rules Amendment) (No. 4) (Simple Procedure) 2016 (SSI 2016/315) para.7 (effective 28 November 2016).

"a decision which orders the respondent to do something for the claimant" means a decree ad factum praestandum;

"advocate" means a practising member of the Faculty of Advocates;

"any time before the decision of the sheriff has been fully implemented" means, where a charge or arrestment has been executed, any time within 14 days of that execution (or, where there has been more than one, the first such execution);

"a person otherwise entitled to conduct proceedings in the sheriff court" means any person so entitled, including a member of a body which has made a successful application under section 25 of the Law Reform (Miscellaneous Provisions) (Scotland) Act 1990, but only to the extent that the member is exercising rights acquired by virtue of section 27 of that Act;

"a question of EU law" means a question which might lead to a reference to the Court of Justice of the European Union for—

    (a)   a preliminary ruling under Article 267 of the Treaty on the Functioning of the European Union;

    (b)   a ruling on the interpretation of the Conventions mentioned in Article 1 of Schedule 2 to the Civil Jurisdiction and Judgments Act 1982 under Article 3 of that Schedule; or

    (c)   a preliminary ruling on the interpretation of the instruments mentioned in Article 1 of Schedule 3 to the Contracts (Applicable Law) Act 1990 under Article 2 of that Schedule;

"child's property administration order" means an order under section 11(1)(d) of the Children (Scotland) Act 1995;

"Child Witness Notice" means a child witness notice under section 12(2) of the Vulnerable Witnesses (Scotland) Act 2004;

"damages management order" means an order about how a sum of money awarded as damages is to be paid to and managed for a person under a legal disability;

"Equality Act 2010 claim" means a claim which, in Scotland, the sheriff has jurisdiction to determine as a result of section 114(1) of the Equality Act 2010;

"EU member state" means a state which is a member of the European Union, within the meaning of Part II of Schedule 1 to the European Communities Act 1972;

"Hague Convention country" means a country in respect of which the Convention of 15 November 1965 on the Service Abroad of Judicial and Extrajudicial Documents in Civil or Commercial Matters is in force, other than an EU member state;

"independent person" means a commissioner before whom evidence is taken in accordance with section 19 of the Vulnerable Witnesses (Scotland) Act 2004;

"next-day postal service which records delivery" means a postal service which—

    (a)   seeks to deliver documents or other things by post no later than the next working day in all or the majority of cases; and

    (b)   provides for the delivery of documents or other things by post to be recorded;

"order for time to pay" means—

    (a)   a time to pay direction under section 1 of the Debtors (Scotland) Act 1987;

    (b)   a time to pay order under section 5 of of the Debtors (Scotland) Act 1987;

(c)   a time order under section 129 of the Consumer Credit Act 1974.

"ordinary cause" means an action under the Ordinary Cause Rules 1993;

"pause a case" means sist a case;

"postal service which records delivery" means a postal service which provides for the delivery of documents or other things by post to be recorded;

"provisional order" means a warrant for—

(a)   arrestment on the dependence or inhibition on the dependence under section 15A(1) of the Debtors (Scotland) Act 1987; or

(b)   interim attachment under section 9A(1) of the Debt Arrangement and Attachment (Scotland) Act 2002;

"Provisional Orders Reconsideration Application" means an application under—

(a)   section 15K(2) or 15L(1) of the Debtors (Scotland) Act 1987; or

(b)   section 9M(2) or 9N(1) of the Debt Arrangement and Attachment (Scotland) Act 2002;

"provisional orders review hearing" means a hearing under—

(a)   section 15K(4) or 15L(3) of the Debtors (Scotland) Act 1987; or

(b)   section 9M(4) or 9N(3) of the Debt Arrangement and Attachment (Scotland) Act 2002;

"restart the case" means recall a sist;

"schedule of inhibition" means a schedule of inhibition in the form prescribed by regulation 3(1)(a) of and Schedule 1 to the Diligence (Scotland) Regulations 2009;

"Service Regulation" means Regulation (EC) No. 1393/2007 of the European Parliament and of the Council of 13 November 2007 on the service in the Member States of judicial and extrajudicial documents in civil or commercial matters (service of documents), and repealing Council Regulation (EC) No. 1348/2000, as amended from time to time and as applied by the Agreement made on 19 October 2005 between the European Community and the Kingdom of Denmark on the service of judicial and extrajudicial documents in civil and commercial matters;

"Sheriff Personal Injury Court" means the all-Scotland sheriff court sitting by virtue of the All-Scotland Sheriff Court (Sheriff Personal Injury Court) Order 2015;

"Special Measures Review Application" means an application under section 13 of the Vulnerable Witness (Scotland) Act 2004;

"solicitor" means a qualified solicitor under section 4 of the Solicitors (Scotland) Act 1980;

"standard order" means one of the standard orders in Schedule 3;

"the principles of simple procedure" means the principles in rule 1.2;

"trading name" means the trading or descriptive name of a person, partnership, limited liability partnership or company;

"trainee solicitor"[1] means a person who is training to be a solicitor and is supervised by a solicitor in accordance with regulations made by the Council of the Law Society of Scotland under section 5 of the Solicitors (Scotland) Act 1980;

"Vulnerable Witness Application" means a vulnerable witness application under section 12(6) of the Vulnerable Witnesses (Scotland) Act 2004.

---

[1] As amended by the Act of Sederunt (Sheriff Court Rules Amendment) (Miscellaneous) 2016 (SSI 2016/367) para.5 (effective 28 November 2016).

(2)   In Part 2 of the Simple Procedure Rules, "other legislation" means any enactment which entitles a person to act as a lay representative in a simple procedure case.

(3)   In Part 11 of the Simple Procedure Rules, "supporter" means a supporter within the meaning of section 22(1) of the Vulnerable Witnesses (Scotland) Act 2004.

(4)   In Part 17 of the Simple Procedure Rules, "initial writ", "intimate", "defences", "options hearing" and "lodging" have the meaning they have in the Ordinary Cause Rules 1993.

Warrants

D2.51.4   **4.**—(1)   In the Simple Procedure Rules—

   (a)   a claim being registered—
      (i)   is warrant for the service of the Claim Form on the respondent;
      (ii)   is warrant for the citation of witnesses;
   (b)   a Response Form being registered is warrant for the citation of witnesses;
   (c)   a certified copy of a written order granting a provisional order is sufficient authority for execution of the diligence specified in the provisional order;
   (d)   in Part 11, a sheriff ordering a witness to be brought to court—
      (i)   is warrant for the apprehension of that witness and for having that witness brought to court,
      (ii)   that warrant is effective in all sheriffdoms without endorsation, and
      (iii)   the expenses of that warrant may be awarded against the witness.

(2)   In a claim for delivery in a simple procedure case, the court may—

   (a)   grant warrant to search for and take possession of goods and to open shut and lockfast places, and
   (b)   that warrant only applies to premises occupied by the respondent.

Arrestment to found jurisdiction

D2.51.5   **5.**—(1)   This paragraph applies to a simple procedure case where the claimant has used an arrestment to found jurisdiction before the Claim Form is formally served on the respondent.

(2)   The service of the arrestment must be reported to the sheriff clerk as soon as possible.

(3)   The arrestment ceases to have effect unless the Claim Form is formally served on the respondent within 21 days from the date of formal service of the arrestment.

SCHEDULE 1   D2.51.6

THE SIMPLE PROCEDURE RULES

Paragraph 2(1)

Part 1 An overview of simple procedure

1.1 *The simple procedure is a court process designed to provide a speedy, inexpensive and informal court way to resolve disputes.*

1.2 What are the principles of simple procedure?

1.3 Who takes part in a simple procedure case?

1.4 What are the sheriff's responsibilities?

1.5 What are parties' responsibilities?

1.6 What are representatives' responsibilities?

1.7 What are the sheriff clerk's responsibilities?

1.8 What are the sheriff's powers?

Part 2 Representation and support

2.1 *This Part is about who may represent a party, and what that representative may and may not do.*

This Part is also about who may provide support to a party in the courtroom, and what that courtroom supporter may and may not do.

Representation

2.2 Who can be a representative?

2.3 What can a representative do?

2.4 Who is entitled by these Rules to be a lay representative?

Support

2.5 Who can be a courtroom supporter?

2.6 What can a courtroom supporter do?

Part 3 How to make a claim

3.1 *This Part is about how the claimant makes a claim and what the court will do with that claim.*

3.2 How is a claim made?

3.3 How do you complete a Claim Form?

3.4 What if there is more than one claimant?

3.5 What if there are more than two respondents?

3.6 What if the respondent uses a trading name?

3.7 What do you do with a completed Claim Form?

3.8 How do you ask for provisional orders to be made?

3.9 What will the court do with the Claim Form?

3.10 What happens next?

3.11 What is the last date for service?

3.12 What is the last date for a response?

3.13 How can the timetable be changed?

Part 4 How to respond to a claim

PART 1: AN OVERVIEW OF SIMPLE PROCEDURE

What is simple procedure?

1.1.—(1) Simple procedure is a court process designed to provide a speedy, inexpensive and informal way to resolve disputes.

What are the principles of simple procedure?

1.2.—(1) Cases are to be resolved as quickly as possible, at the least expense to parties and the courts.

(2) The approach of the court to a case is to be as informal as is appropriate, taking into account the nature and complexity of the dispute.

(3) Parties are to be treated even-handedly by the court.

(4) Parties are to be encouraged to settle their disputes by negotiation or alternative dispute resolution, and should be able to do so throughout the progress of a case.

(5) Parties should only have to come to court when it is necessary to do so to progress or resolve their dispute.

Who takes part in a simple procedure case?

1.3.—(1) A simple procedure case involves a claim being made in the sheriff court.

(2) The person who makes the claim is the claimant.

(3) The person the claim is made against is the respondent.

(4) The claimant and the respondents are the parties.

(5) The case will be decided by the sheriff, who is in charge of the court.

(6) The sheriff clerk provides administrative support to the sheriff.

(7) A claim which is registered by the sheriff clerk is a simple procedure case.

(8) Parties may represent themselves or have representatives.

(9) Parties may be assisted by courtroom supporters.

What are the sheriff's responsibilities?

1.4.—(1) The sheriff must take into account the principles of simple procedure when managing cases and when interpreting these rules.

(2) The sheriff must ensure that parties who are not represented, or parties who do not have legal representation, are not unfairly disadvantaged.

(3) The sheriff must encourage cases to be resolved by negotiation or alternative dispute resolution, where possible.

(4) If a case cannot be resolved by negotiation or alternative dispute resolution, the sheriff must decide the case.

What are parties' responsibilities?

1.5.—(1) Parties must respect the principles of simple procedure.

(2) Parties must be honest with each other, with representatives and with the sheriff.

(3) Parties must be respectful and courteous to each other, to representatives, to witnesses and to the sheriff.

(4) Parties must not try to make a witness give misleading evidence.

(5) Parties must consider throughout the progress of a case whether their dispute could be resolved by negotiation or alternative dispute resolution.

(6) Parties must approach any negotiation or alternative dispute resolution with an open and constructive attitude.

(7) Parties must follow the sheriff's orders.

What are representatives' responsibilities?

1.6.—(1) Representatives must respect the principles of simple procedure.

(2) Representatives must be honest with each other, with parties and with the sheriff.

(3) Representatives must be respectful and courteous to each other, to parties, to witnesses and to the sheriff.

(4) Representatives must act in the best interests of the person being represented, and not allow any personal interest to influence their advice or actions.

(5) Representatives must not knowingly make claims or arguments which have no factual or legal basis.

(6) Representatives must maintain client confidentiality.

(7) Representatives must not try to make a witness give misleading evidence.

(8) Representatives must not act where they have a conflict of interest.

(9) When appearing against a party who is not represented, or who is not legally represented, representatives must not take advantage of that party.

(10) When appearing against a party who is not represented, or who is not legally represented, representatives must help the court to allow that person to argue a case fairly.

(11) Representatives must follow the sheriff's orders.

What are the sheriff clerk's responsibilities?

1.7.—(1) The sheriff clerk must maintain a register of simple procedure cases.

(2) The sheriff clerk must send the sheriff's written orders to the parties.

What are the sheriff's powers?

1.8.—(1) The sheriff may give orders to the parties, either in person or by giving written orders.

(2) The sheriff may do anything or give any order considered necessary to encourage negotiation or alternative dispute resolution between the parties.

(3) The sheriff may do anything or give any order considered necessary to decide the case.

(4) The sheriff may relieve a party from the consequences of failing to comply with any of the Simple Procedure Rules. When doing so, the sheriff may impose conditions or make orders about expenses.

(5) The sheriff may give orders which vary a deadline or period of time set out in the Simple Procedure Rules.

(6) The sheriff may make decisions about the form, location and conduct of a discussion in court, case management discussion or hearing. The sheriff must explain to parties why these decisions were made.

(7) The sheriff may combine separate cases, so that any discussion in court, case management discussion or hearing in the cases is held at the same time.

(8) The sheriff may continue any discussion in court, case management discussion or hearing to another day only if it is necessary to do so.

(9) The sheriff may pause and restart the progress of a case.

(10) The sheriff may decide a case without a hearing.

(11) If a claim, or part of a claim, obviously has no real prospect of success, the sheriff may dismiss the claim or that part of it at any time.

(12)[1] If a claim, or part of a claim, obviously will not succeed because it is incompetent, the sheriff may dismiss the claim or that part of it at any time.

---

[1] As amended by the Act of Sederunt (Rules of the Court of Session 1994 and Sheriff Court Rules Amendment) (No. 4) (Simple Procedure) 2016 (SSI 2016/315) para.7 (effective 28 November 2016).

(13)   If a response, or part of a response, obviously will not succeed because it is incompetent, the sheriff may decide a case, or that part of it, at any time.

(14)   The sheriff may make provisional orders or interim orders which protect or secure a claimant's position before a hearing.

(15)   The sheriff may order an authenticated copy of any document to be treated as an original, where the original is lost or destroyed.

(16)   The sheriff may transfer a simple procedure case to another court, whether in the same sheriffdom or not.

(17)   If a claim should have been raised in a different sheriff court the sheriff must transfer the claim to a court in which the claim could have been raised, unless the sheriff is satisfied that there is a good reason not to.

What is this Part about?

2.1.—(1) This Part is about who may represent a party, and what that representative may and may not do.

(2) This Part is also about who may provide support to a party in the courtroom, and what that courtroom supporter may and may not do.

Representation

Who can be a representative?

2.2.—(1) A party may be represented by a legal representative or a lay representative.

(2)[1] A legal representative is a person who is an advocate, a solicitor, trainee solicitor or a person otherwise entitled to conduct proceedings in the sheriff court.

(3) A lay representative is a person who is not a legal representative but is entitled to be a lay representative, either by these Rules or by other legislation.

What can a representative do?

2.3.—(1) A representative may do anything involved in the preparation or conduct of a case that a party can do.

Who is entitled by these Rules to be a lay representative?

2.4.—(1)[2] If a party wants to be represented by a lay representative throughout a case, then that lay representative must complete a Lay Representation Form and send it to the court when the Claim Form, Response Form or Time to Pay Application is sent to court.

(2) If a party wants to be represented by a lay representative during a particular discussion or hearing only, then the lay representative must complete a Lay Representation Form and give it to the sheriff clerk in person at court at that discussion or hearing.

(3) The sheriff may at any time order a person to stop acting as a lay representative if the sheriff considers that person unsuitable.

(4) For the purposes of considering suitability, the sheriff may take into account any interest that person has in the case and whether that person has been declared a vexatious litigant.

(5) A person is unsuitable to act as a lay representative if their behaviour does not respect the principles of simple procedure.

(6) A person may only act as a lay representative if that person agrees not to receive any remuneration from the party, whether directly or indirectly, for acting as a lay representative. This rule does not apply where the party is a company, limited liability partnership or partnership.

---

[1] As amended by the Act of Sederunt (Sheriff Court Rules Amendment) (Miscellaneous) 2016 (SSI 2016/367) para.5 (effective 28 November 2016).

[2] As amended by the Act of Sederunt ((Simple Procedure Amendment) (Miscellaneous) 2018 (SSI 2018/191) art.2(2)(a) (effective effective 30 July 2018).

Support

Who can be a courtroom supporter?

2.5.—(1) A courtroom supporter is a person (for example, a family member, friend or colleague) who may accompany a party in court in order to provide quiet support, encouragement and advice during a hearing.

(2) A party may ask the sheriff in court for permission for someone to be a courtroom supporter.

(3) The sheriff may permit a person to act as a courtroom supporter only if that person agrees not to receive any remuneration from the party, whether directly or indirectly, for acting as a courtroom supporter.

(4) If at any point the sheriff considers that a person is not suitable to act as a courtroom supporter, the sheriff may withdraw permission to act as a courtroom supporter.

(5) A person is unsuitable to act as a courtroom supporter if their behaviour does not respect the principles of simple procedure.

What can a courtroom supporter do?

2.6.—(1) A courtroom supporter may sit beside or behind the party in court.

(2) A courtroom supporter may provide moral support to the party.

(3) A courtroom supporter may help to manage the party's court documents and other papers.

(4) A courtroom supporter may take notes in court.

(5) A courtroom supporter may quietly advise the party on points of law and procedure, on issues the party might wish to raise with the sheriff or on questions the party might want to ask any witness.

(6) A courtroom supporter may be given any document or information connected to the case.

(7) However, if disclosure of that document or that information is prohibited or restricted in any way, then the courtroom supporter must respect that prohibition or restriction.

PART 3: HOW TO MAKE A CLAIM

What is this Part about?

3.1.—(1) This Part is about how the claimant makes a claim and what the court will do with that claim.

How is a claim made?

3.2.—(1) The process for making a claim is:

(a) the claimant completes a Claim Form (see rule 3.3),

(b) the claimant sends the Claim Form to the court (see rule 3.7),

(c) the sheriff clerk checks and registers the Claim Form (see 3.9),

(d) the sheriff clerk issues a timetable for the case (see rule 3.10), and

(e) the Claim Form is formally served on the respondent, either by the sheriff clerk, a solicitor or a sheriff officer (see Part 6).

How do you complete a Claim Form?

3.3.—(1) The claimant must set out the following information in the Claim Form:

(a) the identity of the claimant, including the claimant's address and whether the claimant is an individual, a company or another type of organisation,

(b) the identity of the respondent, including the respondent's address (where known) and whether the respondent is an individual, a company or another type of organisation,

(c) the essential factual background to the dispute,

(d) what the claimant wants from the respondent if the claim is successful,

(e) why the claim should succeed,

(f) what steps the claimant has already taken (if any) to try to resolve the dispute with the respondent.

(2) The claimant must list in the Claim Form any documents or other evidence that the claimant thinks support the claim.

(3) The claimant must list in the Claim Form any witnesses (other than the claimant and the respondent) that the claimant thinks support the claim.

What if there is more than one claimant?

3.4.—(1) If there is more than one claimant, the claimant must complete a Further Claimant Form for each further claimant.

(2) The Further Claimant Form must identify the further claimant, including the further claimant's address and whether the further claimant is an individual, a company or another type of organisation.

What if there are more than two respondents?

3.5.—(1) If there are more than two respondents, the claimant must set out the claim against all respondents in the Claim Form.

(2) The claimant must also complete a Further Respondent Form for each further respondent.

(3) The Further Respondent Form must identify the further respondent, including the further respondent's address (where known) and whether the further respondent is an individual, a company or another type of organisation.

What if the respondent uses a trading name?

3.6.—(1) If the respondent uses a trading name, a claim may be made against them using that trading name.

What do you do with a completed Claim Form?

3.7.—[1](1)[2] The completed Claim Form must be sent to the sheriff court by submitting it to the court using:

(a) the portal on the Scottish Courts and Tribunals Service website (see rule 6.6(1)(c)), or

(b) the Scottish Courts and Tribunals Service's internet interface to its case management system (see rule 6.6(2)).

(1A) Where the completed Claim Form cannot be sent in either of the ways mentioned in paragraph (1), it may be sent by one of the other ways mentioned in rule 6.6(1), but the claim will only be registered where:

(a) the Claim Form is accompanied with a note explaining why it could not have been sent in either of the ways mentioned in paragraph (1), and

(b) the sheriff considers, from the explanation in the note, that the claimant could not have sent it in either of those ways.

(2) If the Claim Form has been completed on paper then two copies must be sent to the sheriff court.

How do you ask for provisional orders to be made?

3.8.—(1) Provisional orders are orders which protect or secure the claimant's position before the sheriff makes a final decision in a case.

(2) There are three types of provisional order:

(a) an arrestment on the dependence under section 15A(1) of the Debtors (Scotland) Act 1987 (this is an order freezing the respondent's goods or money held by a third party),

(b) an inhibition on the dependence under section 15A(1) of the Debtors (Scotland) Act 1987 (this is an order preventing the respondent from selling their home or other land, or taking out a secured loan), and

(c) an interim attachment under section 9A(1) of the Debt Arrangement and Attachment (Scotland) Act 2002 (this is an order preventing the respondent from selling or removing their goods).

(3) Part 20 of these Rules is about how the claimant may apply for provisional orders.

What will the court do with the Claim Form?

3.9.—(1) The sheriff clerk will check the Claim Form for problems which mean that it cannot be registered. Such problems might include:

(a) the Claim Form not being accompanied by the correct fee,

(b) the Claim Form being sent to the wrong sheriff court,

(c) the Claim Form asking for something that is not possible in simple procedure, such as making a claim for over £5,000,

(d) the Claim Form being incomplete.

(2) If there are no such problems, the sheriff clerk must register the claim.

(3) The sheriff clerk must ask for the approval of the sheriff before registering the claim if:

(a) the respondent's address is unknown,

(aa)[3] the Claim Form has been sent by submitting it to the court using neither

---

[1] As amended by the Act of Sederunt (Simple Procedure Amendment) (Civil Online) 2020 (SSI 2020/293) art.2(3)(a) (effective 1 December 2020).

[2] Paragraphs (1), (1A) substituted for para.(1) by the Act of Sederunt (Simple Procedure Amendment) (Civil Online) 2022 (SSI 2022/81) r.2(3)(a) (effective 31 March 2022).

[3] Inserted by the Act of Sederunt (Simple Procedure Amendment) (Civil Online) 2022 (SSI 2022/81) r.2(3)(b) (effective 31 March 2022).

the portal on the Scottish Courts and Tribunals Service website nor the Scottish Courts and Tribunals Service's internet interface to its case management system,

(b) the claimant is seeking provisional orders or interim orders, or

(c) the sheriff clerk thinks that the claim requires the attention of the sheriff for some other reason.

What happens next?

3.10.—(1) After registering a claim, the sheriff clerk must send the claimant a Timetable.

(2) The Timetable must set out the timetable for the case, including:

(a) the last date for service, and

(b) the last date for a response.

What is the last date for service?

3.11.—(1) The last date for service is the date by which the Claim Form must be formally served on the respondent.

(2) This must normally be 3 weeks before the last date for a response.

(3) If the respondent does not live in an EU member state, the last date for service must normally be 6 weeks before the last date for a response.

(4) If the respondent is a business with no place of business in an EU member state, the last date for service must normally be 6 weeks before the last date for a response.

What is the last date for a response?

3.12.—[1](1) The last date for a response is the date by which the respondent must respond to the claim (see rule 4.2).

How can the timetable be changed?

3.13.—(1) The sheriff may change the timetable at the request of the sheriff clerk or at the request of one of the parties.

(2) The claimant may request a change (if, for example, there has been a difficulty serving the Claim Form on the respondent) by sending the court a Change of Timetable Application.

(3) The respondent may request a change (if, for example, the Claim Form was formally served on them late) by sending the court a Change of Timetable Application.

(4) If the sheriff changes the timetable, the sheriff clerk must send a new Timetable to the claimant or to the parties.

---

[1] As amended by the Act of Sederunt (Sheriff Court Rules Amendment) (Miscellaneous) 2016 (SSI 2016/367) para.5 (effective 28 November 2016).

What is this Part about?

4.1.—(1) This Part is about how the respondent responds to a claim and what the court will do with that response.

How do you respond to a claim?

4.2.—[1](1) The respondent must respond to the claim by the last date for a response.

(2) The respondent may respond to a claim in one of two ways:

(a) by completing a Response Form and sending it to the court and the claimant, or

(b) if the respondent wants to admit the claim and ask for time to pay, by completing a Time to Pay Application and sending it to the court.

What responses can you make?

4.3.—(1) There are three ways in which the respondent may respond to the claim.

(2) The respondent may:

(a) admit the claim and settle it before the last date for a response,

(b) admit the claim and ask the court for time to pay (see Part 5), or

(c) dispute the claim or part of the claim (such as the amount the respondent should pay the claimant).

(3)[2,3] This flow-chart sets out how the respondent may respond to a claim:

---

[1] As substituted by the Act of Sederunt (Simple Procedure Amendment) (Miscellaneous) 2018 (SSI 2018/191) art.2(2)(c) (effective 30 July 2018).

[2] As amended by the Act of Sederunt (Sheriff Court Rules Amendment) (Miscellaneous) 2017 (SSI 2017/154) para.2 (effective 15 June 2017).

[3] As amended by the Act of Sederunt (Simple Procedure Amendment) (Miscellaneous) 2018 (SSI 2018/191) art.2(2)(c) (effective 30 July 2018).

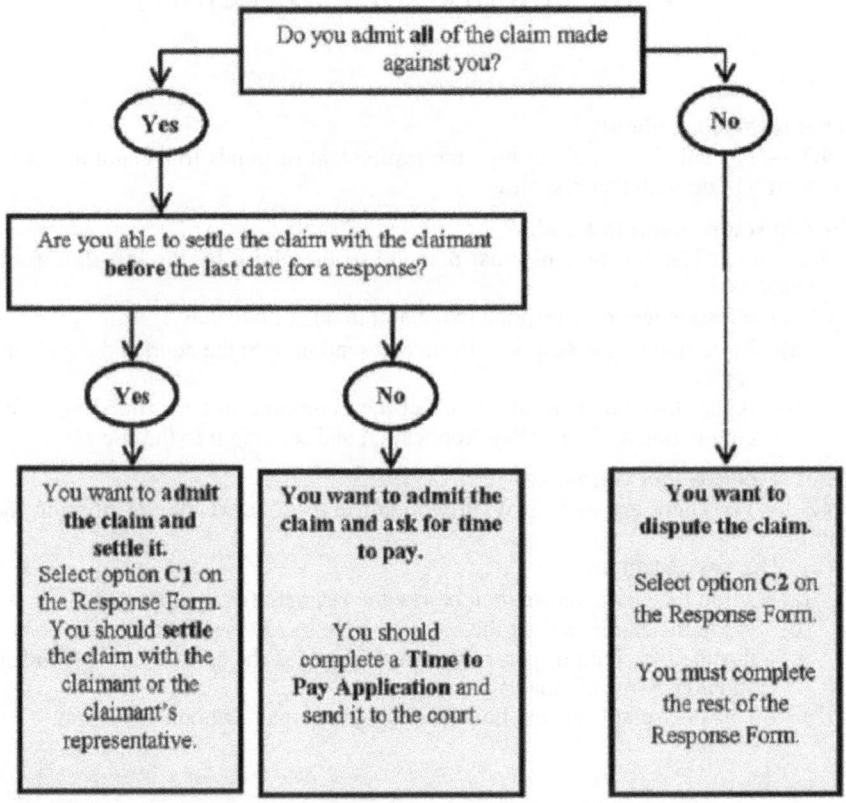

What has to go in the Response Form?

4.4.—(1) The respondent must set out in the Response Form the following information:

(a) which facts (if any) set out in the Claim Form that the respondent agrees with,

(b) which facts (if any) set out in the Claim Form that the respondent disagrees with and why,

(c) why the respondent thinks that the claimant should not get what was asked for in the Claim Form, or why the claimant should only get some of what was asked for in the Claim Form,

(d) what steps the respondent has already taken (if any) to try to resolve the dispute with the claimant.

(2) The respondent must indicate in the Response Form if the respondent thinks that there should be any additional respondents.

(3) The respondent must list in the Response Form any documents, files, or other evidence that the respondent thinks support the response.

(4) The respondent must list in the Response Form any witnesses that the respondent thinks support the response.

What will the court do with the Response Form?

4.5.—(1) When the court receives a Response Form, the sheriff clerk must register it.

(2) The sheriff clerk must then present the Claim Form, the Confirmation of Formal Service and the Response Form to the sheriff (see Part 7).

What is this Part about?

5.1.—(1)   This Part is about how the respondent may ask for time to pay if a claim for payment of a sum of money is admitted, and how the claimant can consent or object to that.

What is an order for time to pay?

5.2.—(1)   An order for time to pay is an order of the sheriff that the respondent must pay the claimant a sum of money in a particular way, such as by instalments or by a delayed payment.

How can a respondent ask for time to pay?

5.3.—(1)   The respondent may ask for time to pay in three ways:

   (a)[1] by completing a Time to Pay Application and sending it to court by the last date for a response,

   (b) by completing a Time to Pay Application and giving it to the sheriff clerk at a discussion in court, case management discussion or a hearing, or

   (c) by completing a Time to Pay Application and sending it to court after the sheriff has made a decision.

What will the court do with a Time to Pay Application?

5.4.—(1)   If the respondent sends a Time to Pay Application to the court, the sheriff clerk must send a copy of it to the claimant along with a Time to Pay Notice.

How can the claimant consent to a Time to Pay Application?

5.5.—(1)   To consent to a Time to Pay Application, the claimant must indicate consent on the Time to Pay Notice and send it to the court within 2 weeks after the claimant is sent the Time to Pay Notice.

(2)   The sheriff may then grant the Time to Pay Application and decide the case.

How can the claimant object to a Time to Pay Application?

5.6.—(1)   To object to a Time to Pay Application, the claimant must indicate objection on the Time to Pay Notice and send it to the court within 2 weeks after the claimant is sent the Time to Pay Notice.

(2)[2]   When the court receives an objection to a Time to Pay Application, the sheriff must give the parties an order arranging a time to pay hearing.

(3)   At a time to pay hearing, the sheriff must decide the case and decide whether to grant or refuse the Time to Pay Application.

What if the claimant does not consent or object to a Time to Pay Application?

5.7.—(1)   If the claimant has not consented or objected to a Time to Pay Application within 2 weeks after the claimant is sent the Time to Pay Notice, the sheriff must decide the case (if the case has not yet been decided) and grant or refuse the Time to Pay Application.

---

[1] As amended by the Act of Sederunt (Simple Procedure Amendment) (Miscellaneous) 2018 (SSI 2018/191) art.2(2)(e) (effective 30 July 2018).

[2] As amended by the Act of Sederunt (Rules of the Court of Session 1994 and Sheriff Court Rules Amendment) (No. 4) (Simple Procedure) 2016 (SSI 2016/315) para.7 (effective 28 November 2016).

What is this Part about?

6.1.—(1) This Part is about what has to be done when these Rules require something to be sent to someone.

(2) This Part is also about what has to be done when these Rules require a document to be formally served on someone.

What is the difference between sending and formally serving?

6.2.—(1) When these Rules require something to be "sent", that may be done by anyone and in a number of ways.

(2) When these Rules require a document to be "formally served" on someone, that may only be done by certain people (sheriff officers, sheriff clerks or solicitors) and may only be done in certain ways.

When must something be sent or formally served?

6.3.—(1) If these Rules say that something must be sent or formally served within a period or number of days, it must be sent or formally served in time for it to arrive before the end of that period or the last day.

(2) If these Rules say that something must be sent or formally served by a particular day, it must be sent or formally served in time for it to arrive before the end of that day.

(3) If these Rules say that something must be sent to court within a period, number of days or by a particular day and the end of that period or that day is a Saturday, Sunday, public holiday or court holiday, then it must be sent so that it will be received before the end of the next working day.

Can a party object to how sending or formal service was done?

6.4.—(1) A party who responds to something (such as sending a Response Form in response to a Claim Form or objecting to an application) may not object to how that thing was sent or formally served.

Sending

How can the court send something to a party?

6.5.—(1)[1] The court may send something to a party in one of 5 ways:

    (a)   handing it to that party or to that party's representative in person,

    (b)   posting it to that party or that party's representative,

    (c)[2] emailing it to that party or that party's representative, using an email address given on the Claim Form or Response Form,

    (d)   making it available to that party using the portal on the Scottish Courts and Tribunals Service website.

    (e)[3] delivering it to a document exchange of which that party or that party's representative is a member.

---

[1] As amended by the Act of Sederunt (Rules of the Court of Session 1994 and Sheriff Court Rules Amendment) (No. 4) (Simple Procedure) 2016 (SSI 2016/315) para.7 (effective 28 November 2016).

[2] As amended by the Act of Sederunt (Simple Procedure Amendment) (Miscellaneous) 2018 (SSI 2018/191) art.2(2)(f) (effective 30 July 2018).

[3] As inserted by the Act of Sederunt (Rules of the Court of Session 1994 and Sheriff Court Rules Amendment) (No. 4) (Simple Procedure) 2016 (SSI 2016/315) para.7 (effective 28 November 2016).

How can a party send something to the court?

6.6—(1)[1] A party may send something to the court in one of 4 ways:

  (a) handing it in to the court in person,

  (b) posting it to the court using a postal service which records delivery,

  (c) submitting it to the court using the portal on the Scottish Courts and Tribunals Service website.

  (d)[2] delivering it to a document exchange of which the sheriff clerk is a member.

(2)[3] A claimant may also send a Claim Form to the court by submitting it to the court using the Scottish Courts and Tribunals Service's internet interface to its case management system.

How can a party send something to another party?

6.7—(1)[4, 5] A party may send something to another party in one of 4 ways:

  (a) posting it to that party or that party's representative using a next-day postal service which records delivery,

  (b) emailing it to that party or that party's representative, using an email address given on the Claim Form, Response Form or Time to Pay Application,

  (c) making it available to that party or that party's representative using the portal on the Scottish Courts and Tribunals Service website.

  (d)[6] delivering it to a document exchange of which that party or that party's representative is a member.

(2)[7] If none of those ways has worked, a party may send it to another party by sheriff officer using one of the methods of formal service mentioned in rule 18.3.

Formal service

How can you formally serve a document on someone living within Scotland?

6.8—(1) Part 18 of these Rules is about formal service on someone living in Scotland.

How can you formally serve a document on someone living outside Scotland?

6.9—(1) Part 19 of these Rules is about formal service on someone living outside Scotland.

What if a person uses a trading name?

6.10—(1) If a person uses a trading name, a document may be formally served on that person at any place of business or office at which that business is carried on within the sheriffdom.

---

[1] As amended by the Act of Sederunt (Rules of the Court of Session 1994 and Sheriff Court Rules Amendment) (No. 4) (Simple Procedure) 2016 (SSI 2016/315) para.7 (effective 28 November 2016).

[2] As inserted by the Act of Sederunt (Rules of the Court of Session 1994 and Sheriff Court Rules Amendment) (No. 4) (Simple Procedure) 2016 (SSI 2016/315) para.7 (effective 28 November 2016).

[3] Inserted by the Act of Sederunt (Simple Procedure Amendment) (Civil Online) 2022 (SSI 2022/81) r.2(3)(c) (effective 31 March 2022).

[4] As amended by the Act of Sederunt (Rules of the Court of Session 1994 and Sheriff Court Rules Amendment) (No. 4) (Simple Procedure) 2016 (SSI 2016/315) para.7 (effective 28 November 2016).

[5] As amended by the Act of Sederunt (Simple Procedure Amendment) (Miscellaneous) 2018 (SSI 2018/191) art.2(2)(g) (effective 30 July 2018).

[6] As inserted by the Act of Sederunt (Rules of the Court of Session 1994 and Sheriff Court Rules Amendment) (No. 4) (Simple Procedure) 2016 (SSI 2016/315) para.7 (effective 28 November 2016).

[7] As inserted by the Act of Sederunt (Sheriff Court Rules Amendment) (Miscellaneous) 2017 (SSI 2017/154) para.2 (effective 15 June 2017).

(2)   If that person does not have a place of business or office within the sheriffdom, a document may be formally served on that person at any place where that business is carried on (including the office of the clerk or secretary of a company, association or firm).

How can the Claim Form be formally served on the respondent?

6.11—(1)   As well as following the rules for formal service in Part 18 or Part 19, there are some additional requirements when formally serving the Claim Form.

(2)   The sheriff clerk may formally serve the Claim Form if:

    (a)   the claimant is not a company, limited liability partnership or partnership, and

    (b)   the claimant is not legally represented.

(3)   When formally serving a Claim Form, the envelope must contain only the following:

    (a)   a copy of the Claim Form,

    (b)   any Further Claimant Forms or Further Respondent Forms,

    (c)   a blank Response Form,

    (d)   a copy of the Notice of Claim,

    (e)   a copy of the Timetable,

    (f)   if the respondent can apply for time to pay, a blank Time to Pay Application, and

    (g)   any other document approved by the sheriff principal in that sheriffdom.

(4)   If a solicitor or sheriff officer has formally served the Claim Form, then a Confirmation of Formal Service must be sent to the court at least 2 days before the last date for a response.

What if the claimant does not know the respondent's address?

6.12—(1)   The claimant must take all reasonable steps to find out the respondent's address.

(2)   If the claimant does not know the respondent's address and cannot find it out, then the claimant does not need to formally serve a copy of the Claim Form on the respondent.

(3)   The claimant must instead complete a Service by Advertisement Application and send it to court with the Claim Form.

(4)   The sheriff may order the details of the claim to be publicised by advertisement on the Scottish Courts and Tribunals Service website.

(5)   The sheriff clerk must make a copy of the Claim Form available for the respondent to collect at the sheriff court.

(6)   If the respondent's address becomes known, the sheriff must order:

    (a)   the Claim Form to be amended,

    (b)   the claimant to formally serve the Claim Form on the respondent,

    (c)   a change to the timetable.

What if the sheriff considers that formal service of the Claim Form has not been done properly?

6.13.—(1)   If the sheriff considers that formal service of the Claim Form was not done correctly, then the sheriff may change the timetable.

(2)   If the sheriff changes the timetable, the sheriff clerk must send a new Timetable to the claimant or to the parties.

What is this Part about?

7.1.—(1)[1] This Part is about what happens after a Response Form has been received and what happens if no Response Form or Time to Pay Application is received by the last date for a response.

Admitted claims

What if parties settle the claim before the last date for a response?

7.2.—[2](1) If the Response Form indicates that the respondent admits the claim and will settle it before the last date for a response, then the sheriff does not have to send written orders to the parties.

(2) If the claimant then sends an Application for a Decision to the court within 2 weeks from the last date for a response, the sheriff may do one of three things:

    (a)   dismiss the claim,

    (b)   make a decision awarding the claimant some or all of what was asked for in the Claim Form,

    (c)   if the sheriff considers that a decision cannot be made awarding the claimant some or all of what was asked for in the Claim Form, order the claimant to come to court to discuss the terms of the decision.

(3) The claimant must, at the same time, send the court evidence that the Claim Form was formally served on the respondent.

(4) If the claimant does not send an Application for a Decision to the court within 2 weeks from the last date for a response, the sheriff must dismiss the claim.

What if the respondent makes a Time to Pay Application?

7.3.—(1) If the respondent admits the claim and asks for time to pay, then the sheriff does not have to send written orders to the parties.

(2) Part 5 of these Rules is about what happens when a Time to Pay Application is made.

What if no Response Form or Time to Pay Application is received by the court?

7.4.—[3](1) If no Response Form or Time to Pay Application has been received by the court by the last date for a response, then the sheriff does not have to send written orders to the parties.

(2) If the claimant sends an Application for a Decision to the court within 2 weeks from the last date for a response, then the sheriff may make a decision awarding the claimant some or all of what was asked for in the Claim Form.

(3) If the sheriff considers that a decision cannot be made awarding the claimant some or all of what was asked for in the Claim Form, then the sheriff may order the claimant to come to court to discuss the terms of the decision.

---

[1] As amended by the Act of Sederunt (Simple Procedure Amendment) (Miscellaneous) 2018 (SSI 2018/191) art.2(2)(h) (effective 30 July 2018).
[2] As amended by the Act of Sederunt (Simple Procedure Amendment) (Miscellaneous) 2018 (SSI 2018/191) art.2(2)(i) (effective 30 July 2018).
[3] As amended by the Act of Sederunt (Simple Procedure Amendment) (Miscellaneous) 2018 (SSI 2018/191) art.2(2)(j) (effective 30 July 2018).

(4) If the claimant does not send an Application for a Decision to the court within 2 weeks from the last date for a response, then the sheriff must dismiss the claim.

Disputed claims

What if the respondent disputes the claim?

7.5.—(1) If the respondent disputes the claim, the sheriff must consider the case in private.

(2) The sheriff must then send the parties the first written orders within 2 weeks from the date the court received the Response Form.

(3) If the Response Form indicates that the respondent thinks that there should be additional respondents, then the sheriff does not have to send first written orders to the parties.

(4)[1] Instead, the sheriff may order that the Claim Form and Response Form should be formally served on those persons by the respondent before the sheriff issues the first written orders.

What will be in the first written orders?

7.6.—(1) The first written orders may do any of 5 things:

    (a)   refer parties to alternative dispute resolution,

    (b)   arrange a case management discussion,

    (c)   arrange a hearing,

    (d)   if the sheriff thinks that a decision could be made without a hearing, indicate that the sheriff is considering doing so,

    (e)   use the sheriff's powers to dismiss a claim or decide a case under rule 1.8(11), (12) and (13).

What is a case management discussion?

7.7.—(1) A case management discussion may take place in a courtroom, by videoconference, conference call, or in any other form or location ordered by the sheriff.

(2) The purpose of a case management discussion is so that the sheriff may:

    (a)   discuss the claim and response with the parties and clarify any concerns the sheriff has,

    (b)   discuss negotiation and alternative dispute resolution with the parties,

    (c)   give the parties, in person, guidance and orders about the witnesses, documents and other evidence which they need to bring to a hearing,

    (d)   give the parties, in person, orders which arrange a hearing.

(3) The sheriff may refer parties to alternative dispute resolution at a case management discussion.

(4) The sheriff may do anything at a case management discussion that can be done at a hearing, including making a decision in a case or part of a case.

What is a hearing?

7.8.—(1) The purpose of a hearing is to help the sheriff to resolve the dispute between the parties.

(2) Part 12 of these Rules is about hearings.

---

[1] As amended by the Act of Sederunt (Rules of the Court of Session 1994 and Sheriff Court Rules Amendment) (No. 4) (Simple Procedure) 2016 (SSI 2016/315) para.7 (effective 28 November 2016).

What is this Part about?

8.1.—(1)   This Part is about the orders which the sheriff can give to manage or decide a case.

What are orders?

8.2.—(1)   Orders are the way that the sheriff uses the powers of the sheriff to manage or decide a case.

(2)   Orders may be given to the parties in writing, using the Order of the Sheriff Form.

(3)   Orders may be given to the parties in person at a hearing, case management discussion or discussion in court.

(4)   Written orders must be signed or authenticated electronically by either the sheriff or the sheriff clerk.

What are standard orders?

8.3.—(1)   There are standard orders which the sheriff may give in typical situations.

(2)   The sheriff may do one of three things:

   (a)   give parties a standard order,

   (b)   give parties an amended version of a standard order, or

   (c)   give parties an order customised to their case.

What are unless orders?

8.4.—(1)   The sheriff may give a party an order which states that unless that party does something or takes a step, then the sheriff will make a decision in the case, including:

   (a)   dismissing the claim,

   (b)   awarding the claimant some or all of what was asked for in the Claim Form.

(2)   If that party does not do the thing or take the step that the party was ordered to, then the decision in the case must be made.

What if a party does not follow an order?

8.5.—(1)   Where a party does not follow an order the sheriff may make a decision in the case, including:

   (a)   dismissing the claim or part of the claim,

   (b)   awarding the claimant some or all of what was asked for in the Claim Form.

What is this Part about?

9.1.—(1)   This Part is about applications which parties may make to the court to ask for things to be done in a case.

Pausing and restarting cases

How can a party ask for the progress of a case to be paused?

9.2.—(1)   A party may apply to have the progress of a case paused by sending the other party an Application to Pause.

(2)   That party must at the same time send the court a copy of the Application to Pause with evidence that it was sent to the other party (for example a postal receipt or a copy of an email).

(3)   The Application to Pause must set out why the progress of a case should be paused.

(4)   If the party who has been sent the Application to Pause objects to having the progress of the case paused, that party must send that Application to Pause to the court within 10 days of it being sent, setting out that objection.

(5)   After considering the Application to Pause, and any objection that may have been sent, the sheriff may do one of three things:

    (a)   grant the application, and pause the progress of the case,

    (b)   refuse the application, and the progress of the case continues, or

    (c)   order both parties to appear at a discussion in court, where the sheriff will consider whether to pause the progress of the case.

What happens if the progress of a case is paused?

9.3.—(1)   If the progress of a case is paused, then any discussions or hearings in the case are cancelled and the case will not progress until it is restarted.

How can a party ask for a paused case to be restarted?

9.4.—(1)   A party may apply to have a paused case restarted by sending the other party an Application to Restart.

(2)   That party must at the same time send the court a copy of the Application to Restart with evidence that it was sent to the other party (for example a postal receipt or a copy of an email).

(3)   The Application to Restart must set out why the paused case should be restarted.

(4)   If the party who has been sent the Application to Restart objects to having the paused case restarted, that party must send that Application to Restart to the court within 10 days of it being sent, setting out that objection.

(5)   After considering the Application to Restart, and any objection that may have been sent, the sheriff may do one of three things:

    (a)   grant the application, and restart the case,

    (b)   refuse the application, and the case continues to be paused, or

    (c)   order both parties to appear at a discussion in court, where the sheriff will consider whether to restart the case.

What can the court do with a paused case?

9.5.—(1)   The sheriff clerk must present to the sheriff a case which has been paused for 6 months or more.

(2)   The sheriff may then send the parties written orders that unless a party (or parties) does something or takes a step, then the sheriff will dismiss the claim.

(3)   If that party (or the parties) does not do the thing or take the step ordered, then the claim must be dismissed.

Miscellaneous applications

How can a person become an additional respondent in a case?

9.6.—(1)   A person who is not a respondent may apply to become a respondent in a case by sending an Additional Respondent Application to the court.

(2)   The Additional Respondent Application must set out why that person has an interest in becoming a respondent.

(3)   The Additional Respondent Application must have attached to it a draft Response Form.

(4)   The sheriff may grant the application without a discussion in court, but must order a discussion in court if considering refusing the application.

(5)   If ordering a discussion in court, the sheriff must also order the person wishing to become a respondent to formally serve a copy of the Additional Respondent Application, the draft Response Form and notice of the discussion on all parties.

(6)   If granting the application, the sheriff must give orders that allow the additional respondent to participate in the case as a respondent.

How can a party ask to amend the Claim Form or the Response Form?

9.7.—(1)   A claimant may apply to amend a Claim Form by sending the respondent an Application to Amend.

(2)   The claimant must at the same time send the court a copy of the Application to Amend with evidence that it was sent to the respondent (for example a postal receipt or a copy of an email).

(3)   A respondent may apply to amend a Response Form by sending the claimant an Application to Amend.

(4)   The respondent must at the same time send the court a copy of the Application to Amend with evidence that it was sent to the claimant (for example a postal receipt or a copy of an email).

(5)   The Application to Amend must set out why the form should be amended.

(6)   The Application to Amend must set out the proposed amendments.

(7)   If the party who has been sent the Application to Amend objects to the proposed amendments, that party must send that Application to Amend to the court within 10 days of it being sent, setting out that objection.

(8)   After considering the Application to Amend, and any objection that may have been sent, the sheriff may do one of three things:

    (a)   grant the application, and allow the proposed amendments (or some of them),

    (b)   refuse the application, and not allow any amendment, or

    (c)   order both parties to appear at a discussion in court, where the sheriff will consider whether to allow the proposed amendments.

How can a claimant abandon a claim?

9.8.—(1)   A claimant may abandon a claim any time before the sheriff decides a case by sending an Abandonment Notice to the respondent.

(2)   That claimant must at the same time send the court a copy of the Abandonment Notice with evidence that it was sent to the respondent (for example a postal receipt or a copy of an email).

(3)   When the court receives the Abandonment Notice, the sheriff must give the parties written orders.

(4) Those orders may dismiss the claim.

(5) Those orders may do one of three further things:

   (a) order that no expenses are to be awarded to any party,

   (b) order that a sum of money is to be paid to a party or to a party's solicitor, as assessed by the sheriff clerk, or

   (c)[1] arrange an expenses hearing (see Part 14).

What can happen if a party dies or becomes legally incapacitated?

9.9.—(1) If a party dies or becomes legally incapacitated before a sheriff decides a case, then a person who asserts a right to represent that party or that party's estate may apply to represent that party, by sending an Application to Represent to the other party.

(2) That person must at the same time send the court a copy of the Application to Represent with evidence that it was sent to other parties (for example a postal receipt or a copy of an email).

(3) If the party who has been sent the Application to Represent objects to the proposed representation, that party must send that Application to Represent to the court within 10 days of it being sent, setting out that objection.

(4) After considering the Application to Represent, and any objection that may have been sent, the sheriff may do one of three things:

   (a) grant the application, and allow the person to represent that party,

   (b) refuse the application, and not allow the person to represent that party, or

   (c) order the parties and the person making the application to appear at a discussion in court, where the sheriff will consider whether to allow the person to represent that party.

How can a party ask the sheriff to make any other orders?

9.10.—(1) A party may ask the sheriff to make any other orders by sending an Incidental Orders Application to the other party.

(2)[2] That party must at the same time send the court a copy of the Incidental Orders Application with evidence that it was sent to the other party (for example a postal receipt or a copy of an email).

(3) If the party who has been sent the Incidental Orders Application objects to the proposed orders, that party must send that Incidental Orders Application to the court within 10 days of it being sent, setting out that objection.

(4) After considering the Incidental Orders Application, and any objection that may have been sent, the sheriff may do one of three things:

   (a) grant the application, and send written orders to the parties,

   (b) refuse the application, and make no orders, or

   (c) order the parties to appear at a discussion in court, where the sheriff will consider whether to make any orders.

---

[1] As amended by the Act of Sederunt (Rules of the Court of Session 1994 and Sheriff Court Rules Amendment) (No. 4) (Simple Procedure) 2016 (SSI 2016/315) para.7 (effective 28 November 2016).

[2] As amended by the Act of Sederunt (Rules of the Court of Session 1994 and Sheriff Court Rules Amendment) (No. 4) (Simple Procedure) 2016 (SSI 2016/315) para.7 (effective 28 November 2016).

PART 10: DOCUMENTS AND OTHER EVIDENCE

What is this Part about?

10.1.—(1) This Part is about how parties should lodge documents and other evidence with the court before a hearing.

(2) This Part is also about how parties can apply for orders to recover documents from other people.

Lodging documents and other evidence

How can you lodge documents and other evidence with the court?

10.2.—(1) Parties must send each other and the court a List of Evidence Form at least 2 weeks before the hearing.

(2) The List of Evidence Form must set out the documents and other evidence that they are lodging with the court.

(3) All documents and other evidence must be lodged with the court at least 2 weeks before the hearing.

(4) Documents and other evidence may be lodged with the court by sending them to the sheriff clerk.

(5) If a party considers that there would be practical difficulties involved in sending evidence to the sheriff clerk, that party must contact the sheriff clerk.

(6) In that situation, the sheriff clerk may give that party permission to lodge only a brief description of the evidence. The party must bring the evidence to any hearing.

What documents and other evidence can a party bring to a hearing?

10.3.—(1) A party may bring to a hearing documents and other evidence which have not been lodged with the court.

(2) The sheriff may refuse to consider these.

How can other parties borrow or inspect documents and other evidence lodged with the court?

10.4.—(1) A solicitor, or the authorised assistant of a solicitor, may borrow any documents or other evidence which have been lodged with the court.

(2) Any documents or other evidence borrowed must be returned to the court before midday (1200 hours) on the last day the court is open before the hearing.

(3) A party who is not represented by a solicitor may, during normal business hours, inspect documents or other evidence at the sheriff clerk's office.

(4) Where it is possible to do so, that party may take copies or photographs of documents or other evidence.

How long will the court keep documents and other evidence for?

10.5.—(1) The court must keep the documents and other evidence for at least 4 weeks after the sheriff has made a decision.

(2) If a party has appealed the sheriff's decision, the court must keep the documents and other evidence until that appeal has been decided.

(3)[1] Each party must collect the documents or other evidence which that party lodged with the court within 2 weeks of:

---

[1] As substituted by the Act of Sederunt (Sheriff Court Rules Amendment) (Miscellaneous) 2017 (SSI 2017/154) para.2 (effective 15 June 2017).

    (a)   the end of the 4 week period, or

    (b)   if the decision is appealed, the date of the appeal decision.

(4) If a party has not collected the documents and other evidence by the end of that 2 weeks, the sheriff clerk must send the party a warning that if the documents and other evidence is not collected within 2 weeks of the warning, then it will be destroyed or disposed of.

(5) If the documents and other evidence are not collected by the end of that further 2 weeks, the sheriff must order it to be destroyed or disposed of.

Orders to recover documents

How can a party recover documents to lodge them with the court?

10.6.—(1) Where a party wants to lodge a document which they do not possess, the sheriff may make an order to recover a document from the person who possesses it.

(2) A party may ask the sheriff to make an order to recover documents by sending a Recovery of Documents Application to the court and the other party.

(3) A party may object to the proposed recovery of documents by returning that Recovery of Documents Application to the court within 10 days of it being sent, setting out that objection.

(4) After considering the Recovery of Documents Application, and any objection that may have been sent, the sheriff may do one of 4 things:

    (a)   grant the application, and make an order to recover documents,

    (b)   grant the application in part, and make an order to recover documents,

    (c)   refuse the application,

    (d)   order the parties to appear at a discussion in court, where the sheriff will consider whether to make an order to recover documents.

What happens when an order to recover documents is made?

10.7.—(1) A party who has been granted an order to recover documents must formally serve it on the person who is named in the order.

(2) When the sheriff clerk receives documents in response to an order to recover documents, the sheriff clerk must lodge them and send the parties a notice indicating that the documents have been received and lodged.

What happens if the person who has the documents claims they are confidential?

10.8.—(1) A person who has documents mentioned in an order to recover documents must tell the court if that person believes them to be confidential.

(2) This is done by:

    (a)   sealing the confidential documents in an envelope, marked as confidential,

    (b)   completing the confidential documents part of the order to recover documents, and

    (c)   sending these to the court.

(3) If the party who obtained the order to recover documents wishes to open the sealed envelope containing the confidential document, the party must send an Application to Open Confidential Document to the court, the other party and the person who sent the document to the court.

(4) If a person who has been sent the Application to Open Confidential Document objects to the confidential document being seen by the parties, that party must send that Application to Open Confidential Document to the court within 10 days of it being sent, setting out that objection.

(5) After considering the Application to Open Confidential Document, and any objection that may have been sent, the sheriff may do one of three things:

(a)   grant the application, and allow the sealed envelope containing the confidential document to be opened,

(b)   refuse the application,

(c)   order the parties and the person who sent the document to the court to appear at a discussion in court, where the sheriff will consider whether to allow the sealed envelope containing the confidential document to be opened.

(6)   When granting an application, the sheriff may order parts of the document to be redacted.

What happens if an order to recover documents has not been complied with?

10.9.—[1](1)   The party who obtained the order to recover documents can ask the sheriff to make a special order to recover documents by sending a Special Recovery of Documents Application to the court and the other party.

(2)   If the party who has been sent the Special Recovery of Documents Application objects to the proposed recovery of documents, that party must send that Special Recovery of Documents Application to the court within 10 days of it being sent, setting out that objection.

(3)   After considering the Special Recovery of Documents Application, and any objection that may have been sent, the sheriff may do one of three things:

(a)   grant the application, and send a special order to recover documents to the parties,

(b)   refuse the application,

(c)   order the parties to appear at a discussion in court, where the sheriff will consider whether to make a special order to recover documents.

What happens when a special order to recover documents is made?

10.10.—(1)   A special order to recover documents appoints a person to recover the documents mentioned in the order for the court. This person is called a commissioner.

(2)   The party who obtained the special order to recover documents must send it to the commissioner.

(3)   The commissioner must carry out the recovery of documents mentioned in the order.

(4)   When the sheriff clerk receives documents from the commissioner, the sheriff clerk must lodge them and send the parties a notice explaining that the documents have been received and lodged.

What happens if the person who has the documents claims they are confidential?

10.11.—[2](1)   A person who has documents mentioned in a special order to recover documents must tell the court if the person believes them to be confidential

(2)   This is done by telling the commissioner why the document is considered to be confidential and giving the commissioner the confidential document in a sealed envelope.

(3)   If the party who obtained the special order to recover documents wishes to open the sealed envelope containing the confidential document, the party must send

---

[1] As amended by the Act of Sederunt (Rules of the Court of Session 1994 and Sheriff Court Rules Amendment) (No. 4) (Simple Procedure) 2016 (SSI 2016/315) para.7 (effective 28 November 2016).
[2] As amended by the Act of Sederunt (Rules of the Court of Session 1994 and Sheriff Court Rules Amendment) (No. 4) (Simple Procedure) 2016 (SSI 2016/315) para.7 (effective 28 November 2016).

an Application to Open Confidential Document to the court, the other party and the person who sent the document to the commissioner.

(4)   If anyone who has been sent the Application to Open Confidential Document objects to the confidential document being seen by the parties, that party must send that Application to Open Confidential Document to the court within 10 days of it being sent, setting out that objection.

(5)   After considering the Application to Open Confidential Document, and any objection that may have been sent, the sheriff may do one of three things:

    (a)   grant the application, and allow the sealed envelope containing the confidential document to be opened,

    (b)   refuse the application,

    (c)   order the parties and the person who sent the document to the commissioner to appear at a discussion in court, where the sheriff will consider whether to allow the sealed envelope containing the confidential document to be opened.

(6)   When granting an application, the sheriff may order parts of the document to be redacted.

PART 11: WITNESSES

What is this Part about?

11.1.—(1)   This Part is about the citation of witnesses and their attendance at hearings.

(2)   This Part is also about measures that the court can take to assist vulnerable witnesses in giving evidence.

The citation of witnesses

How can a party arrange the attendance of witnesses at a hearing?

11.2.—(1)   Parties must send each other and the court a List of Witnesses Form at least 2 weeks before the hearing.

(2)   The List of Witnesses Form must set out the witnesses that they want to appear at a hearing.

(3)   A party only needs to cite a witness to appear at a hearing if the party is unable otherwise to arrange for that witness to appear.

(4)   A witness may be cited to appear at a hearing by formally serving on that witness a Witness Citation Notice.

(5)   The Witness Citation Notice must be formally served on the witness at least 3 weeks before the hearing.

What if a witness does not appear at a hearing?

11.3—(1)   If a witness is cited to appear at a hearing, the witness must appear at that hearing.

(2)   If a witness who has been cited does not appear at a hearing, the sheriff may order the witness to be brought to court.

(3)   [1]

Vulnerable witnesses

How will the court treat a child witness?

11.4—(1)   If a party cites (or intends to arrange the attendance of) a child as a witness, that party must send the court and the other party a Child Witness Notice.

(2)   A Child Witness Notice asks the sheriff to authorise the use of a special measure in taking the child witness's evidence, or to decide that the child witness is to give evidence without the benefit of any special measure.

(3)   Before the sheriff decides how to deal with the Child Witness Notice, the sheriff may order the parties to provide further information.

(4)   The sheriff may decide to make the orders requested in the Child Witness Notice with or without ordering a discussion in court.

(5)   Where the sheriff decides to have a discussion, the sheriff clerk must send the parties notice of when it will be held.

(6)   At the discussion, the sheriff must consider the Child Witness Notice and decide whether to authorise the use of a special measure in taking the child witness's evidence, or that the child witness is to give evidence without the benefit of any special measure.

---

[1] Omitted by the Act of Sederunt (Rules of the Court of Session 1994 and Sheriff Court Rules Amendment) (No. 4) (Simple Procedure) 2016 (SSI 2016/315) para.7 (effective 28 November 2016).

How will the court treat other vulnerable witnesses?

11.5—(1) If a party cites (or intends to arrange the attendance of) a witness who is not a child, but the party thinks that the witness is a vulnerable witness, that party may send the court and the other party a Vulnerable Witness Application.

(2) A Vulnerable Witness Application asks the sheriff to decide whether the witness is a vulnerable witness. If the sheriff agrees, the sheriff may authorise the use of a special measure in taking the vulnerable witness's evidence.

(3) Before the sheriff decides how to deal with the Vulnerable Witness Application, the sheriff may order the parties to provide further information.

(4) The sheriff may decide to make the orders requested in the Vulnerable Witness Application with or without a discussion in court.

(5) Where the sheriff decides to have a discussion, the sheriff clerk must send the parties notice of when it will be held.

(6) At the discussion, the sheriff must consider the Vulnerable Witness Application and decide whether the witness is a vulnerable witness. If the sheriff agrees, the sheriff may authorise the use of a special measure in taking the vulnerable witness's evidence.

What are special measures?

11.6—(1) Special measures are ways of taking the evidence of a child witness or a vulnerable witness.

(2) The sheriff may authorise the use of any of these special measures:

(a) allowing that witness to give evidence before an independent person,

(b) allowing that witness to give evidence by live television link,

(c) allowing that witness to use a screen while giving evidence,

(d) allowing that witness to be supported by someone while giving evidence.

How can a party ask the court to review the arrangements for a child witness or a vulnerable witness?

11.7—(1) The party who sent a Child Witness Notice or Vulnerable Witness Application to the court may ask the sheriff to review the arrangements for the child witness or vulnerable witness to give evidence by sending the court and the other party a Special Measures Review Application.

(2) A Special Measures Review Application asks the sheriff to vary or revoke the current arrangements for the child witness or vulnerable witness to give evidence.

(3)[1] When a Special Measures Review Application is received, the sheriff may do one of 5 things:

(a) vary a special measure,

(b) add a new special measure,

(c) substitute a new special measure for an existing one,

(d) delete a special measure, or

(e) revoke the order authorising the use of special measures entirely.

(4) Before the sheriff decides how to deal with the Special Measures Review Application, the sheriff may order the parties to provide further information.

(5) The sheriff may decide to make the orders requested in the Special Measures Review Application with or without a discussion in court.

(6) Where the sheriff decides to have a discussion, the sheriff clerk must send the parties notice of when it will be held.

---

[1] As substituted by the Act of Sederunt (Rules of the Court of Session 1994 and Sheriff Court Rules Amendment) (No. 4) (Simple Procedure) 2016 (SSI 2016/315) para.7 (effective 28 November 2016).

(7) At the discussion, the sheriff must consider the Special Measures Review Application and decide whether to vary or revoke the current arrangements for the child witness or vulnerable witness to give evidence.

What happens when evidence is to be given before an independent person?

11.8—(1) Where the sheriff authorises a child witness or a vulnerable witness to give evidence before an independent person, the hearing at which the evidence is taken is to be video recorded.

(2) A party may be present when a child witness or vulnerable witness gives evidence before an independent person only if the sheriff has given permission for this to happen.

(3) The independent person must send the video recording and any relevant documents from the hearing to the sheriff clerk.

(4) The sheriff clerk must send the parties a notice indicating that the video recording has been received.

(5) If any relevant documents or other evidence are also received, the sheriff clerk must send the parties notice of what they are and when they were received.

What is this Part about?

12.1.—(1) This Part is about the hearing at which the dispute between the parties should be resolved.

What is the purpose of the hearing?

12.2.—(1) The purpose of the hearing is to help the sheriff to resolve the dispute between the parties.

How will the dispute between the parties be resolved?

12.3.—(1) The sheriff may refer parties to alternative dispute resolution at a hearing.

(2) If the sheriff thinks a negotiated settlement is possible, the sheriff must help the parties to negotiate a settlement to the dispute.

(3) If no negotiated settlement is possible, the sheriff must resolve the dispute by deciding it at that hearing.

(4) The sheriff may continue the hearing to another day without resolving the dispute only if it is necessary to do so.

(5)[1] But the sheriff must not continue a hearing to another day solely because a witness did not appear.

What will the sheriff do at the hearing?

12.4.—(1) The sheriff must ask the parties about their attitudes to negotiation and alternative dispute resolution.

(2) The sheriff must identify the factual basis and legal basis of the claim and the response to the claim.

(3) The sheriff must identify the factual and legal matters genuinely in dispute between the parties.

(4) The sheriff must take a note of the hearing. This note is for the sheriff's own purposes and must be kept until any appeal is no longer possible or until any appeal has been concluded.

What if a party does not come to the hearing?

12.5.—(1) If the claimant does not come to the hearing or is not represented at the hearing, the sheriff may dismiss the claim.

(2) If the respondent does not come to the hearing or is not represented at the hearing, the sheriff may make a decision in the case at that hearing.

(3) If neither party comes to the hearing and neither party is represented at the hearing, the sheriff must dismiss the claim.

How will evidence be given at the hearing?

12.6.—(1) Before evidence is heard, the sheriff must explain to the parties the way the sheriff has decided to consider evidence at the hearing.

(2) The sheriff may impose conditions on how evidence is presented or dealt with, including conditions on how witnesses are questioned or setting time limits on how long witnesses may be questioned.

(3) The sheriff may decide whether the evidence of a witness is to be taken on oath or affirmation or not.

---

[1] As inserted by the Act of Sederunt (Rules of the Court of Session 1994 and Sheriff Court Rules Amendment) (No. 4) (Simple Procedure) 2016 (SSI 2016/315) para.7 (effective 28 November 2016).

(4)   The sheriff may ask questions to the parties or to witnesses.

(5)   The sheriff may inspect any evidence with the parties or their representatives present.

(6)   The sheriff may inspect any place with the parties or their representatives present.

PART 13: THE DECISION

What is this Part about?

13.1.—(1)   This Part is about the decisions which the sheriff can make to resolve a dispute.

(2)   This Part is also about the circumstances in which a party can apply to have a decision recalled.

When must the sheriff make the decision?

13.2.—(1)   At the end of the hearing, the sheriff may either make a decision there and then, or may take time to consider before making a decision.

(2)   If the sheriff takes time to consider a decision, the decision must be made within 4 weeks from the date of the hearing.

How will the sheriff make the decision?

13.3.—(1)   If the sheriff makes a decision there and then, the sheriff must explain the reasons for that decision to the parties in person.

(2)   If the sheriff takes time to consider a decision, the sheriff must prepare a note of the reasons for the decision, and the sheriff clerk must send that note to the parties.

(3)   In every case, the sheriff must set out the decision in the case in a Decision Form.

(4)   The sheriff may correct any errors in a Decision Form before it is sent to a party.

What sort of decisions can the sheriff make?

13.4.—(1)   The sheriff may make any decision which resolves the dispute between the parties, including a decision which:

  (a)   orders the respondent to pay the claimant a sum of money,
  (b)   orders the respondent to deliver something to the claimant,
  (c)   orders the respondent to do something for the claimant,
  (d)   dismisses the claim (or part of the claim) made by the claimant,
  (e)   absolves the respondent of the claim (or part of the claim) made by the claimant.

(2)   A decision which absolves the respondent in a claim means that the claimant cannot make a claim about the same subject against the respondent again.

Recalling a decision

When can a decision of the sheriff be recalled?

13.5—(1)[1]   A party may apply to have a decision of the sheriff recalled in 5 situations:

  (a)   where the sheriff dismissed a claim because the claimant did not send the court an Application for a Decision within 2 weeks from the last date for a response,
  (b)   where the sheriff made a decision because the respondent did not send the court a Response Form or Time to Pay Application by the last date for a response,

---

[1] As substituted by the Act of Sederunt (Simple Procedure Amendment) (Miscellaneous) 2018 (SSI 2018/191) art.2(2)(k) (effective 30 July 2018).

    (c)   where the sheriff dismissed a claim because the claimant did not attend a discussion or hearing,

    (d)   where the sheriff has made a decision because the respondent did not attend a discussion or hearing, and

    (e)   where the sheriff dismissed a claim because neither party attended a discussion or hearing.

(2) If the sheriff dismissed the claim, a party may only apply for recall within 2 weeks of the claim being dismissed.

(3) If the sheriff made a decision (other than dismissal) in the case, a party may apply for recall at any time before the decision of the sheriff has been fully implemented.

(4)[1] A party may only apply to have a decision of the sheriff recalled in a case once.

How can a party apply to have a decision of the sheriff recalled?

13.6—[2](1) A party may apply to have a decision of the sheriff recalled by completing an Application to Recall and sending it to the court.

(2) If the sheriff made a decision following an Application for a Decision and the respondent wants to dispute the claim or part of the claim, the respondent must include a completed Response Form with the Application to Recall.

(3) The sheriff clerk will check whether the Application to Recall is the first Application to Recall in the case by the party making the application.

(4) If it is the first Application to Recall by that party, the sheriff must send the parties an order arranging a discussion in court at which the sheriff will consider whether to recall the decision.

(5) The party making the application must send a copy of the Application to Recall and any Response Form to the other party at least 5 days before the date of the discussion in court.

What happens when a sheriff decides to recall a decision?

13.7—(1) If the sheriff recalls a decision then the sheriff must give each party orders setting out the next steps they are to take to allow the dispute to be resolved.

---

[1] As inserted by the Act of Sederunt (Sheriff Court Rules Amendment) (Miscellaneous) 2017 (SSI 2017/154) para.2 (effective 15 June 2017).

[2] As substituted by the Act of Sederunt (Simple Procedure Amendment) (Miscellaneous) 2018 (SSI 2018/191) art.2(2)(l) (effective 30 July 2018).

PART 14: EXPENSES

What is this Part about?

14.1.—(1) This Part is about the expenses of a claim which the sheriff can order a party to pay for.

What orders about expenses can the sheriff make?

14.2.—(1) Once a claim has been resolved, the sheriff must make an order about expenses, such as:

    (a)   that no payments are to be made in respect of the expenses of any party,

    (b)   that a payment is to be made to a party or to a party's solicitor.

(2) Expenses incurred by a party to do with a courtroom supporter may not be part of an order about expenses.

When will the sheriff make an order about expenses?

14.3.—(1) In a case where the expenses of a claim are capped, the sheriff must make an order about expenses when deciding the claim.

(2) In any other case, the sheriff must, if able to, make an order about expenses when deciding the claim.

(3) If not able to make an order about expenses when deciding the claim, the sheriff may make an order about expenses after deciding the claim.

What if the sheriff does not make an order about expenses when deciding the claim?

14.4.—(1) If the sheriff makes an order about expenses after deciding the claim, then the sheriff must not set out the final decision in a case in a Decision Form until the order about expenses is made.

(2) If the sheriff does not make an order about expenses when deciding the claim, the sheriff must give the parties written orders.

(3) Those orders must arrange an expenses hearing.

(4) Those orders may require a party to send an account of expenses to the court and to each other before the expenses hearing.

(5) Those orders may then require the sheriff clerk to assess the level of expenses (if any) that should be awarded to a party and to send notice of that assessment to the parties before the expenses hearing.

What is an expenses hearing?

14.5.—(1) The purpose of an expenses hearing is to assess the level of expenses (if any) that should be awarded to a party.

(2) At the expenses hearing, the sheriff must make an order about expenses, such as:

    (a)   that no payments are to be made in respect of the expenses of any party,

    (b)   that a payment is to be made to a party or to a party's solicitor.

D2.51.21

What is this Part about?

15.1.—(1) This Part is about the steps which a successful party must take to enforce a decision.

When can a party enforce a decision?

15.2.—(1) After the Decision Form is sent, a party must wait 4 weeks before enforcing a decision.

(2) A party must not enforce a decision if that decision is being appealed (see Part 16).

(3)[1] A party who is sent an order arranging a discussion in court at which the sheriff will consider an Application to Recall must not enforce a decision until the sheriff has decided whether to recall the decision.

(4) A party must not enforce a decision which has been recalled.

How can a party enforce a decision?

15.3.—(1) If a party uses a trading name, a decision which names the party using that trading name may be enforced against the party by that name.

(2)[2] Before enforcing a decision for the payment of a sum of money in the following ways:

(a) an earnings arrestment (which is where a deduction is made from the earnings of the other party as a way of paying that sum of money),

(b) an attachment (which is where certain goods owned by the other party are seized and sold as a way of paying that sum of money),

(c) a money attachment (which is where money in the possession of the other party is seized as a way of paying that sum of money),

the successful party must formally serve a Charge on the other party by sheriff officer using a method of formal service mentioned in rule 18.3.

(3) The purpose of formally serving the Charge is to give the other party one last chance to pay the sum of money ordered by the court.

(4) The Charge must demand payment:

(a) within 2 weeks if the other party is in the United Kingdom,

(b) within 4 weeks if the other party is outside the United Kingdom,

(c) within 4 weeks if the other party's address is unknown.

(5) If the demand in the Charge is not complied with, then the successful party may instruct a sheriff officer to enforce the decision.

(6)[3] The requirement to formally serve by sheriff officer is subject to the exceptions in sections 2 and 3 of the Execution of Diligence (Scotland) Act 1926.

(7)[4] The Charge must be in the form set out in the schedule of the Act of Sederunt (Form of charge for payment) 1988.

---

[1] As substituted by the Act of Sederunt (Simple Procedure Amendment) (Miscellaneous) 2018 (SSI 2018/191) art.2(2)(m) (effective 30 July 2018).

[2] As substituted by the Act of Sederunt (Sheriff Court Rules Amendment) (Miscellaneous) 2017 (SSI 2017/154) para.2 (effective 15 June 2017).

[3] As inserted by the Act of Sederunt (Sheriff Court Rules Amendment) (Miscellaneous) 2016 (SSI 2016/367) para.5 (effective 28 November 2016).

[4] As inserted by the Act of Sederunt (Sheriff Court Rules Amendment) (Miscellaneous) 2017 (SSI 2017/154) para.2 (effective 15 June 2017).

(8)[1] Where the Charge is formally served, the sheriff officer is not required to send a Confirmation of Formal Service to the court.

What if the claimant does not know the respondent's address?

15.4—[2](1) Where the claimant is successful but does not know the respondent's address, the claimant must take all reasonable steps to find out the respondent's address.

(2)[3] If the claimant does not know the respondent's address, then instead of formally serving the Charge on the respondent, the claimant must formally serve it by sheriff officer on the sheriff clerk in the sheriff court district where the respondent's last known address was.

(3) The sheriff clerk must then publicise the Charge by advertising its details on the Scottish Courts and Tribunals Service website for 4 weeks.

(4) After that 4 weeks, the sheriff clerk must certify on the Charge that the advertisement took place and send it to the person who formally served it.

(5) The claimant may then instruct a sheriff officer to enforce the decision.

What if the respondent does not comply with a decision?

15.5—[4](1) A claimant may make an Alternative Decision Application where the respondent does not comply with a decision which:

    (a) orders the respondent to deliver something to the claimant, or

    (b) orders the respondent to do something for the claimant.

(2) An Alternative Decision Application may only be made where the sheriff alternatively ordered the respondent to pay the claimant a sum of money.

(3) The application is made by sending an Alternative Decision Application to the court.

(4) After considering the Alternative Decision Application the sheriff may do one of three things:

    (a) grant the application, and order the respondent to pay the claimant a sum of money,

    (b) refuse the application,

    (c) order the claimant to appear at a discussion in court, where the sheriff will consider whether to make any orders.

---

[1] As inserted by the Act of Sederunt (Simple Procedure Amendment) (Miscellaneous) 2018 (SSI 2018/191) art.2(2)(n) (effective 30 July 2018).

[2] As amended by the Act of Sederunt (Rules of the Court of Session 1994 and Sheriff Court Rules Amendment) (No. 4) (Simple Procedure) 2016 (SSI 2016/315) para.7 (effective 28 November 2016).

[3] As amended by the Act of Sederunt (Sheriff Court Rules Amendment) (Miscellaneous) 2016 (SSI 2016/367) para.5 (effective 28 November 2016).

[4] As amended by the Act of Sederunt (Rules of the Court of Session 1994 and Sheriff Court Rules Amendment) (No. 4) (Simple Procedure) 2016 (SSI 2016/315) para.7 (effective 28 November 2016).

What is this Part about?

16.1.—(1)   This Part is about how a party can appeal a decision and how the sheriff and Sheriff Appeal Court will deal with an appeal.

How do you appeal a decision?

16.2.—(1)   A party may appeal a decision within 4 weeks from the Decision Form being sent.

(2)   A party may appeal a decision by sending a completed Appeal Form to the sheriff court.

(3)   That party must at the same time send a copy of the completed Appeal Form to the other party.

(4)   The Appeal Form must set out the legal points which the party making the appeal wants the Sheriff Appeal Court to answer.

(5)   A party may not appeal a decision if that party can apply to have that decision recalled (see Part 13).

What will the sheriff do with an appeal?

16.3.—(1)   The sheriff must prepare a draft Appeal Report within 4 weeks of the court receiving an Appeal Form.

(2)   The draft Appeal Report must set out the factual and legal basis for the decision which the sheriff came to.

(3)   The draft Appeal Report must set out legal questions for the Sheriff Appeal Court to answer.

(4)   The sheriff clerk must send the draft Appeal Report to all parties.

(5)   All parties may, within 2 weeks of the draft Appeal Report being sent to them, send the sheriff a note of any other legal points they wish the Sheriff Appeal Court to answer and any factual points in the draft Appeal Report they disagree with.

(6)   The sheriff may order a discussion in court to consider whether amendments should be made to the Appeal Report.

(7)   The sheriff may then amend the Appeal Report.

(8)[1]   The sheriff must then sign or authenticate electronically the Appeal Report.

(9)   The sheriff clerk must send a copy of the signed Appeal Report to each party.

(10)   The sheriff clerk must transmit the following to the Clerk of the Sheriff Appeal Court:

   (a)   the note of the reasons for the sheriff's decision (if one was prepared),

   (b)   a copy of the Decision Form,

   (c)   all written orders,

   (d)   the signed Appeal Report, and

   (e)   any note sent to the court by a party.

What will the Sheriff Appeal Court do with an appeal?

16.4.—(1)   The Clerk of the Sheriff Appeal Court must, within 2 weeks of receiving the signed Appeal Report, arrange an appeal hearing and send all parties notice of where and when the appeal hearing is to be held.

---

[1] As amended by the Act of Sederunt (Rules of the Court of Session 1994 and Sheriff Court Rules Amendment) (No. 4) (Simple Procedure) 2016 (SSI 2016/315) r.7(3) (effective 28 November 2016).

(2)   Unless the Sheriff Appeal Court orders otherwise, an appeal hearing must be before one Appeal Sheriff.

(3)   At the end of the appeal hearing, the Sheriff Appeal Court may either make a decision there and then, or may take time to consider the decision.

(4)   If the Sheriff Appeal Court takes time to consider the decision, the decision must be made within 4 weeks from the date of the appeal hearing.

(5)   If the Sheriff Appeal Court makes a decision there and then, it must explain the reasons for that decision to the parties in person.

(6)   If the Sheriff Appeal Court takes time to consider a decision, the court must prepare a note of the reasons for the decision, and the Clerk of the Sheriff Appeal Court must send that note to the parties.

(7)   The Sheriff Appeal Court may alter the decision which the sheriff made by either amending the Decision Form or issuing a new Decision Form.

(8)[1]   Parts 2, 4, 5 and 6 of the Act of Sederunt (Sheriff Appeal Court Rules) 2015 apply to the appeal.

---

[1] As amended by the Act of Sederunt (Rules of the Court of Session 1994 and Sheriff Court Rules Amendment) (No. 4) (Simple Procedure) 2016 (SSI 2016/315) para.7 (effective 28 November 2016).

PART 17: MISCELLANEOUS MATTERS

What is this Part about?

17.1.—(1) This Part is about some miscellaneous matters which can arise during a case.

How can a case be transferred out of the simple procedure?

17.2.—(1) Where a sheriff orders that a case should no longer proceed subject to these rules, that order must identify the procedure under which the case is to continue.

(2) If the sheriff orders that the case should proceed as an ordinary cause, the sheriff must also order three things:

    (a) that the claimant must lodge an initial writ and intimate it to every other party within 2 weeks from the date of the order,

    (b) that the respondent must lodge defences within 4 weeks from the date of the order, and

    (c) that an options hearing is to be held on the first suitable court day occurring not sooner than 10 weeks (or such lesser period as the sheriff considers appropriate) after the last date for lodging the initial writ.

(3) If the sheriff orders that the case should proceed as an ordinary cause the sheriff may also certify in the order that the importance or difficulty of the proceedings makes it appropriate to transfer the case to the Sheriff Personal Injury Court.

How can the sheriff make a reference to the Court of Justice of the European Union?

17.3—(1) If a question of EU law arises in a case, the sheriff may refer that question to the Court of Justice of the European Union using the CJEU Reference Form.

(2) The sheriff may decide to do this when asked to by a party, or without being asked.

(3) The sheriff must draft the reference within 4 weeks of deciding to do so.

(4) Once a reference has been drafted, the sheriff clerk must send a copy to the parties.

(5) Once the draft reference has been sent to the parties, each party has 4 weeks to send suggested amendments of that reference to the sheriff.

(6) Once that 4 weeks has passed, the sheriff has 2 weeks to consider any suggested amendments.

(7) At the end of that period of 2 weeks, the sheriff must finalise and sign the reference.

(8) The sheriff clerk must transmit the reference to the Court of Justice of the European Union and inform parties that the reference has been made.

How can the Commission for Equality and Human Rights ("CEHR") or the Scottish Commission for Human Rights ("SCHR") intervene?

17.4—(1) The CEHR and the SCHR may apply to the sheriff to intervene in a case by sending to the court and to the parties an Application to Intervene.

(2) The Application to Intervene must set out the reasons for the proposed intervention, the issues which the intervention would address, and the reasons why the intervention would assist the sheriff.

(3) The sheriff may grant the application with or without a discussion, but there must be a discussion if a party asks for one.

(4)   The sheriff may grant the Application to Intervene only if satisfied that:

    (a)   the case has a relevant connection to one of the functions of the CEHR or the SCHR,

    (b)   the intervention is likely to assist the sheriff, and

    (c)   the intervention will not unduly delay or otherwise prejudice the interests of the parties, including their liability for expenses.

(5)   The sheriff may impose conditions on the intervention.

(6)   The sheriff may invite the CEHR or SCHR to intervene in a simple procedure case by sending to the CEHR or SCHR and to all parties an Invitation to Intervene.

(7)   An Invitation to Intervene must be accompanied by a copy of the Claim Form and the Response Form, and any other documents relevant to the reasons for the proposed intervention.

(8)   The sheriff may impose conditions on an intervention when making an invitation.

What can the CEHR or the SCHR do in an intervention?

17.5—(1)   An intervention is a written submission of 5,000 words or less (including any appendices).

(2)   A copy of the intervention must be sent to all parties.

(3)   In exceptional circumstances, the sheriff may allow a longer written submission or an oral submission.

Management of damages

When is a damages management order available?

17.6—(1)   Damages management orders are available:

    (a)   where a claimant who is under a legal disability asks for the payment of a sum of money as damages,

    (b)   where another person makes a claim on behalf of a person who is under a legal disability asking for the payment of a sum of money as damages.

(2)   In either case, a damages management order is only available if the person who is under a legal disability is 16 years of age or older.

When must the sheriff make a damages management order?

17.7—(1)   The sheriff must make a damages management order if the sheriff orders the respondent to pay the claimant a sum of money as damages.

(2)   The sheriff must also make a damages management order if the claimant accepts an offer from the respondent to pay a sum of money as damages to settle the claim.

What can the sheriff do in a damages management order?

17.8—(1)   The sheriff must make an order about how the money is to be paid to and managed for the person under a legal disability.

(2)   The sheriff may order the money to be paid to different people to be managed for the benefit of the person under a legal disability.

(3)   The sheriff may order the money to be paid to:

    (a)   the Accountant of Court,

    (b)   the sheriff clerk, or

    (c)   the guardian of the person who is under a legal disability.

(4)   Alternatively, the sheriff may decide that the person under a legal disability is capable of managing the money and order that the money is paid directly to that person.

(5)   Where the sheriff orders the money to be paid to the sheriff clerk or a guardian, the sheriff may also tell that person how to manage the money for the benefit of the person under a legal disability.

How can the damages management order be changed?

17.9—(1)   An interested person can ask the sheriff to change the damages management order by sending an Application to Change a Damages Management Order to the court and every party.

(2)   If a person who has been sent the Application to Change a Damages Management Order objects to the proposed orders, that person must send that Application to Change a Damages Management Order to the court within 10 days of it being sent, setting out that objection.

(3)   After considering the Application to Change a Damages Management Order, and any objection that may have been sent, the sheriff may do one of three things:

(a)   grant the application, and send written orders to the parties and the interested person,

(b)   refuse the application,

(c)   order the parties and the interested person to appear at a discussion in court, where the sheriff will consider whether to make any orders.

How can further instructions about managing the money be given?

17.10—(1)   An interested person can also ask the sheriff to tell the sheriff clerk or a guardian how to manage the money by sending an Application for Instructions about a Damages Management Order to the court and every party.

(2)   If a guardian is managing the money, the Application for Instructions about a Damages Management Order must also be sent to the guardian.

(3)   If a person who has been sent the Application for Instructions about a Damages Management Order, objects to the proposed instructions, that person must send that Application for Instructions about a Damages Management Order to the court within 10 days of it being sent, with a note setting out that objection.

(4)   After considering the Application for Instructions about a Damages Management Order, and any objection that may have been sent, the sheriff may do one of three things:

(a)   grant the application, and send further instructions to the parties, the interested person and the sheriff clerk or guardian,

(b)   refuse the application,

(c)   order the parties, the interested person and the guardian (if there is one) to appear at a discussion in court, where the sheriff will consider whether to give further instructions.

When can someone apply for a child's property administration order?

17.11—(1)   A person may ask the sheriff to make a child's property administration order in any simple procedure case where the sheriff has made an order under section 13 of the Children (Scotland) Act 1995 (section 13 is about the payment and management of money to (or for the benefit of) a child).

How can someone apply for a child's property administration order?

17.12—(1)   A person can ask the sheriff to make a child's property administration order by sending an Application for a Child's Property Administration Order to the court and every party.

(2)   If a person who has been sent the Application for a Child's Property Administration Order objects to the proposed orders, that person must send that Application for a Child's Property Administration Order to the court within 10 days of it being sent, setting out that objection.

(3) After considering the Application for a Child's Property Administration Order, and any objection that may have been sent, the sheriff may do one of three things:

    (a) grant the application, and send written orders to the parties and the applicant,

    (b) refuse the application,

    (c) order the parties and the applicant to appear at a discussion in court, where the sheriff will consider whether to make any orders.

The Equality Act 2010

What is an Equality Act 2010 claim?

17.13—(1) An Equality Act 2010 claim is a claim made under section 114(1) of the Equality Act 2010 (section 114 is about claims related to the provision of services, the exercise of public functions, the disposal and management of premises, education (other than in relation to disability), and associations).

How can the Commission for Equality and Human Rights ("the CEHR") be notified of an Equality Act 2010 claim?

17.14.—(1) The claimant must send a copy of the Claim Form in an Equality Act 2010 claim to the CEHR.

How can an Equality Act 2010 claim be transferred to the Employment Tribunal?

17.15.—(1) The sheriff may order an Equality Act 2010 claim to be transferred to the Employment Tribunal.

(2) The sheriff must state in that order the reasons for making it.

(3) That order may include an order about expenses.

(4) When the sheriff makes that order, the sheriff clerk must transmit, within one week of the order, the following things to the Employment Tribunal:

    (a) the Claim Form,

    (b) the Response Form,

    (c) any written orders, and

    (d) any other document the sheriff orders to be transmitted.

How can an Employment Tribunal case be transferred to simple procedure?

17.16.—(1) When proceedings are transferred to simple procedure from the Employment Tribunal under section 140(3) of the Equality Act 2010, the sheriff clerk must register those proceedings as a claim.

(2) The sheriff must, within 2 weeks of the claim being registered, order a case management discussion.

What if a question of national security arises in an Equality Act 2010 claim?

17.17.—(1) Where the sheriff considers it expedient in the interests of national security, the sheriff may order any of the following persons to be excluded from any or all hearings, case management discussions or discussions in court of an Equality Act 2010 claim:

    (a) the claimant,

    (b) the claimant's representative,

    (c) the claimant's courtroom supporter.

(2) That order may allow an excluded claimant or representative to send a written statement to the court before the case (or part of the case) from which they have been excluded.

(3) When the sheriff makes an order excluding persons, the sheriff clerk must send a copy of the order to the Advocate General for Scotland.

(4) Where the sheriff considers it expedient in the interests of national security, the sheriff may take any steps or make any order required to keep secret any or all of the reasons for the sheriff's decision in an Equality Act 2010 claim.

FORMAL SERVICE IN SCOTLAND

What is this Part about?

18.1.—(1) This Part is about how to formally serve a document on someone living in Scotland.

How can you formally serve a document on someone who lives in Scotland?

18.2—(1) When these Rules require a document to be formally served, the first attempt must be by a next-day postal service which records delivery.

(2) That may only be done by one of three persons:

    (a) the party's solicitor,

    (b) a sheriff officer instructed by the party,

    (c)[1] the sheriff clerk (where provided for by rule 6.11(2)).

(3) The envelope which contains the document must have the following label written or printed on it:

> **THIS ENVELOPE CONTAINS A [NAME OF DOCUMENT] FROM**
> **[NAME OF SHERIFF COURT]**
> **IF DELIVERY CANNOT BE MADE, THE LETTER MUST BE**
> **RETURNED TO THE SHERIFF CLERK AT**
> **[FULL ADDRESS OF SHERIFF COURT]**

(4) After formally serving a document, a Confirmation of Formal Service must be completed and any evidence of delivery attached to it.

(5) Where a solicitor or sheriff officer has formally served the document, then the Confirmation of Formal Service must be sent to the sheriff court within one week of service taking place.

What if service by post does not work?

18.3—(1) If service by post has not worked, a sheriff officer may formally serve a document in one of three ways:

    (a) delivering it personally,

    (b) leaving it in the hands of a resident at the person's home,

    (c) leaving it in the hands of an employee at the person's place of business.

(2) If none of those ways has worked, the sheriff officer must make diligent inquiries about the person's whereabouts and current residence, and may then formally serve the document in one of two ways:

    (a) depositing it in the person's home or place of business by means of a letter box or other lawful way of doing so, or

    (b) leaving it at the person's home or place of business in such a way that it is likely to come to the attention of that person.

(3) If formal service is done in either of those ways, the sheriff officer must also do two more things:

    (a) send a copy of the document to the person by post to the address at which the sheriff officer thinks the person is most likely to be found, and

    (b) write or print on the envelope containing the document the following label:

---

[1] As amended by the Act of Sederunt (Rules of the Court of Session 1994 and Sheriff Court Rules Amendment) (No. 4) (Simple Procedure) 2016 (SSI 2016/315) para.7 (effective 28 November 2016).

THIS ENVELOPE CONTAINS A [NAME OF DOCUMENT] FROM
[NAME OF SHERIFF COURT]

What is this Part about?

19.1.—(1) This Part is about how to formally serve a document on someone   **D2.51.20**
outside Scotland.

How can you formally serve a document on someone who lives outside Scotland?

19.2.—(1) Different rules apply depending on the country that the person lives in.

(2) If the person lives in England and Wales, Northern Ireland, the Isle of Man or the Channel Islands, see rule 19.3.

(3) If the person lives in an EU member state (including Denmark), see rule 19.4.

(4) If the person lives in a Hague Convention country (other than an EU member state), see rule 19.5.

(5) If the person lives in a country with which the United Kingdom has a convention about how to serve court documents (such as Algeria, Libya and the United Arab Emirates), see rule 19.6.

(6) If none of the above applies, see rule 19.7.

How can you formally serve a document on someone who lives in England and Wales, Northern Ireland, the Isle of Man or the Channel Islands?

19.3.—[1] *Method*

(1) There are two ways to formally serve a document on someone who lives in England and Wales, Northern Ireland, the Isle of Man or the Channel Islands.

(2) It may be done by posting the document to the person's home or business address using a postal service which records delivery. This is called postal service.

(3) It may also be done by using the rules for personal service under the domestic law of the country where the document is to be served. This is called personal service.

Who can formally serve the document?

(4) The sheriff clerk may formally serve a Claim Form on the respondent by postal service only if:

    (a) the claimant is not a company or a partnership, and

    (b) the claimant is not legally represented.

(5) Otherwise, postal service may only be done by one of two persons:

    (a) the party's solicitor,

    (b) a sheriff officer instructed by the party.

(6) Personal service may be done by a person who is authorised to do so under the domestic law of the country where the document is to be served.

Additional requirements

(7) Where postal service is used, the envelope containing the document must have the following label printed or written on it:

> **THIS ENVELOPE CONTAINS A [NAME OF DOCUMENT] FROM [NAME OF SHERIFF COURT], SCOTLAND**

---

[1] As amended by the Act of Sederunt (Rules of the Court of Session 1994 and Sheriff Court Rules Amendment) (No. 4) (Simple Procedure) 2016 (SSI 2016/315) para.7 (effective 28 November 2016).

> **IF DELIVERY CANNOT BE MADE, THE LETTER MUST BE RETURNED TO THE SHERIFF CLERK AT [FULL ADDRESS OF SHERIFF COURT]**

(8)   After formally serving a document, a Confirmation of Formal Service must be completed by the person who served it.

(9)   If postal service has been used, any postal receipts must be attached to the Confirmation of Formal Service.

(10)   If a solicitor or a sheriff officer has formally served a document, the Confirmation of Formal Service must be sent to the sheriff court within one week of service taking place.

How can you formally serve a document on someone who lives in an EU member state (including Denmark) under the Service Regulation?

19.4—[1] *Method*

(1)   There are up to 4 ways to formally serve a document on someone who lives in an EU member state (including Denmark) under the Service Regulation, depending on what the law of that member state permits.

(2)   It may be done by posting the document to the person's home or business address using a postal service which records delivery. This is called postal service.

(3)   It may be done by sending the document to a messenger-at-arms and asking them to arrange for it to be served. This is called service by transmitting agency.

(4)[2]   It may be done by sending the document to a person who is entitled to serve court documents in that member state and asking them to arrange for it to be formally served. This is called direct service. This method can only be used if the law of the member state permits it.

(5)   It may be done by sending the document to the Secretary of State for Foreign, Commonwealth and Development Affairs and asking the Secretary of State to arrange for it to be formally served by a British consular authority. This is called consular service. This method can always be used if the document is being served on a British national. Otherwise, it can only be used if the law of the member state permits it.

Who can formally serve the document?

(6)   The sheriff clerk may formally serve a Claim Form on the respondent by postal service only if:

    (a)   the claimant is not a company or a partnership, and

    (b)   the claimant is not legally represented.

(7)   Otherwise, postal service may only be done by one of two persons:

    (a)   the party's solicitor,

    (b)   a sheriff officer instructed by the party.

(8)[3]   For the other methods of formal service, the party sends the document to the Secretary of State for Foreign, Commonwealth and Development Affairs or a person who is entitled to serve court documents in the country where the Form or Notice is to be formally served. That person will make the necessary arrangements for formal service.

---

[1] As amended by the Act of Sederunt (Rules of the Court of Session 1994 and Sheriff Court Rules Amendment) (No. 4) (Simple Procedure) 2016 (SSI 2016/315) para.7 (effective 28 November 2016).

[2] As amended by the Transfer of Functions (Secretary of State for Foreign, Commonwealth and Development Affairs) Order 2020 (SI 2020/942) Sch.1(2) para.25(a) (effective 30 September 2020).

[3] As amended by the Transfer of Functions (Secretary of State for Foreign, Commonwealth and Development Affairs) Order 2020 (SI 2020/942) Sch.1(2) para.25(a) (effective 30 September 2020).

Additional requirements

(9)　Where a party chooses service by transmitting agency, the party must give the messenger-at-arms a translation of the document into a language which the recipient understands or an official language of the member state where the document is to be served.

(10)　After translating a document, the translator must complete a Translation Certificate and give it to the party who is formally serving the document.

(11)　Where postal service is used, the envelope containing the document must have the following label printed or written on it:

**THIS ENVELOPE CONTAINS A [NAME OF DOCUMENT] FROM
[NAME OF SHERIFF COURT], SCOTLAND
IF DELIVERY CANNOT BE MADE, THE LETTER MUST BE
RETURNED TO THE SHERIFF CLERK AT
[FULL ADDRESS OF SHERIFF COURT]**

---

(12)　That label must also be translated into an official language of the country where the document is to be served, unless English is an official language of that country.

(13)　After formally serving a document by postal service, a Confirmation of Formal Service must be completed by the person who formally served it.

(14)　Any postal receipts must be attached to the Confirmation of Formal Service.

(15)　If a solicitor or a sheriff officer has used postal service, the Confirmation of Formal Service must be sent to the sheriff court within one week of formal service taking place.

(16)　If any other method of formal service was used, the party who requested service of the document must send the certificate that the party receives from the person who served the document to the sheriff court within one week of receiving it.

(17)　If the document was translated into another language, the Translation Certificate must be sent to the sheriff court with the Confirmation of Formal Service or the certificate from the person who served the document.

How can you formally serve a document on someone who lives in a Hague Convention country (other than an EU member state)?

19.5—[1]　*Method*

(1)　There are up to 4 ways to formally serve a document on someone who lives in a Hague Convention country, depending on what the law of that country permits.

(2)　It may be done by posting the document to the person's home or business address using a postal service which records delivery. This is called postal service. This method can only be used if the law of the country permits it.

(3)　It may be done by sending the document to the Scottish Ministers and asking them to arrange for it to be formally served. This is called service via central authority. This method can always be used.

(4)[2]　It may be done by sending the document to the Secretary of State for Foreign, Commonwealth and Development Affairs and asking the Secretary of State to arrange for it to be formally served by a British consular authority. This is called

---

[1] As amended by the Act of Sederunt (Rules of the Court of Session 1994 and Sheriff Court Rules Amendment) (No.4) (Simple Procedure) 2016 (SSI 2016/315) para.7 (effective 28 November 2016).
[2] As amended by the Transfer of Functions (Secretary of State for Foreign, Commonwealth and Development Affairs) Order 2020 (SI 2020/942) Sch.1(2) para.25(b) (effective 30 September 2020).

consular service. This method can always be used if the document is being formally served on a British national. Otherwise, it can only be used if the law of the country permits it.

(5)　It may be done by sending the document to a person who is entitled to serve court documents in that country and asking them to arrange for it to be formally served. This is called service by competent person. This method can only be used if the law of the country permits it.

Who can formally serve the document?

(6)　The sheriff clerk may formally serve a Claim Form on the respondent by postal service only if:

    (a)　the claimant is not a company or a partnership, and

    (b)　the claimant is not legally represented.

(7)　Otherwise, postal service may only be done by one of two persons:

    (a)　the party's solicitor,

    (b)　a sheriff officer instructed by the party.

(8)[1]　For the other methods of formal service, the party sends the Form or Notice to the Scottish Ministers, the Secretary of State for Foreign, Commonwealth and Development Affairs or a person who is entitled to serve court documents in the country where the Form or Notice is to be formally served. That person will make the necessary arrangements for formal service.

Additional requirements

(9)　Any document must be accompanied by a translation into an official language of the country where it is to be formally served, unless English is an official language of that country.

(10)　After translating a document, the translator must complete a Translation Certificate and give it to the party who is formally serving the Form or Notice.

(11)　Where postal service is used, the envelope containing the document must have the following label printed or written on it:

> **THIS ENVELOPE CONTAINS A [NAME OF DOCUMENT] FROM**
> **[NAME OF SHERIFF COURT], SCOTLAND**
> **IF DELIVERY CANNOT BE MADE, THE LETTER MUST BE**
> **RETURNED TO THE SHERIFF CLERK AT**
> **[FULL ADDRESS OF SHERIFF COURT]**

(12)　That label must also be translated into an official language of the country where the Form or Notice is to be served, unless English is an official language of that country.

(13)　After formally serving a document by postal service, a Confirmation of Formal Service must be completed by the person who served it.

(14)　Any postal receipts must be attached to the Confirmation of Formal Service.

(15)　If a solicitor or a sheriff officer has used postal service, the Confirmation of Formal Service must be sent to the sheriff court within one week of service taking place.

(16)　If any other method of formal service was used, the party who requested formal service of the document must send the certificate that the party receives from the person who formally served the document to the sheriff court within one week of receiving it.

---

[1] As amended by the Transfer of Functions (Secretary of State for Foreign, Commonwealth and Development Affairs) Order 2020 (SI 2020/942) Sch.1(2) para.25(b) (effective 30 September 2020).

(17) If the document was translated into another language, the Translation Certificate must be sent to the sheriff court with the Confirmation of Formal Service or the certificate from the person who served the document.

How can you formally serve a document on someone who lives in a country with which the United Kingdom has a convention about how to serve court documents?

19.6— [1] *Method*

(1) The ways of formally serving a document on someone who lives in a country with which the United Kingdom has a convention about how to serve court documents depends on the convention between the United Kingdom and that country.

(2) Accordingly, a document can be formally served in any way that is allowed in the convention between the United Kingdom and the country where it is to be served.

Who can formally serve the document?

(3) A document can be formally served by a person who is authorised to do so by the convention between the United Kingdom and the country where it is to be served.

Additional requirements

(4) Where the convention requires that a document must be accompanied by a translation into an official language of the country where it is to be served, the translator must complete a Translation Certificate and give it to the party who is serving the document.

(5) The party who requested formal service of the document must send the certificate that the party receives from the person who served the document to the sheriff court within one week of receiving it.

(6) If the document was translated into another language, the Translation Certificate must be sent to the sheriff court with the certificate from the person who served the document.

How can you formally serve a document on someone who lives in any other country?

19.7— [2] *Method*

(1) There are two ways to formally serve a document on someone who lives in a country where none of the other rules apply.

(2) It can be done by posting the document to the person's home or business address using a postal service which records delivery. This is called postal service.

(3) It can also be done by using the rules for personal service under the domestic law of the country where the document is to be served. This is called personal service.

Who can formally serve the document?

(4) The sheriff clerk may formally serve a Claim Form on the respondent by postal service only if:

(a) the claimant is not a company or a partnership, and

(b) the claimant is not legally represented.

(5) Otherwise, postal service many only be done by one of two persons:

(a) the party's solicitor,

(b) a sheriff officer instructed by the party.

---

[1] As amended by the Act of Sederunt (Rules of the Court of Session 1994 and Sheriff Court Rules Amendment) (No.4) (Simple Procedure) 2016 (SSI 2016/315) para.7 (effective 28 November 2016).
[2] As amended by the Act of Sederunt (Rules of the Court of Session 1994 and Sheriff Court Rules Amendment) (No.4) (Simple Procedure) 2016 (SSI 2016/315) para.7 (effective 28 November 2016).

(6)   Personal service may be done by a person who is authorised to do so under the domestic law of the country where the document is to be served.

Additional requirements

(7)   Any document must be accompanied by a translation into an official language of the country where it is to be formally served, unless English is an official language of that country.

(8)   After translating a document, the translator must complete a Translation Certificate and give it to the party who is formally serving the Form or Notice.

(9)   Where postal service is used, the envelope containing the document must have the following label printed or written on it:

> **THIS ENVELOPE CONTAINS A [NAME OF DOCUMENT] FROM [NAME OF SHERIFF COURT], SCOTLAND IF DELIVERY CANNOT BE MADE, THE LETTER MUST BE RETURNED TO THE SHERIFF CLERK AT [FULL ADDRESS OF SHERIFF COURT]**

(10)   That label must also be translated into an official language of the country where the document is to be served, unless English is an official language of that country.

(11)   After formally serving a document by postal service, a Confirmation of Formal Service must be completed by the person who served it.

(12)   Any postal receipts must be attached to the Confirmation of Formal Service.

(13)   If a solicitor or a sheriff officer has used postal service, the Confirmation of Formal Service must be sent to the sheriff court within one week of service taking place.

(14)   If any other method of formal service was used, the party who requested formal service of the document must send the certificate that the party receives from the person who formally served the document to the sheriff court within one week of receiving it.

(15)   If any other method of formal service was used, the party who requested formal service of the document must also send a Method of Service Abroad Certificate to the sheriff court with the certificate that the party receives from the person who served the document to the sheriff court within one one week of receiving it.

(16)   If the document was translated into another language, the Translation Certificate must be sent to the sheriff court with the Confirmation of Formal Service or the certificate from the person who formally served the document.

PROVISIONAL ORDERS

What is this Part about?

20.1.—(1) This Part is about provisional orders which protect or secure the claimant's position before the sheriff makes a final decision in a case.

When can a claimant ask for provisional orders to be made?

20.2—(1) The claimant may apply for provisional orders to be made by completing a Provisional Orders Application and sending it to the sheriff court with the Claim Form.

(2) The claimant may also apply for provisional orders at any time before the sheriff makes a final decision in a case by completing a Provisional Orders Application and sending it to the sheriff court.

(3) The claimant must also send the Provisional Orders Application to the respondent and any interested person, unless the claimant has asked the court to make the provisional orders without holding a provisional orders hearing.

What happens when the court receives a Provisional Orders Application?

20.3—[1](1) The next steps depend on whether the claimant has asked the court to grant the Provisional Orders Application with or without holding a hearing.

(2) If the claimant has asked the court to hold a hearing, before deciding whether to grant the Provisional Orders Application, the sheriff must—

    (a) send the claimant notice of when and where the hearing is to be held, and

    (b) order the claimant to tell the respondent and any interested person when and where it is to be held.

(3) If the claimant has asked the court to grant the Provisional Orders Application without holding a hearing, the sheriff may do one of 3 things:

    (a) grant the Provisional Orders Application and send the claimant written orders containing the provisional orders,

    (b) refuse to grant the Provisional Orders Application without holding a hearing and send the claimant notice of when and where the hearing is to be held, or

    (c) where the claimant has indicated in Form 20A that they do not want the court to arrange a hearing under paragraph (3)(b), refuse the Provisional Orders Application.

(4) Where the sheriff grants the Provisional Orders Application without holding a hearing, the sheriff must also fix a provisional orders review hearing and order the claimant to tell the respondent and any interested person when and where it is to be held.

(5) If the sheriff refuses to grant the Provisional Orders Application without holding a hearing, the sheriff must also order the claimant to send the respondent and any interested person notice of when and where the hearing is to be held.

How can the claimant tell the respondent or an interested party about a hearing?

20.4—(1) The claimant can tell the respondent or an interested party about any hearing under this Part by sending a Provisional Orders Hearing Notice to the respondent or interested party.

---

[1] As substituted by the Act of Sederunt (Rules of the Court of Session 1994 and Sheriff Court Rules Amendment) (No. 4) (Simple Procedure) 2016 (SSI 2016/315) para.7 (effective 28 November 2016).

How can you ask the court to reconsider provisional orders that it has made?

20.5—(1)   The respondent can ask the sheriff to reconsider a provisional order by sending a Provisional Orders Reconsideration Application to the court, the claimant and any interested person.

(2)   An interested person can ask the sheriff to reconsider a provisional order by sending a Provisional Orders Reconsideration Application to the court, the claimant, the respondent and any other interested person.

(3)   When the court receives a Provisional Orders Reconsideration Application, the sheriff must order every person to whom the application was sent to appear at a provisional orders review hearing where the sheriff will consider whether to change the provisional order.

(4)   The sheriff may also order notice of the provisional orders review hearing to be given to any other person that the sheriff is satisfied has an interest.

How can you ask the court to consider other applications about provisional orders?

20.6—(1)   A party may make any other application mentioned in Part 1A of the Debtors (Scotland) Act 1987 or Part 1A of the Debt Arrangement and Attachment (Scotland) Act 2002 by sending an Incidental Orders Application to the court, the other party and any interested person.

(2)   An interested person may make any other application mentioned in Part 1A of the Debtors (Scotland) Act 1987 or Part 1A of the Debt Arrangement and Attachment (Scotland) Act 2002 by sending an Incidental Orders Application to the court, the parties and any other interested person.

(3)   When the court receives such an Incidental Orders Application, the sheriff must order every person to whom the application was sent to appear at a provisional orders discussion in court, where the sheriff will consider whether to make any orders.

How are provisional orders made effective?

20.7—(1)   The method for making a provisional order effective depends on the type of provisional order.

(2)[1]   An arrestment on the dependence (see rule 3.8(2)(a)) is made effective in accordance with rule 20.8.

(3)   An inhibition on the dependence (see rule 3.8(2)(b)) is made effective in accordance with section 148(3)(b) of the Bankruptcy and Diligence (Scotland) Act 2007 and the Diligence (Scotland) Regulations 2009 (but see rule 20.9 if the respondent's address is not known).

(4)   An interim attachment (see rule 3.8(2)(c)) is made effective in accordance with Chapter 1A of the Rules for Applications in the Sheriff Court under the Debt Arrangement and Attachment (Scotland) Act 2002.

How is an arrestment on the dependence made effective?

20.8—(1)   An arrestment on the dependence is made effective by formally serving an Arrestment Notice on the person named in the provisional order who holds the respondent's goods or money.

(2)   An Arrestment Notice must be formally served by a sheriff officer. The sheriff officer must use one of the methods of formal service mentioned in rule 18.3.

---

[1] As substituted by the Act of Sederunt (Rules of the Court of Session 1994 and Sheriff Court Rules Amendment) (No. 4) (Simple Procedure) 2016 (SSI 2016/315) para.7 (effective 28 November 2016).

(3) After formally serving an Arrestment Notice, the sheriff officer must complete a Confirmation of Formal Service of Arrestment Notice and send it to the sheriff court within one week of service taking place.

(4)[1] The requirement to formally serve by sheriff officer is subject to the exceptions in sections 2 and 3 of the Execution of Diligence (Scotland) Act 1926.

How is an inhibition on the dependence made effective if the claimant does not know the respondent's address?

20.9.—(1) If the claimant does not know the respondent's address, an inhibition on the dependence is made effective if the sheriff officer does two additional things:

(a) send the schedule of inhibition to the sheriff clerk of the sheriff court district where the respondent's last known address is located;

(b) send a copy of the schedule of inhibition by post to the respondent's last known address.

---

[1] As inserted by the Act of Sederunt (Sheriff Court Rules Amendment) (Miscellaneous) 2016 (SSI 2016/367) para.5 (effective 28 November 2016).

What is this Part about?

21.1.—(1)[1] This Part contains a guide for litigants, lay representatives and courtroom supporters to the meaning of certain legal words and expressions used in these rules.

Word or expression	Meaning
Additional respondent	A person who is not named as a respondent by the claimant in the Claim Form but who enters the case later.
Admitting a claim	Where the respondent accepts the claim made by the claimant, including the things which the claimant wants from the respondent.
Appeal	Asking the Sheriff Appeal Court to reverse or vary the decision of a sheriff on a point of law.
Application	A way for a party to ask the court to do something by sending it and other parties a written application in a special form.
Arrestment on the dependence	An order freezing the respondent's funds or good held by a third party (typically money held in a bank account), in advance of the sheriff making a decision in a case.
Case management discussion	An informal discussion of how a case is progressing, involving the sheriff and the parties.
Cite a witness	Demand that a witness attend a hearing by an officer of court formally serving a Witness Citation Notice.
Claim	The things which the claimant wants from the respondent.
Claimant	The person making a claim.
Courtroom supporter	A person who may accompany a party in court to provide moral support.
Decision	The final order which the sheriff makes about the merits of a case, setting out who has been successful.
Discussion	A discussion of a particular issue (such as an application), involving the sheriff

---

[1] As inserted by the Act of Sederunt (Simple Procedure Amendment) (Miscellaneous) 2018 (SSI 2018/191) art.2(2)(o) (effective 30 July 2018).

Word or expression	Meaning
	and the parties, which may take place in court.
Dismissing a claim	An order by the sheriff ending the case without deciding which party has been successful.
Expenses	The contribution the court can order one party to make towards how much it costs another party to conduct a case.
Formal service	The formal process of sending a copy of a court document to a party or other person.
Hearing	An appearance by both parties in court at which witnesses and evidence can be considered and the sheriff will make a decision.
Last date for a response	The date by which the Respondent must respond to the claim by sending a Response Form to the court and to the claimant, or respond to the claim by sending a Time to Pay Application to the court.
Last date for service	The date by which the Claim Form must be formally served on the respondent.
Lay representative	A representative who is not a lawyer.
Legal representative	A representative who is a lawyer.
Lodge	To deposit documents and other evidence to the sheriff clerk before a hearing, for their use at that hearing.
Order	A direction given by the sheriff to the parties telling them what they must do or what will happen next in a case.
Party	A person involved on one side of a simple procedure case – either a claimant or a respondent.
Pause	Temporarily suspend the progress of a case.
Portal on the Scottish Courts and Tribunals Service website	The portal for conducting a simple procedure case at http://www.scotcourts.gov.uk/.
Principles of simple procedure	The 5 principles listed in rule 1.2.
Provisional order	An order which protects or secures a claimant's position before a hearing, such as freezing a sum of money in the respondent's bank account.
Recall	An order cancelling a decision made by the sheriff.

Word or expression	Meaning
Representative	A person who assists a party and speaks on their behalf in court, who may be either a legal representative or a lay representative.
Respondent	The person a claim is made against. Response The respondent's reasons why the claim should not be successful.
Restart	Resuming the progress of a paused case.
Send	Sending something in a way provided for in Part 6 of the rules.
Sheriff	The judge who will decide a simple procedure case.
Sheriff clerk	A court official who provides administrative support to the sheriff.
Sheriff officer	A court officer who may formally serve court documents.
Simple procedure case	A claim which is registered by the sheriff clerk.
Timetable	The dates by which the first two steps that the parties must take in a simple procedure case are to be completed – the last date for service and the last date for a response.
Time to pay	An order giving the respondent time to pay the claimant in instalments or in a deferred lump sum.
Trading name	A name under which a person, partner-ship or company carries out its business.

SCHEDULE 2 FORMS

SCHEDULE 2

FORMS

Paragraph 2(2)

PART 2
2A.[1] Lay Representation Form
PART 3
3A.[2, 3] Claim Form
3B.[4] Further Claimant Form
3C.[5] Further Respondent Form
3D.[6] Timetable
3E. Change of Timetable Application
PART 4
4A.[7, 8, 9, 10]Response Form
PART 5
5A.[11] Time to Pay Application
5B.[12, 13] Time to Pay Notice
PART 6
6A.[14, 15] Notice of Claim

---

[1] As amended by the Act of Sederunt (Simple Procedure Amendment) (Miscellaneous) (SSI 2018/191) art. 2(3)(a) (effective 30 July 2018).

[2] As amended by the Act of Sederunt (Rules of the Court of Session 1994 and Sheriff Court Rules Amendment) (No. 4) (Simple Procedure) 2016 (SSI 2016/315) para.7 (effective 28 November 2016).

[3] As amended by the Act of Sederunt (Simple Procedure Amendment) (Miscellaneous) (SSI 2018/191) art. 2(3)(b) (effective 30 July 2018).

[4] As amended by the Act of Sederunt (Sheriff Court Rules Amendment) (Miscellaneous) 2017 (SSI 2017/154) para.2 (effective 15 June 2017).

[5] As amended by the Act of Sederunt (Rules of the Court of Session 1994 and Sheriff Court Rules Amendment) (No. 4) (Simple Procedure) 2016 (SSI 2016/315) para.7 (effective 28 November 2016).

[6] As amended by the Act of Sederunt (Simple Procedure Amendment) (Miscellaneous) (SSI 2018/191) art. 2(3)(c) (effective 30 July 2018).

[7] As amended by the Act of Sederunt (Rules of the Court of Session 1994 and Sheriff Court Rules Amendment) (No. 4) (Simple Procedure) 2016 (SSI 2016/315) para.7 (effective 28 November 2016).

[8] As amended by the Act of Sederunt (Sheriff Court Rules Amendment) (Miscellaneous) 2017 (SSI 2017/154) para.2 (effective 15 June 2017).

[9] As substituted by the Act of Sederunt (Simple Procedure Amendment) (Miscellaneous) (SSI 2018/191) art. 2(3)(d) (effective 30 July 2018).

[10] As amended by the Act of Sederunt (Simple Procedure Amendment)(Civil Online) 2019 (SSI 2019/122) para.2 (effective 25 April 2019).

[11] As substituted by the Act of Sederunt (Simple Procedure Amendment) (Miscellaneous) (SSI 2018/191) art. 2(3)(e) (effective 30 July 2018).

[12] As amended by the Act of Sederunt (Rules of the Court of Session 1994 and Sheriff Court Rules Amendment) (No. 4) (Simple Procedure) 2016 (SSI 2016/315) para.7 (effective 28 November 2016).

[13] As amended by the Act of Sederunt (Simple Procedure Amendment) (Miscellaneous) (SSI 2018/191) art. 2(3)(f) (effective 30 July 2018).

[14] As amended by the Act of Sederunt (Sheriff Court Rules Amendment) (Miscellaneous) 2017 (SSI 2017/154) para.2 (effective 15 June 2017).

6B.[1, 2] Service by Advertisement Application

6C.[3, 4] Confirmation of Formal Service

PART 7

7A.[5, 6] Application for a Decision

PART 8

8A.[7] Order of the Sheriff

PART 9

9A.[8] Application to Pause

9B.[9] Application to Restart

9C.[10] Additional Respondent Application

9D.[11] Application to Amend

9E.[12] Abandonment Notice

9F. Application to Represent

9G.[13] Incidental Orders Application

PART 10

10A. List of Evidence Form

10B.[14] Recovery of Documents Application

10C.[15] Application to Open Confidential Document

10D.[16] Special Recovery of Documents Application

---

[15] As amended by the Act of Sederunt (Simple Procedure Amendment) (Miscellaneous) (SSI 2018/191) art. 2(3)(g) (effective 30 July 2018).

[1] As amended by the Act of Sederunt (Rules of the Court of Session 1994 and Sheriff Court Rules Amendment) (No. 4) (Simple Procedure) 2016 (SSI 2016/315) para.7 (effective 28 November 2016).

[2] As amended by the Act of Sederunt (Simple Procedure Amendment)(Civil Online) 2019 (SSI 2019/122) para.2 (effective 25 April 2019).

[3] As amended by the Act of Sederunt (Rules of the Court of Session 1994 and Sheriff Court Rules Amendment) (No. 4) (Simple Procedure) 2016 (SSI 2016/315) para.7 (effective 28 November 2016).

[4] As amended by the Act of Sederunt (Sheriff Court Rules Amendment) (Miscellaneous) 2017 (SSI 2017/154) para.2 (effective 15 June 2017).

[5] As amended by the Act of Sederunt (Rules of the Court of Session 1994 and Sheriff Court Rules Amendment) (No. 4) (Simple Procedure) 2016 (SSI 2016/315) para.7 (effective 28 November 2016).

[6] As amended by the Act of Sederunt (Simple Procedure Amendment) (Miscellaneous) (SSI 2018/191) art. 2(3)(h) (effective 30 July 2018).

[7] As amended by the Act of Sederunt (Rules of the Court of Session 1994 and Sheriff Court Rules Amendment) (No. 4) (Simple Procedure) 2016 (SSI 2016/315) para.7 (effective 28 November 2016).

[8] As amended by the Act of Sederunt (Rules of the Court of Session 1994 and Sheriff Court Rules Amendment) (No. 4) (Simple Procedure) 2016 (SSI 2016/315) para.7 (effective 28 November 2016).

[9] As amended by the Act of Sederunt (Rules of the Court of Session 1994 and Sheriff Court Rules Amendment) (No. 4) (Simple Procedure) 2016 (SSI 2016/315) para.7 (effective 28 November 2016).

[10] As amended by the Act of Sederunt (Rules of the Court of Session 1994 and Sheriff Court Rules Amendment) (No. 4) (Simple Procedure) 2016 (SSI 2016/315) para.7 (effective 28 November 2016).

[11] As amended by the Act of Sederunt (Rules of the Court of Session 1994 and Sheriff Court Rules Amendment) (No. 4) (Simple Procedure) 2016 (SSI 2016/315) para.7 (effective 28 November 2016).

[12] As amended by the Act of Sederunt (Rules of the Court of Session 1994 and Sheriff Court Rules Amendment) (No. 4) (Simple Procedure) 2016 (SSI 2016/315) para.7 (effective 28 November 2016).

[13] As amended by the Act of Sederunt (Rules of the Court of Session 1994 and Sheriff Court Rules Amendment) (No. 4) (Simple Procedure) 2016 (SSI 2016/315) para.7 (effective 28 November 2016).

[14] As amended by the Act of Sederunt (Rules of the Court of Session 1994 and Sheriff Court Rules Amendment) (No. 4) (Simple Procedure) 2016 (SSI 2016/315) para.7 (effective 28 November 2016).

[15] As amended by the Act of Sederunt (Rules of the Court of Session 1994 and Sheriff Court Rules Amendment) (No. 4) (Simple Procedure) 2016 (SSI 2016/315) para.7 (effective 28 November 2016).

[16] As amended by the Act of Sederunt (Rules of the Court of Session 1994 and Sheriff Court Rules Amendment) (No. 4) (Simple Procedure) 2016 (SSI 2016/315) para.7 (effective 28 November 2016).

PART 11

11A. List of Witnesses Form

11B.[1,2] Witness Citation Notice

11C.[3] Child Witness Notice

11D.[4] Vulnerable Witness Application

11E.[5] Special Measures Review Application

PART 13

13A.[6,7] Decision Form

13B. Application to Recall

PART 15

15A.[8] Charge to Pay

15B. Alternative Decision Application

PART 16

16A. Appeal Form

16B. Appeal Report

PART 17

17A. CJEU Reference Form

17B. Application to Intervene

17C.[9] Invitation to Intervene

17D.[10] Application to Change a Damages Management Order

17E.[11] Application for Instructions about a Damages Management Order

17F.[12] Application for a Child's Property Administration Order

PART 19

19A. Translation Certificate

---

[1] As amended by the Act of Sederunt (Rules of the Court of Session 1994 and Sheriff Court Rules Amendment) (No. 4) (Simple Procedure) 2016 (SSI 2016/315) para.7 (effective 28 November 2016).

[2] As amended by the Act of Sederunt (Sheriff Court Rules Amendment) (Miscellaneous) 2017 (SSI 2017/154) para.2 (effective 15 June 2017).

[3] As amended by the Act of Sederunt (Rules of the Court of Session 1994 and Sheriff Court Rules Amendment) (No. 4) (Simple Procedure) 2016 (SSI 2016/315) para.7 (effective 28 November 2016).

[4] As amended by the Act of Sederunt (Rules of the Court of Session 1994 and Sheriff Court Rules Amendment) (No. 4) (Simple Procedure) 2016 (SSI 2016/315) para.7 (effective 28 November 2016).

[5] As amended by the Act of Sederunt (Rules of the Court of Session 1994 and Sheriff Court Rules Amendment) (No. 4) (Simple Procedure) 2016 (SSI 2016/315) para.7 (effective 28 November 2016).

[6] As amended by the Act of Sederunt (Sheriff Court Rules Amendment) (Miscellaneous) 2017 (SSI 2017/154) para.2 (effective 15 June 2017).

[7] As substituted by the Act of Sederunt (Simple Procedure Amendment) (Miscellaneous) (SSI 2018/191) art. 2(3)(i) (effective 30 July 2018).

[8] As amended by the Act of Sederunt (Rules of the Court of Session 1994 and Sheriff Court Rules Amendment) (No. 4) (Simple Procedure) 2016 (SSI 2016/315) para.7 (effective 28 November 2016).

[9] As amended by the Act of Sederunt (Rules of the Court of Session 1994 and Sheriff Court Rules Amendment) (No. 4) (Simple Procedure) 2016 (SSI 2016/315) para.7 (effective 28 November 2016).

[10] As amended by the Act of Sederunt (Rules of the Court of Session 1994 and Sheriff Court Rules Amendment) (No. 4) (Simple Procedure) 2016 (SSI 2016/315) para.7 (effective 28 November 2016).

[11] As amended by the Act of Sederunt (Rules of the Court of Session 1994 and Sheriff Court Rules Amendment) (No. 4) (Simple Procedure) 2016 (SSI 2016/315) para.7 (effective 28 November 2016).

[12] As amended by the Act of Sederunt (Rules of the Court of Session 1994 and Sheriff Court Rules Amendment) (No. 4) (Simple Procedure) 2016 (SSI 2016/315) para.7 (effective 28 November 2016).

19B.[1] Method of Service Abroad Certificate
PART 20
20A. Provisional Orders Application
20B. Provisional Orders Hearing Notice
20C.[2] Provisional Orders Reconsideration Application
20D.[3] Arrestment Notice
20E. Confirmation of Formal Service of Arrestment Notice

---

[1] As amended by the Act of Sederunt (Rules of the Court of Session 1994 and Sheriff Court Rules Amendment) (No. 4) (Simple Procedure) 2016 (SSI 2016/315) para.7 (effective 28 November 2016).
[2] As amended by the Act of Sederunt (Rules of the Court of Session 1994 and Sheriff Court Rules Amendment) (No. 4) (Simple Procedure) 2016 (SSI 2016/315) para.7 (effective 28 November 2016).
[3] As amended by the Act of Sederunt (Sheriff Court Rules Amendment) (Miscellaneous) 2017 (SSI 2017/154) para.2 (effective 15 June 2017).

FORM 2A

The Simple Procedure
Lay Representation Form

This is the Lay Representation Form. You must complete it if you are acting as a lay representative in a simple procedure case.

Before completing this form, you should read Part 2 of the Simple Procedure Rules, which is about lay representation.

If you are representing a party throughout a simple procedure case, you must complete this form and send it to the court with the Claim Form, Response Form or Time to Pay Application.

Otherwise, if you are representing a person only during a particular discussion or hearing in a simple procedure case, you must complete this form and give it to the sheriff clerk in person at court.

If you are representing an individual, you must complete Parts A to C. If you are representing a company, limited liability partnership, partnership or unincorporated association, you must also complete Part D.

A. ABOUT THE CASE

Sheriff Court	
Claimant	
Respondent	
Case reference number (if known)	

B. ABOUT YOU

B1. What is your full name?

Name	
Middle name	
Surname	

B2. Are you from an advice or advocacy organisation?

ⓘ A lay representative may be a family member or friend, may be someone from an advice or advocacy organisation, or may be someone else.

☐ Yes

☐ No

B3. If you have answered 'Yes', which organisation are you from?

Name of organisation [   ]

B4. Are you representing a non-natural person?

ⓘ A non-natural person is a company, limited liability partnership, partnership or unincorporated association.

ⓘ If you are representing a non-natural person, then as well as completing part C, you must also complete part D.

☐ Yes

☐ No

C. DECLARATIONS

ⓘ To comply with simple procedure rules, and so that the sheriff can decide if you are a suitable person to act as a lay representative, you must complete this section.

ⓘ Tick the box next to each declaration that applies to you and complete any sections that apply to you.

☐ I am authorised by the person to conduct these proceedings.

☐ I am not receiving and will not receive from the person I represent any remuneration, whether directly or indirectly, for acting as a lay representative.

☐ I accept that documents and information are provided to me by the parties on a confidential basis and I undertake to keep them confidential.

☐ I have not been declared a vexatious litigant under the Vexatious Litigants (Scotland) Act 1898.

☐ I was declared a vexatious litigant on: [   ]

☐ I have no financial interest in the outcome of this case.

998

☐ I have the
following
financial interest
in the outcome
of this case:

D. ADDITIONAL DECLARATIONS: REPRESENTING A NON-NATURAL PERSON

ⓘ If you selected 'Yes' at B4, you must complete this Part, so that the sheriff
can decide if you are a suitable person to act as a lay representative.

ⓘ Tick the box next to each declaration that applies to you and complete any
sections that apply to you.

☐ The relevant
position I hold
with the non-
natural person
is:

[director / secretary of the company, a member of the
limited liability partnership or partnership, or a
member or office holder of the association]

☐ My responsibilities do not consist wholly or mainly of conducting legal
proceedings on behalf of the non-natural person or another person.

☐ I do not have a personal interest in the subject matter of the proceedings.

Signature

Date

C4. What is the first respondent's company name or organisation name?

ⓘ If the respondent is a company (which might be indicated by 'Limited', 'Ltd' or 'plc' after its name), please give the full name of that company and the company registration number.

ⓘ You can check the name of a company on the Companies House website.

Name	
Company type	
Company registration number (if limited company or LLP)	
Trading name (if any)	

C5. What are the first respondent's contact details?

Address	
City	
Postcode	
Email address	

C6. Is the second respondent an individual, a company or an organisation?

☐ An individual (including a sole trader) (please complete C7)

☐ A company or organisation (please complete C8)

C7. What is the second respondent's full name?

ⓘ If the respondent is an individual trading under a name, please also give that name.

Name	
Middle name	
Surname	
Trading name (if any)	

FORM 3A

The Simple Procedure Claim Form

The Simple Procedure is a speedy, inexpensive and informal court procedure for settling or determining disputes with a value of **£5,000 or less**.

The Simple Procedure Rules should be read alongside this form. They can be found on the Scottish Courts and Tribunals Service website. Please **read the whole Claim Form** before beginning to complete it. There are guidance notes above each section of the form.

To make a claim using the Simple Procedure, you must **complete this Claim Form** and send it to the sheriff court to register your case. You should either complete the form yourself or, if you have someone assisting or representing you, you should complete the form with them.

A. ABOUT YOU

ⓘ Set out information about you, so that the court knows who you are and how to contact you.

A1. Are you an individual, a company or an organisation?

☐ An individual (including a sole trader) (please fill out A2)

☐ A company or organisation (please fill out A3)

A2. What is your full name?

Name	
Middle name	
Surname	
Trading name or representative capacity (if any)	

A3. What is the name of the company or organisation?

Name	
Company type	
Company registration number (if limited company or LLP)	
Trading name (if any)	

A4. What are your contact details?

Address	
City	
Postcode	
Email address	

A5. How would you prefer the court and the respondent to contact you?

☐ By post

☐ Online

B. ABOUT YOUR REPRESENTATION

ⓘ Set out information about how you will be represented.

B1. How will you be represented during this case?

☐ I will represent myself

☐ I will be represented by a solicitor

☐ I will be represented by a non-solicitor (e.g. a family member, friend, or someone from an advice or advocacy organisation)

B2. Who is your representative?

ⓘ If a family member or friend, please give their full name. If someone from an advice or advocacy organisation, please also give the name of that organisation.

Name	
Surname	
Organisation / firm name	

B3. What is the address of your representative?

ⓘ If your representative works for a solicitors' firm or an advocacy organisation, please give the address of that firm or organisation.

Address	
City	
Postcode	
Email address	

B4. Would you like us to contact you through your representative?

ⓘ If you select 'yes', then the court will send orders and information in this case to your representative.

☐ Yes

☐ No

B5. How would your representative prefer the court to contact them?

☐ By post

☐ Online

C. ABOUT THE RESPONDENT(S)

ⓘ The person who you are making the claim against is called the respondent. this part, you must fill in information about that person so that the court kno who they are and how to contact them.

ⓘ If there are more than two respondents, you must select 'more than two respondents' at C1 and complete a Further Respondent Form for each fu respondent.

C1. Is there one respondent, two respondents or more than two respondents?

☐ One respondent

☐ Two respondents

☐ More than two respondents

C2. Is the first respondent an individual, a company or an organisation?

☐ An individual (including a sole trader) (please complete C3)

☐ A company or organisation (please complete C4)

C3. What is the first respondent's full name?

ⓘ If the respondent is an individual trading under a name, please al name.

Name	
Middle name	
Surname	
Trading name (if any)	

C8. What is the second respondent's company name or organisation name?

ⓘ If the respondent is a company (which might be indicated by 'Limited', 'Ltd' or 'plc' after its name), please give the full name of that company and the company registration number.

ⓘ You can check the name of a company on the Companies House website.

Name	
Company type	
Company registration number (if limited company or LLP)	
Trading name (if any)	

C9. What are the second respondent's contact details?

Address	
City	
Postcode	
Email address	

C10. Would you like the court to formally serve this Claim Form on your behalf?

ⓘ The court cannot formally serve this Claim Form on your behalf if you are a company or if you are represented by a solicitor. You will have to arrange formal service yourself.

☐ Yes

☐ No

D. ABOUT YOUR CLAIM

ⓘ In this part, you must fill in information about the claim you are making against the respondent.

D1. What is the background to your claim?

ⓘ In this section, you should briefly describe the essential facts about the story behind your claim. You do not need to set out every detail of the story. You should focus on the parts which are important for you to establish your claim.

ⓘ You should include:

– key dates,

– if there was an agreement, what you agreed to do and what the respondent agreed to do,

– when you became aware of the problem or dispute,

- whether any payments have been made so far, and if so what,

- whether any services have been provided so far, and if so what.

ⓘ If this is insufficient space to describe the essential factual background, you may use another sheet of paper, which must be headed 'D1' and must be attached to the Claim Form.

D2. Where did this take place?

ⓘ You should set out where the events described above took place. If any part happened online, please state this.

ⓘ This is so that the court and the respondent can make sure that this is the right court to hear this claim.

Address	
City	
Postcode	
Details	

D3. Does this claim relate to a consumer credit agreement?

ⓘ You should select 'Yes' if the claim is about an agreement between you and the respondent in which you provided the respondent with credit of any amount.

☐ Yes (please complete D4)

☐ No

D4. What are the details of the consumer credit agreement?

ⓘ Set out the following information:

- the date of the agreement and its reference number

- the name and address of any person who acted as guarantor

FORM 3A

The Simple Procedure
Claim Form

The Simple Procedure is a speedy, inexpensive and informal court procedure for settling or determining disputes with a value of **£5,000 or less**.

The Simple Procedure Rules should be read alongside this form. They can be found on the Scottish Courts and Tribunals Service website. Please **read the whole Claim Form** before beginning to complete it. There are guidance notes above each section of the form.

To make a claim using the Simple Procedure, you must **complete this Claim Form** and send it to the sheriff court to register your case. You should either complete the form yourself or, if you have someone assisting or representing you, you should complete the form with them.

A. ABOUT YOU

ⓘ Set out information about you, so that the court knows who you are and how to contact you.

A1. Are you an individual, a company or an organisation?

☐ An individual (including a sole trader) (please fill out A2)

☐ A company or organisation (please fill out A3)

A2. What is your full name?

Name	
Middle name	
Surname	
Trading name or representative capacity (if any)	

A3. What is the name of the company or organisation?

Name	
Company type	
Company registration number (if limited company or LLP)	
Trading name (if any)	

A4. What are your contact details?

Address	
City	
Postcode	
Email address	

A5. How would you prefer the court and the respondent to contact you?

☐ By post

☐ Online

B. ABOUT YOUR REPRESENTATION

ⓘ Set out information about how you will be represented.

B1. How will you be represented during this case?

☐ I will represent myself

☐ I will be represented by a solicitor

☐ I will be represented by a non-solicitor (e.g. a family member, friend, or someone from an advice or advocacy organisation)

B2. Who is your representative?

ⓘ If a family member or friend, please give their full name. If someone from an advice or advocacy organisation, please also give the name of that organisation.

Name	
Surname	
Organisation / firm name	

B3. What is the address of your representative?

ⓘ If your representative works for a solicitors' firm or an advocacy organisation, please give the address of that firm or organisation.

Address	
City	
Postcode	
Email address	

B4. Would you like us to contact you through your representative?

ⓘ If you select 'yes', then the court will send orders and information in this case to your representative.

☐ Yes

☐ No

B5. How would your representative prefer the court to contact them?

☐ By post

☐ Online

C. ABOUT THE RESPONDENT(S)

ⓘ The person who you are making the claim against is called the respondent. In this part, you must fill in information about that person so that the court knows who they are and how to contact them.

ⓘ If there are more than two respondents, you must select 'more than two respondents' at C1 and complete a Further Respondent Form for each further respondent.

C1. Is there one respondent, two respondents or more than two respondents?

☐ One respondent

☐ Two respondents

☐ More than two respondents

C2. Is the first respondent an individual, a company or an organisation?

☐ An individual (including a sole trader) (please complete C3)

☐ A company or organisation (please complete C4)

C3. What is the first respondent's full name?

ⓘ If the respondent is an individual trading under a name, please also give that name.

Name	
Middle name	
Surname	
Trading name (if any)	

C4. What is the first respondent's company name or organisation name?

ⓘ If the respondent is a company (which might be indicated by 'Limited', 'Ltd' or 'plc' after its name), please give the full name of that company and the company registration number.

ⓘ You can check the name of a company on the Companies House website.

Name	
Company type	
Company registration number (if limited company or LLP)	
Trading name (if any)	

C5. What are the first respondent's contact details?

Address	
City	
Postcode	
Email address	

C6. Is the second respondent an individual, a company or an organisation?

☐ An individual (including a sole trader) (please complete C7)

☐ A company or organisation (please complete C8)

C7. What is the second respondent's full name?

ⓘ If the respondent is an individual trading under a name, please also give that name.

Name	
Middle name	
Surname	
Trading name (if any)	

C8. What is the second respondent's company name or organisation name?

ⓘ If the respondent is a company (which might be indicated by 'Limited', 'Ltd' or 'plc' after its name), please give the full name of that company and the company registration number.

ⓘ You can check the name of a company on the Companies House website.

Name	
Company type	
Company registration number (if limited company or LLP)	
Trading name (if any)	

C9. What are the second respondent's contact details?

Address	
City	
Postcode	
Email address	

C10. Would you like the court to formally serve this Claim Form on your behalf?

ⓘ The court cannot formally serve this Claim Form on your behalf if you are a company or if you are represented by a solicitor. You will have to arrange formal service yourself.

☐ Yes

☐ No

D. ABOUT YOUR CLAIM

ⓘ In this part, you must fill in information about the claim you are making against the respondent.

D1. What is the background to your claim?

ⓘ In this section, you should briefly describe the essential facts about the story behind your claim. You do not need to set out every detail of the story. You should focus on the parts which are important for you to establish your claim.

ⓘ You should include:

- key dates,

- if there was an agreement, what you agreed to do and what the respondent agreed to do,

- when you became aware of the problem or dispute,

- whether any payments have been made so far, and if so what,

- whether any services have been provided so far, and if so what.

ⓘ If this is insufficient space to describe the essential factual background, you may use another sheet of paper, which must be headed 'D1' and must be attached to the Claim Form.

D2. Where did this take place?

ⓘ You should set out where the events described above took place. If any part happened online, please state this.

ⓘ This is so that the court and the respondent can make sure that this is the right court to hear this claim.

Address	
City	
Postcode	
Details	

D3. Does this claim relate to a consumer credit agreement?

ⓘ You should select 'Yes' if the claim is about an agreement between you and the respondent in which you provided the respondent with credit of any amount.

☐ Yes (please complete D4)

☐ No

D4. What are the details of the consumer credit agreement?

ⓘ Set out the following information:

- the date of the agreement and its reference number

- the name and address of any person who acted as guarantor

– the details of the agreed repayment arrangements

– the unpaid balance or amount of arrears.

D5. If your claim is successful, what do you want from the respondent?

ⓘ You should select the option(s) that best describes the type of order you would like the court to make if your claim is successful. You can ask for more than one type of order to be made in a claim.

ⓘ You can also ask for alternative orders. For example, you could ask for the respondent to be ordered to repair something of yours or, failing that, to give you money to buy a new item.

ⓘ You should set out the detail of what you would like the court to order next to each option that you select.

☐ I want the respondent to be ordered by the court to pay me a sum of money:

> I want the court to order the respondent to pay me the sum of £_____.___.
>
> I want the court to order the respondent to pay me interest on that sum at the rate of __% annually from the last date for service.

ⓘ You should provide a breakdown to explain the sum of money you are claiming

ⓘ You should also set out the date from which you would like the court to order interest to run from and the rate of interest you would like the court to order.

☐ I want the respondent to be ordered by the court to deliver something to me:

> I want the court to order the respondent to deliver to me the following items:
>   1. [list]
>
> Alternatively, if the respondent does not deliver [that item / those items], I want the court to order the respondent to pay me the sum of £_____.__, with interest on that sum at the rate of __% annually from the last date for service.

ⓘ Set out the item(s) you want to be delivered to you.

ⓘ You may want to set out an alternative claim for payment of a sum of money in case the respondent does not deliver the items to you.

☐ I want the respondent to be ordered by the court to do something for me:

> I want the court to order the respondent to do the following:
>   1. [list]
>
> Alternatively, if the respondent does not do that, I want the court to order the respondent to pay me the sum of £_____.__, with interest on that sum at the rate of __% annually from the last date for service.

ⓘ Set out exactly what you want the respondent to be ordered to do.

ⓘ You may want to set out an alternative claim for payment of a sum of money in case the respondent does not do what the court has ordered.

D6. If your claim is successful, would you like the court to order the respondent to pay you a sum of money for the expenses of the claim?

ⓘ If your claim is successful, the court can order the respondent to pay you a sum of money to compensate you for the expense of making this claim.

☐ Yes

☐ No

D7. Why should your claim be successful?

ⓘ ⓘ You should set out briefly the reasons why your claim should be successful, and the court should make the orders which you have asked for, for example:

– "The respondent breached a contract with me by not completing work satisfactorily"

– "The respondent caused damage or financial loss to me by breaking something belonging to me"

- "The respondent has kept something belonging to me without the right to do."

> My claim should be successful because...

D8. What steps have you taken, if any, to try to settle the dispute with the respondent?

ⓘ It is an important principle of simple procedure that parties should be encouraged to settle their disputes by negotiation, where possible.

ⓘ You should set out any steps you have taken, if any, to try to settle the dispute with the respondent.

ⓘ The court will use this information to assess whether more negotiation would help you and the respondent settle your dispute.

> To try and settle the dispute I have taken the following steps...

E. WITNESSES, DOCUMENTS AND EVIDENCE

E1. Set out in a numbered list any witnesses you might to bring to a hearing to support your claim, their name and address, and what their relationship to the claim is.

ⓘ You should list any witnesses you think you might bring to a hearing. You do not need to list yourself or the respondent.

ⓘ You should provide the full name and address of any witnesses.

ⓘ Your claim may require no witnesses other than you and the respondent. You do not need to bring a witness if the evidence which they might give can be shown in some other way, e.g. by photographs.

ⓘ You should describe the relationship of each witness to the claim. For example, you might indicate that a witness:

- was the person with whom you made an agreement

- was present when damage took place

- inspected some work which you consider to have not been completed satisfactorily.

ⓘ If the court orders a hearing, Part 11 of the Simple Procedure Rules tells you what you need to do to arrange the attendance of your witnesses.

1. [Name]
   [Address]
   [Relationship to claim]

2.

E2. Set out in a numbered list any documents you might bring to court to support your claim.

ⓘ You should list any documents you think you might bring to a hearing. This includes photographs and other printed material which may be kept in a file.

ⓘ When preparing these documents for a hearing, it is useful if they are indexed with numbers.

ⓘ If the court orders a hearing, Part 10 of the Simple Procedure Rules tells you what you need to do to lodge documents.

1.
2.
3.
4.

E3. Set out any other pieces of evidence you intend to bring to a hearing to support your claim.

ⓘ You should list any other evidence you think you might bring to a hearing.

ⓘ This includes objects, but not printed material.

ⓘ For example, if the claim was about damage caused to an item of clothing, you might list the item of clothing. You do not need to bring a piece of evidence if the important point can be shown in some other way, e.g. by photographs.

ⓘ If the court orders a hearing, Part 10 of the Simple Procedure Rules tells you
what you need to do to lodge evidence.

> 1.
> 2.
> 3.
> 4.

PLEASE CHECK THIS FORM BEFORE SENDING IT.

FORM 3B

The Simple Procedure
Further Claimant Form

To make a claim for more than one claimant, you must complete a Further Claimant Form for each extra claimant after the claimant you named in the Claim Form and send it to the sheriff court along with the Claim Form.

A. ABOUT THE FIRST CLAIMANT

i Fill in information about the claimant named on the Claim Form, so that the court knows who you are and how to contact you.

A1. Are you an individual, a company or an organisation?

☐ An individual (including a sole trader) (please fill out A2)
☐ A company or organisation (please fill out A3)

A2. What is your full name?

Name	
Middle name	
Surname	
Trading name or representative capacity (if any)	

A3. What is the name of the company or organisation?

Name	
Company type	
Company registration number (if limited company or LLP)	
Trading name (if any)	

1011

A4. What is your address?

Address	
City	
Postcode	
Email address	

B. ABOUT THE FURTHER CLAIMANT

B1. Is the further claimant an individual, a company or an organisation?

☐ An individual (including a sole trader) (please complete B2)

☐ A company or organisation (please complete B3)

B2. What is the further claimant's full name?

i If the further claimant is an individual trading under a business name, please also give that name.

Name	
Middle name	
Surname	
Trading name (if any)	

B3. What is the further claimant's company name or organisation name?

i If the further claimant is a company (which might be indicated by 'Limited', 'Ltd' or 'plc' after its name), please give the full name of that company and the company registration number.

i You can check the name of a company on the Companies House website.

Name	
Company type	
Company registration number (if limited company or LLP)	
Trading name (if any)	

B4. What are the further claimant's contact details?

Address	

City	

Postcode	

Email address	

FORM 3C

The Simple Procedure
Further Respondent Form

To make a claim against more than two respondents, you must complete a Further Respondent Form for each extra respondent after the two respondents you named in the Claim Form and send it to the sheriff court along with the Claim Form.

A. ABOUT THE FIRST CLAIMANT

ⓘ Fill in information about the claimant named on the Claim Form, so that the court knows who you are and how to contact you.

A1. Are you an individual, a company or an organisation?

☐ An individual (including a sole trader) (please fill out A2)

☐ A company or organisation (please fill out A3)

A2. What is your full name?

Name	
Middle name	
Surname	
Trading name or representative capacity (if any)	

A3. What is the name of the company or organisation?

Name	
Company type	
Company registration number (if limited company or LLP)	
Trading name (if any)	

A4. What is your address?

Address	
City	
Postcode	
Email address	

B. ABOUT THE FURTHER RESPONDENT

B1. What is the first respondent's full name or company name?

ⓘ You must fill in information about the first respondent you named in part C of the Claim Form so that the court knows which claim this relates to.

B2. What is the second respondent's full name or company name?

ⓘ You must fill in information about the second respondent you named in part C of the Claim Form so that the court knows which claim this relates to.

B3. Is the further respondent an individual, a company or an organisation?

☐ An individual (including a sole trader) (please complete B4)

☐ A company or organisation (please complete B5)

B4. What is the further respondent's full name?

ⓘ If the further respondent is an individual trading under a business name, please also give that name.

Name	
Middle name	
Surname	
Trading name (if any)	

B5. What is the further respondent's company name or organisation name?

ⓘ If the further respondent is a company (which might be indicated by 'Limited', 'Ltd' or 'plc' after its name), please give the full name of that company and the company registration number.

ⓘ You can check the name of a company on the Companies House website.

Name

Company type

Company registration number (if limited company or LLP)

Trading name (if any)

B6. What are the further respondent's contact details?

Address

City

Postcode

Email address

FORM 3D

The Simple Procedure Timetable

Your claim has been registered.

This is the timetable for your case. It sets out the two important dates by which certain things must be done in this simple procedure case

A. ABOUT THE CASE

Sheriff Court	
Claimant	
Respondent	
Case reference number	

B. LAST DATE FOR SERVICE

ⓘ The last date for service is the date by which the Claim Form must be formally served on the respondent.

ⓘ Part 6 of the Simple Procedure Rules is about how formal service can be arranged.

Last date for service:

C. LAST DATE FOR A RESPONSE

ⓘ The last date for a response is the date by which the respondent must do one of two things:

(a) send a Response Form to the court and to the claimant, or

(b) if the respondent wants to admit the claim and ask for time to pay, send a Time to Pay Application to the court.

ⓘ Part 7 of the Simple Procedure Rules is about what happens if the respondent sends the court a Response Form and what can happen if they don't.

Last date for a response:

FORM 3E

The Simple Procedure Change of Timetable Application

This is a Change of Timetable Application. You can use this Application to ask to change the timetable in a simple procedure case, including:

- changing the last date for service, or

- changing the last date for a response.

Before completing this form, you should read rule 3.13 of the Simple Procedure Rules, which is about how to apply for a change of timetable.

A. ABOUT THE CASE

Sheriff Court	
Claimant	
Respondent	
Case reference number	

B. ABOUT YOU

B1. What is your full name?

Name	
Middle name	
Surname	
Trading name or representative capacity (if any)	

B2. Which party in this case are you?

☐ Claimant

☐ Respondent

C. THE APPLICATION

C1. Why does the timetable for this case need to be changed?

C1. Why does the timetable for this case need to be changed?

ⓘ Set out why the original timetable for this case can no longer be complied with (e.g. because of difficulties with service).

C2. What new timetable would allow this case to progress?

ⓘ Set out your suggestion for new dates which would allow this case to progress (e.g. how long do you think it will take you to formally serve something?).

FORM 4A
The Simple Procedure
Response Form

The Simple Procedure is a speedy, inexpensive and informal court procedure for settling or determining disputes with a value of **£5,000 or less**.

A claim has been raised against you under the Simple Procedure. You have been provided with a copy of the Claim Form which sets out the claim made against you.

The Simple Procedure Rules should be read alongside this form. They can be found on the Scottish Courts and Tribunals Service website. Please **read the whole Response Form** before beginning to complete it. There are guidance notes for each part of the form.

You can **respond to this claim online** using the Civil Online portal on the Scottish Courts and Tribunals Service website.

If you want to admit the claim against you and **apply for time to pay**, you do not need to complete this Response Form. Instead, you should **complete a Time to Pay Application** and send it to the court by the last date for a response. Only an individual (not a company or another type of organisation) may ask for time to pay.

Please note that if you **do nothing**, the court will almost certainly, if appropriate, award the claim to the claimant and order you to make a payment, including interest and expenses.

Case reference number	

A. ABOUT YOU

ⓘ Set out information about you, so that the court knows who you are and how to contact you.

A1. Are you an individual, a company or an organisation?

☐ An individual (including a sole trader) (please fill out A2)

☐ A company or organisation (please fill out A3)

A2. What is your full name?

Name	
Middle name	
Surname	
Trading name or representative capacity (if any)	

1019

A3. What is the name of the company or organisation?

Name	
Company type	
Company registration number (if limited company or LLP)	
Trading name (if any)	

A4. What are your contact details?

Address	
City	
Postcode	
Email address	

A5. How would you prefer the court and the claimant to contact you?

☐   By post

☐   Online

B. ABOUT YOUR REPRESENTATION

ⓘ Set out information about how you will be represented.

B1. How will you be represented during this case?

☐   I will represent myself

☐   I will be represented by a solicitor

☐   I will be represented by a non-solicitor (e.g. a family member, friend, or someone from an advice or advocacy organisation)

B2. Who is your representative?

ⓘ If a family member or friend, give their full name. If someone from an advice or advocacy organisation, also give the name of that organisation.

Name	
Surname	
Organisation / firm name	

B3. What are the contact details of your representative?

ⓘ If your representative works for a solicitors' firm or an advice or advocacy organisation, give the address of that firm or organisation.

Address	
City	
Postcode	
Email address	

B4. Would you like us to contact you through your representative?

ⓘ If you select 'yes', then the court will send orders and information in this case to your representative.

☐ Yes

☐ No

B5. How would your representative prefer the court to contact them?

☐ By post

☐ Online

C. YOUR RESPONSE TO THE CLAIM

ⓘ You should decide now how you intend to respond to this claim. There are three options. The flow-chart sets out the options on how you might respond. You should follow the instructions for the option you choose.

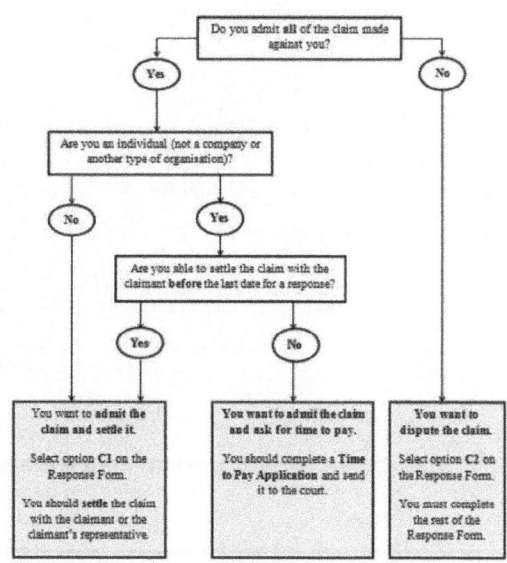

☐ **C1. I want to admit the claim** and settle it before the last date for a response.

ⓘ You should select this option if you accept that the claim against you is correct and you are able to settle it with the claimant now.

ⓘ You do not need to complete Parts D and E.

ⓘ You should send this Response Form to the court and to the claimant. You should settle the claim with the claimant or the claimant's representative by the last date for a response.

☐ **C2. I want to dispute the claim.**

ⓘ You should select this option if you do not accept that the claim against you is correct, and you want to:

– argue that the court does not have jurisdiction,

– dispute the entire claim, or

– dispute the amount that is being claimed.

ⓘ You should complete this Response Form and send it to the court and to the claimant by the last date for a response. You will be sent written orders by the court telling you how to proceed.

D. ABOUT YOUR RESPONSE

D1. What is the background to this claim?

ⓘ In this part, you should set out the essential factual background to the claim. The claimant has set out their understanding in section D1 of the Claim Form. In particular, you should set out anything in section D1 of the Claim Form which you disagree with.

ⓘ For example, you should include:

– key dates,

– if there was an agreement, what was agreed,

– when you became aware of the problem or dispute,

– whether any payments have been made so far and, if so, what payments,

– whether any services have been provided so far and, if so, what services.

ⓘ If this is insufficient space to describe the essential factual background, you may use another sheet of paper, which must be headed 'D1' and must be attached to the Response Form.

D2. Why should the claim not be successful?

(i) You should set out briefly the reasons why the claim made against you should not be successful, and why the court should not make the orders which the claimant has asked for in the Claim Form.

(i) For example, reasons might include:

- that you did not breach a contract with the claimant (e.g. work was completed satisfactorily),

- that you did not cause the claimant damage or financial loss,

- that you have the right to keep something belonging to the claimant (e.g. because a repair has not been paid for).

(i) If this is insufficient space to set out these reasons, you may use another sheet of paper, which must be headed 'D2' and must be attached to the Response Form.

D3. Are there any additional respondents you think should be responding to this claim?

(i) You should complete this section if you think that:

- you have a right of contribution, relief or indemnity against someone who is already a respondent,

- someone else should be made a respondent in this claim, as they are solely, jointly, or jointly and severally liable with you for the claim made against you,

- someone else should be made a respondent in this claim as they are liable to you for the claim made against you.

ⓘ If you complete this section then the court may order you to formally serve the Claim Form and the Response Form on any additional respondents.

☐ Yes (please complete D4)

☐ No

D4. Which additional respondents do you think should be responding to this claim?

ⓘ Set out below the full names and addresses of any additional respondents you think should be responding to the claim made against you.

ⓘ Set out the reasons why each person should be an additional respondent to the claim made against you.

> 1. [Name]
>
> [Address]
>
> [Reasons why this person should be an additional respondent]
>
> 2. [Name]
>
> [Address]
>
> [Reasons why this person should be an additional respondent]
>
> [...]

D5. What steps have you taken, if any, to try to settle the dispute with the claimant?

ⓘ It is an important principle of simple procedure that parties should be encouraged to settle their disputes by negotiation, where possible.

ⓘ The court will use this information to assess whether more negotiation would help you and the claimant settle your dispute.

E. WITNESSES, DOCUMENTS AND EVIDENCE

E1. Set out in a numbered list any witnesses you might bring to a hearing to support your response, their name and address, and what their relationship to the claim or response is.

ⓘ You should list any witnesses you think you might bring to a hearing. You do not need to list yourself or the claimant.

ⓘ You should provide the full name and address of any witnesses.

ⓘ Your claim may require no witnesses other than you and the claimant. You do not need to bring a witness if the evidence which they might give can be shown in some other way (e.g. by photographs).

ⓘ You should describe the relationship of each witness to the claim or response. For example, you might indicate that a witness:

– was the person with whom you made an agreement,

– was present when the alleged damage took place,

– inspected some work which you consider to have been completed satisfactorily.

ⓘ If the court orders a hearing, Part 11 of the Simple Procedure Rules tells you what you need to do to arrange the attendance of your witnesses.

1. [Name]
   [Address]
   [Relationship to the claim or response]

2. [Name]
   [Address]
   [Relationship to the claim or response]

3. [Name]
   [Address]
   [Relationship to the claim or response]

[...]

E2. Set out in a numbered list any documents you might bring to court to support your response.

ⓘ You should list any documents you think you might bring to a hearing. This includes photographs and other printed material which may be kept in a file.

ⓘ When preparing these documents for a hearing, it is useful if they are indexed with numbers.

ⓘ If the court orders a hearing, Part 10 of the Simple Procedure Rules tells you what you need to do to lodge documents before that hearing.

1.
2.
3.
4.
5.
[...]

E3. Set out any other pieces of evidence you intend to bring to a hearing to support your response.

ⓘ You should list any other evidence you think you might bring to a hearing.

(i) This includes objects, but not printed material. For example, if the claim was about damage caused to an item of clothing, you might list the item of clothing. You do not need to bring a piece of evidence if the important point can be shown in some other way (e.g. by photographs).

(i) If the court orders a hearing, Part 10 of the Simple Procedure Rules tells you what you need to do to lodge other evidence before that hearing.

```
1.
2.
3.
4.
5.
[...]
```

PLEASE CHECK THIS FORM BEFORE SENDING IT.

FORM 5A

The Simple Procedure
Time to Pay Application

Sheriff Court	
Claimant	
Respondent	
Case reference number	

This is a Time to Pay Application. It is used to ask the sheriff to make an order for time to pay.

If you would like debt advice or financial guidance, you may wish to contact the Citizens Advice Bureau or another advisory or assistance organisation.

If you complete a Time to Pay Application it means that you are admitting the claim made against you by the claimant for the payment of a sum of money.

Only an individual (not a company or another type of organisation) may ask for time to pay. If you are a company or another type of organisation and accept that the claim against you is correct, you should try to settle the claim with the claimant.

The respondent may ask for time to pay by completing this application and either:

(a) sending it to court, or

(b) bringing it to court at any discussion, case management discussion or hearing.

Before completing this form, you should read Part 5 of the Simple Procedure Rules, which is about asking for time to pay.

There are two situations in which the court can make an order for time to pay: under the Debtors (Scotland) Act 1987 and under the Consumer Credit Act 1974.

Time to pay under the Debtors (Scotland) Act 1987

The Debtors (Scotland) Act 1987 gives you the right to apply to the court for an order which allows you to pay any sum which the court orders you to pay either in instalments or by deferred lump sum. A "deferred lump sum" means that you will be ordered by the court to pay the whole amount at one time within a period which the court will specify.

If the court makes an order, it may also recall or restrict any arrestment made on your property by the claimant in connection with the claim or debt (for example, your bank account may have been frozen).

If an order is made, a copy of the Decision Form will be sent to you telling you when payment should start or when it is you have to pay the lump sum.

If an order is not made, and an order for immediate payment is made against you, a Charge may be served on you if you do not pay.

Under the Debtors (Scotland) Act 1987, the court is required to make an order if satisfied that it is reasonable in the circumstances to do so, and having regard in particular to the following matters:

- the nature of and reasons for the debt in relation to which the order is requested,

- any action taken by the creditor to assist the debtor in paying the debt,

- the debtor's financial position,

- the reasonableness of any proposal by the debtor to pay that debt,

- the reasonableness of any refusal or objection by the creditor to any proposal or offer by the debtor to pay the debt.

Time to pay under the Consumer Credit Act 1974

The Consumer Credit Act 1974 allows you to apply to the court for an order asking the court to give you more time to pay a loan agreement. This order can only be applied for where the claim is about a credit agreement regulated by the Consumer Credit Act 1974. The court has power to make an order in respect of a regulated agreement to reschedule payment of the sum owed. This means that an order can change:

- the amount you have to pay each month,

- how long the loan will last,

- in some cases, the interest rate payable.

An order can also stop the creditor taking away any item bought by you on hire purchase or conditional sale under the regulated agreement, so long as you continue to pay the instalments agreed.

A. ABOUT YOU

A1. What is your full name?

Name	
Middle name	
Surname	
Trading name or representative capacity (if any)	
Date of application	

A2. What are your contact details?

Address	
City	
Postcode	
Email address	

A3. How would you prefer the court and the claimant to contact you?

☐ By post

☐ Online

B. ABOUT YOUR REPRESENTATION

ⓘ Set out information about how you will be represented.

B1. How will you be represented during this case?

☐ I will represent myself

☐ I will be represented by a solicitor

☐ I will be represented by a non-solicitor (e.g. a family member, friend, or someone from an advice or advocacy organisation)

B2. Who is your representative?

ⓘ If a family member or friend, give their full name. If someone from an advice or advocacy organisation, also give the name of that organisation.

Name	
Surname	
Organisation / firm name	

B3. What are the contact details of your representative?

ⓘ If your representative works for a solicitors' firm or an advice or advocacy organisation, give the address of that firm or organisation.

Address	
City	
Postcode	
Email address	

B4. Would you like us to contact you through your representative?

ⓘ If you select 'yes', then the court will send orders in this case to your representative.

☐ Yes

☐ No

B5. How would your representative prefer the court to contact them?

☐ By post

☐ Online

C. ABOUT YOUR APPLICATION

ⓘ Set out how you think that you are able to pay the claimant the sum of money owed.

C1. I admit the claim for a sum of money and would like to apply to pay the sum as follows:

☐ By instalments of: £_____ **per** week / fortnight / month

☐ In one lump sum within: [ ] weeks/ months **from today.**

C2. How did you get into this debt?

ⓘ Set out the reasons for you getting into this debt.

C3. Why should the court give you time to pay?

ⓘ Set out the reasons why the court should give you time to pay.

C4. Why is the payment offer you have made reasonable?

ⓘ Set out any information which explains why the offer you have made is a reasonable one (i.e. why you can afford that offer but not a higher one).

C5. Are you applying to have an arrestment recalled or restricted?

ⓘ When making an order the court may recall or restrict an arrestment (i.e. unfreeze your bank account if it has been frozen).

☐ Yes (explain below)

☐ No

ⓘ Set out the details of the arrestment, including the date on which it occurred.

```



```

C6. If this claim relates to a consumer credit agreement, are you applying for additional orders?

ⓘ When making an order for time to pay in relation to a consumer credit agreement the court has power to reschedule payment of the sum of money owed. This means that the court can change:

- – the amount you have to pay each month,
- – how long the loan will last,
- – in some cases, the interest rate payable.

☐ Yes (explain below)

☐ No

ⓘ Set out the details of the orders sought, including why those orders are sought.

ⓘ If you have a copy of the agreement, please send a copy of it with this application.

```



```

D. ABOUT YOUR FINANCES

ⓘ To help the court decide whether to make an order and what that order should be, please provide some details of your financial situation.

D1. What is your employment situation?

☐ Employed

☐ Self-employed

☐ Unemployed

D2. What are your outgoings?

ⓘ Set out any regular payments you have to make and whether these are made weekly, fortnightly or monthly.

Rent or mortgage £___ **each** week / fortnight / month

Council tax	£___	**each**	week / fortnight / month
Utilities (gas, electricity, etc.)	£___	**each**	week / fortnight / month
Food	£___	**each**	week / fortnight / month
Loans and credit agreements	£___	**each**	week / fortnight / month
Phone	£___	**each**	week / fortnight / month
Other	£___	**each**	week / fortnight / month
Total	£___	**each**	week / fortnight / month

D3. What income do you receive?

ⓘ Set out any regular income and whether it is weekly, fortnightly or monthly.

Wages or pension	£___	**each**	week / fortnight / month
Benefits	£___	**each**	week / fortnight / month
Tax credits	£___	**each**	week / fortnight / month
Other	£___	**each**	week / fortnight / month
Total	£___	**each**	week / fortnight / month

D4. Does anyone rely on your income?

ⓘ Set out how many people (if any) rely on your income and who they are (e.g. spouse / civil partner / children).

D5. Do you have any capital?

ⓘ Set out any capital which you hold. For example, money in savings accounts, shares, investments or houses owned.

1032

FORM 5B

The Simple Procedure
Time to Pay Notice

The respondent has admitted the claim you made against them and applied to the court for time to pay the sum of money which you claimed.

A copy of the Time to Pay Application is attached.

Before completing this form, you should read Part 5 of the Simple Procedure Rules, which is about asking for time to pay.

You must send this Time to Pay Notice back to the court within 2 weeks of it being sent to you or else the court will decide whether to grant the application without hearing from you.

A. ABOUT THE CASE

Sheriff Court	
Name of claimant	
Name of respondent	
Case reference number	
Date notice sent	

B. ABOUT YOU

ⓘ This is so that the court knows who you are.

B1. What is your full name?

Name	
Middle name	
Surname	

Trading name or representative capacity (if any)	

C. YOUR RESPONSE

ⓘ This will assist the court in deciding whether or not to grant the respondent time to pay.

C1. How do you respond to the Time to Pay Application?

ⓘ Set out whether you are content or not for the court to give the respondent time to pay the sum of money in your claim.

☐ I am **content** with the proposal for time to pay.

☐ I am **not content** with the proposal for time to pay.

FORM 6A

The Simple Procedure
Notice of Claim

The Simple Procedure is a speedy, inexpensive and informal court procedure for settling or determining disputes with a value of **£5,000 or less**.

You have been **formally served** with a simple procedure claim.

A. ABOUT THE CASE

Sheriff Court	
Claimant	
Respondent	
Case reference number	

B. ABOUT THIS NOTICE OF CLAIM

What is this envelope?

You have received this envelope because a claim is being made against you in court. The claim is being made under the Simple Procedure. The Simple Procedure is a speedy, inexpensive and informal court procedure for settling or determining disputes with a value of £5,000 or less. The Simple Procedure Rules are available on the Scottish Courts and Tribunals Service website.

In the Simple Procedure, the person who is making a claim against you is known as the claimant. You, the person the claim is being made against, are known as the respondent.

This envelope should contain:

- this Notice of Claim,

- a Timetable,

- a completed Claim Form,

- if you are able to apply to the court for time to pay, a Time to Pay Application,
- a blank Response Form.

What should you do next?

You should read the completed Claim Form carefully, because it sets out the claim being made against you, including the identity of the claimant, what the claimant says happened and what the claimant wants from you if their claim is successful in court.

You should read the Timetable carefully. This sets out what the last date for a response is. This is the date by which, you must do one of two things:

(a)   send a Response Form to the court and the claimant, or;

(b)   if you want to admit the claim and ask for time to pay, send a Time to Pay Application to the court.

You can **respond to this claim online** using the Civil Online portal on the Scottish Courts and Tribunals Service website.

If you do not do this, the court will almost certainly, if appropriate, award the claim to the claimant and order you to make a payment, including interest and expenses.

What help is available?

If you are not sure what to do next, you can contact the office of the sheriff clerk at the sheriff court.

If you need help to decide how to respond to the claim, how to complete the Response Form or Time to Pay Application or help by representing you in court at a hearing, you should contact a solicitor, the Citizens Advice Bureau or another advocacy or assistance organisation.

C. ABOUT FORMAL SERVICE

C1. Who formally served this Notice of Claim?

ⓘ This section will set out the details of the person who formally served this Notice.

Name	
Address	
Firm or organisation	
Signature	
Date of formal service	

FORM 6B

The Simple Procedure Service by Advertisement Application

This is a Service by Advertisement Application. You should complete this application if, after taking all reasonable steps to find out the respondent's address, you do not know what the respondent's address is.

If you complete this application and send it to court with the Claim Form, then the court may order the details of the claim to be publicised by advertisement on the Scottish Courts and Tribunals Service website.

Before completing this form, you should read rule 6.12 of the Simple Procedure Rules, which is about service by advertisement.

A. ABOUT THE CASE

Sheriff Court	
Claimant	
Respondent	
Case reference number	

B. ABOUT YOU

ⓘ Fill in information about you, so that the court knows who you are and how to contact you.

B1. Are you an individual, a company or an organisation?

☐ An individual (including a sole trader) (please fill out B2)

☐ A company or organisation (please fill out B3)

B2. What is your full name?

Name	
Middle name	
Surname	

Trading name or representative capacity (if any)	

B3. What is the name of the company or organisation?

Name	
Company type	
Company registration number (if limited company or LLP)	
Trading name (if any)	

B4. What are your contact details?

Address	
City	
Postcode	
Email address	

C. SERVICE BY ADVERTISEMENT

C1. What steps have you taken to find out the respondent's address?

ⓘ The court will only grant this application if you have taken all reasonable steps to find out the respondent's address.

FORM 6C

The Simple Procedure Confirmation of Formal Service

This is a Confirmation of Formal Service. It is used to inform the court when and how something has been formally served.

It must be completed and sent to the court whenever you are required to formally serve something on someone under the rules.

A. ABOUT THE CASE

Sheriff Court	
Claimant	
Respondent	
Case reference number	

B. ABOUT YOU

B1. What is your full name?

Name	
Middle name	
Surname	
Firm or organisation	

B2. What is your profession?

☐ Sheriff officer

☐ Sheriff clerk

☐ Solicitor

C. ABOUT FORMAL SERVICE

C1. Who did you formally serve something on?

(i) You must identify the person who you were required to serve something on.

C2. What did you formally serve?

(i) You must identify the form or document formally served.

C3. How did you formally serve it?

(i) You must describe the method of formal service used.

☐ By a next-day postal service which records delivery

☐ Delivering it personally

☐ Leaving it in the hands of a resident or employee

☐ Depositing it in a home or place of business by letter box or other lawful way

☐ Leaving it at a home or place of business in a way likely to come to the person's attention

☐ Other

(i) If you have selected 'Other' or need to give more details about the manner of formal service, please set this out below.

C4. When did you formally serve it?

(i) You must identify when service was performed.

FORM 7A

The Simple Procedure
Application for a Decision

This is an Application for a Decision. You can use this Application in two situations:

- to ask the court to make the orders which you asked for in your Claim Form if the respondent has not returned a Response Form or Time to Pay Application to the court by the last date for a response, or

- to ask the court to dismiss a claim or make a decision awarding you some or all of your claim if the claim has been settled before the last date for a response.

Before completing this form, you should read rules 7.2 to 7.4 of the Simple Procedure Rules, which are about applying for a decision.

A. ABOUT THE CASE

Sheriff Court	
Claimant	
Respondent	
Case reference number	

B. ABOUT YOU

B1. What is your full name?

Name	
Middle name	
Surname	
Trading name or representative capacity (if any)	

C. ABOUT THE APPLICATION

ⓘ Set out what has happened that entitles you to make this Application.

☐ No Response Form or Time to Pay Application has been sent to the court by the last date for a response.

☐ The respondent has admitted the claim and wants to settle it by the last date for a response.

D. ABOUT THE DECISION

ⓘ You must set out which orders you would like the sheriff to make.

☐ I would like the sheriff to dismiss the claim.

☐ I would like the sheriff to make all of the orders I asked for in the Claim Form.

☐ I would like the sheriff to make the following orders I asked for in the Claim Form:

FORM 8A

The Simple Procedure
Order of the Sheriff

This is an order of the sheriff in a case which you are a party in. You should **read it** and **follow it**.

You should also read Part 8 of the Simple Procedure Rules, which is about orders of the sheriff.

Sheriff Court:

Date of order:

Claimant:

Respondent:

Case reference number:

[Text of order]

Signed by:

Sheriff of [sheriffdom] at [sheriff court]

FORM 9A

The Simple Procedure
Application to Pause

Before completing this form, you should read rule 9.2 of the Simple Procedure Rules, which is about applying to have a case paused.

If you are applying to have the case paused:

This is an Application to Pause.

If the court grants this application then any hearings arranged in this case will be cancelled and the case will not progress until it is restarted.

You must fill in parts A, B and C of this application and send it to the court and to the other party in this case. So if you are the claimant, it must be sent to respondents. If you are a respondent it must be sent to the claimant.

If you have been sent this application:

This is an Application to Pause.

If the court grants this application then any hearings arranged in this case will be cancelled and the case will not progress until it is restarted.

You have received this application because someone has applied to have a simple procedure case you are involved in paused.

You must fill in part D of this application ('the reply') and return it to the court within 10 days of it being sent to you. The court will then do one of three things: pause the case, refuse to pause the case, or order a discussion in court.

A. ABOUT THE CASE

Sheriff Court	
Claimant	
Respondent	
Case reference number	

B. ABOUT YOU

B1. What is your full name?

Name	
Middle name	
Surname	
Trading name or representative capacity (if any)	

B2. Which party in this case are you?

☐ Claimant

☐ Respondent

C. THE APPLICATION

ⓘ If you are the party replying to this application, do not fill in this part. You should fill in part D.

C1. Why should this case be paused?

ⓘ The party making the application must set out why the court should pause the case.

C2. When was this application sent to the court?

ⓘ Set out the date on which the application was sent to the court (i.e. the date on which the email was sent, or the date on which the application was posted).

ⓘ Any reply to this application must be sent to the court within 10 days of this application being sent.

D. THE REPLY

ⓘ If you are the party making this application, do not fill in this part. You should fill in parts A, B and C.

D1. What is your full name?

Name

Middle name

Surname

Trading name or representative capacity (if any)

D2. Should this case be paused?

☐ Yes

☐ No

D3. If you answered 'no', why should this case not be paused?

ⓘ If the party replying to the application objects to the case being paused, they should set out why the court should not pause the case.

FORM 9B

The Simple Procedure Application to Restart

Before completing this form, you should read rule 9.4 of the Simple Procedure Rules, which is about applying to have a paused case restarted.

If you are applying to have the case restarted:

This is an Application to Restart.

If the court grants this application then the progress of this case will resume and a hearing may be arranged.

You must fill in parts A, B and C of this application and send it to the court and to the other party in this case. So if you are the claimant, it must be sent to the responding party. If you are the responding party it must be sent to the claimant.

If you have been sent this application:

This is an Application to Restart.

If the court grants this application then the progress of this case will resume and a hearing may be arranged.

You have received this application because someone has applied to have a simple procedure case you are involved in restarted.

You must fill in part D of this application ('the reply') and return it to the court within 10 days. The court will then do one of three things: restart the case, refuse to restart the case, or order a discussion in court.

A. ABOUT THE CASE

Sheriff Court	
Claimant	
Respondent	
Case reference number	

B. ABOUT YOU

B1. What is your full name?

Name	
Middle name	
Surname	
Trading name or representative capacity (if any)	

B2. Which party in this case are you?

☐ Claimant

☐ Respondent

C. THE APPLICATION

ⓘ If you are the party replying to this application, do not fill in this part. You should fill in part D.

C1. Why should this case be restarted?

ⓘ The party making the application must set out why the court should restart the case.

C2. When was this application sent to the court?

ⓘ Set out the date on which the application was sent to the court (i.e. the date on which the email was sent, or the date on which the application was posted).

ⓘ Any reply to this application must be sent to the court within 10 days of this application being sent.

D. THE REPLY

ⓘ If you are the party making this application, do not fill in this part. You should fill in parts A, B and C.

D1. What is your full name?

Name	
Middle name	
Surname	
Trading name or representative capacity (if any)	

D2. Should this case be restarted?

☐ Yes

☐ No

D3. If you answered 'no', why should this case not be restarted?

ⓘ If the party replying to the application objects to the case being restarted, they should set out why the court should not restart the case.

FORM 9C

The Simple Procedure Additional Respondent Application

Before completing this form, you should read rule 9.6 of the Simple Procedure Rules, which is about applying to be an additional respondent.

This is an Additional Respondent Application. If the court grants this application then the person making it will become a respondent in this simple procedure case. The court cannot refuse this application without ordering a discussion in court.

A draft Response Form must be attached to this application.

A. ABOUT THE CASE

Sheriff Court	
Claimant	
Respondent	
Case reference number	

B. ABOUT YOU

B1. What is your full name?

Name	
Middle name	
Surname	
Trading name or representative capacity (if any)	

C. THE APPLICATION

C1. What is your interest in becoming a respondent?

ⓘ You must set out what your interest in this simple procedure case is and why the court should allow you to participate in it as a respondent.

FORM 9D

The Simple Procedure
Application to Amend

Before completing this form, you should read rule 9.7 of the Simple Procedure Rules, which is about applying to amend a Claim Form or Response Form.

If you are applying to have a Form amended:

This is an Application to Amend.

If the court grants this application then it will make the amendments you have asked for.

You must fill in parts A, B and C of this application and send it to the court and to the other party in this case. So if you are the claimant, it must be sent to the respondent. If you are the respondent it must be sent to the claimant.

If you have been sent this application:

This is an Application to Amend.

If the court grants this application then it will make the amendments which have been asked for.

You have received this application because someone has applied to have a Form amended in a simple procedure case you are involved in.

You must fill in part D of this application ('the reply') and return it to the court within 10 days of it being sent to you. The court will then do one of three things: allow the amendment, refuse the amendment, or order a discussion in court.

A. ABOUT THE CASE

Sheriff Court	
Claimant	
Respondent	
Case reference number	

B. ABOUT YOU

B1. What is your full name?

Name

Middle name

Surname

Trading name or
representative capacity (if
any)

B2. Which party in this case are you?

☐ Claimant

☐ Respondent

C. THE APPLICATION

ⓘ If you are the party replying to this application, do not fill in this part. You should fill in part D.

C1. What amendments should be made?

ⓘ The party making the application must set out the amendments they want to be made to the Claim Form or Response Form.

ⓘ It might be best to do this as a track-changes version of the original text, attached to this application.

C2. Why should these amendments be made?

ⓘ Set out why the court should allow these amendments to be made?

C3. When was this application sent to the court?

ⓘ Set out the date on which the application was sent to the court (i.e. the date on which the email was sent, or the date on which the application was posted).

ⓘ Any reply to this application must be sent to the court within 10 days of this application being sent.

D. THE REPLY

ⓘ If you are the party making this application, do not fill in this part. You should fill in parts A, B and C.

D1. What is your full name?

Name	
Middle name	
Surname	
Trading name or representative capacity (if any)	

D2. Should these amendments be allowed?

☐ Yes

☐ No

D3. If you answered 'no', why should these amendments not be allowed?

ⓘ If the party replying to the application objects to these amendments, they should set out why.

FORM 9E

The Simple Procedure
Abandonment Notice

Before completing this form, you should read rule 9.8 of the Simple Procedure Rules, which is about applying to abandon a case.

If you are abandoning your claim:

This is an Abandonment Notice.

You must fill in this Notice and sent it to the court and the respondent.

You will be sent written orders.

If you have been sent this notice:

This is an Abandonment Notice.

You have been sent it because the claimant has abandoned a claim made against you.

You will be sent further written orders.

A. ABOUT THE CASE

Sheriff Court	
Claimant	
Respondent	
Case reference number	

B. ABOUT YOU

B1. What is your full name?

Name	
Middle name	
Surname	
Trading name or representative capacity (if any)	

C. ABANDONMENT

C1. Which respondent are you abandoning your claim against?

Name of respondent [   ]

ⓘ You must check the box below to confirm that you are abandoning your claim against this respondent and that you are aware that this will normally mean that you are ordered to pay that respondent a sum of expenses.

[ ] I am abandoning my claim against this respondent.

FORM 9F

The Simple Procedure Application to Represent

Before completing this form, you should read rule 9.9 of the Simple Procedure Rules, which is about applying to represent a deceased or incapacitated party.

If you are applying to represent a party:

This is an Application to Represent.

If the court grants this application then you will be allowed to represent a deceased or legally incapacitated party in this simple procedure case.

You must send fill in parts A, B and C of this application and send it to the court and to the other party in this case. So if you are the claimant, it must be sent to the respondent. If you are the respondent it must be sent to the claimant.

If you have been sent this application:

This is an Application to Represent.

If the court grants this application then it will allow someone to represent a deceased or legally incapacitated party in this simple procedure case.

You have received this application because someone has applied to represent a dead or legally incapacitated party in a simple procedure case you are involved in.

You must fill in part D of this application ('the reply') and return it to the court within 10 days of it being sent to you. The court will then do one of three things: allow that person to represent the party, not allow that person to represent that party, or order a discussion in court.

A. ABOUT THE CASE

Sheriff Court	
Claimant	
Respondent	
Case reference number	

B. ABOUT YOU

B1. What is your full name?

Name	

Middle name	
Surname	
Trading name or representative capacity (if any)	

B2. Which party in this case would you like to represent?

Name	
Middle name	
Surname	
Trading name (if any)	

B3. Which party in this case is that person?

☐ Claimant

☐ Respondent

C. THE APPLICATION

ⓘ If you are the party replying to this application, do not fill in this part. You should fill in part D.

C1. Why should the court let you represent that person in this case?

ⓘ Set out what has happened to the party in this simple procedure case, and why you represent that person or that person's estate.

ⓘ If you have any documents (e.g. a death certificate) which might help the court make a decision in this application, you should send them to the court with this application.

C2. When was this application sent to the court?

ⓘ Set out the date on which the application was sent to the court (i.e. the date on which the email was sent, or the date on which the application was posted).

ⓘ Any reply to this application must be sent to the court within 10 days of this application being sent.

D. THE REPLY

ⓘ If you are the party making this application, do not fill in this part. You should fill in parts A, B and C.

D1. What is your full name?

Name	
Middle name	
Surname	
Trading name or representative capacity (if any)	

D2. Should this person be allowed to represent this party?

☐ Yes

☐ No

D3. If you answered 'no', why should this person not be allowed to represent this party?

ⓘ If the party replying to the application objects, they should set out why the court should not allow this person to represent this party.

FORM 9G

The Simple Procedure
Incidental Orders
Application

Before completing this form, you should read rule 9.10 and rule 20.6 of the Simple Procedure Rules, which is about applying for the sheriff to make incidental orders.

If you are applying for the sheriff to make orders:

This is an Incidental Orders Application.

You can use this Application to ask the sheriff to make any orders that are not specifically provided for by the Simple Procedure Rules.

If you have been sent this application:

This is an Incidental Orders Application.

If the court grants this application then it will make the orders which have been asked for below.

You must fill in part D of this application ('the reply') and return it to court within 10 days of it being sent to you. The court will then either grant the application and send written orders to the parties, or make no orders.

A. ABOUT THE CASE

Sheriff Court	
Claimant	
Respondent	
Case reference number	

B. ABOUT YOU

B1. What is your full name?

Name	
Middle name	
Surname	
Trading name or representative capacity (if any)	

B2. Which party or interested person in this case are you?

☐ Claimant

☐ Respondent

☐ Interested Party

C. THE APPLICATION

ⓘ If you are the party replying to this application, do not fill in this part. You should fill in part D.

C1. What orders would you like the court to make?

ⓘ The party making the application must set out the terms of the orders the court is being asked to make.

C2. Why should the court make these orders?

ⓘ The party making the application must set out why the court should make the orders asked for.

C3. When was this application sent to the court?

ⓘ Set out the date on which the application was sent to the court (i.e. the date on which the email was sent, or the date on which the application was posted).

ⓘ Any reply to this application must be sent to the court within 10 days of this application being sent.

D. THE REPLY

ⓘ If you are the party making this application, do not fill in this part. You should fill in parts A, B and C.

D1. What is your full name?

Name	
Middle name	
Surname	
Trading name or representative capacity (if any)	

D2. Should the court make these orders?

☐ Yes

☐ No

D3. If you answered 'no', why should the court not make these orders?

ⓘ If the party replying to the application objects to proposed orders, they should set out why the court should not make these orders.

FORM 10A

The Simple Procedure
List of Evidence Form

Before completing this form, you should read Part 10 of the Simple Procedure Rules, which is about documents and other evidence.

This is the List of Evidence Form. Parties must send a copy to each other and to the court at least 14 days before the hearing.

All documents and other evidence must be lodged with the court by sending them to the sheriff clerk at least 14 days before the hearing. If you think that there will be practical difficulties involved with sending evidence to the court (e.g. because of size, or because something might go off) you must contact the sheriff clerk before sending that evidence to be lodged.

A. ABOUT THE CASE

Sheriff Court	
Claimant	
Respondent	
Case reference number	

B. ABOUT YOU

B1. What is your full name?

Name	
Middle name	
Surname	
Trading name or representative capacity (if any)	

B2. Which party in this case are you?

☐ Claimant

☐ Respondent

C. LIST OF EVIDENCE

ⓘ Set out all evidence or other documents you are lodging with the court.

ⓘ Set out a brief description of each item of evidence and explain its relationship to the case. This means the reason why you think this item of evidence is necessary for the court to make a decision in this case.

ⓘ It is useful to the court if documents and other evidence being lodged can be numbered using the numbers (C1, C2, etc) below. If bigger documents do not already have page numbers, then adding page numbers can help the court read and understand these documents.

ⓘ If you think that you need more than 10 items of evidence, please fill out a further List of Evidence Form and attach it to this one.

C1. Item of evidence

Brief description of document or other evidence

Relationship to the case

C2. Item of evidence

Brief description of document or other evidence

Relationship to the case

C3. Item of evidence

Brief description of document or other evidence

Relationship to the case

C4. Item of evidence

Brief description of document or other evidence

Relationship to the case

C5. Item of evidence

Brief description of document or other evidence

Relationship to the case

C6. Item of evidence

Brief description of
document or other evidence

Relationship to the case

C7. Item of evidence

Brief description of
document or other evidence

Relationship to the case

C8. Item of evidence

Brief description of
document or other evidence

Relationship to the case

C9. Item of evidence

Brief description of
document or other evidence

Relationship to the case

C10. Item of evidence

Brief description of
document or other evidence

Relationship to the case

FORM 10B

The Simple Procedure
Recovery of Documents
Application

If you are applying for the sheriff to make orders:

This is a Recovery of Documents Application.

If you do not possess a document that you want to lodge with the court, you can use this Application to ask the court for an order to recover documents.

That order tells the person who has the document to send it to the court.

If you have been sent this Application:

This is a Recovery of Documents Application.

If the court grants this application then it will make the orders which have been asked for below.

You must fill in part D of this application ('the reply') and return it to court within 10 days of it being sent to you.

The court will then either grant the application and send an order to recover documents to the parties, refuse the application and make no orders, or order you to appear at a discussion in court where the sheriff will consider whether to make an order.

A. ABOUT THE CASE

Sheriff Court	
Claimant	
Respondent	
Case reference number	

B. ABOUT YOU

B1. What is your full name?

Name	
Middle name	
Surname	
Trading name or representative capacity (if any)	

B2. Which party in this case are you?

☐ Claimant

☐ Respondent

C. THE APPLICATION

ⓘ If you are the party replying to this application, do not fill in this part. You should fill in part D.

C1. What documents would you like to recover?

ⓘ The party making the application must identify every document that the party wants to recover. Use a new line for each document.

C2. Who has these documents?

ⓘ The party making the application must set out who possesses each of the documents.

C3. Why should the court make an order to recover these documents?

ⓘ The party making the application must set out why the court should make an order for recovery of these documents.

C4. When was this application sent to the court?

ⓘ Set out the date on which the application was sent to the court (i.e. the date on which the email was sent, or the date on which the application was posted).

ⓘ Any reply to this application must be sent to the court within 10 days of this application being sent.

D. THE REPLY

ⓘ If you are the party making this application, do not fill in this part. You should fill in parts A, B and C.

D1. What is your full name?

Name	
Middle name	
Surname	
Trading name or representative capacity (if any)	

D2. Should the court make an order to recover these documents?

☐ Yes

☐ No

D3. If you answered 'no', why should the court not make an order to recover these documents?

ⓘ If the party replying to the application objects to the proposed order, they should set out why the court should not make an order to recover these documents.

FORM 10C

The Simple Procedure Application to Open Confidential Document

If you are applying for the sheriff to make orders:

This is an Application to Open Confidential Document.

It is used where someone has claimed that documents are confidential in response to an order to recover documents or a special order to recover documents. That person has given the documents to the court in a sealed envelope.

You can use this Application to ask the court to open the sealed envelope so that the documents can be used in your simple procedure case.

If you have been sent this Application:

This is an Application to Open Confidential Document.

If the court grants this application then it will make the orders which have been asked for below.

You must fill in part D of this application ('the reply') and return it to court within 10 days of it being sent to you.

The court will then either grant the application and allow the sealed envelope containing the confidential document to be opened, refuse the application and make no orders, or order you to appear at a discussion in court where the sheriff will consider whether to make an order.

A. ABOUT THE CASE

Sheriff Court	
Claimant	
Respondent	
Case reference number	

B. ABOUT YOU

B1. What is your full name?

Name	
Middle name	
Surname	
Trading name or representative capacity (if any)	

B2. What is your role in this case?

☐ Claimant

☐ Respondent

C. THE APPLICATION

ⓘ If you are replying to this application, do not fill in this part. You should fill in part D.

C1. Which sealed envelope would you like to open?

ⓘ The party making the application must identify which sealed envelope they wish to have opened.

[Include the date on which the envelope was sent to the court and who sent it]

C2. Why should the court make an order allowing this sealed envelope to be opened?

ⓘ The party making the application must set out why the court should make an order allowing the sealed envelope to be opened.

[Give reasons why the envelope should be opened]

C3. When was this application sent to the court?

ⓘ Set out the date on which the application was sent to the court (i.e. the date on which the email was sent, or the date on which the application was posted).

ⓘ Any reply to this application must be sent to the court within 10 days of this application being sent.

D. THE REPLY

ⓘ If you are the party making this application, do not fill in this part. You should fill in parts A, B and C.

D1. What is your full name?

Name	
Middle name	
Surname	
Trading name or representative capacity (if any)	

D2. What is your role in this case?

☐ Claimant

☐ Respondent

☐ The person who claimed that the document is confidential

D3. Should the court make an order allowing the sealed envelope to be opened?

☐ Yes

☐ No

1074

D4. If you answered 'no', why should the court not make an order allowing the sealed envelope to be opened?

ⓘ If the party replying to the application objects to the proposed order, they should set out why the court should not make an order allowing the sealed envelope to be opened.

FORM 10D

The Simple Procedure Special Recovery of Documents Application

If you are applying for the sheriff to make orders:

This is a Special Recovery of Documents Application.

You can use this Application to ask the court for a special order to recover documents. The court will only grant the Application if it has already made an order to recover documents but that has been unsuccessful.

The special order appoints someone to recover the documents on behalf of the court. The person appointed is normally a solicitor.

If you have been sent this Application:

This is a Special Recovery of Documents Application.

If the court grants this application then it will make the orders which have been asked for below.

You must fill in part D of this application ('the reply') and return it to court within 10 days of it being sent to you.

The court will then either grant the application and send a special order to recover documents to the parties, refuse the application and make no orders, or order you to appear at a discussion in court where the sheriff will consider whether to make an order.

A. ABOUT THE CASE

Sheriff Court	
Claimant	
Respondent	
Case reference number	

B. ABOUT YOU

B1. What is your full name?

Name	

Middle name	

Surname	

Trading name or representative capacity (if any)	

B2. Which party in this case are you?

☐ Claimant

☐ Respondent

C. THE APPLICATION

ⓘ If you are the party replying to this application, do not fill in this part. You should fill in part D.

C1. When did the court make an order to recover documents?

ⓘ Set out the date of the court's order.

C2. When did you serve the order to recover documents on the person who possesses the documents?

ⓘ Set out the date of formal service on that person.

C3. Why was the order to recover documents unsuccessful?

ⓘ Tick the appropriate box.

☐ The person who possesses the documents did not reply to the order.

☐ The person who possesses the documents sent some documents to the court, but these are not all of the documents I want to recover.

☐ I am not satisfied with the explanation given by the person who possesses the documents for not producing them to the court. These are my reasons:

[set out reasons why you are not satisfied with the explanation]

C4. Who do you want the court to appoint as the commissioner?

ⓘ The commissioner is the person appointed by the court to carry out the recovery under a special order to recover documents.

ⓘ The commissioner is usually a solicitor, but the court may appoint any suitable person.

ⓘ The court may decide not to appoint the person you propose, and appoint someone else instead.

Name	
Middle name	
Surname	
Profession	

C5. When was this application sent to the court?

ⓘ Set out the date on which the application was sent to the court (i.e. the date on which the email was sent, or the date on which the application was posted).

ⓘ Any reply to this application must be sent to the court within 10 days of this application being sent.

D. THE REPLY

ⓘ If you are the party making this application, do not fill in this part. You should fill in parts A, B and C.

D1. What is your full name?

Name	
Middle name	
Surname	
Trading name or representative capacity (if any)	

D2. Should the court make a special order to recover these documents?

☐ Yes

☐ Yes, but I object to the appointment of the proposed commissioner

☐ No

D3. If you answered 'yes, but I object to the appointment of the proposed commissioner', why should the court not appoint that person as commissioner?

ⓘ If the party replying to the application objects to the proposed order, they should set out why the court should not appoint that person as commissioner.

D4. If you answered 'no', why should the court not make a special order to recover these documents?

ⓘ If the party replying to the application objects to the proposed order, they should set out why the court should not make a special order to recover these documents.

FORM 11B
The Simple Procedure
Witness Citation Notice

 u have been cited as a witness in a case in the sheriff court. The details of the case and date on which you should come to court are set out below.

s very important that you attend court and you should note that failure to do may result in a warrant being granted for your arrest.

u may claim back money which you have had to spend and any earnings you have lost in certain specified limits, because you have to come to court. These may be paid to you u claim within specified time limits. Claims should be made to the person who has ed you to attend court. Proof of any loss of earnings should be given to that person.

u wish your travelling expenses to be paid before you go to court, you should apply for ment to the person who has asked you to attend court (listed below at D1).

u:

- would like to know more about being a witness,

- are a child under the age of 18,

- think you may be a vulnerable witness within the meaning of section 11(1) of the Vulnerable Witnesses (Scotland) Act 2004 (that is someone the court conside rs may be less able to give their evidence due to mental disorder or fear or distress connected to giving your evidence at the court hearing),

should contact the person who cited you (listed below at D1) for further information.

u are a vulnerable witness (including a child under the age of 18) then you should be to use a special measure (such measures include use of a screen, a live TV link or a porter, or a commissioner) to help you give evidence.

BOUT THE CASE

Sheriff Court	
Claimant	
Respondent	

FORM 11A
The Simple Procedure
List of Witnesses Form

Before completing this form, you should read Part 11 of the Simple Procedure Rules, which is about witnesses.

This is the List of Witnesses Form. Parties must send a copy to each other and to the court at least 14 days before the hearing.

A. ABOUT THE CASE

Sheriff Court	
Claimant	
Respondent	
Case reference number	

B. ABOUT YOU

B1. What is your full name?

Name	
Middle name	
Surname	
Trading name or representative capacity (if any)	

B2. Which party in this case are you?

☐ Claimant

☐ Respondent

C. LIST OF WITNESSES

ⓘ Set out any witnesses you want to appear at the hearing. You do not need to list yourself or the other party.

ⓘ You may need to cite witnesses using the Witness Citation Form, but you should only cite a witness if you cannot otherwise arrange for that witness to appear at the hearing.

(i) Set out the name and address of each witness and explain their relationship to the case. This means the reason why you think this witness's evidence is necessary for the court to make a decision in this case.

(i) If you think that you need more than 4 witnesses, please fill out a further List of Witnesses Form and attach it to this one.

C1. Witness

Name of witness	
Address of witness	
Relationship of the witness to the case	

C2. Witness

Name of witness	
Address of witness	
Relationship of the witness to the case	

C3. Witness

Name of witness	
Address of witness	
Relationship of the witness to the case	

C4. Witness

Name of witness	
Address of witness	
Relationship of the witness to the case	

FORM 11A

The Simple Procedure
List of Witnesses Form

Before completing this form, you should read Part 11 of the Simple Procedure Rules, which is about witnesses.

This is the List of Witnesses Form. Parties must send a copy to each other and to the court at least 14 days before the hearing.

A. ABOUT THE CASE

Sheriff Court	
Claimant	
Respondent	
Case reference number	

B. ABOUT YOU

B1. What is your full name?

Name	
Middle name	
Surname	
Trading name or representative capacity (if any)	

B2. Which party in this case are you?

☐ Claimant

☐ Respondent

C. LIST OF WITNESSES

ⓘ Set out any witnesses you want to appear at the hearing. You do not need to list yourself or the other party.

ⓘ You may need to cite witnesses using the Witness Citation Form, but you should only cite a witness if you cannot otherwise arrange for that witness to appear at the hearing.

ⓘ Set out the name and address of each witness and explain their relationship to the case. This means the reason why you think this witness's evidence is necessary for the court to make a decision in this case.

ⓘ If you think that you need more than 4 witnesses, please fill out a further List of Witnesses Form and attach it to this one.

C1. Witness

Name of witness	
Address of witness	
Relationship of the witness to the case	

C2. Witness

Name of witness	
Address of witness	
Relationship of the witness to the case	

C3. Witness

Name of witness	
Address of witness	
Relationship of the witness to the case	

C4. Witness

Name of witness	
Address of witness	
Relationship of the witness to the case	

FORM 11B

The Simple Procedure
Witness Citation Notice

You have been cited as a witness in a case in the sheriff court. The details of the case and the date on which you should come to court are set out below.

It is very important that you attend court and you should note that failure to do so may result in a warrant being granted for your arrest.

You may claim back money which you have had to spend and any earnings you have lost within certain specified limits, because you have to come to court. These may be paid to you if you claim within specified time limits. Claims should be made to the person who has asked you to attend court. Proof of any loss of earnings should be given to that person.

If you wish your travelling expenses to be paid before you go to court, you should apply for payment to the person who has asked you to attend court (listed below at D1).

If you:

- would like to know more about being a witness,

- are a child under the age of 18,

- think you may be a vulnerable witness within the meaning of section 11(1) of the Vulnerable Witnesses (Scotland) Act 2004 (that is someone the court considers may be less able to give their evidence due to mental disorder or fear or distress connected to giving your evidence at the court hearing),

you should contact the person who cited you (listed below at D1) for further information.

If you are a vulnerable witness (including a child under the age of 18) then you should be able to use a special measure (such measures include use of a screen, a live TV link or a supporter, or a commissioner) to help you give evidence.

A. ABOUT THE CASE

Sheriff Court	
Claimant	
Respondent	

Case reference number	

B. ABOUT THE WITNESS

B1. What is the full name of the witness?

Name	
Middle name	
Surname	

C. WHEN AND WHERE YOU MUST COME TO COURT

ⓘ The witness must come to the court listed below on the date and time listed below.

The Sheriff Court you must come to is:	
Address	
Postcode	
You must come to the Sheriff Court on:	

D. ABOUT THIS CITATION

ⓘ This part contains information about the party who has cited you as a witness.

D1. Who is citing you as a witness?

ⓘ If the person who cited you is represented by a solicitor, they should list the solicitor's details here. If they do not, they should list their own details.

Name	
Address	
Firm or organisation	
Email address	

D2. Which party is citing you as a witness?

☐ Claimant

☐ Respondent

D3. Who formally served this Witness Citation Notice?

Name	
Address	

Firm or organisation

Solicitor or sheriff officer

Signature

Date of formal service

FORM 11C

The Simple Procedure
Child Witness Notice

This is a Child Witness Notice.

It is used to tell the court that a witness who is to give evidence in the simple procedure case is a child witness (someone who is under 18 when the simple procedure case begins).

It asks the sheriff to authorise the use of special measures to take the child witness's evidence, or to decide that the child witness is to give evidence without any special measures.

A. ABOUT THE CASE

Sheriff Court	
Claimant	
Respondent	
Case reference number	

B. ABOUT YOU

B1. What is your full name?

Name	
Middle name	
Surname	
Trading name or representative capacity (if any)	

B2. What is your role in this case?

☐ Claimant

☐ Respondent

C. THE NOTICE

C1. What is the full name of the child witness?

Name

Middle name

Surname

C2. What is the child witness's date of birth?

Date of birth

C3. If the child witness is over 18 when this Notice is completed, was the child witness under 18 when the simple procedure case began?

☐ Yes

☐ No

C4. What order should the court make about the child witness?

☐ The court should authorise the use of the special measure(s) mentioned in part D

ⓘ You should also complete parts D and E.

☐ The court should order that the child witness is to give evidence without the benefit of any special measure

ⓘ You should also complete part E.

C5. Why should the court make this order?

ⓘ You should set out the reasons why the court should make this order.

C6. When was this Notice sent to the court?

ⓘ Set out the date on which the notice was sent to the court (i.e. the date on which the email was sent, or the date on which the notice was posted).

D. THE SPECIAL MEASURES

ⓘ The special measures that the court may make are listed in rule 11.6 of the Simple Procedure Rules.

D1. What special measures would be most appropriate for taking the evidence of this child witness?

ⓘ You may select as many special measures as you think are appropriate.

☐ allowing the child witness to give evidence before an independent person

ⓘ This means that the child witness would give evidence before an independent person appointed by the court, rather than coming to court to give evidence.

☐ allowing the child witness to give evidence by live television link

☐ allowing the child witness to use a screen while giving evidence

☐ allowing the child witness to be supported by someone while giving evidence

D2. Why do you think the special measures you have selected would be most appropriate for taking the evidence of this child witness?

E. VIEWS OF THE CHILD WITNESS AND PARENT

ⓘ In completing this Notice, you must take into account the views of the child witness (if the child witness is of sufficient age and maturity to form a view) and the child witness's parent.

ⓘ The parent of a child witness is any person who has parental responsibilities within the meaning of section 1(3) of the Children (Scotland) Act 1995.

ⓘ Section 15(3)(a) of the Vulnerable Witnesses (Scotland) Act 2004 says that a child witness is presumed to be of sufficient age and maturity to form a view if aged 12 or older.

ⓘ Section 15(3)(b) says that if the views of the child witness and the views of the witness's parent are inconsistent, the views of the witness are to be given greater weight.

E1. Has the child witness expressed a view about how they should give evidence?

☐ Yes

ⓘ If the answer is 'yes', complete E3.

☐ No

ⓘ If the answer is 'no', complete E2.

E2. Why has the child witness not expressed a view about how they should give evidence?

ⓘ Set out why no view has been expressed. For example:

- the child witness may not be of sufficient age or maturity to do so

- the child witness may not wish to do so

E3. What are the views of the child witness?

ⓘ Set out the views of the child witness. In particular, set out:

- whether the child witness wishes to use a special measure to give evidence

- the special measure that the child considers most appropriate

- whether the child witness wishes to give evidence without the benefit of any special measures

E4. What are the views of the child witness's parent?

ⓘ Set out the views of the child witness's parent. In particular, set out:

- whether the parent considers that the child witness should use a special measure to give evidence

- the special measure that the parent considers most appropriate

- whether the parent considers that the child witness should give evidence without the benefit of any special measures

FORM 11D
The Simple Procedure Vulnerable Witness Application

This is a Vulnerable Witness Application.

It is used to ask the court to decide if a witness who is to give evidence in the simple procedure case is a vulnerable witness.

If the sheriff agrees that the witness is a vulnerable witness, it also asks the sheriff to authorise the use of special measures to take the vulnerable witness's evidence.

A. ABOUT THE CASE

Sheriff Court	
Claimant	
Respondent	
Case reference number	

B. ABOUT YOU

B1. What is your full name?

Name	
Middle name	
Surname	
Trading name or representative capacity (if any)	

B2. What is your role in this case?

☐ Claimant

☐ Respondent

C. THE APPLICATION

C1. What is the full name of the witness?

Name	
Middle name	
Surname	

C2. Why do you think that the witness is a vulnerable witness?

ⓘ You should set out the reasons why you think the witness is a vulnerable witness.

ⓘ The matters that the court must take into account in deciding whether the witness is a vulnerable witness are set out in section 11(2) of the Vulnerable Witnesses (Scotland) Act 2004.

C3. When was this Application sent to the court?

ⓘ Set out the date on which the Application was sent to the court (i.e. the date on which the email was sent, or the date on which the notice was posted).

D. THE SPECIAL MEASURES

ⓘ The special measures that the court may make are listed in rule 11.6 of the Simple Procedure Rules.

D1. What special measures would be most appropriate for taking the evidence of the witness?

ⓘ You may select as many special measures as you think are appropriate.

☐ allowing the witness to give evidence before an independent person

ⓘ This means that the witness would give evidence before an independent person appointed by the court, rather than coming to court to give evidence.

☐ allowing the witness to give evidence by live television link

☐ allowing the witness to use a screen while giving evidence

☐ allowing the witness to be supported by someone while giving evidence

D2. Why do you think the special measures you have selected would be most appropriate for taking the evidence of the witness?

```
```

E. VIEWS OF THE WITNESS

ⓘ In completing this Application, you must take into account the views of the witness.

E1. Has the witness expressed a view about how they should give evidence?

☐ Yes

ⓘ If the answer is 'yes', complete E3.

☐ No

ⓘ If the answer is 'no', complete E2.

E2. Why has the witness not expressed a view about how they should give evidence?

ⓘ Set out why no view has been expressed. For example, the witness may not wish to do so.

```
```

E3. What are the views of the witness?

① Set out the views of the witness. In particular, set out:

  – whether the witness wishes to use a special measure to give evidence

  – the special measure that the witness considers most appropriate

FORM 11E

The Simple Procedure
Special Measures Review
Application

This is a Special Measures Review Application.

It is used where the court has decided that a child witness or a vulnerable witness should use a special measure to give evidence.

Its purpose is to ask the court to change the arrangements that have been made for the witness to give evidence.

A. ABOUT THE CASE

Sheriff Court	
Claimant	
Respondent	
Case reference number	

B. ABOUT YOU

B1. What is your full name?

Name	
Middle name	
Surname	
Trading name or representative capacity (if any)	

B2. What is your role in this case?

☐ Claimant

☐ Respondent

C. ABOUT THE WITNESS

C1. What is the full name of the witness?

Name

Middle name

Surname

C2. Is the witness a child witness or a vulnerable witness?

☐ Child witness

☐ Vulnerable witness

C3. What special measures has the court authorised to be used in taking the evidence of the witness?

ⓘ Select as many special measures as the court has authorised.

☐ allowing the witness to give evidence before an independent person

☐ allowing the witness to give evidence by live television link

☐ allowing the witness to use a screen while giving evidence

☐ allowing the witness to be supported by someone while giving evidence

D. THE APPLICATION

D1. How should the court change the current arrangements?

ⓘ Set out the changes you want the court to make.

The court may:

- vary a special measure
- add a new special measure
- substitute a new special measure for an existing one
- delete a special measure
- revoke the order authorising the use of special measures entirely

D2. Why do you think the proposed changes would be most appropriate for taking the evidence of the witness?

D3. When was this Application sent to the court?

ⓘ Set out the date on which the Application was sent to the court (i.e. the date on which the email was sent, or the date on which the notice was posted).

E. VIEWS OF THE WITNESS

ⓘ In completing this Application, you must take into account the views of the witness.

ⓘ You only need to complete E4 if the witness is a child witness.

ⓘ The parent of a child witness is any person who has parental responsibilities within the meaning of section 1(3) of the Children (Scotland) Act 1995.

ⓘ Section 15(3)(a) of the Vulnerable Witnesses (Scotland) Act 2004 says that a child witness is presumed to be of sufficient age and maturity to form a view if aged 12 or older.

ⓘ Section 15(3)(b) says that if the views of the child witness and the views of the witness's parent are inconsistent, the views of the witness are to be given greater weight.

E1. Has the witness expressed a view about the proposed changes to how they should give evidence?

☐ Yes

ⓘ If the answer is 'yes', complete E3.

☐ No

ⓘ If the answer is 'no', complete E2.

E2. Why has the witness not expressed a view about the proposed changes to how they should give evidence?

ⓘ Set out why no view has been expressed. For example:

- a child witness may not be of sufficient age or maturity to do so

- the witness may not wish to do so

E3. What are the views of the witness?

ⓘ Set out the views of the witness. In particular, set out whether the witness agrees with the proposed changes.

E4. If the witness is a child witness, what are the views of the child witness's parent?

ⓘ Set out the views of the child witness's parent. In particular, set out whether the parent agrees with the proposed changes.

PART 13

Part 13

FORM 13A

The Simple Procedure
Decision Form

This is the Decision Form. It contains the terms of the decision that the sheriff has made at the end of the simple procedure case. Part 13 of the Simple Procedure Rules is about the decision of the sheriff.

This Decision Form can be used to enforce the decision made by the sheriff. Part 15 of the Simple Procedure Rules is about how to enforce this decision.

THIS EXTRACT DECREE IS WARRANT FOR ALL LAWFUL EXECUTION THEREON.

Execution of this decree is not lawful:
- within 28 days from the date the Decision Form was sent
- where the decision is being appealed
- where the decision has been recalled.

A. ABOUT THE CASE

Sheriff Court	
Claimant	
Address	
City	
Postcode	
Respondent	
Address	
City	
Postcode	
Case reference number	
Date of decision	

B. THE DECISION OF THE SHERIFF

ⓘ This part sets out the orders which the sheriff has made when deciding the case.

C. EXPENSES

ⓘ This part sets out any orders which the sheriff has made about the expenses of the case.

D. SIGNATURE

Signature of sheriff clerk	
Date sent	

FORM 13B

The Simple Procedure
Application to Recall

This is an Application to Recall.

Before completing this form, you should read rules 13.5 to 13.7 of the Simple Procedure Rules, which are about recalling a decision.

You can use this Application to ask the sheriff to recall a decision made because of your failure to attend court or take a step in simple procedure.

If the sheriff made a decision because you did not respond to the claim by the last date for a response, and you would now like to dispute the claim, or part of the claim, you must also include a completed Response Form with this Application.

A. ABOUT THE CASE

Sheriff Court	
Claimant	
Respondent	
Case reference number	

B. ABOUT YOU

B1. What is your full name?

Name	
Middle name	
Surname	
Trading name or representative capacity (if any)	

B2. Which party in this case are you?

☐   Claimant

☐   Respondent

C. THE APPLICATION

C1. Why should the decision be recalled?

ⓘ The party making the application must set out why the court should recall the decision and the reason for their failure to take a step or attend court.

C2. When was this application sent to the court?

ⓘ Set out the date on which the application was sent to the court (i.e. the date on which the application was submitted online or posted).

FORM 15A

The Simple Procedure
Charge to Pay

This is a Charge to Pay. The purpose of this Charge to Pay is to give you one last chance to comply with a decision made in a simple procedure case.

A. ABOUT THE CASE

Sheriff Court	
Claimant	
Respondent	
Case reference number	

B. ABOUT THE CHARGE

Name of sheriff officer/solicitor	
Address	
Method of formal service	

C. ABOUT THE DECISION

ⓘ This Part contains information about the decision which the court made.

ⓘ You must comply with this decision within the period set out below or there may be enforcement action taken against you and your property.

ⓘ If you do not comply with this decision, you may have your bank accounts frozen or earnings arrested. If you have debts amounting to over £3,000, you may be sequestrated (made bankrupt).

ⓘ Note that interest will continue to run on any sum set out below until you pay this sum.

Date of decision	

Details of decision	The sum now due to the claimant is: Principal Sum Interest to date Expenses TOTAL Less paid Agent's fee Expenses of sheriff officer TOTAL SUM NOW DUE

D. THE CHARGE

YOU ARE CHARGED TO COMPLY WITH THIS DECISION WITHIN	14 / 28 days

IF YOU ARE NOT SURE WHAT TO DO ABOUT THIS CHARGE YOU SHOULD CONSULT A SOLICITOR, CITIZENS ADVICE BUREAU OR OTHER LOCAL ADVICE AGENCY IMMEDIATELY

FORM 15B

The Simple Procedure Alternative Decision Application

Before completing this form, you should read rule 15.5 of the Simple Procedure Rules, which is about applying to ask the court to make an alternative decision.

If you are applying for an alternative order:

This is an Alternative Decision Application. It can be used when the sheriff made a decision ordering the respondent to deliver something to the claimant or do something for the claimant. If the court alternatively ordered the respondent to pay the claimant a sum of money, then this application can be used to ask the court to make that order.

You must fill in parts A, B and C of this application and send it to the court.

A. ABOUT THE CASE

Sheriff Court	
Claimant	
Respondent	
Case reference number	
Date of Decision Form	

B. ABOUT YOU

B1. What is your full name?

Name	
Middle name	
Surname	
Trading name or representative capacity (if any)	

B2. Which party in this case are you?

☐ Claimant

☐ Respondent

C. THE APPLICATION

C1. What alternative order should be made?

ⓘ The party making the application must set out which alternative order for payment from the Decision Form the court is being asked to make.

C2. Why should this alternative order be made?

ⓘ The party making the application must set out why the court should make that alternative order for payment

C3. When was this application sent to the court?

ⓘ Set out the date on which the application was sent to the court (i.e. the date on which the email was sent, or the date on which the application was posted).

FORM 16A
The Simple Procedure
Appeal Form

Before completing this form, you should read Part 16 of the Simple Procedure Rules, which is about appeals.

This is an Appeal Form. You can use this to appeal the decision made by the sheriff at the end of a simple procedure case. You may only do this within 28 days from the Decision Form being sent.

A. ABOUT THE CASE

Sheriff Court	
Claimant	
Respondent	
Case reference number	
Date of Decision Form	

B. ABOUT YOU

B1. What is your full name?

Name	
Middle name	
Surname	
Trading name or representative capacity (if any)	

B2. Which party in the simple procedure case were you?

☐   Claimant

☐   Respondent

C. GROUNDS OF APPEAL

ⓘ Set out the legal points which you want the Sheriff Appeal Court to consider in this appeal.

ⓘ These must be points of law. You cannot appeal simply because you disagree with a matter of fact which the sheriff made a decision on.

I appeal to the Sheriff Appeal Court on the following points of law:

1.

2.

[...]

FORM 16B

The Simple Procedure
Appeal Report

This is an Appeal Report. It sets out the legal questions which the Sheriff Appeal Court will answer in this appeal.

A. ABOUT THE CASE

Sheriff Court	
Claimant	
Respondent	
Case reference number	
Date of Decision Form	
Date of appeal	

B. ABOUT THE DECISION

ⓘ Set out the factual and legal basis for the decision which you came to in this case.

C. QUESTIONS FOR THE SHERIFF APPEAL COURT

ⓘ Set out the legal questions for the Sheriff Appeal Court to answer in this appeal.

Signature

Sheriff of [sheriffdom] at [sheriff court]

FORM 17A

The Simple Procedure
CJEU Reference Form

Before completing this form, you should read rule 17.3 of the Simple Procedure Rules, which is about references to the CJEU.

This is the form of reference for a preliminary ruling of the Court of Justice of the European Union.

A. ABOUT THE CASE

Sheriff Court	
Claimant	
Respondent	
Case reference number	
Date of reference	

B. THE REFERENCE

ⓘ Set out a clear and succinct statement of the case giving rise to the request for a ruling of the CJEU in order to enable the court to consider and understand the issues of EU law raised and to enable governments of Member States and other interested parties to submit observations.

Include:

- particulars of the parties
- the history of the dispute
- the relevant facts as agreed by the parties or found by the court or (failing such agreement or finding) the contentions of the parties
- the nature of the issues of law and fact between the parties
- the State law, so far as relevant
- the Treaty provisions, or other acts, instruments or rules of EU law concerned
- an explanation of why the reference is being made.

C. THE QUESTIONS

C1. The preliminary ruling of the CJEU is accordingly requested on the following questions.

ⓘ Set out the question(s) on which a ruling is sought, identifying the Treaty provisions, or other acts, instruments or rules of EU law concerned.

FORM 17B
The Simple Procedure
Application to Intervene

Before completing this form, you should read rules 17.4 and 17.5 of the Simple Procedure Rules, which are about interventions by the CEHR and SCHR.

This application is used by the Commission for Equality and Human Rights and the Scottish Commission for Human Rights to apply to be allowed to intervene in a simple procedure case.

A. ABOUT THE CASE

Sheriff Court	
Claimant	
Respondent	
Case reference number	
Date of application	

B. ABOUT THE INTERVENER

B1. Who is the proposed intervener in this case?

☐ The Commission for Equality and Human Rights

☐ The Scottish Commission for Human Rights

C. ABOUT THE INTERVENTION

C1. Why is the Commission proposing to intervene?

ⓘ Set out the Commission's reasons for believing that the simple procedure case is relevant to a matter in connection with which the Commission has a function.

C2. What issue does the Commission want to address?

ⓘ Set out the issue in the simple procedure case which the Commission wants to address.

C3. What intervention does the Commission want to make?

ⓘ Set out the propositions to be advanced by the Commission and the Commission's reasons for believing that they would assist the court.

FORM 17C

The Simple Procedure
Invitation to Intervene

This Invitation to Intervene is used by the sheriff to invite the Commission for Equality and Human Rights or the Scottish Commission for Human Rights to intervene in a simple procedure case.

A. ABOUT THE CASE

Sheriff Court	
Claimant	
Respondent	
Case reference number	
Date of invitation	

B. ABOUT THE INVITATION

B1. Who is the sheriff inviting to intervene?

☐ The Commission for Equality and Human Rights

☐ The Scottish Commission for Human Rights

C. THE INVITATION

C1. What is the simple procedure case about?

ⓘ Set out briefly the facts, procedural history and issues in the simple procedure case.

C2. What is the sheriff inviting the Commission to address in an intervention?

ⓘ Set out the issue(s) in the simple procedure case on which the court would like a submission.

FORM 17D

The Simple Procedure Application to Change a Damages Management Order

If you are applying for the sheriff to make orders:

This is an Application to Change a Damages Management Order.

It is used where the court has made a damages management order (which is about how a sum of money awarded as damages is to be paid to and managed for a person under a legal disability), but you want the court to change the order.

You must fill in parts A, B and C of this application and send it to the court. If you are one of the parties, you must send a copy to the other party in this case. If you are an interested person, you must send a copy to every party.

If you have been sent this Application:

This is an Application to Change a Damages Management Order.

If the court grants this application, the damages management order will be changed as proposed in the application.

You have received the application because you are one of the parties in the case.

You must fill in part D of this application ('the reply') and return it to the court within 10 days of it being sent to you.

The court will then either grant the application and send written orders to the parties and the interested person, refuse the application and make no orders, or order you to appear at a discussion in court where the sheriff will consider whether to make any orders.

A. ABOUT THE CASE

Sheriff Court	
Claimant	
Respondent	
Case reference number	

B. ABOUT YOU

B1. What is your full name?

Name

Middle name

Surname

Trading name or
representative capacity (if
any)

B2. Which is your role in this case?

☐ Claimant

☐ Respondent

☐ Interested person

B3. If you are an interested person, what is your interest in this case?

ⓘ Explain why you have an interest in this case. For example:

– the damages management order might tell you to do certain things

– you might be responsible for looking after the person to whom the damages have been awarded.

C. THE APPLICATION

ⓘ If you are replying to this application, do not fill in this part. You should fill in part D.

C1. How should the court change the damages management order?

ⓘ Set out the changes you want the court to make. For example, you could ask the court to:

- – appoint someone else to manage the money

- – order the money to be paid directly to the person under legal disability.

C2. Why should the court change the damages management order?

ⓘ Set out why the court should change the damages management order.

C3. When was this application sent to the court?

ⓘ Set out the date on which the application was sent to the court (i.e. the date on which the email was sent, or the date on which the application was posted).

ⓘ Any reply to this application must be sent to the court within 10 days of this application being sent.

D. THE REPLY

ⓘ If you are the person making this application, do not fill in this part. You should fill in parts A, B and C.

D1. What is your full name?

Name

Middle name

Surname

Trading name or representative capacity (if any)

D2. Should the court change the damages management order?

☐ Yes

☐ No

D3. If you answered 'no', why should the court not change the damages management order?

ⓘ If you object to the proposed order, you should set out why the court should not change the damages management order.

FORM 17E

The Simple Procedure Application for Instructions about a Damages Management Order

If you are applying for the sheriff to make orders:

This is an Application for Instructions about a Damages Management Order.

It is used where the court has made a damages management order (which is about how a sum of money awarded as damages is to be paid to and managed for a person under a legal disability) and you want the court to tell the person appointed to manage the money how to go about doing that.

You must fill in parts A, B and C of this application and send it to the court. If you are one of the parties, you must send a copy to the other party in this case. If you are an interested person, you must send a copy to every party.

If you have been sent this Application:

This is an Application for Instructions about a Damages Management Order.

If the court grants this application, the court will give instructions about how to manage the money to the person appointed to manage it.

You have received the application because you are one of the parties in the case or because you are the guardian appointed to manage the money.

You must fill in part D of this application ('the reply') and return it to the court within 10 days of it being sent to you.

The court will then either grant the application and send written instructions to the parties, the interested person and the sheriff clerk or guardian, refuse the application and make no orders, or order you to appear at a discussion in court where the sheriff will consider whether to give instructions.

A. ABOUT THE CASE

Sheriff Court	
Claimant	
Respondent	
Case reference number	

B. ABOUT YOU

B1. What is your full name?

Name

Middle name

Surname

Trading name or
representative capacity (if
any)

B2. Which is your role in this case?

☐ Claimant

☐ Respondent

☐ Interested person

B3. If you are an interested person, what is your interest in this case?

ⓘ Explain why you have an interest in this case. For example:

– the damages management order might tell you to do certain things

– you might be responsible for looking after the person to whom the damages have
been awarded.

C. THE APPLICATION

ⓘ If you are replying to this application, do not fill in this part. You should fill in part D.

C1. What instructions about the damages management order should the court give?

ⓘ Set out the proposed instructions you want the court to give. For example, you could
ask the court to give instructions about how the money is to be spent or invested.

C2. Why should the court give instructions about the damages management order?

ⓘ Set out why the court should give the proposed instructions.

C3. When was this application sent to the court?

ⓘ Set out the date on which the application was sent to the court (i.e. the date on which the email was sent, or the date on which the application was posted).

ⓘ Any reply to this application must be sent to the court within 10 days of this application being sent.

D. THE REPLY

ⓘ If you are the person making this application, do not fill in this part. You should fill in parts A, B and C.

D1. What is your full name?

Name	
Middle name	
Surname	
Trading name or representative capacity (if any)	

D2. Should the court give instructions about the damages management order?

☐ Yes

☐ No

D3. If you answered 'no', why should the court not give instructions about the damages management order?

ⓘ If you object to the proposed instructions, you should set out why the court should not give them.

FORM 17F

The Simple Procedure Application for a Child's Property Administration Order

If you are applying for the sheriff to make orders:

This is an Application for a Child's Property Administration Order.

It is used where the court has made an order under section 13 of the Children (Scotland) Act 1995 (section 13 is about the payment and management of money to (or for the benefit of) a child).

You must fill in parts A, B and C of this application and send it to the court. If you are one of the parties, you must send a copy to the other party in this case. If you are an interested person, you must send a copy to every party.

If you have been sent this Application:

This is an Application for a Child's Property Administration Order.

If the court grants this application, it will make the proposed order which regulates how the child's property is to be administered.

You have received the application because you are one of the parties in the case.

You must fill in part D of this application ('the reply') and return it to the court within 10 days of it being sent to you.

The court will then either grant the application and send written orders to the parties and the interested person, refuse the application and make no orders, or order you to appear at a discussion in court where the sheriff will consider whether to make any orders.

A. ABOUT THE CASE

Sheriff Court	
Claimant	
Respondent	
Case reference number	

B. ABOUT YOU

B1. What is your full name?

Name

Middle name

Surname

Trading name or
representative capacity (if
any)

B2. Which is your role in this case?

☐ Claimant

☐ Respondent

☐ Interested person

B3. If you are an interested person, what is your interest in this case?

ⓘ Explain why you have an interest in this case: see section 11(3) of the Children (Scotland) Act 1995.

C. THE APPLICATION

ⓘ If you are replying to this application, do not fill in this part. You should fill in part D.

C1. What order should the court make about administering the child's property?

ⓘ Set out the things you want the Child's Property Administration Order to contain.

C2. Why should the court make the Child's Property Administration Order?

ⓘ Set out why the court should make the proposed order.

C3. When was this application sent to the court?

ⓘ Set out the date on which the application was sent to the court (i.e. the date on which the email was sent, or the date on which the application was posted).

ⓘ Any reply to this application must be sent to the court within 10 days of this application being sent.

D. THE REPLY

ⓘ If you are the person making this application, do not fill in this part. You should fill in parts A, B and C.

D1. What is your full name?

Name	
Middle name	
Surname	
Trading name or representative capacity (if any)	

D2. Should the court make the proposed Child's Property Administration Order?

☐ Yes

☐ No

D3. If you answered 'no', why should the court not make the Child's Property Administration Order?

① If you object to the proposed order, you should set out why the court should not make it.

FORM 19A

The Simple Procedure
Translation Certificate

Before completing this form, you should read Part 19 of the Simple Procedure Rules, which is about international service.

This is a Translation Certificate. It is used to confirm to the court that a document which is formally served in a foreign country has been correctly translated into an official language of the foreign country. It is completed by the translator.

It must be sent to the court at the same time as the Confirmation of Service Notice (or the certificate given by the person who served the document abroad).

A. ABOUT THE CASE

Sheriff Court	
Claimant	
Respondent	
Case reference number	

B. ABOUT YOU

B1. What is your full name?

Name	
Middle name	
Surname	
Trading name or representative capacity (if any)	

B2. What is your address?

Address	
Town	
Postcode	

B3. What are your professional qualifications?

ⓘ Fill in information about your qualifications as a translator.

C. DECLARATION

ⓘ You must certify that your translation is a correct translation of the Form or Notice.

☐   I certify that the translation of the Form or Notice is a correct translation.

FORM 19B

The Simple Procedure
Method of Service Abroad
Certificate

Before completing this form, you should read Part 19 of the Simple Procedure Rules, which is about international service.

This is a Method of Service Abroad Certificate. It is used to tell the court about the way a document has been served in a foreign country. It is only used if no other method of service is available. It must be completed by a person who practises (or has practised) law in that country, or by a representative of that country's government.

A. ABOUT THE CASE

Sheriff Court	
Claimant	
Respondent	
Case reference number	

B. ABOUT YOU

B1. What is your full name?

Name	
Middle name	
Surname	
Trading name or representative capacity (if any)	

B2. What is your address?

Address	
Town	
Postcode	

B3. What is your qualification to provide this certificate?

☐ I practice law in: [country where Form or Notice served]

☐ I practised law in: [country where Form or Notice served]

between these dates: [dates when in practice]

☐ I am a representative of the government of: [country where Form or Notice served]

C. ABOUT THE FORMAL SERVICE

C1. Who was the document served on?

ⓘ You must identify the person on whom it was served.

C2. Who served it?

ⓘ You must give the following information about the person who served it:

– the person's full name

– the person's address

– the capacity in which the person served the Form or Notice

C3. How was it served?

ⓘ You must describe the method of service used.

D. DECLARATION

ⓘ You must certify that the method of service used is in accordance with the law of the country where the document has been served.

☐ I certify that the method by which the document was served is in accordance with the law of the country where it was served.

FORM 20A
The Simple Procedure Provisional Orders Application

If you are applying for the sheriff to make orders:

This is a Provisional Orders Application.

You can use this Application to ask the court to make orders that will protect your position until the sheriff makes a final decision in this case.

If you are asking the court to make a provisional order **without a provisional orders hearing**, you do not have to send the Application to anyone except the court.

Otherwise, you have to send a copy of the Application to the respondent and every interested person as well as sending it to the court.

If you have been sent this Application:

This is a Provisional Orders Application.

The claimant has asked the court to make orders to protect the claimant's position until the sheriff makes a final decision in this case.

The sheriff must hear from the claimant, the respondent and any interested person at a provisional orders hearing before deciding whether to make the provisional orders.

A. ABOUT THE CASE

Sheriff Court	
Claimant	
Respondent	
Case reference number	

B. ABOUT THE CLAIMANT

B1. What is your full name?

Name	
Middle name	
Surname	

Trading name or representative capacity (if any)	

C. THE APPLICATION

ⓘ You should complete this Part, Part D and Part F.

ⓘ Only complete Part E if you are asking for an arrestment on the dependence.

C1. What type of provisional order would you like the court to make?

☐ an arrestment on the dependence under section 15A(1) of the Debtors (Scotland) Act 1987

ⓘ This is an order freezing the respondent's goods or money held by a third party.

☐ an inhibition on the dependence under section 15A(1) of the Debtors (Scotland) Act 1987

ⓘ This is an order preventing the respondent from selling their home or other land, or taking out a secured loan.

☐ an interim attachment under section 9A(1) of the Debt Arrangement and Attachment (Scotland) Act 2002

ⓘ This is an order preventing the respondent from selling or removing their goods.

C2. Why should the court make this provisional order?

ⓘ The court will have to be satisfied about certain matters before it makes the order. The matters that are considered depend on the type of order and on whether you are asking the court to make the order without holding a provisional orders hearing or not.

   – If you are asking for arrestment or inhibition on the dependence and you want the court to make a decision about the application without a hearing, see section 15E(2) of the Debtors (Scotland) Act 1987.

   – If you are asking for arrestment or inhibition on the dependence and you want the court to make a decision about the application at a hearing, see section 15F(3) of the Debtors (Scotland) Act 1987.

   – If you are asking for an interim attachment and you want the court to make a decision without a hearing, see section 9D(2) of the Debt Arrangement and Attachment (Scotland) Act 2002.

   – If you are asking for an interim attachment and you want the court to make a decision at a hearing, see section 9E(3) of the Debt Arrangement and Attachment (Scotland) Act 2002.

1136

D. HOW THE APPLICATION SHOULD BE DEALT WITH

D1. How do you want the court to deal with your Application?

☐ I want the court to consider whether to grant the Application without holding a hearing

ⓘ Please complete D2.

☐ I want the court to hold a hearing before deciding whether to grant the Application

D2. If the court refuses to grant the Application without holding a hearing, what should happen to the Application?

ⓘ You can decide to go ahead with a hearing where the sheriff will decide whether to grant the Application after hearing from you, the respondent and any interested person. If you do not want a hearing, the Application will be refused.

☐ I want the court to arrange a hearing

☐ I do not want the court to arrange a hearing

E. ARRESTMENT ON THE DEPENDENCE: INFORMATION ABOUT THIRD PARTY

ⓘ You should only complete this part of the Application if you are asking for an arrestment on the dependence.

ⓘ The third party is the person who holds goods or money that belongs to the respondent.

E1. Is the third party an individual, a company or an organisation?

☐ An individual (including a sole trader)

ⓘ Please complete E2.

☐ A company or organisation

ⓘ Please complete E3.

E2. What is the third party's full name?

ⓘ If the third party is an individual trading under a business name, please also give that name.

Name	
Middle name	
Surname	
Trading name (if any)	

E3. What is the third party's company name or organisation name?

ⓘ If the third party is a company (which might be indicated by 'Limited', 'Ltd' or 'plc' after its name), please give the full name of that company and the company registration number.

ⓘ You can check the name of a company on the Companies House website.

Name	
Company type	
Company registration number (if limited company or LLP)	
Trading name (if any)	

E4. What are the third party's contact details?

Address	
City	
Postcode	
Email address	

F. INTERESTED PERSONS

(i) This Part tells the court about any person who has an interest in the Application.

(i) You do not need to include details for:

– the respondent

– anyone whose details you have given in Part E.

F1. Does any person have an interest in the Application?

☐ Yes

☐ No

F2. Is the interested person an individual, a company or an organisation?

☐ An individual (including a sole trader)

(i) Please complete F3.

☐ A company or organisation

(i) Please complete F4.

F3. What is the interested person's full name?

(i) If the interested person is an individual trading under a business name, please also give that name.

Name	
Middle name	
Surname	
Trading name (if any)	

F4. What is the interested person's company name or organisation name?

ⓘ If the interested person is a company (which might be indicated by 'Limited', 'Ltd' or 'plc' after its name), please give the full name of that company and the company registration number.

ⓘ You can check the name of a company on the Companies House website.

Name [   ]

Company type [   ]

Company registration number (if limited company or LLP) [   ]

Trading name (if any) [   ]

F5. What are the interested person's contact details?

Address [   ]

City [   ]

Postcode [   ]

Email address [   ]

FORM 20B

The Simple Procedure
Provisional Orders
Hearing Notice

The claimant has asked the court to make orders to protect the claimant's position until the sheriff makes a final decision in this case.

The sheriff has arranged a hearing about that application. The sheriff has also ordered the claimant to tell you about the date, time and place where the hearing will be held so that you can make your views known to the sheriff.

A. ABOUT THE CASE

Sheriff Court	
Claimant	
Respondent	
Case reference number	

B. ABOUT THE RECIPIENT

B1. Who is this Notice being sent to?

Name	
Middle name	
Surname	
Trading name or representative capacity (if any)	

B2. What is that person's role in this case?

☐ Respondent

☐ Interested person

C. ABOUT THE HEARING

C1. What type of hearing has the sheriff arranged?

☐   A provisional orders hearing

ⓘ This is a hearing under section 15F of the Debtors (Scotland) Act 1987 or section 9E of the Debt Arrangement and Attachment (Scotland) Act 2002.

☐   A provisional orders review hearing

ⓘ This is a hearing under section 15K of the Debtors (Scotland) Act 1987 or section 9M of the Debt Arrangement and Attachment (Scotland) Act 2002.

C2. When will the hearing take place?

Date of hearing	
Time of hearing	

C3. Where will the hearing take place?

Place of hearing	

FORM 20C

The Simple Procedure Provisional Orders Reconsideration Application

If you are applying for the sheriff to reconsider a provisional order:

This is a Provisional Orders Reconsideration Application.

You can use this Application to ask the court to reconsider a provisional order.

If you are the respondent, you have to send the Application to the court, the claimant and any interested person.

If you are an interested person, you have to send the Application to the court, the claimant, the respondent and any other interested person.

The court will then arrange a provisional orders review hearing. At the hearing, the sheriff must give anyone who was sent the Application an opportunity to be heard before deciding whether to make an order reconsidering the provisional order.

If you have been sent this Application:

This is a Provisional Orders Reconsideration Application.

The respondent or an interested person has asked the court to reconsider a provisional order.

The court will arrange a provisional orders review hearing. At the hearing, you will have an opportunity to be heard before the sheriff decides whether to make an order reconsidering the provisional order.

A. ABOUT THE CASE

Sheriff Court	
Claimant	
Respondent	
Case reference number	

B. ABOUT YOU

B1. What is your full name?

Name	
Middle name	
Surname	
Trading name or representative capacity (if any)	

B2. What is your role in this case?

☐ Respondent

☐ Interested party

C. THE APPLICATION

C1. What type of provisional order would you like the court to reconsider?

☐ an arrestment on the dependence under section 15A(1) of the Debtors (Scotland) Act 1987

ⓘ This is an order freezing the respondent's goods or money held by a third party.

☐ an inhibition on the dependence under section 15A(1) of the Debtors (Scotland) Act 1987

ⓘ This is an order preventing the respondent from selling their home or other land, or taking out a secured loan.

☐ an interim attachment under section 9A(1) of the Debt Arrangement and Attachment (Scotland) Act 2002

ⓘ This is an order preventing the respondent from selling or removing their goods.

C2. When was the provisional order made?

ⓘ Set out the date on which the court made the provisional order?

C3. What do you want the court to do with the provisional order?

   ⓘ Set out the way in which you want the court to reconsider the provisional order.

   ⓘ If the order was made under section 15A(1) of the Debtors (Scotland) Act 1987, section 15K of that Act sets out what the court can do on reconsidering it.

   ⓘ If the order was made under section 9A(1) of the Debt Arrangement and Attachment (Scotland) Act 2002, section 9M of that Act sets out what the court can do on reconsidering it.

C4. Why should the court reconsider the provisional order?

   ⓘ You must set out why the court should reconsider the provisional order.

FORM 20D

The Simple Procedure
Arrestment Notice

This is an Arrestment Notice. It is used when the court makes a provisional order and the provisional order is an arrestment on the dependence.

The purpose of the Arrestment Notice is to inform the third party who holds the respondent's goods or money that they have been frozen by the court. It is formally served on that person by a sheriff officer.

A. ABOUT THE CASE

Sheriff Court	
Claimant	
Respondent	
Case reference number	

B. ABOUT THE THIRD PARTY

B1. Is the third party an individual, a company or an organisation?

☐ An individual (including a sole trader)

ⓘ Please complete B2.

☐ A company or organisation

ⓘ Please complete B3.

B2. What is the third party's full name?

ⓘ If the third party is an individual trading under a business name, please also give that name.

Name	
Middle name	
Surname	
Trading name (if any)	

B3. What is the third party's company name or organisation name?

    ⓘ If the third party is a company (which might be indicated by 'Limited', 'Ltd' or 'plc' after its name), please give the full name of that company and the company registration number.

    ⓘ You can check the name of a company on the Companies House website.

Name	
Company type	
Company registration number (if limited company or LLP)	
Trading name (if any)	

B4. What are the third party's contact details?

Address	
City	
Postcode	
Email address	

C. PROTECTED MINIMUM BALANCE

    ⓘ Section 73F of the Debtors (Scotland) Act 1987 prevents the arrestment of money held by a bank or other financial institution below a certain minimum balance if various conditions are met.

    ⓘ This Part of the Form identifies whether the Protected Minimum Balance applies to this arrestment.

C1. Is the respondent an individual?

☐ Yes

    ⓘ Please complete C2.

☐ No

    ⓘ The Protected Minimum Balance does not apply. Go to Part D.

C2. Is the third party a bank or other financial institution?

ⓘ See section 73F(5) of the Debtors (Scotland) Act 1987 for a definition of bank or other financial institution.

☐ Yes

ⓘ Please complete C3.

☐ No

ⓘ The Protected Minimum Balance does not apply. Go to Part D.

C3. Is the bank account one to which section 73F of the Debtors (Scotland) Act 1987 applies?

ⓘ See section 73F(2).

☐ Yes

ⓘ The Protected Minimum Balance applies. Please complete C4.

☐ No

ⓘ The Protected Minimum Balance does not apply. Go to Part D.

C4. If it applies, what is the Protected Minimum Balance?

ⓘ Insert the Protected Minimum Balance, which is calculated in accordance with section 73F(4).

Protected Minimum Balance, if applicable.

D. ABOUT THE ARRESTMENT ON THE DEPENDENCE

Date of order for arrestment on the dependence

Name of sheriff officer

Address

Witness

Method of formal service

Date and time of formal service

Signature of sheriff officer

IN HER MAJESTY'S NAME AND AUTHORITY AND IN NAME AND AUTHORITY OF THE SHERIFF, the sheriff officer arrests in your hands:

- any moveable property that belongs to the respondent, and

- the following sum of money, more or less, that is due by you to the respondent or to another person on behalf of the respondent

Sum arrested	The sum arrested, in excess of the Protected Minimum Balance where applicable.

E. DUTIES OF THE THIRD PARTY

E1. Compliance with the arrestment

You must retain anything that has been arrested in your hands under arrestment until one of the following things happens:

- the court makes an order transferring them to the claimant, or

- the court makes another order telling you what to do with them.

- ⓘ You should take legal advice before you hand over any goods to the respondent or pay any money to the respondent or someone else on behalf of the respondent.

E2. Duty of disclosure

ⓘ Section 73G of the Debtors (Scotland) Act 1987 requires you to disclose certain information to the claimant.

You must disclose to the claimant the nature and value of the goods and money which have been attached by this arrestment.

You must do this within the period of 3 weeks beginning with the day on which this arrestment is formally served on you.

You must make your disclosure using the form in Schedule 8 to the Diligence (Scotland) Regulations 2009.

You must also send a copy of the disclosure to:

- the respondent, and

- so far as known to you, any other relevant person.

A relevant person is someone (either solely or in common with the respondent):

- who owns or claims to own the attached goods, or

- to whom the attached money is or is claimed to be due.

ⓘ Failure to comply with this duty may lead to a financial penalty under section 73H of the Debtors (Scotland) Act 1987.

ⓘ Failure to comply may also be dealt with as a contempt of court.

If you wish further advice, please contact any Citizens Advice Bureau, local advice centre, sheriff clerk or solicitor.

1

---

[1] As amended by the Act of Sederunt (Rules of the Court of Session 1994 and Sheriff Court Rules Amendment) (No. 4) (Simple Procedure) 2016 (SSI 2016/315) para.7 (effective 28 November 2016).

FORM 20E

The Simple Procedure
Confirmation of Formal
Service
of Arrestment Notice

This is a Confirmation of Formal Service of an Arrestment Notice. It is used to inform the court when and how an Arrestment Notice has been formally served.

It must be completed and sent to the court whenever a sheriff officer formally serves an Arrestment Notice.

A. ABOUT THE CASE

Sheriff Court	
Claimant	
Respondent	
Case reference number	

B. ABOUT THE SHERIFF OFFICER

B1. What is your full name?

Name	
Middle name	
Surname	
Firm or organisation	

C. ABOUT FORMAL SERVICE OF ARRESTMENT NOTICE

C1. Who did you formally serve the Arrestment Notice on?

ⓘ You must identify the person who you were required to serve something on.

C2.How did you formally serve it?

ⓘ You must describe the method of formal service used.

☐ Delivering it personally

☐ Leaving it in the hands of a resident or employee

☐ Depositing it in a home or place of business by letter box or another lawful way

☐ Leaving it at a home or place of business in a way likely to come to the person's attention

ⓘ If you need to give more details about the manner of formal service, please set this out below.

C3. When did you formally serve it?

ⓘ You must identify when service was performed.

SCHEDULE 3 STANDARD ORDERS

SCHEDULE 3[1,2]

STANDARD ORDERS

Paragraph 3(1)

---

[1] As substituted by the Act of Sederunt (Rules of the Court of Session 1994 and Sheriff Court Rules Amendment) (No. 4) (Simple Procedure) 2016 (SSI 2016/315) para.7 (effective 28 November 2016).
[2] As amended by the Act of Sederunt (Simple Procedure Amendment) (Miscellaneous) (SSI 2018/191) art.2(4)(a) (effective 30 July 2018).

SO1

The Simple Procedure
Order of the Sheriff

Response Form received: ordering a case management discussion

This is an order of the sheriff in a case which you are a party in. You should **read it** and **follow it**.

You should also read Part 8 of the Simple Procedure Rules, which is about orders of the sheriff.

Sheriff Court:	
Date of order:	
Claimant:	
Respondent:	
Case reference number:	

The respondent has indicated to the court that this claim will be disputed.

The sheriff has considered the Claim Form and the Response Form and has **given the following orders**:–

Settlement and negotiation
The claimant and the respondent are **encouraged** to contact each other to seek to settle the case or to narrow the issues in dispute, **before** the case management discussion. If the case is settled before the case management discussion date then the parties must contact the court immediately.

Case management discussion

The sheriff would like to discuss this case with **both parties** before ordering a formal court hearing. Both parties are therefore **ordered** to attend a case management discussion in the sheriff court.

The purpose of a case management discussion is to allow the sheriff to discuss the claim and response with both parties and to clarify any concerns which the sheriff has. At the case management discussion, the sheriff will also discuss with both parties their attitudes to negotiation and alternative dispute resolution.

At the case management discussion, the sheriff will give both parties orders in person arranging a hearing at which the case will be considered and their dispute resolved. The sheriff may make a decision at a case management discussion.

Clarification

The claimant is **ordered** to write to the court and to the respondent at least **14 days** before the date of the case management discussion to clarify these issues:

```
1. [list]
2.
3.
```

The respondent is **ordered** to write to the court and to the claimant at least **14 days** before the date of the case management discussion to clarify these issues:

```
1. [list]
2.
3.
```

Documents and other evidence

The claimant is **ordered** to bring the following documents or other evidence to the case management discussion:

```
1. [list]
2.
3.
```

The respondent is **ordered** to bring the following documents or other evidence to the case management discussion:

```
1. [list]
2.
3.
```

Date

Both parties are **ordered** to attend a case management discussion at [Sheriff court] on   at   . Both parties should arrive in good time at the sheriff court building.

At the case management discussion, the sheriff expects both parties to be prepared to discuss the case and to have an open and constructive attitude to the possibility of negotiation or alternative dispute resolution.

Signed by:

> Sheriff of [sheriffdom] at [sheriff court]

SO2

The Simple Procedure
Order of the Sheriff

Response Form received: ordering a hearing

This is an order of the sheriff in a case which you are a party in. You should **read it** and **follow it**.

You should also read Part 8 of the Simple Procedure Rules, which is about orders of the sheriff.

Sheriff Court:	
Date of order:	
Claimant:	
Respondent:	
Case reference number:	

The respondent has indicated to the court that this claim will be disputed.

The sheriff has considered the Claim Form and the Response Form and has **given the following orders**:–

Settlement and negotiation
The claimant and the respondent are **encouraged** to contact each other to seek to settle the case or to narrow the issues in dispute, **before** the hearing date. If the case is settled before the hearing date then the parties must contact the court immediately.

Documents and other evidence
The sheriff has considered the evidence and other documents which the claimant thinks would support the claim.

The claimant is **ordered** to **also** lodge the following documents or other evidence at least 14 days before the hearing date, as the sheriff considers them necessary to support their claim:
1. [list]

The claimant is **ordered** not to lodge the following documents or other evidence, as the sheriff considers them unnecessary to support the claim:
1. [list]

The sheriff has considered the evidence and other documents which the respondent thinks would support the response.

The respondent is **ordered** to **also** lodge the following documents or other evidence at least 14 days before the hearing date, as the sheriff considers them necessary to support their response:
1. [list]

The respondent is **ordered** not to lodge the following documents or other evidence, as the sheriff considers them unnecessary to support the response:
1. [list]

Both parties are **ordered** to bring two copies of every document that is lodged to the hearing.

Clarification
The claimant is **ordered** to write to the court and to the respondent at least **14 days** before the hearing date to clarify these issues:
1. [list]

The respondent is **ordered** to write to the court and to the claimant at least **14 days** before the hearing date to clarify these issues:
1. [list]

Hearing Date
Both parties are **ordered** to attend a hearing at [sheriff court] on [date] at [time]. Both parties should arrive in good time at the sheriff court building.

At this hearing, the sheriff will expect both parties to be prepared to argue their case in full. Both parties should be aware that the sheriff may make a decision in their case even if they are not fully prepared to argue their case.

The case may be decided or dismissed in the absence of a party, if that party fails to attend the hearing.

Signed by:

Sheriff of [sheriffdom] at [sheriff court]

SO3

The Simple Procedure
Order of the Sheriff

Response Form received: considering making a decision without a hearing

This is an order of the sheriff in a case which you are a party in. You should **read it** and **follow it**.

You should also read Part 8 of the Simple Procedure Rules, which is about orders of the sheriff.

Sheriff Court:	
Date of order:	
Claimant:	
Respondent:	
Case reference number:	

The respondent has indicated to the court that this claim will be disputed.

The sheriff has considered the Claim Form and the Response Form and has **given the following orders**:–

Settlement and negotiation
The claimant and the respondent are **encouraged** to contact each other to seek to settle the case or to narrow the issues in dispute. If the case is settled before the date on which the sheriff intends to make a decision then the parties must contact the court immediately.

A decision without a hearing
The sheriff considers that the dispute between the parties is capable of being resolved without a hearing. This is because the dispute appears only to involve a question of law [or because the dispute appears capable of being resolved based only on consideration of the documents and other evidence listed in the Claim Form and Response Form]. If the dispute is resolved without a hearing then the sheriff will give parties an opportunity to write to the court setting out their arguments in the case in advance of making a decision.

Opportunity to object

Both parties are being given an opportunity to object to this dispute being resolved without a hearing.

Both parties are **ordered** to write to the sheriff by [date] stating whether they are content for a decision to be made without a hearing. If parties are not content for a decision to be made without a hearing, they must set out the reasons why a hearing will be necessary to resolve this dispute.

Parties should be aware that failing to write to the sheriff may result in the sheriff deciding to resolve this dispute without a hearing.

Next steps

The sheriff will issue further written orders within 14 days of [date]. These written orders will state whether the sheriff has decided to resolve this dispute without a hearing.

Signed by:

Sheriff of [sheriffdom] at [sheriff court]

The Simple Procedure
Order of the Sheriff

Response Form received: making a decision without a hearing

This is an order of the sheriff in a case which you are a party in. You should **read it** and **follow it**.

You should also read Part 8 of the Simple Procedure Rules, which is about orders of the sheriff.

Sheriff Court:	
Date of order:	
Claimant:	
Respondent:	
Case reference number:	

The sheriff sent the parties written orders stating that the sheriff was considering making a decision in this case without a hearing.

The sheriff has considered the responses received [or no responses were received] and has **given the following orders**:—

Settlement and negotiation

The claimant and the respondent are **encouraged** to contact each other to seek to settle the case or to narrow the issues in dispute. If the case is settled before the date on which the sheriff intends to make a decision (below) then the parties must contact the court immediately.

A decision without a hearing

The sheriff has decided to make a decision in this case without a hearing.

The sheriff will make this decision on [date].

Clarification

The claimant is **ordered** to write to the court and to the respondent at least **14 days** before the decision date to clarify these issues:

    1. [list]

The respondent is **ordered** to write to the court and to the claimant at least **14 days** before the decision date to clarify these issues:

    1. [list]

Notes of argument

Parties are **ordered** to send the court notes of argument at least 14 days before the decision date. These notes should set out any legal points which they wish to make to the sheriff and should comment on any aspect of the evidence which they wish the sheriff to consider.

Documents and other evidence

Documents and other evidence may be lodged by sending copies to the sheriff clerk.

The claimant is **ordered** to lodge the following documents or other evidence at least 14 days before the decision date, as the sheriff considers them necessary to support their claim:

    1. [list]

The respondent is **ordered** to lodge the following documents or other evidence at least 14 days before the decision date, as the sheriff considers them necessary to support their response:

    1. [list]

Both parties should be aware that the sheriff may make a decision in this case on [date] even if they do not follow the orders above.

Signed by:

Sheriff of [sheriffdom] at [sheriff court]

The Simple Procedure
Order of the Sheriff

Transferring a case between courts

This is an order of the sheriff in a case which you are a party in. You should **read it** and **follow it**.

You should also read Part 8 of the Simple Procedure Rules, which is about orders of the sheriff.

Sheriff Court:	
Date of order:	
Claimant:	
Respondent:	
Case reference number:	

The sheriff has considered this simple procedure case and has **given the following orders**:-

Transfer to a different sheriff court

[The sheriff considers that this claim ought to have been raised in a different sheriff court.]

The case is **ordered** to be transferred to [*name of sheriff court*].

What happens next

You will be contacted by the sheriff clerk at [*name of sheriff court*] with the next orders in this case.

Signed by:	
	Sheriff of [sheriffdom] at [sheriff court]

The Simple Procedure
Order of the Sheriff

Unless order

This is an order of the sheriff in a case which you are a party in. You should **read it** and **follow it**.

You should also read Part 8 of the Simple Procedure Rules, which is about orders of the sheriff.

Sheriff Court:	
Date of order:	
Claimant:	
Respondent:	
Case reference number:	

Order

The sheriff orders [the claimant / the respondent] to take the following step[s] by [date]:
1. [list].

Possibility of dismissal

The sheriff considers that taking the steps listed above is necessary for the progress of this case. The claimant is **warned** that unless these steps are taken, this case will be **dismissed** without further warning.

If the step[s] listed above are not taken then the sheriff **dismisses** the claim against the respondent.

Signed by:	Sheriff of [sheriffdom] at [sheriff court]

SO7
The Simple Procedure
Order of the Sheriff

Application to Pause

This is an order of the sheriff in a case which you are a party in. You should **read it** and **follow it**.

You should also read Part 8 of the Simple Procedure Rules, which is about orders of the sheriff.

Sheriff Court:	
Date of order:	
Claimant:	
Respondent:	
Case reference number:	

The court has received an Application to Pause.

The sheriff has considered the Application and has **given the following orders**:–

[*The order below can be used where the sheriff has decided to grant the application, without a discussion in court*:]

Pausing Order

The sheriff **orders** the progress of this case to be paused.

This means that all upcoming hearings in this case have been cancelled. No procedural steps may be taken in this case until the case has been restarted. Either party can ask for this to happen by sending an Application to Restart Form to the court and to the other party.

Both parties should be aware that after six months, the sheriff clerk may write to you directing that a particular step should be taken. If this is not done, the claim may be dismissed.

[*The order below can be used where the sheriff has decided to refuse the application, without a discussion in court*:]

Refusing a Pausing Order

The sheriff **has not** ordered the progress of this case to be paused.

This means that all upcoming hearings in this case are still to go ahead. Parties may continue to progress this case.

[*The order below can be used where the sheriff has decided that a discussion in court is necessary to decide the application:*]

Discussion in court

The sheriff wants to hear from both parties before deciding whether to pause the progress of this case.

Both parties are **ordered** to attend a discussion at [sheriff court] on [date] at [time]. Both parties should arrive in good time at the sheriff court building.

At this discussion, the sheriff will expect both parties to be prepared to discuss whether the progress of the case should be paused. Both parties should be aware that the sheriff may make a decision in their case even where they are not fully prepared to discuss this.

The application may be decided in the absence of a party, if that party fails to attend the discussion.

Signed by:

Sheriff of [sheriffdom] at [sheriff court]

SO8

The Simple Procedure
Order of the Sheriff

Application to Restart

This is an order of the sheriff in a case which you are a party in. You should **read it** and **follow it**.

You should also read Part 8 of the Simple Procedure Rules, which is about orders of the sheriff.

Sheriff Court:	
Date of order:	
Claimant:	
Respondent:	
Case reference number:	

The court has received an Application to Restart.

The sheriff has considered the Application and has **given the following orders**:–

[*The order below can be used where the sheriff has decided to grant the application, without a discussion in court.*]

Restarting Order

The sheriff **orders** the progress of this case to be restarted.

Both parties are **ordered** to attend a discussion at [sheriff court] on [date] at [time]. Both parties should arrive in good time at the sheriff court building.

[*The order below can be used where the sheriff has decided to refuse the application, without a discussion in court.*]

Refusing a Restarting Order

The sheriff **has not** ordered the progress of this case to be restarted.

This means that the progress of the case continues to be paused. There are no upcoming hearings or discussions arranged in this case.

[*The order below can be used where the sheriff has decided that a discussion in court is necessary to decide the application:*]

Discussion in court

The sheriff wants to hear from both parties before deciding whether to restart the progress of this case.

Both parties are **ordered** to attend a discussion at [sheriff court] on [date] at [time]. Both parties should arrive in good time at the sheriff court building.

At this discussion, the sheriff will expect both parties to be prepared to discuss whether the progress of the case should be restarted. Both parties should be aware that the sheriff may make a decision in their case even where they are not fully prepared to discuss this.

The application may be decided in the absence of a party, if that party fails to attend the discussion.

Signed by:

Sheriff of [sheriffdom] at [sheriff court]

SO9

The Simple Procedure
Order of the Sheriff

Paused case – unless order

This is an order of the sheriff in a case which you are a party in. You should **read it** and **follow it**.

You should also read Part 8 of the Simple Procedure Rules, which is about orders of the sheriff.

Sheriff Court:	
Date of order:	
Claimant:	
Respondent:	
Case reference number:	

The sheriff clerk has presented this case to the sheriff because it has been paused for over 6 months.

The sheriff has considered the case and has **given the following orders**:-

Possibility of dismissal

This case has now been paused for over 6 months. Both parties are **warned** that the sheriff will dismiss this claim unless the following steps are taken:

[Both parties / the claimant / the respondent] must write to the sheriff to explain what they would like to happen to this case. If they would like the case to continue to be paused, they must explain why.

[or

The sheriff wants to hear from both parties before deciding what the next steps in this case should be.

Both parties are **ordered** to attend a discussion at [sheriff court] on [date] at [time]. Both parties should arrive in good time at the sheriff court building. At this discussion, the sheriff will expect both parties to be prepared to discuss the progress of the case.]

Signed by:

Sheriff of [sheriffdom] at [sheriff court]

SO10
The Simple Procedure
Order of the Sheriff
Order to recover documents

This is an order of the sheriff in a case which you are a party in. You should **read it** and **follow it**.

You should also read Part 8 of the Simple Procedure Rules, which is about orders of the sheriff.

Sheriff Court:

Address:

Date of order:

Claimant:

Respondent:

Case reference number:

The court has received a Recovery of Documents Application.

The sheriff has considered the Application and has **given the following orders:-**

Order to recover documents

[*This order can be used where the sheriff has decided to grant the application (in whole or in part) without a discussion in court*]

The sheriff **orders** the person mentioned in column 2 of the table below to send the document mentioned in column 1 to the court within [number of days] after this order is formally served.

Column 1	Column 2
Description of document	Name of person who has the document

The sheriff also **orders** that person to fill in part A of this order ('the reply') and return it to the court within [number of days] after this order is formally served.

Refusal of Recovery of Documents Application

[*This order can be used where the sheriff has decided to refuse the application without a discussion in court*]

The sheriff **refuses to make** an order to recover documents.

Discussion in court

[*This order can be used where the sheriff has decided that a discussion in court is necessary to decide the application*]

The sheriff wants to hear from both parties before deciding whether to make an order to recover documents.

Both parties are **ordered** to attend a discussion at [sheriff court] on [date] at [time]. Both parties should arrive in good time at the sheriff court building.

At this discussion, the sheriff will expect both parties to be prepared to discuss whether an order to recover documents should be made. Both parties should be aware that the sheriff may make a decision in their case even where they are not fully prepared to discuss this.

The application may be decided in the absence of a party, if that party fails to attend the discussion.

Signed by:

Sheriff of [sheriffdom] at [sheriff court]

THE REPLY
[*for use only where the sheriff makes an order to recover documents*]
A. ABOUT YOU

A1. What is your full name?

Name	
Middle name	
Surname	
Trading name or	

representative capacity (if
any)

B. DECLARATIONS

B1. How have you complied with the order to recover documents?

ⓘ Tick the box next to the appropriate declaration.

☐ I enclose the following documents.
They are all the documents in my
possession which fall within the
description above.

[list documents enclosed with the reply]

☐ I have no documents in my possession which fall within the description above.

B2. Do you have any additional information about the order to recover documents?

ⓘ Tick the box next to the appropriate declaration.

☐ I believe that there are other
documents which fall within the
description above but they are not
in my possession. I have the
following information about them:

[set out the documents, the date on which you last
saw them and the details of the person who you
believe possesses them]

☐ I have no additional information about documents which fall within the description
above.

B3. Do you believe that any of the documents that you possess are confidential?

ⓘ If your answer is yes, you must still send the document to the court. You should:

   – put it in an envelope and seal it

   – mark "CONFIDENTIAL" on the front of the envelope

ⓘ If the party who obtained the order to recover documents wants to open the envelope, the party has to
make an application to the court first. You will be told about any application and you can explain to the
sheriff why you think the document is confidential before the sheriff decides whether to grant the
application.

☐ Yes

☐ No

SO11

The Simple Procedure
Order of the Sheriff

Special order to recover documents

This is an order of the sheriff in a case which you are a party in. You should **read it** and **follow it**.

You should also read Part 8 of the Simple Procedure Rules, which is about orders of the sheriff.

Sheriff Court:

Address:

Date of order:

Claimant:

Respondent:

Case reference number:

The court has received a Special Recovery of Documents Application.

The sheriff has considered the Application and has **given the following orders:-**

Special order to recover documents

[This order can be used where the sheriff has decided to grant the application (in whole or in part) without a discussion in court]

The sheriff **grants commission** to [name], solicitor, [address] ('the commissioner') to recover the documents mentioned in column 1 from the person mentioned in column 2.

Column 1	Column 2
Description of document	*Name of person who has the document*

The sheriff also **appoints** the commissioner to send a report to the court, together with any documents recovered, as soon as possible.

Refusal of Special Recovery of Documents Application

[*This order can be used where the sheriff has decided to refuse the application without a discussion in court*]

The sheriff **refuses to make** a special order to recover documents.

Discussion in court

[*This order can be used where the sheriff has decided that a discussion in court is necessary to decide the application*]

The sheriff wants to hear from both parties before deciding whether to make a special order to recover documents.

Both parties are **ordered** to attend a discussion at [sheriff court] on [date] at [time]. Both parties should arrive in good time at the sheriff court building.

At this discussion, the sheriff will expect both parties to be prepared to discuss whether a special order to recover documents should be made. Both parties should be aware that the sheriff may make a decision in their case even where they are not fully prepared to discuss this.

The application may be decided in the absence of a party, if that party fails to attend the discussion.

Signed by:

Sheriff of [sheriffdom] at [sheriff court]

The Simple Procedure
Order of the Sheriff

Ordering an expenses hearing

This is an order of the sheriff in a case which you are a party in. You should **read it** and **follow it**.

You should also read Part 8 of the Simple Procedure Rules, which is about orders of the sheriff.

Sheriff Court:	
Date of order:	
Claimant:	
Respondent:	
Case reference number:	

The sheriff has decided the case and is going to make an order about expenses. The sheriff has **given the following orders**:–

Account of expenses
The sheriff orders the [claimant / respondent] to send an account of expenses to the court and to the other party by [date 4 weeks before the expenses hearing].

Assessment of expenses
The sheriff orders the sheriff clerk to assess that account of expenses and send both parties a notice of that assessment by [date 2 weeks before the expenses hearing].

Expenses hearing
The sheriff orders both parties to attend an expenses hearing at [sheriff court] on [date] at [time]. Both parties should arrive in good time at the sheriff court building. If either party does not intend to challenge the assessment of expenses made by the sheriff clerk, they should contact the sheriff clerk by [date before the expenses hearing].

A failure to attend the expenses hearing will be considered an acceptance of the expenses as assessed by the sheriff clerk.

Signed by:	
	Sheriff of [sheriffdom] at [sheriff court]

SO13

The Simple Procedure
Order of the Sheriff

Application to Recall received: ordering a discussion in court

This is an order of the sheriff in a case you are a party in. You should **read it** and **follow it**.

You should also read Part 8 of the Simple Procedure Rules, which is about orders of the sheriff.

Sheriff Court:	
Date of order:	
Claimant:	
Respondent:	
Case reference number:	

The court has received an Application to Recall.

The sheriff has **given the following orders**:–

Discussion in court

The sheriff wants to hear from both parties before deciding whether to recall the decision.

Both parties are **ordered** to attend a discussion at [sheriff court] on [date] at [time]. Both parties should arrive in good time at the sheriff court building.

The party making the application **must send the other party** a copy of the Application to Recall [and the Response Form] at least 5 days before the date of the discussion.

The parties **must bring with them** the Decision Form in this case. If the sheriff decides to recall the decision, the Decision Form must be given to the sheriff clerk.

The decision **must not be enforced** until the sheriff has decided the application.

At this discussion, the sheriff will expect parties to be prepared to discuss whether the decision should be recalled and what should happen next in the case if the decision is recalled. Both parties should be aware that the sheriff may decide the application even where they are not fully prepared to discuss it or in the absence of a party.

The case may be decided or dismissed in the absence of a party if that party fails to attend.

Signed by: Sheriff of [sheriffdom] at [sheriff court]

---

[1] As inserted by the Act of Sederunt (Simple Procedure Amendment) (Miscellaneous) (SSI 2018/191) art. 2(4)(b) (effective 30 July 2018).

DIVISION S

SHERIFF APPEAL COURT PRACTICE

PRACTICE NOTES AND DIRECTIONS

Made 9 December 2021.
Laid before the Scottish Parliament 10 December 2021.
Coming into force 6 January 2022.

CONTENTS

S1.2   In accordance with section 4 of the Scottish Civil Justice Council and Criminal Legal Assistance Act 2013, the Court of Session has approved draft rules submitted to it by the Scottish Civil Justice Council with such modifications as it thinks appropriate.

The Court of Session therefore makes this Act of Sederunt under the powers conferred by section 14(7) of the Scottish Commission for Human Rights Act 2006, section 104(1) of the Courts Reform (Scotland) Act 2014 and all other powers enabling it to do so.

CHAPTER 1 CITATION, COMMENCEMENT AND APPLICATION ETC.

PART 1

PRELIMINARY MATTERS

Chapter 1

Citation, Commencement and Application etc.

Citation and commencement, etc.

1.1.—(1)   This Act of Sederunt may be cited as the Act of Sederunt (Sheriff Appeal Court Rules) 2021.

(2)   It comes into force on 6th January 2022.

(3)   A certified copy is to be inserted in the Books of Sederunt.

S1.3

Application

1.2.   These Rules apply to any appeal or application made under chapters 6 and 29 to 33 of these Rules.

S1.4

Interpretation

1.3.—(1)   In this Act of Sederunt—

S1.5

"the 2014 Act" means the Courts Reform (Scotland) Act 2014;

"advocate" means a practising member of the Faculty of Advocates;

"Chapter 7 procedure" has the meaning given by rule 7.1;

"Chapter 8 procedure" has the meaning given by rule 8.1;

"the Clerk" means the Clerk of the Sheriff Appeal Court;

"the Court" means the Sheriff Appeal Court;

"grounds of appeal" is to be construed in accordance with rule 6.2(2)(b);

"party litigant" has the meaning given by rule 4.1;

"procedural Appeal Sheriff" has the meaning given by paragraph 2(1) of schedule 1;

"procedural hearing" means a hearing under rule 7.9 or rule 29.13;

"sheriff court process" means—

    (a)   the sheriff court process for the cause that is appealed to the Court; or

    (b)   where the cause is recorded in an official book of the sheriff court, a copy of the record in that book certified by the sheriff clerk;

"sheriff's note" means a note setting out the reasons for the decision appealed against;

"solicitor" means a person qualified to practise as a solicitor under section 4 of the Solicitors (Scotland) Act 1980;

"timetable" means a timetable in—

    (a)   Form 7.2 issued under—

        (i)   rule 6.12(5)(a);

        (ii)   rule 7.2(1); or

        (iii)   rule 7.3(4)(b); or

    (b)   Form 29.5 issued under—

        (i)   rule 29.5(1);

        (ii)   rule 29.6(6)(a); or

(iii)   rule 29.6(7)(b).

(2)   In relation to an application under section 69(1) or 71(2) of the 2014 Act—

"appeal" includes that application;
"appellant" includes the applicant;
"note of appeal" includes an application in Form 29.2 or Form 29.14.

Computation of periods of time

S1.6 **1.4.**   If any period of time specified in these Rules expires on a Saturday, Sunday or public or court holiday, it is extended to expire on the next day that the office of the Clerk is open for civil business.

Administrative provisions

S1.7 **1.5.**   Schedule 1 makes provision about administrative arrangements for the Court, including its quorum.

Forms

S1.8 **1.6.**—(1)   Where there is a reference in these Rules to a form, it is a reference to that form in schedule 2.

(2)   Where these Rules require a form to be used, that form may be varied where the circumstances require it.

CHAPTER 2 RELIEF FOR FAILURE TO COMPLY

Part 2

General Provisions

Chapter 2

Relief for Failure to Comply

Relief for failure to comply with rules

2.1.—(1)   The Court may relieve a party from the consequences of a failure to comply with a provision in these Rules.   **S1.9**

(2)   The Court may do so only where the party shows that the failure is due to—

   (a)   mistake;

   (b)   oversight; or

   (c)   any other excusable cause.

(3)   Where relief is granted, the Court may—

   (a)   impose conditions that must be satisfied before relief is granted;

   (b)   make an order to enable the appeal to proceed as if the failure had not occurred.

Chapter 3

Sanctions for Failure to Comply

Circumstances where a party is in default

3.1.— A party is in default if that party fails—   **S1.10**
  (a) to comply with the timetable;
  (b) to implement an order of the Court within the period specified in the order;
  (c) to appear or be represented at any hearing; or
  (d) otherwise to comply with any requirement imposed on that party by these Rules.

Sanctions where a party is in default

3.2.—(1) This rule—   **S1.11**
  (a) applies where a party is in default;
  (b) but does not apply where a party is in default because the party has failed to comply with rule 18.4(1).

(2) The Court may make any order to secure the expeditious disposal of the appeal.

(3) In particular, the Court may either—
  (a) refuse the appeal, where the party in default is the appellant; or
  (b) allow the appeal, if the condition in paragraph (4) is satisfied, where either—
      (i) the party in default is the sole respondent; or
      (ii) every respondent is in default.

(4) The condition is that the appellant must show cause why the appeal should be allowed.

Chapter 4

Representation and support

Representation and support

4.1.—(1)   A natural person who is a party to proceedings may appear and act on that party's behalf.   **S1.12**

(2)   That person is to be known as a party litigant.

(3)   A party may be represented in any proceedings by—

(a)   a legal representative (see rule 4.2); or

(b)   a lay representative (see rule 4.3).

(4)   A lay supporter (see rule 4.5) may assist a party litigant with the conduct of any proceedings.

Legal representation

4.2.   A party is represented by a legal representative if that party is represented by an advocate or a solicitor.   **S1.13**

Lay representation: applications

4.3.—(1)   This rule does not apply where any other enactment makes provision for a party to a particular type of case to be represented by a lay representative.   **S1.14**

(2)   A party is represented by a lay representative if that party is represented by a person who is not a legal representative.

(3)   A party litigant may apply to the Court for permission to be represented by a lay representative.

(4)   An application is to be—

(a)   made by motion;

(b)   accompanied by a document in Form 4.3 signed by the prospective lay representative.

(5)   The Court may grant an application only if it considers that it would be in the interests of justice to do so.

(6)   Where the Court grants permission, it may—

(a)   do so in respect of one or more specified hearings;

(b)   withdraw permission of its own accord or on the motion of any party.

Lay representation: functions, conditions and duties

4.4.—(1)   A lay representative may represent a party at any hearing at which permission has been granted under rule 4.3 or where any other enactment makes provision for a party to be represented by a lay representative.   **S1.15**

(2)   The party must appear along with the lay representative at any hearing where the lay representative is to represent the party.

(3)   Where permission is granted under rule 4.3, the lay representative may do anything in the preparation or conduct of the hearing that the party may do.

(4)   A party may show any document (including a court document) or communicate any information about the proceedings to that party's lay representative without contravening any prohibition or restriction on the disclosure of the document or information.

(5)   Where a document or information is disclosed under paragraph (4), the lay representative is subject to any prohibition or restriction on the disclosure in the same way that the party is.

(6)   A lay representative must not receive, directly or indirectly, from the party any remuneration or other reward for assisting the party.

(7)   Any expenses incurred by a party in connection with a lay representative are not recoverable expenses in the proceedings.

Lay support: applications

S1.16   **4.5.**—(1)   A party litigant may apply to the Court for permission for a named person to assist the party litigant in the conduct of proceedings, and such a person is to be known as a lay supporter.

(2)   An application is to be made by motion.

(3)   The Court may refuse an application only if it is of the opinion that—

    (a)   the named person is an unsuitable person to act as a lay supporter (whether generally or in the proceedings concerned); or

    (b)   it would be contrary to the efficient administration of justice to grant it.

(4)   The Court, if satisfied that it would be contrary to the efficient administration of justice for permission to continue, may withdraw permission—

    (a)   of its own accord; or

    (b)   on the motion of any party.

Lay support: functions, conditions and duties

S1.17   **4.6.**—(1)   A lay supporter may assist a party by accompanying the party at hearings in court or in chambers.

(2)   A lay supporter may, if authorised by the party, assist the party by—

    (a)   providing moral support;

    (b)   helping to manage court documents and other papers;

    (c)   taking notes of the proceedings;

    (d)   quietly advising on—

        (i)   points of law and procedure;

        (ii)   issues which the party litigant might wish to raise with the Court.

(3)   A party may show any document (including a court document) or communicate any information about the proceedings to that party's lay supporter without contravening any prohibition or restriction on the disclosure of the document or information.

(4)   Where a document or information is disclosed under paragraph (3), the lay supporter is subject to any prohibition or restriction on the disclosure in the same way that the party is.

(5)   A lay supporter must not receive, directly or indirectly, from the party any remuneration or other reward for assisting the party.

(6)   Any expenses incurred by a party in connection with a lay supporter are not recoverable expenses in the proceedings.

CHAPTER 5 INTIMATION AND LODGING ETC.

Chapter 5

Intimation and Lodging etc.

Interpretation of this Chapter

5.1.—(1)   In this Chapter— S1.18

"first class post" means a postal service which seeks to deliver documents or other things by post no later than the next working day in all or the majority of cases;

"intimating party" means any party who has to give intimation in accordance with rule 5.2(1);

"receiving party" means any party to whom intimation is to be given in accordance with rule 5.2;

"recorded delivery" means a postal service which provides for the delivery of documents or other things by post to be recorded.

(2)   Where this Chapter authorises intimation to be given by electronic means—

    (a)   intimation may only be given by this method if the intimating party and the solicitor for the receiving party have notified the Court that they will accept intimation by electronic means at a specified email address;

    (b)   the intimation is to be sent to the specified email address of the solicitor for the receiving party.

(3)   Where this Chapter authorises a document to be lodged by electronic means, it must be sent to the email address of the Court.

Intimation

5.2.—(1)   Unless the Court orders otherwise, where— S1.19

    (a)   any provision in these Rules requires a party to—

        (i)   lodge any document;

        (ii)   intimate any other matter; or

    (b)   the Court orders a party to intimate something,

intimation must be given to every other party.

(2)   Where intimation relates to the lodging of a document, a copy of that document must be provided at the same time as intimation is made.

(3)   Where the Court makes an order, the Clerk is to intimate the order to every party.

Methods of intimation

5.3.—(1)   Intimation may be given to a receiving party who is a party litigant by— S1.20

    (a)   the method specified in rule 5.4;

    (b)   any of the methods specified in rule 5.5.

(2)   Intimation may be given to a receiving party who is represented by a solicitor by—

    (a)   the method specified in rule 5.4;

    (b)   any of the methods specified in rule 5.5;

    (c)   any of the methods specified in rule 5.6.

Methods of intimation: recorded delivery

S1.21

5.4. An intimating party may give intimation by recorded delivery to the receiving party.

Methods of intimation: by sheriff officer

S1.22

5.5.—(1) A sheriff officer may give intimation on behalf of an intimating party by—

    (a) delivering it personally to the receiving party; or

    (b) leaving it in the hands of—

        (i) a resident at the receiving party's dwelling place; or

        (ii) an employee at the receiving party's place of business.

  (2) Where a sheriff officer has been unsuccessful in giving intimation in accordance with paragraph (1), the sheriff officer may give intimation by—

    (a) depositing it in the receiving party's dwelling place or place of business; or

    (b) leaving it at the receiving party's dwelling place or place of business in such a way that it is likely to come to the attention of that party.

Additional methods of intimation where receiving party represented by solicitor

S1.23

5.6.—(1) An intimating party may give intimation to the solicitor for the receiving party by—

    (a) delivering it personally to the solicitor;

    (b) delivering it to a document exchange of which the solicitor is a member;

    (c) first class post;

    (d) fax;

    (e) electronic means.

  (2) Where intimation is given by the method in paragraph (1)(a), (d) or (e) no later than 1700 hours on any day, the date of intimation is that day.

  (3) Where intimation is given by the method in—

    (a) paragraph (1)(b) or (c); or

    (b) paragraph (1)(a), (d) or (e) after 1700 hours on any day,

the date of intimation is the next day.

Lodging

S1.24

5.7.—(1) Where any provision in these Rules requires a party to lodge a document, it is to be lodged with the Clerk.

  (2) A document may be lodged by—

    (a) delivering it personally to the office of the Clerk;

    (b) delivering it to a document exchange of which the Clerk is a member;

    (c) first class post;

    (d) fax;

    (e) electronic means, provided that parties have provided an email address in terms of rule 13.5.

Part 3

Initiation and Progress of an Appeal

Chapter 6

Initiation and Progress of an Appeal

Application of this Chapter

6.1. This Chapter applies to an appeal against a decision of a sheriff in civil proceedings except—   **S1.25**

- (a) an application for a new trial under section 69(1) of the 2014 Act (see Chapter 29);
- (b) an application to enter a jury verdict under section 71(2) of the 2014 Act (see Chapter 29);
- (c) an appeal under section 38 of the Sheriff Courts (Scotland) Act 1971 (see Chapter 30);
- (d) an appeal under section 82 of the 2014 Act (see Chapter 31);
- (e) an appeal by stated case under section 163(1), 164(1), 165(1) or 167(1) of the Children's Hearings (Scotland) Act 2011 (see Chapter 32);
- (f)[1] an appeal under section 38(3), 46(3) or 67(3) of the Age of Criminal Responsibility (Scotland) Act 2019 (see Chapter 33);
- (g) an appeal against an interlocutor granting decree of divorce in a simplified divorce application (see rule 33.81 of the Ordinary Cause Rules 1993);
- (h) an appeal against an interlocutor granting decree of dissolution of civil partnership in a simplified dissolution of civil partnership application (see rule 33A.74 of the Ordinary Cause Rules 1993).

Form of appeal

6.2.—(1) An appeal is made by lodging a note of appeal in Form 6.2.   **S1.26**

(2) The note of appeal must—

- (a) specify—
    - (i) the decision complained of;
    - (ii) the date on which the decision was made;
    - (iii) the date on which it was intimated to the appellant;
    - (iv) any other relevant information;
- (b) state the grounds of appeal in brief specific numbered paragraphs setting out concisely the grounds on which it is proposed that the appeal should be allowed;
- (c) have appended to it a copy of the interlocutor containing the decision appealed against;
- (d) where the sheriff's note is available, have appended to it a copy of the note;
- (e) where the sheriff's note is not available, indicate whether the appellant—

---

[1] As amended by Act of Sederunt (Rules of the Court of Session 1994 and Sheriff Appeal Court Rules Amendment) (Miscellaneous) 2022 (SSI 2022/135) para.(3).

> (i) has requested that the sheriff writes a note and is awaiting its production;
> (ii) requests that the sheriff write a note; or
> (iii) considers that the appeal is sufficiently urgent that the Court should hear and determine the appeal without the sheriff's note;

(f) state whether, taking into account the matters in rule 6.11(3), the appellant considers that the appeal should be appointed to Chapter 7 procedure or Chapter 8 procedure;

(g) be signed;

(h) where the appellant is represented by a solicitor, specify the name and business address of the solicitor.

Time for appeal

S1.27

6.3.—(1) An appeal must be made either—

(a) within 28 days after the date on which the decision appealed against was given; or

(b) where permission to appeal is required, within 7 days after the date on which permission was granted if that results in a later date.

(2) This rule does not apply where the enactment under which the appeal is made specifies a period within which the appeal must be made.

Applications to appeal out of time

S1.28

6.4.—(1) This rule applies where the enactment under which the appeal is made—

(a) specifies a period within which the appeal must be made; and

(b) provides that a party may apply to the Court to allow an appeal to be made outwith that period.

(2) An application to allow an appeal to be received out of time is to be made by motion.

(3) That motion is to be made when the note of appeal is lodged.

(4) The application is to be determined by a procedural Appeal Sheriff.

(5) Where a motion to allow an appeal to be received out of time is determined—

(a) the Clerk is to—

> (i) notify the sheriff clerk of the outcome of the application;
> (ii) transmit the note of appeal and the Court's interlocutor to the sheriff clerk;

(b) the sheriff clerk is to place the note of appeal in the process.

(6) Where an application to allow an appeal to proceed out of time is granted, the appeal will proceed as if it had been made in time.

Order for intimation and answers

S1.29

6.5.—(1) Subject to paragraph (2), on the first available court day after the appeal is lodged, the Clerk must make an order for—

(a) intimation of the appeal, within 7 days after the date of the order, to be given to—

> (i) the respondent;
> (ii) any other person who appears to have an interest in the appeal;

(b) any person on whom the appeal is intimated to lodge answers in Form 6.5, if so advised, within 14 days after the date of intimation.

(2) The procedural Appeal Sheriff may vary the periods of 7 days and 14 days mentioned in paragraph (1)—

    (a)   of the procedural Appeal Sheriff's own accord; or

    (b)   on cause shown, on the application of the appellant.

    (3)   That application must—

    (a)   be included in the note of appeal;

    (b)   give reasons for varying the period.

    (4)   Where an appeal is intimated under this rule, the appellant must lodge a certificate of intimation in Form 6.5-A within 14 days after the date of intimation, or such other period as the procedural Appeal Sheriff may direct.

    (5)   In the answers, the respondent or other interested party must state—

    (a)   his or her view on whether the appeal should be appointed to Chapter 7 procedure or Chapter 8 procedure;

    (b)   why he or she has reached that view, taking into account the matters mentioned in rule 6.11(3).

Cross-appeals

6.6.—(1)   A respondent who seeks to—   **S1.30**

    (a)   appeal against any decision of the sheriff; or

    (b)   challenge the grounds on which the sheriff made the decision appealed against,

may lodge grounds of cross-appeal in Form 6.6 within the period for lodging answers in accordance with an order under rule 6.5(1)(b) or, as the case may be, rule 6.5(2), together with a certificate of intimation in Form 6.5-A.

    (2)   The appellant may lodge answers to the respondent's grounds of cross-appeal within 14 days after the grounds are intimated to the appellant.

Urgent disposal procedure

6.7.—(1)   The procedural Appeal Sheriff may order urgent disposal of an appeal—   **S1.31**

    (a)   of the procedural Appeal Sheriff's own accord; or

    (b)   on the application of the appellant or a respondent.

    (2)   The Clerk may refer an appeal to the procedural Appeal Sheriff to consider ordering urgent disposal.

    (3)   Where the appellant or a respondent seeks urgent disposal, an application for urgent disposal is to be made by motion.

    (4)   An application may be made—

    (a)   by the appellant, when the note of appeal is lodged;

    (b)   by the respondent, no later than the expiry of the period for lodging answers specified in rule 6.5(1)(b).

    (5)   Where the decision appealed against concerns an order made by the sheriff—

    (a)   under section 11(1) of the Children (Scotland) Act 1995 (court orders relating to parental responsibilities etc.);

    (b)   in relation to adoption; or

    (c)   in relation to permanence,

the appellant must seek urgent disposal.

    (6)   Where the procedural Appeal Sheriff proposes to order urgent disposal of the procedural Appeal Sheriff's own accord—

    (a)   the Clerk must notify every party to the appeal;

    (b)   any party who objects to urgent disposal may make representations within such time and in such manner as the procedural Appeal Sheriff orders.

Urgent disposal objection: determination

S1.32

6.8.—(1)   Where an application for urgent disposal made under rule 6.7(4) is opposed or a party makes representations objecting to urgent disposal in accordance with rule 6.7(6)(b), before ordering urgent disposal the procedural Appeal Sheriff must—

    (a)   give parties an opportunity to be heard on the matter; or

    (b)   order the Clerk to intimate to parties that the matter will be considered on written submissions and specify the date by which such submissions are to be lodged.

(2)   At a hearing under paragraph (1)(a) or in written submissions lodged under paragraph (1)(b), the parties must provide the procedural Appeal Sheriff with an assessment of the likely duration of the hearing to determine the appeal.

(3)   When ordering urgent disposal of an appeal, the procedural Appeal Sheriff must make an order specifying—

    (a)   the procedure to be followed in the appeal;

    (b)   the number of appeal sheriffs who will hear the appeal, taking into account the matters mentioned in rule 6.11(3); and

    (c)   where the appeal is to proceed under Chapter 7 procedure, the periods for complying with each procedural step.

(4)   The procedural Appeal Sheriff must not make an order under rule 6.11(2) until the matter of urgent disposal has been determined.

Questions about competency

S1.33

6.9.—(1)   A question about the competency of an appeal or cross-appeal may be referred to the procedural Appeal Sheriff by—

    (a)   any party; or

    (b)   the Clerk.

(2)   A party may refer a question by lodging a reference in Form 6.9.

(3)   A party may refer a question within the period for lodging answers, in accordance with rule 6.5(1)(b) or, as the case may be, rule 6.6(2).

(4)   The Clerk may refer a question at any time until the procedural Appeal Sheriff makes an order under rule 6.11(2).

(5)   When a reference is made, the Clerk must fix a hearing and intimate the date and time of that hearing to the parties.

(6)   When a reference is made by the Clerk and the procedural Appeal Sheriff considers that a question of competency arises, the order fixing the hearing must specify the question about the competency of the appeal or cross-appeal.

(7)   The order fixing the hearing on a reference must specify the date by which notes of argument are to be lodged.

(8)   The note of argument must—

    (a)   give fair notice of the submissions the party intends to make on the question of competency; and

    (b)   comply with the requirements in rule 7.7(3).

(9)   Paragraphs (4) and (5) of rule 7.7 apply to the note of argument.

Questions about competency: determination

S1.34

6.10.—(1)   At a hearing on the competency of an appeal, the procedural Appeal Sheriff may—

    (a)   refuse the appeal as incompetent;

    (b)   find the appeal to be competent; or

    (c)   refer the question of competency to the Court.

(2)   The procedural Appeal Sheriff may make an order as to the expenses of the reference.

(3)   Where the question of competency is referred to the Court, it may—

    (a)   refuse the appeal as incompetent; or

    (b)   find the appeal to be competent.

(4)   The Court may make an order as to the expenses of the reference.

Initial case management of appeals

6.11.—(1)   This rule does not apply to an appeal that has been ordered for urgent disposal.   **S1.35**

(2)   Subject to rule 6.8(4), on expiry of the period for lodging answers and any grounds of cross-appeal, the procedural Appeal Sheriff must appoint an appeal to—

    (a)   Chapter 7 procedure; or

    (b)   Chapter 8 procedure.

(3)   An appeal is to be appointed to such procedure as the procedural Appeal Sheriff considers proportionate for the disposal of the appeal, having regard to the following—

    (a)   any representations made by the parties;

    (b)   the value and importance of the claim;

    (c)   the complexity of the issues of fact and law raised by the appeal or the cross appeal;

    (d)   the presumption in paragraph (4).

(4)   Without prejudice to the generality of paragraph (3), the following are presumed to be appropriate for Chapter 8 procedure in the absence of special circumstances—

    (a)   appeals from procedural decisions;

    (b)   appeals against decisions—

        (i)   granting decree by default;

        (ii)   refusing a reponing note;

        (iii)   granting interim or summary decree;

        (iv)   sisting an action.

(5)   The Clerk must intimate an order under this rule to parties.

Sist of appeals

6.12.—(1)   Any party may apply by motion to—   **S1.36**

    (a)   sist the appeal for a specified period; or

    (b)   recall the sist.

(2)   An application to sist the appeal may only be granted on cause shown.

(3)   The procedural Appeal Sheriff may—

    (a)   grant the application;

    (b)   refuse the application; or

    (c)   make an order not sought in the application, where the procedural Appeal Sheriff considers that doing so would secure the expeditious disposal of the appeal.

(4)   Where the procedural Appeal Sheriff makes an order sisting the appeal, the Clerk must discharge any hearing already fixed under rule 7.2(2), rule 7.9(3)(a) or rule 8.2(1)(a).

(5)   When a sist in an appeal under Chapter 7 procedure is recalled or expires, the Clerk must—

    (a)   issue a revised timetable in Form 7.2; and

    (b)   fix a procedural hearing.

(6)   When a sist in an appeal under Chapter 8 procedure is recalled or expires, the Clerk must—

    (a)   fix a procedural hearing or a hearing of the appeal; and

    (b)   intimate the date and time of the procedural hearing or appeal to parties.

Chapter 7

Procedure Before Three Appeal Sheriffs

Application of this Chapter

7.1. This Chapter applies to an appeal which has been appointed to proceed under procedure before three Appeal Sheriffs, to be known as Chapter 7 procedure.

S1.37

Timetable in appeal

7.2.—(1) The Clerk must issue a timetable in Form 7.2 when an appeal is appointed to Chapter 7 procedure.

S1.38

(2) When the Clerk issues a timetable, the Clerk must also fix a procedural hearing to take place after completion of the procedural steps specified in paragraph (4).

(3) The timetable specifies—

    (a) the dates by which parties must comply with those procedural steps;

    (b) the date and time of the procedural hearing.

(4) The procedural steps are the steps mentioned in the first column of the following table, provision in respect of which is found in the rule mentioned in the second column—

Procedural step	Rule
Lodging of appeal print	7.4(1)
Lodging of appendices to appeal print	7.5(1)
Giving notice that the appellant considers appendix unnecessary	7.6(1)
Lodging of notes of argument	7.7(1)
Lodging of estimates of duration of appeal hearing	7.8

Variation of timetable

7.3.—(1) Any party may apply by motion to vary the timetable.

S1.39

(2) An application to vary the timetable may only be granted on cause shown.

(3) The procedural Appeal Sheriff may—

    (a) grant the application;

    (b) refuse the application; or

    (c) make an order not sought in the application, where the procedural Appeal Sheriff considers that doing so would secure the expeditious disposal of the appeal.

(4) Where the procedural Appeal Sheriff makes an order varying the timetable, the Clerk must—

    (a) discharge the procedural hearing fixed under rule 7.2(2);

    (b) issue a revised timetable in Form 7.2;

    (c) fix a procedural hearing.

Appeal print

7.4.—(1) The appellant must lodge an appeal print within 21 days after the timetable is issued under rule 7.2(1).

S1.40

(2)   An appeal print must contain—

    (a)   the pleadings in the sheriff court process;

    (b)   the interlocutors in the sheriff court process;

    (c)   the sheriff's note setting out the reasons for the decision appealed against, if it is available.

(3)   Where the appeal is directed at the refusal of the sheriff to allow the pleadings to be amended, the appeal print must also contain the text of the proposed amendment.

Appendix to appeal print: contents

S1.41
    7.5.—(1)   The appellant must lodge an appendix to the appeal print no later than 14 days before the procedural hearing, unless rule 7.6(1) is complied with.

(2)   The appendix must contain—

    (a)   any document lodged in the sheriff court process that is founded upon in the grounds of appeal;

    (b)   the notes of evidence from any proof, if it is sought to submit them for consideration by the Court.

(3)   Where the sheriff's note has not been included in the appeal print and it subsequently becomes available, the appellant must—

    (a)   include it in the appendix where the appendix has not yet been lodged; or

    (b)   lodge a supplementary appendix containing the sheriff's note.

(4)   The parties must—

    (a)   discuss the contents of the appendix;

    (b)   co-operate in making up the appendix.

(5)   Where the Court at any stage considers further documents are necessary for the determination of the appeal, the appellant must lodge a supplementary appendix containing those documents.

Appendix to appeal print considered unnecessary

S1.42
    7.6.—(1)   Where the appellant considers that it is not necessary to lodge an appendix, the appellant must, no later than 14 days before the procedural hearing—

    (a)   give written notice of that fact to the Clerk;

    (b)   intimate that notice to every respondent.

(2)   Where the appellant complies with paragraph (1), the respondent may apply by motion for an order requiring the appellant to lodge an appendix.

(3)   An application under paragraph (2) must specify the documents or notes of evidence that the respondent considers should be included in the appendix.

(4)   In disposing of an application, the procedural Appeal Sheriff may—

    (a)   grant the application and make an order requiring the appellant to lodge an appendix;

    (b)   refuse the application and make an order requiring the respondent to lodge an appendix; or

    (c)   refuse the application and make no order.

(5)   Where the procedural Appeal Sheriff makes an order under paragraph (4)(a) or (b), that order must specify—

    (a)   the documents or notes or evidence to be included in the appendix;

    (b)   the time within which the appendix must be lodged.

Notes of argument

7.7.—(1) The parties must lodge notes of argument no later than 14 days before the procedural hearing.   **S1.43**

(2) A note of argument must summarise briefly the submissions the party intends to develop at the appeal hearing.

(3) A note of argument must—
- (a) state, in brief numbered paragraphs, the points that the party intends to make;
- (b) after each point, identify by means of a page or paragraph reference the relevant passage in any notes of evidence or other document on which the party relies in support of the point;
- (c) for every authority that is cited—
    - (i) state the proposition of law that the authority demonstrates;
    - (ii) identify the page or paragraph references for the parts of the authority that support the proposition;
- (d) cite only one authority for each proposition of law, unless additional citation is necessary for a proper presentation of the argument.

(4) Where a note of argument has been lodged and the party lodging it subsequently becomes aware that an argument in the note is not to be insisted upon, that party must—
- (a) give written notice of that fact to the Clerk;
- (b) intimate that notice to every other party.

(5) Where a party wishes to advance an argument at a hearing that is not contained in that party's note of argument, the party must apply by motion for leave to advance the argument.

Estimates of duration of appeal hearing

7.8. The parties must lodge estimates of the duration of any appeal hearing required to dispose of the appeal in Form 7.8 no later than 14 days before the procedural hearing.   **S1.44**

Procedural hearing

7.9.—(1) At a procedural hearing, the procedural Appeal Sheriff must ascertain the state of preparation of the parties, so far as reasonably practicable.   **S1.45**

(2) The procedural Appeal Sheriff may—
- (a) determine that parties are ready to proceed to an appeal hearing; or
- (b) determine that further procedure is required.

(3) Where the procedural Appeal Sheriff determines that parties are ready to proceed—
- (a) the procedural Appeal Sheriff must fix an appeal hearing;
- (b) the Clerk must intimate the date and time of that hearing to the parties;
- (c) the procedural Appeal Sheriff may make an order specifying further steps to be taken by the parties before the hearing.

(4) Where the procedural Appeal Sheriff determines that further procedure is required, the procedural Appeal Sheriff—
- (a) must make an order to secure the expeditious disposal of the appeal;
- (b) may direct the Clerk to fix a further procedural hearing and intimate the date and time of that hearing to parties.

Authorities

S1.46

7.10.—(1) When an appeal hearing is fixed, the appellant must, after consultation with the respondent and any other party to the appeal, lodge a joint list of authorities upon which each party intends to rely at the hearing.

(2) The appellant must lodge the joint list by the date specified in the interlocutor that fixes the appeal hearing.

(3) The joint list of authorities must not include—

    (a) authorities for propositions not in dispute;

    (b) more than 10 authorities, unless permission has previously been granted by the Court on cause shown for the lodging of additional authorities.

(4) The Court may make an order requiring parties to lodge a joint bundle of photocopies or electronic versions of the authorities or digital links to them.

(5) Joint lists of authorities which do not conform with this rule may be rejected.

(6) The Court may find no expenses are payable, or may modify any expenses, where authorities are included unnecessarily.

Transmission of sheriff court process

S1.47

7.11.—(1) The Court may order—

    (a) of its own accord;

    (b) on cause shown, where any party to the appeal applies for such an order by motion,

that the sheriff court process, or any part of it, must be transmitted to the Clerk.

(2) Where the procedural Appeal Sheriff makes such an order, the Clerk must send a copy of the order to the sheriff clerk.

(3) Within 4 days after receipt of the order, the sheriff clerk must—

    (a) send written notice to each party to the cause;

    (b) certify on the interlocutor sheet that sub-paragraph (a) has been complied with;

    (c) transmit the sheriff court process, or the specified part of it, to the Clerk.

(4) On receipt of the sheriff court process, the Clerk must—

    (a) mark the date of receipt on—

        (i) the interlocutor sheet, where the entire process is transmitted;

        (ii) the part of process that has been transmitted, where the procedural Appeal Sheriff has specified that only part of the process is to be transmitted;

    (b) send written notice of that date to the parties.

(5) Where the Clerk or a sheriff clerk fails to comply with this rule—

    (a) that does not affect the validity of the appeal;

    (b) the procedural Appeal Sheriff may, as the procedural Appeal Sheriff thinks fit, make an order to enable the appeal to proceed as if the failure had not occurred.

Extension of notes of evidence

S1.48

7.12. It is not necessary to produce notes of evidence in relation to any issue in respect of which the parties are agreed that the decision appealed against is not to be submitted to review.

Referral to family mediation

S1.49

7.13.—(1) Where the decision appealed against concerns an order made by the sheriff under section 11(1) of the Children (Scotland) Act 1995 (court orders relating to parental responsibilities etc.), the procedural Appeal Sheriff may refer that matter to a family mediator.

(2)   In this rule, "family mediator" means a person accredited as a mediator in family mediation to an organisation which is concerned with such mediation and which is approved for the purposes of the Civil Evidence (Family Mediation) (Scotland) Act 1995 by the Lord President of the Court of Session.

Application to transfer appeal to Chapter 8 procedure

7.14.—(1)   The procedural Appeal Sheriff may—   **S1.50**

    (a)   of the procedural Appeal Sheriff's own accord; or

    (b)   on the application of any party,

order that an appeal is to proceed under Chapter 8 procedure instead of Chapter 7 procedure.

(2)   An application is to be made by motion.

(3)   The procedural Appeal Sheriff may only make such an order if satisfied that, taking into account the matters in rule 6.11(3), it is no longer appropriate for the appeal to proceed under Chapter 7 procedure.

(4)   That order must appoint the appeal to proceed under Chapter 8 procedure and specify—

    (a)   the procedure to be followed in the appeal;

    (b)   the periods for complying with each procedural step.

Chapter 8

Procedure Before One Appeal Sheriff

Application of this Chapter

8.1. This Chapter applies to an appeal which has been appointed to proceed under procedure before one Appeal Sheriff, to be known as Chapter 8 procedure.

S1.51

Hearing of appeal

8.2.—(1) When an appeal has been appointed to proceed under Chapter 8 procedure, the Court must order the Clerk to—

S1.52

(a) fix a hearing and intimate the date and time of that hearing to parties; or
(b) intimate to parties that the appeal will be considered on written submissions and specify the date by which such submissions are to be lodged.

(2) The Court may make any order required to regulate procedure in the appeal.

Notes of argument

8.3.—(1) This rule applies where parties are ordered to lodge notes of argument.

S1.53

(2) The parties must lodge notes of argument by the date specified in the order that fixes the hearing or in such other order the Court may make to regulate procedure in the appeal.

(3) A note of argument must summarise briefly the submissions the party intends to develop at the hearing.

(4) A note of argument must—

(a) state, in brief numbered paragraphs, the points that the party intends to make;
(b) after each point, identify by means of a page or paragraph reference the relevant passage in any notes of evidence or other document on which the party relies in support of the point;
(c) for every authority that is cited—
    (i) state the proposition of law that the authority demonstrates;
    (ii) identify the page or paragraph references for the parts of the authority that support the proposition;
(d) cite only one authority for each proposition of law, unless additional citation is necessary for a proper presentation of the argument.

(5) Where a note of argument has been lodged and the party lodging it subsequently becomes aware that an argument in the note is not to be insisted upon, that party must—

(a) give written notice of that fact to the Clerk;
(b) intimate that notice to every other party.

(6) Where a party wishes to advance an argument at a hearing that is not contained in that party's note of argument, the party must apply by motion for leave to advance the argument.

Authorities

8.4.—(1) This rule applies where parties are ordered to lodge authorities.

S1.54

(2)   The appellant must, after consultation with the respondent and any other party to the appeal, lodge a joint list of authorities upon which each party intends to rely at the hearing.

(3)   The appellant must lodge the joint list by the date specified in the order that fixes the hearing or in such other order the Court may make to regulate procedure in the appeal.

(4)   The joint list of authorities must not include—

    (a)   authorities for propositions not in dispute;

    (b)   more than 10 authorities, unless permission has previously been granted by the Court on cause shown for the lodging of additional authorities.

(5)   The Court may make an order requiring parties to lodge a joint bundle of photocopies or electronic versions of the authorities or digital links to them.

(6)   Joint lists of authorities which do not conform with this rule may be rejected.

(7)   The Court may find no expenses are payable, or may modify any award of expenses, where authorities are included unnecessarily.

Application to transfer appeal to Chapter 7 procedure

S1.55

8.5.—(1)   The procedural Appeal Sheriff may—

    (a)   of the procedural Appeal Sheriff's own accord; or

    (b)   on the application of any party,

order that an appeal is to proceed as an appeal under Chapter 7 procedure instead of Chapter 8 procedure.

(2)   An application is to be made by motion.

(3)   The procedural Appeal Sheriff may only make such an order if satisfied that, taking into account the matters in rule 6.11(3), it is no longer appropriate for the appeal to proceed under Chapter 8 procedure.

(4)   That order must appoint the appeal to proceed under Chapter 7 procedure and specify the procedure to be followed in the appeal.

PART 4

DISPOSAL OF AN APPEAL

Chapter 9

Refusal of Appeal Due to Delay

Application to refuse appeal due to delay

9.1.—(1)   Any party may apply to the procedural Appeal Sheriff to refuse the appeal if the conditions in paragraph (2) are met.

(2)   The conditions are that—

   (a)   there has been an inordinate and inexcusable delay by—

      (i)   another party;

      (ii)   another party's solicitor, lay representative or other agent; and

   (b)   unfairness has resulted from that delay.

(3)   An application is to be made by motion.

(4)   That motion must specify the grounds on which refusal of the appeal is sought.

S1.56

Determination of application to refuse appeal due to delay

9.2.—(1)   The procedural Appeal Sheriff may refuse the appeal if the procedural Appeal Sheriff considers that—

   (a)   there has been an inordinate and inexcusable delay on the part of—

      (i)   any party;

      (ii)   any party's solicitor, lay representative or other agent; and

   (b)   such delay results in unfairness specific to the factual circumstances, including the procedural circumstances, of the appeal.

(2)   The procedural Appeal Sheriff must take into account the procedural consequences of allowing the appeal to proceed for—

   (a)   the parties to the appeal;

   (b)   the efficient disposal of business in the Court.

S1.57

CHAPTER 10 ABANDONMENT OF APPEAL

Chapter 10

Abandonment of Appeal

Application to abandon appeal

10.1.—(1)   An appellant may apply to the Court to abandon an appeal by lodging a minute of abandonment.

S1.58

(2)   The appellant must, at the same time as lodging a minute of abandonment, apply by motion to abandon in terms of the minute of abandonment.

(3)   Where all of the parties consent to the abandonment of the appeal, the Court must refuse the appeal.

(4)   Where the other parties do not consent to the abandonment of the appeal, the Court may either—

    (a)   refuse the application; or

    (b)   grant the application and refuse the appeal.

(5)   If the Court refuses an appeal under this rule, it may make an order as to the expenses of the appeal.

(6)   If the Court refuses an application, it may make an order as to the expenses of the application.

Chapter 11

Remit to the Court of Session

Application to remit appeal to the Court of Session

11.1.—(1)   An application under section 112 of the 2014 Act (remit of appeal   **S1.59**
from the Sheriff Appeal Court to the Court of Session) is to be made by motion.

(2)   Within 4 days after the Court has made an order remitting an appeal to the
Court of Session, the Clerk must—

   (a)   give notice of the remit to each party;

   (b)   certify on the interlocutor sheet that sub-paragraph (a) has been
      complied with;

   (c)   transmit the process to the Deputy Principal Clerk of Session.

(3)   Failure by the Clerk to comply with paragraph (2)(a) or (b) does not affect
the validity of a remit.

CHAPTER 12 APPLICATIONS FOR PERMISSION TO APPEAL TO THE COURT OF SESSION

Chapter 12

Applications for Permission to Appeal to the Court of Session

Application of this Chapter

12.1. This Chapter applies where a party seeks the permission of the Court to appeal to the Court of Session against a decision of the Court constituting final judgment in civil proceedings under section 113 of the 2014 Act (appeal from the Sheriff Appeal Court to the Court of Session). **S1.60**

Applications for permission to appeal

12.2.—(1) An application to the Court for permission to appeal to the Court of Session is to be made in Form 12.2. **S1.61**

(2) Such an application must be lodged within 14 days after the date on which the Court gave its final judgment on the appeal.

(3) When an application is made, the Court must order the Clerk to either—

    (a) fix a hearing and intimate the time and date of that hearing to the parties to the appeal; or

    (b) intimate to parties that the application is to be considered on written submissions and specify the date by which such submissions are to be lodged.

(4) The application is, so far as reasonably practicable, to be considered by the Appeal Sheriff or Appeal Sheriffs who made the decision in respect of which permission to appeal is sought.

Applications for leave to appeal

12.3.—(1) In any appeal to which section 113(4) of the Courts Reform (Scotland) Act 2014 applies and leave to appeal is required, a motion seeking leave of the Court must be lodged within 14 days after the date on which the Court gave its final judgment on the appeal. **S1.62**

(2) When such a motion is lodged, the Court must order the Clerk to either—

    (a) fix a hearing and intimate the time and date of that hearing to the parties to the appeal; or

    (b) intimate to parties that the motion is to be considered on written submissions and specify the date by which such submissions are to be lodged.

(3) The motion is, so far as reasonably practicable, to be considered by the Appeal Sheriff or Appeal Sheriffs who made the decision in respect of which leave to appeal is sought.

Part 5

Incidental Procedure: Standard Procedures

Chapter 13

Motions: General

Interpretation

13.1.—(1)   In this Chapter, Chapter 14 and Chapter 15—   **S1.63**

"court day" means a day on which the office of the Clerk is open;

"court day 1" means the court day on which a motion is treated as being intimated under rule 14.1;

"court day 3" means the second court day after court day 1;

"court day 4" means the third court day after court day 1;

"lodging party" means the party lodging the motion;

"receiving party" means a party receiving the intimation of the motion from the lodging party;

"transacting motion business" means—

      (a)   intimating and lodging motions;

      (b)   receiving intimation of motions;

      (c)   intimating consent or opposition to motions;

      (d)   receiving intimation of opposition to motions.

(2)   In this Chapter and Chapter 14, a reference to—

  (a)   the address of a party is a reference to the email address included in the list maintained under rule 13.5(4) of either—

      (i)   that party's solicitor; or

      (ii)   that party;

  (b)   the address of the court is a reference to the email address of the court included in that list under rule 13.5(5).

Making of motions

13.2.   A motion may be made either—   **S1.64**

  (a)   orally, in accordance with rule 13.3; or

  (b)   in writing, in accordance with rule 13.4.

Oral motions

13.3.—(1)   A motion may be made orally during any hearing.   **S1.65**

(2)   Such a motion may only be made with leave of the Court.

Written motions

13.4.—(1)   A motion in writing is made by lodging it with the Clerk in accordance with Chapter 14 or Chapter 15.   **S1.66**

(2)   Chapter 14 applies where each party to an appeal has provided to the Clerk an email address for the purpose of transacting motion business.

(3)   Chapter 15 applies where a party to an appeal has not provided to the Clerk an email address for the purpose of transacting motion business.

Provision of email addresses to the Clerk

S1.67   **13.5.**—(1)   A solicitor representing a party in an appeal must provide to the Clerk an email address for the purpose of transacting motion business.

(2)   A solicitor who does not have suitable facilities for transacting motion business by email may make a declaration in writing to that effect, which must be—

(a)   sent to the Clerk;

(b)   intimated to each of the other parties to the appeal.

(3)   A party who is not represented by a solicitor may provide to the Clerk an email address for the purpose of transacting motion business.

(4)   The Clerk must maintain a list of the email addresses provided for the purpose of transacting motion business, which must be published in up to date form on the website of the Scottish Courts and Tribunals Service.

(5)   The Clerk must also include on that list an email address of the Court for the purpose of lodging motions.

Grounds for written motion

S1.68   **13.6.**   A motion in writing must specify the grounds on which it is made.

Determination of unopposed motions in writing

S1.69   **13.7.**—(1)   The Clerk may determine any unopposed motion in writing other than a motion which seeks a final interlocutor.

(2)   Where the Clerk considers that such a motion should not be granted, the Clerk must refer the motion to the procedural Appeal Sheriff.

(3)   The procedural Appeal Sheriff is to determine—

(a)   a motion referred under paragraph (2);

(b)   an unopposed motion which seeks a final interlocutor,

in chambers without the appearance of parties, unless the procedural Appeal Sheriff otherwise determines.

Issuing of orders by email

S1.70   **13.8.**   Where the Court makes an order determining a motion which was lodged in accordance with Chapter 14, the Clerk must email a copy of the order to the addresses of the lodging party and every receiving party.

Chapter 14

Motions Lodged By Email

Intimation of motions by email

14.1.—(1)   The lodging party must give intimation of that party's intention to   **S1.71**
lodge the motion, and of the terms of the motion, to every other party by sending an
email in Form 14.1 to the addresses of every party.

(2)   The requirement under paragraph (1) to give intimation of a motion to a
party by email does not apply where that party—

  (a)   has not lodged answers within the period of notice for lodging those
        answers;
  (b)   has withdrawn or is deemed to have withdrawn those answers; or
  (c)   became a party to the appeal by minute, but has withdrawn or is deemed
        to have withdrawn that minute.

(3)   A motion intimated under this rule must be intimated no later than 1700
hours on a court day.

Opposition to motions

14.2.—(1)   A receiving party must intimate any opposition to a motion by send-   **S1.72**
ing an email in Form 14.2 to the address of the lodging party.

(2)   Any opposition to a motion must be intimated to the lodging party no later
than 1700 hours on court day 3.

(3)   Late opposition to a motion must be sent to the address of the Court and
may only be allowed with the leave of the procedural Appeal Sheriff, on cause
shown.

Consent to motions

14.3.   Where a receiving party seeks to consent to a motion, that party may do so   **S1.73**
by sending an email confirming the consent to the address of the lodging party.

Lodging unopposed motions

14.4.—(1)   This rule applies where no opposition to a motion has been intimated.   **S1.74**

(2)   The motion must be lodged by the lodging party no later than 1230 hours on
court day 4 by sending an email in Form 14.1 headed "Unopposed motion" to the
address of the court.

(3)   That motion is to be determined by 1700 hours on court day 4.

(4)   Where for any reason it is not possible for that motion to be determined in
accordance with paragraph (3), the Clerk must advise the parties of that fact and
give reasons.

Lodging opposed motions by email

14.5.—(1)   This rule applies where opposition to a motion has been intimated.   **S1.75**

(2)   The motion must be lodged by the lodging party no later than 1230 hours on
court day 4 by—

  (a)   sending an email in Form 14.1 headed "Opposed motion", to the ad-
        dress of the court; and

(b) attaching to that email the opposition in Form 14.2 intimated by the receiving party to the lodging party.

(3) That motion is to be heard by the procedural Appeal Sheriff on the first suitable court day after court day 4.

(4) The Clerk must intimate the date and time of the hearing to the parties.

Variation of periods of intimation

S1.76   **14.6.** Where either—

    (a) every receiving party in an appeal consents to a shorter period of intimation; or

    (b) the Court shortens the period of intimation,

the motion may be lodged by the lodging party, or heard or otherwise determined by the Court at an earlier time and date than that which is specified in this Chapter.

CHAPTER 15 MOTIONS LODGED BY OTHER MEANS

Chapter 15

Motions Lodged by Other Means

Intimation of motions by other means

15.1.—(1) The lodging party must give intimation of that party's intention to lodge the motion, and of the terms of the motion, to every other party in Form 15.1.

(2) That intimation must be accompanied by a copy of any document referred to in the motion.

S1.77

Opposition to motions

15.2.—(1) A receiving party may oppose a motion by lodging a notice of opposition in Form 15.2.

(2) Any notice of opposition must be lodged within 7 days after the date of intimation of the motion.

(3) The procedural Appeal Sheriff may, on the application of the lodging party, either—

    (a) vary the period of 7 days mentioned in paragraph (2); or

    (b) dispense with intimation on any party.

(4) An application mentioned in paragraph (3) must—

    (a) be included in the motion;

    (b) give reasons for varying the period or dispensing with intimation, as the case may be.

(5) The procedural Appeal Sheriff may allow a notice of opposition to be lodged late, on cause shown.

S1.78

Consent to motions

15.3. Where a receiving party seeks to consent to a motion, that party may do so by lodging a notice to that effect.

S1.79

Lodging of motions

15.4.—(1) The motion must be lodged by the lodging party within 5 days after the date of intimation of the motion, unless paragraph (3) applies.

(2) The lodging party must also lodge—

    (a) a certificate of intimation in Form 6.5-A;

    (b) so far as practicable, any document referred to in the motion that has not already been lodged.

(3) Where the procedural Appeal Sheriff varies the period for lodging a notice of opposition to a period of 5 days or less, the motion must be lodged no later than the day on which that period expires.

S1.80

Joint motions

15.5.—(1) A joint motion by all parties need not be intimated.

(2) Such a motion is to be lodged by any of the parties.

S1.81

Hearing of opposed motions

S1.82   **15.6.**—(1)   Where a notice of opposition in Form 15.2 is lodged, the motion is to be heard by the procedural Appeal Sheriff on the first suitable court day after the lodging of the notice of opposition.

(2)   The Clerk must intimate the date and time of the hearing to the parties.

Modification of Chapter 5

S1.83   **15.7.**   For the purposes of this Chapter, the following provisions in Chapter 5 do not apply—

      (a)   rule 5.6(1)(e);

      (b)   rule 5.7(2)(e).

CHAPTER 16 MINUTES

Chapter 16

Minutes

Application of this Chapter

16.1. This Chapter applies to any application to the Court that is made by minute, other than a joint minute, a minute of abandonment or a minute of amendment.

S1.84

Form and lodging of minute

16.2.—(1) A minute is to be made in Form 16.

S1.85

(2) A minute must—

   (a) specify the order sought from the Court;

   (b) contain a statement of facts supporting the granting of that order;

   (c) where appropriate, contain pleas-in-law.

(3) A minute is to be lodged in the process of the appeal to which it relates.

Orders for intimation and answers

16.3.—(1) On the first available court day after being lodged, a minute must be brought before the procedural Appeal Sheriff for an order—

S1.86

   (a) for intimation, within 7 days after the date of the order, to—

      (i) every other party to the appeal;

      (ii) any other person who appears to have an interest in the minute;

   (b) for any person to whom the minute is intimated to lodge answers, if so advised, within 14 days after the date of intimation;

   (c) fixing a hearing on the minute and any answers no sooner than 28 days after the date of the order.

(2) The procedural Appeal Sheriff may vary the periods of 7 days, 14 days and 28 days mentioned in paragraph (1) either—

   (a) of the procedural Appeal Sheriff's own accord; or

   (b) on cause shown, on the application of the applicant.

(3) An application mentioned in paragraph (2)(b) must—

   (a) be included in the minute;

   (b) give reasons for varying the period.

(4) Where a minute is intimated in accordance with an order under this rule, the applicant must lodge a certificate of intimation in Form 6.5-A within 14 days after the date of intimation.

Consent to minute

16.4.—(1) Where a person to whom a minute is intimated seeks to consent to the minute, that person may do so by lodging a notice to that effect.

S1.87

(2) Where every person to whom a minute is intimated consents to the minute, the procedural Appeal Sheriff is to determine the minute in chambers without the appearance of those persons, unless the procedural Appeal Sheriff otherwise determines.

Minutes of sist and transference

S1.88

16.5.—(1)   This rule applies where a party to an appeal ("P") dies or comes under legal incapacity while the appeal is depending before the Court.

(2)   Any person who claims to represent P or P's estate may apply to the Court by minute to be sisted as a party to the appeal.

(3)   If no person makes an application under paragraph (2), any other party may apply to the Court by minute to transfer the appeal in favour of or against (as the case may be) the person who represents P or P's estate.

(4)   An application under paragraph (3) must be intimated to the person specified in the minute as representing P or P's estate.

Applications to enter process as respondent

S1.89

16.6.—(1)   A person to whom the appeal has not been intimated may apply by minute for leave to enter the process as a party minuter and lodge answers.

(2)   A minute under paragraph (1) must specify—

    (a)   the applicant's title and interest to enter the process;

    (b)   the basis for the answers that the applicant proposes to lodge.

(3)   At the hearing fixed under rule 16.3(1)(c), the procedural Appeal Sheriff must determine whether the applicant has shown title and interest to enter the process.

(4)   If the procedural Appeal Sheriff is satisfied, the procedural Appeal Sheriff may grant the applicant leave to enter the process and lodge answers.

(5)   Where leave is granted, the procedural Appeal Sheriff is to make such further order as the procedural Appeal Sheriff thinks fit.

(6)   In particular, such an order may include an order—

    (a)   varying any timetable;

    (b)   as to the expenses of the application.

CHAPTER 17 AMENDMENT OF PLEADINGS

Chapter 17

Amendment of Pleadings

Amendment of sheriff court pleadings

17.1.—(1) Any party to an appeal may apply by motion to amend the pleadings   **S1.90**
in the sheriff court process.

(2) A party seeking to amend must lodge a minute of amendment setting out the
proposed amendment and, at the same time, lodge a motion to allow—

    (a) the minute of amendment to be received;

    (b) any other person to lodge answers, if so advised, within a specified
period.

(3) Where the procedural Appeal Sheriff makes an order allowing a minute of
amendment to be received and answered, the procedural Appeal Sheriff may—

    (a) allow a period of adjustment of the minute of amendment and answers;
and

    (b) fix a hearing on the minute of amendment and answers as adjusted.

(4) Each party must, no later than 2 days before the hearing fixed under
paragraph (3)(b), lodge a copy of their minute of amendment or answers with any
adjustments made thereto in italic or bold type, or underlined.

(5) The procedural Appeal Sheriff may make such order in relation to expenses,
and may impose such conditions, as the procedural Appeal Sheriff thinks fit.

(6) Where the procedural Appeal Sheriff—

    (a) allows an amendment to the pleadings in the sheriff court process; and

    (b) considers that the amendment makes a material change to the pleadings,
the procedural Appeal Sheriff may recall the decision appealed against and remit the
matter to the sheriff for a further hearing.

Amendment of note of appeal and answers etc.

17.2.—(1) A party who has lodged a document specified in paragraph (2) may   **S1.91**
apply by motion to amend that document.

(2) The documents are—

    (a) a note of appeal;

    (b) answers to a note of appeal;

    (c) grounds of appeal in a cross-appeal;

    (d) answers to grounds of appeal in a cross-appeal.

(3) Such a motion must include the text of the proposed amendment.

(4) An application under paragraph (1) must be accompanied by an application
to vary the timetable under rule 7.3(1) or rule 29.6(1)(c) if such an application is
necessary.

Chapter 18

Withdrawal of Solicitors

Interpretation of this Chapter

18.1. In this Chapter, "peremptory hearing" means a hearing at which a party whose solicitor has withdrawn from acting must appear or be represented in order to state whether or not the party intends to proceed.

S1.92

Giving notice of withdrawal to the Court

18.2.—(1) Where a solicitor withdraws from acting on behalf of a party, the solicitor must give notice in writing to the Clerk and to every other party.

S1.93

(2) Paragraph (1) does not apply if the solicitor withdraws from acting at a hearing in the presence of the other parties or their representatives.

(3) Paragraph (4) applies if a solicitor who withdraws from acting is aware that the address of the party for whom the solicitor acted has changed from that specified in the instance of the note of appeal or answers to the note of appeal.

(4) The solicitor must disclose to the Clerk and every other party the last known address of the party for whom the solicitor acted.

Arrangements for peremptory hearing

18.3.—(1) On the first available court day after notice is given under rule 18.2(1), the procedural Appeal Sheriff must make an order—

S1.94

    (a) ordaining the party whose solicitor has withdrawn from acting to appear or be represented at a peremptory hearing;

    (b) fixing a date and time for the peremptory hearing;

    (c) appointing any other party to the appeal to intimate the order and a notice in Form 18.3 to that party within 7 days after the date of the order.

(2) A peremptory hearing must be fixed no sooner than 14 days after the date on which an order is made under paragraph (1).

(3) The procedural Appeal Sheriff may vary the period of 7 days mentioned in paragraph (1) or the period of 14 days mentioned in paragraph (2) either—

    (a) of the procedural Appeal Sheriff's own accord; or

    (b) on cause shown, on the application of any other party to the appeal.

(4) Where any previously fixed hearing is to occur within 14 days after the date on which the procedural Appeal Sheriff is to make an order under paragraph (1), the procedural Appeal Sheriff may continue consideration of the matter to the previously fixed hearing instead of making an order under paragraph (1).

(5) Where an order and a notice in Form 18.3 are intimated under this rule, the party appointed to intimate them must lodge a certificate of intimation in Form 6.5-A either—

    (a) within 14 days after the date of intimation; or

    (b) before the peremptory hearing,

whichever is sooner.

Peremptory hearing

S1.95   **18.4.**—(1) At a peremptory hearing, the party must appear or be represented in order to state whether the party intends to proceed.

(2) Where the party fails to comply with paragraph (1), the Court may make an order mentioned in paragraph (3) only if it is satisfied that the order and notice in Form 18.3 have been intimated to that party.

(3) The orders are either—

    (a) if the party is the appellant, an order refusing the appeal; or

    (b) if the party is the respondent and the condition in paragraph (4) is satisfied, an order allowing the appeal.

(4) The condition is that the appellant must show cause why the appeal should be allowed.

(5) If the Court is not satisfied that the order and notice in Form 18.3 have been intimated to that party, it may make—

    (a) an order fixing a further peremptory hearing;

    (b) any other order that the Court considers appropriate to secure the expeditious disposal of the appeal.

CHAPTER 19 CAUTION AND SECURITY

Chapter 19

Caution and Security

Application of this Chapter

19.1. This Chapter applies to any appeal in which the Court has power to order a person to find caution or give other security. **S1.96**

Form of application to find caution or give security

19.2. An application— **S1.97**
  (a) for an order for caution or other security;
  (b) to vary or recall such an order,
is to be made by motion.

Orders for caution or other security: time for compliance

19.3. Where the Court makes an order for caution or to give other security, the order must specify the period within which caution is to be found or security given. **S1.98**

Methods of finding caution or giving security

19.4.—(1) A person who is ordered to find caution must do so by obtaining a bond of caution. **S1.99**

(2) A person who is ordered to consign a sum of money into court must do so by consignation under the Sheriff Courts Consignations (Scotland) Act 1893 in the name of the Clerk.

(3) The Court may order a person to give security by—
  (a) a method other than those mentioned in paragraphs (1) and (2);
  (b) a combination of two or more methods of security.

(4) Any document by which an order to find caution or give security is satisfied must be lodged in process.

(5) A document lodged under paragraph (4) may not be borrowed from process.

Cautioners and other guarantors

19.5. A bond of caution or other security may only be given by a person who is an authorised person within the meaning of section 31 of the Financial Services and Markets Act 2000 (authorised persons). **S1.100**

Form of bond of caution

19.6.—(1) A bond of caution must oblige the cautioner to make payment of the sums as validly and in the same manner as the party is obliged. **S1.101**

(2) In this rule—

  "cautioner" includes the cautioner's heirs and executors;
  "party" means the person to whom the cautioner is bound, and that person's heirs and successors;
  "the sums" are the sums for which the cautioner is bound to the party.

Caution or other security: sufficiency and objections

S1.102   **19.7.**—(1)   The Clerk must be satisfied that any document lodged in process under rule 19.4(4) is in proper form.

(2)   A party who is dissatisfied with the sufficiency or form of any document lodged in process under rule 19.4(4) may apply to the Court by motion for an order under rule 19.9(1).

Insolvency or death of cautioner or guarantor

S1.103   **19.8.**—(1)   This rule applies where caution has been found by bond of caution or security has been given by guarantee.

(2)   Where one of the events specified in paragraph (3) occurs, the party entitled to benefit from the caution or guarantee may apply to the Court by motion for further caution to be found or further security to be given.

(3)   The events are that the cautioner or guarantor—

    (a)   becomes apparently insolvent within the meaning of section 16 of the Bankruptcy (Scotland) Act 2016 (meaning of "apparent insolvency");

    (b)   calls a meeting of the cautioner or guarantor's creditors to consider the state of that person's affairs;

    (c)   dies unrepresented; or

    (d)   is a company and—

        (i)   an administration, bank administration or building society special administration order has been made in respect of it;

        (ii)   a winding up, bank insolvency or building society insolvency order has been made in respect of it;

        (iii)   a resolution for its voluntary winding up has been passed;

        (iv)   a receiver of all or any part of its undertaking has been appointed;

        (v)   a voluntary arrangement within the meaning of section 1(1) of the Insolvency Act 1986 (those who may propose an arrangement) has been approved under Part I of that Act.

Failure to find caution or give security

S1.104   **19.9.**—(1)   Where a person who has been ordered to find caution or give security fails to do so, any other party may apply to the Court by motion for a finding that the person is in default.

(2)   Despite rule 3.1, a person who fails to find caution or give security is only in default if the Court grants a motion under paragraph (1) and makes a finding that the person is in default.

Chapter 20

Expenses

Taxation of expenses

20.1.—(1)   Where the Court makes an award of expenses in any appeal, those **S1.105**
expenses must be taxed before decree is granted for them.

(2)   This rule does not apply where the Court modifies those expenses to a fixed
sum.

Time for lodging account of expenses

20.2.—(1)   A party found entitled to expenses must lodge an account of expenses **S1.106**
in process—

(a)   no later than 4 months after the final judgment; or

(b)   at any time with permission of the court, but subject to such conditions,
if any, as the Court thinks fit to impose.

(2)   Where the account of expenses is lodged by the Scottish Legal Aid Board in
reliance on regulation 39(2)(a) of the Civil Legal Aid (Scotland) Regulations 2002
(recovery of expenses), paragraph (1)(a) applies as if the period specified there is 8
months.

(3)   In this rule, "final judgment" has the meaning assigned by section 136(1) of
the 2014 Act (interpretation).

Diet of taxation

20.3.—(1)   Where an account of expenses is lodged for taxation, the Clerk must **S1.107**
transmit the account and the process to the auditor of court.

(2)   Subject to paragraph (3), the auditor of court must fix a diet of taxation on
receipt of—

(a)   the account of expenses;

(b)   the process;

(c)   vouchers in respect of all outlays claimed in the account, including
counsel's fees; and

(d)   a letter addressed to the auditor of court—

(i)   confirming that the items referred to in sub-paragraphs (a) and
(c) have been intimated to the party found liable in expenses;
and

(ii)   providing such information as is required to enable the auditor
of court to give intimation to the party found liable in expenses
in accordance with paragraph (4)(b).

(3)   The auditor of court may fix a diet of taxation where paragraph (2)(c) or (d),
or both, have not been complied with.

(4)   The auditor of court must intimate the diet of taxation to—

(a)   the party found entitled to expenses;

(b)   the party found liable in expenses.

(5)   The party found liable in expenses must, no later than 1600 hours on the
fourth business day before the diet of taxation, intimate to the auditor of court and to
the party found entitled to expenses particular points of objection, specifying each
item objected to and stating concisely the nature and ground of objection.

(6) Subject to paragraph (7), if the party found liable in expenses fails to intimate points of objection under paragraph (5) within the time limit set out there, the auditor of court must not take account of them at the diet of taxation.

(7) Where a failure to comply with the requirement contained in paragraph (5) was due to mistake, oversight or other excusable cause, the auditor of court may relieve a party of the consequences of such failure on such conditions, if any, as the auditor thinks fit.

(8) At the diet of taxation, or within such reasonable period of time thereafter that the auditor of court may allow, the party found entitled to expenses must make available to the auditor of court all documents, drafts or copies of such documents sought by the auditor and relevant to the taxation.

(9) In this rule, a "business day" means any day other than a Saturday, Sunday or public or court holiday.

Auditor's statement

S1.108
20.4.—(1) The auditor of court must—
- (a) prepare a statement of the amount of expenses as taxed;
- (b) transmit the process, the taxed account and the statement to the Clerk;
- (c) on the day on which the documents referred to in sub-paragraph (b) are transmitted, intimate that fact and the date of the report to each party to whom the auditor intimated the diet of taxation.

(2) The party found entitled to expenses must, within 7 days after the receipt of intimation under paragraph (1)(c), send a copy of the taxed account to the party found liable in expenses.

(3) Where no objections are lodged under rule 20.5(1), the court may grant decree for the expenses as taxed.

Objections to taxed account

S1.109
20.5.—(1) A party to an appeal who has appeared or been represented at a diet of taxation may object to the auditor of court's statement by lodging in process a note of objection within 14 days after the date of the statement.

(2) The party lodging a note of objection is referred to in this rule as "the objecting party".

(3) On lodging the note of objection the objecting party must apply by motion for an order—
- (a) allowing the note to be received;
- (b) allowing a hearing on the note of objection.

(4) On the granting of the order mentioned in paragraph (3), the objecting party must intimate to the auditor of court—
- (a) the note of objection;
- (b) the interlocutor containing the order.

(5) Within 14 days after receipt of intimation of the items mentioned in paragraph (4), the auditor of court must lodge in process a statement of reasons in the form of a minute stating the reasons for the auditor's decision in relation to the items to which objection is taken in the note.

(6) On the lodging of the statement of reasons, the Clerk must fix a hearing on the note of objection.

(7) At the hearing, the Court may—
- (a) sustain or repel any objection in the note of objection or remit the account of expenses to the auditor of court for further consideration;

(b) find any party liable in the expenses of the procedure on the note of objection.

Decree for expenses in name of solicitor

20.6. The Court may allow a decree for expenses to be extracted in the name of the solicitor who conducted the appeal. **S1.110**

Expenses of curator ad litem appointed to a respondent

20.7.—(1) This rule applies where a curator ad litem is appointed to any respondent to an appeal. **S1.111**

(2) The appellant is responsible in the first instance for the payment of the expenses of a curator ad litem mentioned in paragraph (3).

(3) Those expenses are any fees of the curator ad litem and any outlays incurred by the curator from the date of appointment until any of the following steps occur—

(a) the lodging of a minute stating that the curator does not intend to lodge answers to the note of appeal;

(b) the lodging of answers by the curator, or the adoption of answers that have already been lodged; or

(c) the discharge of the curator before either of the steps in sub-paragraphs (a) or (b) occurs.

CHAPTER 21 QUALIFIED ONE-WAY COSTS SHIFTING

Chapter 21

Qualified One-way Costs Shifting

Application and interpretation of this Chapter

21.1.—(1)   This Chapter applies in civil proceedings, where either or both—   **S1.112**
  (a)   an application for an award of expenses is made to the Court;
  (b)   such an award is made by the Court.
  (2)   Where this Chapter applies—
  (a)   rules 10.1(5) and (6);
  (b)   any common law rule entitling a pursuer to abandon an appeal, to the
    extent that it concerns expenses,
are disapplied.
  (3)   In this Chapter—

   "the 2018 Act" means the Civil Litigation (Expenses and Group Proceedings)
     (Scotland) Act 2018;
   "the applicant" has the meaning given in rule 21.2(1), and"applicants" is
     construed accordingly;
   "civil proceedings" means civil proceedings to which section 8 of the 2018 Act
     (restriction on pursuer's liability for expenses in personal injury claims)
     applies.

Application for an award of expenses

21.2.—(1)   Where civil proceedings have been brought by a pursuer, another   **S1.113**
party to the action ("the applicant") may make an application to the Court for an
award of expenses to be made against the pursuer, on one or more of the grounds
specified in either or both—
  (a)   section 8(4)(a) to (c) of the 2018 Act;
  (b)   paragraph (2) of this rule.
  (2)   The grounds specified in this paragraph, which are exceptions to section
8(2) of the 2018 Act, are as follows—
  (a)   failure by the pursuer to obtain an award of damages greater than the
    sum offered by way of a tender lodged in process;
  (b)   unreasonable delay on the part of the pursuer in accepting a sum of-
    fered by way of a tender lodged in process;
  (c)   abandonment of the appeal by the pursuer in terms of rule 10.1(1) to
    (4), or at common law.

Award of expenses

21.3.—(1)   Subject to paragraph (2), the determination of an application made   **S1.114**
under rule 21.2(1) is at the discretion of the Court.
  (2)   Where, having determined an application made under rule 21.2(1), the Court
makes an award of expenses against the pursuer on the ground specified in rule
21.2(2)(a) or (b)—
  (a)   the pursuer's liability is not to exceed the amount of expenses the ap-
    plicant has incurred after the date of the tender;
  (b)   the liability of the pursuer to the applicant, or applicants, who lodged
    the tender is to be limited to an aggregate sum, payable to all applicants
    (if more than one) of 75% of the amount of damages awarded to the

pursuer and that sum is to be calculated without offsetting against those expenses any expenses due to the pursuer by the applicant, or applicants, before the date of the tender;

(c) the Court must order that the pursuer's liability is not to exceed the sum referred to in sub-paragraph (b), notwithstanding that any sum assessed by the Auditor of Court as payable under the tender procedure may be greater or, if modifying those expenses to a fixed sum in terms of rule 20.1(2), that such sum does not exceed that referred to in sub-paragraph (b);

(d) where the award of expenses is in favour of more than one applicant the Court, failing agreement between the applicants, must apportion the award of expenses recoverable under the tender procedure between them.

(3) In the event that the Court makes an award of expenses against the pursuer on the ground specified in rule 21.2(2)(c), the Court may make such orders in respect of expenses, subject to such conditions, if any, as it considers appropriate.

Procedure

S1.115   **21.4.**—(1)   An application under rule 21.2(1)—

(a) must be made by motion, in writing;

(b) may be made at any stage in the case prior to the granting of an order disposing of the expenses of the appeal.

(2)   Where an application under rule 21.2(1) is made, the Court may make such orders as it thinks fit for dealing with the application, including an order—

(a) requiring the applicant to intimate the application to any other person;

(b) requiring any party to lodge a written response;

(c) requiring the lodging of any document;

(d) fixing a hearing.

Award against legal representatives

S1.116   **21.5.**   Section 8(2) of the 2018 Act does not prevent the Court from making an award of expenses against a pursuer's legal representative in terms of section 11 (awards of expenses against legal representatives) of that Act.

CHAPTER 22 DEVOLUTION ISSUES

INCIDENTAL PROCEDURE: SPECIAL PROCEDURES

Chapter 22

Devolution Issues

Interpretation

22.1. In this Chapter—   **S1.117**
"devolution issue" means a devolution issue under—
  (a) Schedule 6 to the Scotland Act 1998;
  (b) Schedule 10 to the Northern Ireland Act 1998;
  (c) Schedule 9 to the Government of Wales Act 2006;
and any reference to Schedule 6, Schedule 10 or Schedule 9 is a reference to
that Schedule in that Act;
"relevant authority" means—
  (a) the Advocate General;
  (b) in the case of a devolution issue under Schedule 6, the Lord
       Advocate;
  (c) in the case of a devolution issue under Schedule 10, the Attorney
       General for Northern Ireland, and the First Minister and deputy
       First Minister acting jointly;
  (d) in the case of a devolution issue under Schedule 9, the Counsel
       General to the Welsh Government.

Raising a devolution issue
22.2.—(1) A devolution issue is raised by specifying a devolution issue in Form   **S1.118**
22.2.
  (2) A devolution issue in Form 22.2 is to be lodged—
  (a) by an appellant, when the note of appeal is lodged;
  (b) by a respondent, when answers to the note of appeal are lodged,
unless the Court allows an appellant or a respondent to raise a devolution issue at a
later stage in proceedings.
  (3) An application to allow a devolution issue to be raised after the note of appeal has been lodged or answers to the note of appeal have been lodged, as the case
may be, is to be made by motion.
  (4) The party raising a devolution issue must specify, in sufficient detail to enable the Court to determine whether a devolution issue arises—
  (a) the facts and circumstances;
  (b) the contentions of law,
on the basis of which it is alleged that the devolution issue arises in the appeal.
  (5) The Court may not determine a devolution issue unless permission has been
given for the devolution issue to proceed.

Raising a devolution issue: intimation and service
22.3.—(1) This rule applies to the intimation of a devolution issue on a relevant   **S1.119**
authority under—
  (a) paragraph 5 of Schedule 6;

(b)   paragraph 23 of Schedule 10;

(c)   paragraph 14(1) of Schedule 9.

(2)   When a devolution issue is raised, the party raising it must intimate the devolution issue to the relevant authority unless the relevant authority is a party to the appeal.

(3)   Within 14 days after intimation, the relevant authority may give notice to the Clerk that it intends to take part in the appeal as a party under—

(a)   paragraph 6 of Schedule 6;

(b)   paragraph 24 of Schedule 10;

(c)   paragraph 14(2) of Schedule 9.

Raising a devolution issue: permission to proceed

S1.120

22.4.—(1)   When a devolution issue is raised, the Clerk must fix a hearing and intimate the date and time of that hearing to the parties.

(2)   Within 14 days after the Clerk intimates the date and time of the hearing, each party must lodge a note of argument.

(3)   That note of argument must summarise the submissions the party intends to make on the question of whether a devolution issue arises in the appeal.

(4)   At the hearing, the procedural Appeal Sheriff must determine whether a devolution issue arises in the appeal.

(5)   Where the procedural Appeal Sheriff determines that a devolution issue arises, the procedural Appeal Sheriff must grant permission for the devolution issue to proceed.

(6)   Where the procedural Appeal Sheriff determines that no devolution issue arises, the procedural Appeal Sheriff must refuse permission for the devolution issue to proceed.

(7)   At the hearing the procedural Appeal Sheriff may make any order, including an order concerning expenses.

(8)   In this rule, "party" includes a relevant authority that has given notice to the Clerk that it intends to take part in the appeal as a party, and "parties" is construed accordingly.

Participation by the relevant authority

S1.121

22.5.—(1)   Paragraph (2) applies where a relevant authority has given notice to the Clerk that it intends to take part in the appeal as a party.

(2)   Within 7 days after permission to proceed is given, the relevant authority must lodge a minute containing the relevant authority's written submissions in respect of the devolution issue.

Reference to the Inner House or Supreme Court

S1.122

22.6.—(1)   This rule applies to the reference of a devolution issue to the Inner House of the Court of Session for determination under—

(a)   paragraph 7 of Schedule 6;

(b)   paragraph 25 of Schedule 10;

(c)   paragraph 15 of Schedule 9.

(2)   This rule also applies where the Court has been required by a relevant authority to refer a devolution issue to the Supreme Court under—

(a)   paragraph 33 of Schedule 6;

(b)   paragraph 33 of Schedule 10;

(c)   paragraph 29 of Schedule 9.

(3)   The Court is to make an order concerning the drafting and adjustment of the reference.

(4)   The reference must specify—

(a)   the questions for the Inner House or the Supreme Court;

(b)   the addresses of the parties;

(c)   a concise statement of the background to the matter, including—

  (i)   the facts of the case, including any relevant findings of fact;

  (ii)   the main issues in the case and contentions of the parties with regard to them;

(d)   the relevant law including the relevant provisions of the Scotland Act 1998, the Northern Ireland Act 1998 or the Government of Wales Act 2006;

(e)   the reasons why an answer to the questions is considered necessary for the purpose of disposing of the proceedings.

(5)   The reference must have annexed to it—

(a)   a copy of all orders made in the appeal;

(b)   a copy of any judgments in the proceedings.

(6)   When the reference has been drafted and adjusted, the Court is to make and sign the reference.

(7)   The Clerk must—

(a)   send a copy of the reference to the parties to the proceedings;

(b)   certify on the back of the principal reference that sub-paragraph (a) has been complied with.

Reference to the Inner House or Supreme Court: further procedure

22.7.—(1)   On a reference being made, the appeal must, unless the Court orders otherwise, be sisted until the devolution issue has been determined.   **S1.123**

(2)   Despite a reference being made, the Court continues to have the power to make any interim order required in the interests of the parties.

(3)   The Court may recall a sist for the purpose of making such interim orders.

(4)   On a reference being made the Clerk must send the principal copy of the reference to either (as the case may be)—

(a)   the Deputy Principal Clerk of the Court of Session; or

(b)   the Registrar of the Supreme Court (together with 7 copies).

(5)   Unless the Court orders otherwise, the Clerk must not send the principal copy of the reference where an appeal against the making of the reference is pending.

(6)   An appeal is to be treated as pending either—

(a)   until the expiry of the time for making that appeal; or

(b)   where an appeal has been made, until that appeal has been determined.

Reference to the Inner House or Supreme Court: procedure following determination

22.8.—(1)   This rule applies where either the Inner House of the Court of Session or the Supreme Court has determined a devolution issue.   **S1.124**

(2)   Upon receipt of the determination, the Clerk must place a copy of the determination before the Court.

(3)   The Court may, on the motion of any party or otherwise, order such further procedure as may be required.

(4)   Where the Court makes an order other than on the motion of a party, the Clerk must intimate a copy of the order on all parties to the appeal.

Chapter 23

Preliminary References to the CJEU – Citizens' Rights

Interpretation of this Chapter

23.1.   In this Chapter, "reference" means a reference to the European Court for a   **S1.125**
preliminary ruling under Article 158 of the Agreement between the European Union
and the European Atomic Energy Community and the United Kingdom of Great
Britain and Northern Ireland on the withdrawal of the United Kingdom of Great
Britain and Northern Ireland from the European Union and the European Atomic
Energy Community.

Applications for a reference

23.2.—(1)   An application for a reference by a party is to be made by motion.   **S1.126**
(2)   The Court may make a reference of its own accord.

Preparation of reference

23.3.—(1)   Where the Court decides that a reference is to be made, it must make   **S1.127**
an order specifying—
    (a)   by whom the reference is to be drafted and adjusted;
    (b)   the periods within which the reference is to be drafted and adjusted.
(2)   A reference is to be drafted in Form 23.3 unless the Court directs otherwise
when it makes an order under paragraph (1).
(3)   In drafting and adjusting the reference, parties are to have regard to the
Recommendations to national courts and tribunals in relation to the initiation of
preliminary ruling proceedings issued by the European Court.
(4)   When the reference has been drafted and any adjustments required by the
Court have been made, the Court must make and sign the reference.
(5)   When the reference is made, the Clerk must notify the parties.

Transmission of reference to European Court

23.4.   A copy of the reference is to be certified by the Clerk and sent to the   **S1.128**
Registrar of the European Court.

Sist of appeal

23.5.—(1)   When a reference is made, the Court is to sist the appeal until the   **S1.129**
European Court determines the reference, unless the Court orders otherwise.
(2)   Where an appeal is sisted under paragraph (1), the Court may recall the sist
for the purposes of making an interim order.

CHAPTER 24 INTERVENTIONS BY CEHR AND SCHR

Chapter 24

Interventions by CEHR and SCHR

Application and interpretation of this Chapter

24.1.—(1)   This Chapter applies to—

    (a)   interventions in legal proceedings by the CEHR under section 30(1) of the Equality Act 2006 (judicial review and other legal proceedings);

    (b)   interventions in civil proceedings (other than children's hearing proceedings) by the SCHR under section 14(2) of the Scottish Commission for Human Rights Act 2006 (power to intervene).

(2)   In this Chapter—

"the CEHR" means the Commission for Equality and Human Rights;
"the SCHR" means the Scottish Commission for Human Rights.

Applications to intervene

24.2.—(1)   An application for leave to intervene is to be made in Form 24.2.

S1.131

(2)   Such an application must be lodged in the process of the appeal to which it relates.

(3)   When an application is lodged, rule 5.2(1) applies as if the applicant were a party.

(4)   The parties may request a hearing on the application within 14 days after the application is lodged.

(5)   Where a hearing is requested—

    (a)   the Court must appoint a date and time for a hearing;

    (b)   the Clerk must notify the date and time of the hearing to the parties and the applicant.

(6)   Where no hearing is requested, the Court may appoint a date and time for a hearing of its own accord and the Clerk must notify the date and time of the hearing to the parties and the applicant.

Applications to intervene: determination

24.3.—(1)   The Court may determine an application for leave to intervene without a hearing, unless a hearing is fixed under rule 24.2(5) or (6).

S1.132

(2)   In an application for leave to intervene under section 30(1) of the Equality Act 2006, the Court may grant leave only if it is satisfied that the proposed submissions are likely to assist the Court.

(3)   Where the Court grants leave to intervene, it may impose any conditions that it considers desirable in the interests of justice.

(4)   In particular, the Court may make provision about any additional expenses incurred by the parties as a result of the intervention.

(5)   When an application is determined, the Clerk must notify the parties and the applicant of the outcome.

Invitations to intervene

24.4.—(1)   An invitation to intervene under section 14(2)(b) of the Scottish Commission for Human Rights Act 2006 is to be in Form 24.4.

S1.133

(2)   The Clerk must send a copy of Form 24.4 to the parties to the proceedings and to the SCHR.

(3)   When the Clerk sends a copy of Form 24.4 to the SCHR, the Clerk must also send—

    (a)   a copy of the note of appeal and any answers to it;

    (b)   the appeal print, if it is available;

    (c)   any other documents relating to the appeal that the Court thinks are relevant.

(4)   Where the Court invites the SCHR to intervene, it may impose any conditions that it considers desirable in the interests of justice.

(5)   In particular, the Court may make provision about any additional expenses incurred by the parties as a result of the intervention.

Form of intervention

S1.134

24.5.—(1)   An intervention is to be by way of written submission.

(2)   A written submission (including any appendices) must not exceed 5,000 words.

(3)   The intervener must lodge the written submission within such time as the Court may direct.

(4)   In exceptional circumstances, the Court may allow—

    (a)   a written submission exceeding 5,000 words to be made;

    (b)   an oral submission to be made.

(5)   Where the Court allows an oral submission to be made, it must appoint a date and time for the submission to be made.

(6)   The Clerk must notify that date and time to the parties and the intervener.

CHAPTER 25 PROOF

Chapter 25

Proof

Taking proof in the course of an appeal

25.1.—(1)   If it is considered necessary, proof or additional proof may be ordered—

    (a) by the procedural Appeal Sheriff at a procedural hearing;

    (b) by the Court in the course of an appeal hearing.

(2)   Where the procedural Appeal Sheriff orders that proof or additional proof is to be taken—

    (a) the procedural Appeal Sheriff must appoint a date and time for a hearing for that to be done;

    (b) so far as reasonably practicable, the hearing is to be before the procedural Appeal Sheriff who made the order.

(3)   Where the Court orders that proof or additional proof is to be taken, the Court must—

    (a) remit the proof to be taken before any Appeal Sheriff;

    (b) appoint a date and time for a hearing for that to be done;

    (c) continue the appeal hearing until the Appeal Sheriff reports the proof to the Court.

(4)   Where a hearing is fixed under this rule, the Clerk must notify the date and time of the hearing to the parties.

S1.135

Preparation for proof

25.2.—(1)   Where a proof or additional proof is ordered, the Appeal Sheriff before whom it is to be taken must make an order specifying—

    (a) the witnesses whose evidence is to be taken;

    (b) how those witnesses are to be cited to the hearing.

(2)   An order under paragraph (1) may include provision as to liability for the fees and expenses of a witness.

S1.136

Conduct of proof

25.3.   A proof is to be taken continuously so far as possible, but the Appeal Sheriff may adjourn the hearing from time to time.

S1.137

Administration of oath or affirmation to witnesses

25.4.—(1)   The Appeal Sheriff is to administer the oath to a witness in Form 25.4-A unless the witness elects to affirm.

(2)   Where a witness elects to affirm, the Appeal Sheriff must administer the affirmation in Form 25.4-B.

S1.138

Recording of evidence

25.5.—(1)   The evidence given at a hearing is to be recorded, unless the parties agree to dispense with the recording of evidence and the Appeal Sheriff considers that it is appropriate to do so.

(2)   The evidence must be recorded by—

S1.139

(a) a shorthand writer to whom the oath *de fideli administratione* has been administered in connection with the Court; or

(b) by tape recording or other mechanical means approved by the Court.

(3)   In the first instance, the solicitors for the parties are personally liable to pay, in equal shares—

(a) the fees of a shorthand writer; or

(b) the fee payable for recording evidence by tape recording or other mechanical means.

(4)   The record of evidence is to include—

(a) any objection taken to a question or to the line of evidence;

(b) any submission made in relation to such an objection;

(c) the ruling of the Appeal Sheriff in relation to the objection and submission.

Transcripts of evidence

S1.140

25.6.—(1)   A transcript of the record of the evidence is to be made only where the Appeal Sheriff orders it to be made.

(2)   In the first instance, the solicitors for the parties are personally liable, in equal shares, for the cost of making the transcript.

(3)   The transcript provided for the use of the Court must be certified as a faithful record of the evidence by—

(a) the shorthand writer who recorded the evidence; or

(b) where the evidence was recorded by tape recording or other mechanical means, by the person who transcribed the record.

(4)   The Appeal Sheriff may alter the transcript where the Appeal Sheriff considers it necessary to do so, but only after hearing parties on the proposed alterations.

(5)   Where the Appeal Sheriff alters the transcript, the Appeal Sheriff must authenticate the alterations.

(6)   The transcript may only be borrowed from process on cause shown.

(7)   Where a transcript is required for the purpose of an appeal but the Appeal Sheriff has not directed that it be made—

(a) the appellant may request a transcript from the shorthand writer or the person in whose possession the recording of the evidence is;

(b) in the first instance, the solicitor for the appellant is liable for the cost of the transcript;

(c) the appellant must lodge the transcript in process; and

(d) any party may obtain a copy by paying the fee of the person who made the transcript.

Recording objections where recording of evidence dispensed with

S1.141

25.7.   Where the recording of evidence has been dispensed with under rule 25.5(1), a party may request that the Appeal Sheriff record in the report of the proof—

(a) any objection taken to a question or to the line of evidence;

(b) any submission made in relation to such an objection; and

(c) the ruling of the Appeal Sheriff in relation to the objection and submission.

Chapter 26

Vulnerable Witnesses

Application and interpretation of this Chapter

26.1.—(1)   This Chapter applies where a proof or an additional proof is ordered to be taken under rule 25.1(1).

(2)   In this Chapter—

"the 2004 Act" means the Vulnerable Witnesses (Scotland) Act 2004;

"child witness notice" has the meaning given by section 12(2) of the 2004 Act (orders authorising the use of special measures for vulnerable witnesses);

"review application" means an application under section 13(1)(a) of the 2004 Act (review of arrangements for vulnerable witnesses);

"vulnerable witness application" has the meaning given by section 12(6) of the 2004 Act (orders authorising the use of special measures for vulnerable witnesses).

S1.142

Form of notices and applications

26.2.—(1)   A child witness notice is to be made in Form 26.2–A.

(2)   A vulnerable witness application is to be made in Form 26.2–B.

(3)   A review application is to be made—

    (a)   in Form 26.2–C; or

    (b)   orally, if the Court grants leave.

S1.143

Determination of notices and applications

26.3.—(1)   When a notice or application under this Chapter is lodged, the Court may require any of the parties to provide further information before determining the notice or application.

(2)   The Court may—

    (a)   determine the notice or application by making an order under section 12(1) or (6) or 13(2) of the 2004 Act without holding a hearing;

    (b)   fix a hearing at which parties are to be heard on the notice or application before determining it.

(3)   The Court may make an order altering the date of the proof in order that the notice or application may be determined.

S1.144

Determination of notices and applications: supplementary orders

26.4.   Where the Court determines a notice or application under this Chapter and makes an order under section 12(1) or (6) or 13(2) of the 2004 Act, the Court may make further orders to secure the expeditious disposal of the appeal.

S1.145

Intimation of orders

26.5.—(1)   Where the Court makes an order—

    (a)   fixing a hearing under rule 26.3(2)(b);

    (b)   altering the date of a proof or other hearing under rule 26.3(3); or

    (c)   under section 12(1) or (6) or 13(2) of the 2004 Act,

the Clerk must intimate the order in accordance with this rule.

(2)   Intimation must be given to—

S1.146

    (a)   every party to the proceedings;

    (b)   any other person named in the order.

  (3)   Intimation must be made—

    (a)   on the day that the hearing is fixed or the order is made;

    (b)   in the manner ordered by the Court.

Taking of evidence by commissioner: preparatory steps

S1.147   **26.6.**—(1)   This rule applies where the Court authorises the special measure of taking evidence by a commissioner under section 19(1) of the 2004 Act (taking of evidence by a commissioner).

  (2)   The commission is to proceed without interrogatories unless the Court otherwise orders.

  (3)   The order of the Court authorising the special measure is sufficient authority for citing the vulnerable witness to appear before the commissioner.

  (4)   The party who cited the vulnerable witness—

    (a)   must give the commissioner—

        (i)   a certified copy of the order of the Court appointing the commissioner;

        (ii)   a copy of the appeal documents;

        (iii)   where rule 26.7 applies, the approved interrogatories and cross-interrogatories;

    (b)   must instruct the clerk to the commission;

    (c)   is responsible in the first instance for the fee of the commissioner and the clerk.

  (5)   The commissioner is to fix a hearing at which the commission will be carried out.

  (6)   The commissioner must consult the parties before fixing the hearing.

  (7)   An application by a party for leave to be present in the room where the commission is carried out is to be made by motion.

  (8)   In this rule, "appeal documents" means any of the following documents that have been lodged in process by the time the use of the special measure is authorised—

    (a)   the note of appeal and answers;

    (b)   where there is a cross-appeal, the grounds of appeal and answers;

    (c)   the appeal print and appendices;

    (d)   the notes of argument.

Taking of evidence by commissioner: interrogatories

S1.148   **26.7.**—(1)   This rule applies where the Court—

    (a)   authorises the special measure of taking evidence by a commissioner under section 19(1) of the 2004 Act; and

    (b)   orders that interrogatories are to be prepared.

  (2)   The party who cited the vulnerable witness must lodge draft interrogatories in process.

  (3)   Any other party may lodge cross-interrogatories.

  (4)   The parties may adjust their interrogatories and cross-interrogatories.

  (5)   At the expiry of the adjustment period, the parties must lodge the interrogatories and cross-interrogatories as adjusted in process.

  (6)   The Court is to resolve any dispute as to the content of the interrogatories and cross-interrogatories, and approve them.

(7)   When the Court makes an order for interrogatories to be prepared, it is to specify the periods within which parties must comply with the steps in this rule.

Taking of evidence by commissioner: conduct of commission

26.8.—(1)   The commissioner must administer the oath *de fideli administratione* to the clerk.

S1.149

(2)   The commissioner is to administer the oath to the vulnerable witness in Form 25.4-A unless the witness elects to affirm.

(3)   Where the witness elects to affirm, the commissioner must administer the affirmation in Form 25.4-B.

Taking of evidence by commissioner: lodging and custody of video record and documents

26.9.—(1)   The commissioner must lodge the video record of the commission and any relevant documents with the Clerk.

S1.150

(2)   When the video record and any relevant document are lodged, the Clerk must notify every party—
  (a)   that the video record has been lodged;
  (b)   whether any relevant documents have been lodged;
  (c)   of the date on which they were lodged.

(3)   The video record and any relevant documents must be kept by the Clerk.

(4)   Where the video record has been lodged—
  (a)   the name and address of the vulnerable witness and the record of the witness's evidence are to be treated as being in the knowledge of the parties;
  (b)   the parties need not include—
    (i)   the name of the witness in any list of witnesses; or
    (ii)   the record of evidence in any list of productions.

Chapter 27

Use of Live Links

Interpretation

27.1.   In this Chapter—   **S1.151**

"evidence" means the evidence of—
- (a)   the party; or
- (b)   a person who has been or may be cited to appear before the court as a witness;

"live link" means—
- (a)   a live television link; or
- (b)   where the Court gives permission in accordance with rule 27.2(4), an alternative arrangement;

"submission" means any oral submission which would otherwise be made to the Court by a party or that party's representative, including an oral submission in support of a motion.

Application for use of live link

(1)   A party may apply to the Court to use a live link to make a submission or to give evidence.

(2)   An application to use a live link is to be made by motion.

(3)   Where a party seeks to use a live link other than a live television link, the motion must specify the proposed arrangement.

(4)   The Court must not grant a motion to use a live link other than a live television link unless the proposed arrangement meets the requirements in paragraph (5).

(5)   The requirements are that the person using the live link is able to—
- (a)   be seen and heard, or heard without being seen, in the courtroom; and
- (b)   see and hear, or hear without seeing, the proceedings in the courtroom.

CHAPTER 28 REPORTING RESTRICTIONS

Chapter 28

Reporting Restrictions

Application and interpretation of this Chapter

28.1.—(1)   This Chapter applies to orders which restrict the reporting of proceedings.

    (2)   In this Chapter "interested person" means a person—

        (a)   who has asked to see any order made by the Court which restricts the reporting of proceedings, including an interim order; and

        (b)   whose name is included on a list kept by the Lord President for the purposes of this Chapter.

S1.153

Interim orders

28.2.—(1)   Where the Court is considering making an order, the Court must first make an interim order.

    (2)   The Clerk must immediately send a copy of the interim order to any interested person.

    (3)   The Court must specify in the interim order why the Court is considering making an order.

S1.154

Representations

28.3.—(1)   An interested person who would be directly affected by the making of an order must be given an opportunity to make representations to the Court before the order is made.

    (2)   Representations must—

        (a)   be made in Form 28.3;

        (b)   include reasons why an urgent hearing is necessary, if an urgent hearing is sought;

        (c)   be lodged no later than 2 days after the interim order is sent to interested persons in accordance with rule 28.2(2).

    (3)   If representations are made—

        (a)   the Court must appoint a date and time for a hearing—

            (i)   on the first suitable court day; or

            (ii)   where the Court considers that an urgent hearing is necessary, at an earlier date and time;

        (b)   the Clerk must—

            (i)   notify the date and time of the hearing to the parties to the proceedings and any person who has made representations;

            (ii)   send a copy of the representations to the parties.

    (4)   Where no interested person makes representations in accordance with paragraph (3), the Clerk must put the interim order before the Court in chambers in order that the Court may resume consideration of whether to make an order.

    (5)   Where the Court, having resumed consideration, makes no order, it must recall the interim order.

    (6)   Where the Court recalls an interim order, the Clerk must immediately notify any interested person.

S1.155

Notification of reporting restrictions

S1.156

28.4. Where the Court makes an order, the Clerk must immediately—

    (a)   send a copy of the order to any interested person;

    (b)   arrange for the publication of the making of the order on the Scottish Courts and Tribunals Service website.

Applications for variation or revocation

S1.157

28.5.—(1)   A person aggrieved by an order may apply to the Court for its variation or revocation.

(2)   An application is to be made in Form 28.5.

(3)   When an application is made—

    (a)   the Court must appoint a date and time for a hearing;

    (b)   the Clerk must—

        (i)   notify the date and time of the hearing to the parties to the proceedings and the applicant;

        (ii)   send a copy of the application to the parties.

(4)   The hearing is, so far as reasonably practicable, to be before the Appeal Sheriff or Appeal Sheriffs who made the order.

CHAPTER 29 APPLICATION FOR NEW JURY TRIAL OR TO ENTER JURY VERDICT

SPECIAL APPEAL PROCEEDINGS

Chapter 29

Application for New Jury Trial or to Enter Jury Verdict

Application of this Chapter

29.1. This Chapter applies to an application—

    (a) for a new trial under section 69(1) of the 2014 Act (application for new trial);

    (b) to enter a verdict under section 71(2) of the 2014 Act (verdict subject to opinion of the Sheriff Appeal Court).

S1.158

Form of application for new trial

29.2.—(1) An application for a new trial is to be made in Form 29.2.

(2) Such an application must be made within 7 days after the date on which the jury have returned their verdict.

(3) The application must specify the grounds on which the application is made.

(4) When an application for a new trial is lodged, the party lodging it must also lodge—

    (a) a print containing—

        (i) the pleadings in the sheriff court process;

        (ii) the interlocutors in the sheriff court process;

        (iii) the issues and counter-issues;

    (b) the verdict of the jury;

    (c) any exception and the determination on it of the sheriff presiding at the trial.

S1.159

Application for new trial: restrictions

29.3.—(1) An application for a new trial which specifies the ground in section 69(2)(a) of the 2014 Act (misdirection by sheriff) may not be made unless the procedure in rule 36B.8 of the Ordinary Cause Rules 1993 (exceptions to sheriff's charge) has been complied with.

(2) An application for a new trial which specifies the ground in section 69(2)(b) of the 2014 Act (undue admission or rejection of evidence) may not be made unless objection was taken to the admission or rejection of evidence at the trial and recorded in the notes of evidence under the direction of the sheriff presiding at the trial.

(3) An application for a new trial which specifies the ground in section 69(2)(c) of the 2014 Act (verdict contrary to evidence) may not be made unless it sets out in brief specific numbered propositions the reasons the verdict is said to be contrary to the evidence.

S1.160

Applications out of time

29.4.—(1) An application to allow an application for a new trial to be lodged outwith the period specified in rule 29.2(2) is to be included in the application made under rule 29.2(1).

S1.161

(2)   Where the procedural Appeal Sheriff allows such an application, the application for a new trial is to be received on such conditions as to expenses or otherwise as the procedural Appeal Sheriff thinks fit.

Timetable in application for new trial

S1.162   **29.5.**—(1)   The Clerk must issue a timetable in Form 29.5 when an application is lodged under rule 29.2(1).

(2)   When the Clerk issues a timetable, the Clerk must also fix a procedural hearing to take place after completion of the procedural steps specified in paragraph (4).

(3)   The timetable specifies—

(a)   the dates by which parties must comply with those procedural steps; and

(b)   the date and time of the procedural hearing.

(4)   The procedural steps are the steps mentioned in the first column of the following table, provision in respect of which is found in the rule mentioned in the second column—

Procedural step	Rule
Referral of question about competency of application	29.7(3)
Lodging of appendices to print	29.9(1)
Giving notice that the applicant considers appendix unnecessary	29.10(1)
Lodging of notes of argument	29.11(1)
Lodging of estimates of duration of hearing of application for new trial	29.12

Sist of application for new trial and variation of timetable

S1.163   **29.6.**—(1)   Any party may apply by motion to—

(a)   sist the application for a new trial for a specified period;

(b)   recall a sist;

(c)   vary the timetable.

(2)   An application is to be determined by the procedural Appeal Sheriff.

(3)   An application to sist the application for a new trial or to vary the timetable may only be granted on special cause shown.

(4)   The procedural Appeal Sheriff may—

(a)   grant the application;

(b)   refuse the application; or

(c)   make an order not sought in the application, where the procedural Appeal Sheriff considers that doing so would secure the expeditious disposal of the appeal.

(5)   Where the procedural Appeal Sheriff makes an order sisting the application for a new trial, the Clerk must discharge the procedural hearing fixed under rule 29.5(2).

(6)   When a sist is recalled or expires, the Clerk must—

(a)   issue a revised timetable in Form 29.5;

(b)   fix a procedural hearing.

(7)   Where the procedural Appeal Sheriff makes an order varying the timetable, the Clerk must—

(a)   discharge the procedural hearing fixed under rule 29.5(2);

(b)   issue a revised timetable in Form 29.5;

(c)   fix a procedural hearing.

Questions about competency of application

29.7.—(1)   A question about the competency of an application for a new trial   **S1.164**
may be referred to the procedural Appeal Sheriff by a party, other than the applicant.

(2)   A question is referred by lodging a reference in Form 29.7.

(3)   A question may be referred within 7 days after the date on which the application for a new trial was lodged.

(4)   Where a reference is lodged, the Clerk must fix a hearing and intimate the time and date of that hearing to the parties.

(5)   Within 7 days after the date on which the reference is lodged, each party must lodge a note of argument.

(6)   That note of argument must—

(a)   give fair notice of the submissions the party intends to make on the question of competency;

(b)   comply with the requirements in rule 29.11(3).

(7)   Paragraphs (4) and (5) of rule 29.11 apply to a note of argument lodged under paragraph (5).

Questions about competency: determination

29.8.—(1)   At a hearing on the competency of an application for a new trial, the   **S1.165**
procedural Appeal Sheriff may—

(a)   refuse the application as incompetent;

(b)   find the application to be competent;

(c)   reserve the question of competency until the hearing of the application; or

(d)   refer the question of competency to the Court.

(2)   The procedural Appeal Sheriff may make an order as to the expenses of the reference.

(3)   Where the question of competency is referred to the Court, it may—

(a)   refuse the application as incompetent;

(b)   find the application to be competent; or

(c)   reserve the question of competency until the hearing of the application.

(4)   The Court may make an order as to the expenses of the reference.

Appendices to print: contents

29.9.—(1)   The applicant must lodge an appendix to the print mentioned in rule   **S1.166**
29.2(4)(a) no later than 7 days before the procedural hearing, unless rule 29.10(1) is complied with.

(2)   The appendix must contain—

(a)   any document lodged in the sheriff court process that is founded upon in the application for a new trial;

(b)   the notes of evidence from the trial, if it is sought to submit them for consideration by the Court.

(3)   Where the sheriff's note has not been included in the print and it subsequently becomes available, the applicant must—

(a)   include it in the appendix where the appendix has not yet been lodged; or

(b)   lodge a supplementary appendix containing the sheriff's note.

(4)   The parties must—

(a)   discuss the contents of the appendix;

(b)   so far as possible, co-operate in making up the appendix.

Appendices to print considered unnecessary

S1.167
29.10.—(1) Where the applicant considers that it is not necessary to lodge an appendix, the applicant must, no later than 7 days before the procedural hearing—

(a) give written notice of that fact to the Clerk;

(b) intimate that notice to every respondent.

(2) Where the applicant complies with paragraph (1), the respondent may apply by motion for an order requiring the applicant to lodge an appendix.

(3) An application under paragraph (2) must specify the documents or notes of evidence that the respondent considers should be included in the appendix.

(4) In disposing of an application under paragraph (2), the procedural Appeal Sheriff may—

(a) grant the application and make an order requiring the applicant to lodge an appendix;

(b) refuse the application and make an order requiring the respondent to lodge an appendix; or

(c) refuse the application and make no order.

(5) Where the procedural Appeal Sheriff makes an order requiring the applicant or the respondent to lodge an appendix, that order must specify—

(a) the documents or notes or evidence to be included in the appendix;

(b) the time within which the appendix must be lodged.

Notes of argument

S1.168
29.11.—(1) The parties must lodge notes of argument no later than 7 days before the procedural hearing.

(2) A note of argument must summarise briefly the submissions the party intends to develop at the hearing of the application for a new trial.

(3) A note of argument must—

(a) state, in brief numbered paragraphs, the points that the party intends to make;

(b) after each point, identify by means of a page or paragraph reference the relevant passage in any notes of evidence or other document on which the party relies in support of the point;

(c) for every authority that is cited—

(i) state the proposition of law that the authority demonstrates;

(ii) identify the page or paragraph references for the parts of the authority that support the proposition;

(d) cite only one authority for each proposition of law, unless additional citation is necessary for a proper presentation of the argument.

(4) Where a note of argument has been lodged and the party lodging it subsequently becomes aware that an argument in the note is not to be insisted upon, that party must—

(a) give written notice of that fact to the Clerk;

(b) intimate that notice to every other party.

(5) Where a party wishes to advance an argument at a hearing that is not contained in that party's note of argument, the party must apply by motion for leave to advance the argument.

Estimates of duration of hearing of application for new trial

S1.169
29.12. The parties must lodge estimates of the duration of any hearing required to dispose of the application for a new trial in Form 29.12 no later than 7 days before the procedural hearing.

Procedural hearing

29.13.—(1)   At the procedural hearing, the procedural Appeal Sheriff must ascertain the state of preparation of the parties, so far as reasonably practicable.   **S1.170**

(2)   The procedural Appeal Sheriff may—

   (a)   determine that parties are ready to proceed to a hearing of the application for a new trial; or

   (b)   determine that further procedure is required.

(3)   Where the procedural Appeal Sheriff determines that parties are ready to proceed—

   (a)   the procedural Appeal Sheriff must fix a hearing of the application for a new trial;

   (b)   the Clerk is to intimate the date and time of that hearing to the parties;

   (c)   the procedural Appeal Sheriff may make an order specifying further steps to be taken by the parties before the hearing.

(4)   Where the procedural Appeal Sheriff determines that further procedure is required, the procedural Appeal Sheriff—

   (a)   must make an order to secure the expeditious disposal of the appeal;

   (b)   may direct the Clerk to fix a further procedural hearing and intimate the date and time of that hearing to parties.

Application to enter jury verdict

29.14.—(1)   This rule applies to an application under section 71(2) of the 2014 Act (verdict subject to opinion of the Court).   **S1.171**

(2)   Such an application is to be made in Form 29.14.

(3)   When an application is lodged, the party lodging it must also lodge—

   (a)   a print containing—

      (i)   the pleadings in the sheriff court process;

      (ii)   the interlocutors in the sheriff court process;

      (iii)   the issues and counter-issues;

   (b)   the verdict of the jury;

   (c)   any exception and the determination on it of the sheriff presiding at the trial.

(4)   Unless the procedural Appeal Sheriff otherwise directs—

   (a)   it is not necessary for the purposes of such a motion to print the notes of evidence;

   (b)   but the notes of the sheriff presiding at the trial may be produced at any time if required.

(5)   The procedural Appeal Sheriff may refer an application referred to in paragraph (1) to the Court in cases of complexity or difficulty.

CHAPTER 30 APPEALS FROM SUMMARY CAUSES

Chapter 30

Appeals from Summary Causes

Application of this Chapter

30.1. This Chapter applies to an appeal under section 38 of the Sheriff Courts (Scotland) Act 1971 (appeal in summary causes) arising from the decision of a sheriff in proceedings under the Summary Cause Rules 2002.

S1.172

Transmission of appeal

30.2.—(1) Within 4 days after the sheriff has signed the stated case, the sheriff clerk must—

S1.173

    (a) send the parties a copy of the stated case;

    (b) transmit to the Clerk—

        (i) the stated case;

        (ii) all documents and productions in the case.

(2) On receipt of the stated case, the Clerk must fix a hearing and intimate the date, time and place of that hearing to the parties.

Transmission of appeal: time to pay direction

30.3.—(1) Within 4 days after the sheriff states in writing the reasons for the sheriff's original decision in accordance with rule 25.4(4) of the Summary Cause Rules 2002 (appeal in relation to time to pay direction), the sheriff clerk must transmit to the Clerk—

S1.174

    (a) the appeal in Form 33 of the Summary Cause Rules 2002;

    (b) the sheriff's written reasons for the sheriff's original decision.

(2) On receipt of those documents, the Clerk must fix a hearing and intimate the date, time and place of that hearing to the parties.

Hearing of appeal

30.4.—(1) Any party may apply by motion for the question of liability for expenses to be heard after the Court gives its decision on the appeal.

S1.175

(2) At the hearing, a party may only raise questions of law of which notice has not been given if the Court permits the party to do so.

(3) The Court may permit a party to amend any question of law or to add any new question of law.

(4) Where the Court grants permission under paragraph (2) or (3), it may do so on such conditions as to expenses or otherwise as the Court thinks fit.

Determination of appeal

30.5.—(1) At the conclusion of the hearing, the Court may either give its decision orally or reserve judgment.

S1.176

(2) Where the Court reserves judgment, it must give its decision in writing within 28 days.

(3) The President of the Sheriff Appeal Court may vary the period in paragraph (2).

(4) The Court may—

    (a) adhere to or vary the decision appealed against;

   (b)   recall the decision and substitute another decision for it; or

   (c)   remit the matter to the sheriff for further procedure.

(5)   The Court may not remit the matter to the sheriff in order that further evidence may be led.

Appeal to the Court of Session: certification

S1.177

30.6.—(1)   This rule applies where the Court has determined an appeal arising from the decision of a sheriff in proceedings under the Summary Cause Rules 2002.

(2)   An application under section 38(b) of the Sheriff Courts (Scotland) Act 1971 (appeal in summary causes) for a certificate that a cause is suitable for appeal to the Court of Session is to be made in Form 30.6.

(3)   Such an application must be lodged within 14 days after the date on which the Court gave its decision on the appeal.

(4)   An application may only be disposed of after the procedural Appeal Sheriff has heard parties on it.

CHAPTER 31 APPEALS FROM SIMPLE PROCEDURE

Chapter 31

Appeals From Simple Procedure

Appeals from Simple Procedure

31.1.   Part 16 of the Simple Procedure Rules applies to an appeal of a decision made under the simple procedure.   **S1.178**

CHAPTER 32 APPEALS BY STATED CASE UNDER PART 15 OF THE CHILDREN'S HEARINGS (SCOTLAND) ACT 2011

Chapter 32

Appeals by Stated Case Under Part 15 of the Children's Hearings (Scotland) Act 2011

Application and interpretation of this Chapter

32.1.—(1)   This Chapter applies to an appeal by stated case under section 163(1)   **S1.179**
(appeals to sheriff principal and Court of Session: children's hearings etc.), 164(1)
(appeals to sheriff principal and Court of Session: relevant persons), 165(1) (appeals
to sheriff principal and Court of Session: contact and permanence orders) and 167(1)
(appeals to sheriff principal: section 166) of the Children's Hearings (Scotland) Act
2011.

(2)   In this Chapter, "parties" means the parties specified in rule 3.59(2) of the
Act of Sederunt (Child Care and Maintenance Rules) 1997 (appeals: applications
for stated case).

Transmission of appeal

32.2.—(1)   Within 4 days after the sheriff has signed the stated case, the sheriff   **S1.180**
clerk must—
- (a)   send the parties a copy of the stated case;
- (b)   transmit to the Clerk—
    - (i)   the stated case;
    - (ii)   all documents and productions in the case.

(2)   On receipt of the stated case, the Clerk must fix a hearing and intimate the
date, time and place of that hearing to the parties.

Hearing of appeal

32.3.—(1)   At the hearing, a party may only raise questions of law or procedural   **S1.181**
irregularities of which notice has not been given if the Court permits the party to do
so.

(2)   Where the Court grants permission, it may do so on such conditions as to
expenses or otherwise as the Court thinks fit.

Determination of appeal

32.4.—(1)   At the conclusion of the hearing, the Court may either give its deci-   **S1.182**
sion orally or reserve judgment.

(2)   Where the Court reserves judgment, it must give its decision in writing
within 28 days.

(3)   The President of the Sheriff Appeal Court may vary the period in paragraph
(2).

Leave to appeal to the Court of Session

32.5.—(1)   This rule applies to applications for leave to appeal to the Court of   **S1.183**
Session under sections 163(2), 164(2) or 165(2) of the Children's Hearings
(Scotland) Act 2011.

(2)   An application is to be made in Form 32.5.

(3)   Such an application must be lodged within 7 days after the date on which
the Court gave its decision on the appeal.

(4) On receipt of an application, the Clerk must—

    (a) fix a hearing to take place before the procedural Appeal Sheriff no later than 14 days after the application is received;

    (b) intimate the date, time and place of that hearing to the parties.

CHAPTER 33 APPEALS UNDER PART 4 OF THE AGE OF CRIMINAL RESPONSIBILITY (SCOTLAND) ACT 2019

Chapter 33

Appeals under Part 4 of the Age of Criminal Responsibility (Scotland) Act 2019

Application of this Chapter

33.1.[1] This Chapter applies to an appeal against the decision of a sheriff under section 38(3), 46(3) and 67(3) of the Age of Criminal Responsibility (Scotland) Act 2019.

S1.184

Form of appeal

33.2.—(1) An appeal is made by lodging a note of appeal in Form 33.2.

(2) Rule 6.2(2)(a) to (c) and (g) to (h) applies for the purpose of making an appeal under this rule.

S1.185

Hearing of appeal

33.3. On receipt of the appeal, the Clerk must fix forthwith a hearing to take place within 3 working days (within the meaning of section 76 of the Age of Criminal Responsibility (Scotland) Act 2019) and intimate the date, time and place of that hearing to—

(a) the constable who applied for the order to which the decision relates;

(b) the child or person acting on behalf of the child to whom the decision relates;

(c) any other person the court considers has an interest in proceedings.

S1.186

Determination of appeal

33.4.—(1) At the conclusion of the hearing, the Court may either give its decision orally or reserve judgment.

(2) Where the Court reserves judgment, it must give its decision in writing within 28 days.

(3) The President of the Sheriff Appeal Court may vary the period in paragraph (2).

S1.187

---

[1] As amended by Act of Sederunt (Rules of the Court of Session 1994 and Sheriff Appeal Court Rules Amendment) (Miscellaneous) 2022 (SSI 2022/135) para.(3).

CHAPTER 34 ANCILLARY PROVISIONS

Chapter 34

Ancillary Provisions

Revocation

34.1. Act of Sederunt (Sheriff Appeal Court Rules) 2015 is revoked.　　　**S1.188**

Consequential amendment

34.2.—(1)　The Simple Procedure Rules are amended in accordance with this　**S1.189**
paragraph.

(2)　In rule 16.4(8) (what will the Sheriff Appeal Court do with an appeal?), for
"Act of Sederunt (Sheriff Appeal Court Rules) 2015" substitute "Act of Sederunt
(Sheriff Appeal Court Rules) 2021".

Saving provision

34.3.—(1)　Subject to paragraphs (2) to (4), Act of Sederunt (Sheriff Appeal　**S1.190**
Court Rules) 2015 ("the 2015 Rules") is saved in so far as it applies to any proceedings commenced before the coming into force of this Act of Sederunt.

(2)　Rules 21.1 and 21.5 of the 2015 Rules are saved in respect of appeals in
which a reference to the European Court is made before IP completion day.

(3)　In paragraph (2), "reference" has the meaning given in rule 21.1 of the 2015
Rules.

(4)　Paragraph (1) does not apply to rules 21.2 to 21.4 of the 2015 Rules.

Transitional provision

34.4.　The Appeal Sheriff may direct that this Act of Sederunt applies to any　**S1.191**
proceedings commenced before the coming into force of this Act of Sederunt but
only after giving the parties an opportunity to be heard.

SCHEDULE 1

ADMINISTRATIVE PROVISIONS

Rule 1.5

Quorum of the Court

1.—(1) The quorum of the Court for the types of business specified in sub-paragraph (3) is one Appeal Sheriff but more than one Appeal Sheriff may sit where the Court considers that to be appropriate.

S1.192

(2) The quorum of the Court for any other business is three Appeal Sheriffs but more than three Appeal Sheriffs may sit where the Court considers that to be appropriate.

(3) The types of business are—

  (a) relieving a party from the consequences of a failure to comply with a provision in these Rules under rule 2.1(1);

  (b) making an order to secure the expeditious disposal of the appeal under rule 3.2(2);

  (c) granting permission for lay representation under rule 4.3;

  (d) granting an application for lay support under rule 4.5;

  (e) ordering otherwise where a party is to intimate to every other party under rule 5.2;

  (f) disposing of an application for leave to receive an appeal out of time under rule 6.4(2);

  (g) a hearing fixed under rule 6.7;

  (h) a hearing fixed under rule 6.8;

  (i) a hearing fixed under Chapter 8;

  (j) disposing of an application to abandon an appeal under rule 10.1;

  (k) disposing of an application for permission to appeal to the Court of Session under rule 12.2(1), where the decision in respect of which permission to appeal is sought was made by one Appeal Sheriff;

  (l) a peremptory hearing under rule 18.4;

  (m) disposing of an application for sanction for the employment of counsel, unless the application seeks sanction in respect of appearing at a hearing before more than one Appeal Sheriff;

  (n) ordering caution or giving security under rule 19.3;

  (o) ordering caution or giving security under rule 19.4;

  (p) ordering further caution to be found or further security to be given under rule 19.8(2);

  (q) granting a motion for a finding that a person is in default under rule 19.9(1);

  (r) granting decree for expenses as taxed under rule 20.4(3);

  (s) disposing of a note of objections under rule 20.5(7), where the order allowing expenses was made by one Appeal Sheriff;

  (t) allowing decree for expenses to be extracted in the name of the solicitor who conducted the appeal under rule 20.6;

  (u) disposing of an application to allow a devolution issue to be raised after the note of appeal has been lodged or answers to the note of appeal have been lodged under rule 22.2(3);

(v)   making an order concerning the drafting and adjustment of a reference to the Inner House of the Court of Session or to the Supreme Court under rule 22.6(3);

(w)   making and signing a reference under rule 22.6(6);

(x)   ordering a sist under rule 22.7;

(y)   ordering further procedure under rule 22.8;

(z)   appointing a hearing under rule 24.2(5);

(aa)   determining an application under rule 24.3;

(bb)   making an order under rule 24.5;

(cc)   ordering a party to provide further information under Chapter 26;

(dd)   determining an application to use a live link under Chapter 27;

(ee)   making an interim order under Chapter 28;

(ff)   a hearing fixed under Chapter 30;

(gg)   a hearing fixed by virtue of Chapter 31;

(hh)   a hearing fixed under Chapter 33;

(ii)   disposing of an application for authority to address the Court in Gaelic or to give oral evidence in Gaelic under paragraph 5 of this schedule;

(jj)   any business where the Rules provide for that business to be disposed of by the procedural Appeal Sheriff.

Procedural Appeal Sheriff

2.—(1) Every Appeal Sheriff is a procedural Appeal Sheriff.

(2) Where the Court considers it appropriate to do so, the Court may dispose of any business where the Rules provide for that business to be disposed of by the procedural Appeal Sheriff.

Signature of interlocutors etc.

3.—(1) Any order made by the Court under these Rules is to be contained in an interlocutor.

(2) An interlocutor must be signed in accordance with sub-paragraphs (3) to (5).

(3) Where the Court is constituted by more than one Appeal Sheriff when an order is made, the interlocutor must be signed by either—

(a)   the Appeal Sheriff who presided over the Court when the order was made; or

(b)   in the event of the death, disability or absence of that Appeal Sheriff, the next senior Appeal Sheriff who sat on that occasion, after such consultation with the other Appeal Sheriffs who sat as may be necessary.

(4) Where the Court is constituted by one Appeal Sheriff, the interlocutor must be signed by that Appeal Sheriff.

(5) Where the Clerk determines an unopposed motion in writing in accordance with rule 13.7(1), the interlocutor must be signed by the Clerk unless the procedural Appeal Sheriff directs otherwise.

(6) The Clerk may sign any other interlocutor if directed to do so by the procedural Appeal Sheriff.

(7) A direction under sub-paragraph (6) need not be in writing.

(8) An interlocutor signed in accordance with sub-paragraphs (5) and (6) is to be treated for all purposes as if it had been signed by an Appeal Sheriff.

(9) An extract of an interlocutor which is not signed in accordance with the provisions of this rule is void and has no effect.

(10) An interlocutor may, on cause shown, be corrected or altered at any time before extract by either—

(a)   the Appeal Sheriff who signed it;

(b)   in the event of the death, disability or absence of that Appeal Sheriff, by any other Appeal Sheriff; or

(c)   where the interlocutor was signed by the Clerk, by any Appeal Sheriff.

Decrees, extracts and execution

4.—(1)   In this paragraph, "decree" includes any order or interlocutor which may be extracted.

(2)   A decree may be extracted at any time after whichever is the later of—

(a)   the expiry of the period within which an application for leave to appeal may be made, if no such application is made;

(b)   the date on which leave to appeal is refused, if there is no right to appeal from that decision;

(c)   the expiry of the period within which an appeal may be made, if no such appeal is made; or

(d)   the date on which an appeal is finally disposed of.

(3)   A party may apply by motion to the procedural Appeal Sheriff to allow an extract to be issued earlier than a date referred to in sub-paragraph (2).

(4)   Nothing in this paragraph affects the power of the Court to supersede extract.

(5)   Where execution may follow on an extract decree, the decree is to include the warrant for execution specified in sub-paragraph (6).

(6)   That warrant is "This extract is warrant for all lawful execution hereon.".

(7)   Where interest is included in, or payable under, a decree, the rate of interest is 8 per cent a year unless otherwise stated.

Use of Gaelic

5.—(1)   This paragraph applies where the use of Gaelic by a party has been authorised by the sheriff in the proceedings out of which an appeal arises.

(2)   That party may apply by motion for authority to address the Court in Gaelic at—

(a)   an appeal hearing fixed under rule 7.9(3)(a) or rule 8.2(1)(a);

(b)   a hearing under rule 30.4.

(3)   Where proof or additional proof is ordered in accordance with rule 25.1 and that party wishes to give oral evidence in Gaelic, the party may apply by motion for authority to do so.

(4)   Where the Court grants authority under sub-paragraph (2) or (3), an interpreter must be provided by the Court.

SCHEDULE 2

FORMS

Rule 1.6(1)

Form 4.3

S1.193

Rule 4.3(4)(b)

Statement of prospective lay representative for appellant or respondent
IN THE SHERIFF APPEAL COURT
STATEMENT
by
PROSPECTIVE LAY REPRESENTATIVE FOR APPELLANT *[or* RESPOND-
ENT]
in the appeal in the cause
[A.B.] (*designation and address*)
PURSUER and [APPELLANT/RESPONDENT]
against
[C.D.] (*designation and address*)
DEFENDER and [RESPONDENT/APPELLANT]

Name and address of prospective lay representative who requests permission to represent party litigant:

Identify hearing(s) in respect of which permission for lay representation is sought:

The prospective lay representative declares that:

(a)   I have no financial interest in the outcome of the case.

[or I have the following financial interest in the outcome of the case: (*state briefly the financial interest*).]

(b)   I am not receiving remuneration or other reward directly or indirectly from the litigant for my assistance and will not receive directly or indirectly such remuneration or other reward from the litigant.

(c)   I accept that documents and information are provided to me by the litigant on a confidential basis and I undertake to keep them confidential.

(d)   I have no previous convictions.

[or I have the following convictions: (*list the convictions*).]

(e)   I have not been declared a vexatious litigant under the Vexatious Actions (Scotland) Act 1898.

[or I was declared a vexatious litigant under the Vexatious Actions (Scotland) Act 1898 on (*date*).]

(*Signed*)
[X.Y.], Prospective lay representative

Form 6.2

S1.194

Rule 6.2(1)

Note of appeal
APPEAL
to
THE SHERIFF APPEAL COURT
[A.B.] (*designation and address*)
PURSUER and [APPELLANT/RESPONDENT]
against
[C.D.] (*designation and address*)
DEFENDER and [RESPONDENT/APPELLANT]

1. The appellant appeals to the Sheriff Appeal Court against the decision of the sheriff at (*place*) (*specify nature of decision*) made on (*date*). The court reference number is (*insert court reference number*).

GROUNDS OF APPEAL

2. (*State briefly (in numbered paragraphs) the ground(s) of appeal.*)

AVAILABILITY OF SHERIFF'S NOTE

3. The sheriff has provided a note setting out the reasons for the decision appealed against, and a copy is appended.

[*or* The appellant has requested that the sheriff write a note, but the note is not yet available.]

[*or* The sheriff has not provided a note setting out the reasons for the decision appealed against, and the appellant requests that the sheriff write a note.]

[*or* The sheriff has not provided a note setting out the reasons for the decision appealed against. The appellant considers that the appeal is sufficiently urgent that the Sheriff Appeal Court should hear and determine the appeal without the sheriff's note. (*State briefly (in numbered paragraphs) why the appeal is sufficiently urgent to justify its determination without the sheriff's note*).]

INITIAL CASE MANAGEMENT: APPELLANT'S VIEWS

4. The appellant considers that the appeal should be appointed to procedure before three Appeal Sheriffs (Chapter 7 procedure) [or procedure before one Appeal Sheriff (Chapter 8 procedure)] because:

(*state briefly (in numbered paragraphs) why the appellant considers that the appeal should be appointed to that procedure, taking into account the matters mentioned in rule 6.11(3).*)

IN RESPECT WHEREOF
[A.B.] [*or*[C.D.]], Appellant
[*or* [X.Y.], Solicitor for Appellant
(*insert business address of solicitor*)]

S1.195

Form 6.5

Rule 6.5(1)(b)

IN THE SHERIFF APPEAL COURT
ANSWERS
in the appeal in the cause
[A.B.] (*designation and address*)
PURSUER and [APPELLANT/RESPONDENT]
against
[C.D.] (*designation and address*)
DEFENDER and [RESPONDENT/APPELLANT]

1. The appellant has appealed to the Sheriff Appeal Court against the decision of the sheriff at (*place*) (*specify nature of decision*) made on (*date*).

2. The respondent answers the appeal. (*State briefly (in numbered paragraphs) the answers to the ground(s) of appeal.*)

INITIAL CASE MANAGERMENT: RESPONDENT'S VIEWS

3. The respondent considers that the appeal should be appointed to procedure before three Appeal Sheriffs (Chapter 7 procedure) [*or* procedure before one Appeal Sheriff (Chapter 8 procedure)] because:

(*state briefly (in numbered paragraphs) why the respondent considers that the appeal should be appointed to that procedure, taking into account the matters mentioned in rule 6.11(3).*)

IN RESPECT WHEREOF
[A.B.] [*or*[C.D.]], Respondent
[*or* [X.Y.], Solicitor for Respondent

(insert business address of solicitor)]

Form 6.5-A

S1.196

Rules 6.5(4), 6.6(1), 15.4(2)(a), 16.3(4) and 18.3(5)

Certificate of intimation

IN THE SHERIFF APPEAL COURT

CERTIFICATE OF INTIMATION

in the appeal in the cause

[A.B.] *(designation and address)*

PURSUER and [APPELLANT/RESPONDENT]

against

[C.D.] *(designation and address)*

DEFENDER and [RESPONDENT/APPELLANT]

1. I certify that I gave intimation of *(specify document or other matter to be intimated)* to *(insert name of receiving party)*.
2. Intimation was given by *(specify method of intimation authorised by rule 5.3)*.
3. Intimation was given on *(insert date)*.

[A.B.] *[or*C.D.]], [Appellant/Respondent]

[or [X.Y.], Solicitor for [Appellant/Respondent]]

[or [P.Q.], Sheriff Officer]

(insert business address of solicitor or sheriff officer)]

Form 6.6

S1.197

Rule 6.6(1)

Grounds of cross-appeal

IN THE SHERIFF APPEAL COURT

GROUNDS OF APPEAL FOR RESPONDENT

in the appeal in the cause

[A.B.] *(designation and address)*

PURSUER and [APPELLANT/RESPONDENT]

against

[C.D.] *(designation and address)*

DEFENDER and [RESPONDENT/APPELLANT]

1. The appellant has appealed to the Sheriff Appeal Court against the decision of the sheriff at *(place)* to *(specify nature of decision)* made on *(date)*.
2. The respondent appeals against the decision of the sheriff at *(place)* to *(specify nature of decision)* made on *(date)*.

[or The respondent challenges the grounds on which the sheriff made the decision against which the appellant has appealed.]

3. *(State briefly (in numbered paragraphs) the ground(s) of appeal)*.

IN RESPECT WHEREOF

[A.B.] *[or*[C.D.]], Respondent

[or [X.Y.], Solicitor for Respondent

(insert business address of solicitor)]

Form 6.9

S1.198

Rule 6.9(2)

Reference of question about competency of appeal

IN THE SHERIFF APPEAL COURT

REFERENCE OF QUESTION ABOUT COMPETENCY OF APPEAL

by

[A.B.] *[or*[C.D.]] *(designation and address)*

RESPONDENT

in the appeal in the cause

1279

[A.B.] (*designation and address*)
PURSUER and [APPELLANT/RESPONDENT]
against
[C.D.] (*designation and address*)
DEFENDER and [RESPONDENT/APPELLANT]

1. The respondent refers the following question about the competency of the appeal to the procedural Appeal Sheriff:

(*state briefly (in numbered paragraphs) the question(s) about the competency of the appeal*).

2. (*State briefly (in numbered paragraphs) the grounds for referring the question(s).*)

[A.B.] [*or*[C.D.]], Respondent
[*or* [X.Y.], Solicitor for Respondent
(*insert business address of solicitor*)]

S1.199

Form 7.2

Rules 6.12(5)(a), 7.2(1) and 7.3(4)(b)

Timetable in appeal
IN THE SHERIFF APPEAL COURT
TIMETABLE IN APPEAL
in the cause
[A.B.] (*designation and address*)
PURSUER and [APPELLANT/RESPONDENT]
against
[C.D.] (*designation and address*)
DEFENDER and [RESPONDENT/APPELLANT]

Date of issue of timetable: (*date*)

[This is a revised timetable issued under rule 6.12(5)(a) [*or* rule 7.3(4)(b)] which replaces the timetable issued on (*date*).]

1. The appellant must lodge the appeal print under rule 7.4(1) no later than (*date*).
2. The appellant must lodge the appendix to the appeal print under rule 7.5(1) no later than (*date*).
3. If the appellant does not consider that it is necessary to lodge an appendix to the appeal print, the appellant must lodge written notice under rule 7.6(1) no later than (*date*).
4. The parties must lodge notes of argument under rule 7.7(1) no later than (*date*).
5. The parties must lodge estimates of the duration of any appeal hearing required to dispose of the appeal under rule 7.8 no later than (*date*).
6. A procedural hearing will take place at (*place*) on (*date and time*).

S1.200

Form 7.8

Rule 7.8

Estimate of duration of appeal hearing
IN THE SHERIFF APPEAL COURT
ESTIMATE OF DURATION OF APPEAL HEARING
in the appeal in the cause
[A.B.] (*designation and address*)
PURSUER and [APPELLANT/RESPONDENT]
against
[C.D.] (*designation and address*)
DEFENDER and [RESPONDENT/APPELLANT]

I, (*name and designation*) estimate that the likely duration of an appeal hearing in this appeal is (*state estimated duration*).

[A.B.] [*or*[C.D.]], [Appellant/Respondent]
[*or* [X.Y.], Solicitor for [Appellant/Respondent]
(*insert business address of solicitor*)]

Form 12.2

S1.201

Rule 12.2(1)

Form of application for permission to appeal to the Court of Session
IN THE SHERIFF APPEAL COURT
APPLICATION
for
PERMISSION TO APPEAL TO THE COURT OF SESSION
under section 113 of the Courts Reform (Scotland) Act 2014
by
[A.B.] (*designation and address*)

APPLICANT

against
A DECISION OF THE SHERIFF APPEAL COURT

1. On (*date*) the Sheriff Appeal Court (*briefly describe decision in respect of which permission to appeal to the Court of Session is sought*).

GROUNDS OF APPEAL

2. (*State briefly (in numbered paragraphs) the ground(s).*)

PERMISSION TO APPEAL

3. The appeal raises an important point of principle or practice because (*state briefly the reasons*).

[*or* The appeal does not raise an important point of principle or practice but there is some other compelling reason for the Court of Session to hear the appeal because (*state briefly the reasons*).]

[A.B.], Applicant
[*or* [X.Y.], Solicitor for Applicant
(*insert business address of solicitor*)]

Form 14.1

S1.202

Rules 14.1(1), 14.4(2), and 14.5(2)(a)

Form of motion by email
IN THE SHERIFF APPEAL COURT
Unopposed[*or* Opposed]motion

To: (email address of the Court)
1. Case name:
2. Court ref number:
3. Is the case in court in the next 7 days?
4. Solicitors or party lodging motion:
    (a) Reference:
    (b) Telephone number:
    (c) Email address:
5. Lodging motion on behalf of:
6. Motion (in brief terms):
7. Submissions in support of motion (if required):
8. Date of lodging of motion:
9. Intimation made to:
    (a) Provided email address(es):
    (b) Additional email address(es) of fee-earner or other person(s) dealing

1281

with the case on behalf of a receiving party (if applicable):

10. Date intimations sent:
11. Opposition must be intimated to opponent no later than 1700 hours on:
12. Is motion opposed or unopposed?
13. Has consent to the motion been provided?
14. Document(s) intimated and lodged with motion:

EXPLANATORY NOTE TO BE ADDED WHERE RECEIVING PARTY IS NOT LEGALLY REPRESENTED

OPPOSITION TO THE MOTION MAY BE MADE by completing Form 14.2 (Form of opposition to motion by email) and intimating it to the party intending to lodge the motion (insert email address) on or before the last date for intimating opposition (see paragraph 11 above).

IN THE EVENT OF A FORM OF OPPOSITION BEING INTIMATED, the party intending to lodge the motion will lodge an opposed motion and the clerk of the Sheriff Appeal Court will assign a date, time and place for hearing parties on the motion. Intimation of this hearing will be sent to parties by the clerk.

IF NO NOTICE OF OPPOSITION IS LODGED, OR IF CONSENT TO THE MOTION IS INTIMATED TO THE PARTY INTENDING TO LODGE THE MOTION, the motion will be considered without the attendance of parties.

IF YOU ARE UNCERTAIN WHAT ACTION TO TAKE you should consult a solicitor. You may also obtain advice from a Citizens Advice Bureau or other advice agency.

S1.203

Form 14.2

Rules 14.2(1) and 14.5(2)(b)

Form of opposition to motion by email
IN THE SHERIFF APPEAL COURT
TO BE INTIMATED TO THE PARTY INTENDING TO LODGE THE MOTION

1. Case name:
2. Court ref number:
3. Date of intimation of motion:
4. Date of intimation of opposition to motion:
5. Solicitors or party opposing motion:
    (a) Reference:
    (b) Telephone number:
    (c) Email address:
6. Opposing motion on behalf of:
7. Grounds of opposition:
8. Estimated duration of hearing:

S1.204

Form 15.1

Rule 15.1(1)

Form of motion
IN THE SHERIFF APPEAL COURT
MOTION FOR THE APPELLANT [or RESPONDENT]
in the appeal in the cause
[A.B.] (*designation and address*)
PURSUER and [APPELLANT/RESPONDENT]
against
[C.D.] (*designation and address*)
DEFENDER and [RESPONDENT/APPELLANT]

Date: (*insert date of intimation*)

1. The appellant (*or* respondent) moves the Court to (*insert details of the motion*).
2. (*State briefly (in numbered paragraphs) the grounds for the motion*).
3. The last date for lodging opposition to the motion is (*insert last date for lodging opposition*).
4. (*Where a copy of a document accompanies the motion in accordance with rule 15.1(2), list the document(s) in question.*)

[A.B.] *[or*[C.D.]], [Appellant/Respondent]
[or [X.Y.], Solicitor for [Appellant/Respondent]
(*insert business address of solicitor*)]

EXPLANATORY NOTE TO BE INSERTED WHERE RECEIVING PARTY IS NOT LEGALLY REPRESENTED.

YOU MAY OPPOSE THE MOTION BY COMPLETING FORM 15.2 (Form of Opposition to Motion) and lodging it with the Clerk of the Sheriff Appeal Court.

You must do so on or before the last date for lodging opposition.

IF YOU OPPOSE THE MOTION, the Clerk will arrange a hearing. The Clerk will tell you the date, time and place for the hearing. You will have to attend the hearing or be represented at it.

IF YOU DO NOT OPPOSE THE MOTION, the Court may decide how to dispose of the motion without a hearing.

IF YOU ARE UNCERTAIN WHAT ACTION TO TAKE, you should consult a solicitor. You may also obtain advice from a Citizens Advice Bureau or other advice agency.

Form 15.2

S1.205

Rule 15.2(1)

Form of opposition to motion
IN THE SHERIFF APPEAL COURT
OPPOSITION BY APPELLANT *[or* RESPONDENT] TO MOTION
in the appeal in the cause
[A.B.] (*designation and address*)
PURSUER and [APPELLANT/RESPONDENT]
against
[C.D.] (*designation and address*)
DEFENDER and [RESPONDENT/APPELLANT]

Date of intimation of motion: (*insert date of intimation*)
Date of intimation of opposition to motion: (*insert date of intimation*)

1. The appellant (*or* respondent) opposes the motion by the respondent [*or* appellant].
2. (*State briefly (in numbered paragraphs) the grounds for opposing the motion.*)

[A.B.] *[or*[C.D.]], [Appellant/Respondent]
[or [X.Y.], Solicitor for [Appellant/Respondent]
(*insert business address of solicitor*)]

Form 16

S1.206

Rule 16.2(1)

IN THE SHERIFF APPEAL COURT
MINUTE
in the appeal in the cause
[A.B.] (*designation and address*)
PURSUER and [APPELLANT/RESPONDENT]
against

[C.D.] (*designation and address*)

DEFENDER and [RESPONDENT/APPELLANT]

1. The minuter asks the Court to make the following order:

(*state briefly (in numbered paragraphs) the order sought from the Court*).

2. (*State briefly (in numbered paragraphs) the facts supporting the making of that order.*)

3. (*Where appropriate, state the pleas-in-law.*)

IN RESPECT WHEREOF

[A.B.], Minuter

[*or* [X.Y.], Solicitor for Minuter

(*insert business address of solicitor*)]

S1.207

Form 18.3

Rule 18.3(1)(c)

Notice of peremptory hearing

IN THE SHERIFF APPEAL COURT

NOTICE OF PEREMPTORY HEARING

in the appeal in the cause

[A.B.] (*designation and address*)

PURSUER and [APPELLANT/RESPONDENT]

against

[C.D.] (*designation and address*)

DEFENDER and [RESPONDENT/APPELLANT]

1. The Court has been informed that your solicitor no longer represents you.

2. As a result, the Court has made an order that you should attend or be represented at a peremptory hearing at (*insert place*) on (*insert date and time*).

3. At the peremptory hearing, you will have to tell the Court whether you intend to continue with the appeal [*or* your answers to the appeal].

[A.B.] [*or*[C.D.]], [Appellant/Respondent]

[*or* [X.Y.], Solicitor for [Appellant/Respondent]

(*insert business address of solicitor*)]

IF YOU ARE UNCERTAIN WHAT ACTION TO TAKE, you should consult a solicitor. You may also obtain advice from a Citizens Advice Bureau or other advice agency.

S1.208

Form 22.2

Rule 22.2(1)

Devolution issue

IN THE SHERIFF APPEAL COURT

DEVOLUTION ISSUE

in the appeal in the cause

[A.B.] (*designation and address*)

PURSUER and [APPELLANT/RESPONDENT]

against

[C.D.] (*designation and address*)

DEFENDER and [RESPONDENT/APPELLANT]

The appellant [*or* respondent] wishes to raise a devolution issue in this appeal.

(*State briefly (in numbered paragraphs) the following information—*

(a) *the facts and circumstances and contentions of law on the basis of which it is alleged that the devolution issue arises;*

(b) *details of the relevant law (including the relevant provisions of the Scotland Act 1998, the Northern Ireland Act 1998 or the Government of Wales Act 2006, as the case may be).*)

[A.B.] *[or*[C.D.]], [Appellant/Respondent]
[or [X.Y.], Solicitor for [Appellant/Respondent]
(*insert business address of solicitor*)]

Form 23.3

Rule 23.3(2)

S1.209

Reference to the European Court
REQUEST
for
PRELIMINARY RULING
of
THE COURT OF JUSTICE OF THE EUROPEAN UNION
from
THE SHERIFF APPEAL COURT IN SCOTLAND
in the appeal in the cause
[A.B.] (*designation and address*)
PURSUER and [APPELLANT/RESPONDENT]
against
[C.D.] (*designation and address*)
DEFENDER and [RESPONDENT/APPELLANT]

(*Set out a clear and succinct statement of the case giving rise to the request for the ruling of the European Court in order to enable the European Court to consider and understand the issues of EU law raised and to enable governments of Member States and other interested parties to submit observations. The statement of case should include:*

(a) *particulars of the parties;*
(b) *the history of the dispute between the parties;*
(c) *the history of the proceedings;*
(d) *the relevant facts as agreed by the parties or found by the court or, failing such agreement or finding, the contentions of the parties on such facts;*
(e) *the nature of the issues of law and fact between the parties;*
(f) *the Scots law, so far as it is relevant;*
(g) *the Treaty provisions or other acts, instruments or rules of EU law concerned; and*
(h) *an explanation of why the reference is being made.*)

The preliminary ruling of the Court of Justice of the European Union is accordingly requested on the following questions:

(*state (in numbered paragraphs) the questions on which the ruling is sought*).

Dated the (*day*) day of (*month and year*).

Appeal Sheriff

Form 24.2

Rule 24.2(1)

S1.210

Application for leave to intervene by the CEHR or SCHR
IN THE SHERIFF APPEAL COURT
APPLICATION FOR LEAVE TO INTERVENE
by
THE COMMISSION FOR EQUALITY AND HUMAN RIGHTS ("the CEHR")
[or THE SCOTTISH COMMISSION FOR HUMAN RIGHTS ("the SCHR")]
in the appeal in the cause
[A.B.] (*designation and address*)
PURSUER and [APPELLANT/RESPONDENT]
against
[C.D.] (*designation and address*)

DEFENDER and [RESPONDENT/APPELLANT]

1. The CEHR *[or* The SCHR] seeks leave to intervene in this appeal under section 30(1) of the Equality Act 2006 *[or* section 14(2) of the Scottish Commission for Human Rights Act 2006].

2. The CEHR considers that this appeal is relevant to a matter in connection with which it has a function because:

(state briefly (in numbered paragraphs) the reasons).

[or The SCHR considers that an issue arising in this appeal is relevant to its general duty and raises a matter of public interest because:

(state briefly (in numbered paragraphs) the reasons).]

3. The issue in this appeal which the CEHR *[or* the SCHR] intends to address is:

(state briefly (in numbered paragraphs) the reasons).

4. The CEHR *[or* The SCHR] intends to make the following submission if leave to intervene is granted:

(state briefly (in numbered paragraphs) a summary of the proposed submissions).

[X.Y.], Solicitor for the CEHR *[or* the SCHR]

(insert business address of solicitor)

S1.211

Form 24.4

Rule 24.4(1)

Invitation to the SCHR to intervene
IN THE SHERIFF APPEAL COURT
INVITATION

to

THE SCOTTISH COMMISSION FOR HUMAN RIGHTS ("the SCHR")

TO INTERVENE

in the appeal in the cause

[A.B.] *(designation and address)*

PURSUER and [APPELLANT/RESPONDENT]

against

[C.D.] *(designation and address)*

DEFENDER and [RESPONDENT/APPELLANT]

1. The Sheriff Appeal Court invites the SCHR to intervene in this appeal under section 14(2)(b) of the Scottish Commission for Human Rights Act 2006.

2. *(State briefly (in numbered paragraphs) the procedural history, facts and issues in the appeal.)*

3. The Court seeks a submission from the SCHR on the following issue:

(state briefly (in numbered paragraphs) the issue).

Appeal Sheriff

S1.212

Form 25.4–A

Rules 25.4(1) and 26.8(2)

Form of oath for witness

I swear by Almighty God that I will tell the truth, the whole truth and nothing but the truth.

S1.213

Form 25.4–B

Rules 25.4(2) and 26.8(3)

Form of affirmation for witness

I solemnly, sincerely and truly declare and affirm that I will tell the truth, the whole truth and nothing but the truth.

S1.214

Form 26.2–A

Rule 26.2(1)

Child witness notice

IN THE SHERIFF APPEAL COURT
CHILD WITNESS NOTICE
under section 12 of the Vulnerable Witnesses (Scotland) Act 2004
in the appeal in the cause
[A.B.] (*designation and address*)
PURSUER and [APPELLANT/RESPONDENT]
against
[C.D.] (*designation and address*)
DEFENDER and [RESPONDENT/APPELLANT]

1. The applicant is the appellant [*or* respondent].
2. The applicant has cited [*or* intends to cite] [E.F.] (*date of birth*) as a witness.
3. [E.F.] is a child witness under section 11 of the Vulnerable Witnesses (Scotland) Act 2004 [and was under the age of eighteen on the date of the commencement of proceedings.]
4. The applicant considers that the following special measure[s] is [are] the most appropriate for the purpose of taking the evidence of [E.F.] [*or* that [E.F.] should give evidence without the benefit of any special measure]:
(*specify any special measure(s) sought*).
5. The reason[s] this [these] special measure[s] is [are] considered the most appropriate is [are] as follows:
(*specify the reason(s) for the special measure(s) sought*).
[*or* The reason[s] it is considered that [E.F.] should give evidence without the benefit of any special measure is [are]:
(*explain why it is felt that no special measures are required*).]
6. [E.F.] and the parent[s] of [*or* [person[s] with parental responsibility for] [E.F.] has [have] expressed the following view[s] on the special measure[s] that is [are] considered most appropriate [*or* [the appropriateness of [E.F.] giving evidence without the benefit of any special measure]:
(*specify the view(s) expressed and how they were obtained*).
7. Other information considered relevant to this application is as follows:
(*state briefly any other information relevant to the child witness notice*).
8. The applicant asks the Court to—
    (a) consider this child witness notice; and
    (b) make an order authorising the special measure[s] sought;
    [*or* make an order authorising the giving of evidence by [E.F.] without the benefit of special measures.]

[A.B.] [*or*[C.D.]], Applicant
[*or* [X.Y.], Solicitor for Applicant
(*insert business address of solicitor*)]

Form 26.2–B   **S1.215**

Rule 26.2(2)

Vulnerable witness application
IN THE SHERIFF APPEAL COURT
VULNERABLE WITNESS APPLICATION
under section 12 of the Vulnerable Witnesses (Scotland) Act 2004
in the appeal in the cause
[A.B.] (*designation and address*)
PURSUER and [APPELLANT/RESPONDENT]
against
[C.D.] (*designation and address*)
DEFENDER and [RESPONDENT/APPELLANT]

1. The applicant is the appellant [*or* respondent].

2. The applicant has cited *[or* intends to cite] [E.F.] *(date of birth)* as a witness.
3. The applicant considers that [E.F.] is a vulnerable witness under section 11(1)(b) of the Vulnerable Witnesses (Scotland) Act 2004 for the following reasons:
(specify why the witness is considered to be a vulnerable witness).
4. The applicant considers that the following special measure[s] is [are] the most appropriate for the purpose of taking the evidence of [E.F.]:
(specify any special measure(s) sought).
5. The reason[s] this [these] special measure[s] is [are] considered the most appropriate is [are] as follows:
(specify the reason(s) for the special measure(s) sought).
6. [E.F.] has expressed the following view[s] on the special measure[s] that is [are] considered most appropriate:
(specify the view(s) expressed and how they were obtained).
7. Other information considered relevant to this application is as follows:
(state briefly any other information relevant to the vulnerable witness application).
8. The applicant asks the Court to—
    (a) consider this vulnerable witness application; and
    (b) make an order authorising the special measure[s] sought.

[A.B.] *[or*[C.D.]], Applicant
[or [X.Y.], Solicitor for Applicant
(insert business address of solicitor)]

S1.216

Form 26.2–C

Rule 26.2(3)(a)

Application for review of arrangements for vulnerable witness
IN THE SHERIFF APPEAL COURT
APPLICATION FOR REVIEW OF ARRANGEMENTS FOR VULNERABLE WITNESSES
under section 13 of the Vulnerable Witnesses (Scotland) Act 2004
in the appeal in the cause
[A.B.] *(designation and address)*
PURSUER and [APPELLANT/RESPONDENT]
against
[C.D.] *(designation and address)*
DEFENDER and [RESPONDENT/APPELLANT]

1. The applicant is the appellant *[or* respondent].
2. A proof *[or* hearing] is fixed for *(date)* at *(time)*.
3. [E.F.] is a witness who is to give evidence at, or for the purposes of, the proof *[or* hearing]. [E.F.] is a child witness *[or* vulnerable witness] under section 11 of the Vulnerable Witnesses (Scotland) Act 2004.
4. The current arrangements for taking the evidence of [E.F.] are *(specify the current arrangements).*
5. The current arrangements should be reviewed because *(specify reasons for review).*
6. [E.F.] [and the parent[s] of *[or* person[s] with parental responsibility for] [E.F.]] has [have] expressed the following view[s] on [the special measure[s] that is [are] considered most appropriate] *[or* the appropriateness of [E.F.] giving evidence without the benefit of any special measure]:
(specify the view(s) expressed and how they were obtained).
7. The applicant seeks *(specify the order sought).*

[A.B.] *[or*[C.D.]], Applicant

[or [X.Y.], Solicitor for Applicant
(insert business address of solicitor)]
Form 28.3   **S1.217**

Rule 28.3(2)(a)

Representations about a proposed order restricting the reporting of proceedings

IN THE SHERIFF APPEAL COURT
REPRESENTATIONS
by
[A.B.] *(designation and address)*

APPLICANT

1.   On *(date)* the Sheriff Appeal Court made an interim order under rule 28.2(1) of the Act of Sederunt (Sheriff Appeal Court Rules) 2021.
2.   The applicant is a person who would be directly affected by an order restricting the reporting of proceedings because:
(state briefly (in numbered paragraphs) the reasons).
3.   The applicant wishes to make the following representations:
(state briefly (in numbered paragraphs) the representations).
4.   The applicant seeks an urgent hearing on these representations because:
(state briefly (in numbered paragraphs) why an urgent hearing is necessary).]

[A.B.], Applicant
[or [X.Y.], Solicitor for Applicant
(insert business address of solicitor)]
Form 28.5   **S1.218**

Rule 28.5(2)

Application for variation or revocation of an order restricting the reporting of proceedings

IN THE SHERIFF APPEAL COURT
APPLICATION
by
[A.B.] *(designation and address)*

APPLICANT

1.   On *(date)* the Sheriff Appeal Court made an order restricting the reporting of proceedings in *(name of case (and court reference, if known)).*
2.   The applicant seeks variation [or revocation] of the order because:
(state briefly (in numbered paragraphs) the reasons for the application).
3.   The applicant seeks to vary the order by:
(state briefly (in numbered paragraphs) the proposed variation(s)).]

[A.B.], Applicant
[or [X.Y.], Solicitor for Applicant
(insert business address of solicitor)]
Form 29.2   **S1.219**

Rule 29.2(1)

Application for new trial
APPLICATION
to
THE SHERIFF APPEAL COURT
for
A NEW TRIAL
under section 69 of the Courts Reform (Scotland) Act 2014
by
[A.B.] *(designation and address)*

APPLICANT

[C.D.] (*designation and address*)

RESPONDENT

1. On (*date*), a jury trial was held before the Sheriff of Lothian and Borders at Edinburgh in the cause [A.B.] (*designation and address*), pursuer, against [C.D.] (*designation and address*), defender. The court reference number is (*insert court reference number*).

2. The verdict of the jury was (*state the verdict returned in accordance with section 68 of the Courts Reform (Scotland) Act 2014*).

3. The applicant applies to the Sheriff Appeal Court for a new trial under section 69(1) of the Court Reform (Scotland) Act 2014.

GROUNDS FOR APPLICATION

(*State briefly (in numbered paragraphs) the ground(s) for the application including references to section 69(2) of the Court Reform (Scotland) Act 2014*).

IN RESPECT WHEREOF

[A.B.], Applicant

[or [X.Y.], Solicitor for Applicant

(*insert business address of solicitor*)]

S1.220

Form 29.5

Rules 29.5(1), 29.6(6)(a) and (7)(b)

Timetable in application for new trial

IN THE SHERIFF APPEAL COURT

TIMETABLE IN APPLICATION FOR NEW TRIAL

by

[A.B.] (*designation and address*)

APPLICANT

against

[C.D.] (*designation and address*)

RESPONDENT

Date of issue of timetable: (*date*)

[This is a revised timetable issued under rule 29.6(6)(a) [*or* rule 29.6(7)(b)] which replaces the timetable issued on (*date*).]

1. The respondent may refer a question of competency under rule 29.7(3) no later than (*date*).

Note: if a reference is lodged, parties must lodge notes of argument under rule 29.7(5) within 7 days after the date on which the reference is lodged.

2. The applicant must lodge the appendix to the print under rule 29.9(1) no later than (*date*).

3. If the applicant does not consider that it is necessary to lodge an appendix to the print, the applicant must lodge written notice under rule 29.10(1) no later than (*date*).

4. The parties must lodge notes of argument under rule 29.11(1) no later than (*date*).

5. The parties must lodge estimates of the duration of any hearing required to dispose of the application for a new trial under rule 29.12 no later than (*date*).

6. A procedural hearing will take place at (*place*) on (*date and time*).

S1.221

Form 29.7

Rule 29.7(2)

Reference of question about competency of application for new trial

IN THE SHERIFF APPEAL COURT

REFERENCE OF QUESTION ABOUT COMPETENCY OF APPLICATION FOR NEW TRIAL

by
[C.D.] (*designation and address*)

RESPONDENT

in the appeal by
[A.B.] (*designation and address*)

APPLICANT

against
[C.D.] (*designation and address*)

RESPONDENT

1. The respondent refers the following question about the competency of the application for a new trial to the procedural Appeal Sheriff:
(*state briefly (in numbered paragraphs) the question(s) about the competency of the application for a new trial*).
2. (*State briefly (in numbered paragraphs) the grounds for referring the question(s).*)

[C.D.], Respondent
[or [X.Y.], Solicitor for Respondent
(*insert business address of solicitor*)]

Form 29.12

S1.222

Rule 29.12

Estimate of duration of hearing
IN THE SHERIFF APPEAL COURT
ESTIMATE OF DURATION OF HEARING
in the application for a new trial
[A.B.] (*designation and address*)

APPLICANT

against
[C.D.] (*designation and address*)

RESPONDENT

I, (name and designation) estimate that the likely duration of a hearing to dispose of this application for a new trial is (state estimated duration).

[A.B.], *[or*[C.D.]] [Applicant/Respondent]
[or [X.Y.], Solicitor for [Applicant/Respondent]
(*insert business address of solicitor*)]

Form 29.14

S1.223

Rule 29.14(2)

Application to enter jury verdict
APPLICATION
to
THE SHERIFF APPEAL COURT
to
ENTER JURY VERDICT
under section 71(2) of the Courts Reform (Scotland) Act 2014
by
[A.B.] (*designation and address*)

APPLICANT

[C.D.] (*designation and address*)

RESPONDENT

1. On (*date*), a jury trial was held before the Sheriff of Lothian and Borders at Edinburgh in the cause [A.B.] (*designation and address*), pursuer, against [C.D.] (*designation and address*), defender. The court reference number is (*insert court reference number*).

2. The verdict of the jury was (*state the verdict returned in accordance with section 68 of the Courts Reform (Scotland) Act 2014*).

3. The applicant applies to the Sheriff Appeal Court for the verdict instead to be entered in the applicant's favour under section 71(2) of the Court Reform (Scotland) Act 2014.

GROUNDS FOR APPLICATION

(*State briefly (in numbered paragraphs) the ground(s) for the application*).

IN RESPECT WHEREOF

[A.B.], [*or* C.D.] Applicant

[*or* [X.Y.], Solicitor for Applicant

(*insert business address of solicitor*)]

S1.224

Form 30.6

Rule 30.6(2)

Application for certificate of suitability for appeal to the Court of Session

IN THE SHERIFF APPEAL COURT

APPLICATION FOR CERTIFICATE OF SUITABILITY FOR APPEAL TO THE COURT OF SESSION

in the appeal in the cause

[A.B.] (*designation and address*)

PURSUER and [APPELLANT/RESPONDENT]

against

[C.D.] (*designation and address*)

DEFENDER and [RESPONDENT/APPELLANT]

1. The appellant [*or* respondent] asks the Sheriff Appeal Court to certify that this appeal is suitable for appeal to the Court of Session under section 38(b) of the Sheriff Courts (Scotland) Act 1971.

2. The appellant [*or* respondent] considers that this appeal is suitable for appeal to the Court of Session because:

(*state briefly (in numbered paragraphs) the reasons*).

[A.B.] [*or*[C.D.]], [Appellant/Respondent]

[*or* [X.Y.], Solicitor for [Appellant/Respondent]

(*insert business address of solicitor*)]

S1.225

Form 32.5

Rule 32.5(2)

Application for leave to appeal to the Court of Session

IN THE SHERIFF APPEAL COURT

APPLICATION FOR LEAVE TO APPEAL TO THE COURT OF SESSION

under

SECTION 163(2) [*or* 164(2)] [*or* 165(2)] OF THE CHILDREN'S HEARINGS (SCOTLAND) ACT 2011

in the appeal in the cause

[A.B.] (*designation and address*)

PURSUER and [APPELLANT/RESPONDENT]

against

[C.D.] (*designation and address*)

DEFENDER and [RESPONDENT/APPELLANT]

1. The appellant [*or* respondent] asks the Sheriff Appeal Court to grant leave to appeal to the Court of Session under section 163(2) [*or* 164(2)] [*or* 165(2)] of the Children's Hearings (Scotland) Act 2011.

GROUNDS OF APPEAL

2. (*State briefly (in numbered paragraphs) the point(s) of law or procedural irregularity on which the appeal is to proceed.*)

[A.B.] *[or*[C.D.]], [Appellant/Respondent]
[or [X.Y.], Solicitor for [Appellant/Respondent]
(*insert business address of solicitor*)]
Form 33.2

S1.226

Rule 33.2(1)

Note of appeal
APPEAL
to
THE SHERIFF APPEAL COURT
[A.B.] (*designation and address*)
APPLICANT and [APPELLANT/RESPONDENT]
[C.D.] (*designation and address*)
RESPONDENT and [RESPONDENT/APPELLANT]

1. The appellant appeals to the Sheriff Appeal Court against the decision of the sheriff at (*place*) (*specify nature of decision*) made on (*date*). The court reference number is (*insert court reference number*). [The appellant's email address is (*insert contact email address of the appellant, if the appellant has one*).] [The respondent's email address is (*insert contact email address of the respondent, if known*).] [The following person[s] [is/are] considered to have an interest in the proceedings: (*insert names and addresses of any parties with an interest in the proceedings and, if known, their contact email addresses*).]

GROUNDS OF APPEAL

2. (*State briefly (in numbered paragraphs) the ground(s) of appeal.*)

AVAILABILITY OF SHERIFF'S NOTE

3. The sheriff has provided a note setting out the reasons for the decision appealed against, and a copy is appended.

[or The appellant has requested that the sheriff write a note, but the note is not yet available.]

[or The sheriff has not provided a note setting out the reasons for the decision appealed against, and the appellant requests that the sheriff write a note.]

[or The sheriff has not provided a note setting out the reasons for the decision appealed against. The appellant considers that the appeal is sufficiently urgent that the Sheriff Appeal Court should hear and determine the appeal without the sheriff's note. (*State briefly (in numbered paragraphs) why the appeal is sufficiently urgent to justify its determination without the sheriff's note*).]

IN RESPECT WHEREOF

[P.Q.] (Applicant)
[A.B.] *[or*[C.D.]], Appellant
[or [X.Y.] Solicitor for Appellant
(*insert business address of solicitor*)]

1293

PRACTICE NOTE NO.1 OF 2016

Contents

Introduction

1. The purpose of this Practice Note is to set out the practice of the Sheriff Appeal Court ("the Court") in dealing with civil appeals. It comes into force on 29 March 2015.

2. This Practice Note follows the general structure of the Sheriff Appeal Court Rules ("the Rules"). Miscellaneous procedural matters are dealt with towards the end. The Court intends to review its practice once it begins to hear appeals. Where no provision is made in the Rules or this Practice Note about any aspect of procedure in relation to civil appeals, practitioners may have regard to the practice of the Court of Session in relation to that type of business.

Part 2: general provisions

Chapter 3: sanctions for failure to comply

3. Where a party considers that any other party is in default for any of the reasons set out in rule 3.1, that party should bring the matter to the attention of the procedural Appeal Sheriff by lodging a motion in writing.

Rule 4.2: legal representation

4. Where a party is legally represented, it is expected that the advocate or solicitor who will conduct the appeal hearing should appear at the procedural hearing. That person should be authorised to take any necessary decisions on substantive or procedural questions about the appeal. The Court considers that continuity of representation at procedural and appeal hearings is an important factor in minimising late settlements and the discharge of appeal hearings.

Part 3: initiation and progress of an appeal

Rule 6.2(2)(d): request for sheriff's note

5. Appellants are reminded that it is their responsibility to request a note from the sheriff where one has not already been produced. The note of appeal requires to include information about the availability of the sheriff's note and any steps taken to obtain one.

6. Where an appellant fails to take the necessary steps to obtain the sheriff's note and the appeal proceedings are delayed as a result, this may be taken into account in the determination of any question of expenses.

Rule 6.5(1)(b): answers to note of appeal

7. When the procedural Appeal Sheriff makes an order for intimation and answers, any person who receives intimation may lodge answers, if so advised. The lodging of answers makes the Court and all other parties aware of a respondent's case and the Court considers that answers serve an important function in framing a respondent's lines of argument. Accordingly, it considers them to be compulsory where a respondent wishes to oppose an appeal.

8. Answers need not be elaborate, but they may mirror the format of the grounds of appeal specified in the note of appeal.

Rule 7.3: cross-appeals

9. Where the grounds of appeal in a cross-appeal have not been dealt with in the sheriff's note, the respondent should include in the grounds of appeal a request that the sheriff write a further note.

10. Where grounds of appeal in a cross-appeal are lodged, it may not be possible for all of the procedural steps to take place in accordance with the timetable issued under rule 7.2. Accordingly, the respondent should discuss with the appellant whether some variation of the timetable is necessary to allow the cross appeal to be taken into account in preparing for the procedural hearing. Where the parties consider that a variation is required as a result of the cross-appeal, a motion under rule 7.6 should be made.

Rule 7.6: sist or variation of timetable

11. A motion under this rule must, like all motions in writing, specify the grounds on which it is made (rule 12.6). Full details of the grounds on which the motion is based should be given, accompanied where relevant by appropriate evidence. Any such motion should be made as soon as possible after the need for variation or a sist is identified. Variation of the timetable may be either by extension or acceleration.

12. A motion to sist must specify the period of sist sought, but parties are reminded that it is for the procedural Appeal Sheriff to determine the period of sist that will be granted. The procedural Appeal Sheriff will seek to avoid any unnecessary delay in carrying out the procedural steps set out in the timetable. Where an appeal is sisted pending the outcome of an application for legal aid, the expectation is that the period of sist will not exceed 6 weeks.

13. It should be noted that motions for sist or for variation of the timetable will not be granted, even if made of consent, unless sufficient information to justify them is placed before the procedural Appeal Sheriff. Any party opposing such an application will be required to demonstrate that their opposition is well founded.

Special cause

14. A motion to sist the appeal or vary the timetable may only be granted on special cause shown (rule 7.6(2)). The procedural Appeal Sheriff will determine, in the particular circumstances of a case, whether or not special cause has been shown.

15. Special cause might arise for example, where there is a need for a party to obtain:

(a)   transcripts of evidence;

(b)   legal aid;

(c)   the sheriff's note, if it cannot be obtained in time to comply with the timetable.

16. The procedural Appeal Sheriff may require to hear parties on an unopposed motion to sist the appeal or vary the timetable if:

(a)   the Scottish Legal Aid Board take issue with what is stated to be the current position in relation to an application for legal aid;

(b)   the procedural Appeal Sheriff is not satisfied that special cause has been shown.

Legal aid

17. The Court will expect parties to consider at the earliest possible stage whether they may require to apply for legal aid for the appeal. Delay in making an application for legal aid or in then making a motion under this rule may lead to the motion being refused. Generally, the Court will expect parties to adhere to guidance issued by the Scottish Legal Aid Board. Parties are reminded that the Board may make legal aid available for specially urgent work undertaken before a legal aid application is determined. This may obviate the need to sist the appeal or vary the timetable. Further information can be obtained in the Special Urgency Chapter of the Civil Legal Aid Handbook[1].

18. Where a party makes a motion under rule 7.6 pending the outcome of an application for legal aid, that party should notify the Board electronically within the same period as that party requires to intimate it to other parties. In specifying the grounds for the motion, the party should set out the current position in relation to the application for legal aid.

Rule 7.10: appendix to appeal print

19. The appendix should be made up in accordance with rule 7.10. However, it should only contain such material as is necessary for understanding the legal issues and the argument to be presented to the Court.

Notes of evidence from proof

20. Where the parties seek to submit the notes of evidence from a proof for consideration by the Court, they are reminded of the terms of rule 29.18(11) of the Ordinary Cause Rules 1993. Where the evidence has been recorded by tape recording, the appellant must request from the sheriff clerk a transcript of the record. In the rare cases where a shorthand writer has been instructed, the appellant must inform the shorthand writer that the notes require to be extended for the purpose of the appeal. If the recording will not be transcribed or the notes will not be extended before the appendix must be lodged, the appellant should inform the Clerk as soon as possible.

Form of appendix

21. The appendix should be paginated, each page being numbered individually and consecutively, with page numbers being inserted in a form which can be clearly distinguished from any other pagination on the document. Where any marking or writing in colour on a document is important, the document should be copied in colour or marked up correctly in colour. Documents which are not easily legible should be transcribed and the transcription placed adjacent to the document transcribed.

22. Any questions as to the contents or form of the appendix may be raised with the procedural Appeal Sheriff.

23. An appendix which does not conform to rule 7.10 and this Practice Note may be rejected by the Court, which may also find that no expenses are payable, or modify any award of expenses, in respect of the rejected appendix.

24. Where documents are included in an appendix unnecessarily, the Court may

---

[1] *http://www.slab.org.uk/handbooks/Civil%20handbook/wwhelp/wwhimpl/js/html/wwhelp.htm#href=Part%20V%20AA%20acs/Part%20V%20AA%20acs.html*

also find that no expenses are payable, or modify any award of expenses, in respect of the appendix.

Rule 7.12: notes of argument

25. Parties are reminded that rule 7.12 makes detailed provision about how notes of argument are to be prepared. A note of argument which does not comply with that rule may be rejected by the Court, which may also find that no expenses are payable, or modify any award of expenses, in respect of the rejected note of argument.

26. Any questions as to the form of notes of argument may be raised with the procedural Appeal Sheriff.

27. A single date will be specified in the timetable for the lodging of notes of argument. As a matter of good practice, parties should exchange draft versions of their notes of argument in advance of the date referred to in the timetable. Whenever possible, the drafts should be exchanged in sufficient time to enable each party to answer, in its note of argument, the arguments advanced by the other parties.

Rule 7.13: estimates of length of hearings

28. Where a party is legally represented, the certificate of estimate of the length of the hearing in Form 7.13 should be given by the advocate or solicitor who will conduct the appeal hearing. Where a party is not legally represented, it should be given by the party.

29. Any estimate exceeding one day should be fully explained in writing.

30. The Court expects that persons making oral submissions at an appeal hearing will confine their submissions so as to enable the hearing to be completed within the time indicated in the estimate. If additional time is required, that person must seek the Court's permission.

Rule 7.14: procedural hearing

31. The procedural hearing is an important aspect of the standard appeal procedure. It is intended to be the final procedural step and is dealt with by the procedural Appeal Sheriff.

32. The primary purpose of the procedural hearing is to make sure that no case is sent for an appeal hearing (i.e. a hearing on its merits) unless the procedural Appeal Sheriff is satisfied that the parties are prepared for it.

33. Where a party is legally represented, the Court expects that the advocate or solicitor who will conduct the appeal hearing should appear at the procedural hearing (see paragraph 4 above).

34. At the procedural hearing, the Court expects that parties will be in a position to discuss the issues involved in the appeal and how they can be disposed of. Parties should address the procedural Appeal Sheriff on their state of preparation.

35. If the procedural Appeal Sheriff is satisfied that parties are prepared to proceed to an appeal hearing, the procedural Appeal Sheriff will fix the appeal hearing and determine its length.

36. If the procedural Appeal Sheriff is not satisfied that parties are prepared to proceed to an appeal hearing, the procedural Appeal Sheriff will make an order to secure the expeditious disposal of the appeal. The procedural Appeal Sheriff may direct the Clerk to fix a further procedural hearing.

37. The Court considers that it is important that further procedural hearings be avoided unless they are necessary. If any difficulty arises in complying with the order of the procedural Appeal Sheriff, the parties should bring this to the attention of the Court. The parties should confirm whether:

  (a) the order has been complied with (and if not, why not);
  (b) further time is required (and if so, why);
  (c) a further hearing is genuinely required.

Part 5: incidental procedure: standard procedures

Chapter 19: expenses

38. The closing submissions for each party in an appeal hearing should deal with expenses: parties should either make their submissions about expenses at that point, or invite the Court to reserve all questions of expenses to a further hearing after it has determined the appeal.

Part 7: special appeal proceedings

Chapter 28: applications for new trial

39. The procedure in an application for a new trial is closely modelled on the standard appeal procedure. Accordingly, the guidance on the standard appeal procedure given in paragraphs 9 to 37 above applies equally (with any necessary modifications of terminology) to applications for a new trial under section 69 of the Courts Reform (Scotland) Act 2014.

Chapters 29 and 30: appeals by stated case

40. The procedure for requesting a stated case continues to be governed by the Summary Cause Rules 2002, the Small Claim Rules 2002 or the Act of Sederunt (Child Care and Maintenance Rules) 1997.

41. The Court reminds parties that great care should be taken to focus as precisely as possible the question of law (or procedural irregularity, in Chapter 30 appeals) on which the appeal is to proceed. If an advocate is to be instructed to conduct the appeal before the Court, it may be prudent to consult that advocate about the formulation of the question of law and any proposed adjustments to the draft stated case.

42. Parties are also reminded that the permission of the Court must be obtained if a party wishes at the appeal hearing to raise a question of law of which notice has not been given (see rules 29.4(3) to (5) and 30.3).

43. Where parties disagree about the occurrence of events in the sheriff court proceedings, the Court will normally accept the account of events which is given in the stated case.

Schedule 1: administrative provisions

Paragraph 4: form of process

44. Paragraph 4 prescribes the steps of process that must be included when a process is made up. Styles for each step of process are in the Schedule to this Practice Note. Processes which do not conform substantially to these styles may be rejected by the Court.

Miscellaneous procedural matters

Communication with the Court

45.   The Court considers that it is important to avoid unnecessary hearings: hearings in court should not take place unless the matter in issue cannot otherwise be resolved. Hearings can often be avoided by means of email or other communication between solicitors and the Clerk, with the involvement of the procedural Appeal Sheriff where necessary.

Communication where appeal is not to proceed

46.   Parties are reminded that those involved in litigation have an obligation to take reasonable care to avoid situations where court time would be wasted. Where a party or that party's legal representative considers that it is likely that the appeal may not proceed, the Clerk must be informed immediately.

Core bundles

47.   In cases where the appendix comprises more than 500 pages (exclusive of notes of evidence) the appellant should, after consultation with the respondent, also lodge a core bundle. The core bundle should be lodged at least 7 days prior to the procedural hearing. It should contain the documents which are central to the appeal and it should not ordinarily exceed 150 pages. As with the appendix, the core bundle should be paginated, each page being numbered individually and consecutively, with page numbers being inserted in a form which can be clearly distinguished from any other pagination on the document.

48.   Any questions as to the contents or form of the core bundle may be raised with the procedural Appeal Sheriff.

Authorities

49.   When an appeal hearing is fixed, the appellant should, after consultation with the respondent, lodge a bundle containing photocopies of the authorities cited in the notes of argument upon which each party will rely at the hearing.

Contents of bundle of authorities

50.   The bundle of authorities should not include:
  (a)   authorities for propositions not in dispute;
  (b)   more than 10 authorities, unless the Court gives permission for additional authorities to be included.

Form of bundle of authorities

51.   If a case is reported in Session Cases or the Law Reports published by the Incorporated Council of Law Reporting for England and Wales, it should be cited from those sources. Where a case is not reported in Session Cases or the Law Reports, references to other recognised reports may be given.

52.   Unreported judgments should only be cited if they contain an authoritative statement of a relevant principle of law not to be found in a reported case or if they are necessary for the understanding of some other authority.

53. The bundle of authorities should be assembled in chronological order, with an index page.

54. The bundle of authorities should be paginated, each page being numbered individually and consecutively, with page numbers being inserted in a form which can be clearly distinguished from any other pagination on the document.

55. The passages on which each party intends to rely (as specified in that party's note of argument) should be marked or highlighted.

56. Any questions as to the contents or form of the bundle of authorities may be raised with the procedural Appeal Sheriff.

57. A bundle of authorities which does not conform to this Practice Note may be rejected by the Court, which may also find that no expenses are payable, or modify any award of expenses, in respect of the rejected bundle.

58. Where authorities are included in a bundle unnecessarily, the Court may also find that no expenses are payable, or modify any award of expenses, in respect of the bundle.

Appeal hearings: preparation by the Court

59. Before the appeal hearing, the Appeal Sheriff(s) who will hear the appeal will normally have read:

   (a)   the appeal print;

   (b)   the note of appeal and answers to the note of appeal;

   (c)   any grounds of appeal (and answers) in a cross-appeal;

   (d)   the appendix;

   (e)   parties' notes of argument;

   (f)   any core bundle;

   (g)   the bundle of authorities.

60. Accordingly, one copy of each of these documents will be required for each Appeal Sheriff who sits for the appeal hearing. The precise number will depend upon the composition of the Court, which will be confirmed at the procedural hearing.

61. Parties will be ordered to lodge these copies by a date specified in the order. That date will be determined by the procedural Appeal Sheriff. Normally these documents will require to be lodged no later than 14 days prior to the hearing.

62. The timeous lodging of these copies is critical if the Appeal Sheriffs are to undertake pre-reading in preparation for the appeal hearing. The Court considers that this preparation is essential to the efficient disposal of business. Accordingly, parties and their legal representatives must inform the Clerk at the earliest possible opportunity if any difficulty in complying with the order is anticipated. This will enable the Court to consider whether further orders are required.

Documents generally

63. Documents, particularly appendices, core bundles and bundles of authorities, must be presented in a form which is robust, manageable and not excessively heavy. All documents must be easily legible.

Disposal by consent

64. If the parties have reached agreement as to how the appeal should be disposed of, they may prepare and lodge a joint minute setting out that agreement in clear and comprehensive terms. It should include terms as to expenses. It should also state the terms of the interlocutor that the parties wish the Court to pronounce.

65. Where the parties have agreed that the appeal should be allowed and the sheriff's decision recalled or varied because it is wrong, the joint minute must also explain why cause has been shown for the appeal to be allowed. Detailed submissions should be made, with appropriate reference to authority.

66. Where the parties have agreed that the appeal should be allowed because they wish the sheriff's interlocutor to be recalled or varied for practical reasons (but they do not consider that it was wrong), the joint minute must explain those practical reasons. It must also state that the parties do not seek a determination of the merits of the appeal.

21 March 2016

Schedule

Style steps of process

Style minute of proceedings

IN THE SHERIFF APPEAL COURT

MINUTE OF PROCEEDINGS

in the appeal by

[A.B.] (*designation and address*)

PURSUER and APPELLANT [*or* RESPONDENT]

against

[C.D.] (*designation and address*)

DEFENDER and RESPONDENT [*or* APPELLANT]

Date   *Clerk*

Style inventory of process

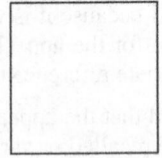

IN THE SHERIFF APPEAL COURT

INVENTORY OF PROCESS

in the appeal by

[A.B.] *(designation and address)*

PURSUER and APPELLANT [*or* RESPONDENT]

against

[C.D.] *(designation and address)*

DEFENDER and RESPONDENT [*or* APPELLANT]

1.   Note of appeal.

2.

3.

4.

5.

6.

7.

8.

9.

10.

PRACTICE NOTE: NO.1 OF 2017

1. The purpose of this Practice Note is to set out the practice of the Sheriff Appeal Court in dealing with the auditing of Accounts of Expenses arising out of civil appeals in the Court.

2. It comes into force on 10 February 2017.

3. Such Accounts of Expenses are to be lodged for taxation with the Clerk of the Sheriff Appeal Court within the court offices in Parliament House for onward transmission to the auditor as required by Chapter 19 of the Sheriff Appeal Court Rules 2015.

4. Such Accounts of Expenses are to be taxed by the Auditor of the Sheriff Appeal Court (Mr Kenneth Cumming W.S.) Parliament House Parliament Square, Edinburgh EH1 1RQ (office entered though 120 Cowgate, Edinburgh). Tel: 0131 240 6789. Fax: 0131 220 0137.

5. All cheques and other remittances in respect of audit fees are to be made payable to 'The Auditor of the Sheriff Appeal Court'.

9 February 2017